Professional
ASP.NET 2.0 Databases

Professional
ASP.NET 2.0 Databases

Thiru Thangarathinam

Wiley Publishing, Inc.

Professional ASP.NET 2.0 Databases

Published by
Wiley Publishing, Inc.
10475 Crosspoint Boulevard
Indianapolis, IN 46256
www.wiley.com

Published simultaneously in Canada

ISBN: 978-0-470-04179-6

Manufactured in the United States of America

10 9 8 7 6 5 4 3 2 1

For general information on our other products and services or to obtain technical support, please contact our Customer Care Department within the U.S. at (800) 762-2974, outside the U.S. at (317) 572-3993 or fax (317) 572-4002.

Library of Congress Catalog Publication Data is available from the Publisher.

About the Author

Thiru Thangarathinam works for Intel Corporation in Phoenix, Arizona. He is an MVP and specializes in architecting, designing, and developing distributed enterprise-class applications using .NET-related technologies. He is the author of *Professional ASP.NET 2.0 XML* from Wiley and has also coauthored a number of books in .NET-related technologies. Thiru has also been a frequent contributor to leading technology-related online publications. At Intel, he is part of the team that is focused on developing the Enterprise Architecture and Service Oriented Architectures for Intel. He can be reached at thiruthangarathinam@yahoo.com.

Credits

Senior Acquisitions Editor
Jim Minatel

Development Editor
Brian Herrmann

Technical Editor
Cody Reichenau

Production Editor
Felicia Robinson

Copy Editor
Foxxe Editorial Services

Editorial Manager
Mary Beth Wakefield

Production Manager
Tim Tate

Vice President and Executive Group Publisher
Richard Swadley

Vice President and Executive Publisher
Joseph B. Wikert

Project Coordinator
Erin Smith

Graphics and Production Specialists
Carrie A. Foster
Brooke Graczyk
Jennifer Mayberry
Barry Offringa
Alicia B. South

Quality Control Technician
John Greenough

Proofreading
Sean Medlock

Indexing
Broccoli Information Management

Wiley Bicentennial Logo
Richard J. Pacafico

Contents

Acknowledgments

I would like to acknowledge my wife Thamiya, my parents and my family for their constant support and encouragement while I spent nights and weekends working on this book.

Introduction

Who This Book Is For

This book is aimed at intermediate or experienced programmers who have started on their journey toward ASP.NET development and who are already familiar with relational databases such as SQL Server. While readers won't be introduced to many new ASP.NET 2.0 concepts in Chapter 1, this book is not intended to be a first port of call for the developer looking at ASP.NET, since there are already many books and articles covering this area. Instead, this book cuts straight to the heart of accessing data from within ASP.NET web applications. To get the most out of the book, you should have some basic knowledge of C#. All the code examples will be explained in C#.

In a similar vein, there are many books and articles that cover in depth the data access technologies that you will need to use this book. General knowledge of ADO.NET and XML, and a basic understanding of relational databases are assumed.

What This Book Covers

This book explores the array of ADO.NET 2.0 features and how they can be used in ASP.NET for developing web applications. Data access is a key component of .NET Framework and is present everywhere in the .NET Framework, from data source controls to data bound controls that consume data all the way from objects to relational data stores. In the first part of this book, you'll find in-depth coverage of the data source controls that enable data binding in the ASP.NET platform. Data source controls, data bound controls, and caching support built in to the data source controls are discussed with ASP.NET samples and reference information. Next, the book moves on to advanced features such as site navigation, implementing sorting and paging, and displaying and editing data in templates.

The final part of this book focuses on transactions in ADO.NET 2.0, advanced ADO.NET features for data display, and SQL Server 2005 XML features. You'll also find a couple of case studies on the use of data source and data bound controls in ASP.NET and XML features that provide you with a real-life example on how to leverage these features.

How This Book Is Structured

The book consists of 15 chapters, including two case studies. The book is structured to walk the reader through the process of XML development in ASP.NET 2.0. It takes a focused approach, teaching readers only what they need at each stage without using an excessive level of ancillary detail, overly complex technical jargon, or unnecessary digressions into detailed discussion of specifications and standards. A brief explanation of each of the chapters follows.

Chapter 1: Introduction to ASP.NET 2.0

This chapter gives the reader an overview of the new features of ASP.NET 2.0. It will highlight the new ASP.NET page architecture, new data controls, and code-sharing features. It also discusses the master pages and goes onto talk about how master pages and themes aid in creating consistent web sites. Later on, this chapter discusses the new security controls and web parts framework and illustrates how ASP.NET 2.0 enables 70% code reduction. Finally, this chapter will look at the new caching and administration and management functionalities of ASP.NET 2.0.

Chapter 2: Introduction to ADO.NET 2.0

This chapter describes the architecture of ADO.NET and the ADO.NET data providers. You will learn about ADO.NET basics such as opening a connection, executing a SQL statement or stored procedure, and retrieving the results of a query. Specifically, this chapter examines how to programmatically interact with relational databases using your data provider of choice. This chapter also discusses the role of connection objects, command objects, data readers, data adapters, and numerous types within the `System.Data` namespace (specifically, `DataSet`, `DataTable`, `DataRow`, `DataColumn`, `DataView`, and `DataRelation`).

Chapter 3: ASP.NET 2.0 Data Controls

ASP.NET offers server-side controls that provide various behaviors such as a drop-down list or a button. As part of this suite of controls, ASP.NET 2.0 offers two sets of controls that are specific to working with data. The first set is data source controls that allow a page to connect to a source of data and to read from and write to that source. However, a data source control has no means to display data on an ASP.NET 2.0 page, which is where data bound controls come into play. Data bound controls display data to the user by rendering data on a page. This chapter provides an introduction to the data source controls and the reading behaviors of data bound controls. The subsequent chapters in this book will build on the data controls foundation provided in this chapter.

Chapter 4: Data Binding with the SqlDataSource Control

This chapter focuses on the `SqlDataSource` control that provides a new layer of abstraction for accessing relational data. This chapter focuses on this control to easily and quickly bind data to data bound controls. This chapter also focuses on the advanced features of the `SqlDataSource` control such as handling events and exceptions with `SqlDataSource` control, renaming parameters sent to the command, programmatically adding a `SqlDataSource` at runtime, and so on.

Chapter 5: Data Binding with XML Data

This chapter builds on the previous chapter and starts discussing the `XmlDataSource` control that allows you to work with hierarchical XML data. This chapter will explore the application of the `XmlDataSource` control by looking at various examples that process XML data. This chapter demonstrates how the `XmlDataSource` control can be used to directly display the XML data using data bound controls or transform that XML data using an XSLT style sheet. In addition, this chapter will also describe the caching techniques that you can use to cache XML data using the `XmlDataSource` control.

Chapter 6: Data Binding with Objects

This chapter focuses on one of the most interesting and promising data source controls, the `ObjectDataSource` control, that complements the n-tier application design. This chapter discusses the use of the `ObjectDataSource` control in enabling you to bind the values returned by the middle-tier objects directly onto data bound controls such as `GridView`, `FormView`, `DetailsView`, and so on. Through examples, this chapter will take a detailed look at the features of the `ObjectDataSource` control such as passing parameters to a middle-tier method; handling events; performing insertions, updates, and deletions; invoking a web service; and so on.

Chapter 7: ASP.NET 2.0 Site Navigation

ASP.NET 2.0 tackles the nagging site navigation problem with the introduction of a navigation system that makes it quite trivial to manage how end users work through the web sites you create. This chapter focuses on the ASP.NET 2.0 navigation system that includes the capability to define your entire site in an XML file, which is called a site map. This chapter takes a look at all of these components in the new ASP.NET 2.0 navigation system by looking at both declarative and programmatic use of the site navigation system.

Chapter 8: Displaying and Editing Data Using Templates

This chapter takes a closer look at the `GridView`, `DetailsView`, and `FormView` controls and demonstrates how to fine-tune formatting with templates. In addition, this chapter also focuses on features such as display, selection, and editing of data using templates.

Chapter 9: GridView Sorting and Paging

This chapter focuses on the paging and sorting in the `GridView` control that represents the archetype of the advances in ASP.NET version 2.0. This chapter starts by discussing the basics of sorting and paging and then moves on to some embellishments that solve common real-world problems. Specifically, this chapter covers the sorting and paging features such as codeless scenarios, sorting using the middle-tier object, sorting using visual clues, customizing page templates, and using callbacks in conjunction with sorting and paging.

Chapter 10: Advanced Data Source and Data Bound Controls

This chapter shifts gears to focus on the advanced usage of data source controls and data bound controls for creating rich data-driven web applications. Specifically, this chapter discusses features such as generating master/detail display, displaying parent/child view in a single `GridView`, displaying selected rows in a `GridView`, retrieving and displaying images from the database, creating custom templates, performing two-way data binding and extending the `GridView` control.

Chapter 11: Transactions

Virtually all business applications require some level of transaction support. ADO.NET 2.0 provides excellent support for transaction processing through the transaction engine that enables you to easily create resource managers for any type of resource you want to participate in a transaction. This chapter starts by providing an overview of transactions and then goes onto discuss the transaction features of .NET 1.x and 2.0 versions.

Chapter 12: Case Study: Creating an Online Rental Reservation System Using N-Tier Architecture with ASP.NET 2.0 and SQL Server 2005

This case study focuses on incorporating all the features such as `XmlDataSource`, `SqlDataSource`, `ObjectDataSource`, `SiteMapDataSource`, XML data display, and XML support in SQL Server 2005, and so on, that you have learned from previous chapters. This case study will not only discuss the application of these features in a web site but also demonstrate the best practices of using these features.

Chapter 13: Advanced ADO.NET for ASP.NET Data Display

This chapter explores the advanced features of ADO.NET 2.0 and demonstrates how they can be utilized from an ASP.NET page, enabling you to create high-performance web sites. Specifically, this chapter discusses the ADO.NET 2.0 features such as MARS (Multiple Active Result Sets), asynchronous execution of commands, provider-independent data access code, serializing a `DataSet`, creating and working with strongly typed `DataSets`, and so on.

Chapter 14: Accessing Data from SQL Server 2005

This chapter discusses the new SQL Server 2005 features by focusing on the CLR integration and XML-specific features of SQL Server 2005. This chapter also looks into the new `XML` data type in SQL Server 2005 and shows how you can use that to build better architected applications. This chapter also showcases the steps involved in working with `XML` data-typed columns using ADO.NET.

Chapter 15: Case Study: Best Practices for Creating ASP.NET Web Sites

This case study puts together all the lessons in this book to create a scalable n-tier web site showcasing the wide range of ADO.NET and ASP.NET features. This chapter also shows the use of enterprise library application blocks supplied with Enterprise Library 2.0 for plumbing functionalities such as exception management, data access, and configuration management. In addition, this chapter also leverages the generics collection object as a data transport mechanism to transfer data between different layers of the n-tier web site.

What You Need to Use This Book

All of the examples in this book are ASP.NET samples. The key requirements for running these applications are the .NET Framework 2.0 and Microsoft Visual Studio 2005. You also need to have SQL Server

2005 server along with the AdventureWorks sample database installed to make most of the samples work, and a few examples make use of SQL Server 2005 Express database.

The SQL Server examples in this book utilize integrated security to connect to the SQL Server database, so remember to enable integrated authentication in your SQL Server. This will also require you to turn on integrated Windows authentication (as well as impersonation, depending on your configuration) in ASP.NET web sites.

Conventions

To help you get the most from the text and keep track of what's happening, a number of conventions have been used throughout the book.

> **Boxes like this one hold important, not-to-be forgotten information that is directly relevant to the surrounding text.**

Tips, hints, tricks, and asides to the current discussion are offset and placed in italics like this.

As for styles in the text:

- New terms and important words are *italicized* when they are introduced.
- Keyboard strokes are shown like this: Ctrl+A.

Code is presented in the following format:

```
In code examples new and important code is highlighted with a gray background.
```

Source Code

As you work through the examples in this book, you may choose either to type in all the code manually or to use the source code files that accompany the book. All of the source code used in this book is available for downloading at `www.wrox.com`. Once at the site, simply locate the book's title (either by using the Search box or by using one of the title lists) and click the Download Code link on the book's detail page to obtain all the source code for the book.

Because many books have similar titles, you may find it easiest to search by ISBN; this book's ISBN is 0-470-04179-x (changing to 978-0-4700-4179-6 as the new industry-wide 13-digit ISBN numbering system is phased in by January 2007).

Once you download the code, just decompress it with your favorite compression tool. Alternately, you can go to the main Wrox code download page at `www.wrox.com/dynamic/books/download.aspx` to see the code available for this book and all other Wrox books.

Errata

Every effort is made to ensure that there are no errors in the text or in the code. However, no one is perfect, and mistakes do occur. If you find an error in one of our books, such as a spelling mistake or faulty piece of code, we would be very grateful for your feedback. By sending in errata, you may save another reader hours of frustration and at the same time you will be helping us provide even higher-quality information.

To find the errata page for this book, go to `www.wrox.com` and locate the title using the Search box or one of the title lists. Then, on the book details page, click the Book Errata link. On this page, you can view all errata that has been submitted for this book and posted by Wrox editors. A complete book list, including links to each book's errata, is also available at `www.wrox.com/misc-pages/booklist.shtml`.

If you don't spot "your" error on the Book Errata page, go to `www.wrox.com/contact/techsupport.shtml` and complete the form there to send us the error you have found. We'll check the information and, if appropriate, post a message to the book's errata page and fix the problem in subsequent editions of the book.

p2p.wrox.com

For author and peer discussion, join the P2P forums at `http://p2p.wrox.com`. The forums are a web-based system for you to post messages relating to Wrox books and related technologies and interact with other readers and technology users. The forums offer a subscription feature to email you topics of interest of your choosing when new posts are made to the forums. Wrox authors, editors, other industry experts, and your fellow readers are present on these forums.

At `http://p2p.wrox.com` you will find a number of different forums that will help you not only as you read this book but also as you develop your own applications. To join the forums, just follow these steps:

1. Go to `http://p2p.wrox.com` and click the Register link.
2. Read the terms of use and click Agree.
3. Complete the required information to join as well as any optional information you wish to provide and click Submit.
4. You will receive an email with information describing how to verify your account and complete the joining process.

You can read messages in the forums without joining P2P but in order to post your own messages, you must join.

Once you join, you can post new messages and respond to messages other users post. You can read messages at any time on the web. If you would like to have new messages from a particular forum emailed to you, click the Subscribe to this Forum icon by the forum name in the forum listing.

For more information about how to use the Wrox P2P, be sure to read the P2P FAQs for answers to questions about how the forum software works as well as many common questions specific to P2P and Wrox books. To read the FAQs, click the FAQ link on any P2P page.

Part I
Introduction

1

Introduction to ASP.NET 2.0

With the release of ASP.NET 1.0, Microsoft revolutionized web application development by providing a rich set of features aimed at increasing the productivity of developers. Now with ASP.NET 2.0, Microsoft has raised the bar to a much higher level by providing excellent out-of-the-box features that are not only geared toward increasing the productivity of developers but also toward simplifying the administration and management of ASP.NET 2.0 applications. These new features, combined with the increased speed and performance of ASP.NET 2.0, arm developers with a powerful platform that can make a significant impact on the way web applications are developed, deployed, and maintained.

This chapter takes a quick tour of the new ASP.NET 2.0 features. Specifically, this chapter will discuss the features of this new, improved platform that will help you in designing, developing, and deploying enterprise-class web applications.

ASP.NET 2.0 Features

If you have worked with ASP.NET 1.x versions, you will undoubtedly agree that it was a great product that provided huge improvements in the way web applications were designed and deployed. If ASP.NET 1.x was a great product, then what's wrong with it? Well, nothing, actually, but when developing software, there is always a trade-off between how much can be done, how many resources you have, and how much time you have to do it. There is an almost never-ending supply of features you can add, but at some stage you have to ship the product. You cannot doubt that ASP.NET 1.0 shipped with an impressive array of features, but the ASP.NET team members are ambitious, and they not only had plans of their own but also listened to their users. ASP.NET 2.0 addresses the areas that both the development team and users wanted to improve. The aims of the new version are:

- **Reduce the number of lines of code required by 70%:** The declarative programming model freed developers from having to write reams of code, but there are still many scenarios where this cannot be avoided. Data access is a great example, where the same Connection, `DataAdapter/DataSet`, and `Command/DataReader` code is used regularly.

- **Increase developer productivity:** This partly relates to reducing the amount of code required, but is also affected by more server controls encompassing complex functionality, as well as providing better solutions for common web site scenarios (such as portals and personalized sites).
- **Provide the fastest web server platform:** Although ASP.NET 1.x offered a fast server platform, ASP.NET 2.0 will improve areas such as application start-up times and provide better application tracing and performance data. Innovative caching features will enhance application performance, especially when SQL Server is used.
- **Support for mobile development:** In ASP.NET 1.0, the Microsoft Mobile Internet Toolkit (MMIT in version 1.0 and ASP.NET Mobile Controls in version 1.1) provided this support, including separate controls for building web pages suitable for small screen browsers. In ASP.NET 2.0, the MMIT is no longer required because mobile support is built into all controls. This reduces the amount of code required, as well as the need for specialist knowledge about mobile platforms.
- **Provide the best hosting solution:** With the large number of Internet applications being hosted, it's important to provide better solutions for hosters. For example, better management features to identify and stop rogue applications will give hosters more control over their current environment. More control can also be given to hosted companies by use of the new web-based administration tool, allowing users to easily control the configuration of applications remotely.
- **Provide easier and more sophisticated management features:** Administration of ASP.NET applications under version 1.x required manual editing of the XML configuration file, which is not a great solution for administrators. Version 2.0 brings a graphical user interface–based administration tool that is integrated with the Internet Information Services (IIS) administration tool.
- **Easy implementation of entire scenarios:** The better management features are built on top of a management application programming interface (API), allowing custom administration programs to be created. Along with application packaging, this will provide support for easily deployable applications, with or without source.

Even from this broad set of aims, you can see that ASP.NET 2.0 is a great advance from 1.x for both developers and administrators. For the purposes of this chapter, the features of ASP.NET 2.0 based on the following three core themes are examined:

- Developer productivity
- Administration and management
- Speed and performance

Note that this chapter isn't an in-depth look at any specific feature — instead it gives you a taste of what's to come so that you can see how much easier web development is going to be.

Developer Productivity

One of the goals of ASP.NET 2.0 is to enable developers to easily and quickly build feature-rich web applications. To accomplish this, Microsoft looked at the existing ASP.NET 1.x applications to identify the common features, patterns, and code that developers build over and over today. Once they identified those features, they componentized those features and included them as built-in functionality of ASP.NET. With ASP.NET 2.0, the ASP.NET team has a goal of reducing the number of lines of code required for an application by a whopping 70%. To this end, Microsoft has introduced a collective arsenal of new features that are now available to developers in ASP.NET 2.0.

Using these features, you can spend your time building richer, more fully featured applications by leveraging the new controls and infrastructure services built into the core platform, as opposed to writing a lot of infrastructure code as is the case with ASP.NET 1.x. For example, ASP.NET 2.0 now includes built-in support for membership (username/password credential storage) and role management services out of the box. The new personalization service provides for quick storage/retrieval of user settings and preferences, enabling rich customization with minimal code. With ASP.NET 2.0, Microsoft has introduced a new concept known as master pages that now enable flexible page user interface (UI) inheritance across sites. The new site navigation system enables developers to quickly build link structures consistently across a site. Site counters enable rich logging and instrumentation of client browser access patterns. Themes enable flexible UI skinning of controls and pages. And the new ASP.NET Web Part Framework enables rich portal-style layout and end user customization features that would require tens of thousands of lines of code to write today. Along with all these features, ASP.NET 2.0 also brings with it 45 new server controls that enable powerful declarative support for data access, login security, wizard navigation, image generation, menus, treeviews, portals, and more. The next few sections will provide you with a glimpse of these features.

Master Pages

ASP.NET 2.0 introduces a new concept known as master pages, in which a common base master file contains the common look and feel and standard behavior for all the pages in your application. Once the common content is placed in the master page, the content pages (child pages) can inherit content from the master pages apart from adding their content to the final output. To allow the content page to add its own content, you add placeholders (known as `ContentPlaceHolder` control) in the master page that will be utilized by the content pages to add their custom content. When users request the content pages, the output of the content pages are merged with the output of the master page, resulting in an output that combines the layout of the master page with the output of the content page.

In ASP.NET 1.x, you could achieve similar effects by creating user controls that abstract the common look and behavior of all the pages in the application and then declaring the user control in each and every page. Even though this approach was useful, it required a lot of cutting and pasting of code across all the pages in a web application. Master pages take this approach of reusable user controls to the next level by providing a much cleaner approach to reusing a common look and feel across all the pages.

Master pages are saved with the file extension `.master`. Apart from containing all the contents that are required for defining the standard look and feel of the application, the master pages also contain all the top-level HTML elements for a page, such as `<html>`, `<head>`, and `<form>`. As mentioned previously, the master pages also contain one or more content placeholders that are used to define regions that will be rendered through the content pages.

Now that you have had a general understanding of master pages, take a look at an example. First, create a master page named `CommonPage.master` and add the code shown in Listing 1-1.

Listing 1-1: A Master Page Example

```
<%@ master language="C#" %>
<html>
<head runat="server">
```

(continued)

Listing 1-1: *(continued)*

```
    <title>Master Page</title>
  </head>
  <body>
    <form runat="server">
      Master Page Content
      <br/>
      <b>
        <asp:ContentPlaceHolder id="MiddleContent" runat="server">
        </asp:ContentPlaceHolder>
      </b>
    </form>
  </body>
  </html>
```

Apart from looking at the file extension, you can also identify a master file by looking at the new page directive named `master` at the top of the page. This declarative is used to identify that the current page is a master page and prevents users from requesting the page from a browser. Inside the code, the code contains an element named `asp:ContentPlaceHolder`, which will be used by all the content pages to render appropriate content that is specific to their pages. That's all there is to creating the master page. To create a content page, add a new ASP.NET page named `ContentPage.aspx` and modify the code as follows:

```
<%@ page language="c#" MasterPageFile="~/CommonPage.master" %>
<asp:Content id="Content1" ContentPlaceHolderID="MiddleContent"
  runat="server">
  Child Page Content
</asp:Content>
```

The code required for the content page is very simple and straightforward. As part of the `page` directive, specify a new attribute named `MasterPageFile` that is used to identify the name of the master page that you want to utilize. This example uses the master page created in Listing 1-1. Next, you have a new element named `asp:Content` that is used to associate the `asp:ContentPlaceHolder` element in the master page with the content page. This is done through the use of the `ContentPlaceHolderID` attribute. That's all that is there to creating a master page and using the master page from a content page. Now, if you request the content page from a browser, you will get the output that is produced by merging the master page with the content page.

New Code-Behind Model in ASP.NET 2.0

ASP.NET 1.x supports two coding models: the inline model, in which markup and code coexist in the same ASPX file, and the code-behind model, which places markup in ASPX files and code in source code files. ASP.NET 2.0 introduces a third model: a new form of code-behind that relies on the new partial classes support in the Visual C# and Visual Basic compilers. Code-behind in ASP.NET 2.0 fixes a nagging problem with version 1.x: the requirement that code-behind classes contain protected fields whose types and names map to controls declared in the ASPX file.

The following code listing shows the `.aspx` file named `HelloWorld.aspx`:

```
<%@ Page Language="C#" CodeFile="HelloWorld.aspx.cs" Inherits="HelloWorld" %>
<html>
<body>
```

```
  <form id="form1" runat="server">
    <asp:TextBox ID="TextBox1" runat="server"></asp:TextBox>
    <asp:Button ID="Button1" runat="server" OnClick="Button1_Click" Text="Button"/>
    <asp:Label ID="Label1" runat="server"></asp:Label>
  </form>
</body>
</html>
```

The code-behind file referenced by `HelloWorld.aspx` file is `HelloWorld.aspx.cs`, which is defined as follows:

```
using System;
using System.Web.UI;
using System.Web.UI.WebControls;
public partial class HelloWorld : System.Web.UI.Page
{
  protected void Button1_Click(object sender, EventArgs e)
  {
    Label1.Text = TextBox1.Text;
  }
}
```

As you can see, `HelloWorld.aspx` contains the markup and `HelloWorld.aspx.cs` contains the code. The `Inherits` attribute in the `@Page` directive identifies the code-behind class, while the `CodeFile` attribute identifies the file containing the class. Note the absence of any fields in the `HelloWorld` class providing mappings to controls in the ASPX file. Old-style code-behind is still supported, but this new model is now the preferred one. Not surprisingly, Visual Studio 2005 supports the new model natively.

Creating and Sharing Reusable Components in ASP.NET 2.0

Prior to ASP.NET 2.0, if you were to reference a reusable component from your ASP.NET application, you had to compile the assembly and place it in the bin folder (or place it in the GAC) of the web application. But now with ASP.NET 2.0, creating a reusable component is very simple and straightforward. All you need to do is create the component in a predefined subdirectory called `App_Code`. Any component placed in this directory will be automatically compiled at runtime into a single assembly. This assembly is automatically referenced and will be available to all the pages in the site. Note that you should only put components in the `App_Code` subdirectory.

New ASP.NET 2.0 Controls

ASP.NET 2.0 introduces several new controls that help create data-driven web applications. These controls perform actions, such as connecting to a database, executing commands against the database, and so on, without you even having to write a single line of code. ASP.NET 2.0 introduces more than 40 new control types to help you build rich web UIs while insulating you from the vagaries of HTML, client-side script, and browser DOMs. The following table lists the new control types.

Control Category	Controls
Data source controls	`SqlDataSource`, `ObjectDataSource`, `XmlDataSource`, `AccessDataSource`, `SiteMapDataSource`
Data-bound controls	`GridView`, `DetailsView`, `FormView`, `TreeView`, `Menu`

Table continued on following page

Control Category	Controls
Login controls	`Login`, `LoginName`, `LoginStatus`, `LoginView`, `CreateUser Wizard`, `ChangePassword`, `PasswordRecovery`
Navigation controls	`Menu`, `TreeView`, `SiteMapPath`
Web Parts controls	`WebPartManager`, `WebPartZone`, `CatalogZone`, `EditorZone`, `ConnectionsZone`, `DeclarativeCatalogPart`, `PageCatalog-Part`, `ImportCatalogPart`, `AppearanceEditorPart`, `Behavior EditorPart`, `LayoutEditorPart`, `PropertyGridEditorPart`
Other controls	`BulletedList`, `FileUpload`, `HiddenField`, `ImageMap`, `Wizard`, `WizardStep`, `MultiView`, `View`, `Substitution`, `Content`, `ContentPlaceHolder`

To start with, the next section will explore the new data source controls supplied with ASP.NET 2.0.

Data Controls

As mentioned previously, one of the important goals of ASP.NET 2.0 is 70% code reduction. The data controls supplied with ASP.NET 2.0 play an important role in making this ambitious goal a reality. Data source controls provide a consistent and extensible method for declaratively accessing data from web pages. Data source controls supplied with ASP.NET 2.0 are as follows:

- `<asp:SqlDataSource>`: This data source control is designed to work with SQL Server, OLE DB, Open DataBase Connectivity (ODBC), and Oracle databases. Using this control, you can also select, update, delete, and insert data using SQL commands.
- `<asp:ObjectDataSource>`: N-tier methodology allows you to create web applications that are not only scalable but also easier to maintain. N-tier principle also enables clean separation, thereby allowing you to easily add new functionalities. In an n-tier application, the middle-tier objects may return complex objects that you have to process in your ASP.NET presentation layer. Keeping this requirement in mind, Microsoft has created this new control that allows you to seamlessly integrate the data returned from the middle-layer objects with the ASP.NET presentation layer.
- `<asp:AccessDataSource>`: This is very similar to the `SqlDataSource` control, except for the difference that it is designed to work with Access databases.
- `<asp:XmlDataSource>`: Allows you to bind to XML data, which can come from a variety of sources, such as an external XML file, a `DataSet` object, and so on. Once the XML data is bound to the `XmlDataSource` control, this control can then act as a source of data for data-bound controls such as `TreeView` and `Menu`.
- `<asp:SiteMapDataSource>`: Provides a site navigation framework that makes the creation of a site navigation system a breezy experience. Accomplishing this requires the use of a new XML file named `web.sitemap` that lays out the pages of the site in a hierarchical XML structure. Once you have the site hierarchy in the `web.sitemap` file, you can then data-bind the `SiteMap DataSource` control with the `web.sitemap` file. Then the contents of the `SiteMapDataSource` control can be bound to data-aware controls such as `TreeView`, `Menu`, and so on.

Now that you have had a look at the data source controls supplied with ASP.NET 2.0, this section will examine the data-bound controls that you will normally use to display data that is contained in the data source controls. These data-bound controls bind data automatically.

One of the neat things about data-bound controls is that the development environment automatically guides developers through the process of binding a data control to a data source. Developers are prompted to select the particular data source to use for selecting, inserting, updating, and deleting data. The feature that walks the developers through this process is called Smart Tasks. This is explained in detail in the "Visual Studio 2005 Improvements" section later in this chapter.

The `DataGrid` is one of the most popular data-bound controls in ASP.NET, but in some ways it is a victim of its own success: It is so rich in functionality that it leaves ASP.NET developers wanting even more. The `DataGrid` control does not change much in ASP.NET 2.0, but the new `GridView` control offers features commonly requested in `DataGrid` and adds a few surprises of its own. In addition, new controls named `DetailsView` and `FormView` simplify the building of master-detail views and web-editable user interfaces. The new data-bound controls introduced in ASP .NET 2.0 are:

- `<asp:GridView>`: This control is the successor to the `DataGrid` control that was part of ASP.NET 1.x, and is used to display multiple records in a web page. However, the `GridView` also enables you to add, update, and delete a record in a database without writing a single line of code. Similarly to the `DataGrid` control, in a `GridView` control each column represents a field, while each row represents a record. As you would expect, you can bind a `GridView` control to a `SqlDataSource` control, as well as to any data source control as long as that control implements the `System.Collections.IEnumerable` interface.
- `<asp:DetailsView>`: Can be used in conjunction with the `GridView` control to display a specific record in the data source.
- `<asp:FormView>`: Provides a user interface to display and modify the data stored in a database. The `FormView` control provides different templates, such as `ItemTemplate` and `EditItemTemplate`, that you can use to view and modify the database records.
- `<asp:TreeView>`: Provides a seamless way to consume information from hierarchical data sources, such as an XML file, and then display that information. You can use the `TreeView` control to display information from a wide variety of data sources, such as an XML file, a sitemap file, a string, or a database.
- `<asp:Menu>`: Like the `TreeView` control, the `Menu` control can be used to display hierarchical data. You can use the `Menu` control to display static data, sitemap data, and database data. The main difference between the two controls is their appearance.

Listing 1-2 shows you an example of how to use the combination of `SqlDataSource` and `GridView` controls to retrieve and display data from the ProductCategory table in the AdventureWorks database without even having a single line of code.

Listing 1-2: Using the SqlDataSource Control to Retrieve Categories Information

```
<%@ page language="C#" %>
<html>
<head id="Head1" runat="server">
  <title>Data Binding using SqlDataSource control</title>
</head>
```

(continued)

Listing 1-2: *(continued)*

```
<body>
  <form id="Form1" runat="server">
    <asp:SqlDataSource id="categorySource" runat="server"
      ConnectionString="server=localhost;database=AdventureWorks;uid=user;pwd=word"
      SelectCommand="SELECT * From Production.ProductCategory">
    </asp:SqlDataSource>
    <asp:GridView DataSourceID="categorySource" runat="server" id="gridCategories">
    </asp:GridView>
  </form>
</body>
</html>
```

The code declares a `SqlDataSource` control and a `GridView` control. The `SqlDataSource` control declaration also specifies the connection string and the SQL statement to be executed as attributes. The `DataSourceID` attribute in the `GridView` is the one that links the `SqlDataSource` control to the `GridView` control. That's all there is to retrieving the data from the database and displaying it in a web page. Figure 1-1 shows the output produced by the page when requested from the browser.

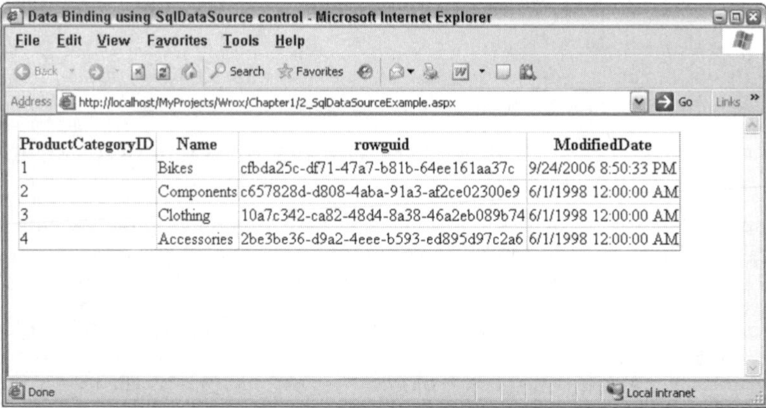

Figure 1-1

Security Controls

With the large amount of business being done on the web, security is vitally important for protecting not only confidential information such as credit card numbers, but also users' personal details and preferences. Thus, most of the web applications require the capability to authenticate users on their web sites. Although this was easy to do in ASP.NET 1.x, you still had to write code. With ASP.NET 2.0, things have changed for the better. For security-related functionalities, ASP.NET 2.0 introduces a wide range of new controls:

- `<asp:Login>`: Provides a standard login capability that allows the users to enter their credentials
- `<asp:LoginName>`: Allows you to display the name of the logged-in user
- `<asp:LoginStatus>`: Displays whether the user is authenticated or not

- `<asp:LoginView>`: Provides various login views depending on the selected template
- `<asp:PasswordRecovery>`: Provides the web site administrators with the capability to email the users their lost password

The login controls described here abstract most of the common tasks for which developers have to manually write code for a secured web site. Although this could be achieved in ASP.NET 1.x, you still had to add controls manually and write code. Apart from providing the user interface, ASP.NET 2.0 also provides the capability to retrieve and validate user information using Membership functionality. To this end, ASP.NET ships with a new Membership API, the aim of which is to abstract the required membership functionality from the storage of the member information.

Other New Controls

In addition to the new controls, ASP.NET 2.0 also provides numerous enhancements to existing controls that make these controls more versatile than ever before in building component-based web pages. For example, the `Panel` control now has a `DefaultButton` property that specifies which button should be clicked if the user presses the Enter key while the panel has the focus.

There is also a new `Wizard` control, which simplifies the task of building web UIs that step users through sequential operations. Individual steps are defined by `WizardStep` controls. The `Wizard` control serves as a container for `WizardStep` and provides a default interface for stepping backward and forward. It is also capable of displaying a list of steps, enabling users to randomly navigate between them, and it fires events that can be used to programmatically control step ordering. A simple `Wizard` control declaration is:

```
<asp:Wizard ID="Wizard1" runat="server">
  <WizardSteps>
    <asp:WizardStep ID="WizardStep1" runat="server" Title="Step 1">
      Wizard Step 1
    </asp:WizardStep>
    <asp:WizardStep ID="WizardStep2" runat="server" Title="Step 2"
      StepType="Complete">
      Wizard Step 2
    </asp:WizardStep>
  </WizardSteps>
</asp:Wizard>
```

Another interesting and potentially very useful control debuting in ASP.NET 2.0 is the `MultiView` control. Paired with `View` controls, `MultiView` controls can be used to create pages containing multiple logical views. Only one view (the one whose index is assigned to the `MultiView` control's `ActiveViewIndex` property) is displayed at a time, but you can switch views by changing the active view index.

Validation Groups

In ASP.NET 1.x, you would assign validation controls to input controls such as text boxes, password fields, radio buttons, and check boxes, and the validation controls would automatically validate the data entered by an end user to input controls. With ASP.NET 2.0, Microsoft introduces a new feature known as validation groups, which enables you to create different groups of validation controls and assign them to input controls, such as text boxes. You can assign a validation group to a collection of input controls if you want to validate the collection of input controls on the same criteria. For example, you can assign the button control to a group of input controls and validate the data entered to each group of input controls on a criterion. This feature is very handy when you have multiple forms on a single web page. For example, you can create a web page that contains login and password text boxes for registered end users, and another set of controls for new end users to register with the web site. In this case, you can use the validation group property to perform different actions, such as logging on to the web site and registering an end user.

Themes

One of the neat features of ASP.NET 2.0 is *themes*, which enable you to define the appearance of a set of controls once and apply the appearance to your entire web application. For example, you can utilize themes to define a common appearance for all of the `CheckBox` controls in your application, such as the background and foreground color, in one central location. By leveraging themes, you can easily create and maintain a consistent look throughout your web site. Themes are extremely flexible in that they can be applied to an entire web application, to a page, or to an individual control. Theme files are stored with the extension `.skin`, and all the themes for a web application are stored in the special folder named `App_Themes`.

> **As you read this, you might be wondering if themes are another variation of CSS stylesheets. Themes are not the same thing as Cascading Style Sheets. Using Cascading Style Sheets, you can control the appearance of HTML tags on the browser. Whereas themes are applied on the server and they apply to the properties of ASP.NET controls. Another difference is that themes can also include external files, such as images and so on.**

The implementation of themes in ASP.NET 2.0 is built around two areas: skins and themes. A *skin* is a set of properties and templates that can be applied to controls. A *theme* is a set of skins and any other associated files (such as images or stylesheets). Skins are control-specific, so for a given theme there could be a separate skin for each control within that theme. Any controls without a skin inherit the default look. There are two types of themes:

- **Customization themes:** These types of themes are applied after the properties of the control are applied, meaning that the properties of the themes override the properties of the control itself.
- **Stylesheet themes:** You can apply this type of theme to a page in exactly the same manner as a customization theme. However, stylesheet themes don't override control properties, thus allowing the control to use the theme properties or override them.

Characteristics of ASP.NET 2.0 Themes

Some of the important characteristics of ASP.NET 2.0 themes are:

- Themes make it simple to customize the appearance of a site or page using the same design tools and methods used when developing the page itself, thus obviating the need to learn any special tools or techniques to add and apply themes to a site.
- As mentioned previously, you can apply themes to controls, pages, and even entire sites. You can leverage this feature to customize parts of a web site while retaining the identity of the other parts of the site.
- Themes allow all visual properties to be customized, thus ensuring that when themed, pages and controls can achieve a consistent style.

- Customization themes override control definitions, thus changing the look and feel of controls. Customization themes are applied with the `Theme` attribute of the `Page` directive.
- Stylesheet themes don't override control definitions, thus allowing the control to use the theme properties or override them. Stylesheet themes are applied with the `StylesheetTheme` attribute of the `Page` directive.

Now that you have an understanding of the concepts behind themes, the next section provides you with a quick example of creating a theme and utilizing it from an ASP.NET page.

Creating a Simple Theme

To create a theme and apply it to a specific page, go through the following steps:

1. Create a folder called `ControlThemes` under the `App_Themes` folder.
2. Create a file with the extension `.skin` and add all the controls (that you want to use in a page) and their style properties. Or you can also create individual skin files for each and every control. When you are defining skin files, remember to remove the `ID` attribute from all of the controls' declarations. For example, you can use the following code to define the theme for a `Button` control:

```
<asp:Button runat="server" BackColor="Black" ForeColor="White"
  Font-Name="Arial" Font-Size="10px" />
```

3. Name the skin file `Button.skin` and place it under the `ControlThemes` folder. Once you have created the `.skin` file, you can then apply that theme to all the pages in your application by using appropriate settings in the `Web.config` file. To apply the theme to a specific page, all you need to do is to add the `Theme` attribute to the `Page` directive as shown below:

```
<%@Page Theme="ControlThemes" %>
```

That's all there is to creating a theme and utilizing it in an ASP.NET page. It is also possible for you to programmatically access the theme associated with a specific page using the `Page.Theme` property. Similarly, you can also set the `SkinID` property of any of the controls to specify the skin. If the theme does not contain a `SkinID` value for the control type, then no error is thrown and the control simply defaults to its own properties. For dynamic controls, it is possible to set the `SkinID` property after they are created.

Web Parts Framework

There are many times when you would want to allow the users of your web site to be able to customize the content by selecting, removing, and rearranging the contents in the web page. Traditionally, implementing this capability required a lot of custom code, or you had to depend on third-party products to accomplish this. To address this shortcoming, ASP.NET 2.0 ships with a Web Parts Framework that provides the infrastructure and the building blocks required for creating modular web pages that can be easily customized by the users. You can use Web Parts to create portal pages that aggregate different types of content, such as static text, links, and content that can change at runtime. It is also possible for the users to change the layout of the Web Parts by dragging and dropping them from one place to another, providing a rich user experience.

> **Web Parts are reusable pieces of code that allow you to logically group related functionality together into one unit. Once the Web Parts are added to an ASP.NET page, they can then be shown, hidden, moved around, and redesigned, all by the user.**

By taking advantage of Web Parts, you, as a developer, can empower your users with the ability to perform the following operations.

- Users can personalize page content.
- Users can personalize the page layout by allowing the users to drag Web Parts from one zone to another zone, or change its appearance, look and feel, and so on.
- Users can also export and import Web Part controls so the Web Parts can be effectively shared among other sites.
- Users can create connections between two Web Parts by establishing communication between Web Part controls.

As a developer, you will typically work with Web Parts in one of the three ways: creating pages that use Web Parts controls, creating individual Web Parts controls, or creating complete personalizable web portals. You can create two kinds of Web Parts in ASP.NET 2.0:

- **Custom Web Part:** Those Web Part controls that derive from the `System.Web.UI.WebControls.WebParts.WebPart` class.
- **Generic Web Part:** A custom control that does not inherit from the `WebPart` class and is still used as a Web Part is called `GenericWebPart`. For example, if you place a `TextBox` control inside a `WebPartZone` control (a zone on the page that hosts the Web Parts control), the `TextBox` control will be wrapped to a `GenericWebPart` class.

This section provides you with a simple generic Web Part creation example followed by a code examination. Listing 1-3 shows the code required to implement the Web Part.

Listing 1-3: Creating a Simple Generic Web Part

```
<%@ Page Language="C#" %>
<html xmlns="http://www.w3.org/1999/xhtml" >
<head runat="server">
  <title>Example of a GenericWebPart</title>
</head>
<body>
<form id="form1" runat="server">
  <asp:WebPartManager id="WebPartManager1" runat="Server">
  </asp:WebPartManager>
  <table cellspacing="0" cellpadding="0" border="0">
    <tr>
      <td valign="top">
        <asp:WebPartZone id="MainZone" runat="server"
          headertext="Main">
          <ZoneTemplate>
            <asp:Label id="contentPart" runat="server"
              title="GenericWebPart">
              <h4>GenericWebPart that uses a label control
                to generate the contents of the Web Part
               </h4>
            </asp:Label>
          </ZoneTemplate>
        </asp:WebPartZone>
      </td>
```

```
      </tr>
    </table>
  </form>
  </body>
  </html>
```

To start with, you declare a `WebPartManager` control. The `WebPartManager` control is a must for any ASP.NET page that utilizes Web Parts. This control must be the first element in an ASP.NET web form, above all other Web Parts, zones, or any other custom or specialized Web Part controls. The `WebPartManager` has no visual element associated with it; however, it is crucial because of the required plumbing it provides for managing the interactions between Web Parts. Then the code declares a `WebPartZone` control, which in turn includes a `Label` control that consists of all the HTML elements that make up the display of the Web Part. The `WebPartZone` control is the one that provides overall layout for the Web Part controls that compose the main UI of a page. Before navigating to the page using the browser, enable Windows Authentication for the web site through IIS Manager and ensure that SQL Server 2005 Express is installed with Windows authentication enabled. Now run the page, and you will see the output shown in Figure 1-2.

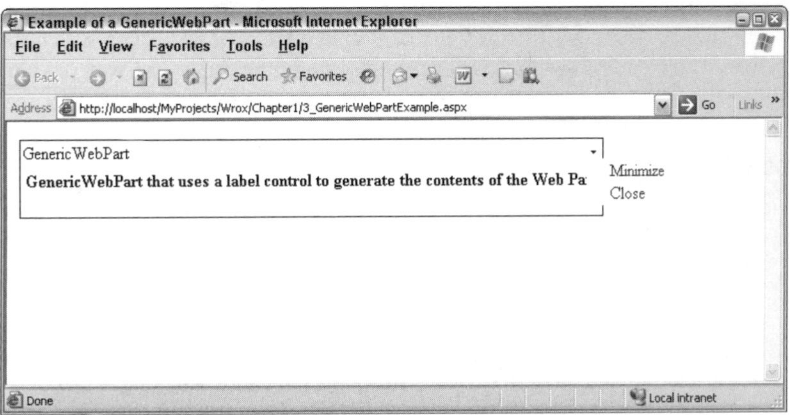

Figure 1-2

In Figure 1-2, you can choose to minimize or close the Web Part by clicking on the corresponding links.

Personalization Framework

There are times when you want to store and present information that is unique to a specific user. For instance, when a user visits your site, you can collect information from the user about his preferences, such as color scheme, styles, and so forth. Once you have that information, you can use it to present the user with a personalized version of your web application. To implement this with ASP.NET 1.x, you had to go through the following steps.

1. Store user information with a unique user identifier, used to identify the user when he visits again.
2. Fetch the user information as needed.
3. Finally, present the user with the personalized content.

Now with the introduction of ASP.NET 2.0 personalization, all of the above complexities are handled by the personalization framework itself. In ASP.NET personalization, information about a specific user is stored in a persistent format. Also, ASP.NET personalization allows you to easily manage user information without requiring you to create and maintain your own database. In addition, the personalization system makes the user information available using a consistent, easy-to-use, strongly typed API that you can access from anywhere in your application. You can also store objects of any type in the personalization system, including user information, user preferences, or business information. The personalization system uses a generic storage system for storing the data and makes that data available to the users in a type-safe manner. By default, ASP.NET 2.0 uses SQL Server as the storage mechanism.

Visual Studio 2005 Improvements

Visual Studio 2005 is the best development tool for building data-driven web applications. As part of the Visual Studio 2005 suite of tools, Microsoft is introducing a new tool called Visual Web Developer (VWD) that is designed to work with the current and next generation of ASP.NET. VWD provides powerful new features for the web developer. VWD is also tuned to the specific needs of the web developer through a new web profile that exposes a menu and window layout optimized for web development. The environment includes a best-of-breed HTML source editor, an improved visual page designer, better IntelliSense support, a new project system, better support for working with data, and full XHTML standards support. Collectively, these features enable you to develop data-driven web applications faster than ever before. The next few sections will explore some of the important web development improvements coming with VWD.

Better Source Code Editing

VWD provides an improved HTML source editor that enables you to write and modify your pages faster. The source editor provides full IntelliSense throughout your files and has new features for navigating and validating your markup.

> **If you are not aware what IntelliSense is, it is the pop-up code hints that automatically appear when you type in the development environment.**

Although Visual Studio.NET provides excellent IntelliSense support, it gets even better with Visual Studio 2005. In Visual Studio 2005, IntelliSense pops up everywhere. For example, you can take full advantage of IntelliSense within the script blocks, `Page` directives, inline CSS style attributes, and `Web.config`, as well as in any generic XML file that contains a DTD or XML Schema reference.

HTML Source Preservation

Visual Studio 2005 preserves the formatting of your HTML markup, including all white space, casing, indention, carriage returns, and word wrapping. The formatting is preserved exactly, even when switching back and forth between the Design View and Source View of the page. This is one of the important features that developers have been clamoring for in the previous versions of Visual Studio.

Tag Navigator

Visual Studio 2005 comes with a new Tag Navigator feature that enables developers to easily track their location in a HTML document, thereby providing excellent navigation support. The Tag Navigator displays the current path within the source of an HTML page by displaying a list of all the HTML tags that contain the tag where your cursor is currently located. Clicking on any of the nodes enables developers to optionally change the source level selection, and quickly move up and down a deep HTML hierarchy. This feature can be very handy, especially when you are editing multiple nested HTML elements. For example, when you are editing multiple nested HTML tables, it is very easy to get lost, and you can leverage Tag Navigator to easily identify the current path within the hierarchy of table elements.

Targeting Specific Browsers and HTML Validation

Using Visual Studio 2005, you can easily target a specific HTML standard or browser when writing your HTML pages. For example, you can target your HTML pages to work with a particular browser, such as Internet Explorer 5.0 or Netscape Navigator 4.0. Alternatively, you can target a particular HTML standard, such as XHTML 1.0 Strict or XHTML 1.0 Transitional. As you type your HTML in the source editor, it will be automatically validated in real time. Invalid HTML will automatically be underlined with a red squiggly line, and all the validation errors are also summarized in real time within the Task List window.

Code Refactoring

Code Refactoring allows you to change the code structure without changing or affecting what the code itself actually does. For example, changing a variable name or packaging a few lines of code into a method are part of Code Refactoring. The main difference between Code Refactoring and a mere edit or find-and-replace is that you can harness the intelligence of the compiler to distinguish between code and comments, and so on. Code Refactoring is supported everywhere that you can write code, including both code-behind and single-file ASP.NET pages.

Smart Tasks

Smart tasks are a new feature that displays a pop-up list of common tasks that you can perform on an ASP.NET control. For example, when you add a `GridView` control to a page, a common task list appears, which allows you to quickly enable sorting, paging, or editing for the `GridView`. Visual Studio 2005 enables you to perform many of the most common programming tasks directly from the designer surface. When you drag new controls onto the designer surface, a pop-up list of common tasks automatically appears. You can use the common tasks list to quickly configure a control's properties, as well as walk through common operations you might perform with it. Smart tasks can go a long way in increasing the productivity of the developers, allowing developers to create feature-rich, database-driven web applications without writing a single line of code.

Creating Web Projects

With Visual Studio 2005, you have more flexibility and features for managing the files in your web projects. When you bring up the New Web Site dialog box and click on the Browse button, you will see the dialog box shown in Figure 1-3.

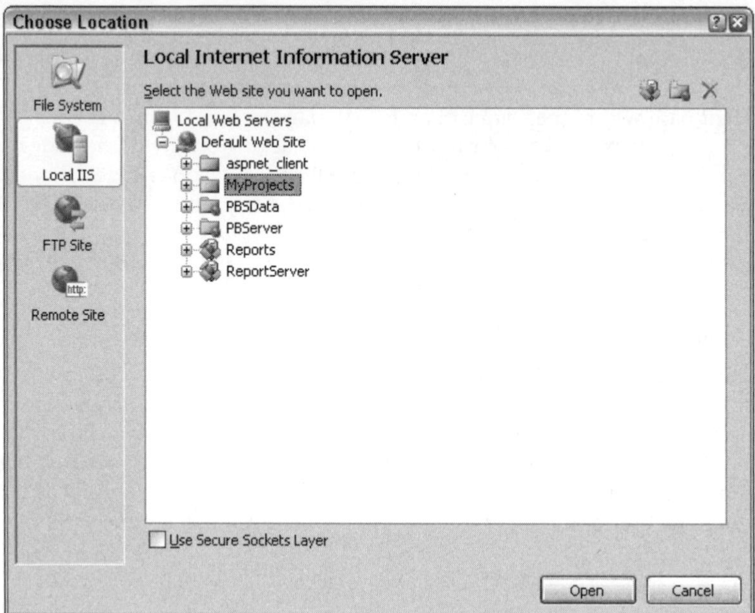

Figure 1-3

As you can see from Figure 1-3, you have the following options when creating web projects:

- **File System Support:** With Visual Studio 2005, you now have the option of creating a new web application within any folder on your computer. Note that neither IIS nor Front Page Server Extensions is required to be installed on your computer. You can simply point the web application to a specific folder and start building web pages. This is made possible through the new built-in ASP.NET enabled web server that ships with Visual Studio 2005. Using this new web server, you can develop and debug web applications without requiring Administrator access. Note that the built-in web server cannot be accessed remotely, and it automatically shuts down when you close the Visual Studio 2005 development environment.
- **Local IIS Support:** In addition to file system projects, Visual Studio 2005 now enables you to more easily manage projects that are hosted on an IIS web server. When you create a new IIS project, you can now view all of the web sites and applications configured on your machine. You can even create new IIS web applications or virtual directories directly from the New Web Site dialog box. Figure 1-3 shows an example of this in action. FrontPage Server Extensions (FPSE) is no longer required for locally developed IIS web applications.
- **FTP Support:** Visual Studio 2005 now has out-of-the-box support for editing and updating remote web projects using the standard File Transfer Protocol (FTP). The New Web Site and Open Web Site dialog boxes allow you to quickly connect to a remote web site using FTP.

Administration and Management

One of the key goals of ASP.NET 2.0 is to ease the effort required to deploy, manage, and operate ASP.NET web sites. To this end, ASP.NET 2.0 features a new Configuration Management API that enables users to programmatically build programs or scripts that create, read, and update configuration files such as `Web.config` and `machine.config`. In addition, there is a new comprehensive admin tool that plugs into the existing IIS Administration MMC, enabling an administrator to graphically read or change any setting within the configuration files. ASP.NET 2.0 also provides new health-monitoring support to enable administrators to be automatically notified when an application on a server starts to experience problems. New tracing features will enable administrators to capture runtime and request data from a production server to better diagnose issues.

Visual Studio 2005 also ships with a new web-based tool that provides a very easy way to administer an ASP.NET web site. You can access this by clicking Website ➪ ASP.NET Configuration in Visual Studio 2005. This web-based tool wraps much of the Management API, thereby providing an easy and effective way to remotely administer a site. Figure 1-4 shows the ASP.NET Web Application Administration tool in action.

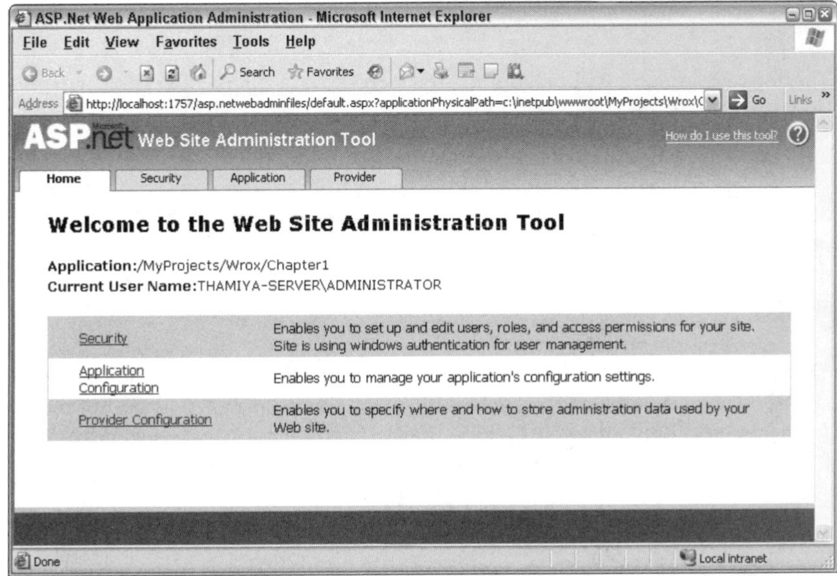

Figure 1-4

As you can see from Figure 1-4, it provides a simple web interface that allows configuration of all aspects of a site. The interface is designed to be customized, so corporations and hosts can give it a company look.

Precompilation

One of the significant improvements in ASP.NET 2.0 is the capability to request a web form (`.aspx` file) from a browser without having to compile the code even once. When the page is first requested, ASP.NET compiles the page on the fly, dynamically generating the assembly. This makes it possible for you to resort to the "Just Hit Save" programming model (similar to ASP), wherein you just develop and test the page without having to compile it. After the initial compilation, the compiled page is cached, which is used to satisfy the subsequent requests for the same page. Although this approach is flexible, it does result in a performance hit, especially when the page is requested for the first time, since ASP.NET requires a bit of extra time to compile the code. You can avoid this overhead by leveraging a new feature known as *precompilation*, using which you can compile an ASP.NET web site before making the web site available to users. Precompilation also allows you to catch all the compilation errors before deploying the application onto the production servers. ASP.NET 2.0 provides the following two options for precompiling a site:

- **In-place precompilation:** When you perform in-place precompilation, all ASP.NET files are compiled and stored in a special folder. The precompilation process follows the same logic that ASP.NET uses for dynamic compilation, also taking into consideration the dependencies between files. During precompilation, the compiler creates assemblies for all executable output and places them in a special folder. After the compiled output is created, ASP.NET fulfills requests for pages using the assemblies contained in this folder. One of the important advantages of precompilation is the ability to check the web site for compilation errors. For example, to precompile a web site named Chapter1, enter the following command at the .NET Framework 2.0 SDK command prompt:

```
aspnet_compiler -v /myprojects/wrox/chapter1
```

  The above command will precompile the web site and display the compilation errors in the browser, if there are any.

- **Precompiling a site for deployment:** Using this option, you can create a special deployable output of your web application that can be deployed to production servers. Once the output is created, you can deploy the output, using various mechanisms such as XCOPY, FTP, or Windows installers, onto the production servers. To precompile a web site for deployment, use the same `aspnet_compiler` utility and specify the target path as an additional argument:

```
aspnet_compiler -v /myprojects/wrox/chapter1 C:\Chapter1\Output
```

  This type of precompilation enables applications to be deployed without any source being stored on the server (even the content of `.aspx` files is removed as part of the precompilation), further protecting your intellectual property. This capability can be very useful in web site hosting scenarios.

Speed and Performance

Although ASP.NET 1.x is the one of the world's fastest web application servers, Microsoft aims to make it even faster by bundling the performance improvements in ASP.NET 2.0. It is now 64-bit-enabled, meaning it can take advantage of the full memory address space of new 64-bit processors and servers. Developers can simply copy existing 32-bit ASP.NET applications onto a 64-bit ASP.NET 2.0 server, and the web applications will be automatically JIT compiled and executed as native 64-bit applications. As part of the performance improvements, ASP.NET 2.0 also enhances the caching feature set by providing new functionalities. The next section provides you with a quick overview of the caching improvements in ASP.NET 2.0.

Caching Feature

Caching is defined as temporary storage of data for faster retrieval on subsequent requests. In ASP .NET 2.0, the caching support is integrated with the `DataSource` controls to cache data in a web page. ASP.NET 2.0 also now includes automatic database server cache invalidation. This powerful and easy-to-use feature allows developers to aggressively output cache database-driven page and partial page content within a site, and have ASP.NET automatically invalidate these cache entries and refresh the content whenever the back-end database changes. ASP .NET 2.0 also introduces the `Substitution` control, which allows you to link dynamic and cached content in a web page.

Caching with the DataSource Controls

The `DataSource` controls enable you to cache database data while connecting a .NET application to a database. The `DataSource` control provides various properties, such as `EnableCaching`, which you can use to automatically cache the data represented by a `DataSource` control. The syntax to cache a database table in a memory for 120 seconds is:

```
<asp:SqlDataSource ID="SqlDataSource1" EnableCaching="True" CacheDuration="120"
ConnectionString="Server=localhost;database=AdventureWorks;uid=user;pwd=word;"
SelectCommand="SELECT * FROM Production.ProductCategory" Runat="server"/>
```

The above syntax caches a database table, `ProductCategory`, by setting the `EnableCaching` property of the `DataSource` control to `True`. The `CacheDuration` property of the `DataSource` control specifies the time, in seconds, for caching the data before it is updated in a database containing the `ProductCategory` table. The value of the `Time` parameter is set to `120` to cache data for two minutes.

Using SQL Cache Invalidation

The Cache API introduced with ASP.NET 1.x was a powerful feature that can be immensely useful in increasing the performance of a web application. The Cache API also allows you to invalidate items in the cache based on some predefined conditions, such as change in an XML file, change in another cache item, and so on. Using this feature, you can remove or invalidate an item from the cache when the data or another cached item changes. However, the Cache API in ASP.NET 1.x versions did not provide a mechanism to invalidate an item in the cache when data in a SQL Server database changed. This is a very common capability that many web applications require. Now with ASP.NET 2.0, Microsoft has introduced a new cache invalidation mechanism that works with SQL Server as well. Using this new capability, you can invalidate an item in the `Cache` object whenever the data in a SQL Server database changes. This built-in cache invalidation mechanism works with SQL Server 7.0 and above. However, with SQL Server 7.0 and 2000, only table-level cache invalidation mechanism is supported. The next release of SQL Server (named SQL Server 2005) will also feature a row-level cache invalidation mechanism, providing a finer level of accuracy over the cached data. To enable the SQL Server–based cache invalidation mechanism, you need to do the following:

1. Add a `<caching>` element to the `Web.config` file, and specify the polling time and the connection string information.
2. Enable SQL cache invalidation at the database and table levels by using either the `aspnet_regsql` utility or the `SqlCacheDependencyAdmin` class. This is not required if you are using SQL Server 2005 as your database.
3. Specify the `SqlCacheDependency` attribute in the `SqlDataSource` control.

That's all you need to do to leverage SQL Server cache invalidation from your ASP.NET pages.

Using the Substitution Control

ASP.NET 2.0 provides a new control called the `Substitution` control, which enables you to insert dynamic content into a cached web page. For example, you can display the name of an end user, which is dynamically generated in a cached web page containing some text or images. The `Substitution` control provides a property called `MethodName`, which represents the method called to return the dynamic content. Listing 1-4 shows an example of the `Substitution` control in action.

Listing 1-4: Partial Page Caching Using Substitution Control

```
<%@ Page Language="C#" %>
<%@ OutputCache Duration="6000" VaryByParam="none" %>
<script runat="server">
  static string GetRandomNumber(HttpContext context)
  {
    int randomNumber;
    randomNumber = new System.Random().Next(1, 10000);
    return randomNumber.ToString();
  }
</script>
<html>
<head>
  <title>Use of Substitution control to implement Partial Caching</title>
</head>
<body>
  <form id="form1" runat="server">
    The random number generated is:
    <asp:Substitution ID="Substitution1" MethodName="GetRandomNumber"
      Runat="Server" />
    <p>
      The current time is <%= DateTime.Now.ToString("t") %>.
      It never changes since the page is cached.
    </p>
  </form>
</body>
</html>
```

At the top of the page, the `OutputCache` directive is used to cache the contents of the page in memory. The `Duration` attribute of the `OutputCache` directive is set to 6000 milliseconds. The `VaryByParam` attribute indicates whether or not ASP.NET should consider the parameters passed to the page when caching. When `VaryByParam` is set to `none`, no parameters will be considered; all users will receive the same page no matter what additional parameters are supplied. The `MethodName` attribute of the `Substitution` control is set to a method named `GetRandomNumber`, which simply returns a random number between 1 and 10,000. Note that the return value of the `GetRandomNumber` method is a string, because the `HttpResponseSubstitutionCallback` delegate always requires a return type of string. When you make a request for the page through the browser, you will find that the displayed current time always remains the same, whereas the portion of the page that is generated by the substitution control keeps changing every time. In this case, it displays a random number between 1 and 10,000 every time someone requests the page.

Summary

This chapter has provided you with a quick tour of the features of ASP.NET 2.0. Specifically, this chapter discussed the number of new productivity enhancements of ASP.NET 2.0 that are exciting for the developers. In addition, this chapter has also discussed the configuration and management of ASP.NET web applications, as well as the performance improvement features. Apart from the features discussed so far, ASP.NET 2.0 also provides the following features:

- ASP.NET 2.0 is 64-bit enabled.
- ASP.NET 2.0 is almost completely backward compatible with ASP.NET 1.0 and ASP.NET 1.1.
- You can also define a single class in multiple files, and at runtime they will be compiled together to create a single assembly.

Now that you have had a quick tour of ASP.NET 2.0, the next chapter focuses on the features of ADO.NET 2.0.

2

Introduction to ADO.NET 2.0

A large number of computer applications — both desktop and web applications — are data-driven. These applications are largely concerned with retrieving, displaying, and modifying data. As you would expect, the .NET platform defines a number of namespaces that allow you to interact with local and remote data stores. Collectively speaking, these namespaces are known as ADO.NET. The small miracle of ADO.NET is that it allows you to write more or less the same data access code in web applications that you write for client-server desktop applications, or even single-user applications that connect to a local database.

This chapter describes the architecture of ADO.NET and the ADO.NET data providers. You will learn about ADO.NET basics such as opening a connection, executing a SQL statement or stored procedure, and retrieving the results of a query. Specifically, this chapter examines how to programmatically interact with relational databases using your data provider of choice. As you will see, ADO.NET provides two distinct ways to interface with a data source, often termed the connected layer and disconnected layer. You will come to know the role of connection objects, command objects, data readers, data adapters, and numerous types within the `System.Data` namespace (specifically, `DataSet`, `DataTable`, `DataRow`, `DataColumn`, `DataView`, and `DataRelation`).

What's New with ADO.NET 2.0

If you're a seasoned .NET 1.x programmer, you're probably wondering what's new in the latest iteration of ADO.NET. Without a doubt, the greatest change for ASP.NET applications is the new data-binding model, which allows you to reduce the amount of code you write for data display, and it can even allow you avoid writing any data access code at all. Even with the advent of the new data-binding model, the underlying ADO.NET object model does not change that much. Here are the new ADO.NET features:

- **Provider factories:** The dream of generic data access code (code you can write once and use with multiple different databases without rewriting the code) takes a giant leap forward in .NET 2.0 thanks to provider factories — new components that can create strongly typed `Connection`, `Command`, and `DataAdapter` objects on the fly.

- **Change notification:** To build truly scalable web applications, you need to cache data that is retrieved from a database, so it can be reused without connecting to the data source each time. However, caching introduces the possibility of out-of-date information. ADO.NET includes a new change notification feature that you can use to automatically remove cached data when the related records in the database change.
- **Connection statistics:** It is a small frill, but the new connection-tracking features of the `SqlConnection` object might help you profile different data access strategies.

In addition to these features, ADO.NET 2.0 also provides support for few features that are limited to SQL Server 2005. These features include the following:

- **MARS (Multiple Active Result Sets):** This allows you to have more than one query on the go at the same time. For example, you could query a list of customers and then query a list of orders without closing the first query. This technique is occasionally useful, but it is better if you can avoid the extra overhead.
- **User-defined data types:** Using .NET code, you can define a custom class and then store instances of that class directly in a column of the database. This saves you the work of examining several fields in a row and then manually creating a corresponding data object to use in your application.
- **Managed stored procedures:** SQL Server 2005 can host the CLR, which gives you the ability to write stored procedures in the database using pure C# code.
- **SQL notifications:** Notifications allow your code to respond when specific changes are made in a database. In ASP.NET, this feature is most commonly used to invalidate a cached data object when one or more records are updated. This is the only SQL Server 2005 feature that is also supported in SQL Server 7 and SQL Server 2000, albeit through a different mechanism.
- **Snapshot transaction isolation:** This is a new transaction level that allows you to improve concurrency. It allows transactions to see a slightly older version of data while it's being updated by another transaction.

For the most part, this chapter concentrates on programming techniques that work with SQL Server 2005 database. Now that you have an idea of the new features, you can examine the fundamental ADO.NET 2.0 namespaces.

Fundamental ADO.NET 2.0 Namespaces

Note that an ADO.NET provider is simply a set of ADO.NET classes (with an implementation of `Connection`, `Command`, `DataAdapter`, and `DataReader`) that is distributed in a class library assembly. Usually, all the classes in the data provider use the same prefix. For example, the prefix `Oracle` is used for the ADO.NET `Oracle` provider, and it provides an implementation of the `Connection` object named `OracleConnection`.

Simply put, a data provider is a set of types defined in a given namespace that understand how to communicate with a specific data source. Regardless of which data provider you make use of, each defines a set of class types that provide core functionality.

The ADO.NET classes are grouped into several namespaces. Each provider has its own namespace, and generic classes such as the `DataSet` are stored in the `System.Data` namespaces. The following table describes the namespaces.

Namespace	Description
`System.Data`	Contains the key data container classes that model columns, relations, tables, datasets, rows, views, and constraints. In addition, contains the key interfaces that are implemented by the connection-based data objects.
`System.Data.Common`	Contains base, mostly abstract classes that implement some of the interfaces from `System.Data` and define the core ADO.NET functionality. Data providers inherit from these classes to create their own specialized versions.
`System.Data.OleDb`	Contains the classes used to connect to an OLE DB provider, including `OleDbCommand`, `OleDbConnection`, and `OleDbDataAdapter`. These classes support most OLE DB providers, but not those that require OLE DB version 2.5 interfaces.
`System.Data.SqlClient`	Contains the classes you use to connect to a Microsoft SQL Server database, including `SqlCommand`, `SqlConnection`, and `SqlDataAdapter`. These classes are optimized to use the native TDS (tabular data stream) interface to SQL Server.
`System.Data.OracleClient`	Contains the classes required to connect to an Oracle database: `OracleConnection` and `OracleDataAdapter`. These classes utilize the optimized Oracle Call Interface (OCI).
`System.Data.Odbc`	Contains the classes required to connect to most ODBC drivers. These classes include `OdbcCommand`, `OdbcConnection`, and `OdbcDataAdapter`. ODBC drivers are included for all kinds of data sources and are configured through the Data Sources icon in the Control Panel.
`System.Data.SqlTypes`	Contains structures that match the native data types in SQL Server. These classes aren't required but provide an alternative to using standard .NET data types, which require automatic conversion.

The OLE DB data provider, which is composed of the types defined in the `System.Data.OleDb` namespace, allows you to access data located in any data store that supports the classic COM-based OLE DB protocol. Using this provider, you may communicate with any OLE DB–compliant database simply by tweaking the Provider segment of your connection string. Be aware, however, that the OLE DB provider interacts with various COM objects behind the scenes, which can affect the performance of your application. By and large, the OLE DB data provider is only useful if you are interacting with a DBMS that does not define a specific .NET data provider.

No specific data provider maps directly to the Jet engine (and therefore Microsoft Access). If you wish to interact with an Access data file, you can do so using the OLE DB or ODBC data provider.

The Microsoft SQL Server data provider offers direct access to Microsoft SQL Server data stores, and only SQL Server data stores (version 7.0 and greater). The `System.Data.SqlClient` namespace contains the types used by the SQL Server provider and offers the same basic functionality as the OLE DB provider. The key difference is that the SQL Server provider bypasses the OLE DB layer (by using the TDS interface directly) and thus gives numerous performance benefits. As well, the Microsoft SQL Server data provider allows you to gain access to the unique features of this particular DBMS.

The System.Data Namespace

Of all the ADO.NET namespaces, `System.Data` is the lowest common denominator. You simply cannot build ADO.NET applications without specifying this namespace in your data access applications. This namespace contains types that are shared among all ADO.NET data providers, regardless of the underlying data store. In addition to a number of database-centric exceptions (`NoNullAllowedException`, `RowNotInTableException`, `MissingPrimaryKeyException`, and the like), `System.Data` contains types that represent various database primitives (tables, rows, columns, constraints, and so forth), as well as the common interfaces implemented by data provider objects. The following table lists some of the core types to be aware of.

Type	Description
`Constraint`	Represents a constraint for a given `DataColumn` object.
`DataColumn`	Represents a single column within a `DataTable` object.
`DataRelation`	Represents a parent/child relationship between two `DataTable` objects.
`DataRow`	Represents a single row within a `DataTable` object.
`DataSet`	Represents an in-memory cache of data consisting of any number of interrelated `DataTable` objects.
`DataTable`	Represents a tabular block of in-memory data.
`DataTableReader`	Allows you to treat a `DataTable` as a fire-hose cursor (forward only, read-only data access). This class is new in .NET 2.0.
`DataView`	Represents a customized view of a `DataTable` for sorting, filtering, searching, editing, and navigation.

Now that you have had a look at the core members of the `System.Data` namespace, your next task is to examine the core ADO.NET 2.0 objects.

Understanding ADO.NET 2.0 Core Objects

As mentioned previously, ADO.NET does not provide a single set of types that communicate with multiple database management systems (DBMSs). ADO.NET supports multiple data providers, each of which is optimized to interact with a specific DBMS. The first benefit of this approach is that a specific data provider can be programmed to access any unique features of the DBMS. Another benefit is that a specific data provider is able to directly connect to the underlying engine of the DBMS without an intermediate mapping layer standing between the tiers.

The following table documents some (but not all) of the core common objects, their base class (all defined in the `System.Data.Common` namespace), and their implemented data-centric interfaces (each defined in the `System.Data` namespace).

Class	Base Class	Implemented Interfaces	Purpose
`Connection`	`DbConnection`	`IDbConnection`	Provides the ability to connect to and disconnect from the data store. Connection objects also provide access to a related transaction object.
`Command`	`DbCommand`	`IDbCommand`	Represents a SQL query or name of a stored procedure. `Command` objects also provide access to the provider's data reader object.
`DataReader`	`DbDataReader`	`IDataReader`, `IDataRecord`	Provides forward-only, read-only access to data.
`DataAdapter`	`DbDataAdapter`	`IDataAdapter`, `IDbDataAdapter`	Transfers `DataSets` between the caller and the data store. `Data Adapters` contain a set of four internal command objects used to select, insert, update, and delete information from the data store.
`Parameter`	`DbParameter`	`IDataParameter`, `IdbDataParameter`	Represents a named parameter within a parameterized query.
`Transaction`	`DbTransaction`	`IDbTransaction`	Performs the database transaction.

Although the names of these types will differ among data providers (for example, `SqlConnection` versus `OracleConnection` versus `OdbcConnection`), each object derives from the same base class that implements identical interfaces. Given this, you are correct to assume that once you learn how to work with one data provider, the remaining providers are quite straightforward.

> *Note that as a naming convention, the objects in a specific data provider are prefixed with the name of the related DBMS. For example, the Oracle provider connection object is referred to as* `OracleConnection`.

Figure 2-1 illustrates the big picture behind ADO.NET data providers. Note that in the diagram, the client assembly can literally be any type of .NET application: console program, Windows Forms application, ASP.NET web page, XML web service, .NET code library, and so on.

Now, to be sure, a data provider will supply you with other types beyond the objects shown in Figure 2-1. However, these core objects define a common baseline across all data providers.

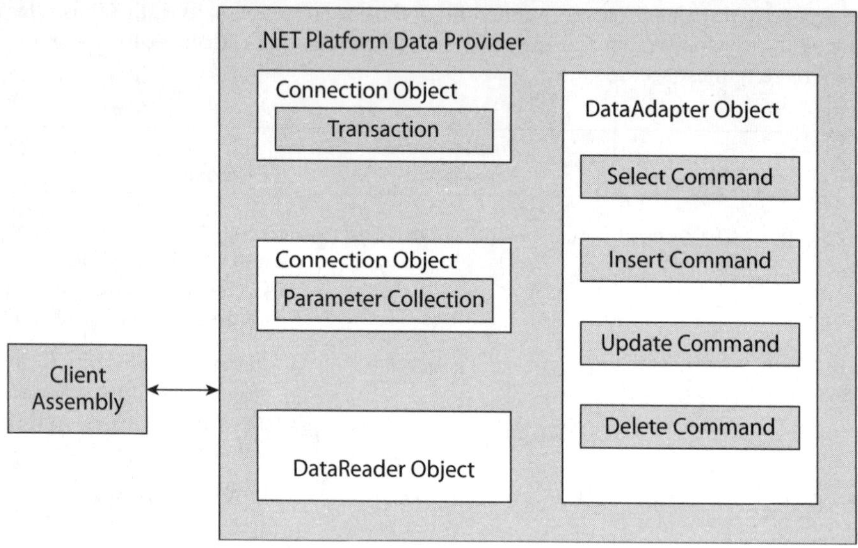

Figure 2-1

Fundamental ADO.NET Classes

You can divide the ADO.NET objects into two types of objects: connection-based and content-based.

- **Connection-based objects:** These are the data provider objects such as `Connection`, `Command`, `DataAdapter`, and `DataReader`. They execute SQL statements, connect to a database, or fill a `DataSet`. The connection-based objects are specific to the type of data source.
- **Content-based objects:** These objects are really just packages for data. They include the `DataSet`, `DataColumn`, `DataRow`, `DataRelation`, and several others. They are completely independent of the type of data source and are found in the `System.Data` namespace.

Figure 2-2 shows where the various connected and disconnected objects fit into the bigger picture.

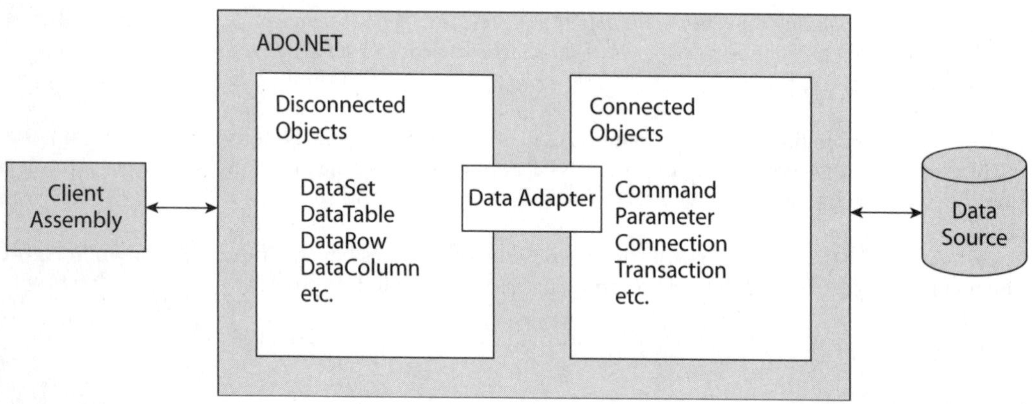

Figure 2-2

Note that in Figure 2-2, your program talks with ADO.NET as a whole. In other words, it can choose to use the disconnected objects, the `DataAdapter`, the connected objects, or a combination thereof. Since the connected objects need to work directly with the underlying database, connected objects typically need to implement database-specific code. On the other hand, disconnected objects are meant to be database-agnostic; thus, it is logical to assume that they can be shared between different databases.

The Connected Objects

The Connected Objects portion of Figure 2-2 represents the objects that insist on having an open connection available for them to work and interact with the data source. Under the connected part of ADO.NET, there are the following main objects:

- **Connection:** This is the object that allows you to establish a connection with the data source. Depending on the actual .NET data provider involved, connection objects automatically pool physical database connections for you. It is important to realize that they don't pool connection object instances, but they try to recycle physical database connections. Examples of connection objects are `OleDbConnection`, `SqlConnection`, and `OracleConnection`.
- **Transaction:** There are times when you would want to execute a group of commands together as a group or as an atomic operation — as an all-or-nothing execution. An example might be a banking application where a credit must not occur if a corresponding debit cannot be done. Transaction objects let you group together such groups of commands and execute them atomically. Examples of transaction objects are `OleDbTransaction`, `SqlTransaction`, and `OracleTransaction`. In ADO.NET 2.0, you also have the ability to run distributed transactions and enlist in non-database transactions via the classes in the `System.Transactions` namespace. In ADO.NET 1.0 and 1.1, this was possible as a less than ideal solution using the `System.EnterpriseServices` namespace.
- **DataAdapter:** This object acts as a gateway between the disconnected and connected flavors of ADO.NET. It establishes the connection for you, or, given an established connection, it has enough information specified to itself to enable it to understand a disconnected object's data and act upon the database in a predetermined manner. Examples of `DataAdapters` are `SqlDataAdapter` and `OracleDataAdapter`.
- **Command:** This object represents an executable command on the underlying data source. This command may or may not return any results. These commands can be used to manipulate existing data, query existing data, and update or even delete existing data. In addition, these commands can be used to manipulate underlying table structures. Examples of command objects are `SqlCommand` and `OracleCommand`.
- **Parameter:** A command needs to be able to accept parameters. This allows commands to be more flexible and accept input values and act accordingly. These parameters could be input/output or return values of stored procedures, or `?` arguments passed to a SQL query, or simply named parameters to a dynamic query. Examples of parameters are `SqlParameter` and `OracleParameter`.
- **DataReader:** The `DataReader` object is the equivalent of a read-only/forward-only fire-hose cursor that allows you to fetch data from a database at an extremely high speed, but in a forward-only and read-only mode.

The Disconnected Objects

Constantly connected applications alone do not fulfill the demands of modern-day distributed applications. Disconnected applications built using ADO.NET, however, take a different approach. Disconnected applications typically connect as late as possible and disconnect as early as they can. While they are working in a disconnected fashion, ADO.NET pools the actual physical connection between various requests. The various objects in consideration under the disconnected model of ADO.NET are:

- **DataSet:** The `DataSet` is at the central core of the disconnected mode of ADO.NET data access. The best way to think of a `DataSet` is that it is like having your own very mini–relational database management system (RDBMS) completely represented in memory. While it isn't quite an RDBMS and should never be thought to replace an RDBMS, it helps one to understand a `DataSet` if its various components are connected on a one-to-one basis with most major RDBMS objects. A `DataSet` can also be thought of as a logical collection of `DataTable` and `DataRelation` objects.
- **DataTable:** A `DataTable` is most similar to a table in a database. It consists of `DataColumns`, `DataRows`, and various constraints set upon them. It stores data in a row/column format. Starting with ADO.NET 2.0, a `DataTable` is fully convertible to XML and can be serialized just like a `DataSet`. For data access needs where your `DataSet` might contain only one `DataTable`, it may make more sense to use a `DataTable` instead. As you will see in future chapters, this is not only more convenient, but it is also better performing.
- **DataRow:** One of the properties of `DataTable` is rows of the `DataRowCollection` type, which represents an enumerable collection of `DataRow` objects. As data is filled into a `DataTable`, the `DataRowCollection` gets new `DataRow` objects added to it. The best logical equivalent of a `DataRow` in a database is a row in a table.
- **DataColumn:** A `DataTable` also contains a `Columns` property of `DataColumnCollection` type. Essentially, this represents the structure of a `DataTable`. The best logical equivalent of a `DataColumn` object in a database is an individual column in a given table in a database.
- **DataView:** A `DataView` is most similar to a view in a database. A `DataView` allows you to create a view on a `DataTable` and view a subset of the data based on a preset condition specified in its `Filter` property. You could also use the `Sort` property to sort the filtered subset of the `DataTable` object's data. One `DataTable` can have multiple views defined on it.
- **Constraint:** A `DataTable` contains yet another property called `Constraints`, of `ConstraintsCollection` type. This lets you create `ForeignKeyConstraint` or `UniqueConstraint` objects and associate various columns with certain conditions based on which data in the `DataTable` must pass for it to exist in the `DataTable`. The most logical equivalent of a `ForeignKeyConstraint` is a foreign key in a database, and `UniqueConstraint` specifies a unique condition on a given column in a database.
- **DataRelation:** A `DataSet`, like a database, might contain various interrelated tables. A `DataRelation` object lets you specify relations between various tables that allow you to both validate data across tables and browse parent and child rows in various `DataTable` objects. Its most logical equivalent is a foreign key specified between two tables in a database. The difference between a `ForeignKeyConstraint` and a `DataRelation` is that a `DataRelation`, in addition to validating data, gives you a convenient mechanism to browse parent and child rows in a `DataSet`.

Now that you have an understanding of the connected and disconnected objects, the next sections discuss them in detail through code examples.

Understanding the Connected Layer of ADO.NET

Recall that the connected layer of ADO.NET allows you to interact with a database using the connection, command, and data reader objects of your data provider. When you wish to connect to a database and read the records using a data reader object, you need to perform the following steps:

1. Allocate, configure, and open your connection object.
2. Allocate and configure a command object, specifying the connection object as a constructor argument or via the `Connection` property.
3. Call `ExecuteReader()` on the configured command object.
4. Process each record using the `Read()` method of the data reader.

The next few sections examine each of the connected layer objects in detail. Note that all of these examples will utilize the classes contained in the `System.Data.SqlClient` namespace and connect to a SQL Server 2005 AdventureWorks database.

Working with Connection Objects

The first step to take when working with a data provider is to establish a session with the data source using the `Connection` object (which, as you recall, derives from `DbConnection`). .NET connection types are provided with a formatted connection string, which contains a number of name/value pairs separated by semicolons. This information is used to identify the name of the machine you wish to connect to, the required security settings, the name of the database on that machine, and other data provider-specific information.

Once your connection string has been established, a call to `Open()` establishes your connection with the DBMS. In addition to the `ConnectionString`, `Open()`, and `Close()` members, a `Connection` object provides a number of members that let you configure attritional settings regarding your connection, such as timeout settings and transactional information. The following table lists some (but not all) members of the `DbConnection` base class.

Type	Description
`BeginTransaction`	Begins a database transaction.
`ChangeDatabase`	Changes the database on an open connection.
`ConnectionTimeout`	Read-only property that determines the amount of time to wait before terminating and generating an error.
`Database`	Gets the name of the database maintained by the `Connection` object.
`DataSource`	Gets the name of the database server to connect to.
`State`	Returns the current state of the connection string in the form of a `ConnectionString` enumeration, which can take any one of these values: `Broken`, `Closed`, `Connecting`, `Executing`, `Fetching`, or `Open`.

As you can see, the properties of the `DbConnection` type are typically read-only in nature and are only useful when you wish to obtain the characteristics of a connection at runtime. When you wish to override default settings, you must alter the connection string itself. For example, the connection string sets the connection timeout setting from 15 seconds to 30 seconds (via the `Connect Timeout` segment of the connection string):

```
SqlConnection conn = new SqlConnection();
conn.ConnectionString = "uid=user;pwd=word;Initial Catalog=AdventureWorks;" +
  "server=localhost;Connect Timeout=30";
conn.Open();
//Show various stats about current connection object.
Response.Write ("Database location: " + conn.DataSource);
Response.Write ("Database name: " + conn.Database);
Response.Write ("Timeout: " + conn.ConnectionTimeout);
```

Working with .NET 2.0 ConnectionStringBuilders

Working with connection strings programmatically can be a bit clunky, given that they are often represented as string literals, which are difficult to maintain and error-prone at best. Under .NET 2.0, the Microsoft-supplied ADO.NET data providers now support connection string builder objects, which allow you to establish the name/value pairs using strongly typed properties. Consider the following update to the code shown in previous section:

```
SqlConnection conn = new SqlConnection();
SqlConnectionStringBuilder builder = new SqlConnectionStringBuilder();
builder.UserID = "user";
builder.Password = "word";
builder.InitialCatalog = "AdventureWorks";
builder.DataSource = "localhost";
builder.ConnectTimeout = 30;
conn.ConnectionString = builder.ConnectionString;
conn.Open();
```

In this iteration, you create an instance of `SqlConnectionStringBuilder`, set the properties accordingly, and obtain the internal string via the `ConnectionString` property. Also note that you make use of the default constructor of the type. If you so choose, you can also create an instance of your data provider's connection string builder object by passing in an existing connection string as a starting point (which can be helpful when you are reading these values dynamically from an `app.config` file). Once you have hydrated the object with the initial string data, you can change specific name/value pairs using the related properties as well.

Working with Command Objects

Now that you better understand the role of the `Connection` object, the next order of business is to check out how to submit SQL queries to the database in question. The `SqlCommand` type (which derives from `DbCommand`) is an OO representation of a SQL query, table name, or stored procedure. The type of command is specified using the `CommandType` property, which may take any value from the `CommandType` enum:

```
public enum System.Data.CommandType
{
  StoredProcedure,
  TableDirect,
  Text   //Default value
}
```

When creating a command object, you may establish the SQL query as a constructor parameter or directly via the `CommandText` property. Also, when you are creating a `Command` object, you need to specify the connection to be used. Again, you may do so as a constructor parameter or via the `Connection` property:

```
SqlConnection conn = new SqlConnection();
//Create another command object via properties
string sql = "Select * from HumanResources.Employee";
SqlCommand command = new SqlCommand();
command.Connection = conn;
command.CommandText = sql;
```

Realize that at this point, you have not literally submitted the SQL query to the Cars database, but rather prepped the state of the command type for future use. The following table highlights some additional members of the `DbCommand` type.

Type	Description
`CommandTimeout`	Gets or sets the time to wait while executing the command before terminating the attempt and generating an error. The default is 30 seconds.
`Connection`	Gets or sets the `DbConnection` used by this instance of the `DbCommand`.
`Parameters`	Gets the collection of `DbParameter` types used for a parameterized query.
`Cancel`	Cancels the execution of a command.
`ExecuteReader`	Returns the data provider's `DbDataReader` object, which provides forward-only, read-only access to the underlying data.
`ExecuteNonQuery`	Issues the command text to the database.
`ExecuteScalar`	A lightweight version of the `ExecuteNonQuery()` method, designed specifically for singleton queries (such as obtaining a record count).
`ExecuteXmlReader`	Returns the XML output in the form of a `System.Xml.XmlReader` object.

Note that in .NET 2.0, the `SqlCommand` object has been updated with additional members that facilitate asynchronous database interactions.

Working with DataReaders

Once you have established the active connection and SQL command, the next step is to submit the query to the data source. As you might guess, you have a number of ways to do so. The `DbDataReader` type (which implements `IDataReader`) is the simplest and fastest way to obtain information from a data store. Recall that data readers represent a read-only, forward-only stream of data returned one record at a time. Given this, it should stand to reason that data readers are useful only when submitting SQL selection statements to the underlying data store.

Data readers are useful when you need to iterate over large amounts of data very quickly and have no need to maintain an in-memory representation. For example, if you request 20,000 records from a table to store in a text file, it would be rather memory-intensive to hold this information in a `DataSet`. A better approach is to create a data reader that spins over each record as rapidly as possible. Be aware, however, that data reader objects (unlike data adapter objects, which you'll examine later) maintain an open connection to their data source until you explicitly close the session.

Data reader objects are obtained from the command object via a call to `ExecuteReader()`. When invoking this method, you may optionally instruct the reader to automatically close down the related `Connection` object by specifying `CommandBehavior.CloseConnection`.

The following use of the data reader leverages the `Read()` method to determine when you have reached the end of your records (via a false return value). For each incoming record, you are making use of the type indexer to print out the make, pet name, and color of each automobile. Also note that you call `Close()` as soon as you are finished processing the records, to free up the `Connection` object:

```
SqlDataReader reader;
reader= command.ExecuteReader(CommandBehavior.CloseConnection);
while (reader.Read())
{
  Response.Write("Employee ID: " + reader["EmployeeID"] + "<br>");
  Response.Write("NationalID: " + reader["NationalIDNumber"] + "<br>");
}
reader.Close();
```

The indexer of a data reader object has been overloaded to take either a string (representing the name of the column) or an integer (representing the column's ordinal position).

Executing a Stored Procedure Using DbCommand

A stored procedure is a named block of SQL code stored in the database. Stored procedures can be constructed to return a set of rows or scalar data types and may take any number of optional parameters. The end result is a unit of work that behaves like a typical function, with the obvious difference of being located on a data store rather than a binary business object.

It is worth pointing out that the SQL Server 2005 is a CLR host. Therefore, stored procedures (and other database atoms) can be authored using managed languages (such as C# or VB.NET) rather than traditional SQL.

To illustrate the process, create a stored procedure named `GetEmployeeTitle` that allows the caller to look up the title of an employee based on the employee ID:

```
CREATE PROCEDURE GetEmployeeTitle
  @EmployeeID int,
  @Title nvarchar(50) output
```

```
AS
  SELECT @Title = Title from HumanResources.Employee
  where EmployeeID = @EmployeeID
```

Before you execute the stored procedure, it is time to get to know the `DbParameter` type (which is the base class to a provider's specific `Parameter` object). This class maintains a number of properties that allow you to configure the name, size, and data type of the parameter, as well as other characteristics such as the parameter's direction of travel. The following table describes some key properties of the `DbParameter` type.

Property	Description
`DbType`	Gets or sets the native data type from the data source, represented as CLR data type.
`Direction`	Gets or sets whether the parameter is input-only, output-only, bidirectional, or a return value parameter.
`IsNullable`	Gets or sets whether the parameter accepts null values.
`ParameterName`	Gets or sets the name of the `DbParameter`.
`Size`	Gets or sets the maximum parameter size of the data.
`Value`	Gets or sets the value of the parameter.

When you wish to execute a stored procedure, you begin as always by creating a new `Connection` object, configuring your connection string, and opening the session. However, when you create your `Command` object, the `CommandText` property is set to the name of the stored procedure (rather than a SQL query). As well, you must be sure to set the `CommandType` property to `CommandType.StoredProcedure` (the default is `CommandType.Text`). Given that this stored procedure has one input and one output parameter, your goal is to build a `Command` object that contains two `SqlParameter` objects within its parameter collection:

```
string storedproc = "GetEmployeeTitle";
int employeeID = 1;
SqlCommand command = new SqlCommand();
command.Connection = conn;
command.CommandText = storedproc;
command.CommandType = CommandType.StoredProcedure;

//EmployeeID input parameter
SqlParameter employeeIDParam = new SqlParameter();
employeeIDParam.ParameterName = "@EmployeeID";
employeeIDParam.SqlDbType = SqlDbType.Int;
employeeIDParam.Value = employeeID;
employeeIDParam.Direction = ParameterDirection.Input;
command.Parameters.Add(employeeIDParam);

//Title output parameter
SqlParameter titleParam = new SqlParameter();
titleParam.ParameterName = "@Title";
titleParam.SqlDbType = SqlDbType.NVarChar;
```

```
titleParam.Size = 50;
titleParam.Direction = ParameterDirection.Output;
command.Parameters.Add(titleParam);
command.ExecuteNonQuery();
Response.Write("Title : " + command.Parameters["@Title"].Value);
```

Notice that the `Direction` property of the `Parameter` object allows you to specify `input` and `output` parameters. Once the stored procedure completes via a call to `ExecuteNonQuery()`, you are able to obtain the value of the `output` parameter by investigating the `Command` object's parameter collection.

In the previous example, you used the synchronous version of the `ExecuteNonQuery()` method. As of .NET 2.0, the SQL data provider (represented by the `System.Data.SqlClient` namespace) has been enhanced to support asynchronous database interactions via the following new members of `SqlCommand`:

- `BeginExecuteReader()` **and** `EndExecuteReader()`
- `BeginExecuteNonQuery()` **and** `EndExecuteNonQuery()`
- `BeginExecuteXmlReader()` **and** `EndExecuteXmlReader()`

As the name suggests, the .NET asynchronous delegate pattern makes use of a `Begin()` method to execute a task on a secondary thread, whereas the `End()` method can be used to obtain the result of the asynchronous invocation using the members of `IAsyncResult` and the optional `AsyncCallback` delegate. More information on this can be found in the later chapters.

Understanding the Disconnected Layer of ADO.NET

As you have seen, working with the connected layer allows you to interact with a database using `Connection`, `Command`, and `DataReader` objects. With this small handful of types, you are able to select, insert, update, and delete records in your database. In reality, however, you have seen only half of the ADO.NET story. Recall that the ADO.NET object model can be used in a disconnected manner.

When you work with the disconnected layer of ADO.NET, you will still make use of `Connection` and `Command` objects. In addition, you will leverage a specific object named a `DataAdapter` (which extends the abstract `DbDataAdapter`) to fetch and update data. Unlike the connected layer, data obtained via a `DataAdapter` is not processed using `DataReader` objects. Rather, `DataAdapter` objects make use of `DataSet` objects to move data between the caller and data source. The `DataSet` type is a container for any number of `DataTable` objects, each of which contains a collection of `DataRow` and `DataColumn` objects.

The `DataAdapter` object of your data provider handles the database connection automatically. In an attempt to increase scalability, `DataAdapter` objects keep the connection open for the shortest possible amount of time. Once the caller receives the `DataSet` object, the caller is completely disconnected from the DBMS and left with a local copy of the remote data. The caller is free to insert, delete, or update rows in a given `DataTable`, but the physical database is not updated until the caller explicitly passes the `DataSet` to the `DataAdapter` for updating. In a nutshell, `DataSet` objects allow the clients to pretend they are indeed always connected, when in fact they are operating on an in-memory database.

Given that the centerpiece of the disconnected layer is the `DataSet` type, the next section examines the `DataSet` object.

Working with the DataSet

Simply put, a `DataSet` is an in-memory representation of external data. More specifically, a `DataSet` is a class type that maintains three internal strongly typed collections. They are `DataTablesCollection`, `DataRelationCollection`, and `PropertyCollection`.

The `Tables` property of the `DataSet` allows you to access the `DataTableCollection` that contains the individual `DataTable` objects. Another important collection used by the `DataSet` is the `DataRelation Collection`. Given that a `DataSet` is a disconnected version of a database schema, it can programmatically represent the parent/child relationships between its tables. For example, a relation can be created between two tables to model a foreign key constraint using the `DataRelation` type. This object can then be added to the `DataRelationCollection` through the `Relations` property. At this point, you can navigate between the connected tables as you search for data. Before exploring too many other programmatic details, take a look at some core members of the `DataSet` in the following table.

Property	Description
`CaseSensitive`	Indicates whether or not string comparisons in `DataTable` objects are case sensitive.
`DataSetName`	Represents the friendly name of this `DataSet`. Typically, this value is established as a constructor parameter.
`EnforceConstraints`	Gets or sets a value indicating whether constraint rules are followed when attempting any update operation.
`ExtendedProperties`	Gets the collection of name/value properties that provide more information on the `DataSet`.
`HasErrors`	Gets a value indicating whether there are errors in any of the rows in any of the `DataTable` objects of the `DataSet`.
`RemotingFormat`	This new .NET 2.0 property allows you to define how the `DataSet` should serialize its content (binary or XML) for the .NET remoting layer.

The methods of the `DataSet` mimic some of the functionality provided by the aforementioned properties. In addition to interacting with XML streams, the `DataSet` provides methods that allow you to copy/clone the contents of your `DataSet`, as well as establish the beginning and ending points of a batch of updates. This table describes some core methods.

Method	Description
`AcceptChanges`	Commits all the changes made to this `DataSet` since it was loaded or the last time `AcceptChanges()` was called.
`Clear`	Completely clears the `DataSet` data by removing every row in each `DataTable`.

Method	Description
`Clone`	Clones the structure of the `DataSet`, including all `DataTable` objects, as well as all relations and any constraints.
`Copy`	Copies both the structure and data for this `DataSet`.
`GetChanges`	Returns a copy of the `DataSet` containing all changes made to it since it was last loaded, or since `AcceptChanges()` was last called.
`GetChildRelations`	Returns the collection of child relations that belong to a specified table.
`GetParentRelations`	Gets the collection of parent relations that belong to a specified table.
`HasChanges`	Gets a value indicating whether the `DataSet` has changes, including new, deleted, or modified rows.
`Merge`	Merges this `DataSet` with a specified `DataSet`.
`ReadXml`	Allows you to read XML data from a valid stream (file-based, memory-based, or network-based) into the `DataSet`.
`ReadXmlSchema`	Reads an XML schema into a `DataSet`.
`RejectChanges`	Rolls back all the changes made to this `DataSet` since it was created or the last time `AcceptChanges()` was called.
`WriteXml`	Writes XML data contained in the `DataSet` object to either file-based, memory-based, or network-based stream.
`WriteXmlSchema`	Writes the `DataSet` structure as an XML schema.

Now that you have a better understanding of the role of the `DataSet` (and some idea of what you can do with one), you should understand the code required to create an instance of a `DataSet` object. After creating the `DataSet` object, add two extended properties representing your company name and timestamp:

```
//Create the DataSet object.
  DataSet addressDataSet = new DataSet("Address");
  addressDataSet.ExtendedProperties["TimeStamp"] = DateTime.Now;
  addressDataSet.ExtendedProperties["Company"] = "Wrox Press";
```

Note that the `DataSet` is contained in the `System.Data` namespace. A `DataSet` without `DataTable` objects does not stand on its own. Therefore, the next task is to examine the internal composition of the `DataTable`, beginning with the `DataColumn` type.

Working with DataColumns

The `DataColumn` type represents a single column within a `DataTable`. Collectively speaking, the set of all `DataColumn` types bound to a given `DataTable` represents the foundation of a table's schema information. For example, if you were to model the Address table, you would create four `DataColumn` objects, one for each column (AddressID, City, State, and Zip). Once you have created your `DataColumn` objects, they are typically added into the columns collection of the `DataTable` type (via the `Columns` property).

If you have a background in relational database theory, you know that a given column in a data table can be assigned a set of constraints (for example, configured as a primary key, assigned a default value, and so forth). Also, every column in a table must map to an underlying data type. For example, the Address table's schema requires that the AddressID column maps to an integer, while City, State, and Zip map to an array of characters. The `DataColumn` class has numerous properties that allow you to configure these very things. The following table provides a rundown of some core properties.

Property	Description
`AllowDBNull`	Used to indicate if a row can specify null values in this column. The default value is `true`.
`AutoIncrement`, `AutoIncrementSeed`, `AutoIncrementStep`	Used to configure the auto increment behavior for a given column. This can be helpful when you wish to ensure unique values in a given `DataColumn` (such as a primary key). By default, a `DataColumn` does not support auto increment behavior.
`Caption`	Gets or sets the caption to be displayed for this column (what the end user sees in a `DataGridView`).
`ColumnMapping`	Determines how a `DataColumn` is represented when a `DataSet` is saved as an XML document using the `DataSet.WriteXml()` method.
`ColumnName`	This property gets or sets the name of the column in the `Columns` collection (meaning how it is represented internally by the `DataTable`). If you do not set the `ColumnName` explicitly, the default values are Column with (n + 1) numerical suffixes (such as `Column1`, `Column2`, `Column3`, and so on).
`DataType`	Defines the data type (Boolean, string, float, and so forth) stored in the column.
`DefaultValue`	This property gets or sets the default value assigned to this column when inserting new rows. This is used if not otherwise specified
`Expression`	This property gets or sets the expression used to filter rows, calculate a column's value, or create an aggregate column.
`Ordinal`	Gets the numerical position of the column in the `Columns` collection maintained by the `DataTable`.
`ReadOnly`	Determines if this column can be modified once a row has been added to the table. The default is `false`.
`Table`	Gets the `DataTable` that contains this `DataColumn`.
`Unique`	Gets or sets a value indicating whether the values in each row of the column must be unique or if repeating values are permissible. If a column is assigned a primary key constraint, the `Unique` property should be set to `true`.

Assume that you wish to model the columns of the Address table. Given that the AddressID column will be the table's primary key, you will configure the `DataColumn` object as unique and non-null (using the `Unique` and `AllowDBNull` properties, respectively).

```
//Create data columns that map to the real columns in the Address table
DataColumn addressIDColumn = new DataColumn("AddressID", typeof(int));
addressIDColumn.Caption = "Address ID";
addressIDColumn.AllowDBNull = false;
addressIDColumn.Unique = true;
DataColumn cityColumn = new DataColumn("City", typeof(string));
DataColumn stateColumn = new DataColumn("State", typeof(string));
DataColumn zipColumn = new DataColumn("Zip", typeof(string));
cityColumn.Caption = "City Name";
```

The `DataColumn` type does not typically exist as a standalone entity, but is instead inserted into a related `DataTable`. To illustrate, create a new `DataTable` type (fully detailed in just a moment) and insert each `DataColumn` object in the columns collection using the `Columns` property:

```
//Now add DataColumns to a DataTable
DataTable addressTable = new DataTable("Address");
addressTable.Columns.AddRange(new DataColumn[]
  {addressIDColumn, cityColumn, stateColumn, zipColumn });
```

Working with DataRows

As you have seen, a collection of `DataColumn` objects represents the schema of a `DataTable`. In contrast, a collection of `DataRow` types represents the actual data in the table. Thus, if you have 20 listings in the Address table, you can represent these records using 20 `DataRow` types. Using the members of the `DataRow` class, you are able to insert, remove, evaluate, and manipulate the values in the table. The following table documents some of the members of the `DataRow` type.

Member	Description
`HasErrors`	Returns a Boolean value indicating if there are errors.
`ClearErrors`	Clears the errors for the row.
`GetErrorColumn`	Returns the error description of a column.
`RowError`	Allows you to configure a textual description of the error for a given row.
`ItemArray`	Gets or sets all of the values for this row using an array of objects.
`RowState`	Used to pinpoint the current state of the `DataRow` using values of the `RowState` enumeration.
`Table`	Used to obtain a reference to the `DataTable` containing this `DataRow`.
`AcceptChanges`, `RejectChanges`	Commits or rejects all changes made to this row since the last time `AcceptChanges()` was called.

Member	Description
BeginEdit, EndEdit, CancelEdit	Begins, ends, or cancels an edit operation on a DataRow object.
Delete	Marks this row to be removed when the AcceptChanges() method is called.
IsNull	Gets a value indicating whether the specified column contains a null value.

Working with a DataRow is a bit different from working with a DataColumn, because you cannot create a direct instance of this type; rather, you obtain a reference from a given DataTable. For example, assume that you wish to insert two rows in the Address table. The DataTable.NewRow() method allows you to obtain the next slot in the table, at which point you can fill each column with new data via the type indexer, as shown here:

```
//Now add a row to the Address Table
DataRow addressRow = addressTable.NewRow();
addressRow["AddressID"] = 1;
addressRow["City"] = "Chandler";
addressRow["State"] = "AZ";
addressRow["Zip"] = "85249";
addressTable.Rows.Add(addressRow);
```

Notice how the DataRow class defines an indexer that can be used to gain access to a given DataColumn by numerical position as well as column name. At this point, you have a single DataTable containing one row.

Working with DataTables

The DataTable defines a good number of members, many of which are identical in name and functionality to those of the DataSet. The following table describes some core properties of the DataTable type beyond rows and columns.

Property	Description
CaseSensitive	Indicates whether or not string comparisons within the table are case sensitive. The default value is false.
ChildRelations	Returns the collection of child relations for this DataTable (if any).
Constraints	Gets the collection of constraints maintained by the table.
DataSet	Gets the DataSet that contains this table (if any).
DefaultView	Gets a customized view of the table that may include a filtered view or a cursor position.
MinimumCapacity	Gets or sets the initial number of rows in this table (the default is 25).
ParentRelations	Gets the collection of parent relations for this DataTable.
PrimaryKey	Gets or sets an array of columns that function as primary keys for the DataTable.

Property	Description
`RemotingFormat`	Allows you to define how the `DataSet` should serialize its content (binary or XML) for the .NET remoting layer. This property is new in .NET 2.0.
`TableName`	Gets or sets the name of the table. This same property may also be specified as a constructor parameter.

For the current example, set the `PrimaryKey` property of the `DataTable` to the `addressIDColumn` `DataColumn` object:

```
//Mark the primary key of this table
addressTable.PrimaryKey = new DataColumn[]{addressTable.Columns[0]};
```

Once you do this, the `DataTable` example is complete. The final step is to insert your `DataTable` into the `addressDataSet` object:

```
//Finally, add Address table to the DataSet
addressDataSet.Tables.Add(addressTable);
```

As of .NET 2.0, `DataTable` objects also now support a method named `CreateDataReader()`. This method allows you to obtain the data within a `DataTable` using a data-reader-like navigation scheme (forward-only, read-only). To illustrate, create a `DataTableReader` object using the previously created `DataTable`:

```
//Get the new .NET 2.0 DataTableReader type.
DataTableReader addressReader = addressTable.CreateDataReader();
 //The DataTableReader works just like the DataReader
 while (addressReader.Read())
 {
   //Process the values contained in the DataReader object
 }
```

Notice that the `DataTableReader` works identically to the `DataReader` object of your data provider. Using a `DataTableReader` can be an ideal choice when you wish to quickly pump out the data within a `DataTable` without needing to traverse the internal row and column collections.

Summary

This chapter gave you a brief introduction to the exciting world of ADO.NET. It introduced you to various important classes and their logical groupings within ADO.NET. It also showed you how ADO.NET is logically grouped into connected and disconnected parts, and how various data sources are supported. In many cases, using simple commands and quick read-only cursors to retrieve results provides the easiest and most efficient way to write data access code for a web application.

3

ASP.NET 2.0 Data Controls

ASP.NET provides server-side controls that offer various behaviors, such as a drop-down list or a button. As part of this suite of controls, ASP.NET 2.0 offers two sets of controls that are specific to working with data. The first set is data source controls that allow a page to connect to a source of data and to read from and write to that source. However, a data source control has no means to display data on an ASP.NET 2.0 page, which is where data-bound controls come into play. Data-bound controls display data to the user by rendering data onto a page. This chapter provides an introduction to the data source controls and the reading behaviors of data-bound controls. The subsequent chapters in this book will build on the data control foundation provided in this chapter.

ASP.NET 2.0 introduces a series of new tools that improve data access, including several data source and data-bound controls. The new assortment of data controls can eliminate a ton of repetitive code that was required in ASP.NET 1.x. Before .NET, building data grids with traditional ASP often required you to write a lot of code to build an HTML table on the fly while looping through an ADO recordset. ASP.NET 1.x made this type of development easier by allowing you to bind a `DataSet` to the ASP.NET `DataGrid` control. This reduced the code required to generate the grid. However, both traditional ASP and ASP.NET 1.x require code to implement paging, sorting, editing, and row-selection features. With the improvements in ASP.NET 2.0, this code can be significantly reduced to produce a data-filled grid with full paging, sorting, and editing features. ASP.NET 2.0 enables this significant code reduction by providing two types of controls. The first type of controls (known as data source controls) focus on the data source-specific features, such as establishing connection, invoking the appropriate commands, and retrieving the results. Once the results are readily available from the data source controls, the second type of controls (known as data-bound controls) are then responsible for displaying that data using different formats, such as tabular and hierarchical and so on. The next section starts the discussion of ASP.NET 2.0 data controls by examining the data source controls.

Introducing Data Source Controls

In ASP.NET 1.x, you typically performed a data-binding operation by writing some data access code to retrieve a `DataReader` or a `DataSet` object, then you bound that data object to a server control, such as a `DataGrid`, `DropDownList`, or `ListBox`. If you wanted to update or delete the bound data, you were then responsible for writing the data access code to do that.

ASP.NET 2.0 introduces an additional layer of abstraction through the use of data source controls. The data source controls abstract the use of an underlying data provider, such as the SQL data provider or the OLE DB data provider. This means that you no longer need to concern yourself with the underlying complexities of using the data providers. Instead, the data source controls do all the heavy lifting for you. All you need to know is the location of your data and, if necessary, how to construct a query for performing CRUD (create, retrieve, update, and delete) operations.

> **Since the data source controls all derive from the `Control` class, you can use them much as you would any other web server control. For instance, you can define and control the behavior of the data source control either declaratively in your HTML or programmatically. This means that you can perform all manner of data access and manipulation without ever having to write one line of code.**

The five built-in data source controls in ASP.NET 2.0 are each used for a specific type of data access. The following table describes each data source control included in ASP.NET 2.0.

Control Name	Description
`SqlDataSource`	Provides access to any data source that has an ADO.NET data provider available. By default, this provides access to ODBC, OLE DB, SQL Server, Oracle, and SQL Server CE providers.
`ObjectDataSource`	Provides data access by allowing you to execute the methods of the business objects or other classes.
`XmlDataSource`	Provides data access to XML documents that may be in the form of physical XML files or in-memory XML data.
`SiteMapDataSource`	Provides access to sitemap data for a web site. By default, sitemap information is stored in the `web.sitemap` file.
`AccessDataSource`	Provides access to data stored in the Access database.

All of the above data source controls are derived from the `DataSourceControl` class, which is derived from `Control` and implements the `IDataSource` and `IListSource` interfaces. This means that although each control is designed for use with specific data sources, all data source controls share a basic set of core functionality. It also means that it is easy for you to create your own custom data source controls based on the structure of your specific data sources. Regardless of which data source control you use, it will enable a set of behaviors for your ASP.NET 2.0 page. These include a connection to the database and the enabling of behaviors such as reading and writing data. These behaviors will be available to data-bound controls that display data and receive input from the user.

If you are familiar with older versions of ASP, the ASP.NET 2.0 data source controls instantiate ADO.NET objects. Therefore, ADO.NET provides the underlying technology for data access. The creation and manipulation of ADO.NET objects for most scenarios is now handled automatically (and correctly and efficiently) by the higher-level data source control objects. In summary, the data source controls create the background infrastructure needed to use data. However, they do not create any rendering on the web page. Rather, they make the data behaviors like reading and writing to data stores available to data-bound controls. The next section begins the in-depth examination of data source controls with the `SqlDataSource` control.

SqlDataSource Control

The `SqlDataSource` control is the data source control to use if your data is stored in a SQL Server, Oracle Server, ODBC data source, OLE DB data source, or Windows SQL CE Database. The `SqlDataSource` represents a database connection that uses an ADO.NET provider. However, this has a catch. The `SqlDataSource` needs a generic way to create the `Connection`, `Command`, and `DataReader` objects it requires. The only way this is possible is if your data provider includes a data provider factory, which has the responsibility of creating the provider-specific objects that the `SqlDataSource` needs in order to access the data source.

As you know, .NET ships with these four provider factories:

- `System.Data.SqlClient`
- `System.Data.OracleClient`
- `System.Data.OleDb`
- `System.Data.Odbc`

These are registered in the `machine.config` file, and as a result you can use any of them with the `SqlDataSource`. You specify the provider name as part of the `SqlDataSource` control declaration. Here is a `SqlDataSource` that connects to a SQL Server database:

```
<asp:SqlDataSource ID="productCategoriesSource"
  ProviderName="System.Data.SqlClient"..../>
```

The next step is to supply the required connection string—without it, you cannot make any connections:

```
<asp:SqlDataSource ProviderName="System.Data.SqlClient"
  ConnectionString="server=localhost;database=AdventureWorks;uid=user;pwd=word"
  ....>
</asp:SqlDataSource>
```

Once you have specified the provider name and connection string, the next step is to add the query logic that the `SqlDataSource` will use when it connects to the database. The complete declaration of the data source control is:

```
<asp:SqlDataSource ID="productCategoriesSource" runat="server"
  ProviderName="System.Data.SqlClient"
  ConnectionString="server=localhost;database=AdventureWorks;uid=user;pwd=word"
  SelectCommand="SELECT ProductCategoryID, Name FROM Production.ProductCategory">
</asp:SqlDataSource>
```

Now that you have the SqlDataSource control with all the attributes, the next step is to add a data-bound control that uses the data from the data source control. In this case, a DropDownList control is used as the data-bound control:

```
<asp:DropDownList ID="productCategoriesSource" runat="server"
  DataSourceID="productCategoriesSource" DataTextField="Name"
  DataValueField="ProductCategoryID" AutoPostBack="True">
</asp:DropDownList>
```

If you browse to the above page, you should see output similar to that in Figure 3-1.

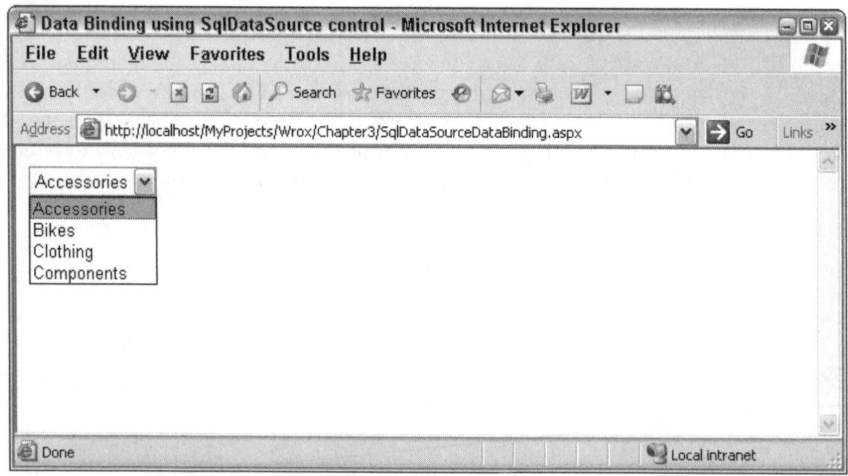

Figure 3-1

Connection Strings from the Configuration File

In ASP.NET 2.0, Microsoft has tried to address the common shortcomings in the Web.config file with ASP.NET 1.x. One such shortcoming is that there is not a well-defined location for storing connection strings. Because database connection information is so frequently stored in the Web.config file, you now have an entirely new configuration section in that file, <connectionStrings>, specifically for storing the connection string information.

Although you can hard-code the connection string directly in the SqlDataSource tag (as shown in the previous section), you should always place it in the <connectionStrings> section of the Web.config file to guarantee greater flexibility and ensure that you won't inadvertently change the connection string, which minimizes the effectiveness of connection pooling. For example, add the below connection string in the Web.config file:

```
<configuration xmlns="http://schemas.microsoft.com/.NetConfiguration/v2.0">
<connectionStrings>
  <add name="AdventureWorks"
   connectionString="server=localhost;database=AdventureWorks;uid=user;pwd=word;"/>
</connectionStrings>
...
</configuration>
```

With the above connection string placed in the Web.config file, you would reference it in the SqlDataSource using the $ expression, as shown below:

```
<asp:SqlDataSource ID="productCategoriesSource" runat="server"
  ProviderName="System.Data.SqlClient"
  ConnectionString="<%$ConnectionStrings:AdventureWorks%>"
  SelectCommand="SELECT ProductCategoryID, Name FROM Production.ProductCategory">
</asp:SqlDataSource>
```

If you navigate to the page again using the browser, you should see the same output as that of Figure 3-1.

The Page Life Cycle with Data Binding

In ASP.NET 1.x, creating data-bound pages was complicated because you needed to understand the page's life cycle, or you risked binding the page at the wrong time. Of course, in ASP.NET 2.0 you still need to understand the basics of the page's life cycle, because you will run into situations where you need to work with or extend the data-binding model. For example, you might want to add data or set a selected item in a control after it has been bound to the data source. Depending on the scenario, you might be able to respond to data source control events, but they are not always fired at the point you need to perform your logic. Essentially, data-binding tasks occur in this order:

1. The page object is created (based on the .aspx file).
2. The page life cycle begins, and the Page.Init and Page.Load events fire.
3. All other control events fire.
4. The data source controls perform any updates. If a row is being updated, the Updating and Updated events fire. If a row is being inserted, the Inserting and Inserted events fire. If a row is being deleted, the Deleting and Deleted events fire.
5. The Page.PreRender event fires.
6. The data source controls perform any queries and insert the retrieved data in the linked controls. The Selecting and Selected events fire at this point.
7. The page is rendered and disposed of.

The data binding is performed on every postback (unless you redirect to another page). If you need to write code that springs into action after the data binding is complete, you can override the Page.OnPreRenderComplete() method. This method is called immediately after the PreRender stage, but just before the view state is serialized and the actual HTML is rendered.

DataSourceMode Property

One of many important properties of the SqlDataSource control is the DataSourceMode property, which enables you to tell the control if it should use a DataSet or a DataReader internally when retrieving the data. This is important when you are designing data-driven ASP.NET pages. If you choose to use a DataReader, data is retrieved using what is commonly known as fire-hose mode, or a forward-only, read-only cursor. This is the fastest way to read data from your data source, because a DataReader does not have the memory and processing overhead of a DataSet. But choosing to use a DataSet makes the data source control more powerful by enabling the control to perform other operations, such as inserting, updating, or deleting data as it is changed in the DataSet. It also enables the built-in caching capabilities of the control. Each option offers distinct advantages and disadvantages, so consider this property carefully when designing your web site. The default value for the `DataSourceMode` property is to use a `DataSet` to retrieve data. The following code shows how to add the `DataSourceMode` property to your `SqlDataSource` control:

```
<asp:SqlDataSource ID="productCategoriesSource" runat="server"
  ProviderName="System.Data.SqlClient"
  ConnectionString="<%$ConnectionStrings:AdventureWorks%>"
  SelectCommand="SELECT ProductCategoryID, Name FROM Production.ProductCategory"
  DataSourceMode="DataSet"/>
```

Filtering Data Using SelectParameters

Of course, when selecting data from your data source, you may not want to get every single row of data from a view or table. You want to be able to specify parameters in your query to limit the data that is returned. The `SqlDataSource` data source control allows you to do this by using the `SelectParameters` collection to create parameters that it can use at runtime to alter the data that is returned from a query.

> **In addition to the `SelectParameters` collection, the `SqlDataSource` control also exposes properties such as `InsertParameters`, `UpdateParameters`, and `DeleteParameters`, which enable you to add parameters to the insert, update, and delete commands, respectively.**

The `SelectParameters` collection consists of controls that are derived from the `Parameters` class. You can combine any number of parameter controls in the collection. The data source control then uses these to create a dynamic SQL query. The following table lists and describes the available parameter controls that can be used in conjunction with the `xxxParameters` collection.

Parameter	Description
`ControlParameter`	Uses the value of the specified control
`CookieParameter`	Uses the key value of a cookie
`FormParameter`	Uses the key value from the `Forms` collection
`QueryStringParameter`	Uses a key value from the query string collection
`ProfileParameter`	Uses a key value from the user's profile collection
`SessionParameter`	Uses a key value from the current user's session

In the previous example, the complete query was hard-coded. Often, you won't have this flexibility. Instead, you will want to retrieve a subset of data, such as all the products in a given category or all the employees in a specific city. The following example extends the previous example by allowing you to select a product category and bring up all the product subcategories. To create this example, you need two data sources. The first data source provides a list of product categories (which was shown in the previous example), and the second data source provides a list of product subcategories based on the selected product category. Listing 3-1 provides the complete code of the page.

Listing 3-1: Using the SqlDataSource Control to Retrieve Categories Information

```
<%@ page language="C#" %>
<html xmlns="http://www.w3.org/1999/xhtml">
<head id="Head1" runat="server">
  <title>Data Binding using SqlDataSource control</title>
</head>
<body>
  <form id="Form1" runat="server">
    <asp:SqlDataSource id="productCategoriesSource"
      ProviderName="System.Data.SqlClient" runat="server"
      ConnectionString="<%$ConnectionStrings:AdventureWorks%>"
      SelectCommand="SELECT * From Production.ProductCategory">
    </asp:SqlDataSource>
    <asp:DropDownList ID="lstCategories" runat="server"
      DataSourceID="productCategoriesSource" DataTextField="Name"
      DataValueField="ProductCategoryID" AutoPostBack="True">
    </asp:DropDownList>
    <asp:SqlDataSource ID="productSubCategoriesSource" runat="server"
      ProviderName="System.Data.SqlClient"
      ConnectionString="<%$ ConnectionStrings:AdventureWorks %>"
      SelectCommand="SELECT ProductSubcategoryID As CategoryID, Name from
      Production.ProductSubcategory
      WHERE ProductCategoryID=@ProductCategoryID">
      <SelectParameters>
        <asp:ControlParameter ControlID="lstCategories" Name="ProductCategoryID"
          PropertyName="SelectedValue" />
      </SelectParameters>
    </asp:SqlDataSource>
    <asp:GridView id="gridCategories" DataSourceID="productSubCategoriesSource"
      runat="server">
    </asp:GridView>
  </form>
</body>
</html>
```

In Listing 3-1, the `DropDownList` control has automatic postback enabled, which ensures that the page is posted back every time the list selection is changed, giving your page the chance to update its data-bound controls accordingly. The other option is to create a dedicated button (such as Select) next to the list control for initiating the postback. When you select a category from the drop-down list, the second data source retrieves all the subcategories that belong to that category.

As you can see, the second data source control has the query written using a parameter. Parameters are always indicated with an at (`@`) symbol, as in `@ProductCategoryID`. You can define as many symbols as you want, but you must map each provider to another value. In this example, the value for the `@ProductCategoryID` parameter is taken from the `lstCategories.SelectedValue` property. However, you could just as easily modify the `ControlParameter` tag to bind to another property or control. Because all the parameter controls are derived from the `Parameters` class, they all contain several useful common properties. These properties are shown in the following table.

Property	Description
`ConvertEmptyToNull`	Indicates if the control should convert the assigned value to `Null` if the value is equal to `System.String.Empty`
`DefaultValue`	Allows you to specify a default value for the parameter if it is evaluated as `Null`
`Name`	Allows you to specify the name of the parameter
`Type`	Allows you to strongly type the value of the parameter
`Size`	Allows you to set or get the size of the parameter

So far this chapter has just provided the basics of the `SqlDataSource` control. For an in-depth treatment of `SqlDataSource` control, please refer to Chapter 4.

Disadvantages of the SqlDataSource

As you have seen, when you use the `SqlDataSource` control, you can often avoid writing any data access code. However, you also sacrifice a fair bit of flexibility. Here are the most significant disadvantages:

- **Data access logic embedded in the page:** To create a `SqlDataSource` control, you need to hard-code the SQL statements in your web page. This means that you cannot fine-tune your query without modifying your web page. In an enterprise application, this limitation is not acceptable, as it is common to revise the queries after the application is deployed in response to profiling, indexes, and expected loads. You can improve this situation a fair bit by restricting your use of the `SqlDataSource` to stored procedures. However, in a large-scale web application, the data access code will be maintained, tested, and refined separately from the business logic (and it may even be coded by different developers). `SqlDataSource` just does not give you that level of flexibility.
- **Maintenance in large applications:** Every page that accesses the database needs its own set of `SqlDataSource` controls. This can turn into a maintenance nightmare, particularly if you have several pages using the same query (each of which requires a duplicate instance of the `SqlDataSource`). In a component-based application, you will use a higher-level model. The web pages will communicate with a data access library, which will contain all the database details.
- **Inapplicability to other data tasks:** The `SqlDataSource` does not properly represent some types of tasks. The `SqlDataSource` is intended for data display and data-editing scenarios. However, this model breaks down if you need to connect to the database and perform another task, such as placing a shipment request into an order pipeline or logging an event. In these situations, you will need custom database code. It will simplify your application if you have a single database library that encapsulates these tasks along with data retrieval and updating operations.

Although the `SqlDataSource` control is powerful, there are a number of other data source controls that might better suit your specific data access scenario. One such control is `XmlDataSource` control, which is the topic of focus in the next section.

XmlDataSource Control

XML data is generally used to represent semistructured or hierarchal data. Using XML documents as your data source allows you to receive XML documents from other sources and format the XML data to be compatible with your application. ASP.NET 1.x let you use XML data sources, but much of that work required manual coding to get the data into a format suitable for displaying. In contrast, ASP.NET 2.0 provides a new `XmlDataSource` control that simplifies binding XML data to controls such as the `TreeView` and `GridView`—and it works with both hierarchical and tabular data.

The `XmlDataSource` control provides you with a simple way of binding XML documents, either in-memory (using the `Data` property) or located on a physical drive (using the `DataFile` property). The control provides you with a number of properties that make it easy to specify an XML file containing data and an XSLT transform file for converting the source XML into a more suitable format. You can also provide an XPath query to select only a certain subset of data. Listing 3-2 shows how you might consume a local RSS file, selecting all the item nodes within it for binding to a bound list control such as the `TreeView`.

Listing 3-2: Using the XmlDataSource Control to Display RSS Feeds

```
<html xmlns="http://www.w3.org/1999/xhtml" >
<head id="Head1" runat="server">
  <title>Using the XmlDataSource control</title>
</head>
<body>
<form id="form1" runat="server">
    <div>
      <asp:XmlDataSource ID="XmlDataSource1" Runat="server"
        XPath="rss/channel/item" DataFile="App_Data/Index.xml"/>
      <asp:TreeView runat="server" ID="TreeView1" DataSourceID="XmlDataSource1"/>
    </div>
  </form>
</body>
</html>
```

Once you have the data available in the `XmlDataSource` control, you can then easily bind it to data-bound controls such as `TreeView`, `Menu`, or `GridView`, as shown in Listing 3-2. Please refer to Chapter 5 of this book for in-depth coverage of `XmlDataSource` control.

ObjectDataSource Control

The `ObjectDataSource` allows you to create a declarative link between your web page controls and a data access component that queries and updates data. The `ObjectDataSource` is remarkably flexible and can work with a variety of different components. However, to use it, your data access class must conform to a few rules:

- It must be stateless. That's because the `ObjectDataSource` will create an instance only when needed and destroy it at the end of every request.
- It must have a default, no-argument constructor.
- All the logic must be contained in a single class. (If you want to use different classes for selecting and updating your data, you will need to wrap them in another, higher-level class.)

- None of the linked methods (for selecting or updating records) can be static.
- It must provide the query results when a single method is called. The query results are several records, which can be represented as a collection, an array, or a list object that implements `IEnumerable`. Each record should be a custom object that exposes all its data through public properties.

You can work around many of these rules by handling `ObjectDataSource` events and writing custom code. However, if you want your data access class to plug into the data-binding model seamlessly without extra work, you should observe these guidelines. The following table provides a listing of the important properties of the `ObjectDataSource` control.

Property	Description
`ConvertNullToDBNull`	Allows you to specify whether the null value supplied to the control should be automatically converted to `DBNull`.
`DataObjectTypeName`	Allows you to set or get the name of a class that the `ObjectDataSource` control uses for passing parameters.
`DeleteMethod`	Allows you to specify the name of the method that the `ObjectDataSource` control uses for delete operation.
`DeleteParameters`	Read-only property that allows you to get the parameter collection used by the `DeleteMethod`.
`InsertMethod`	Allows you to set or get the name of the insert method used by the `ObjectDataSource` control.
`InsertParameters`	Read-only property that allows you to get reference to the parameters used by the `InsertMethod` method.
`SelectCountMethod`	Allows you to specify the name of the business object method that will be used by the `ObjectDataSource` control to get the count of the number of rows. Note that the row count is specifically used to support data source paging.
`SelectMethod`	Allows you to specify the method used by the `ObjectDataSource` control for retrieving data.
`SelectParameters`	Read-only property that gets the reference to the parameters collection used by the `SelectMethod`.
`TypeName`	Allows you to set or get the name of the class that the `ObjectDataSource` control performs all the operations against.
`UpdateMethod`	Allows you to get or set the name of the method used by the `ObjectDataSource` control for updating purposes.
`UpdateParameters`	Read-only property that returns the parameters collection used by the `UpdateMethod` method.

Now that you have an understanding of the properties of the `ObjectDataSource` control, the next section discusses a simple example using the `ObjectDataSource` control.

Selecting Records

In this section, you will replace the `SqlDataSource` control with the `ObjectDataSource` to understand the steps involved in creating and consuming a custom data access class from an ASP.NET page. The custom data access class is named `CategoryDB`, and it is placed in the `App_Code` directory. It is declared as shown in Listing 3-3.

Listing 3-3: Implementation of the CategoryDB Class

```
using System.Data;
using System.Data.SqlClient;
using System.Web.Configuration;

public class CategoryDB
{
public CategoryDB(){}

public DataSet GetCategories()
{
    string connectionString = WebConfigurationManager.ConnectionStrings
      ["AdventureWorks"].ConnectionString;
    using (SqlConnection connection = new SqlConnection(connectionString))
    {
      SqlCommand command = connection.CreateCommand();
      command.CommandText = "Select ProductCategoryID as CategoryID, Name " +
        "from Production.ProductCategory ";
      command.Connection = connection;
      SqlDataAdapter adapter = new SqlDataAdapter(command);
      DataSet categoriesDataSet = new DataSet();
      adapter.Fill(categoriesDataSet);
      return categoriesDataSet;
    }
  }
}
```

Listing 3-3 connects to the AdventureWorks database, executes a query against the `Production.ProductCategory` table, and returns the results to the caller in the form of a `DataSet` object. Now that the data access class is created, you are ready to consume it from an ASP.NET page.

The first step to use this class in your page is to define the `ObjectDataSource` and indicate the name of the class that contains the data access methods. You do this by specifying the fully qualified class name with the `TypeName` property:

```
<asp:ObjectDataSource ID="categoriesSource" runat="server"
  TypeName="CategoryDB".../>
```

For the above code to work, the `CategoryDB` class must exist in the `App_Code` folder. Once you have attached the `ObjectDataSource` to a class, the next step is to point it to the methods it can use to select records. The `ObjectDataSource` defines `SelectMethod`, `DeleteMethod`, `UpdateMethod`, and `InsertMethod` properties that you use to link your data access class to various tasks. Each property takes the name of the method in the data access class. In this example, you simply need to enable querying, so you need to set the `SelectMethod` attribute:

```
<asp:ObjectDataSource ID="categoriesSource" runat="server"
  TypeName="CategoryDB" SelectMethod="GetCategories" />
```

Remember, the `GetCategories()` method returns a `DataSet` object. Once you have set up the `ObjectDataSource`, you can bind your web page controls in the same way you do with the `SqlDataSource`. Listing 3-4 provides the complete page code, without the formatting details for the `GridView`.

Listing 3-4: Binding the ObjectDataSource Control with the CategoryDB Class

```
<html xmlns="http://www.w3.org/1999/xhtml">
<head id="Head1" runat="server">
  <title>Data Binding using ObjectDataSource control</title>
</head>
<body>
  <form id="Form1" runat="server">
    <asp:ObjectDataSource ID="categoriesSource" runat="server"
      SelectMethod="GetCategories" TypeName="CategoryDB" />
    <asp:GridView id="gridCategories" DataKeyNames="CategoryID"
      AutoGenerateColumns="True" DataSourceID="categoriesSource" runat="server">
    </asp:GridView>
  </form>
</body>
</html>
```

As you can see, this example is equivalent to the `SqlDataSource` page shown in Listing 3-1. The apparent similarities conceal some real behind-the-scenes differences. In this example, the web page does not require any hard-coded SQL details. Instead, all the work is handed off to the `CategoryDB` class. When you run the page, the `GridView` will request data from the `ObjectDataSource`, which will call the `CategoryDB.GetCategories()` method to retrieve the data. This data is then bound and displayed, without any code whatsoever.

> **Earlier, you saw how you could use the `SqlDataSource` to execute parameterized commands. The same feat is possible with the `ObjectDataSource`. To accomplish this, you provide a suitable select method that accepts one or more parameters in your data access class. You can then map each parameter to a control value, query string argument, and so on. The name you define for the parameter must match the parameter name you use in the method exactly. When the `ObjectDataSource` calls the method, it uses reflection to examine the method, and it examines the parameter names to determine the order of arguments.**

SiteMapDataSource Control

The `SiteMapDataSource` control enables you to work with data stored in your web site's sitemap configuration file, if you have one. By default, this configuration information is stored in `web.sitemap` file. This can be useful if you are changing your sitemap data at runtime, perhaps based on user privilege or status. The `SiteMapDataSource` control will automatically consume the contents of the `web.sitemap` file and make it readily available for the hierarchical data-bound controls.

In this example, you use the TreeView control to display hierarchical information about the site structure using the contents of the web.sitemap file. For the purposes of this example, use the web.sitemap file shown in Listing 3-5.

Listing 3-5: Web.sitemap File

```
<?xml version="1.0" encoding="utf-8" ?>
<siteMap>
  <siteMapNode title="Default" description="Home" url="Default.aspx" >
    <siteMapNode title="Members" description="Members" url="Members.aspx">
      <siteMapNode title="My Account" description="My Account"
        url="MyAccount.aspx" />
      <siteMapNode title="Products" description="Products" url="Products.aspx" />
    </siteMapNode>
    <siteMapNode title="Administration" description="Administration"
      url="~/Admin/Default.aspx">
      <siteMapNode title="Customer" description="Customer Admin"
        url="~/Admin/Customer/default.aspx" />
      <siteMapNode title="Products Admin" description="Products Admin"
        url="~/Admin/ProductsAdmin.aspx" />
    </siteMapNode>
  </siteMapNode>
</siteMap>
```

As you can see, the web.sitemap file specifies the list of nodes that specifies he navigation structure of the site, which can be completely independent of the site folder layout or other structure. Now that you have the web.sitemap file created, it is very easy to leverage it from an ASP.NET page. Listing 3-6 shows the complete ASP.NET page.

Listing 3-6: Using SiteMapDataSource Control to Display Site Hierarchy

```
<html xmlns="http://www.w3.org/1999/xhtml" >
<head id="Head1" runat="server">
  <title>Using the SiteMapDataSource control</title>
</head>
<body>
<form id="form1" runat="server">
    <div>
      <asp:TreeView ID="TreeView1" Runat="server"
        DataSourceID="SiteMapDataSource1">
      </asp:TreeView>
      <asp:SiteMapDataSource ID="SiteMapDataSource1" Runat="server" />
    </div>
  </form>
</body>
</html>
```

Listing 3-6 declares a SiteMapDataSource control on the ASP.NET page that acts as a data source control for TreeView1. The SiteMapDataSource looks for a file with the name web.sitemap, by default. It will read the contents of the web.sitemap file and consume that information as a data source control. Once the information is available in a SiteMapDataSource control, you can then consume it from a data-bound control such as a TreeView control. Figure 3-2 shows the output produced by the ASP.NET page.

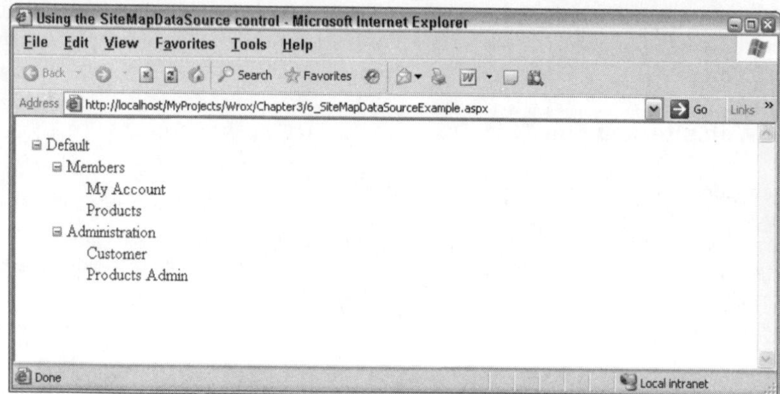

Figure 3-2

It is also possible for you to retrieve site navigation data programmatically in code. One of the important classes that you use for obtaining site navigation data programmatically is the `SiteMap` class. This class provides a number of static methods, the most important one being the `CurrentNode` property. For example, you can invoke `SiteMap.CurrentNode` to reference a piece of navigation data matching the currently executing page. The `CurrentNode` property returns an instance of a `SiteMapNode` object that corresponds to the current page. Once you have an instance of the `SiteMapNode` object instance, you can perform the following tasks:

- Retrieve properties of a node including `Url`, `Title`, and `Description`.
- Obtain a node's parent as well as a node's children.
- Navigate through the sibling nodes before and after the current node.
- Obtain a reference to the `SiteMapProvider` instance that returned this node.

Chapter 7 of this book provides you with a complete discussion of the `SiteMapDataSource` control.

Configuring Data Source Control Caching

Caching is now automatically built into all the data source controls except the `SiteMapDataSource` control. This means that you can easily configure and control data caching using the same declarative syntax. All data source controls (except the `SiteMapDataSource` control) enable you to create basic caching policies, including a cache direction, expiration policies, and key dependencies.

> **Remember that the `SqlDataSource` control's caching features are available only if you have set the `DataSourceMode` property to `DataSet`. If it is set to `DataReader`, the control throws a `NotSupportedException`.**

Cache duration can be set to a specific length of time, such as 3600 seconds (60 minutes), or you can set it to `Infinite` to force the cached data never to expire. The following code shows how you can easily add caching features to a data source control:

```
<asp:SqlDataSource ID="SqlDataSource1" Runat="server"
  SelectCommand="SELECT * FROM Production.ProductCategory"
ConnectionString="<%$ ConnectionStrings:AdventureWorks %>"
  DataSourceMode="DataSet" EnableCaching="True" CacheKeyDependency="SomeKey"
  CacheDuration="Infinite">
</asp:SqlDataSource>
```

Some controls also extend this core set of caching features with additional caching functionality specific to their data sources. For instance, if you are using the `SqlDataSource` control, you can use the `SqlCacheDependency` property to create SQL dependencies. You can learn more about ASP.NET 2.0 caching features in Chapter 11.

Introducing Data-Bound Controls

Data-bound controls provide the link between the data source controls and the user. They take the data and behaviors of the data source control and render them to the visitor. This division of labor works very well. You can select any data source control and link that to any of the data-bound controls. With just a few exceptions, it is a mix-and-match scenario.

Data-bound controls encapsulate remarkable amounts of behavior. For example, the `GridView` control can not only display data in a table, but it also offers sorting, selecting, paging through subsets, and one-click transition to data editing. If your needs extend beyond these capabilities, you can write custom code hooked into events exposed by the `GridView` control.

> **There is one constraint on the compatibility of data source controls and data-bound controls. Each control is optimized for tabular data, tree data, or custom class data. For example, XML data is organized as a tree and thus best accessed with the `XmlDataSource` control and displayed in `Menu` or `TreeView` data-bound controls. SQL Server data is organized into tables, and thus is accessed with the `SqlDataSource` control and displayed in `GridView` (tables) or `DetailsView`. List type data-bound controls can display either source of data. You can twist the controls to cross-utilize types of data, but in general it is best to stick to their intended purpose.**

Note that you can still use the familiar `DataBind()` method to bind data to the list controls. In fact, that method has even been enhanced to include a Boolean overload that allows you to turn the data-binding events on or off. This enables you improve the performance of your application if you are not using any of the binding events. Let us start our discussion of data-bound controls by looking at the new control in town, `GridView`.

GridView

If you have programmed with ASP.NET 1.x, you've probably used the `DataGrid` control. Faced with the challenge of enhancing the `DataGrid` while preserving backward compatibility, the ASP.NET team decided to create an entirely new control to implement their improvements. This control is the `GridView`. The `GridView` is an extremely flexible grid control for showing data. It includes a wide range of hard-wired features, including selection, paging, and editing, and it is extensible through templates.

The great advantage of the GridView over the DataGrid is its support for code-free scenarios. Using the GridView, you can accomplish many common tasks, such as paging and selection, without writing any code. With the DataGrid, you were forced to handle events to implement the same features.

> *The DataGrid is still available in ASP.NET 2.0, and it now supports binding to a data source control. As a rule of thumb, the DataGrid should be used only for backward compatibility and existing ASP.NET web sites (where it still works quite well). When creating a new web site, use the GridView instead.*

Here is a simple GridView declaration that uses a SqlDataSource control named productSub CategoriesSource as its data source:

```
<asp:GridView id="gridCategories" AutoGenerateColumns="true"
  DataSourceID="productSubCategoriesSource" runat="server">
</asp:GridView>
```

Note that the AutoGenerateColumns property is set to true in the above case. This enables all the columns from the data source control to be displayed in the GridView. The default value of AutoGenerateColumns property is true.

Defining Columns

The GridView example you have seen so far has set the GridView.AutoGenerateColumns property to true. When this property is set, the GridView uses reflection to examine that data object and find all the fields (of a record) or properties (of a custom object). It then creates a column for each one, in the order that it finds it.

This automatic column generation is good for creating quick test pages, but it does not give you the flexibility you will usually want. For example, what if you want to hide columns, change their order, or configure some aspect of their display, such as the formatting or heading text? In all of these cases, you will need to set AutoGenerateColumns to false and define the columns yourself in the <Columns> section of the GridView control tag.

> **It is possible to have AutoGenerateColumns set to true and define columns in the <Columns> section. In this case, the columns you explicitly defined are added before the auto-generated columns. However, for the most flexibility, you will usually want to explicitly define every column.**

Each column can be any of several different types, as described in the following table. The order of your column tags determines the right-to-left order of columns in the GridView.

Field	Description
BoundField	Displays the value of a field in a data source. This is the default column type of the GridView control.
CheckBoxField	Displays a check box for each item in the GridView control. This column field type is commonly used to display fields with a Boolean value.

Field	Description
HyperLinkField	Displays the value of a field in a data source as a hyperlink. This column field type allows you to bind a second field to the hyperlink's URL.
ButtonField	Displays a command button for each item in the GridView control. This allows you to create a column of custom button controls, such as an Add or Remove button.
CommandField	Represents a special field that displays command buttons to perform select, edit, insert, or delete operations in a data-bound control.
ImageField	Automatically displays an image when the data in the field represents an image.
TemplateField	Displays user-defined content for each item in the GridView control according to a specified template. This column field type allows you to create a custom column field.

Here is a complete GridView declaration with explicit columns:

```
<asp:GridView id="gridCategories" AutoGenerateColumns="False"
  DataSourceID="productSubCategoriesSource" runat="server">
  <Columns>
    <asp:BoundField DataField="CategoryID" HeaderText="Category ID" />
    <asp:BoundField DataField="Name" HeaderText="Category Name" />
</Columns>
</asp:GridView>
```

When you explicitly declare a bound field, you have the opportunity to set other properties. The following table lists these properties.

Property	Description
DataField	The name of the field (for a row) or property (for an object) of the data item that you want to display in this column.
DataFormatString	A format string that formats the field. This is useful for getting the right representation of numbers and dates.
FooterText, HeaderText	Sets the text in the header and footer region of the grid, if this grid has a header (ShowHeader is true) and footer (ShowFooter is true).
ReadOnly	If true, the value for this column can't be changed in edit mode. No edit control will be provided. Primary key fields are often read-only.
Visible	If false, the column won't be visible in the page (and no HTML will be rendered for it). This property gives you a convenient way to programmatically hide or show specific columns, changing the overall view of the data.
SortExpression	An expression that can be appended to a query to perform a sort based on this column.
ConvertEmpty StringToNull	If true, before an edit is committed, all empty strings will be converted to null values.

The GridView control is also enhanced with the addition of a sorting feature. The capability to sort data is one of the most basic tools users have to navigate through a significant amount of data. The DataGrid control made sorting columns in a grid a relatively easy task, but the GridView control takes it one step further. Unlike using the DataGrid, where you are responsible for coding the sort routine, to enable column sorting in this grid, you just set the AllowSorting attribute to true. The control takes care of all the sorting logic for you internally. Listing 3-7 shows how to add this attribute to your grid.

Listing 3-7: Using the GridView Control to Display Category Information

```
<html xmlns="http://www.w3.org/1999/xhtml">
<head id="Head1" runat="server">
  <title>Data Binding using GridView control</title>
</head>
<body>
  <form id="Form1" runat="server">
    <asp:SqlDataSource ID="productSubCategoriesSource" runat="server"
      ProviderName="System.Data.SqlClient"
      ConnectionString="<%$ ConnectionStrings:AdventureWorks %>"
      SelectCommand="SELECT ProductSubcategoryID As CategoryID, Name from
      Production.ProductSubcategory">
    </asp:SqlDataSource>
    <asp:GridView id="gridCategories" DataKeyNames="CategoryID" AllowSorting="true"
      AutoGenerateColumns="False" DataSourceID="productSubCategoriesSource"
      runat="server">
      <Columns>
        <asp:BoundField SortExpression="CategoryID" DataField="CategoryID"
           HeaderText="Category ID" />
        <asp:BoundField DataField="Name" HeaderText="Category Name" />
      </Columns>
    </asp:GridView>
  </form>
</body>
</html>
```

Figure 3-3 shows what your web page looks like when you execute the code in a browser.

After enabling sorting, you see that the Category ID column has now become hyperlinks. Clicking a column header sorts that specific column. Figure 3-3 shows your grid after the data has been sorted by Category ID. Chapter 8 provides you with more details on the steps involved in inserting, updating, and deleting rows from the GridView.

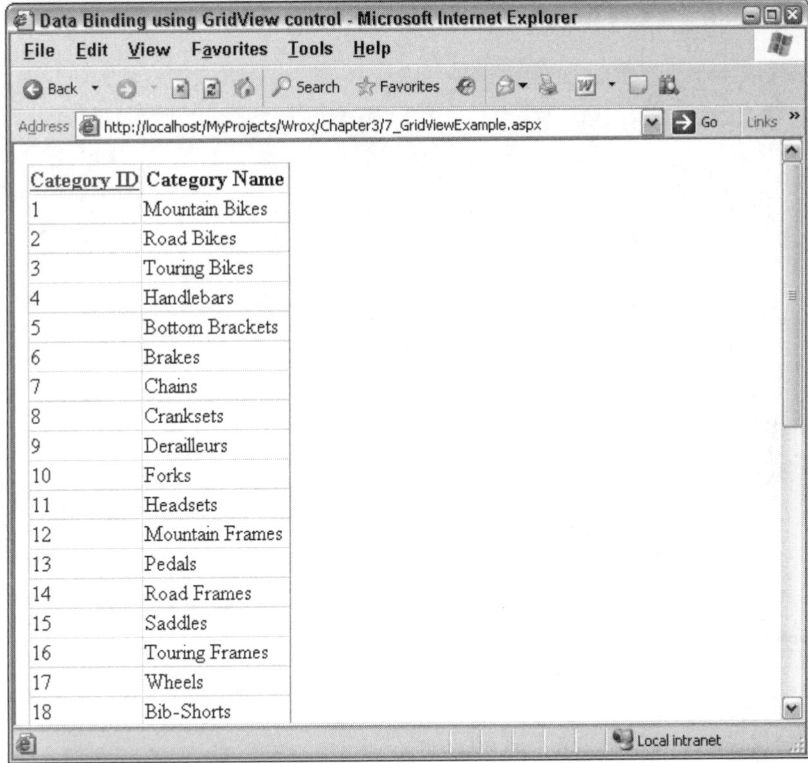

Category ID	Category Name
1	Mountain Bikes
2	Road Bikes
3	Touring Bikes
4	Handlebars
5	Bottom Brackets
6	Brakes
7	Chains
8	Cranksets
9	Derailleurs
10	Forks
11	Headsets
12	Mountain Frames
13	Pedals
14	Road Frames
15	Saddles
16	Touring Frames
17	Wheels
18	Bib-Shorts

Figure 3-3

DetailsView

The `DetailsView` server control is a new data-bound control that enables you to view a single data record at a time. It places each piece of information (be it a field or a property) in a separate row of a table. Although the `GridView` control is an excellent control for viewing a collection of data, many scenarios demand that you be able to drill down into an individual record. The `DetailsView` control allows you to do this and provides many of the same data manipulation and display capabilities as the `GridView`. It allows you to do things such as paging, updating, inserting, and deleting data.

You can customize the appearance of the `DetailsView` control by picking and choosing which fields the control displays. By default, the control displays each column from the table it is working with. Much like the `GridView` control, however, the `DetailsView` control enables you to specify that only certain selected columns are displayed, as illustrated in Listing 3-8.

Listing 3-8: Binding a DetailsView Control to a SqlDataSource Control

```
<html xmlns="http://www.w3.org/1999/xhtml">
<head id="Head1" runat="server">
  <title>Data Binding using DetailsView control</title>
</head>
<body>
  <form id="Form1" runat="server">
    <asp:SqlDataSource ID="productSubCategoriesSource" runat="server"
      ProviderName="System.Data.SqlClient"
      ConnectionString="<%$ ConnectionStrings:AdventureWorks %>"
      SelectCommand="SELECT ProductSubcategoryID As CategoryID, Name from
      Production.ProductSubcategory">
    </asp:SqlDataSource>
    <asp:DetailsView id="detailViewCategories" DataKeyNames="CategoryID"
      AllowPaging="true" AutoGenerateRows="False"
      DataSourceID="productSubCategoriesSource" runat="server">
      <Fields>
        <asp:BoundField SortExpression="CategoryID" DataField="CategoryID"
          HeaderText="Category ID" />
        <asp:BoundField DataField="Name" HeaderText="Category Name" />
      </Fields>
    </asp:DetailsView>
  </form>
</body>
</html>
```

If you run the page at this point, you see that the control displays one record, the first record returned by your query. You can navigate to the remaining records by using the page navigation mechanism. Figure 3-4 shows you what the `DetailsView` looks like in a web page.

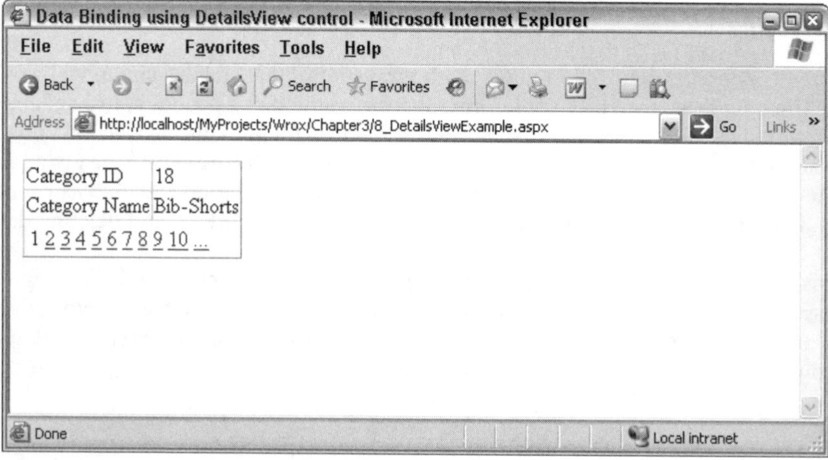

Figure 3-4

Notice that the page navigation mechanism is enabled in the `GridView` control through the `AllowPaging` attribute of the `DetailsView`, which is set to `true` in this case.

FormView

The `FormView` control is a new control included with the ASP.NET 2.0 toolbox. It basically functions like the `DetailsView` control, in that it displays a single data item from a bound data source control and allows adding, editing, and deleting data. What makes it unique is that it displays the data in custom templates, which provides much greater control over how the data is displayed and edited. Listing 3-9 shows a `FormView` control that has the `ItemTemplate` that contains the actual declarations.

Listing 3-9: Binding a FormView Control with a SqlDataSource Control

```
<html xmlns="http://www.w3.org/1999/xhtml">
<head id="Head1" runat="server">
  <title>Data Binding using GridView control</title>
</head>
<body>
  <form id="Form1" runat="server">
    <asp:SqlDataSource ID="productSubCategoriesSource" runat="server"
      ProviderName="System.Data.SqlClient"
      ConnectionString="<%$ ConnectionStrings:AdventureWorks %>"
      SelectCommand="SELECT ProductSubcategoryID As CategoryID, Name from
      Production.ProductSubcategory">
    </asp:SqlDataSource>
    <asp:FormView id="detailViewCategories" DataKeyNames="CategoryID"
      AllowPaging="true" DataSourceID="productSubCategoriesSource" runat="server">
      <ItemTemplate>
        <table border="1">
          <tr>
            <td>
              <asp:Label id="categoryIDLabel" Text='<%# Eval("CategoryID") %>'
                runat="server"/>
            </td>
            <td>
              <asp:Label id="categoryNameLabel" Text='<%# Eval("Name") %>'
                runat="server"/>
            </td>
          </tr>
        </table>
      </ItemTemplate>
      <PagerSettings Mode="NextPrevious" Position="Bottom" />
    </asp:FormView>
  </form>
</body>
</html>
```

You can see that you have complete control over how your data is displayed. The `FormView` control also contains an `EditTemplate` that allows you to determine how the control is displayed when entering Edit or Insert mode.

The beauty of the `FormView` *template model is that it matches the model of the* `TemplateField` *in the* `GridView` *quite closely. This means you have the following templates to work with:* `ItemTemplate`, `EditItemTemplate`, `InsertItemTemplate`, `FooterTemplate`, `HeaderTemplate`, `EmptyData Template`, *and* `PagerTemplate`. *This means you can take the exact template content you put in a* `TemplateField` *in a* `GridView` *and place it inside the* `FormView`.

Menu

The last control in this section is the new `Menu` control. Like the `TreeView` control, it is capable of displaying hierarchical data in a vertical pop-out-style menu. Also like the `TreeView` control, it can be bound only to the `XmlDataSource` and the `SiteMapDataSource` controls. Listing 3-10 shows how you can use the same `SiteMap` data used earlier in the `TreeView` control sample, and modify it to be displayed using the new `Menu` control.

Listing 3-10: Using the Menu Control with a SiteMap

```
<html xmlns="http://www.w3.org/1999/xhtml" >
<head id="Head1" runat="server">
    <title>Using the Menu control</title>
</head>
<body>
    <form id="form1" runat="server">
    <div>
        <asp:Menu ID="Menu1" Runat="server" DataSourceID="SiteMapDataSource1">
        </asp:Menu>
        <asp:SiteMapDataSource ID="SiteMapDataSource1" Runat="server" />
    </div>
    </form>
</body>
</html>
```

Inline Data Binding Syntax

Another feature of data binding that has greatly improved in ASP.NET 2.0 is inline data binding syntax. Inline syntax in ASP.NET 1.x was primarily relegated to templated controls such as the `DataList` or the `Repeater` controls, and even then, it was sometimes difficult and confusing to make it work as you wanted it to. In ASP.NET 1.x, if you needed to use inline data binding, you might have created something like the following code:

```
<asp:Repeater id=Repeater1 runat="server">
<HeaderTemplate>
    <table>
</HeaderTemplate>
<ItemTemplate>
    <tr>
      <td><%# Container.DataItem("CategoryID") %></td>
    </tr>
   </ItemTemplate>
   <FooterTemplate>
     </table>
   </FooterTemplate>
</asp:Repeater>
```

As you can see in this sample, you are using a Repeater control to display a series of categories. Because the Repeater control is a template control, you use data binding to output the category-specific data in the proper location of the template. In ASP.NET 2.0, the content of inline data binding remains basically the same, but you are given a simpler syntax and several powerful new binding tools to use. ASP.NET 2.0 contains three different ways to perform data binding. First, you can continue to use the existing method of binding, employing the Container.DataItem syntax:

```
<%# Container.DataItem("Name") %>
```

This is good because it means you won't have to change your existing web pages if you are migrating from ASP.NET 1.x to ASP.NET 2.0. But if you are creating new web pages, you should probably use the simplest form of binding, employing the Eval method directly:

```
<%# Eval("Name") %>
```

You can also continue to format data using the formatter overload of the Eval method:

```
<%# Eval("HireDate", "{0:mm dd yyyy}" ) %>
```

In addition to these changes, ASP.NET 2.0 introduces a new form of data binding called two-way data binding. In ASP.NET 1.x, using the binding syntax was essentially a read-only form of accessing data. In ASP.NET 2.0, two-way data binding allows you to support both read and write operations for bound data. This is done using the Bind method, which, other than using a different method name, works just like the Eval method:

```
<%# Bind("Name") %>
```

The new Bind method should be used in new controls like the GridView, DetailsView, or FormView, where auto-updates to the data source are implemented.

XML Data Binding Syntax

Because XML is becoming ever more prevalent in applications, ASP.NET 2.0 also introduces several new ways to bind specifically to XML data sources, called XML data binders. These new binders give you powerful ways of working with the hierarchical format of XML. Additionally, except for the different method names, these binding methods work exactly the same as the Eval and Bind methods discussed earlier. These binders should be used when you are using the XmlDataSource control. The first binding format that uses the XPathBinder class is shown in the following code:

```
<% XPathBinder.Eval(Container.DataItem, "Categories/Category/Name") %>
```

Notice that rather than specifying a column name as in the Eval method, the XPathBinder binds the result of an XPath query. Like the standard Eval binder, the XML binder also has a shorthand format:

```
<% XPath("Categories/Category/Name") %>
```

Also, like the Eval method, the XPath binder supports applying formatting to the data:

```
<% XPath("Categories/Category/ModifiedDate", "{0:mm dd yyyy}") %>
```

The XPathBinder returns a single node using the XPath query provided. If you want to return multiple nodes from the XmlDataSource control, you can use the class's Select method. This method returns a list of nodes that match the supplied XPath query:

```
<% XPathBinder.Select(Container.DataItem,"categories/category") %>
```

Or use the shorthand syntax:

```
<% XPathSelect("categories/category") %>
```

DropDownList, ListBox, RadioButtonList, and CheckBoxList

Although the DropDownList, ListBox, and CheckBoxList controls have largely remained the same from ASP.NET 1.x to ASP.NET 2.0, they contain several new properties that you might find useful. Additionally, ASP.NET 2.0 contains the new RadioButtonList and BulletedList controls. One of the new properties available in all these controls is the AppendDataBoundItems property. Setting this property to true tells the DropDownList control to append data-bound list items to any existing statically declared items, rather than overwriting them as the ASP.NET 1.x version would have done. Another useful new property available to all these controls is the DataTextFormatString, which allows you to specify a string format for the display text of the drop-down list items.

Summary

In this chapter, you examined how data binding in ASP.NET 2.0 has been significantly enhanced and improved. The introduction of data source controls such as SqlDataSource and ObjectDataSource makes querying and displaying data from any number of data sources an almost trivial task. You examined how even a novice developer can easily combine the data source controls with the new GridView and DetailsView controls to create powerful data manipulation applications with a minimal amount of coding.

You saw how ASP.NET includes a multitude of controls that can be data-bound, specifically examining the features of the new data-bound controls that are included in ASP.NET 2.0, such as the GridView, DetailsView, FormView, TreeView, and Menu controls. Finally, you looked at how the inline data-binding syntax has been improved and strengthened with the addition of the XML-specific data-binding syntax.

Part II

ASP.NET 2.0 Data Source and Data Bound Controls

Data Binding with the SqlDataSource Control

As discussed in the previous chapter, Microsoft has taken the concept of data binding and expanded it to make data binding even easier to understand and use with ASP.NET 2.0. This is accomplished primarily through the introduction of a new layer of data abstraction called data source controls. One of the key controls in the suite of controls introduced with ASP.NET 2.0 is the `SqlDataSource` control. This chapter focuses on this control to easily and quickly bind data to data-bound controls. This chapter also focuses on the advanced features of the `SqlDataSource` control, such as handling events and exceptions with `SqlDataSource` control, renaming parameters sent to the command, programmatically adding a `SqlDataSource` at runtime, and so on. Specifically, this chapter covers:

- How to execute a stored procedure that returns data from the database
- How to pass parameters to a command using the values from the `QueryString` parameter
- How to process the return parameters from a stored procedure
- How to process the output parameters from a stored procedure
- How to handle null values
- How to handle exceptions raised by the `SqlDataSource` control
- How to perform updates and deletion using the `SqlDataSource` control
- How to detect conflict during updates
- How to encrypt the connection string stored in the `Web.config` file
- How to programmatically add a `SqlDataSource` control to the page
- How to sort the output of the `SqlDataSource` control
- How to cache the output of the `SqlDataSource` control
- How to establish caching dependency with the data in the SQL Server database

The next section starts with an overview of the `SqlDataSource` control, before looking at examples.

Introduction to the SqlDataSource Control

The `SqlDataSource` control enables you to represent a database connection and common database commands declaratively. Simply by declaring an instance of the `SqlDataSource` control in a page, you can represent `SELECT`, `INSERT`, `UPDATE`, and `DELETE` commands that can be executed against a database. This new control makes it entirely too easy to display and manipulate database records in a web page. Without writing a single line of code, you can display and edit database records by using any of the visual data controls such as the new `GridView`, `DetailsView`, or `FormView` controls. The following table discusses the important properties of the `SqlDataSource` control.

Property	Description
`CacheDuration`	Allows you to get or set the length of the time that the data source control caches data.
`CacheExpirationPolicy`	Allows you to set or get the cache expiration behavior; when combined with the duration, describes the behavior of the cache.
`CacheKeyDependency`	Allows you to get or get a user-defined key dependency that is linked to all data cache objects created by the data source control.
`CancelSelectOnNullParameter`	Indicates whether the data retrieval operation is canceled when any of the parameters contained in the `Select Parameters` evaluate to `Null`.
`ConflictDetection`	Gets or sets the value that indicates how the `SqlData Source` control performs updates or deletons when the data changes in the underlying database. This property returns and accepts an enumeration of type `Conflict Options`.
`ConnectionString`	Gets or sets the connection string used by the `SqlData Source` control to connect to an underlying database.
`DataSourceMode`	Specifies whether the control retrieves data as a `DataReader` or `DataSet` through an enumeration of type `SqlDataSourceMode`, which is set to `SqlDataSource Mode.DataSet`.
`DeleteCommand`	Gets or sets the SQL command that the `SqlDataSource` control uses to delete data from the underlying database.
`DeleteCommandType`	Specifies whether the text contained in the `Delete Command` property is a SQL statement or a stored procedure.
`DeleteParameters`	Gets the parameters collection used by the command contained in the `DeleteCommand` property.

Property	Description
EnableCaching	Gets or sets a value indicating whether the data source control has caching enabled.
FilterExpression	Allows you to get or set a filtering expression that is applied at the time when the Select() method is called.
FilterParameters	Gets a collection of parameters that are associated with the parameter placeholders in the FilterExpression.
InsertCommand	Gets or sets the SQL command that the SqlDataSource control uses to insert data into the underlying database.
InsertCommandType	Specifies whether the text contained in the Insert Command property is a SQL statement or a stored procedure.
InsertParameters	Gets the parameters collection used by the command contained in the InsertCommand property.
OldValuesParameterFormatString	Gets or sets a format string to apply to the names of any parameters that are passed to the Delete() or Update() method.
ProviderName	Gets or sets the name of the provider that the SqlData Source control uses to connect to an underlying data source.
SelectCommand	Gets or sets the SQL command that the SqlDataSource control uses to select data from the underlying database.
SelectCommandType	Specifies whether the text contained in the Select Command property is a SQL statement or a stored procedure.
SelectParameters	Gets the parameters collection used by the command contained in the SelectCommand property.
SortParameterName	Gets or sets the name of the stored procedure parameter that is used for sorting when data retrieval is performed using a stored procedure.
SqlCacheDependency	Gets or sets the semicolon-separated string that indicates the databases and tables to use for SQL Server cache dependency.
UpdateCommand	Gets or sets the SQL command that the SqlDataSource control uses to update data in the underlying database.
UpdateCommandType	Specifies whether the text contained in the Update Command property is a SQL statement or a stored procedure.
UpdateParameters	Gets the parameters collection used by the command contained in the UpdateCommand property.

In addition to the properties described in the previous table, the `SqlDataSource` control also exposes the following events.

Event	Description
`Deleting, Deleted`	Occurs before and after the completion of execution of a `DELETE` statement.
`Inserting, Inserted`	Occurs before and after the completion of execution of and `INSERT` statement.
`Selecting, Selected`	Occurs before and after the completion of execution of a `SELECT` statement.
`Updating, Updated`	Occurs before and after the completion of execution of an `UPDATE` statement.
`Filtering`	Occurs before a filtering operation.

The `SqlDataSource` control in ASP.NET 2.0 is all about Rapid Application Development (RAD). Although it is a complete violation of architecture principles in the eyes of architects, who won't entertain the thought of placing data layer components on the UI, you have to appreciate the simplicity associated with dropping the `SqlDataSource` control on a web form, hooking it up to a `GridView`, and having the ability to page and sort through records returned by query. From an architecture theory standpoint, the `SqlDataSource` control does have a role to play in ASP.NET web applications. For example, building a multi-tier application is a necessity when you need your application to be able to support multiple interfaces (such as both a web form interface and a Windows Form interface) or multiple data providers (such as both a Microsoft SQL Server database and an Oracle database). However, there are situations in which building a multi-tier application would be extreme overkill. For example, if you need to build an application that simply consists of a single report page generated from a database, devoting the effort to build a component library would be a tedious waste of time. In these cases, a simple web page with the `SqlDataSource` control that handles all the database communication, results, and so on would fit the bill.

Now that you have an understanding of the properties and events of the `SqlDataSource` control, the next section discusses a simple example using the `SqlDataSource` control.

Selecting Records

In this section, you will understand how to execute stored procedures using the `SqlDataSource` control. Before looking at the ASP.NET page, examine the stored procedures that will be invoked from the ASP.NET page. Basically, two stored procedures are used to retrieve the categories and products information, respectively. The first one, `GetProductSubCategories`, is declared as follows:

```
CREATE PROCEDURE [dbo].[GetProductSubCategories]
AS
  SELECT ProductSubcategoryID, Name FROM Production.ProductSubcategory
  ORDER BY ProductSubcategoryID
```

The second one, `GetProductsByCategoryID`, accepts a specific category ID and returns all the products that belong to that category ID:

```
CREATE PROCEDURE [dbo].[GetProductsByCategoryID]
@ProductSubcategoryID int
  AS
  SELECT ProductID, Name, ProductNumber FROM Production.Product
  WHERE ProductSubcategoryID = @ProductSubcategoryID ORDER By ProductID
```

Listing 4-1 shows the ASP.NET page that invokes these two stored procedures to display categories and products information in a `dropdownlist` and `GridView`.

Listing 4-1: Executing Stored Procedures Using the SqlDataSource Control

```
<%@ Page Language="C#" %>
<html xmlns="http://www.w3.org/1999/xhtml" >
<head runat="server">
  <title>Executing a Stored Procedure using SqlDataSource Control</title>
</head>
<body>
  <form id="form1" runat="server">
    <div>
      <asp:SqlDataSource ID="categoriesSource" runat="server"
        ProviderName="System.Data.SqlClient"
        ConnectionString="<%$ ConnectionStrings:AdventureWorks %>"
        SelectCommand="GetProductSubCategories"
        SelectCommandType="StoredProcedure">
      </asp:SqlDataSource>
      Categories:
      <asp:DropDownList runat="server" DataSourceID="categoriesSource"
        DataValueField="ProductSubcategoryID" DataTextField="Name"
        AutoPostBack="true" ID="lstCategories" />
      <asp:SqlDataSource ID="productsSource" runat="server"
        ProviderName="System.Data.SqlClient"
        ConnectionString="<%$ ConnectionStrings:AdventureWorks %>"
        SelectCommand="GetProductsByCategoryID"
        SelectCommandType="StoredProcedure">
        <SelectParameters>
          <asp:ControlParameter ControlID="lstCategories"
            Name="ProductSubcategoryID" PropertyName="SelectedValue" />
        </SelectParameters>
      </asp:SqlDataSource>
      <asp:GridView runat="server" DataSourceID="productsSource"
        HeaderStyle-HorizontalAlign="Center" HeaderStyle-Font-Bold="True"
        HeaderStyle-BackColor="blue" HeaderStyle-ForeColor="White" />
    </div>
  </form>
</body>
</html>
```

Listing 4-1 connects to the AdventureWorks database, executes the stored procedure to retrieve all the categories data, and displays that in a drop-down list. When you select a particular category from the drop-down list, it then executes another stored procedure that returns all the products that belong to a specific category. This product information is then displayed through a `GridView` control, which is directly bound to the product's data source control. If you navigate to the page again using the browser, you should see the same output as that shown in Figure 4-1.

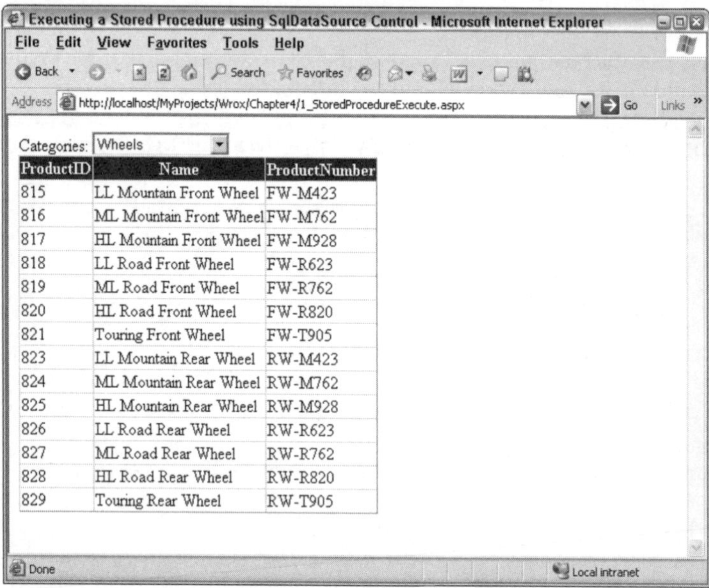

Figure 4-1

Note that Listing 4-1 uses the following connection string, stored in the `Web.config` file:

```
<configuration xmlns="http://schemas.microsoft.com/.NetConfiguration/v2.0">
<connectionStrings>
  <add name="AdventureWorks"
   connectionString="server=localhost;database=AdventureWorks;uid=user;pwd=word;"/>
</connectionStrings>
...
</configuration>
```

With the above connection string placed in the `Web.config` file, you would reference it in the `SqlDataSource` using the `$` expression as follows:

```
<asp:SqlDataSource runat="server"
  ConnectionString="<%$ConnectionStrings:AdventureWorks%>"
  SelectCommand="GetProductsByCategoryID" SelectCommandType="StoredProcedure">
</asp:SqlDataSource>
```

The `SqlDataSource` can return either a `DataSet` or `DataReader`. This option is configurable via the `SqlDataSource` control's `DataSourceMode` property, with the default being `DataSet`. To utilize the `GridView` control's built-in sorting and paging capabilities or the `SqlDataSource` control's caching capabilities, you will need to have the `SqlDataSource` return a `DataSet`. The next section shows how to return a `DataReader` from the `SqlDataSource` control.

Using DataReader with the SqlDataSource Control

As mentioned previously, you can configure the `SqlDataSource` control to return data as a `DataReader` instead by setting the `SqlDataSourceMode` property to `"DataReader"`. Using a `DataReader` is generally more performant than a `DataSet` when you just need forward-only, read-only access to the data. However, note that the sorting capability of `SqlDataSource` will be disabled in this mode. Listing 4-2 shows the code required to use the `DataReader` mode with the `SqlDataSource` control.

Listing 4-2: Using DataReader Mode to Execute the Select Statement

```
<%@ Page Language="C#" %>
<html xmlns="http://www.w3.org/1999/xhtml" >
<head runat="server">
  <title>Using the DataReader mode for executing a SQL Statement</title>
</head>
<body>
  <form id="form1" runat="server">
    <div>
      <asp:SqlDataSource ID="categoriesSource" runat="server"
        ProviderName="System.Data.SqlClient" DataSourceMode="DataReader"
        ConnectionString="<%$ ConnectionStrings:AdventureWorks %>"
        SelectCommand="Select ProductSubcategoryID, Name from
        Production.ProductSubcategory">
      </asp:SqlDataSource>
      Categories:
      <asp:DropDownList runat="server" DataSourceID="categoriesSource"
        DataValueField="ProductSubcategoryID"
        DataTextField="Name"
        AutoPostBack="true" ID="lstCategories" />
      <asp:SqlDataSource ID="productsSource" runat="server"
        ProviderName="System.Data.SqlClient" DataSourceMode="DataReader"
        ConnectionString="<%$ ConnectionStrings:AdventureWorks %>"
        SelectCommand="Select ProductID, Name, ProductNumber, StandardCost from
        Production.Product Where ProductSubcategoryID=@ProductSubcategoryID">
        <SelectParameters>
          <asp:ControlParameter ControlID="lstCategories"
            Name="ProductSubcategoryID" PropertyName="SelectedValue" />
        </SelectParameters>
      </asp:SqlDataSource>
      <asp:GridView runat="server" DataSourceID="productsSource"
        HeaderStyle-HorizontalAlign="Center" HeaderStyle-Font-Bold="True"
        HeaderStyle-BackColor="blue" HeaderStyle-ForeColor="White" />
    </div>
  </form>
</body>
</html>
```

The key thing to note in Listing 4-2 is the addition of the `DataSourceMode` attribute, which is set to `"DataReader"`. This instructs the `SqlDataSource` to execute the `Select` query, and returns the results in the form of a `DataReader` object.

Retrieving Values from the QueryString

So far, you have seen how to retrieve values from a control such as the drop-down list in the page. In this section, you will see how to retrieve the query string values and use them as parameters to the stored procedure. Listing 4-3 shows the code wherein the `SqlDataSource` control invokes a stored procedure, passing in the query string information as an argument.

Listing 4-3: Using QueryString Values as Parameters to the Stored Procedure

```
<%@ Page Language="C#" %>
<html xmlns="http://www.w3.org/1999/xhtml" >
<head runat="server">
  <title>Retrieving Stored Procedure Parameter values from QueryString</title>
</head>
<body>
  <form id="form1" runat="server">
    <div>
      <asp:SqlDataSource ID="productsSource" runat="server"
        ProviderName="System.Data.SqlClient"
        ConnectionString="<%$ ConnectionStrings:AdventureWorks %>"
        SelectCommand="GetProductsByCategoryID"
        SelectCommandType="StoredProcedure">
        <SelectParameters>
          <asp:QueryStringParameter Name="ProductSubcategoryID"
            QueryStringField="CategoryID" />
        </SelectParameters>
      </asp:SqlDataSource>
      <asp:GridView runat="server" DataSourceID="productsSource"
        HeaderStyle-HorizontalAlign="Center" HeaderStyle-Font-Bold="True"
        HeaderStyle-BackColor="blue" HeaderStyle-ForeColor="White" />
    </div>
  </form>
</body>
</html>
```

Notice that the `Name` and `QueryStringField` attributes of the `<asp:QueryStringParameter>` indicate the stored procedure parameter and the query string parameter names, respectively. Figure 4-2 shows the output produced by the page when you append the page name with the query string using the format `"?CategoryID=1"`.

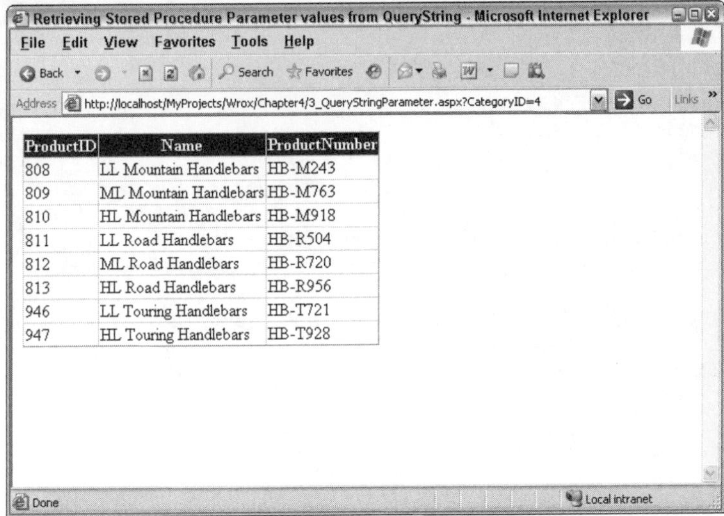

Figure 4-2

Handling Return Parameter Values through the SqlDataSource Control

So far, you have seen how to pass input parameters to a stored procedure through the `Select Parameters` collection. In addition to input parameters, you can also have parameters that are bidirectional, such as input/output, output, and return. These types of parameters are represented by the `Direction` property of the `Parameter` class, which takes any of the following values: `Input`, `Output`, `InputOutput`, and `ReturnValue`. To retrieve the values of these parameters after a data source operation completes, you handle the appropriate post-operation event, such as `Selected`, `Updated`, `Inserted`, or `Deleted`, to obtain the parameter value from the event arguments passed to these events. The `SqlDataSourceStatusEventArgs` has a `Command` property you can use to obtain return value parameters. Before looking at an example of how to handle return parameters, start with the definition of the stored procedure:

```
CREATE PROCEDURE [dbo].[GetDepartments]
  AS
  SELECT DepartmentID, Name, GroupName, ModifiedDate FROM HumanResources.Department
  DECLARE @Count smallint
  SELECT @Count = Count(DepartmentID) FROM HumanResources.Department
  RETURN @Count
```

The `GetDepartments` stored procedure simply returns the department details from the Department table. In addition, it also returns the number of rows contained in that table as a return parameter value. Listing 4-4 demonstrates how to process the department details and the return parameter, using the `SqlDataSource` control.

Listing 4-4: Handling Return Parameter Values from a Stored Procedure

```
<%@ Page Language="C#" AutoEventWireup="true"%>
<%@ Import Namespace="System.Text" %>
<script runat="server">
  void deptSource_Selected(Object sender,
    System.Web.UI.WebControls.SqlDataSourceStatusEventArgs e)
  {
    StringBuilder builder = new StringBuilder();
    foreach (System.Data.SqlClient.SqlParameter param in e.Command.Parameters)
    {
      builder.Append(Server.HtmlEncode(param.ParameterName) + "=");
      builder.Append(Server.HtmlEncode(param.Value.ToString()) + " (");
      builder.Append(Server.HtmlEncode(param.Value.GetType().ToString()) +
        ")<br>");
    }
    lblResult.Text = "Return Parameter : " + builder.ToString();
  }
</script>
<html xmlns="http://www.w3.org/1999/xhtml" >
<head id="Head1" runat="server">
  <title>Handling Return Parameters from a Stored Procedure</title>
</head>
<body>
  <form id="form1" runat="server">
    <asp:GridView ID="deptView" AllowSorting="true" AllowPaging="true"
      Runat="server" DataSourceID="deptSource" DataKeyNames="DepartmentID"
      AutoGenerateColumns="False" HeaderStyle-HorizontalAlign="Center"
      HeaderStyle-Font-Bold="True" HeaderStyle-BackColor="blue"
      HeaderStyle-ForeColor="White">
      <Columns>
        <asp:BoundField ReadOnly="true" HeaderText="Department ID"
          DataField="DepartmentID" SortExpression="DepartmentID" />
        <asp:BoundField HeaderText="Name" DataField="Name" SortExpression="Name"/>
        <asp:BoundField HeaderText="Group Name" DataField="GroupName"
          SortExpression="GroupName" />
        <asp:BoundField HeaderText="ModifiedDate" DataField="ModifiedDate"
          SortExpression="ModifiedDate" />
      </Columns>
    </asp:GridView>
    <asp:SqlDataSource ID="deptSource" Runat="server"
      SelectCommandType="StoredProcedure" SelectCommand="GetDepartments"
      ConnectionString="<%$ ConnectionStrings:AdventureWorks%>"
      OnSelected="deptSource_Selected">
      <SelectParameters>
        <asp:Parameter Direction="ReturnValue" Name="ReturnValue" Type="Int32" />
      </SelectParameters>
    </asp:SqlDataSource>
    <asp:Label runat="server" Font-Bold="true" ID="lblResult" />
  </form>
</body>
</html>
```

Note that the `Direction` property of `<asp:Parameter>` is set to `ReturnValue`, which is used to capture the return value from the stored procedure. You retrieve this return value in the `Selected` event of the `SqlDataSource` control by examining the `Command` property of `SqlDataSourceStatusEventArgs`. Figure 4-3 shows the result of viewing the page in a browser.

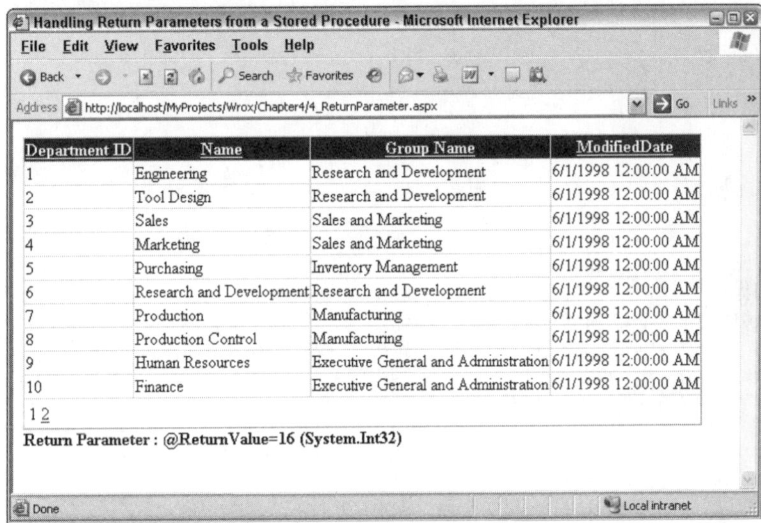

Figure 4-3

Handling Output Parameter Values through the SqlDataSource Control

This section builds on the previous section by showing how to leverage the output parameters (instead of return values) to achieve the same result. The modified `GetDepartments` stored procedure that returns output parameters is:

```
CREATE PROCEDURE GetDepartments
@Count smallint OUTPUT
AS
SELECT DepartmentID, Name, GroupName, ModifiedDate
FROM HumanResources.Department
SELECT @Count = Count(DepartmentID) FROM HumanResources.Department
```

Listing 4-5 shows the code required to handle the output parameter values.

Listing 4-5: Handling Output Parameters Returned by a Stored Procedure

```
<%@ Page Language="C#" AutoEventWireup="true"%>
<%@ Import Namespace="System.Text" %>
<script runat="server">
  void deptSource_Selected(Object sender,
    System.Web.UI.WebControls.SqlDataSourceStatusEventArgs e)
  {
    StringBuilder builder = new StringBuilder();
```

```
    foreach (System.Data.SqlClient.SqlParameter param in e.Command.Parameters)
    {
      builder.Append(Server.HtmlEncode(param.ParameterName) + "=");
      builder.Append(Server.HtmlEncode(param.Value.ToString()) + " (");
      builder.Append(Server.HtmlEncode(param.Value.GetType().ToString()) +
        ")<br>");
    }
    lblResult.Text = "Output Parameter : " + builder.ToString();
  }
</script>
<html xmlns="http://www.w3.org/1999/xhtml" >
<head id="Head1" runat="server">
  <title>Handling Return Parameters from a Stored Procedure</title>
</head>
<body>
  <form id="form1" runat="server">
    <asp:GridView ID="deptView" AllowSorting="true" AllowPaging="true"
      Runat="server" DataSourceID="deptSource" DataKeyNames="DepartmentID"
      AutoGenerateColumns="False" HeaderStyle-HorizontalAlign="Center"
      HeaderStyle-Font-Bold="True" HeaderStyle-BackColor="blue"
      HeaderStyle-ForeColor="White">
      <Columns>
        <asp:BoundField ReadOnly="true" HeaderText="Department ID"
          DataField="DepartmentID" SortExpression="DepartmentID" />
        <asp:BoundField HeaderText="Name" DataField="Name" SortExpression="Name"/>
        <asp:BoundField HeaderText="Group Name" DataField="GroupName"
          SortExpression="GroupName" />
        <asp:BoundField HeaderText="ModifiedDate" DataField="ModifiedDate"
          SortExpression="ModifiedDate" />
      </Columns>
    </asp:GridView>
    <asp:SqlDataSource ID="deptSource" Runat="server"
      SelectCommandType="StoredProcedure" SelectCommand="GetDepartments"
      ConnectionString="<%$ ConnectionStrings:AdventureWorks%>"
      OnSelected="deptSource_Selected">
      <SelectParameters>
        <asp:Parameter Direction="Output" Name="Count" Type="Int32" />
      </SelectParameters>
    </asp:SqlDataSource>
    <asp:Label runat="server" Font-Bold="true" ID="lblResult" />
  </form>
</body>
</html>
```

As you can see, the code is very similar to Listing 4-4, except for the key difference that the `Direction` property is set to `Output` as part of the `<asp:Parameter>` declaration.

Handling Null Values through the SqlDataSource Control

`SqlDataSource` exposes a `CancelSelectOnNullParameter` property, which prevents the data source from executing its `Select` method when any of the parameters in the `Select` query are set to null. This property is set to `true` by default. This property can be handy when you are implementing a drop-down list filter that displays all values from the data source initially until a filter value is selected. This is achieved by adding an item to the drop-down list with an empty string value (with the text set to something like `"ALL"`), and setting the `ConvertEmptyStringToNull` property on the associated `ControlParameter` for the `DropDownList` in the data source. Then, in the data source `SelectCommand`, you can check for a null value in order to return all (unfiltered) values. Listing 4-6 demonstrates this technique using a simple SQL command, although you could also perform the null check in the implementation of a stored procedure.

Listing 4-6: Handling Null Value Parameters in the SqlDataSource Control

```
<%@ Page Language="C#" %>
<html xmlns="http://www.w3.org/1999/xhtml" >
<head runat="server">
  <title>Handling Null values in the SqlDataSource Control</title>
</head>
<body>
  <form id="form1" runat="server">
    <div>
      <asp:SqlDataSource ID="categoriesSource" runat="server"
        ProviderName="System.Data.SqlClient"
        ConnectionString="<%$ ConnectionStrings:AdventureWorks %>"
        SelectCommand="Select ProductSubcategoryID, Name from
        Production.ProductSubcategory">
      </asp:SqlDataSource>
      Categories:
      <asp:DropDownList AppendDataBoundItems="true" runat="server"
        DataSourceID="categoriesSource" DataValueField="ProductSubcategoryID"
        DataTextField="Name" AutoPostBack="true" ID="lstCategories">
        <asp:ListItem Value="">ALL</asp:ListItem>
      </asp:DropDownList>
      <asp:SqlDataSource ID="productsSource" runat="server"
        ProviderName="System.Data.SqlClient" CancelSelectOnNullParameter="false"
        ConnectionString="<%$ ConnectionStrings:AdventureWorks %>"
        SelectCommand="Select ProductID, Name, ProductNumber, StandardCost from
        Production.Product WHERE ProductSubcategoryID =
        IsNull(@ProductSubcategoryID, ProductSubcategoryID)">
        <SelectParameters>
         <asp:ControlParameter ControlID="lstCategories"
           Name="ProductSubcategoryID" ConvertEmptyStringToNull="true"
           PropertyName="SelectedValue" />
        </SelectParameters>
      </asp:SqlDataSource>
      <asp:GridView runat="server" DataSourceID="productsSource"
        HeaderStyle-HorizontalAlign="Center" HeaderStyle-Font-Bold="True"
        HeaderStyle-BackColor="blue" HeaderStyle-ForeColor="White" />
    </div>
  </form>
</body>
</html>
```

Note the use of the `AppendDataBoundItems` property of the `DropDownList`, which allows values obtained from the `DropDownList` data source to be appended to the statically added `"ALL"` item in the `Items` collection. Also note that by default, the `SqlDataSource` does not perform a `Select` operation if any of the associated parameters to the SelectCommand are null. To allow the select operation to execute even when a null parameter is passed, you need to set the CancelSelectOnNullParameter property to false. The ConvertEmptyStringToNull property specified in the SqlDataSource parameter object specifies that String.Empty values posted from the client should be converted to null before invoking the associated data source operation.

Handling Errors in SqlDataSource Control

When you deal with an outside resource such as a database, you need to protect your code with a basic amount of error-handling logic. Even if you have avoided every possible coding mistake, you still need to defend against factors outside your control — for example, if the database server is not running or the network connection is broken.

You can count on the SqlDataSource to properly release any resources (such as connections) if an error occurs. However, the underlying exception won't be handled. Instead, it will bubble up to the page and derail your processing. As with any other unhandled exception, the user will receive a cryptic error message or an error page. This design is unavoidable — if the SqlDataSource suppressed exceptions, it could hide potential problems and make debugging extremely difficult. However, it is a good idea to handle the problem in your web page and show a more suitable error message. To do this, you handle the data source event that occurs immediately after the error. If you are performing a query, that is the Selected event. If you are performing an update, delete, or insert operation, you would handle the Updated, Deleted, or Inserted events instead. (If you do not want to offer customized error messages, you could handle all these events with the same event handler.)

Within the event handler, you can access the exception object through the SqlDataSourceStatusEventArgs.Exception property. If you want to prevent the error from spreading any further, simply set the SqlDataSourceStatusEventArgs.ExceptionHandled property to true. Then, make sure you show an appropriate error message on your web page to inform the user that the command was not completed. Here is an example:

```
protected void categoriesSource_Selected(object sender,
  SqlDataSourceStatusEventArgs e)
{
  if (e.Exception != null)
  {
    //Mask the error with a generic message (for security purposes).
    lblError.Text = "An exception occurred performing the query.";
    //Consider the error handled.
    e.ExceptionHandled = true;
  }
}
```

Updating Records

Selecting data is only half of the equation. The SqlDataSource can also apply changes. The only catch is that not all controls support updating. For example, the ListBox does not provide any way for the user to edit values, delete existing items, or insert new ones. Fortunately, ASP.NET's rich data controls such as GridView, DetailsView, and FormView have editing features that you can switch on.

As you have seen in the select example, the first step is to define suitable commands for the operations you want to perform, such as inserting (`InsertQuery`), deleting (`DeleteQuery`), and updating (`UpdateQuery`). If you know that you will allow the user to perform only certain operations (such as updates) but not others (such as insertions and deletions), you can safely omit the commands you do not need.

You define the `InsertCommand`, `DeleteCommand`, and `UpdateCommand` in the same way that you define the command for the `SelectCommand` property—by using a parameterized query. For example, here is a `SqlDataSource` that defines a basic update command that updates every field:

```
<asp:SqlDataSource ID="deptSource" runat="server"
  ProviderName="System.Data.SqlClient"
  ConnectionString="<%$ ConnectionStrings:AdventureWorks%>"
  SelectCommand="SELECT DepartmentID, Name, GroupName, ModifiedDate FROM
    HumanResources.Department"
  UpdateCommand="UPDATE HumanResources.Department SET Name=@Name,
    GroupName=@GroupName, ModifiedDate=@ModifiedDate
    WHERE DepartmentID=@DepartmentID">
</asp:SqlDataSource>
```

In this example, the parameter names are not chosen arbitrarily. As long as you give each parameter the same name as the field it affects and preface it with the `@` symbol (so `Name` becomes `@Name`), you do not need to define the parameter. That is because the ASP.NET data controls automatically submit a collection of parameters with the new values before triggering the update. Each parameter in the collection uses this naming convention.

To try this, create a page with the `SqlDataSource` shown previously and a linked `GridView` control that is declared as in Listing 4-7.

Listing 4-7: Updating Data through the GridView Control

```
<asp:GridView ID="deptView" AllowPaging="true" Runat="server"
  DataSourceID="deptSource" AutoGenerateEditButton="true"
  DataKeyNames="DepartmentID" AutoGenerateColumns="False"
  HeaderStyle-HorizontalAlign="Center" HeaderStyle-Font-Bold="True"
  HeaderStyle-BackColor="blue" HeaderStyle-ForeColor="White">
  <Columns>
    <asp:BoundField ReadOnly="true" HeaderText="Department ID"
      DataField="DepartmentID"/>
    <asp:BoundField HeaderText="Name" DataField="Name"/>
    <asp:BoundField HeaderText="Group Name" DataField="GroupName"/>
    <asp:BoundField HeaderText="ModifiedDate" DataField="ModifiedDate"/>
  </Columns>
</asp:GridView>
```

Note that the `AutoGenerateEditButton` and `DataKeyNames` are set to `true` and `DepartmentID`, respectively. The `DataKeyNames` property indicates the primary key of the Department table. With the previous code in place, when you run the page and the `GridView` is bound and displayed, the edit column displays an Edit link next to every record, as shown in Figure 4-4.

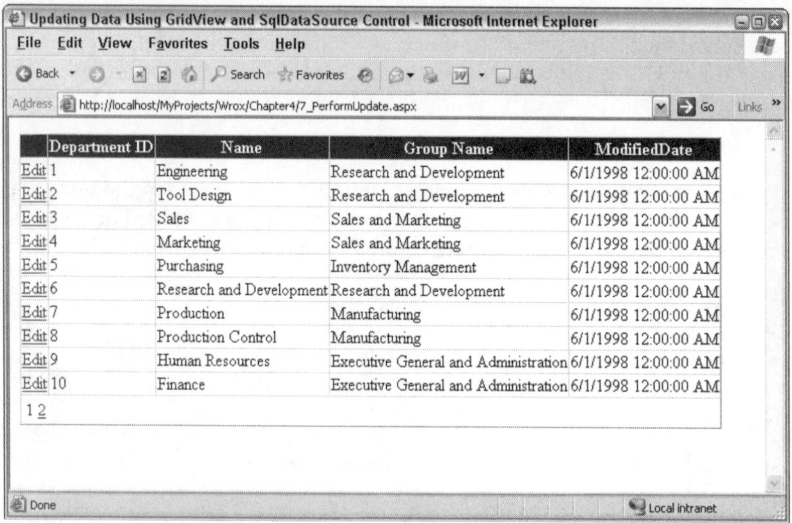

Figure 4-4

When clicked, the Edit link switches the corresponding row into edit mode. All fields are changed to text boxes (with the exception of read-only fields), and the Edit link is replaced with an Update link and a Cancel link, as shown in Figure 4-5.

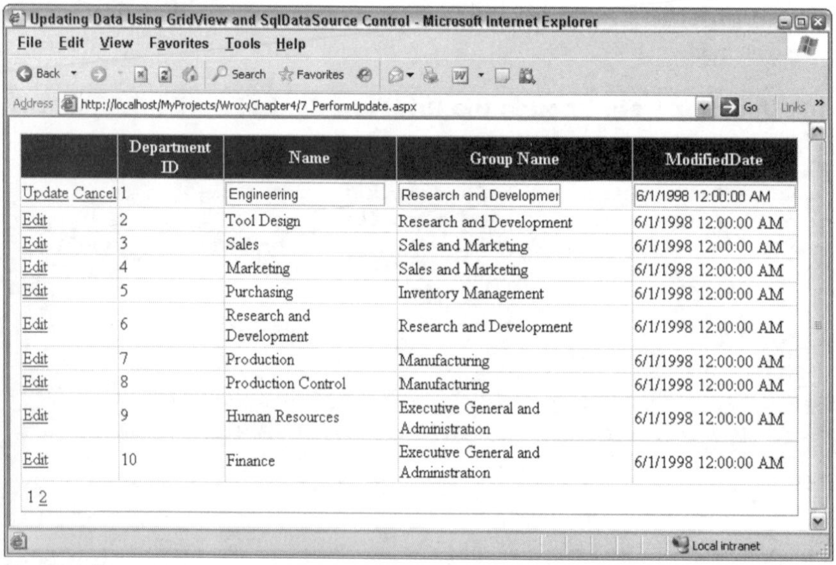

Figure 4-5

The Cancel link returns the row to its initial state. The Update link passes the values to the `SqlDataSource.UpdateParameters` collection (using the field names) and then triggers the

`SqlDataSource.Update()` method to apply the change to the database. Once again, you do not have to write any code.

You can create similar parameterized commands for the `DeleteCommand` and `InsertCommand`. To enable deleting and inserting, you need to add a column to the `GridView` that has the `ShowInsertButton` and `ShowDeleteButton` properties set to `true`.

> *The `GridView` is an extremely flexible control. Templates, one of its many features, allow you to define the controls and markup used when editing a record. This is handy if you want to enable editing through drop-down lists, add validation controls, or just fine-tune the appearance of a row in edit mode. You will learn about templates in Chapter 8.*

Updating and Key Fields

All the rich data controls include a `DataKeyNames` property. This property indicates which field or fields are considered primary keys. To use this feature, you must set the `DataKeyNames` property with a comma-separated list of one or more key fields. In the previous example, `DataKeyNames` was set to `DepartmentID`, since `DepartmentID` is the primary key for the Department table. Often, you will have only one key field, as shown here:

```
<asp:GridView ID="deptView" runat="server" DataSourceID="deptSource"
  DataKeyNames="DepartmentID" ... >
```

Key fields are given special treatment. For example, the `GridView` makes it possible to easily retrieve the key information for a given row. Additionally, when you commit an update to a row, the data control passes the original value of the key fields, as well as the changed value (unless it is read-only). The original value is used in a `WHERE` clause to locate the row so you can perform the update. To avoid confusion, the parameter that contains the original value is automatically given the prefix `original`. For example, the `@DepartmentID` parameter becomes `@original_DepartmentID`.

This difference can lead to a potential problem. You may begin using a parameter name such as `@DepartmentID` and then set the `DataKeyNames` property to get access to another feature, such as selection. When you attempt to perform an update, you will receive an error indicating the parameter `@DepartmentID` can't be found. Now that you understand the problem, the solution is quite simple. Most of the time you will use the `DataKeyNames` property, so you should modify your command to use the original value of any read-only primary keys. Here is an example:

```
UpdateCommand="UPDATE HumanResources.Department SET Name=@Name,
  GroupName=@GroupName, ModifiedDate=@ModifiedDate
  WHERE DepartmentID=@original_DepartmentID"
```

This problem has another workaround. The `@original_` naming convention is configurable. You can use a different prefix by changing the `SqlDataSource.OldValuesParameterFormatString` property. This property takes a string of the form `@original_{0}`, where `{0}` indicates the unadulterated name. If you are sure that your key values are read-only and won't be modified in an update operation, you have no reason to use this convention, because there is no difference between the original name and the current name. So, simply change the `OldValuesParameterFormatString` property to `{0}`, and your commands will continue to work with the unmodified field names. Listing 4-8 shows an example of this in action.

Listing 4-8: Using Key Fields in Update Operations

```
<%@ Page Language="C#" AutoEventWireup="true"%>
<html xmlns="http://www.w3.org/1999/xhtml" >
<head id="Head1" runat="server">
  <title>Updating Data Using GridView and SqlDataSource Control</title>
</head>
<body>
  <form id="form1" runat="server">
    <asp:GridView ID="deptView" AllowPaging="true" Runat="server"
      DataSourceID="deptSource" AutoGenerateEditButton="true"
      DataKeyNames="DepartmentID" AutoGenerateColumns="False"
      HeaderStyle-HorizontalAlign="Center" HeaderStyle-Font-Bold="True"
      HeaderStyle-BackColor="blue" HeaderStyle-ForeColor="White">
      <Columns>
        <asp:BoundField ReadOnly="true" HeaderText="Department ID"
          DataField="DepartmentID"/>
        <asp:BoundField HeaderText="Name" DataField="Name"/>
        <asp:BoundField HeaderText="Group Name" DataField="GroupName" />
        <asp:BoundField HeaderText="ModifiedDate" DataField="ModifiedDate"/>
      </Columns>
    </asp:GridView>
    <asp:SqlDataSource ID="deptSource" Runat="server" SelectCommand="SELECT
      DepartmentID, Name, GroupName, ModifiedDate from HumanResources.Department"
      UpdateCommand="UPDATE HumanResources.Department SET Name = @Name,
      GroupName = @GroupName, ModifiedDate = @ModifiedDate
      Where DepartmentID = @original_DepartmentID"
      OldValuesParameterFormatString="original_{0}"
      ConnectionString="<%$ ConnectionStrings:AdventureWorks%>" />
  </form>
</body>
</html>
```

The important point to note in the above code is the introduction of the `OldValuesParameter FormatString` property and `"@original_"` in the `UpdateCommand` property.

Strict Concurrency Checking

The update command in the previous example matches the record based on its ID. The problem with this approach is that the update command updates every field indiscriminately — it has no way to distinguish between fields that are and are not changed. As a result, you can end up obliterating the changes of another user, if they are made between the time the page is requested and the time the page is updated.

For example, imagine X and Y are viewing the same table of department records. X commits a change to the name of a department. A few seconds later, Y commits a location change to the same department record. However, that update command not only applies the new location, but it also overwrites every field with the values in X's page — effectively replacing the address name entered with the old location.

To defend against this sort of problem, you can enforce stricter concurrency checking. One way to do this is to create a command that performs the update only if every field matches. Here is what that command would look like:

```
UpdateCommand="UPDATE HumanResources.Department SET Name=@Name,
GroupName=@GroupName, ModifiedDate=@ModifiedDate WHERE
DepartmentID=@original_DepartmentID AND Name=@original_Name AND
GroupName=@original_GroupName AND ModifiedDate=@original_ModifiedDate"
```

The problem is that the command does not have access to the original values of every field—instead, it has only the original value of any key fields. You could define every field in the table as a key field, but this is certain to cause confusion. A better solution is to set the `SqlDataSource.ConflictDetection` property to `ConflictOptions.CompareAllValues` instead of `ConflictOptions.OverwriteChanges` (the default). The data control will then supply the original value of every field, and the command will work as written.

Commands that compare values are often inefficient, because they require more data to be sent over the network and mean more comparison work for the database. A better solution is to use a timestamp field. If the row is unchanged, the timestamp will always match. In this case, you would hide the timestamp column from the data control but set the `DataKeyFields` property to include it, so you could use it when constructing your command.

Updating with Stored Procedures

The update example works just as readily with stored procedures. In this case, you simply supply the stored procedure name for the `UpdateCommand`:

```
<asp:SqlDataSource ID="deptSource" Runat="server"
SelectCommand="GetDepartment" SelectCommandType="StoredProcedure"
UpdateCommand="UpdateDepartment" UpdateCommandType="StoredProcedure"
ConnectionString="<%$ ConnectionStrings:AdventureWorks%>" />
```

However, this has a catch. As you have learned, the parameter names are based on the field names. If the stored procedure uses the same parameter names, the update works without a hitch. However, if the stored procedure parameter names are slightly different, the update will fail.

The order of parameters is irrelevant. Only the names are important. The `SqlDataSource` *does a case-insensitive comparison, so your parameters can have different capitalization.*

For example, consider an `UpdateDepartment` stored procedure that takes parameters like this:

```
CREATE PROC [dbo].[UpdateDepartment]
  @DepartmentID smallint,
  @DeptName nvarchar(50),
  @DeptGroupName nvarchar(50),
  @ModifiedDate datetime
AS
  UPDATE HumanResources.Department
    SET Name = @DeptName, GroupName = @DeptGroupName,
    ModifiedDate = @ModifiedDate WHERE DepartmentID = @DepartmentID
```

In this example, the `Name` and `GroupName` fields map to parameters named `@DeptName` and `@DeptGroupName`. Unfortunately, there is no declarative way to correct this problem and map these parameters to their correct names. Instead, you need to define the new parameters and write a little custom code.

The first step is to add two parameters to the `SqlDataSource.UpdateParameters` collection. Unfortunately, you cannot create these while the update is in progress. Instead, you need to add them to the `SqlDataSource` tag:

```
<asp:SqlDataSource ID="deptSource" runat="server"
  ConnectionString="<%$ ConnectionStrings:AdventureWorks%>"
  SelectCommand= "SELECT DepartmentID, Name, GroupName, ModifiedDate from
    HumanResources.Department" UpdateCommand="UpdateDepartment"
  UpdateCommandType="StoredProcedure" OnUpdating="deptSource_Updating" >
  <UpdateParameters>
    <asp:Parameter Name="DeptName" Type="String" />
    <asp:Parameter Name="DeptGroupName" Type="String" />
  </UpdateParameters>
</asp:SqlDataSource>
```

Note that the parameter names do not include the @ symbol when you define them in the `SqlDataSource` tag. The next step is to react to the `SqlDataSource.Updating` event, which fires immediately before the update is committed. You can then set the value for the `@DeptName` and `@DeptGroupName` parameters and remove the `@Name` and `@GroupName` parameters from sight. Listing 4-9 shows the complete code required for renaming parameters.

Listing 4-9: Renaming Parameters to the Stored Procedure Parameters during Update

```
<%@ Page Language="C#"%>
<script runat="server">
  void deptSource_Updating(Object sender,
    System.Web.UI.WebControls.SqlDataSourceCommandEventArgs e)
  {
    e.Command.Parameters["@DeptName"].Value = e.Command.Parameters["@Name"].Value;
    e.Command.Parameters["@DeptGroupName"].Value =
      e.Command.Parameters["@GroupName"].Value;
    e.Command.Parameters.Remove(e.Command.Parameters["@Name"]);
    e.Command.Parameters.Remove(e.Command.Parameters["@GroupName"]);
  }
</script>
<html xmlns="http://www.w3.org/1999/xhtml" >
<head id="Head1" runat="server">
  <title>Renaming Parameters passed to a Stored Procedure by handling the
    SqlDataSource Events
  </title>
</head>
<body>
  <form id="form1" runat="server">
    <asp:GridView ID="deptView" AllowSorting="true" AllowPaging="true"
      Runat="server" DataSourceID="deptSource" AutoGenerateEditButton="true"
      DataKeyNames="DepartmentID" AutoGenerateColumns="False"
      HeaderStyle-HorizontalAlign="Center" HeaderStyle-Font-Bold="True"
```

```
      HeaderStyle-BackColor="blue" HeaderStyle-ForeColor="White">
      <Columns>
        <asp:BoundField ReadOnly="true" HeaderText="Department ID"
          DataField="DepartmentID" SortExpression="DepartmentID" />
        <asp:BoundField HeaderText="Name" DataField="Name" SortExpression="Name"/>
        <asp:BoundField HeaderText="Group Name" DataField="GroupName"
          SortExpression="GroupName" />
        <asp:BoundField HeaderText="ModifiedDate" DataField="ModifiedDate"
          SortExpression="ModifiedDate" />
      </Columns>
    </asp:GridView>
    <asp:SqlDataSource ID="deptSource" runat="server"
      ConnectionString="<%$ ConnectionStrings:AdventureWorks%>"
      SelectCommand= "SELECT DepartmentID, Name, GroupName, ModifiedDate from
      HumanResources.Department" UpdateCommand="UpdateDepartment"
      UpdateCommandType="StoredProcedure" OnUpdating="deptSource_Updating" >
      <UpdateParameters>
        <asp:Parameter Name="DeptName" Type="String" />
        <asp:Parameter Name="DeptGroupName" Type="String" />
      </UpdateParameters>
    </asp:SqlDataSource>
  </form>
</body>
</html>
```

This listing represents a fairly typical scenario in which the no-code data binding will not work. Overall, if you can design your stored procedures and classes to work with the data source controls, you can avoid writing a great deal of code. On the other hand, if you introduce the data source controls to an existing application with a fixed database schema and database components, it may take a fair bit of extra code to fit these pieces together.

Deleting Records

Like the `SelectCommand` and `UpdateCommand`, the `SqlDataSource` control also supports `DeleteCommand`, which is specifically used to delete data from the underlying database. The `DeleteCommand` property can be a SQL string or the name of a stored procedure, if the database supports stored procedures. The `DeleteCommand` should contain parameter placeholders for each value that will be passed by the `GridView` control. You also specify a `DeleteParameters` collection to set properties for each parameter, such as the parameter data type, input/output direction, or default value. Listing 4-10 provides you with an example of how to set the `DeleteCommand` text to delete a department from the Department table in the AdventureWorks database. Data is retrieved from the Department table and displayed in a `GridView` control. Additionally, when the Delete button is clicked, the `GridView` control automatically populates the `DeleteParameters` collection and calls the `Delete` method. Finally, the `Deleted` event of the `SqlDataSource` control is used to determine if the deletion has been completed successfully.

Listing 4-10: Performing Deletions through the SqlDataSource Control

```
<%@ Page Language="C#" %>
<script runat="server">
  void deptSource_Deleted(object sender,SqlDataSourceStatusEventArgs e)
  {
```

(continued)

Listing 4-10: *(continued)*

```
      if (e.Exception == null)
      {
        if (e.AffectedRows == 1)
        {
          lblResult.Text = "Record deleted successfully.";
        }
        else
        {
          lblResult.Text = "An error occurred during the delete operation.";
        }
      }
      else
      {
        lblResult.Text = "An error occurred while attempting to delete the row." +
          e.Exception.Message;
        e.ExceptionHandled = true;
      }
    }
</script>
<html xmlns="http://www.w3.org/1999/xhtml" >
<head runat="server">
  <title>Deletion using SqlDataSource Control</title>
</head>
<body>
  <form id="form1" runat="server">
    <div>
      <asp:SqlDataSource ID="deptSource" runat="server"
        ProviderName="System.Data.SqlClient"
        ConnectionString="<%$ ConnectionStrings:AdventureWorks %>"
        SelectCommand="Select DepartmentID, Name, GroupName, ModifiedDate from
        HumanResources.Department"
        DeleteCommand="Delete from HumanResources.Department Where
        DepartmentID=@original_DepartmentID"
        OldValuesParameterFormatString="original_{0}"
        OnDeleted="deptSource_Deleted">
        <DeleteParameters>
          <asp:Parameter Type="Int32" Name="DepartmentID"></asp:Parameter>
        </DeleteParameters>
      </asp:SqlDataSource>
      <asp:GridView ID="deptView" AutoGenerateColumns="False" runat="server"
        DataSourceID="deptSource"
        HeaderStyle-HorizontalAlign="Center" HeaderStyle-Font-Bold="True"
        HeaderStyle-BackColor="blue" HeaderStyle-ForeColor="White"
        DataKeyNames="DepartmentID">
        <Columns>
          <asp:TemplateField HeaderText="Delete">
            <ItemTemplate>
              <asp:Button ID="btnDelete" Text="Delete" runat="server"
                OnClientClick="return confirm('Are you sure you want to delete this
                record?');" CommandName="Delete" />
            </ItemTemplate>
          </asp:TemplateField>
          <asp:BoundField HeaderText="DepartmentID" DataField="DepartmentID" />
          <asp:BoundField HeaderText="Department Name" DataField="Name" />
```

```
            <asp:BoundField HeaderText="Group Name" DataField="GroupName" />
            <asp:BoundField HeaderText="Last Modified Date"
              DataField="ModifiedDate"/>
          </Columns>
        </asp:GridView>
        <asp:Label ID="lblResult" runat="server" ForeColor="DarkRed"/>
      </div>
    </form>
  </body>
  </html>
```

As you can see from the above, the `GridView` control's `TemplateField` declares an `ItemTemplate`, which in turn contains a `Button` control. Such a button, with the `CommandName` set to `Delete`, will cause the `GridView` to delete the associated row when pressed. To display a confirmation message box before deleting the record, you leverage the `OnClientClick` property of the `Button` control and set it to the JavaScript that displays the confirmation message box for the users.

Similarly to the previous example, the `DataKeyNames` property of the `GridView` control is used to specify the field or fields that represent the primary key of the data source. Next, you set the `SqlDataSource` control's `DeleteCommand` and its parameters. Since the `GridView` needs to locate the row that needs to be located, you use `@original_DepartmentID` after setting the `OldValuesParameterFormatString` property to `"original_{0}"`.

To display a confirmation message to the user after the row has been deleted, you use the `Deleted` event of the `SqlDataSource` control. You can also use this event to display error messages, if there are any. Figure 4-6 shows the output produced by the ASP.NET page when requested through the browser.

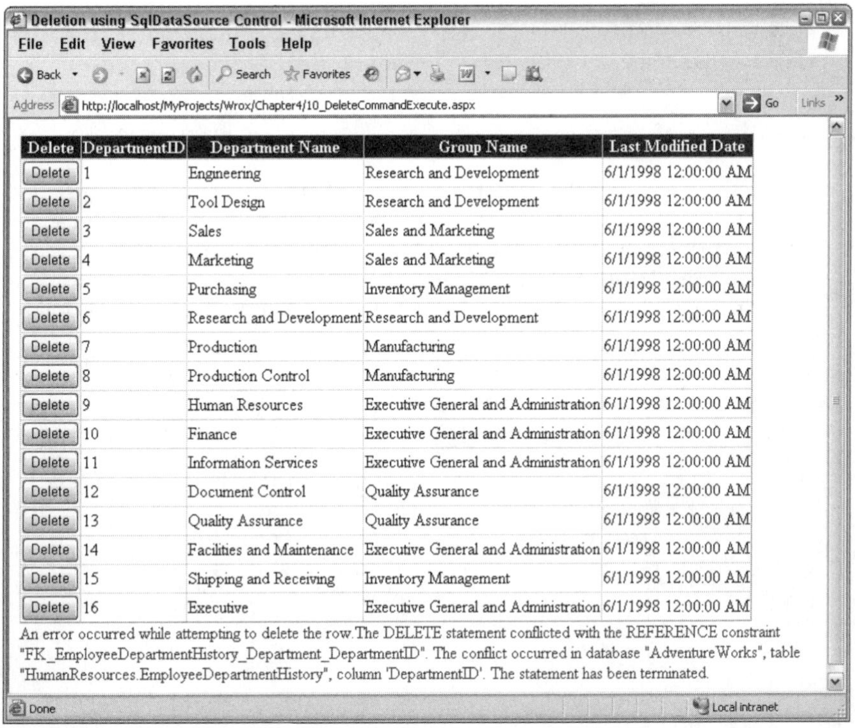

Deletion using SqlDataSource Control - Microsoft Internet Explorer

Address http://localhost/MyProjects/Wrox/Chapter4/10_DeleteCommandExecute.aspx

Delete	DepartmentID	Department Name	Group Name	Last Modified Date
Delete	1	Engineering	Research and Development	6/1/1998 12:00:00 AM
Delete	2	Tool Design	Research and Development	6/1/1998 12:00:00 AM
Delete	3	Sales	Sales and Marketing	6/1/1998 12:00:00 AM
Delete	4	Marketing	Sales and Marketing	6/1/1998 12:00:00 AM
Delete	5	Purchasing	Inventory Management	6/1/1998 12:00:00 AM
Delete	6	Research and Development	Research and Development	6/1/1998 12:00:00 AM
Delete	7	Production	Manufacturing	6/1/1998 12:00:00 AM
Delete	8	Production Control	Manufacturing	6/1/1998 12:00:00 AM
Delete	9	Human Resources	Executive General and Administration	6/1/1998 12:00:00 AM
Delete	10	Finance	Executive General and Administration	6/1/1998 12:00:00 AM
Delete	11	Information Services	Executive General and Administration	6/1/1998 12:00:00 AM
Delete	12	Document Control	Quality Assurance	6/1/1998 12:00:00 AM
Delete	13	Quality Assurance	Quality Assurance	6/1/1998 12:00:00 AM
Delete	14	Facilities and Maintenance	Executive General and Administration	6/1/1998 12:00:00 AM
Delete	15	Shipping and Receiving	Inventory Management	6/1/1998 12:00:00 AM
Delete	16	Executive	Executive General and Administration	6/1/1998 12:00:00 AM

An error occurred while attempting to delete the row.The DELETE statement conflicted with the REFERENCE constraint "FK_EmployeeDepartmentHistory_Department_DepartmentID". The conflict occurred in database "AdventureWorks", table "HumanResources.EmployeeDepartmentHistory", column 'DepartmentID'. The statement has been terminated.

Done — Local intranet

Figure 4-6

Figure 4-6 displays the resultant error message when you try to delete any of the department records, because of the referential integrity violation. If you remove the relationship between HumanResources.Department and HumanResources.EmployeeDepartmentHistory and try the deletion, you will find that it works fine.

> **Note that instead of using ItemTemplate and placing the Delete button inside that, you could have also set the AutoGenerateDeleteButton property of the GridView to true to render the Delete button. But the disadvantage of using the AutoGenerateDeleteButton property is that it does not provide a finer level of control over the deletion process, in that it does not allow you to intercept the Delete button click to prompt the user for confirmation.**

Encrypting the Connection String Stored in the Web.config File

So far in this chapter, you have used the connection string specified in the Web.config file, which is specified in plain text. One of the disadvantages of this approach is that it is stored in plain text and is visible to anyone who has access to the Web.config file. To help alleviate this concern, ASP.NET 2.0 provides a simple way to encrypt the <connectionStrings> section of the Web.config file. At runtime, ASP.NET can automatically decrypt its contents so that it can connect to the appropriate database. For this to work, you need to ensure that the Windows account that your code runs under has access to the RsaProtectedConfigurationProvider container. Here are the steps that need to be followed for setting up encryption and decryption:

1. At the Windows command line, run the ASP.NET IIS registration tool (aspnet_regiis.exe), which is located in the <DriveName>:\[WinDir]\Microsoft.NET\Framework\[Version] directory:

```
aspnet_regiis -pe "connectionStrings" -app "/MyProjects/Wrox/Chapter4"
```

- In this command, the pe option indicates that the contents of the specified section (connectionStrings, in this case) are encrypted. The -app option enables you to pass the name of the application. When the command has finished, open the contents of the Web.config file, and you will find that the connectionStrings configuration section is completely encrypted instead of a clear-text connection string, as follows:

```
<connectionStrings configProtectionProvider="RsaProtectedConfigurationProvider">
  <EncryptedData Type="http://www.w3.org/2001/04/xmlenc#Element"
    xmlns="http://www.w3.org/2001/04/xmlenc#">
    <EncryptionMethod Algorithm="http://www.w3.org/2001/04/xmlenc#tripledes-cbc"/>
    <KeyInfo xmlns="http://www.w3.org/2000/09/xmldsig#">
      <EncryptedKey xmlns="http://www.w3.org/2001/04/xmlenc#">
        <EncryptionMethod Algorithm="http://www.w3.org/2001/04/xmlenc#rsa-1_5" />
        <KeyInfo xmlns="http://www.w3.org/2000/09/xmldsig#">
          <KeyName>Rsa Key</KeyName>
        </KeyInfo>
```

```
        <CipherData>
<CipherValue>k7jbSt59NERjDJRBlCvJcKd64hwU9u0Y4y2U56seuXXohFFWi2Cmrst0gc5NEB11R9tp+q
JGVsieTHKRYKKyP/cx5UVgUIW516xQipP6FHTKPud3PYXRjYdhNT43faUkSKKB/qMxp0fERLaIRSQn8rW1c
/rKPh4/ixHaefSCMMQ=</CipherValue>
        </CipherData>
      </EncryptedKey>
    </KeyInfo>
    <CipherData>
<CipherValue>RLXpz5SnZSLQCvAegfRGEUNTRFHhnovoi6FSDiFxX0vKKSAkMGjFwEHsnLYo67hGXGrSi5
FX5BmSNQOLNvg7XZPTu++x1ANHdQNf0Vg8PRkXnXFet17frzCzcXeTh7BBLB5zSUp9d0kmcJDoVWJh7SBs5
Me4XF1H5Jz3ZU8VXRt1ZBj6zVs2mxVOkkDr9wBYLGQrT96/P79wbELKeamEGdyWRfRGFwrR</CipherValu
e>
    </CipherData>
  </EncryptedData>
</connectionStrings>
```

2. Now that the `<connectionStrings>` section is encrypted, the next step is to give the user account (or identity) under which ASP.NET runs access to the encryption key. By default, in Windows Server 2003 with impersonation disabled for an ASP.NET application, the identity under which the application runs is the NETWORK SERVICE account. In other versions of Windows, ASP.NET runs under the local ASPNET account. At the command prompt, run the `aspnet_regiis.exe` tool with the following options:

```
aspnet_regiis -pa "NetFrameworkConfigurationKey" "NT AUTHORITY\NETWORK SERVICE"
```

- In this command, the `-pa` option enables you to specify the name of the RSA key container for the default `RsaProtectedConfigurationProvider`, as well as the identity of your ASP.NET application. This example uses the default NETWORK SERVICE account. Figure 4-7 shows the output in the command prompt.

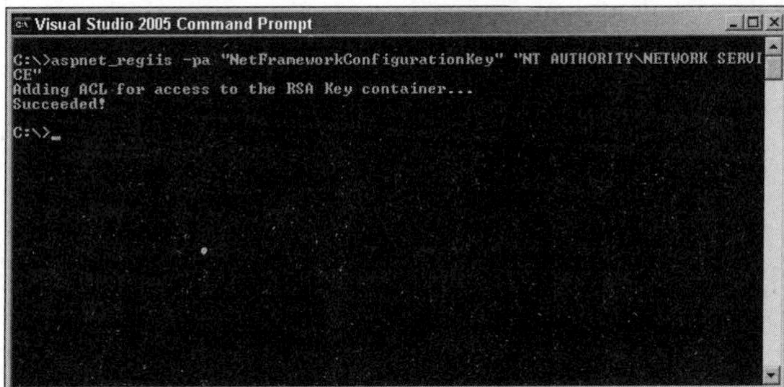

Figure 4-7

3. To decrypt the encrypted `Web.config` file contents, run the `aspnet_regiis.exe` tool with the `-pd` option. The syntax is the same as encrypting `Web.config` file contents, except for the difference that you use the `-pd` option in this case:

```
aspnet_regiis -pd "connectionStrings" -app "/MyProjects/Wrox/Chapter4"
```

Programmatically Adding a SqlDataSource Control to the Page

You can also programmatically create an instance of a SqlDataSource control and work with the data in code. To programmatically access the contents of a SqlDataSource control, call the Select() method. This method expects a single input parameter of type DataSourceSelectArguments. This parameter can be used to pass along requests for the SqlDataSource to message the data before returning it. For example, when working with a sortable GridView, sorting a column calls the Select() method passing in a DataSourceSelectArguments instance, with its SortExpression property set to the column name by which the end user sorted the data. If you don't want the SqlDataSource to sort, filter, or return only a page of data, simply pass in DataSourceSelectArguments.Empty, as shown in the following code example.

The Select() method returns an object that implements the IEnumerable interface. Specifically, it returns a DataView if the DataSourceMode property is set to DataSet, and a DataReader object if it is set to DataReader. Listing 4-11 shows how to programmatically create an instance of the SqlDataSource control, set its properties, and access the data contained in it. When the drop-down list selection changes, you retrieve the products in that category by writing code in the SelectedIndexChanged event to invoke the GetProductsByCategoryID stored procedure using the dynamically created SqlDataSource control. Then the retrieved products list is displayed through a GridView control.

Listing 4-11: Programmatically Adding a SqlDataSource Control to the Page

```
<%@ Page Language="C#" %>
<%@ Import Namespace="System.Web.Configuration" %>
<script runat="server">
  void lstCategories_SelectedIndexChanged(Object sender, EventArgs e)
  {
    SqlDataSource productsSource = new SqlDataSource();
    productsSource.ID = "productsSource";
    Page.Controls.Add(productsSource);
    productsSource.ConnectionString =
      WebConfigurationManager.ConnectionStrings["AdventureWorks"].ConnectionString;
    productsSource.SelectCommand = "GetProductsByCategoryID";
    productsSource.SelectCommandType = SqlDataSourceCommandType.StoredProcedure;
    ControlParameter categoryIdParam = new ControlParameter();
    categoryIdParam.ControlID = "lstCategories";
    categoryIdParam.Name = "ProductSubcategoryID";
    categoryIdParam.PropertyName = "SelectedValue";
    productsSource.SelectParameters.Clear();
    productsSource.SelectParameters.Add(categoryIdParam);
    productsSource.Select(DataSourceSelectArguments.Empty);
    GridView1.DataSource = productsSource;
    GridView1.DataBind();
  }
</script>
<html xmlns="http://www.w3.org/1999/xhtml" >
<head id="Head1" runat="server">
  <title>Programmatically adding a SqlDataSource control to the Page</title>
</head>
<body>
```

```
    <form id="form1" runat="server">
      <div>
        <asp:SqlDataSource ID="categoriesSource" runat="server"
          ProviderName="System.Data.SqlClient"
          ConnectionString="<%$ ConnectionStrings:AdventureWorks %>"
          SelectCommand="GetProductSubCategories"
          SelectCommandType="StoredProcedure">
        </asp:SqlDataSource>
        Categories:
        <asp:DropDownList runat="server" DataSourceID="categoriesSource"
          DataValueField="ProductSubcategoryID"
          OnSelectedIndexChanged="lstCategories_SelectedIndexChanged"
          DataTextField="Name" AutoPostBack="true" ID="lstCategories" />
        <asp:GridView ID="GridView1" runat="server"
          HeaderStyle-HorizontalAlign="Center" HeaderStyle-Font-Bold="True"
          HeaderStyle-BackColor="blue" HeaderStyle-ForeColor="White" />
      </div>
    </form>
  </body>
  </html>
```

The majority of the work occurs in the `SelectedIndexChanged` event of `dropdownlist`. Specifically, you create an instance of the `SqlDataSource` control, set its properties, and invoke its `Select()` method. Finally, you set the `DataSource` property of the `GridView` control to the `SqlDataSource`.

Sorting with the SqlDataSource Control

As you may know, the `GridView` has built-in support ofsorting. In ASP.NET 1.x, there is no `GridView` control. Instead, you have the `DataGrid` control. To handle the sorting of the `DataGrid` control, you have to build your own sorting logic. This is not required with the new `GridView` control.

To enable the built-in sort functionality of the `GridView` control, you set the `AllowSorting` property of the `GridView` to `true`. When the `AllowSorting` property is set to `true`, the `GridView` will add a `LinkButton` for each column header and set the `SortExpression` to the field bound to each column. For example, if the one column is bound to a field (for example, CustomerName), the `SortExpression` property will be `CustomerName`. Setting the grid's `AllowSorting` property allows you to sort columns by default. You can disable sorting for individual fields (BoundColumn or TemplateColumns fields) by setting the `SortExpression` property of the individual column to an empty string.

The sorting is handled by the data source control associated to the `GridView` *control. Not all data source controls can sort data. For example,* `XmlDataSource` *can't sort any data. If the data source control associated to a* `GridView` *control supports sorting, the* `DataView` *object exposed by the data source control will set its* `CanSort` *property to* `true`*. For the* `GridView` *control to be able to display sorted data, the data source control to which it is bound must meet certain criteria.*

Now that you have seen the basics of sorting, the next several paragraphs discuss how sorting works.

When you press the `LinkButton` for the column you want to be sorted, the `Sorting` event will be raised. The `GridView` passes the sort expression to the data source control, and the data source control executes its `SelectCommand` with the sort expression as an argument. When this is done, the `GridView` will rebind itself.

If the SqlDataSource control is used and the DataSourceMode property is set to DataSet, the sort expression will be set to the DataView object's Sort property of the first table in the returned DataSet. If the DataSourceMode is set to DataReader, the SortExpression will not work and an exception will be thrown when you try to use it. To sort a DataReader, the SortParameterName must be used. If you specify a value to the SortParameterName, you must use a stored procedure. The stored procedure must have an input parameter with the same name as the value specified in the SortParameterName property. If you set the SortParameterName to "sort", you must have a "@sort" input parameter added to the stored procedure. The SqlDataSource will pass the sort expression to the stored procedure's parameter.

By default, the sorting of a column in the GridView control will only sort on one column. To sort on several columns, you can use the Sorting event of the GridView to change the sort expression. Listing 4-12 uses a SqlDataSource control with its DataSourceMode set to DataSet. When one of the LinkButtons in the header of the GridView is pressed, the Sorting event will be executed. If the Name column LinkButton is pressed, the sort expression will be changed and an ascending sort on both the Name and GroupName columns will be made.

Listing 4-12: Programmatically Controlling Sorting Behavior

```
<%@ Page Language="C#" %>
<script runat="server">
  void deptView_Sorting(object sender, GridViewSortEventArgs e)
  {
    if (e.SortExpression == "Name")
    {
      e.SortExpression = e.SortExpression + ", GroupName";
    }
  }
</script>
<html xmlns="http://www.w3.org/1999/xhtml" >
<head runat="server">
  <title>Programmatically controlling the Sorting behavior</title>
</head>
<body>
  <form id="form1" runat="server">
    <div>
      <asp:GridView ID="deptView" AllowSorting="true" AllowPaging="true"
        Runat="server" DataSourceID="deptSource" DataKeyNames="DepartmentID"
        AutoGenerateColumns="False" HeaderStyle-HorizontalAlign="Center"
        HeaderStyle-Font-Bold="True" HeaderStyle-BackColor="blue"
        HeaderStyle-ForeColor="White">
        <Columns>
          <asp:BoundField ReadOnly="true" HeaderText="Department ID"
            DataField="DepartmentID" SortExpression="DepartmentID" />
          <asp:BoundField HeaderText="Name" DataField="Name"
            SortExpression="Name" />
          <asp:BoundField HeaderText="Group Name" DataField="GroupName"
            SortExpression="GroupName" />
          <asp:BoundField HeaderText="ModifiedDate" DataField="ModifiedDate"
```

```
            SortExpression="ModifiedDate" />
        </Columns>
      </asp:GridView>
      <asp:SqlDataSource ID="deptSource" Runat="server" SelectCommandType="Text"
        SelectCommand="Select DepartmentID, Name, GroupName, ModifiedDate
        from HumanResources.Department"
        ConnectionString="<%$ConnectionStrings:AdventureWorks%>">
      </asp:SqlDataSource>
    </div>
  </form>
</body>
</html>
```

Figure 4-8 shows the output of the page when it is requested from the browser.

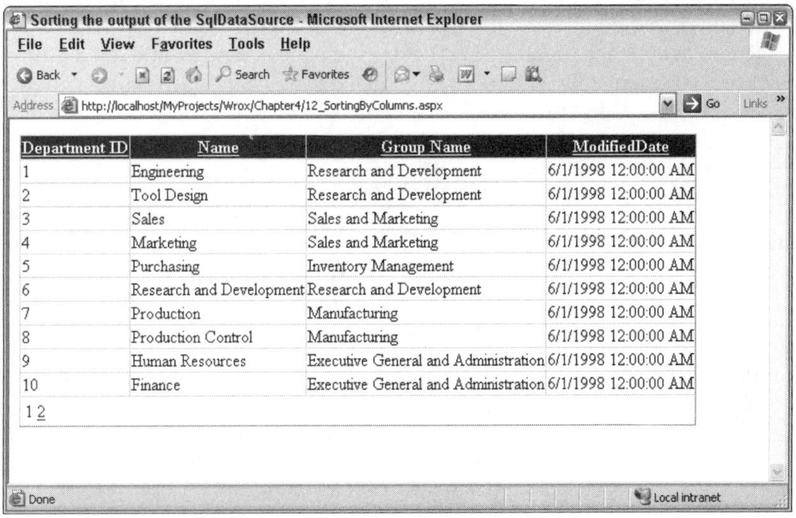
Sorting the output of the SqlDataSource - Microsoft Internet Explorer
File Edit View Favorites Tools Help
Back Search Favorites
Address http://localhost/MyProjects/Wrox/Chapter4/12_SortingByColumns.aspx
Go Links
Department ID | Name | Group Name | ModifiedDate
1 | Engineering | Research and Development | 6/1/1998 12:00:00 AM
2 | Tool Design | Research and Development | 6/1/1998 12:00:00 AM
3 | Sales | Sales and Marketing | 6/1/1998 12:00:00 AM
4 | Marketing | Sales and Marketing | 6/1/1998 12:00:00 AM
5 | Purchasing | Inventory Management | 6/1/1998 12:00:00 AM
6 | Research and Development | Research and Development | 6/1/1998 12:00:00 AM
7 | Production | Manufacturing | 6/1/1998 12:00:00 AM
8 | Production Control | Manufacturing | 6/1/1998 12:00:00 AM
9 | Human Resources | Executive General and Administration | 6/1/1998 12:00:00 AM
10 | Finance | Executive General and Administration | 6/1/1998 12:00:00 AM
1 2
Done
Local intranet

Figure 4-8

As you can see from Figure 4-8, the rows were sorted based on the Name and GroupName columns, when the Name hyperlink was clicked.

Caching

Many developers who learn about caching see it as a bit of a frill, but nothing could be further from the truth. Used intelligently, caching can provide a twofold, threefold, or even tenfold performance improvement by retaining important data for just a short period of time. ASP.NET really has two types of caching. Your applications can and should use both types, because they complement each other:

- **Output caching:** This is the simplest type of caching. It stores a copy of the final rendered HTML page that is sent to the client. The next client that submits a request for this page doesn't actually run the page. Instead, the final HTML output is sent automatically. The time that would have been required to run the page and its code is completely reclaimed.

- **Data caching:** This is carried out manually in your code. To use data caching, you store important pieces of information that are time-consuming to reconstruct (such as a `DataSet` retrieved from a database) in the cache. Other pages can check for the existence of this information and use it, thereby bypassing the steps ordinarily required to retrieve it. Data caching is conceptually the same as using application state, but it's much more server-friendly, because items will be removed from the cache automatically when it grows too large and performance could be affected. Items can also be set to expire automatically,

This sectionwill primarily focus on the caching techniques used with the `SqlDataSource` control.

Caching with the SqlDataSource Control

Of the two types of caching, the `SqlDataSource` supports built-in data caching. Using caching with the `SqlDataSource` control is highly recommended, because unlike your own custom data code, the data source controls always requery the data source in every postback. They also query the data source once for every bound control, so if you have three controls bound to the same data source, three separate queries are executed against the database just before the page is rendered. Even a little caching can reduce this overhead dramatically. The following table discusses the caching-related properties of the `SqlDataSource` control.

Property	Description
`CacheDuration`	The number of seconds to cache the data object. If you are using sliding expiration, the time limit is reset every time the object is retrieved from the cache. The default, `DataSource CacheExpiry.Infinite`, keeps cached items perpetually.
`CacheExpirationPolicy`	Uses a value from the `DataSourceCacheExpiry` enumeration — `Absolute` for absolute expiration (which times out after a fixed interval of time) or `Sliding` for sliding expiration (which resets the time window every time the data object is retrieved from the cache).
`CacheKeyDependency` and `SqlCacheDependency`	Allows you to make a cached item dependent on another item in the data cache (`CacheKeyDependency`) or on a table in your database (`SqlCacheDependency`).
`EnableCaching`	If true, caching is switched on. This property is set to `false` by default.

When you enable caching for the `SqlDataSource` control, you cache the results of the select query. However, if you create a select query that takes parameters, the `SqlDataSource` will cache a separate result for every set of parameter values. For example, imagine that you create a page that allows you to view products by category. The user selects the desired category from a list box, and you use a `SqlDataSource` control to fill in the matching products' records in a grid. As mentioned before, the `SqlDataSource` caching works only when the `DataSourceMode` property is set to `DataSet` (the default). That's because the `DataReader` object cannot be efficiently cached, because it represents a live connection to the database. To fill the grid, you use the following `SqlDataSource`:

```
<asp:SqlDataSource ID="sourceProducts" runat="server"
  ProviderName="System.Data.SqlClient"
```

```
ConnectionString="<%$ConnectionStrings:AdventureWorks %>"
SelectCommand="Select ProductID, Name, ProductNumber, ListPrice,
ProductSubcategoryID from Production.Product"
SelectCommandType="Text" FilterExpression="ProductSubcategoryID='{0}'">
<FilterParameters>
  <asp:ControlParameter ControlID="lstCategories"
    Name="ProductSubcategoryID" PropertyName="SelectedValue" />
 </FilterParameters>
</asp:SqlDataSource>
```

In this example, each time you select a category, a separate query is performed to get just the matching products in that category. The query is used to fill a `DataSet`, which is then cached. If you select a different city, the process is repeated, and the new `DataSet` is cached separately. However, if you pick a city that you or another user has already requested, the appropriate `DataSet` is fetched from the cache (provided that it has not yet expired).

If you explore the `SqlDataSource` control's properties, you will notice the `FilterExpression` and `FilterParameters` properties. You may be wondering how the `FilterParameters` collection differs from the `SelectParameters` collection. `FilterExpression` and `FilterParameters` are properties designed for filtering the results returned by the database. That is, with these two properties, after the records have been returned from the backend database, these results are further filtered by `FilterExpression` and `FilterParameters` before being handed over to the data web control or programmer whose code is requesting the data source's data. Using a parameterized query and `SelectParameters`, on the other hand, performs the filtering on the database side.

As you probably can guess, filtering on the database side is much more efficient than bringing back all data to the data source control and then having it filter the results. However, there are times (as in the caching example shown here) when you would want to use the `FilterExpression` and `FilterParameters` properties.

Caching separate results for different parameter values works well if some parameter values are used much more frequently than others. For example, if the results for Pedals are requested much more often than the results for Wheels, this ensures that the Pedals results stick around in the cache even when the Wheels `DataSet` has been released. Assuming that the full set of results is extremely large, this may be the most efficient approach.

Although many data source controls support caching, it is not a required data source control feature, and you will run into data source controls that do not support it or for which it may not make sense (such as `SiteMapDataSource`).

Caching with Filtering

On the other hand, if the parameter values are all used with similar frequency, caching with filtering is not as suitable. One of the problems it imposesis that when the items in the cache expire, you will need multiple database queries to repopulate the cache (one for each parameter value), which is not as efficient as getting the combined results with a single query.

If you fall into the second situation, you can change the `SqlDataSource` so that it retrieves a `DataSet` with all the employee records and caches that. The `SqlDataSource` can then extract just the records it needs to satisfy each request from the `DataSet`. This way, a single `DataSet` with all the records is cached, which can satisfy any parameter value.

To use this technique, you need to rewrite your `SqlDataSource` to use filtering. First, the select query should return all the rows and not use any `SELECT` parameters:

```
<asp:SqlDataSource runat="server"
  SelectCommand="Select ProductID, Name, ProductNumber, StandardCost from
  Production.Product"
......./>
```

Second, you need to define the filter expression. This is the portion that goes in the `WHERE` clause of a typical SQL query. (In fact, the `SqlDataSource` uses the `DataView` control's row-filtering abilities behind the scenes.) However, this has a catch — if you're supplying the filter value from another source (such as a control), you need to define one or more placeholders, using the syntax `{0}` for the first placeholder, `{1}` for the second, and so on. You then supply the filter values using the `<FilterParameters>` section in much the same way that you supplied the select parameters in the first version.

Here is the completed `SqlDataSource` tag:

```
<asp:SqlDataSource ID="productsSource" runat="server"
  ProviderName="System.Data.SqlClient"
  ConnectionString="<%$ ConnectionStrings:AdventureWorks%>"
  SelectCommand="Select ProductID, Name, ProductNumber, StandardCost from
  Production.Product"
  FilterExpression="ProductSubcategoryID='{0}'" EnableCaching="True">
  <FilterParameters>
    <asp:ControlParameter ControlID="lstCategories" Name="ProductSubcategoryID"
      PropertyName="SelectedValue" />
  </FilterParameters>
</asp:SqlDataSource>
```

Don't use filtering unless you are using caching. If you use filtering without caching, you are essentially retrieving the full result set each time and then extracting a portion of its records. This combines the worst of both worlds — you have to repeat the query with each postback, and you fetch far more data than you need each time.

Cache Dependencies

As time passes, the data source may change in response to other actions. However, if your code uses caching, you may remain unaware of the changes and continue using out-of-date information from the cache. To help mitigate this problem, ASP.NET supports cache dependencies. Cache dependencies allow you to make a cached item dependent on another resource so that when that resource changes, the cached item is removed automatically.

ASP.NET includes two types of dependencies:

- ❑ Dependencies on other cache items or files
- ❑ Dependencies on a database query

In the next section, you will consider the steps involved in setting up a database cache dependency.

Understanding SQL Cache Notifications

SQL cache dependencies are one of the most widely touted new ASP.NET 2.0 features — the ability to automatically invalidate a cached data object (such as a `DataSet`) when the related data is modified in the database. This feature is supported in both SQL Server 2005 and in SQL Server 2000, although the underlying plumbing is quite a bit different.

To understand how SQL cache dependencies work, it is important to understand a couple of flawed solutions that developers have been forced to resort to in the past:

- One common technique is to use a marker file. With this technique, you add the data object to the cache and set up a file dependency. However, the file you use is empty — it is just a marker file intended to indicate when the database state changes. Here is how it works. When the user calls a stored procedure that modifies the table you are interested in, your stored procedure removes or modifies the marker file. ASP.NET immediately detects the file change and removes the corresponding data object. This ugly workaround is not terribly scalable and can introduce concurrency problems if more than one user calls the stored procedure and tries to remove the file at the same time. It also forces you to clutter your stored procedure code, because every stored procedure that modifies the database needs similar file modification logic. Having a database interact with the file system is a bad idea from the start, because it adds to the complexity and reduces the security of your overall system.
- Another common approach is to use a custom HTTP handler that removes cached items at your request. Once again, this only works if you build the appropriate level of support into the stored procedures that modify the corresponding tables. In this case, instead of interacting with a file, these stored procedures call the custom HTTP handler and pass a query string that indicates what change has taken place or what cache key has been affected. The HTTP handler can then use the `Cache.Remove()` method to get rid of the data. The problem with this approach is that it requires the considerable complexity of an extended stored procedure. Also, the request to the HTTP handler must be synchronous, which causes a significant delay. Even worse, this delay happens every time the stored procedure executes, because the stored procedure has no way of determining if the call is necessary or if the cached item has already been removed. As a result, the overall time taken to execute the stored procedure increases significantly, and the overall scalability of the database suffers. Like the marker file approach, it works well in small scenarios but cannot handle large-scale, complex applications. Both of these approaches introduce a whole other set of complications in web farm scenarios with multiple servers.

What is needed is an approach that can deliver notifications asynchronously, and in a scalable and reliable fashion. In other words, the database server should notify ASP.NET without stalling the current connection. Just as importantly, it should be possible to set up the cache dependency in a loosely coupled way so stored procedures do not need to be aware of the caching that is in place. The database server should watch for changes that are committed by any means, including from a script, an inline SQL command, or a batch process. Even if the change does not go through the expected stored procedures, the change should still be noticed, and the notification should still be delivered to ASP.NET. Finally, the notification method needs to support web farms. With all these requirements in mind, Microsoft put together a team of architects from the ASP.NET, SQL Server, ADO.NET, and IIS groups to concoct a solution. They came up with two different architectures, depending on the database server you are using. Both of them use the same `SqlCacheDependency` class, which derives from the `CacheDependency` class.

Using SQL cache dependencies still entails more complexity than just using a time-based expiration policy. If it is acceptable for certain information to be used without reflecting all the most recent changes (and developers often overestimate the importance of up-to-the-millisecond live information), you may not need it at all.

The next two sections examine the database cache dependency with SQL Server 2000, SQL Server 7, and SQL Server 2005 versions.

Cache Notifications in SQL Server 2000 or SQL Server 7

ASP.NET uses a polling model for SQL Server 2000 and SQL Server 7. Older versions of SQL Server and other databases are not supported, although it is possible for third parties to implement their own solutions by creating a custom dependency class.

With the polling model, ASP.NET keeps a connection open to the database and uses a dedicated thread to check periodically if a table has been updated. The effect of tying up one connection in this way is not terribly significant, but the extra database work involved with polling does add some database overhead. For the polling model to be effective, the polling process needs to be quicker and lighter than the original query that extracts the data.

Enabling Notifications

Before you can use SQL Server cache invalidation, you need to enable notifications for the database. This task is performed with the `aspnet_regsql.exe` command-line utility, which is located in the `<DriveName>:\[WinDir]\Microsoft.NET\Framework\[Version]` directory. To enable notifications, you need to use the `-ed` command-line switch. You also need to identify the server (use `-E` for a trusted connection and `-S` to choose a server other than the current computer) and the database (use `-d`). Here is an example that enables notifications for the Northwind database on the current server:

```
aspnet_regsql -ed -E -d AdventureWorks
```

In addition to caching, note that the `aspnet_regsql` *is used for a number of scenarios, such as creating the tables for ASP.NET 2.0 features such as membership, profiles, and role management.*

When you execute the previous command in the command prompt, a new table named SqlCacheTables ForChangeNotification is added to the database named AspNet (which must already exist). The SqlCacheTablesForChangeNotification table has three columns: tableName, notificationCreated, and changeId. This table is used to track changes. Essentially, when a change takes place, a record is written into this table. The SQL Server polling queries this table.

This design achieves a number of benefits:

- Because the change notification table is much smaller than the table with the cached data, it is much faster to query.
- Because the change notification table is not used for other tasks, reading these records won't risk locking and concurrency issues.

- Because multiple tables in the same database will use the same notification table, you can monitor several tables at once without materially increasing the polling overhead.

Even once you have created the SqlCacheTablesForChangeNotification table, you still need to enable notification support for each individual table. You can do this manually using `SqlCacheRegisterTableStoredProcedure`, or you can rely on `aspnet_regsql`, using the `-et` parameter to turn on the notifications and the `-t` parameter to name the table. Here is an example that enables notifications for the DatabaseLog table:

```
aspnet_regsql -et -E -d AdventureWorks -t DatabaseLog
```

This step generates the notification trigger for the DatabaseLog table.

How Notifications Work

Now you have all the ingredients in place to use the notification system. For example, imagine that you cache the results of a query like this:

```
SELECT * FROM DatabaseLog
```

This query retrieves records from the DatabaseLog table. To check for changes that might invalidate your cached object, you need to know if any record in the DatabaseLog table is inserted, deleted, or updated. You can watch for these operations using triggers. For example, here is the trigger on the DatabaseLog table that `aspnet_regsql` creates:

```
CREATE TRIGGER [DatabaseLog_AspNet_SqlCacheNotification_Trigger] ON
  [dbo].[DatabaseLog] FOR INSERT, UPDATE, DELETE AS
  BEGIN
    SET NOCOUNT ON
    EXEC dbo.AspNet_SqlCacheUpdateChangeIdStoredProcedure N'DatabaseLog'
  END
```

The `AspNet_SqlCacheUpdateChangeIdStoredProcedure` stored procedure simply increments the `changeId` for the table:

```
CREATE PROCEDURE dbo.AspNet_SqlCacheUpdateChangeIdStoredProcedure
  @tableName NVARCHAR(450)
AS
  BEGIN
    UPDATE dbo.AspNet_SqlCacheTablesForChangeNotification WITH (ROWLOCK)
      SET changeId = changeId + 1 WHERE tableName = @tableName
  END
```

The `AspNet_SqlCacheTablesForChangeNotification` contains a single record for every table you are monitoring. As you can see, when you make a change in the table (such as inserting a record), the changeIdcolumn is incremented by one. ASP.NET queries this table repeatedly and keeps track of the most recent `changeId` values for every table. When this value changes in a subsequent read, ASP.NET knows that the table has changed.

This hints at one of the major limitations of cache invalidation as implemented in SQL Server 2000 and SQL Server 7. Any change to the table is deemed to invalidate any query for that table. In other words, look at the following query:

```
SELECT * FROM DatabaseLog WHERE Event='CREATE_TABLE'
```

With this query, the caching still works in the same way. That means if any log record is touched, even if the event is some other event (and therefore is not one of the cached records), the notification is still sent and the cached item is considered invalid. Keeping track of what changes do and do not invalidate a cached data object is simply too much work for SQL Server 2000 (although it is possible in SQL Server 2005).

The implementation of cache invalidation with SQL Server 2000 has more overhead than the implementation with SQL Server 2005 and is not as fine-grained. As a result, it does not make sense for tables that change frequently or for narrowly defined queries that retrieve only a small subset of records from a table.

Enabling ASP.NET Polling

Now that you have prepared the database, the next step is to instruct ASP.NET to poll the database. You do this on a per-application basis. In other words, every application that uses cache invalidation will hold a separate connection and poll the notification table on its own.

To enable the polling service, you use the `<sqlCacheDepency>` element in the `Web.config` file. You set the `enabled` attribute to `true` to turn it on, and you set the `pollTime` attribute to the number of milliseconds between each poll. (The higher the poll time, the longer the potential delay before a change is detected.) You also need to supply the connection string information.

For example, this `Web.config` file checks for updated notification information every 15 seconds:

```
<configuration>
  <connectionStrings>
    <add name="AdventureWorks" connectionString=
      "Data Source=localhost;Initial Catalog=AdventureWorks;uid=user;pwd=word;"/>
  </connectionStrings>
  <system.web>
    <caching>
      <sqlCacheDependency enabled="true" pollTime="15000">
        <databases>
          <add name="AdventureWorks" connectionStringName="AdventureWorks" />
        </databases>
      </sqlCacheDependency>
    </caching>
    ...
  </system.web>
</configuration>
```

Creating the Cache Dependency

Now that you have seen how to set up your database to support SQL Server notifications, the only remaining detail is the code, which is quite straightforward. After configuring a SQL cache dependency, you can use it to enable change notification for a data source control. The following declaration of a `SqlDataSource` control uses the AdventureWorks entry:

```
<asp:SqlDataSource id="databaseLogSource" runat="server"
  ConnectionString="<%$ConnectionStrings:AdventureWorks%>"
  SelectCommand="SELECT DatabaseLogID, DatabaseUser, Event FROM DatabaseLog"
  DataSourceMode="DataSet" EnableCaching="True"
  SqlCacheDependency="AdventureWorks:DatabaseLog ">
</asp:SqlDataSource>
```

If you want to base the cached data invalidation on more than one SQL cache dependency, you separate them with semicolons. For example:

```
SqlDependency="AdventureWorks:DatabaseLog;AdventureWorks:ErrorLog"
```

The cached row set data is invalidated automatically when you update the table contents in the database; after updating, the next refresh of the main page will show the new value.

Cache Notifications in SQL Server 2005

SQL Server 2005 gets closest to the ideal notification solution, because the notification infrastructure is built into the database with a messaging system called Service Broker. The Service Broker manages queues, which are database objects that have the same standing as tables, stored procedures, or views.

Essentially, you can instruct SQL Server 2005 to send notifications for specific events using the `CREATE EVENT NOTIFICATION` command. ASP.NET offers a higher-level model — you register a query, and ASP.NET automatically instructs SQL Server 2005 to send notifications for any operations that would affect the results of that query. This mechanism works in a similar way to indexed views. Every time you perform an operation, SQL Server determines whether your operation affects a registered command. If it does, SQL Server sends a notification message and stops the notification process.

When using notification with SQL Server, you get the following benefits over SQL Server 2000:

- **Notification is much more fine-grained:** Instead of invalidating your cached object when the table changes, SQL Server 2005 invalidates your object only when a row that affects your query is inserted, updated, or deleted.
- **Notification is more intelligent:** A notification message is sent the first time the data is changed, but not if the data is changed again (unless you re-register for notification messages by adding an item back to the cache).
- **No special steps are required to set up notification:** You do not run `aspnet_regsql` or add polling settings to the `Web.config` file.

Notifications work with `SELECT` queries and stored procedures. However, some restrictions exist for the `SELECT` syntax you can use. To properly support notifications, your command must adhere to the following rules:

- You must fully qualify table names in the form `[Owner].table`, as in `dbo.AdventureWorks.DatabaseLog` (not just `DatabaseLog`).
- Your query cannot use an aggregate function, such as `COUNT()`, `MAX()`, `MIN()`, or `AVERAGE()`.
- You cannot select all columns with the wildcard `*` (as in `SELECT * FROM Employees`). Instead, you must specifically name each column, so SQL Server can properly track changes that do and do not affect the results of your query.

Here is an acceptable command:

```
SELECT DatabaseLogID, DatabaseUser, Event FROM dbo.AdventureWorks.Employees
```

These are the most important rules, but the SQL Server Books Online has a lengthy list of caveats and exceptions. If you break one of these rules, you will not receive an error. However, the notification message will be sent as soon as you register the command, and the cached item will be invalidated immediately.

Creating the Cache Dependency

You use a different syntax to use SQL cache dependencies with SQL Server 2005. It is not enough to simply identify the database name and table—instead, SQL Server needs to know the exact command. If you are using the `OutputCache` directive or a data source control, ASP.NET takes care of the registration for you. You simply need to supply the string value `CommandNotification`, as shown here:

```
<asp:SqlDataSource id="identifier" runat="server"
  EnableCaching="True"
  SqlCacheDependency="CommandNotification"
  ...
/>
```

Summary

As this chapter has shown, the introduction of the `SqlDataSource` control makes querying and displaying data from any number of data sources an almost trivial task. From this chapter, you have understood the basics of accessing data from databases using the `SqlDataSource` control. In addition to selecting records from the database, you also learned the steps involved in updating and deleting data from the database.

This chapter also demonstrated the steps involved in programmatically adding a `SqlDataSource` control to the page and leveraging its `Select()` method to execute the `SELECT` statement. You also examined how the `SqlDataSource` control can be used to process stored procedure parameters, such as return parameters and output parameters. With the rich set of properties added to the `SqlDataSource` control, handling null values and filtering the result set from the database is now a breezy experience.

Caching is now automatically built into the `SqlDataSource` control. This means that you can easily configure and control data caching using the same declarative syntax.

With the background of relational data binding, the next chapter focuses on data binding with XML data.

5

Data Binding with XML Data

The previous chapter demonstrated how the SqlDataSource control can be used to create rich data-driven web applications. Similar to the way the SqlDataSource control allows you to work with the relational data, the XmlDataSource control enables you to work with hierarchical XML data. Using the XmlDataSource control, you can directly display the XML data using data-bound controls or transform that XML data using an XSLT stylesheet.

This chapter focuses on the techniques of XML data handling of the XmlDataSource control, which are useful in displaying the XML data in a meaningful manner to the users of your web application. This chapter will explore the application of the XmlDataSource control by looking at various examples that process XML data. In addition, this chapter will also describe the caching techniques that you can use to cache XML data using the XmlDataSource control.

By the end of this chapter, you will have a good understanding of the following:

- Support provided by the XmlDataSource control for displaying XML data
- Filtering XML data using the built-in XPath support of the XmlDataSource control
- Applying an XSLT stylesheet to transform XML data using an XmlDataSource control
- Binding an XmlDataSource control to controls such as TreeView, GridView, and DataList
- Updating data through the XmlDataSource control
- Programmatically creating the XmlDataSource control
- Handling the events raised by the XmlDataSource control
- Caching XML data in an XmlDataSource control

Introduction to the XmlDataSource Control

The data controls supplied with ASP.NET support a variety of rich data-binding scenarios. By taking advantage of the new data source controls, you can bind to any data source without writing any code. One such control is `<asp:XmlDatasource>`. This control allows you to bind to XML data, which can come from a variety of sources, such as an external XML file, a `DataSet` object, and so on. Once the XML data is bound to the `XmlDataSource` control, this control can then act as a source of data for other data-bound controls such as `TreeView` and `Menu`. The `XmlDataSource` control can be bound to any of the following data controls:

- `<asp:TreeView>`
- `<asp:GridView>`
- `<asp:DataList>`
- `<asp:DropDownList>`
- `<asp:Repeater>`

The `XmlDataSource` control provides a rich set of properties and methods that can enable sophisticated data-binding scenarios. The following table provides a brief overview of the important properties of the `XmlDataSource` control.

Property	Description
`CacheDuration`	Allows you to get or set the length of the time that the data source control caches data.
`CacheExpirationPolicy`	Allows you to set or get the cache expiration behavior; when combined with the duration, describes the behavior of the cache.
`CacheKeyDependency`	Allows you to get or set a user-defined key dependency that is linked to all data cache objects created by the data source control
`Data`	Allows you to get or set the block of XML that is used by the data source control as an input
`DataFile`	Allows you to specify the name of the XML file that is used as an input by the data source control
`EnableCaching`	Gets or sets a value indicating whether the data source control has caching enabled
`Transform`	Gets or sets the block of XSLT that specifies the XSLT transformation to be performed on the XML data
`TransformArgumentList`	Provides the list of XSLT arguments that are used with the stylesheet defined by the `Transform` or `TransformFile` property
`TransformFile`	Specifies the XSL file that defines the XSLT transformation to be performed on the XML data
`XPath`	Specifies an XPath query to be applied to the XML data contained by the `Data` property, or by the XML file indicated by the `DataFile` property

In addition to these properties, the `XmlDataSource` control also exposes the events shown in the following table.

Event	Description
`DataBinding`	Occurs when the data source control binds to a data source
`Transforming`	Occurs when the XSL stylesheet is applied to the XML data

You will employ most of these properties in the later sections of this chapter. Before looking at how to use `XmlDataSource` control, consider the XML document shown in Listing 5-1, which contains a simple book store that provides information about the various books that are part of the bookstore.

Listing 5-1: Bookstore.xml File

```
<bookstore>
  <genre name="Fiction">
    <book ISBN="10-861003-324" Title="A Tale of Two Cities" Price="19.99">
      <chapter num="1" name="Introduction">
        Abstract...
      </chapter>
      <chapter num="2" name="Body">
        Abstract...
      </chapter>
      <chapter num="3" name="Conclusion">
        Abstract...
      </chapter>
    </book>
    <book ISBN="1-861001-57-5" Title="Pride And Prejudice" Price="24.95">
      <chapter num="1" name="Introduction">
        Abstract...
      </chapter>
      <chapter num="2" name="Body">
        Abstract...
      </chapter>
      <chapter num="3" name="Conclusion">
        Abstract...
      </chapter>
    </book>
  </genre>
  <genre name="NonFiction">
    <book ISBN="10-861003-324" Title="Statistics of Two Cities" Price="19.99">
      <chapter num="1" name="Introduction">
        Abstract...
      </chapter>
      <chapter num="2" name="Body">
        Abstract...
      </chapter>
      <chapter num="3" name="Conclusion">
        Abstract...
      </chapter>
    </book>
```

(continued)

Listing 5-1: *(continued)*

```
      <book ISBN="1-861001-57-6"
        Title="The Sea: becoming an Old Man and the Sea" Price="27.95">
        <chapter num="1" name="Introduction">
          Abstract...
        </chapter>
        <chapter num="2" name="Body">
          Abstract...
        </chapter>
        <chapter num="3" name="Conclusion">
          Abstract...
        </chapter>
      </book>
    </genre>
  </bookstore>
```

Note that the `Bookstore.xml` file shown in Listing 5-1 will be used in most of the examples presented in this chapter. Now that you have created the XML file, it is time to create the stylesheet that will transform the XML into HTML. Listing 5-2 shows the declaration of the XSL stylesheet.

Listing 5-2: Bookstore.xsl File

```
<xsl:stylesheet version="1.0"
  xmlns:xsl="http://www.w3.org/1999/XSL/Transform">
  <xsl:template match="bookstore">
    <bookstore>
      <xsl:apply-templates select="genre"/>
    </bookstore>
  </xsl:template>
  <xsl:template match="genre">
    <genre>
      <xsl:attribute name="name">
        <xsl:value-of select="@name"/>
      </xsl:attribute>
      <xsl:apply-templates select="book"/>
    </genre>
  </xsl:template>
  <xsl:template match="book">
    <book>
      <xsl:attribute name="ISBN">
        <xsl:value-of select="@ISBN"/>
      </xsl:attribute>
      <xsl:element name="title">
        <xsl:value-of select="title"/>
      </xsl:element>
      <xsl:element name="price">
        <xsl:value-of select="price"/>
      </xsl:element>
      <xsl:apply-templates select="chapters/chapter" />
    </book>
  </xsl:template>
  <xsl:template match="chapter">
    <chapter>
```

```
        <xsl:attribute name="num">
          <xsl:value-of select="@num"/>
        </xsl:attribute>
        <xsl:attribute name="name">
          <xsl:value-of select="@name"/>
        </xsl:attribute>
        <xsl:apply-templates/>
      </chapter>
    </xsl:template>
  </xsl:stylesheet>
```

For the purposes of this chapter, note that the `Bookstore.xml` and `Bookstore.xsl` files are stored in the `App_Data` directory. Now that you have had a brief look at the XML and XSL files, the next section dives deep into the process of implementing data binding with the `XmlDataSource` control.

Data Binding with the XmlDataSource Control

Typically, you will want to modify the display of the XML to provide more meaningful information. This section demonstrates how to bind the `XmlDataSource` control with a `TreeView` control. The `TreeView` control exposes bindings that let you specify how each node is rendered. For example, you can create a binding for the `bookstore` element that states that it should be rendered using the static text, Books. The `TreeView` also contains a number of built-in properties that let you easily customize its appearance. For example, you can set the `ImageSet` property to a specific value that will render with predefined graphics so that elements appear as folders. Listing 5-3 shows the code required for data binding an `XmlDataSource` control with a `TreeView` control.

Listing 5-3: Binding a TreeView Control to an XmlDataSource Control

```
<%@ Page Language="C#" %>
<html xmlns="http://www.w3.org/1999/xhtml" >
<head>
  <title>Binding XML Data from an XmlDataSource Control</title>
</head>
<body>
  <form id="form1" runat="server">
    <div>
      <asp:TreeView ID="bookView" Runat="server"
        DataSourceID="bookSource">
        <DataBindings>
          <asp:TreeNodeBinding ImageUrl="~/Images/openbook.gif"
            TextField="Title" DataMember="book"></asp:TreeNodeBinding>
          <asp:TreeNodeBinding ImageUrl="~/Images/notepad.gif"
            TextField="name" DataMember="chapter"></asp:TreeNodeBinding>
        </DataBindings>
      </asp:TreeView>
      <asp:XmlDataSource ID="bookSource" Runat="server"
        DataFile="~/App_Data/Bookstore.xml"
        XPath="bookstore/genre[@name='Fiction']/book">
      </asp:XmlDataSource>
    </div>
  </form>
  XPath="bookstore/genre[@name='Fiction']/book"</body>
</html>
```

In the previous code, you have two controls on the page. The first, `XmlDataSource`, does all of the work, including reading `bookstore.xml` and applying the XPath expression to the contents of the XML file. The second, the `TreeView`, takes that data and displays that information on the page. To bind the `TreeView` to the `XmlDataSource` source, you need to set the `DataSourceID` property of the `TreeView` control to the ID of the `XmlDataSource` control.

As this example shows, the XPath is used to filter out the initial set of matches. For example, if you create a treeview that shows the fiction books, you need to use the XPath support that is built into the `XmlDataSource` to prefilter the results. To use XPath, you supply the XPath expression that selects the data you are interested in by using the `XmlDataSource.XPath` property. This XPath expression extracts an `XmlNodeList`, which is then made available to the bound controls:

```
<asp:XmlDataSource ID="bookSource" runat="server"
DataFile="~/App_Data/Bookstore.xml"
   XPath="/bookstore/genre[@name='Fiction']/book " />
```

If that expression returns a list of nodes, and all the information you need to display is found in attributes, you do not need to perform any extra steps. However, if the information is in element text, you need to create a template.

With the preceding steps, you can see on your page a display of data from your `XmlDataSource` control. The output produced by the page is shown in Figure 5-1.

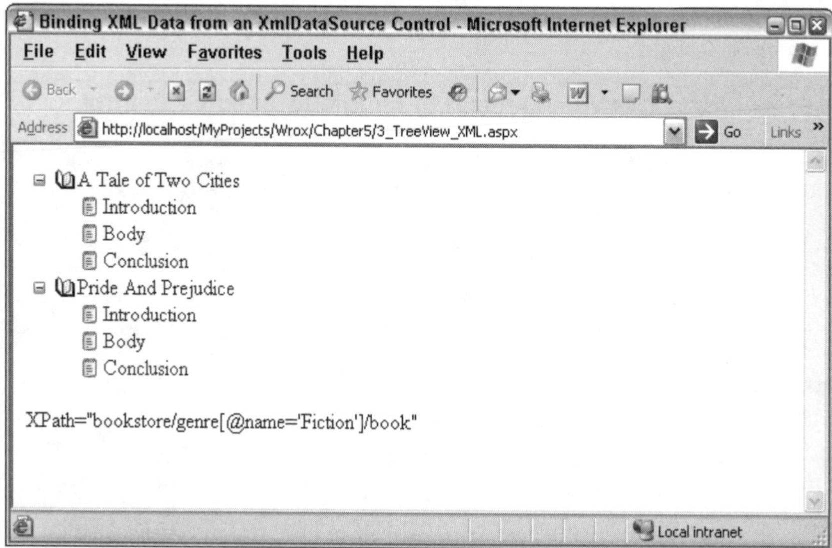

Figure 5-1

Binding an XmlDataSource Control with a GridView Control

Frequently, XML is the source of data in many cases. So, you need a way to be able to display that XML data in other tabular controls apart from the hierarchal `TreeView` control. This section explores how to use an `XmlDataSource` control with a `GridView` control and a `DropDownList` control. Follow these steps to bind the `XmlDataSource` control to a `GridView` control.

The first step is to define the XML data source and point it to the file that has the content you want to use:

```
<asp:XmlDataSource ID="bookSource" runat="server"
  DataFile="~/App_Data/Bookstore.xml " />
```

Now you can bind the `GridView` with automatically generated columns, in the same way that you bind it to any other data source:

```
<asp:GridView ID="bookView" runat="server"
  AutoGenerateColumns="True" DataSourceID="bookSource">
```

Now, when you run the page, the `XmlDataSource` will extract the data from the `Bookstore.xml` file, provide it to the `GridView` as an `XmlDocument` object, and call `DataBind()`. Because the `XmlDocument` implements the `IEnumerable` interface, the `GridView` can walk through its structure in much the same way as it walks through a `DataView`. It traverses the `XmlDocument.Nodes` collection and gets all the attributes for each `XmlNode`.

The complete code for binding an `XmlDataSource` control with a `GridView` control is shown in Listing 5-4.

Listing 5-4: Binding Tabular Controls with an XmlDataSource Control

```
<%@ Page Language="C#" %>
<%@ Import Namespace="System.Xml" %>
<html xmlns="http://www.w3.org/1999/xhtml" >
<head>
  <title>Displaying XML Data in a GridView and a ListBox</title>
</head>
<body>
  <form id="form1" runat="server">
    <div>
       
    </div>
    <div>
      <asp:ListBox ID="lstTitles" Runat="server"
        DataSourceID="bookSource" DataValueField="ISBN"
        DataTextField="Title"/>
    </div>
  <div>
      <asp:GridView ID="bookView" Runat="server"
        DataSourceID="bookSource" AutoGenerateColumns="False">
        <Columns>
          <asp:BoundField HeaderText="ISBN" DataField="ISBN"
            SortExpression="ISBN"></asp:BoundField>
          <asp:BoundField HeaderText="Title" DataField="Title"
            SortExpression="Title"></asp:BoundField>
          <asp:BoundField HeaderText="Price" DataField="Price"
            SortExpression="Price"></asp:BoundField>
        </Columns>
      </asp:GridView>
    </div>
    <div>
      <asp:XmlDataSource ID="bookSource" Runat="server"
```

(continued)

Listing 5-4: *(continued)*

```
            DataFile="~/App_Data/Bookstore.xml"
            XPath="bookstore/genre[@name='Fiction']/book">
          </asp:XmlDataSource>
           
        </div>
        <div>
           
        </div>
      </form>
    </body>
    </html>
```

In Listing 5-4, you have the `GridView` control named `bookView,` and its `DataSourceID` property is set to the ID of the `XmlDataSource` control. Once you have created that association, you can then bind the individual fields in the `XmlDataSource` control to the columns in the `GridView`. Note that `XmlDataSource` control has its `XPath` attribute set to a specific XPath expression, which will be evaluated at runtime.

As part of the `GridView` declaration, three columns are declared: ISBN, Title, and Price. Along with the columns declaration, you also set the `HeaderText`, `SortExpression`, and `DataField` properties to appropriate values. That's all there is to displaying data in a `GridView` control using `XmlDataSource` as the data source. Similarly, the `ListBox` control is also bound to the `XmlDataSource` through the `DataSourceID` property. Apart from setting the `DataSourceID` property, you also set the `DataValueField` and `DataTextField` properties to appropriate values. If you request the page from the browser, you should see the output shown in Figure 5-2.

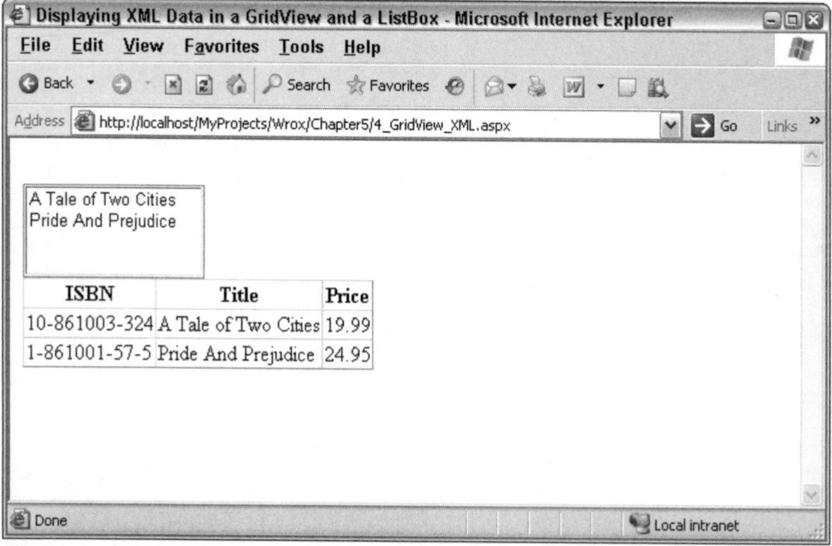

Figure 5-2

Inline XML Data with the XmlDataSource Control

So far, you have seen how to utilize an external XML file to load the required data into the `XmlDataSource` control. However, if you have a relatively simple XML data and you know the XML contents at design time, you might then want to embed the XML data inline along with the `XmlDataSource` control declaration for reasons of simplicity. Listing 5-5 demonstrates how to use an `XmlDataSource` to display inline XML data contained by the `Data` property with a `TreeView` control.

Listing 5-5: Using Inline XML Data

```
<%@ Page Language="C#" %>
<html xmlns="http://www.w3.org/1999/xhtml" >
<head>
  <title>Using Inline XML Data in an XmlDataSource Control</title>
</head>
<body>
  <form id="form1" runat="server">
    <div>
      <asp:TreeView ID="bookView" Runat="server"
        DataSourceID="bookSource">
        <DataBindings>
          <asp:TreeNodeBinding ImageUrl="~/Images/openbook.gif"
            TextField="Title" DataMember="book"></asp:TreeNodeBinding>
          <asp:TreeNodeBinding ImageUrl="~/Images/notepad.gif"
            TextField="name" DataMember="chapter"></asp:TreeNodeBinding>
        </DataBindings>
      </asp:TreeView>
    </div>
    <div>
      <asp:XmlDataSource ID="bookSource" Runat="server" XPath="bookstore/book">
        <Data>
          <bookstore>
            <book ISBN="10-861003-324" Title="A Tale of Two Cities" Price="19.99">
              <chapter num="1" name="Introduction">
                Abstract...
              </chapter>
              <chapter num="2" name="Body">
                Abstract...
              </chapter>
              <chapter num="3" name="Conclusion">
                Abstract...
              </chapter>
            </book>
            <book ISBN="1-861001-57-5" Title="Pride And Prejudice"
              Price="24.95">
              <chapter num="1" name="Introduction">
                Abstract...
              </chapter>
              <chapter num="2" name="Body">
                Abstract...
              </chapter>
              <chapter num="3" name="Conclusion">
                 Abstract...
```

(continued)

Listing 5-5: *(continued)*

```
                </chapter>
              </book>
            </bookstore>
          </Data>
        </asp:XmlDataSource>
      </div>
    </form>
  </body>
  </html>
```

The code in Listing 5-5 is very similar to Listing 5-3, except for the difference that the XML data is embedded within the declaration of the `XmlDataSource` control in this case. In declarative scenarios such as the current one, the `Data` property is specified as a multi-line inner property of the `XmlDataSource` object. An inner property is compatible with XML data, because it enables you to format the XML data in any way and ignore character adding issues, such as padding quote characters. Note that the value of the `Data` property is stored in view state.

> *Similar to the* `Data` *property,* `XmlDataSource` *control also has a property named* `Transform` *that allows you to embed inline XSL stylesheet as part of the* `XmlDataSource` *control declaration. This property defines an XSLT transformation to be performed on the XML data that is contained by the* `Data` *property, or by the XML file indicated by the* `DataFile` *property. The default value is* `System.String.Empty`.

If both the `DataFile` and `Data` properties are set for an `XmlDataSource` control, the `DataFile` property takes precedence and the data in the XML file is used instead of the XML specified in the `Data` property.

XML Data Binders

Because XML is becoming ever more prevalent in applications, ASP.NET 2.0 also introduces several new ways to bind specifically to XML data sources, called *XML data binders*. These new binders give you powerful ways of working with the hierarchical format of XML. Except for the different method names, these binding methods work exactly the same way and provide similar functionality. These binders should be used when you are using the `XmlDataSource` control. The first binding format that uses the `XPathBinder` class is shown in the following code:

```
<% XPathBinder.Eval(Container.DataItem, "bookstore/genre/book") %>
```

Notice that rather than specifying a column name as in the `Eval` method, the `XPathBinder` binds the result of an XPath query. Like the standard `Eval` binder, the XML binder also has a shorthand format:

```
<% XPath("bookstore/genre/book") %>
```

Also, like the `Eval` method, the `XPath` binder supports applying formatting to the data:

```
<% XPath("bookstore/book/publishedDate", "{0:mm dd yyyy}") %>
```

The `XPathBinder` returns a single node using the XPath query provided. If you want to return multiple nodes from the `XmlDataSource` control, you can use the class's `Select` method. This method returns a list of nodes that match the supplied XPath query:

```
<% XPathBinder.Select(Container.DataItem,"bookstore/genre/book") %>
```

Or use the shorthand syntax:

```
<% XPathSelect("bookstore/genre/book") %>
```

The next section provides an example of how to use the XML data binders to retrieve the right set of nodes/data from the XML tree.

Nested DataList Controls with an XmlDataSource Control

Another feature of the `XmlDataSource` control is the capability to support nested elements by nesting one `DataList` control inside another, allowing you to deal with much more complex XML structures. The remarkable part is that ASP.NET provides support for this approach without requiring you to write any code. The `DataList` control is used to display a repeated list of items that are bound to the control. However, the `DataList` control adds a table around the data items by default. The `DataList` control may be bound to a database table, an XML file, or another list of items. The code in Listing 5-6 shows how to bind the `XmlDataSource` control to a `DataList` control.

Listing 5-6: Using the XmlDataSource Control with Nested DataList Controls

```
<%@ Page Language="C#" %>
<html xmlns="http://www.w3.org/1999/xhtml">
<head>
  <title>Displaying XML Data in Nested DataList Controls</title>
</head>
<body>
  <form runat="server">
    <h1>Bookstore: Fiction</h1>
    <asp:XmlDataSource id="bookSource" DataFile="~/App_Data/Bookstore.xml"
      XPath="bookstore/genre[@name='Fiction']/book" runat="server"/>
    <asp:DataList id="bookList" DataSourceID="bookSource" runat="server">
      <ItemTemplate>
        <table>
          <tr>
            <td>
              <img src='<%# "images/" + XPath("@ISBN") + ".jpg" %>'>
            </td>
            <td>
              <h4><%# XPath("@Title") %></h4>
              <b>ISBN:</b> <%# XPath("@ISBN") %><br>
              <b>Price:</b> <%# XPath("@Price") %><br>
            </td>
          </tr>
        </table>
        <asp:DataList id="chapterList" DataSource='<%# XPathSelect("chapter")%>'
          runat="server">
          <ItemTemplate>
            <br>
            <u>
              Chapter <%# XPath("@num") %>: <%# XPath("@name") %>
```

(continued)

Listing 5-6: *(continued)*

```
            </u>
            <br>
              <%# XPath(".") %>
          </ItemTemplate>
        </asp:DataList>
      </ItemTemplate>
    </asp:DataList>
  </form>
</body>
</html>
```

In this example, you have a `DataList` control named `bookList`, and its `DataSourceID` property is set to the ID of the `XmlDataSource` control. In the `DataList` control, the `ItemTemplate` element is used to specify the data fields in the `XmlDataSource` control that will be displayed through the `Label` controls.

As part of the Label controls declaration, you use the XPath expression to identify the element in the `XmlDataSource`. To the XPath expression, you pass in the name of the data element as a parameter. Since the `XmlDataSource` contains elements such as ISBN, Title, and Price, you use them in the XPath expression. In addition to the outer `DataList` control, there is also an inner `DataList` control named `chapterList` for which the outer data source control provides the source data. This is accomplished by setting the `DataSource` property of the `chapterList` control to the output produced by the `XpathSelect()` function:

```
<asp:DataList id="chapterList" DataSource='<%# XPathSelect("chapter")%>'
```

When you call `XPathSelect()`, you supply the XPath expression that retrieves the `XmlNodeList` based on a search starting at the current node. In this case, you need to drill down to the group of `<chapter>` elements. Once you have set the right data source, all you need to do is define a template in the second `DataList` that displays the appropriate information. In this case, you need only a single data-binding expression to get the element text.

Ordinarily, when you bind an `XmlNode`, you display only attribute values. However, you can get the text from nested elements using XPath data-binding expressions. The most flexible way to do this is to use a template that defines XPath data-binding expressions. XPath data-binding expressions are similar to `Eval()` expressions, except that instead of supplying the name of the field you want to display, you supply an XPath expression based on the current node. For example, here is an XPath expression that starts at the current node, looks for a nested node named `Title`, and gets the associated element text:

```
<%# XPath("./Title")%>
```

Here is an XPath expression that filters out the text of an ID attribute for the current node:

```
<%# XPath("./@ID")%>
```

You can use the XPath data-binding syntax with your own custom data objects, but it is not easy. The only requirement is that the data item must implement the `IXPathNavigable` interface.

Output produced by the code Listing 5-6 is shown in Figure 5-3.

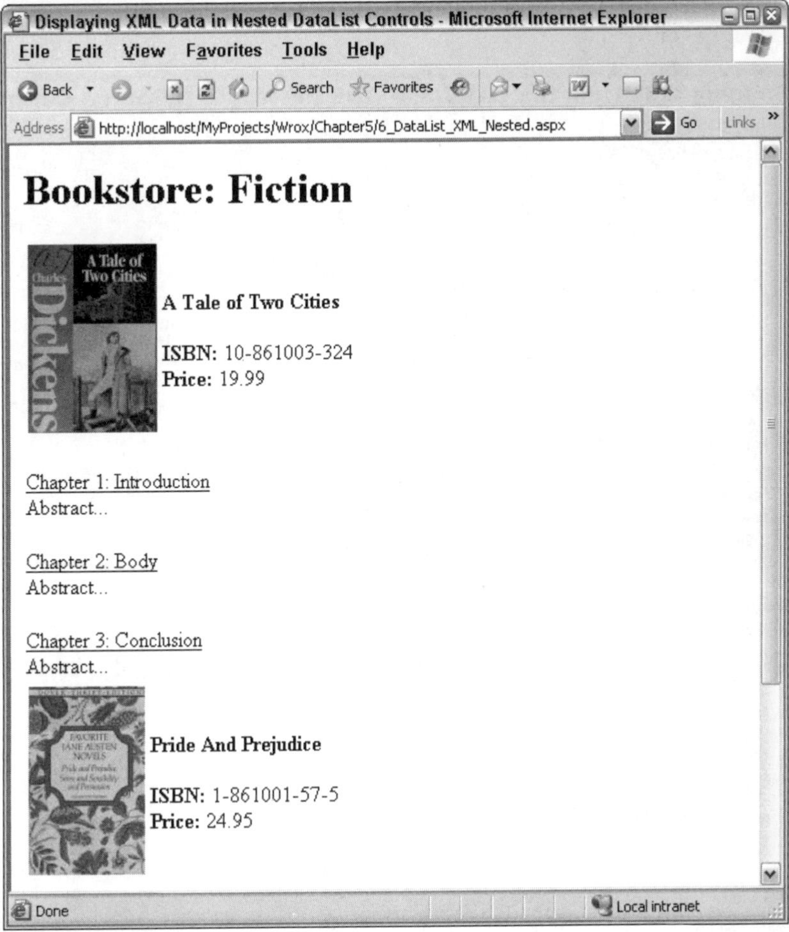

Figure 5-3

XML Binding with Data from Other Sources

So far, all the examples you have seen demonstrate how to bind to XML content in a file or use the inline XML data. This is the standard scenario for the `XmlDataSource` control, but it is not your only possibility. The other option is to supply the XML as text through the `Data` property. You can set the `Data` property at any point before the binding takes place. One convenient time is during the `Page_Load` event, as follows:

```
protected void Page_Load(object sender, EventArgs e)
{
string xmlContent;
//Retrieve data from other location
  bookSource.Data = xmlContent;
}
```

This allows you to read XML content from another source (such as a database) and still work with the bound data controls. However, it requires adding some custom code. Listing 5-7 shows you an example of how to retrieve data from the AdventureWorks database in XML format and use that as an input to the `XmlDataSource` control.

Listing 5-7: Using XML from the Database with the XmlDataSource Control

```
<%@ Page Language="C#" %>
<%@ Import Namespace="System.Data.SqlClient" %>
<%@ Import Namespace="System.Xml" %>
<%@ Import Namespace="System.Web.Configuration" %>
<script runat="server">
protected void Page_Load(object sender, EventArgs e)
{
    string connectionString = WebConfigurationManager.ConnectionStrings
      ["AdventureWorks"].ConnectionString;
    using (SqlConnection connection = new SqlConnection(connectionString))
    {
      connection.Open();
      string sql = "Select ProductID, Name from Production.Product AS Product " +
        "Order by ProductID FOR XML AUTO, ROOT('Products')";
      SqlCommand command = new SqlCommand(sql, connection);
      XmlReader reader = command.ExecuteXmlReader();
      XmlDocument doc = new XmlDocument();
      doc.Load(reader);
      productsSource.Data = doc.OuterXml;
      productsSource.XPath = "Products/Product";
    }
  }
</script>
<html xmlns="http://www.w3.org/1999/xhtml">
<head>
  <title>Binding XML Data from Other Sources</title>
</head>
<body>
<form id="form1" runat="server">
    <asp:XmlDataSource id="productsSource" runat="server"/>
    <asp:GridView ID="productView" Runat="server" DataSourceID="productsSource"
      AutoGenerateColumns="False">
      <Columns>
        <asp:BoundField HeaderText="Product ID" DataField="ProductID">
        </asp:BoundField>
        <asp:BoundField HeaderText="Product Name" DataField="Name">
        </asp:BoundField>
      </Columns>
    </asp:GridView>
  </form>
</body>
</html>
```

First, you execute a `FOR XML` query against the AdventureWorks database using the `ExecuteXmlReader()` method of the `SqlCommand` object. You retrieve the query results into an `XmlReader` object, which is then transferred to an `XmlDocument` object, using the `XmlDocument.Load()` method. Then you retrieve the XML string output from the `XmlDocument` object, using the `OuterXml` property of the `XmlDocument` object. After that, you set the `Data` and `XPath` properties of the `XmlDataSource` to appropriate values. The output of the ASP.NET page when displayed through the browser is shown in Figure 5-4.

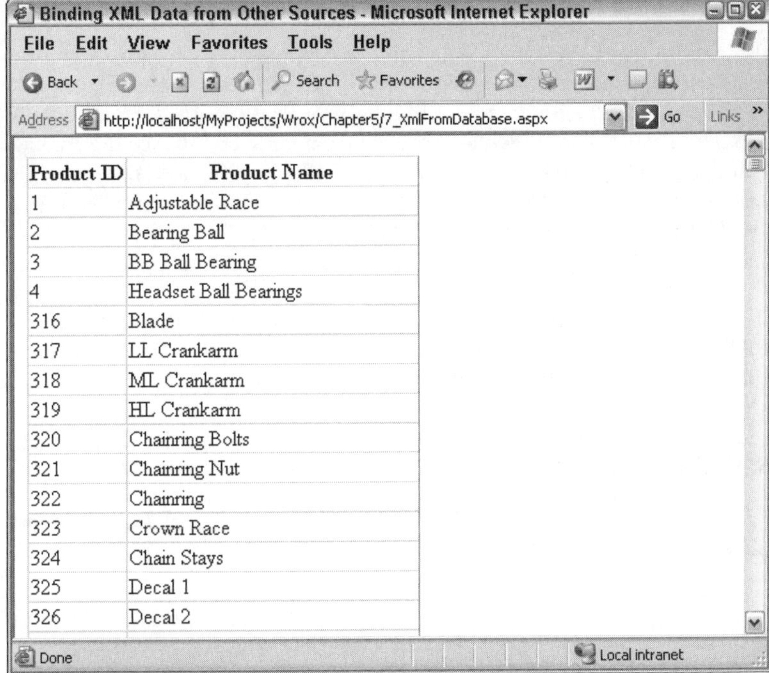

Product ID	Product Name
1	Adjustable Race
2	Bearing Ball
3	BB Ball Bearing
4	Headset Ball Bearings
316	Blade
317	LL Crankarm
318	ML Crankarm
319	HL Crankarm
320	Chainring Bolts
321	Chainring Nut
322	Chainring
323	Crown Race
324	Chain Stays
325	Decal 1
326	Decal 2

Figure 5-4

Even if you do use the `XmlDataSource.Data` property, XML data binding still is not nearly as flexible as the built-in .NET XML classes. One of the key limitations is that the XML content needs to be loaded into memory all at once as a string object. If you are dealing with large XML documents, or if you just need to ensure the best possible scalability for your web application, you might be able to reduce the overhead considerably by using the `XmlReader` instead, even though it will require much more code. Handling the XML parsing process yourself also gives you unlimited flexibility to rearrange and aggregate your data into a meaningful summary, which is not always easy using XSLT alone.

If you do use the `XmlDataSource` to display XML data from a file, make sure that you use caching to reduce the number of times that the file needs to be opened with the `CacheDuration`, `CacheDependency`, and `CachePolicy` properties. If your file changes infrequently, you will be able to keep it in the cache indefinitely, which guarantees good performance. On the other hand, if you need to update the underlying XML document frequently, you are likely to run into multi-user concurrency issues.

Updating XML Data

Unlike the `SqlDataSource` and `ObjectDataSource` controls, the `XmlDataSource` does not support editable binding. You can confirm this fact with a simple test—just bind the `XmlDataSource` to `GridView`, and add a `CommandField` with edit buttons. When you try to commit the update, you will get an error informing you that the data source does not support this feature. However, the `XmlData`

Source does provide a Save() method. This method replaces the file specified in the DataFile property with the current XML content. Although you need to add code to call the Save() method, you could use this technique to provide editable XML data binding.

> **The basic technique to edit XML data using XmlDataSource control is as follows: when the user commits a change in a control, your code retrieves the current XML content as an XmlDocument object by calling the XmlDataSource.GetXmlDocument() method. Then, your code finds the corresponding node and makes the change using the features of XmlDocument. You can find and edit specific nodes, remove nodes, or add nodes. Finally, your code must call the XmlDataSource.Save() method to commit the change.**

Listing 5-8 shows the code required to update Bookstore.xml with the XmlDataSource control. Through the ASP.NET page, you can enter the discount percentage, which is used to calculate the actual discount by multiplying that with the value of the Price attribute. This discount value is then added to the book node as an attribute.

Listing 5-8: Updating XML Data through the XmlDataSource Control

```
<%@ Page Language="C#" %>
<%@ Import NameSpace="System.Xml" %>
<script runat="server" >
  void btnDiscount_Click(Object sender, EventArgs e)
{
    XmlDocument doc = new XmlDocument();
    doc = (XmlDocument)bookSource.GetXmlDocument();
    double discountPercent = Convert.ToInt32(txtDiscountPercent.Text);
    string path = "bookstore/genre/book";
    XmlNodeList nodeList = doc.SelectNodes(path);
    for(int i=0; i< nodeList.Count ; i++)
    {
      XmlNode node = nodeList[i];
      double price = Convert.ToDouble(node.Attributes["Price"].Value);
      double discount = price * (discountPercent/100);
      XmlAttribute discountAttribute = doc.CreateAttribute("Discount");
      discountAttribute.Value = discount.ToString();
      node.Attributes.Append(discountAttribute);
    }
    bookSource.Save();
    bookRepeater.DataBind();
  }
</script>
<html>
<head>
  <title>Updating Data through XmlDataSource Control</title>
</head>
<body>
  <form id="Form1" runat="server" >
  <asp:XmlDataSource runat="server" ID="bookSource" XPath="bookstore/genre/book"
    DataFile="~/App_Data/Bookstore.xml" EnableViewState="True"/>
  <asp:Repeater runat="server" ID="bookRepeater" DataSourceID="bookSource" >
```

```
      <ItemTemplate >
        <h2><%# XPath ("@Title") %> </h2>
        <b>ISBN:</b><%# XPath ("@ISBN") %> <%# XPath ("author/last-name/text()") %>
        <b>Price:</b><%# XPath ("@Price") %>
        <b>Discount:</b><%# XPath ("@Discount") %>
      </ItemTemplate>
    </asp:Repeater>
    <p>
      Enter the discount percentage:
        <asp:TextBox runat="server" ID="txtDiscountPercent" />
      <asp:Button runat="server" ID="btnAddDiscount" onclick="btnDiscount_Click"
        Text="Add Discount" />
    </p>
    </form>
  </body>
  </html>
```

First, you capture the click event of the `btnAddDiscount` control, and inside that event, you get a reference to the `XmlDocument` of the `XmlDataSource` control, using the `GetXmlDocument()` method. Once you have obtained a reference to the `XmlDocument`, you then get a reference to all the book nodes, using an XPath expression. After that, you loop through all the book nodes and add the `Discount` attribute whose value is calculated by multiplying the user-specified percentage by the price of the book. Figure 5-5 shows the output of the page when you enter the discount percentage of 10 and click the Add Discount button.

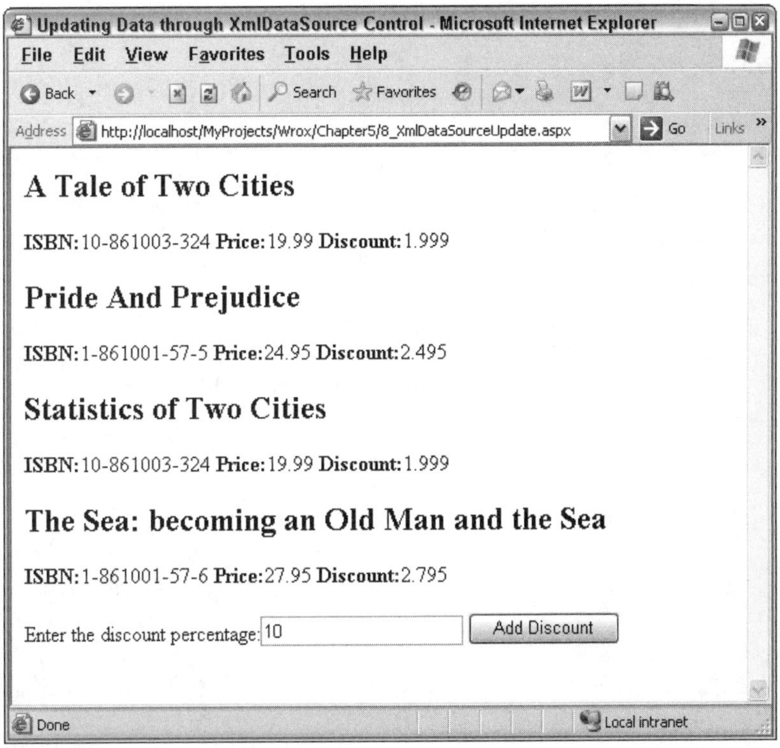

Updating Data through XmlDataSource Control - Microsoft Internet Explorer

File Edit View Favorites Tools Help

Address http://localhost/MyProjects/Wrox/Chapter5/8_XmlDataSourceUpdate.aspx

A Tale of Two Cities

ISBN:10-861003-324 **Price:**19.99 **Discount:**1.999

Pride And Prejudice

ISBN:1-861001-57-5 **Price:**24.95 **Discount:**2.495

Statistics of Two Cities

ISBN:10-861003-324 **Price:**19.99 **Discount:**1.999

The Sea: becoming an Old Man and the Sea

ISBN:1-861001-57-6 **Price:**27.95 **Discount:**2.795

Enter the discount percentage: 10 [Add Discount]

Done | Local intranet

Figure 5-5

Although this approach works perfectly well, it is not necessarily a great way to design a web site. The XML manipulation code can become quite long, and you are likely to run into concurrency headaches if two users make different changes to the same `XmlDocument` at the same time. If you need to change XML content, it is almost always a better idea to implement the logic you need in a separate component, using the .NET XML classes.

Programmatically Creating an XmlDataSource Control

You can also programmatically create an instance of an `XmlDataSource` control and work with the data in code. To programmatically manipulate the contents of an `XmlDataSource` control, call either the `DataFile` or `Data` properties. Once the contents are set, you can then filter the contents, using the `XPath` property. If you need to apply XSL transformation on the XML data, you can then also set either the `TransformFile` or `Transform` properties. With these properties set to appropriate values, you are now ready to bind the `XmlDataSource` control to a `GridView` control. Listing 5-9 shows an example of this in action.

Listing 5-9: Programmatically Adding an XmlDataSource Control to an ASP.NET Page

```
<%@ Page Language="C#" %>
<script runat="server">
protected void Page_Load(object sender, EventArgs e)
{
    XmlDataSource bookSource = new XmlDataSource();
    bookSource.DataFile = "~/App_Data/Bookstore.xml";
    bookSource.XPath = "bookstore/genre[@name ='Fiction']/book";
    bookView.DataSource = bookSource;
    bookView.DataBind();
  }
</script>
<html xmlns="http://www.w3.org/1999/xhtml">
<head>
  <title>Programmatically Creating an XmlDataSource Control</title>
</head>
<body>
<form id="form1" runat="server">
    <div>
      <asp:GridView ID="bookView" Runat="server" AutoGenerateColumns="False">
        <Columns>
          <asp:BoundField HeaderText="ISBN" DataField="ISBN"
            SortExpression="ISBN"></asp:BoundField>
          <asp:BoundField HeaderText="Title" DataField="Title"
            SortExpression="Title"></asp:BoundField>
          <asp:BoundField HeaderText="Price" DataField="Price"
            SortExpression="Price"></asp:BoundField>
        </Columns>
      </asp:GridView>
    </div>
  </form>
</body>
</html>
```

The majority of the work occurs in the `Page_Load` event of the ASP.NET page. Specifically, you create an instance of the `XmlDataSource` control and set its `DataFile` and `XPath` properties. Finally, you set the `DataSource` property of the `GridView` control to the `XmlDataSource` and invoke its `DataBind()` method.

XSL Transformations with XmlDataSource Control

XSL Transformations (XSLT) is the most important part of the eXtensible Stylesheet Language (XSL) Standards. XSLT is that part of XSL that is used to transform an XML document into another XML document, or another type of document that is recognized by a browser, such as HTML and XHTML. Traditionally, performing XSL transformations in the .NET Framework requires you to use the `XslCompiledTransform` class and its methods.

Fortunately with the `XmlDataSource` control, you have an easy and effective way to perform XSL transformations by leveraging the control's built-in attributes. The difference is that you do not use the stylesheet to convert the XML to HTML. Instead, you use it to convert the source XML document into an XML structure that is easier to data bind. For example, you might generate an XML document with just the results you want, and generate a flattened structure (with elements converted into attributes) for easier data binding. To specify a stylesheet, you can set the `TransformFile` property to point to a file with the XSL transform, or you can supply the stylesheet as a single long string using the `Transform` property. You can use both stylesheets and XPath expressions, but the stylesheet is always applied first:

```
<asp:XmlDataSource ID="bookSource" runat="server"
    DataFile="Bookstore.xml" TransformFile="Bookstore.xsl" />
```

One good reason to use the XSLT features of the `XmlDataSource` is to get your XML data ready for display in a hierarchical control such as the `TreeView`. You also want to put all the content into attributes so that it is easy to bind. Listing 5-10 shows you an example of how to utilize XSL to format an XML document into another XML document.

Listing 5-10: Applying an XSL Transformation Using the XmlDataSource Control

```
<%@ Page Language="C#" %>
<html xmlns="http://www.w3.org/1999/xhtml" >
<head>
  <title>Applying XSL Transformation on an XmlDataSource Control</title>
</head>
<body>
  <form id="form1" runat="server">
    <div>
      <asp:TreeView ID="bookView" Runat="server"
        DataSourceID="bookSource" />
      <asp:XmlDataSource ID="bookSource" Runat="server"
        DataFile="~/App_Data/Bookstore.xml"
        TransformFile="~/App_Data/Bookstore.xsl" />
    </div>
  </form>
</body>
</html>
```

You have two controls on the page. The first, `XmlDataSource`, does all of the work, including reading `Bookstore.xsl` and loading XML contents into its memory. Instead of directly using the XML from the `XmlDataSource` control, you transform the XML into another format. This is accomplished using the `TransformFile` property. In this case, you set the value of `TransformFile` property to `Bookstore.xsl`. The second control, the `TreeView`, takes that data and displays that information on the page. To bind the `TreeView` to the `XmlDataSource` source, you set the `DataSourceID` property of the `TreeView` control to the ID of the `XmlDataSource` control. Figure 5-6 shows the output of the page when requested through the browser.

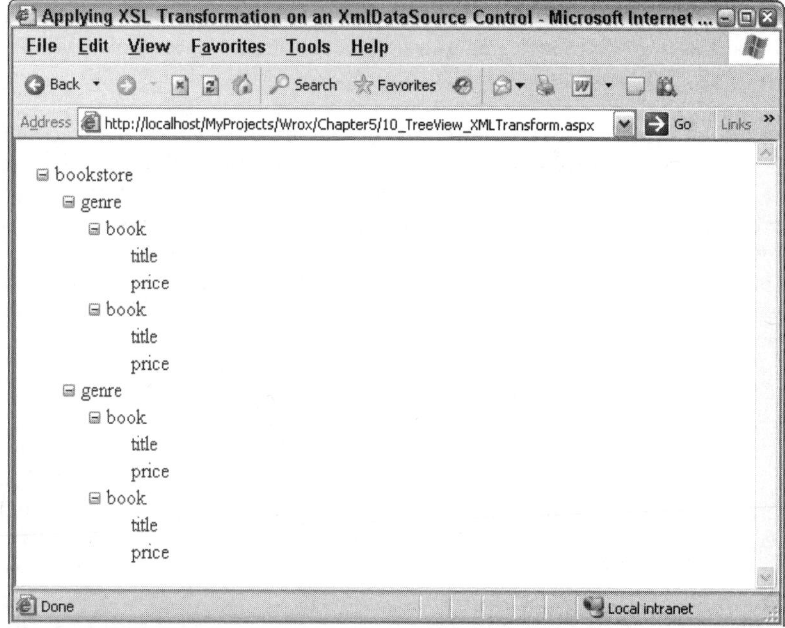

Figure 5-6

As shown in Figure 5-6, when the transformed XML is displayed through the `XmlDataSource` control, it simply displays the node names and attribute names in the `TreeView`.

Handling Events Raised by the XmlDataSource Control

One of the ways you can extend the `XmlDataSource` control is through handling the events generated by the `XmlDataSource` control. For example, by default the `XmlDataSource` allows you to pass parameters to the XSLT stylesheet only if the `XmlDataSource` is created programmatically. However, you can extend the `XmlDataSource` to pass parameters even in the declarative scenario by handling the `Transforming` event of the `XmlDataSource` control.

The first step is to declare the parameter in the XSLT stylesheet, as follows:

```
<xsl:stylesheet version="1.0" xmlns:xsl="http://www.w3.org/1999/XSL/Transform">
<xsl:param name="discount"/>
<xsl:template match="bookstore">
```

```
    ------
    ------
  </xsl:template>
</xsl:stylesheet>
```

Next, associate the event handler with the `Transforming` event of the `XmlDataSource` control:

```
<asp:XmlDataSource ID="bookSource" Runat="server"
 DataFile="~/App_Data/Bookstore.xml" XPath="bookstore/genre[@name ='Fiction']/book"
 TransformFile="~/App_Data/Bookstore_with_parameter.xsl"
 OnTransforming="bookSource_Transforming">
```

Then write the code to handle the `Transforming` event:

```
protected void bookSource_Transforming(object sender, EventArgs e)
{
int discountPercentage = 10;
XsltArgumentList argList = new XsltArgumentList();
argList.AddParam("discount", "", discountPercentage.ToString());
  ((XmlDataSource) sender).TransformArgumentList = argList;
}
```

Note that the `AddParam()` method of the `XsltArgumentList` class contained in the `System.Xml.Xsl` namespace enables you to add parameters to the XSLT stylesheet. Once all the parameters are added to the `XsltArgumentList` object, it can then be assigned to the `TransformArgumentList` property of the `XmlDataSource` control.

Implementing Caching with the XmlDataSource Control

Similarly to the `SqlDataSource` control, the `XmlDataSource` control also supports caching, using which you can cache the output of the `XmlDataSource` control. This will be very useful when you want to cache just the output of a data source control, while recreating the rest of the page every time the page is requested.

Simply by setting a couple of properties on the `XmlDataSource` control, you can automatically cache the data represented by a data source control in memory. For example, if you want to cache the `Bookstore.xml` file in memory for 100 seconds, you can declare an `XmlDataSource` control like this:

```
<asp:XmlDataSource EnableCaching="true" CacheDuration="100"
  ID="bookSource" Runat="server"
  DataFile="~/App_Data/Bookstore.xml">
</asp:XmlDataSource>
```

Listing 5-11 shows the complete code of the page.

Listing 5-11: Caching with the XmlDataSource Control

```
<%@ Page Language="C#" %>
<%@ Import Namespace="System.Xml" %>
<script runat="server">
```

(continued)

Listing 5-11: Caching with the XmlDataSource Control

```
    void Page_Load(object sender, EventArgs e)
    {
      lblCurrentTime.Text = "Current Time is : " +
        DateTime.Now.ToLongTimeString();
    }
  </script>
  <html xmlns="http://www.w3.org/1999/xhtml" >
  <head>
    <title>Caching XML Data in an XmlDataSource Control</title>
  </head>
  <body>
    <form id="form1" runat="server">
      <div>
        <asp:Label Runat="server" ID="lblCurrentTime"></asp:Label>
        <asp:GridView ID="bookView" Runat="server"
          DataSourceID="bookSource" AutoGenerateColumns="False">
          <Columns>
            <asp:BoundField HeaderText="ISBN" DataField="ISBN"
              SortExpression="ISBN"></asp:BoundField>
            <asp:BoundField HeaderText="Title" DataField="Title"
              SortExpression="Title"></asp:BoundField>
            <asp:BoundField HeaderText="Price" DataField="Price"
              SortExpression="Price"></asp:BoundField>
          </Columns>
        </asp:GridView>
        <asp:XmlDataSource EnableCaching="true" CacheDuration="100"
          CacheExpirationPolicy="Absolute"
          ID="bookSource" Runat="server"
          DataFile="~/App_Data/Bookstore.xml"
          XPath="bookstore/genre[@name='Fiction']/book">
        </asp:XmlDataSource>
      </div>
    </form>
  </body>
  </html>
```

Before looking at the code in detail, examine the output produced by the page, which is shown in Figure 5-7.

In Listing 5-11, the `XmlDataSource` control has its `EnableCaching` property set to `true`. When the `EnableCaching` property is set to `true`, the `XmlDataSource` will automatically cache the XML data obtained by evaluating the XPath expression. The `CacheDuration` property enables you to specify, in seconds, how long the data should be cached before it is refreshed from the database. By default, the `XmlDataSource` will cache data using an absolute expiration policy, meaning that the data will be refreshed every so many seconds, as specified in the `CacheDuration` property. You also have the option of enabling a sliding expiration policy. When the `XmlDataSource` is configured to use a sliding expiration policy, the data will not be dropped as long as it continues to be accessed. Employing a sliding expiration policy is useful whenever you have a large number of items that need to be cached, because this expiration policy enables you to keep only the most frequently accessed items in memory. In the preceding example, you cached the results of the XPath expression to 100 seconds by setting the `EnableCaching`, `CacheExpirationPolicy`, and `CacheDuration` attributes to `True`, `Absolute`, and `100`, respectively.

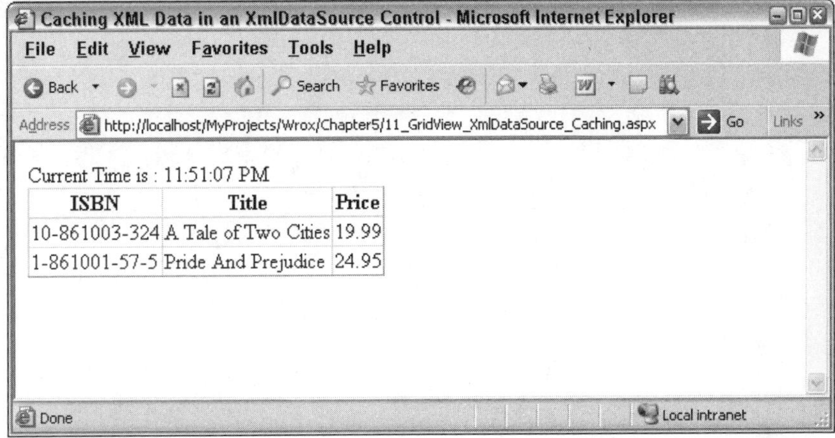

Figure 5-7

Summary

ASP.NET 2.0 provides excellent support for consuming and displaying XML data through a rich set of data source controls and server controls. Exploiting this bounty of features to build dynamic web-based applications is simple and straightforward thanks to the codeless data-binding features of the `XmlDataSource` control. In this chapter, you have learned the features of `XmlDataSource` through discussion and examples. In particular, you have seen:

- How to display XML data by data binding a `TreeView` control with an `XmlDataSource` control
- How an `XmlDataSource` control can also be bound to tabular controls such as `GridView` and `DataList` that are nonhierarchical in nature
- How to retrieve data from external data sources and use `XmlDataSource` control to render that data
- How to update data through the `Save()` method of the `XmlDataSource` control
- How to programmatically create an `XmlDataSource` control
- How to transform XML data before rendering it on the browser by applying an XSLT stylesheet
- How to handle events raised by the `XmlDataSource` control
- How to implement caching using the built-in caching support of the `XmlDataSource` control

Now that you have seen the data binding with XML data, the next chapter builds on the data-binding features of ASP.NET by looking at object data binding.

6

Data Binding with Objects

As you have seen in previous chapters, ASP.NET 2.0 has introduced a host of new data source controls for seamlessly consuming data from a variety of data sources without writing a line of code. To this end, ASP.NET 2.0 features new data source controls such as `SqlDataSource`, `ObjectDataSource`, `AccessDataSource`, `XmlDataSource`, and `SiteMapDataSource`. Of all these controls, the most interesting and promising control is the `ObjectDataSource` control. This is because it complements the n-tier application design (widely used by enterprise-class applications) by allowing you to bind the values returned by the middle-tier objects directly onto data-bound controls such as `GridView`, `FormView`, `DetailsView`, and so on. This chapter will take a detailed look at the features of the `ObjectDataSource` control through examples. Specifically, this chapter covers:

- How to execute a middle-tier method that retrieves data from the database
- How to pass parameters to a middle-tier method using the `ObjectDataSource` control
- How to process the return values from a middle-tier method
- How to handle events fired by the `ObjectDataSource` control
- How to perform inserts, updates, and deletions using the various methods of the `ObjectDataSource` control
- How to programmatically add an `ObjectDataSource` control to the page
- How to perform data binding with generic collections returned by the middle-tier method
- How to invoke a web service method using the `ObjectDataSource` control
- How to cache the outputs of the `ObjectDataSource` control

The next section starts with an overview of the `ObjectDataSource` control before looking at examples.

Introduction to the ObjectDataSource Control

The ASP.NET `ObjectDataSource` control represents a middle-tier object with data retrieval and update capabilities. The `ObjectDataSource` control acts as a data interface for data-bound controls such as the `GridView`, `FormView`, or `DetailsView` controls, and enables those controls to display and edit data from a middle-tier object on an ASP.NET web page. The object model of the `ObjectDataSource` control is similar to that of the `SqlDataSource` control. Instead of a `ConnectionString` property, `ObjectDataSource` exposes a `TypeName` property that specifies an object type (class name) to instantiate for performing operations. Similarly to the command properties of `SqlDataSource`, the `ObjectDataSource` control supports properties such as `SelectMethod`, `UpdateMethod`, `InsertMethod`, and `DeleteMethod` for specifying methods of the associated type to call to perform these data operations.

As mentioned previously, an `ObjectDataSource` control allows you to directly bind the output of the middle-tier object to a data-bound control such as a `GridView` or a `FormView` control. To enable this declarative codeless object binding, the `ObjectDataSource` control exposes a number of properties. The following table outlines the important properties of the `ObjectDataSource` control that you are most likely going to work with.

Property	Description
`CacheDuration`	Allows you to get or set the length of the time that the data source control caches data.
`CacheExpirationPolicy`	Allows you to set or get the cache expiration behavior; when combined with the duration, describes the behavior of the cache.
`CacheKeyDependency`	Allows you to get or set a user-defined key dependency that is linked to all data cache objects created by the data source control.
`ConflictDetection`	Gets or sets the value that indicates how the `ObjectDataSource` control performs updates or deletions when the data changes in the underlying database. This property returns and accepts an enumeration of type `ConflictOptions`.
`ConvertNullToDBNull`	Gets or sets a value indicating whether the `Parameter` values that are passed to an insert, update, or delete operation are automatically converted from a null reference to `DBNull`.
`DataObjectTypeName`	Gets or sets the name of a class that the `ObjectDataSource` control uses for a parameter in an update, insert, or delete data operation. This allows you to reuse an existing object and use it as a parameter instead of passing individual values from the data-bound control.
`DeleteMethod`	Gets or sets the middle-tier method that the `ObjectDataSource` control uses to delete data from the underlying database.
`DeleteParameters`	Gets the parameters collection used by the method contained in the `DeleteMethod` property.
`EnableCaching`	Gets or sets a value indicating whether the data source control has caching enabled.

What Is N-Tier Design?

Simply stated, an n-tier application helps you distribute the overall functionality into various tiers or layers. For example, in a typical implementation you can have one or more of the following layers:

- Presentation layer
- Business rules layer
- Data access layer
- Database/data store

In certain scenarios, some of the layers mentioned above may be split further into one or more sublayers. Each layer can be developed independently of the others, provided that it adheres to the standards and communicates with the other layers as per the specifications. This is one of the biggest advantages of the n-tier application. Each layer can potentially treat the other layers as a *black box*. In other words, each layer does not care how the other layer processes the data, as long as it sends the right data in a correct format.

What Is Object Binding?

Object binding is the ability to bind the output of an object's method to a data-bound control (through a data source control such as an `ObjectDataSource` control) declaratively without writing any lines of code. `ObjectDataSource` belongs to the family of data source controls in ASP.NET, which enables a declarative data-binding model against a variety of underlying data stores and middle-tier objects. Most data source controls encourage a two-tiered application architecture, where the presentation layer (the page) interacts directly with the back-end data provider. However, it is also common for page developers to encapsulate data retrieval (and optionally business logic) into a component object, introducing an additional layer between the presentation page and data provider. The `ObjectDataSource` control allows developers to structure their applications using the proven three-tiered architecture principles and still take advantage of the ease-of-use benefits of the declarative data-binding model in ASP.NET. This approach provides for clean separation and encapsulation of code, thereby eliminating the need to write data access layer code in the presentation layer.

Property	Description
`FilterExpression`	Allows you to get or set a filtering expression that is applied at the time when the `SelectMethod` property is called.
`FilterParameters`	Gets a collection of parameters that are associated with the parameter placeholders in the `FilterExpression`.
`InsertMethod`	Gets or sets the name of the method that the `ObjectDataSource` control uses to insert data.

Table continued on following page

Property	Description
InsertParameters	Gets the parameters collection used by the method contained in the InsertMethod property.
OldValuesParameter FormatString	Gets or sets a format string to apply to the names of any parameters that are passed to the Delete or Update method.
SelectCountMethod	Gets or sets the name of the method that the ObjectDataSource control uses to retrieve a row count.
SelectMethod	Gets or sets the name of the method that the ObjectDataSource control uses to retrieve data.
SelectParameters	Gets the parameters collection used by the method contained in the SelectMethod property.
SortParameterName	Gets or sets the name of the parameter in the business object used by the SelectMethod parameter that is used for sorting.
SqlCacheDependency	Gets or sets the semicolon-separated string that indicates the databases and tables to use for SQL Server cache dependency.
TypeName	Gets or sets the name of the class that the ObjectDataSource control represents.
UpdateMethod	Gets or sets the method that the ObjectDataSource control uses to update data.
UpdateParameters	Gets the parameters collection used by the method contained in the UpdateMethod property.

In addition to the properties described in the previous table, the ObjectDataSource control also exposes the following events.

Event	Description
Deleting, Deleted	Occurs before and after the completion of execution of a delete operation
Inserting, Inserted	Occurs before and after the completion of execution of an insert operation
Selecting, Selected	Occurs before and after the completion of execution of a select operation
Updating, Updated	Occurs before and after the completion of execution of an update operation
Filtering	Occurs before a filtering operation

The ObjectDataSource control is remarkably flexible and can work with a variety of different components. However, to use it, your middle-tier class must conform to a few rules:

- It must be stateless. That is because the `ObjectDataSource` will create an instance only when needed and destroy it at the end of every request.
- It must have a default, no-argument constructor.
- All the logic must be contained in a single class. (If you want to use different classes for selecting and updating your data, you'll need to wrap them in another, higher-level class.)
- None of the linked methods (for selecting or updating records) can be static.
- It must provide the query results when a single method is called.
- When the query results are several records, they must be represented as a collection, an array, or a list object that implements `IEnumerable`. If you are using a collection, each record should be a custom object that exposes all its data through public properties.

You can work around many of these rules by handling `ObjectDataSource` events and writing custom code. However, if you want your data access class to plug into the data-binding model seamlessly without extra work, you should observe these guidelines.

Now that you have an understanding of the properties and events of the `ObjectDataSource` control, the next section discusses a simple example of selecting records using the `ObjectDataSource` control.

Selecting Records

In this section, you will understand how to use the `ObjectDataSource` control to invoke a middle-tier object method. Before looking at the ASP.NET page, it is useful to start with the middle-tier object, which is responsible for performing data access. Listing 6-1 shows the implementation of the `Category` class.

Listing 6-1: Implementation of the Category Class

```
using System;
using System.Collections;
using System.Collections.Generic;
using System.Data;
using System.Data.SqlClient;
using System.Web.Configuration;
using System.Web.UI;
using System.Web.UI.WebControls;

public class Category
{
public Category()
{
}

public SqlDataReader GetCategories()
{
  string connectionString = WebConfigurationManager.ConnectionStrings
      ["AdventureWorks"].ConnectionString;
    SqlConnection connection = new SqlConnection(connectionString);
    string storedProc = "GetCategories";
```

(continued)

Listing 6-1: *(continued)*

```
            SqlCommand command= new SqlCommand(storedProc, connection);
            command.CommandType = CommandType.StoredProcedure;
            connection.Open();
            SqlDataReader reader = command.ExecuteReader(CommandBehavior.CloseConnection);
            return reader;
        }
    }
```

Inside the `GetCategories()` method, a stored procedure named `GetCategories` is invoked to retrieve the categories details from the AdventureWorks database. The `GetCategories` stored procedure is declared as follows:

```
CREATE PROCEDURE [dbo].[GetCategories]
AS
  SELECT ProductSubcategoryID, Name, ModifiedDate FROM
    Production.ProductSubcategory ORDER BY ProductSubcategoryID
```

Now that you have the middle-tier object created, it is time to create the ASP.NET page that leverages the middle-tier functionalities using the `ObjectDataSource` control. Listing 6-2 shows the code of the ASP.NET page.

Listing 6-2: Invoking a Middle-Tier Object Method Using the ObjectDataSource Control

```
<%@ Page Language="C#"%>
<html xmlns="http://www.w3.org/1999/xhtml" >
<head id="Head1" runat="server">
  <title>Invoking a middle tier using ObjectDataSource Control</title>
</head>
<body>
  <form id="form1" runat="server">
    <asp:GridView ID="categoryView" Runat="server"
      DataSourceID="categorySource" AutoGenerateColumns="False"
      HeaderStyle-HorizontalAlign="Center" HeaderStyle-Font-Bold="True"
      HeaderStyle-BackColor="blue" HeaderStyle-ForeColor="White">
        <Columns>
          <asp:BoundField HeaderText="Category ID"
            DataField="ProductSubcategoryID"/>
          <asp:BoundField HeaderText="Name" DataField="Name"/>
          <asp:BoundField HeaderText="ModifiedDate" DataField="ModifiedDate"/>
        </Columns>
      </asp:GridView>
      <asp:ObjectDataSource ID="categorySource" runat="server" TypeName="Category"
        SelectMethod="GetCategories">
      </asp:ObjectDataSource>
    </form>
  </body>
</html>
```

Listing 6-2 shows the `ObjectDataSource` control with its `TypeName` and `SelectMethod` properties set to `"Category"` and `"GetCategories"`, respectively. As mentioned previously, the `TypeName` property indicates the name of the class that contains the middle-tier methods. For the purposes of this example, it is set to the `Category` class, which is placed in the `App_Code` directory. Instead of referencing the class from the `App_Code` directory, you can also reference an external assembly that is referenced from within the ASP.NET application. In that case, you need to specify the fully qualified name of the class in the `TypeName` property.

> **The `App_Code` directory, like the `bin` directory, is a special directory used by ASP.NET, but with the following exceptions: While the `bin` directory is designed for storing precompiled assemblies used by your application, the `App_Code` directory is designed for storing class files to be compiled dynamically at runtime. This allows you to store classes for business logic components, data access components, and so on in a single location in your application, and use them from any page. Because the classes are compiled dynamically at runtime and automatically referenced by the application containing the `App_Code` directory, you don't need to build the project before deploying it, nor do you need to explicitly add a reference to the class. ASP.NET monitors the `App_Code` directory, and when new components are added, it dynamically compiles them. This makes it possible for you to easily make changes to a component and deploy with a simple XCOPY or with a drag-and-drop operation.**

Once you have attached the `ObjectDataSource` to a class, the next step is to point it to the methods it can use to select and update records. The `ObjectDataSource` defines `SelectMethod`, `DeleteMethod`, `UpdateMethod`, and `InsertMethod` properties that you use to link your class to various tasks. Each property takes the name of the method in the middle-tier class. In this example, you simply need to enable querying, so you need to set the `SelectMethod` property:

```
<asp:ObjectDataSource ID="categorySource" runat="server"
  TypeName="Category" SelectMethod="GetCategories">
```

Remember, the `GetCategories()` method returns a `SqlDataReader` object. Once you have set up the `ObjectDataSource`, you can bind your web page controls in the same way you do with the `SqlDataSource`. Specifically, you set the `DataSourceID` property of the `GridView` to the ID of the `ObjectDataSource` control. Figure 6-1 shows the result.

From the user's perspective, this example is equivalent to the `SqlDataSource` page shown in Chapter 4. The apparent similarities conceal some real behind-the-scenes differences. In this example, the web page does not require any hard-coded SQL details. Instead, all the work is handed off to the `Category` class. When you run the page, the `GridView` will request data from the `ObjectDataSource`, which will call the `Category.GetCategories()` method to retrieve the data. This data is then bound and displayed in both controls, with no code required.

> *Remember, the* `GetCategories()` *method of* `Category` *class does not catch exceptions. Best design practices are to let the exception notify the web page, which can then decide how best to inform the user. You can handle errors with the* `ObjectDataSource` *in the same way you handle them with the* `SqlDataSource`*—first, handle the* `Selected`, `Inserted`, `Updated`, *or* `Deleted` *event; second, check for an exception; and third, mark it as handled.*

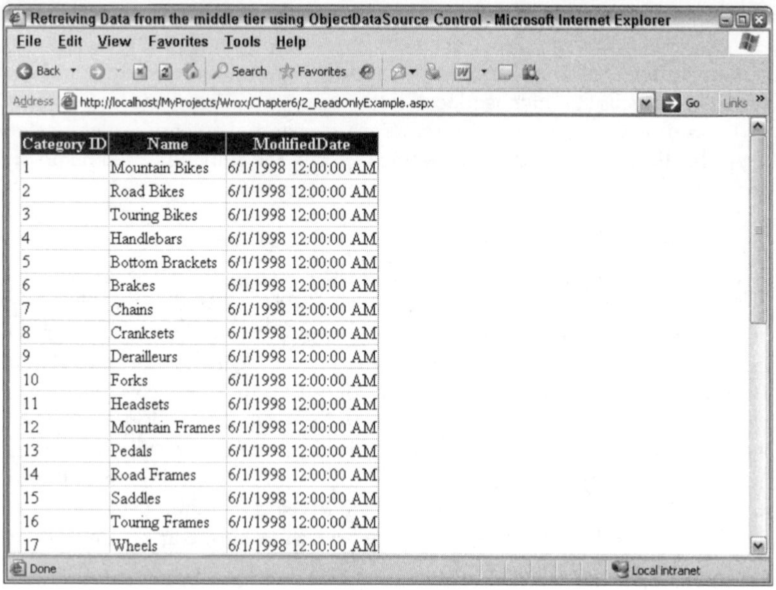
Retreiving Data from the middle tier using ObjectDataSource Control - Microsoft Internet Explorer
File Edit View Favorites Tools Help
Back Search Favorites
Address http://localhost/MyProjects/Wrox/Chapter6/2_ReadOnlyExample.aspx
Go Links
Category ID Name ModifiedDate
1 Mountain Bikes 6/1/1998 12:00:00 AM
2 Road Bikes 6/1/1998 12:00:00 AM
3 Touring Bikes 6/1/1998 12:00:00 AM
4 Handlebars 6/1/1998 12:00:00 AM
5 Bottom Brackets 6/1/1998 12:00:00 AM
6 Brakes 6/1/1998 12:00:00 AM
7 Chains 6/1/1998 12:00:00 AM
8 Cranksets 6/1/1998 12:00:00 AM
9 Derailleurs 6/1/1998 12:00:00 AM
10 Forks 6/1/1998 12:00:00 AM
11 Headsets 6/1/1998 12:00:00 AM
12 Mountain Frames 6/1/1998 12:00:00 AM
13 Pedals 6/1/1998 12:00:00 AM
14 Road Frames 6/1/1998 12:00:00 AM
15 Saddles 6/1/1998 12:00:00 AM
16 Touring Frames 6/1/1998 12:00:00 AM
17 Wheels 6/1/1998 12:00:00 AM
Done
Local intranet

Figure 6-1

Using a Parameterized Constructor

One of the ways you can extend the `ObjectDataSource` control is through handling the events generated by the `ObjectDataSource` control. For example, by default the `ObjectDataSource` is capable of creating your custom middle-tier class only if it provides a zero no-argument constructor. However, you can extend the `ObjectDataSource` to work with middle-tier classes that do not meet this requirement by writing code that reacts to the `ObjectDataSource.ObjectCreating` event.

The current `Category` class retrieves the database connection string directly from the `Web.config` file, as shown here:

```
public SqlDataReader GetCategories()
{
  string connectionString = WebConfigurationManager.ConnectionStrings
    ["AdventureWorks"].ConnectionString;
  SqlConnection connection = new SqlConnection(connectionString);
  ......
}
```

However, you might want to add another constructor that lets the web page supply a specific connection string of its choosing:

```
public Category (string connectionString)
{
  _connectionString = connectionString;
}
```

Note that in the above constructor, the `_connectionString` is a private variable declared at the `Category` class. To force the `ObjectDataSource` to use this constructor, you need to handle the `ObjectCreating` event, create the `Category` instance yourself, and then assign it to the data source using the `ObjectDataSourceEventArgs`:

```
private void categorySource_ObjectCreating(object sender,
  ObjectDataSourceEventArgs e)
{
  string connectionString = WebConfigurationManager.ConnectionStrings
    ["AdventureWorks"].ConnectionString;
  e.ObjectInstance = new Category(connectionString);
}
```

Clearly, you could perform more complex initialization in the `ObjectCreating` event. For example, you could call an initialization method, choose to instantiate one of several derived classes, and so on.

> **The data source controls expose a rich event model. Events tend to fall into two categories. Events ending in -ing, such as `ObjectCreating`, occur while a task is underway and give you the chance to cancel or customize what is happening. Events ending in -ed, such as `ObjectCreated`, occur when the task is finished and are suitable for logging the action, synchronizing other controls, and handling errors.**

You can also react to the `ObjectDisposing` event to perform cleanup. The `ObjectDisposing` event is fired just before the middle-tier object is released (before the page is served). Usually, you will not need to use the `ObjectDisposing` event because a better alternative exists—place your cleanup code in a dedicated `Dispose()` method inside your middle-tier class. As long as you implement `IDisposable`, the `ObjectDataSource` will automatically call your `Dispose()` method. To get a painless implementation of `IDisposable` for free, just derive your middle-tier class from the `System.ComponentModel.Component` class and override the `Dispose()` method.

Using Parameters with ObjectDataSource Control

In Chapter 4, you saw how you could use the `SqlDataSource` to execute parameterized commands. The same feat is possible with the `ObjectDataSource`, if you provide a suitable select method that accepts one or more parameters. You can then map each parameter to a control value, query string argument, and so on. To try this, create an ASP.NET page that displays the categories details in a `DropDownList` and the products details in a `GridView` control. For each selected category, the products `GridView` is refreshed to display the appropriate products that belong to that category. First of all, you need to create the product class that allows you to retrieve the products based on the category.

For the purposes of this example, create another class named `Product` that is responsible for performing operations against the Product table.

Listing 6-3: Implementation of the Product Class

```
using System;
using System.Collections.Generic;
using System.Data;
```

(continued)

Listing 6-3: *(continued)*

```
using System.Data.SqlClient;
using System.Web.Configuration;

public class Product
{
public Product()
{
}

public SqlDataReader GetProductsByCategoryID(int categoryID)
{
    string connectionString = WebConfigurationManager.ConnectionStrings
      ["AdventureWorks"].ConnectionString;
    SqlConnection connection = new SqlConnection(connectionString);
    string storedProc = "GetProductsByCategoryID";
    SqlCommand command = new SqlCommand(storedProc, connection);
    command.CommandType = CommandType.StoredProcedure;
    SqlParameter paramCategoryID = new SqlParameter("@categoryID", SqlDbType.Int);
    paramCategoryID.Value = categoryID;
    command.Parameters.Add(paramCategoryID);
    connection.Open();
    SqlDataReader reader = command.ExecuteReader(CommandBehavior.CloseConnection);
     return reader;
  }
}
```

The `GetProductsByCategoryID()` method of the `Product` class executes a stored procedure that accepts a category ID as an argument and returns a result set of all the products that belong to that category. Once you have created the `Product` class, the next step is to create the ASP.NET page. Whenever there is a change in the category, you then invoke the `GetProductsByCategoryID()` method to get the products that belong to the selected category. Listing 6-4 shows the complete code of the ASP.NET page.

Listing 6-4: Passing Parameters to a Middle-Tier Method

```
<%@ Page Language="C#"%>
<html xmlns="http://www.w3.org/1999/xhtml" >
<head id="Head1" runat="server">
  <title>Passing parameters using an ObjectDataSource Control</title>
</head>
<body>
  <form id="form1" runat="server">
  Categories:
  <asp:DropDownList ID="ddlCategories" runat="server" DataSourceID="categorySource"
    DataTextField="Name" AutoPostBack="true"
    DataValueField="ProductSubcategoryID"/>
  <asp:GridView ID="productsView" Runat="server" DataSourceID="productSource"
    AutoGenerateColumns="False" HeaderStyle-HorizontalAlign="Center"
    HeaderStyle-Font-Bold="True" HeaderStyle-BackColor="blue"
    HeaderStyle-ForeColor="White">
    <Columns>
      <asp:BoundField HeaderText="Product ID" DataField="ProductID"/>
```

```
        <asp:BoundField HeaderText="Name" DataField="Name"/>
        <asp:BoundField HeaderText="Product Number" DataField="ProductNumber"/>
        <asp:BoundField HeaderText="List Price" DataField="ListPrice"/>
      </Columns>
    </asp:GridView>
    <asp:ObjectDataSource ID="productSource" runat="server" TypeName="Product"
      SelectMethod="GetProductsByCategoryID">
      <SelectParameters>
        <asp:ControlParameter ControlID="ddlCategories" PropertyName="SelectedValue"
          Name="categoryID" />
      </SelectParameters>
    </asp:ObjectDataSource>
    <asp:ObjectDataSource ID="categorySource" runat="server" TypeName="Category"
  SelectMethod="GetCategories">
    </asp:ObjectDataSource>
    </form>
  </body>
  </html>
```

The page provides a list with all the categories in the drop-down list. This list control invokes the `GetCategories()` method through the `ObjectDataSource` control that represents the `Category` class.

```
<asp:DropDownList ID="ddlCategories" runat="server" DataSourceID="categorySource"
  DataTextField="Name" AutoPostBack="true" DataValueField="ProductSubcategoryID"/>
<asp:ObjectDataSource ID="categorySource" runat="server"
  TypeName="Category" SelectMethod="GetCategories">
</asp:ObjectDataSource>
```

When you choose a category, the page posts back and uses a second `ObjectDataSource` to call `GetProductsByCategoryID()`. The `categoryID` value is taken from the selected item in the list:

```
<asp:ObjectDataSource ID="productSource" runat="server" TypeName="Product"
  SelectMethod="GetProductsByCategoryID">
  <SelectParameters>
    <asp:ControlParameter ControlID="ddlCategories"
      PropertyName="SelectedValue" Name="categoryID" />
  </SelectParameters>
</asp:ObjectDataSource>
```

The name you define for the parameter must match the parameter name you use in the method exactly. When the `ObjectDataSource` calls the method, it uses reflection to examine the method, and it examines the parameter names to determine the order of the arguments. This system allows you to use overloaded methods, because the `ObjectDataSource` is able to correctly identify the overload you want based on the number of parameters you define and their names.

> **The data types are not used in the "parameters-to-argument" matching process — instead, the `ObjectDataSource` will attempt to convert the parameter value into the data type of the matching parameter using the appropriate type converter for that data type. If this process fails, an exception is raised.**

Now, the products returned from `GetProductsByCategoryID()` are displayed in another rich data control — the `GridView`. Figure 6-2 shows the resultant output produced by the page.

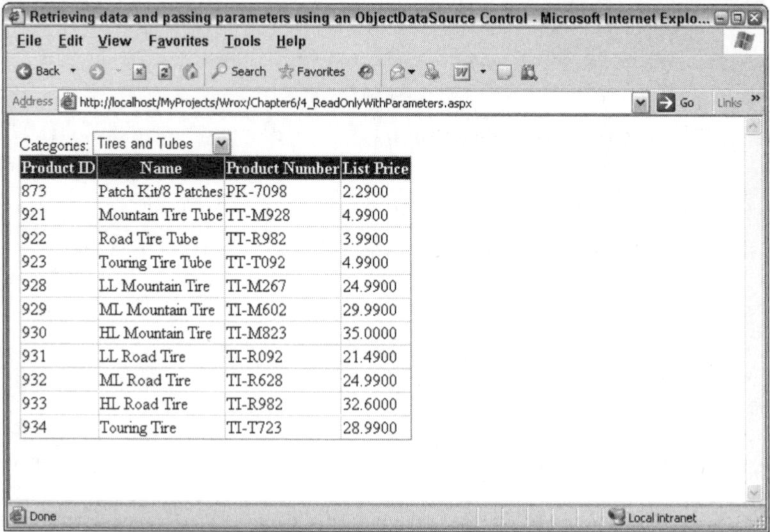

Figure 6-2

Updating Records

The `ObjectDataSource` provides the same type of support for updatable data binding as the `SqlDataSource`. The first step is to specify the `UpdateMethod`, which needs to be a public instance method in the same class:

```
<asp:ObjectDataSource ID="deptSource" runat="server" TypeName="Department"
SelectMethod="GetDepartments" UpdateMethod="UpdateDepartment" />
```

The challenge is in making sure that the `UpdateMethod` has the right signature. As with `SqlDataSource`, updates, inserts, and deletions automatically receive a collection of parameters from the linked data control. These parameters have the same names as the corresponding class properties.

To understand how this works, it helps to consider a basic example. Assume that you create a grid that shows a list of departments. You also add a column with edit links. When the user commits an edit, the `GridView` fills the `ObjectDataSource.UpdateParameters` collection with one parameter for each field in the `GridView`, including `DepartmentID`, `Name`, `GroupName`, and `ModifiedDate`. Then, the `ObjectDataSource` searches for a method named `UpdateDepartment()` in the `Department` class. This method must have the same parameters, with the same names. For example, the following method signature is a match:

```
public void UpdateDepartment(int DepartmentID, string Name,
  string GroupName, DateTime ModifiedDate)
  { ... }
```

Note that the method-matching algorithm is not case sensitive, and it does not consider the order or data type of the parameters. It simply tries to find a method with the right number of parameters and the same names. As long as that method is present, the update can be committed automatically, without any custom code.

To help you understand how to perform an update using `ObjectDataSource`, this section will leverage a class named `Department` that will allow you to update the Department table in the AdventureWorks database. Listing 6-5 shows the code of the `Department` class.

Listing 6-5: Implementation of the Department Class

```
using System;
using System.Data;
using System.Data.SqlClient;
using System.Web.Configuration;

public class Department
{
  public Department()
  {
  }

  public SqlDataReader GetDepartments()
  {
    string connectionString = WebConfigurationManager.ConnectionStrings
      ["AdventureWorks"].ConnectionString;
    SqlConnection connection = new SqlConnection(connectionString);
    string sql = "SELECT * FROM HumanResources.Department";
    SqlCommand command= new SqlCommand(sql, connection);
    connection.Open();
    SqlDataReader reader = command.ExecuteReader(CommandBehavior.CloseConnection);
    return reader;
  }

  public void UpdateDepartment(int DepartmentID, string Name,
    string GroupName, DateTime ModifiedDate)
  {
    string connectionString = WebConfigurationManager.ConnectionStrings
      ["AdventureWorks"].ConnectionString;
    using (SqlConnection connection = new SqlConnection(connectionString))
    {
      string sql = "UpdateDepartment";
      SqlCommand command = new SqlCommand(sql, connection);
      command.CommandType = CommandType.StoredProcedure;
      SqlParameter paramDepartmentID = new SqlParameter
        ("@DepartmentID", SqlDbType.Int);
      paramDepartmentID.Value = DepartmentID;
      command.Parameters.Add(paramDepartmentID);
      SqlParameter paramName = new SqlParameter("@Name", SqlDbType.NVarChar, 50);
```

(continued)

Listing 6-5: *(continued)*

```
        paramName.Value = Name;
        command.Parameters.Add(paramName);
        SqlParameter paramGroupName = new SqlParameter("@GroupName",
paramGroupName.Value = GroupName;
        command.Parameters.Add(paramGroupName);
        SqlParameter paramModifiedDate = new SqlParameter("@ModifiedDate",
          SqlDbType.DateTime);
        paramModifiedDate.Value = ModifiedDate;
        command.Parameters.Add(paramModifiedDate);
        connection.Open();
        command.ExecuteNonQuery();
      }
    }
  }
```

The `Department` class has two methods: `GetDepartments()` and `UpdateDepartment()`. As the names suggest, the `GetDepartments()` method returns all the departments for display purposes, and the `UpdateDepartment()` method updates the Department table with the values entered by the user. Once you have created the `Department` class, Listing 6-6 examines the ASP.NET page that contains the `ObjectDataSource` that represents the `Department` class.

Listing 6-6: Updating Values through the ObjectDataSource Control

```
<%@ Page Language="C#"%>
<html xmlns="http://www.w3.org/1999/xhtml" >
<head id="Head1" runat="server">
<title>Editing Data using ObjectDataSource Control</title>
</head>
<body>
  <form id="form1" runat="server">
    <asp:GridView ID="departmentsView" Runat="server" DataKeyNames="DepartmentID"
      DataSourceID="deptSource" AutoGenerateColumns="False"
      AutoGenerateEditButton="true" HeaderStyle-HorizontalAlign="Center"
      HeaderStyle-Font-Bold="True" HeaderStyle-BackColor="blue"
      HeaderStyle-ForeColor="White">
      <Columns>
        <asp:BoundField ReadOnly="true" HeaderText="Department ID"
          DataField="DepartmentID"/>
        <asp:BoundField HeaderText="Name" DataField="Name"/>
        <asp:BoundField HeaderText="Group Name" DataField="GroupName"/>
        <asp:BoundField HeaderText="ModifiedDate" DataField="ModifiedDate"/>
      </Columns>
    </asp:GridView>
    <asp:ObjectDataSource ID="deptSource" runat="server" TypeName="Department"
      SelectMethod="GetDepartments" UpdateMethod="UpdateDepartment">
    </asp:ObjectDataSource>
  </form>
</body>
</html>
```

Note that the `AutoGenerateEditButton` property of the `GridView` is set to `true` to allow the users to update the details of a specific department. Because of this, an Edit link will appear right next to each of the Department rows, as shown in Figure 6-3.

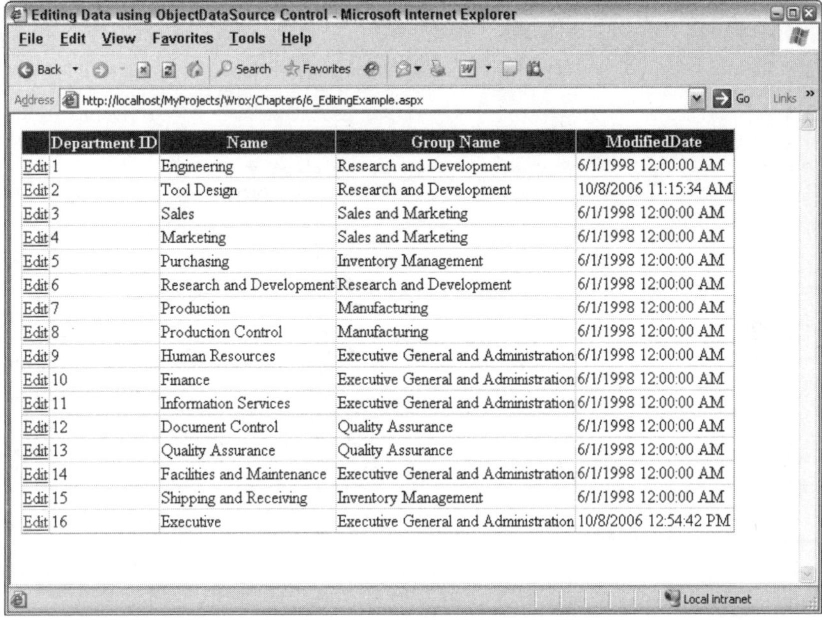

	Department ID	Name	Group Name	ModifiedDate
Edit	1	Engineering	Research and Development	6/1/1998 12:00:00 AM
Edit	2	Tool Design	Research and Development	10/8/2006 11:15:34 AM
Edit	3	Sales	Sales and Marketing	6/1/1998 12:00:00 AM
Edit	4	Marketing	Sales and Marketing	6/1/1998 12:00:00 AM
Edit	5	Purchasing	Inventory Management	6/1/1998 12:00:00 AM
Edit	6	Research and Development	Research and Development	6/1/1998 12:00:00 AM
Edit	7	Production	Manufacturing	6/1/1998 12:00:00 AM
Edit	8	Production Control	Manufacturing	6/1/1998 12:00:00 AM
Edit	9	Human Resources	Executive General and Administration	6/1/1998 12:00:00 AM
Edit	10	Finance	Executive General and Administration	6/1/1998 12:00:00 AM
Edit	11	Information Services	Executive General and Administration	6/1/1998 12:00:00 AM
Edit	12	Document Control	Quality Assurance	6/1/1998 12:00:00 AM
Edit	13	Quality Assurance	Quality Assurance	6/1/1998 12:00:00 AM
Edit	14	Facilities and Maintenance	Executive General and Administration	6/1/1998 12:00:00 AM
Edit	15	Shipping and Receiving	Inventory Management	6/1/1998 12:00:00 AM
Edit	16	Executive	Executive General and Administration	10/8/2006 12:54:42 PM

Figure 6-3

When you click on Edit, a text box appears as a replacement for the label fields for each of the non-read-only columns in the `GridView`, allowing you to enter the new values for those columns. At the end of the editing process, you can either hit the Update or Cancel links to save or cancel the new data. This is shown in Figure 6-4.

When you click the Update link, the page will be refreshed with the latest data from the database through a call to the `GetDepartments()` method of the `Department` class.

Dealing with Nonstandard Method Signatures

Sometimes you may run into a problem in which the property names of your data class do not exactly match the parameter names of your update method. If all you need is a simple renaming job, you can catch the `Updating` event of the `ObjectDataSource` control and change the names of the parameters within that event.

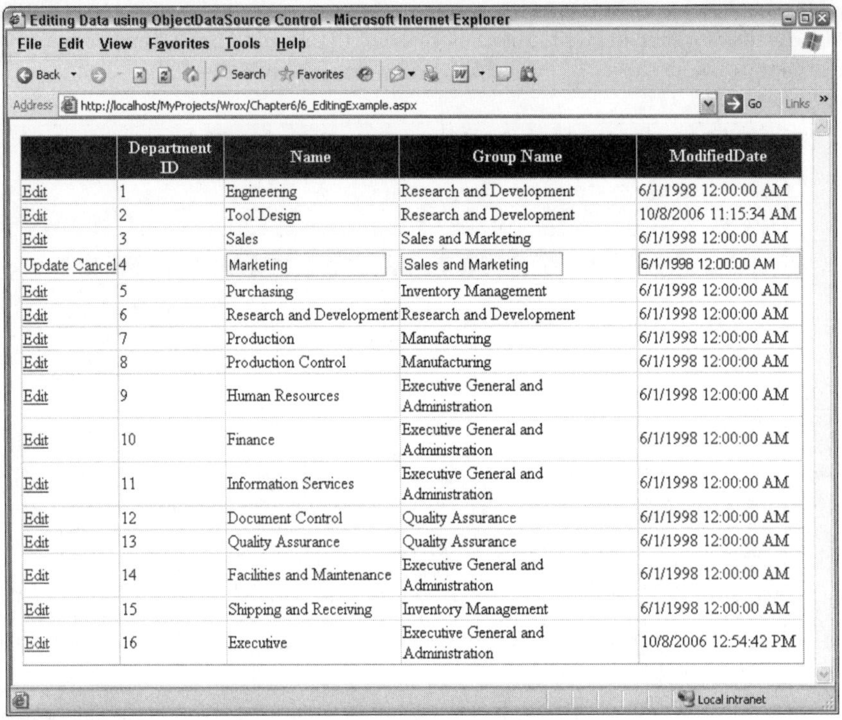

	Department ID	Name	Group Name	ModifiedDate
Edit	1	Engineering	Research and Development	6/1/1998 12:00:00 AM
Edit	2	Tool Design	Research and Development	10/8/2006 11:15:34 AM
Edit	3	Sales	Sales and Marketing	6/1/1998 12:00:00 AM
Update Cancel	4	Marketing	Sales and Marketing	6/1/1998 12:00:00 AM
Edit	5	Purchasing	Inventory Management	6/1/1998 12:00:00 AM
Edit	6	Research and Development	Research and Development	6/1/1998 12:00:00 AM
Edit	7	Production	Manufacturing	6/1/1998 12:00:00 AM
Edit	8	Production Control	Manufacturing	6/1/1998 12:00:00 AM
Edit	9	Human Resources	Executive General and Administration	6/1/1998 12:00:00 AM
Edit	10	Finance	Executive General and Administration	6/1/1998 12:00:00 AM
Edit	11	Information Services	Executive General and Administration	6/1/1998 12:00:00 AM
Edit	12	Document Control	Quality Assurance	6/1/1998 12:00:00 AM
Edit	13	Quality Assurance	Quality Assurance	6/1/1998 12:00:00 AM
Edit	14	Facilities and Maintenance	Executive General and Administration	6/1/1998 12:00:00 AM
Edit	15	Shipping and Receiving	Inventory Management	6/1/1998 12:00:00 AM
Edit	16	Executive	Executive General and Administration	10/8/2006 12:54:42 PM

Figure 6-4

First, you define the additional parameters you need, with the correct names. For example, maybe you need to rename the `DepartmentID` property to a parameter-named ID in the update method. Here is the new parameter you need:

```
<asp:ObjectDataSource ID="deptSource" runat="server"
  TypeName="Department" SelectMethod="GetDepartments"
  UpdateMethod="UpdateDepartment" OnUpdating="deptSource_Updating">
  <UpdateParameters>
    <asp:Parameter Name="id" Type="Int32" />
  </UpdateParameters>
</asp:ObjectDataSource>
```

Second, you react to the `ObjectDataSource`.Updating event, setting the value for these parameters and removing the ones you do not want:

```
protected void deptSource_Updating(object sender,
  ObjectDataSourceMethodEventArgs e)
{
  e.InputParameters["id"] = e.InputParameters["DepartmentID"];
  e.InputParameters.Remove("DepartmentID");
}
```

You can use a similar approach to add extra parameters. For example, if your method requires a parameter with information that's not contained in the linked data control, just define it as one of the `UpdateParameters` and then set the value when the `ObjectDataSource.Updating` event fires.

If you are more ambitious, you can even decide to programmatically point the `ObjectDataSource` to a different update method in the same class:

```
deptSource.UpdateMethod = "UpdateDepartmentStrict";
```

In fact, to get really adventurous, you could set the `ConflictDetection` property to `ConflictOptions.CompareAllValues`, so the old and new values are submitted in the `UpdateParameters` collection. You can then examine these parameters, determine what fields have changed, and call a different method (with different parameters accordingly). Unfortunately, this is not a zero-code scenario, and you might end up writing some awkward code for updating and removing parameters. Still, it gives you a valuable extra layer of flexibility.

Note that the same approach used here for updating applies when you are performing inserts and deletions. The only difference is that you handle the `Inserting` *and* `Deleting` *events instead.*

Updating with an Object

One problem with the `UpdateDepartment()` method shown in Listing 6-5 is that the method signature is a little cumbersome—you need one parameter for each value you want to pass to the `UpdateDepartment()` method. It might be a lot easier if you had one object, such as `DepartmentInfo`, that you could populate with all the values and send to the `UpdateDepartment()` method. As an example, consider the following version of the `UpdateDepartment()` method:

```
public void UpdateDepartment(DepartmentInfo dept)
{
  string connectionString = WebConfigurationManager.ConnectionStrings
    ["AdventureWorks"].ConnectionString;
  using (SqlConnection connection = new SqlConnection(connectionString))
  {
    string sql = "UpdateDepartment";
    SqlCommand command = new SqlCommand(sql, connection);
    command.CommandType = CommandType.StoredProcedure;
    SqlParameter paramDepartmentID = new SqlParameter("@DepartmentID",
      SqlDbType.Int);
    paramDepartmentID.Value = dept.DepartmentID;
    .........
    .........
  }
}
```

The `DepartmentInfo` class basically exposes four public properties: `DepartmentID`, `Name`, `GroupName`, and `ModifiedDate`. Once you have the `UpdateDepartment()` accept a `Department` object, you can then set the `DataObjectTypeName` property of the `ObjectDataSource` to the name of the class you want to use. Here is how it works:

```
<asp:ObjectDataSource ID="deptSource" runat="server"
  TypeName="Department" SelectMethod="GetDepartments"
  DataObjectTypeName="DepartmentInfo" UpdateMethod="UpdateDepartment">
</asp:ObjectDataSource>
```

Once this is in place, the `ObjectDataSource` will match only the `UpdateMethod` if it has a single parameter that accepts the type specified in `DataObjectTypeName`. Additionally, your data object must follow some rules:

- It must provide a default (zero-argument) constructor.
- For every parameter, there must be a property with the same name, and all the public variables are ignored.
- All properties must be public and writable.
- You are free to add code to your middle-tier class. For example, you can add methods, constructors, validation, and event-handling logic in your property procedures, and so on.

Inserting Data

Similar to updating and selecting, the `ObjectDataSource` control is also equally good at performing insert operations by invoking the appropriate middle-tier method. To this end, the `ObjectDataSource` control exposes the `InsertMethod` property. This section will examine the steps involved in inserting new records into the Department table through the `ObjectDataSource` control.

So far, all the examples in the previous section have used parameters to supply values to an update operation. However, you can also create a parameter to return a result. With the `SqlDataSource`, you can use this option to get access to an output parameter. With the `ObjectDataSource`, you can use this technique to capture the return value. To see this in action, it is worth considering the `InsertDepartment()` method, which adds a department record and returns the newly generated unique ID value as an integer:

Listing 6-7: Inserting a Department

```
public int InsertDepartment(DepartmentInfo dept)
{
  string connectionString = WebConfigurationManager.ConnectionStrings
    ["AdventureWorks"].ConnectionString;
  using (SqlConnection connection = new SqlConnection(connectionString))
  {
    string sql = "InsertDepartment";
    SqlCommand command = new SqlCommand(sql, connection);
    command.CommandType = CommandType.StoredProcedure;
    SqlParameter paramReturnValue = new SqlParameter("@DepartmentID",
      SqlDbType.Int);
    paramReturnValue.Direction = ParameterDirection.ReturnValue;
    command.Parameters.Add(paramReturnValue);
    SqlParameter paramName = new SqlParameter("@Name", SqlDbType.NVarChar, 50);
    paramName.Value = dept.Name;
    command.Parameters.Add(paramName);
    SqlParameter paramGroupName = new SqlParameter("@GroupName",
      SqlDbType.NVarChar, 50);
    paramGroupName.Value = dept.GroupName;
    command.Parameters.Add(paramGroupName);
    SqlParameter paramModifiedDate = new SqlParameter("@ModifiedDate",
      SqlDbType.DateTime);
    paramModifiedDate.Value = dept.ModifiedDate;
    command.Parameters.Add(paramModifiedDate);
    connection.Open();
```

```
        command.ExecuteNonQuery();
        return (int)command.Parameters["@DepartmentID"].Value;
    }
}
```

The `InsertDepartment()` method inserts a new department record by invoking the `InsertDepartment` stored procedure, and returns the newly inserted `DepartmentID` (identity value) as a return value to the caller. You can capture this identity value and display this as a confirmation in the ASP.NET page. To add a new department using the `InsertDepartment()` method, create an ASP.NET page as shown in Listing 6-8.

Listing 6-8: Inserting a Department Using a Middle-Tier Method

```
<%@ Page Language="C#"%>
<script runat="server">
  protected void deptSource_Inserted(object sender,
    ObjectDataSourceStatusEventArgs e)
  {
    if (e.Exception == null)
    {
      lblResult.Text = "Inserted Department: " + e.ReturnValue.ToString();
    }
  }
</script>
<html xmlns="http://www.w3.org/1999/xhtml" >
<head id="Head1" runat="server">
  <title>Inserting Data using ObjectDataSource Control</title>
</head>
<body>
  <form id="form1" runat="server">
    <asp:DetailsView ID="departmentsView" Runat="server"
      DataKeyNames="DepartmentID" DataSourceID="deptSource"
      AutoGenerateRows="false" AutoGenerateInsertButton="True"
      HeaderStyle-HorizontalAlign="Center" HeaderStyle-Font-Bold="True"
      HeaderStyle-BackColor="blue" HeaderStyle-ForeColor="White"
      AllowPaging="true" >
      <Fields>
        <asp:BoundField DataField="DepartmentID" HeaderText="Department ID"
          InsertVisible="False" ReadOnly="true"/>
        <asp:BoundField DataField="Name"  HeaderText="Name"/>
        <asp:BoundField DataField="GroupName" HeaderText="Group Name"/>
        <asp:BoundField DataField="ModifiedDate" HeaderText="Modified Date"/>
      </Fields>
    </asp:DetailsView>
    <asp:ObjectDataSource ID="deptSource" runat="server" TypeName="Department"
      SelectMethod="GetDepartmentsAsDataSet" OnInserted="deptSource_Inserted"
      InsertMethod="InsertDepartment" DataObjectTypeName="DepartmentInfo">
      <InsertParameters>
        <asp:Parameter Direction="ReturnValue" Name="DepartmentID" Type="Int32" />
      </InsertParameters>
    </asp:ObjectDataSource>
      <asp:Label ID="lblResult" runat="server" ForeColor="DarkRed"/>
</form>
</body>
</html>
```

For the purposes of inserting a new department, Listing 6-8 uses a `DetailsView` control and is connected to the `Department` class through the `ObjectDataSource` control. To handle the return value from the `InsertDepartment()` method, the `ObjectDataSource` declaration consists of an `InsertParameters` collection as well as the event handler for the `Inserted` event that is responsible for displaying the return value:

```
<asp:ObjectDataSource ID="sourceEmployees" runat="server"
  OnInserted="sourceEmployees_Inserted"
  ......>
  <InsertParameters>
    <asp:Parameter Direction="ReturnValue" Name="DepartmentID" Type="Int32" />
  </InsertParameters>
</asp:ObjectDataSource>
```

Now you can retrieve the parameter by responding to the `Inserted` event, which fires after the insert operation is finished:

```
protected void deptSource_Inserted(object sender,
  ObjectDataSourceStatusEventArgs e)
{
  if (e.Exception == null)
  {
    lblResult.Text = "Inserted Department: " + e.ReturnValue.ToString();
  }
}
```

Figure 6-5 shows the output produced by the after the insert operation has been completed successfully.

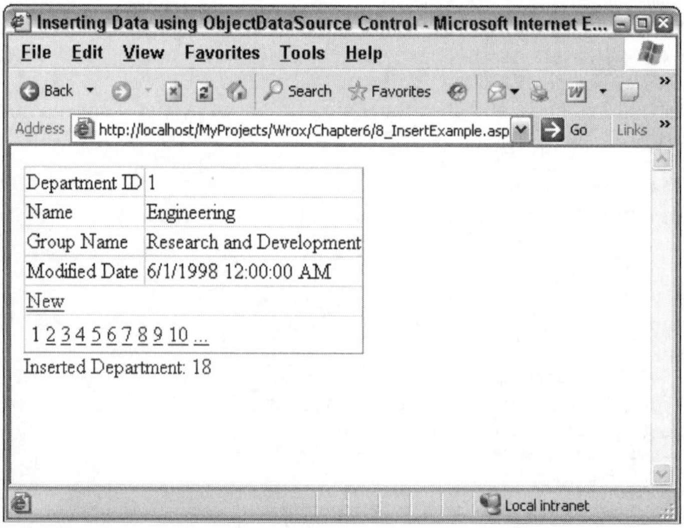

Figure 6-5

In Figure 6-5, the page displays the department ID of the newly added record.

Deleting Records

So far, you have seen the steps involved in inserting and updating records using the `ObjectDataSource` control. This section builds on that foundation by demonstrating the steps involved in performing deletions using the `ObjectDataSource` control, discussing the deletion using the Department table in the AdventureWorks. To start with, define the stored procedure required to delete a department from the Department table:

```
CREATE PROCEDURE [dbo].[DeleteDepartment]
@DepartmentID smallint
AS
BEGIN
  DELETE FROM HumanResources.Department WHERE DepartmentID = @DepartmentID
END
```

Now that the stored procedure is created, the next step is to add the delete method to the `Department` middle-tier class, which is shown in Listing 6-9.

Listing 6-9: Deleting a Department

```
public void DeleteDepartment(int DepartmentID)
{
  string connectionString = WebConfigurationManager.ConnectionStrings
    ["AdventureWorks"].ConnectionString;
  using (SqlConnection connection = new SqlConnection(connectionString))
  {
    string sql = "DeleteDepartment";
    SqlCommand command = new SqlCommand(sql, connection);
    command.CommandType = CommandType.StoredProcedure;
    SqlParameter paramDepartmentID = new SqlParameter("@DepartmentID",
      SqlDbType.Int);
    paramDepartmentID.Value = DepartmentID;
    command.Parameters.Add(paramDepartmentID);
    connection.Open();
    command.ExecuteNonQuery();
  }
}
```

The `DeleteDepartment` method simply executes the `DeleteDepartment` stored procedure using the supplied `DepartmentID` as an argument. Once you have set up the middle-tier method, the next step is to invoke it from the ASP.NET page, as outlined in Listing 6-10.

Listing 6-10: Handling Deletions through the ObjectDataSource Control

```
<%@ Page Language="C#"%>
<script runat="server">
  void deptSource_Deleted(object sender,ObjectDataSourceStatusEventArgs e)
  {
    if (e.Exception == null)
    {
      lblResult.Text = "Record deleted successfully.";
    }
```

(continued)

Listing 6-10: *(continued)*

```
      else
      {
        lblResult.Text = "An error occurred while attempting to delete the row." +
          e.Exception.Message;
        e.ExceptionHandled = true;
      }
    }
</script>
<html xmlns="http://www.w3.org/1999/xhtml" >
<head id="Head1" runat="server">
  <title>Deleting Data using ObjectDataSource Control</title>
</head>
<body>
<form id="form1" runat="server">
    <asp:GridView ID="departmentsView" Runat="server" DataKeyNames="DepartmentID"
      DataSourceID="deptSource" AutoGenerateColumns="False"
      HeaderStyle-HorizontalAlign="Center" HeaderStyle-Font-Bold="True"
      HeaderStyle-BackColor="blue" HeaderStyle-ForeColor="White">
      <Columns>
        <asp:TemplateField HeaderText="Delete">
          <ItemTemplate>
            <asp:Button ID="btnDelete" Text="Delete" runat="server"
              OnClientClick="return confirm('Are you sure you want to delete this
              record?');" CommandName="Delete" />
          </ItemTemplate>
        </asp:TemplateField>
        <asp:BoundField ReadOnly="true" HeaderText="Department ID"
          DataField="DepartmentID"/>
        <asp:BoundField HeaderText="Name" DataField="Name"/>
        <asp:BoundField HeaderText="Group Name" DataField="GroupName"/>
        <asp:BoundField HeaderText="ModifiedDate" DataField="ModifiedDate"/>
      </Columns>
    </asp:GridView>
    <asp:ObjectDataSource ID="deptSource" runat="server" TypeName="Department"
      SelectMethod="GetDepartments" OnDeleted="deptSource_Deleted"
      DeleteMethod="DeleteDepartment">
      <DeleteParameters>
        <asp:Parameter Type="Int32" Name="DepartmentID"></asp:Parameter>
      </DeleteParameters>
    </asp:ObjectDataSource>
    <asp:Label ID="lblResult" runat="server" Font-Bold="true" ForeColor="DarkRed"/>
  </form>
</body>
</html>
```

As you can see from Listing 6-10, the `GridView` control's `TemplateField` declares an `ItemTemplate`, which in turn contains a `Button` control. Such a button, with the `CommandName` set to `Delete`, will cause the `GridView` to delete the associated row when pressed. To display a confirmation message box before deleting the record, you leverage the `OnClientClick` property of the `Button` control and set it to the JavaScript that displays the confirmation message box for the users.

Similar to the previous example, the `DataKeyNames` property of the `GridView` control is used to specify the field or fields that represent the primary key of the data source. Next, you set the `ObjectDataSource` control's `DeleteMethod` and its parameters.

To display a confirmation message to the user after the row has been deleted, you use the `Deleted` event of the `SqlDataSource` control. You can also use this event to display error messages, if there are any:

```
void deptSource_Deleted(object sender,ObjectDataSourceStatusEventArgs e)
{
   .........
   .........
}
```

To test this, add a new record to the Department table, and navigate to the page and delete that newly added record.

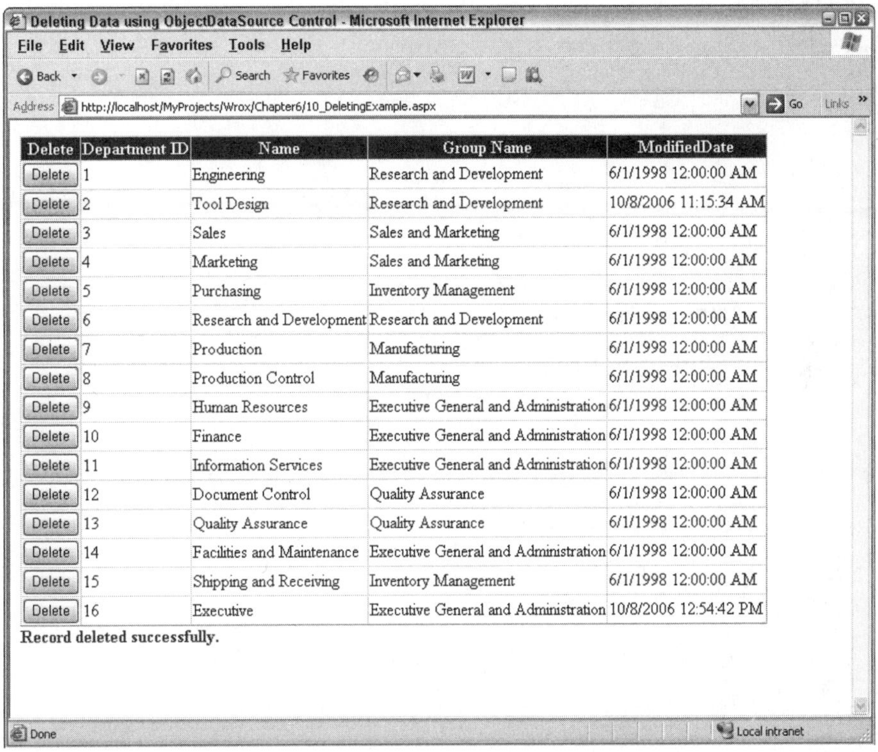

Deleting Data using ObjectDataSource Control - Microsoft Internet Explorer

http://localhost/MyProjects/Wrox/Chapter6/10_DeletingExample.aspx

Delete	Department ID	Name	Group Name	ModifiedDate
Delete	1	Engineering	Research and Development	6/1/1998 12:00:00 AM
Delete	2	Tool Design	Research and Development	10/8/2006 11:15:34 AM
Delete	3	Sales	Sales and Marketing	6/1/1998 12:00:00 AM
Delete	4	Marketing	Sales and Marketing	6/1/1998 12:00:00 AM
Delete	5	Purchasing	Inventory Management	6/1/1998 12:00:00 AM
Delete	6	Research and Development	Research and Development	6/1/1998 12:00:00 AM
Delete	7	Production	Manufacturing	6/1/1998 12:00:00 AM
Delete	8	Production Control	Manufacturing	6/1/1998 12:00:00 AM
Delete	9	Human Resources	Executive General and Administration	6/1/1998 12:00:00 AM
Delete	10	Finance	Executive General and Administration	6/1/1998 12:00:00 AM
Delete	11	Information Services	Executive General and Administration	6/1/1998 12:00:00 AM
Delete	12	Document Control	Quality Assurance	6/1/1998 12:00:00 AM
Delete	13	Quality Assurance	Quality Assurance	6/1/1998 12:00:00 AM
Delete	14	Facilities and Maintenance	Executive General and Administration	6/1/1998 12:00:00 AM
Delete	15	Shipping and Receiving	Inventory Management	6/1/1998 12:00:00 AM
Delete	16	Executive	Executive General and Administration	10/8/2006 12:54:42 PM

Record deleted successfully.

Figure 6-6

Figure 6-6 displays the output message produced when a department record is deleted through the `DeleteDepartment` method.

Programmatically Adding the ObjectDataSource Control

You can also programmatically create an instance of an `ObjectDataSource` control and work with it in the code. To programmatically invoke the `SelectMethod` of the `ObjectDataSource` control, call the `Select()` method. The `Select()` method returns an object that implements `IEnumerable`.

In this example, you will create the master-details capability using the combination of categories and products data in the AdventureWorks database. Specifically, a drop-down list with all the categories is displayed in the page, and whenever the category selection changes, you update the `GridView` to display the products that belong to that category. To accomplish this, create two `ObjectDataSource` controls programmatically: one during the `Page_Load` event to populate the initial list of categories in the `DropDownList` control, and another one during the `SelectedIndexChanged` event (that fires whenever the category selection changes) of the `DropDownList`. The complete code is shown in Listing 6-11.

Listing 6-11: Dynamically Adding an ObjectDataSource Control to the Page

```
<%@ Page Language="C#" %>
<%@ Import Namespace="System.Web.Configuration" %>
<script runat="server">
  void Page_Load(object sender, EventArgs e)
  {
    if (!Page.IsPostBack)
    {
      ObjectDataSource categorySource = new ObjectDataSource();
      categorySource.ID = "categorySource";
      Page.Controls.Add(categorySource);
      categorySource.SelectMethod = "GetCategories";
      categorySource.TypeName = "Category";
      ddlCategories.DataSource = categorySource.Select();
      ddlCategories.DataBind();
    }
  }

  void ddlCategories_SelectedIndexChanged(Object sender, EventArgs e)
  {
    ObjectDataSource productsSource = new ObjectDataSource();
    productsSource.ID = "productsSource";
    Page.Controls.Add(productsSource);
    productsSource.TypeName = "Product";
    productsSource.SelectMethod = "GetProductsByCategoryID";
    ControlParameter categoryIDParam = new ControlParameter();
    categoryIDParam.ControlID = "ddlCategories";
    categoryIDParam.Name = "categoryID";
    categoryIDParam.PropertyName = "SelectedValue";
    productsSource.SelectParameters.Clear();
    productsSource.SelectParameters.Add(categoryIDParam);
    productsView.DataSource = productsSource.Select();
    productsView.DataBind();
  }
</script>
<html xmlns="http://www.w3.org/1999/xhtml" >
```

```
<head id="Head1" runat="server">
  <title>Programmatically adding a ObjectDataSource control to the Page</title>
</head>
<body>
  <form id="form1" runat="server">
    <div>
      Categories:
      <asp:DropDownList runat="server"
        DataValueField="ProductSubcategoryID" DataTextField="Name"
        OnSelectedIndexChanged="ddlCategories_SelectedIndexChanged"
        AutoPostBack="true" AppendDataBoundItems="true" ID="ddlCategories">
        <asp:ListItem Text="Select an Item" Value="0" />
      </asp:DropDownList>
      <asp:GridView ID="productsView" Runat="server"
        AutoGenerateColumns="False"  HeaderStyle-HorizontalAlign="Center"
        HeaderStyle-Font-Bold="True" HeaderStyle-BackColor="blue"
        HeaderStyle-ForeColor="White">
        <Columns>
          <asp:BoundField HeaderText="Product ID" DataField="ProductID"/>
          <asp:BoundField HeaderText="Name" DataField="Name"/>
          <asp:BoundField HeaderText="Product Number" DataField="ProductNumber"/>
          <asp:BoundField HeaderText="List Price" DataField="ListPrice"/>
        </Columns>
      </asp:GridView>
     </div>
  </form>
</body>
</html>
```

In the `Page_Load` event, you dynamically create an `ObjectDataSource` control that represents the `Category` class. You set the `ID`, `SelectMethod`, and `TypeName` properties to appropriate values. However, the majority of the work occurs in the `SelectedIndexChanged` event of the `DropDownList` where the `ObjectDataSource` control that represents the `Product` class is created. Specifically, you create a new `ControlParameter`, set its properties, and add that to the `SelectParameters` collection of the `ObjectDataSource` control before invoking the `GetProductsByCategoryID()` method. Similar to creating `ControlParameter` object, you can also create other parameters, such as `QueryString Parameter`, `ProfileParameter`, `FormParameter`, `CookieParameter`, and `SessionParameter`, dynamically.

Using Generics with the ObjectDataSource Control

One of the new and exciting features introduced with .NET 2.0 is generics which allow you to realize type safety at compile time. They allow you to create a data structure without committing to a specific data type. When the data structure is used, however, the compiler makes sure that the types used with it are consistent for type safety. Generics provide type safety, but without any loss of performance or code bloat. While they are similar to templates in C++ in this regard, they are very different in their implementation.

A generic class is defined using a slightly different notation. The following is the basic code for a generic class named `Compare` that can compare two items of the same type and return the larger or smaller value, depending on the method that is invoked:

```
public class Compare<ItemType, ItemType>
{
  public ItemType ReturnLarger(ItemType data, ItemType data2)
  {
     //logic...
  }

  public ItemType ReturnSmaller  (ItemType data, ItemType data2)
  {
    //logic...
  }
}
```

This generic could be used with any data type, ranging from basic data types such as integers to complex classes and structures. When you use the generic, you identify what data type you are using with it. For example, to use an integer with the previous `Compare` generic, you would write code similar to the following:

```
Compare<int, int> compare = new Compare<int, int>;
int result = compare.ReturnLarger(3,5);
```

In addition to the ability to define generic classes, the .NET Framework 2.0 also provides you with a predefined set of generic collection classes such as `List`, `Queue`, `Stack`, and so on. All these generic collection classes are contained in the `System.Collections.Generic` namespace. These collection classes provide you with the ability to wrap a set of custom objects and can be used as a transport mechanism.

In this section, you will see how to return generic collections from a middle-tier object and bind it directly to the `ObjectDataSource` control. This example will also use the master-detail capabilities using the categories and products information in the AdventureWorks database. To start with, create a class named `CategoryInfo` that acts as the placeholder for capturing attributes related to a Category. The code for the `CategoryInfo` class is provided in Listing 6-12.

Listing 6-12: Implementation of CategoryInfo

```
using System;

public class CategoryInfo
{
  public CategoryInfo()
  {}

  private int _categoryID;
  private string _name;

  public int CategoryID
  {
```

```
      get{_categoryID;}
      set{_categoryID = value;}
    }

    public string Name
    {
      get{return _name;}
      set{_name = value;}
    }
  }
```

Once you have set up the `CategoryInfo` class, the next step is to use it from within the `Category` class for returning the categories information. To this end, add the method `GetCategoriesAsCollection()`, shown in Listing 6-13, to the `Category` class.

Listing 6-13: Returning a Collection of Categories as a Generic Collection

```
public IList<CategoryInfo> GetCategoriesAsCollection()
{
  IList<CategoryInfo> categoryCollection = new List<CategoryInfo>();
  string connectionString = WebConfigurationManager.ConnectionStrings
    ["AdventureWorks"].ConnectionString;
  using (SqlConnection connection = new SqlConnection(connectionString))
  {
    connection.Open();
    SqlCommand command = connection.CreateCommand();
    command.CommandText = "Select ProductSubcategoryID, Name " +
      "from Production.ProductSubcategory";
    using (SqlDataReader reader = command.ExecuteReader())
    {
      while (reader.Read())
      {
        CategoryInfo category = new CategoryInfo();
        category.CategoryID = Convert.ToInt32(reader["ProductSubcategoryID"]);
        category.Name = reader["Name"].ToString();
        categoryCollection.Add(category);
      }
    }
}
return categoryCollection;
}
```

In the previous code, you start by declaring an object of type `IList` generic collection and assigning that to the generic collection of type `List`. Then you open the connection to the database, execute the query, and get the results into a `SqlDataReader` object. Once you have the results in a `SqlDataReader` object, you loop through the `SqlDataReader` object, retrieve its values, and assign that to the `CategoryInfo` object. After that, you add the `CategoryInfo` object to the previously declared generic collection. After adding all the rows in the `SqlDataReader` object to the collection, you finally return the collection object back to the caller.

Similar to the `CategoryInfo` class, Listing 6-14 defines the `ProductInfo` class that acts as the place-holder for product-related attributes.

Listing 6-14: Implementation of ProductInfo

```
using System;

public class ProductInfo
{
  public ProductInfo()
  {}

  private int _productID;
  private string _name;
  private string _productNumber;
  private string _listPrice;

  public int ProductID
  {
    get{return _productID;}
    set{_productID = value;}
  }

  public string Name
  {
    get{return _name;}
    set{_name = value;}
  }

  public string ProductNumber
  {
    get{return _productNumber;}
    set{_productNumber = value; }
  }

  public string ListPrice
  {
    get{return _listPrice;}
    set{_listPrice = value;}
  }
}
```

Now that you have set up the `ProductInfo` class, the next step is to use it from the `Product` class, which is defined as shown in Listing 6-15.

Listing 6-15: Returning a Collection of Products as a Generic Collection

```
using System;
using System.Collections.Generic;
using System.Data;
using System.Data.SqlClient;
using System.Web.Configuration;

public class Product
{
  public Product()
  {
```

```
  }

  public IList<ProductInfo> GetProductsByCategoryIDAsCollection
    (int categoryID)
  {
    IList<ProductInfo> productCollection = new List<ProductInfo>();
    string connectionString = WebConfigurationManager.ConnectionStrings
      ["AdventureWorks"].ConnectionString;
    using (SqlConnection connection = new SqlConnection(connectionString))
    {
      connection.Open();
      SqlCommand command = connection.CreateCommand();
      command.CommandText = "Select ProductID, Name, ProductNumber, ListPrice " +
        " from Production.Product Where ProductSubcategoryID=" +
        categoryID.ToString();
      using (SqlDataReader reader = command.ExecuteReader())
      {
        while (reader.Read())
        {
          ProductInfo product = new ProductInfo();
          product.ProductID = Convert.ToInt32(reader["ProductID"]);
          product.Name = reader["Name"].ToString();
          product.ProductNumber = reader["ProductNumber"].ToString();
          product.ListPrice = reader["ListPrice"].ToString();
          productCollection.Add(product);
        }
      }
    }
    return productCollection;
  }
}
```

The `GetProductsByCategoryIDAsCollection()` method is similar to `GetCategoriesAsCollection()`, in that it also works exactly the same: executing the SQL, retrieving the result set, looping through the result set, populating the generic collection object, and finally returning back to the caller.

Now that you have created the `Category` and `Product` classes, you can now invoke its methods using the `ObjectDataSource` control. Because of the two separate methods that need to be invoked, you need to set up two `ObjectDataSource` controls: one for the `Category.GetCategoriesAsCollection()` and another one for the `Product.GetProductsByCategoryIDAsCollection()`. Listing 6-16 shows the code of the ASP.NET page that uses generic category and product collections.

Listing 6-16: Using Generic Collections with the ObjectDataSource Control

```
<%@ Page Language="C#"%>
<html xmlns="http://www.w3.org/1999/xhtml" >
<head id="Head1" runat="server">
  <title>Retrieving data as Generic Collections ObjectDataSource Control</title>
</head>
<body>
```

(continued)

Listing 6-16: *(continued)*

```
    <form id="form1" runat="server">
      Categories:
      <asp:DropDownList ID="ddlCategories" runat="server"
        DataSourceID="categorySource" DataTextField="Name" AutoPostBack="true"
        DataValueField="CategoryID" />
      <asp:GridView ID="productsView" Runat="server"
        DataSourceID="productSource" AutoGenerateColumns="False"
        HeaderStyle-HorizontalAlign="Center" HeaderStyle-Font-Bold="True"
        HeaderStyle-BackColor="blue" HeaderStyle-ForeColor="White">
        <Columns>
          <asp:BoundField HeaderText="Product ID" DataField="ProductID"/>
          <asp:BoundField HeaderText="Name" DataField="Name"/>
          <asp:BoundField HeaderText="Product Number" DataField="ProductNumber"/>
          <asp:BoundField HeaderText="List Price" DataField="ListPrice"/>
        </Columns>
      </asp:GridView>
      <asp:ObjectDataSource ID="productSource" runat="server"
        TypeName="Product" SelectMethod="GetProductsByCategoryIDAsCollection">
        <SelectParameters>
          <asp:ControlParameter ControlID="ddlCategories"
            PropertyName="SelectedValue" Name="categoryID" />
        </SelectParameters>
      </asp:ObjectDataSource>
      <asp:ObjectDataSource ID="categorySource" runat="server"
        TypeName="Category" SelectMethod="GetCategoriesAsCollection">
      </asp:ObjectDataSource>
    </form>
  </body>
  </html>
```

The category `ObjectDataSource` control is bound to a `DropDownList`, and the product `ObjectDataSource` control is bound to a `GridView` control, so the collection of products returned through the generic collection can be displayed in the `GridView`.

Caching

Using caching with the `ObjectDataSource` control is highly recommended, as it can eliminate the round trips to the database, thereby providing huge improvements in the performance. The following table discusses the caching related properties of the `ObjectDataSource` control.

Property	Description
`CacheDuration`	The number of seconds to cache the output of the `SelectMethod` method of the object. If you are using sliding expiration, the time limit is reset every time the object is retrieved from the cache. The default, `DataSourceCacheExpiry.Infinite`, keeps cached items perpetually.

Property	Description
CacheExpirationPolicy	Uses a value from the DataSourceCacheExpiry enumeration—Absolute for absolute expiration (which times out after a fixed interval of time) or Sliding for sliding expiration (which resets the time window every time the data object is retrieved from the cache).
CacheKeyDependency and SqlCacheDependency	Allows you to make a cached item dependent on another item in the data cache (CacheKeyDependency) or on a table in your database (SqlCacheDependency).
EnableCaching	If true, caching is switched on. This property is set to false by default.

When you enable caching for the ObjectDataSource control, you cache the results of the SelectMethod. However, if you execute a select method that accepts parameters, the ObjectDataSource will cache a separate result for every set of parameter values. For example, imagine you create a page that allows you to view products by category. The user selects the desired category from a list box, and you use an ObjectDataSource control to fill in the matching products records in a grid. In this case, you create a cache entry for each unique value of the category ID that is supplied to the products retrieval method.

Note that the ObjectDataSource control supports caching only when the middle-tier object returns DataSet as the return type. For example, caching is not supported when the middle-tier method returns a SqlDataReader object as its return value.

The following declaration caches the output of the GetCategoriesAsDataSet() method for 60 seconds.

```
<asp:ObjectDataSource EnableCaching="true" CacheDuration="60"
  ID="categorySource" runat="server" TypeName="Category"
  SelectMethod="GetCategoriesAsDataSet">
</asp:ObjectDataSource>
```

Similar to the FilterParameters and FilterExpression properties of the SqlDataSource control (discussed in Chapter 4), the ObjectDataSource control also supports these properties to enable filtering of the results returned by the SelectMethod property.

Using Web Services with the ObjectDataSource Control

So far, you have seen the use of ObjectDataSource control in invoking methods of the classes contained in the App_Code directory. You can also use the ObjectDataSource control to invoke the methods of the classes that are located in a separate assembly, which requires you to specify the fully qualified name of the class in the TypeName property. In addition to using the ObjectDataSource control to invoke local methods, you can also leverage it to invoke remote web service methods. For the purposes of this example, consider the web service named DeptService that exposes a method to return all the departments from the Department table in the AdventureWorks database. Listing 6-17 discusses the code of the DeptService class.

Listing 6-17: Implementation of DeptService

```
<%@ WebService Language="C#" Class="DeptService" %>
using System;
using System.Collections.Generic;
using System.Data;
using System.Data.SqlClient;
using System.Web;
using System.Web.Configuration;
using System.Web.Services;
using System.Web.Services.Protocols;

[WebService(Namespace = "http://tempuri.org/")]
[WebServiceBinding(ConformsTo = WsiProfiles.BasicProfile1_1)]
public class DeptService  : System.Web.Services.WebService
{
  [WebMethod]
  public List<DepartmentInfo> GetDepartments()
  {
    List<DepartmentInfo> deptCollection = new List<DepartmentInfo>();
    string connectionString = WebConfigurationManager.ConnectionStrings
      ["AdventureWorks"].ConnectionString;
    using (SqlConnection connection = new SqlConnection(connectionString))
    {
      connection.Open();
      SqlCommand command = connection.CreateCommand();
      command.CommandText = "SELECT DepartmentID, Name, GroupName, " +
        " ModifiedDate FROM HumanResources.Department";
      using (SqlDataReader reader = command.ExecuteReader())
      {
        while (reader.Read())
        {
          DepartmentInfo dept = new DepartmentInfo();
          dept.DepartmentID = Convert.ToInt32(reader["DepartmentID"]);
          dept.Name = reader["Name"].ToString();
          dept.GroupName = reader["GroupName"].ToString();
          dept.ModifiedDate = Convert.ToDateTime(reader["ModifiedDate"]);
          deptCollection.Add(dept);
        }
      }
    }
    return deptCollection;
  }
}
```

The return value of the `GetDepartments()` method is a generic collection of `DepartmentInfo` objects. The generic collection object is populated by retrieving the department records from the Department table and looping through all the records in the result set. Once you have set up the web service, the next step is to invoke its method using the `ObjectDataSource` control.

To be able to invoke a remote web service method, you need to create a proxy for the web service method, which can be accomplished using either of the following options:

- ❑ Using the Add Web Reference option in Visual Studio 2005
- ❑ Using the `WSDL.exe` utility

To create the proxy using the WSLD.exe utility, open the .NET Framework 2.0 SDK command prompt and enter the following command:

```
WSDL /namespace:DeptServiceProxy
  http://localhost/MyProjects/Wrox/Chapter6/DeptService.asmx
```

The namespace switch allows you to specify the namespace within which the proxy class needs to be created. Once the proxy is created, you can then reference it the same manner as that of a regular class. Listing 6-18 discusses the code required to accomplish this.

Listing 6-18: Invoking the Web Service Methods

```
<%@ Page Language="C#"%>
<html xmlns="http://www.w3.org/1999/xhtml" >
<head id="Head1" runat="server">
  <title>Retrieving data from a Web Service using ObjectDataSource</title>
</head>
<body>
  <form id="form1" runat="server">
    <asp:GridView ID="departmentsView" Runat="server" DataKeyNames="DepartmentID"
      DataSourceID="deptSource" AutoGenerateColumns="False"
      HeaderStyle-HorizontalAlign="Center" HeaderStyle-Font-Bold="True"
      HeaderStyle-BackColor="blue" HeaderStyle-ForeColor="White">
      <Columns>
        <asp:BoundField ReadOnly="true" HeaderText="Department ID"
          DataField="DepartmentID"/>
        <asp:BoundField HeaderText="Name" DataField="Name"/>
        <asp:BoundField HeaderText="Group Name" DataField="GroupName"/>
        <asp:BoundField HeaderText="ModifiedDate" DataField="ModifiedDate"/>
      </Columns>
    </asp:GridView>
    <asp:ObjectDataSource ID="deptSource" runat="server"
      TypeName="DeptServiceProxy.DeptService" SelectMethod="GetDepartments">
    </asp:ObjectDataSource>
  </form>
</body>
</html>
```

The key thing to note in Listing 6-18 is the value of the `TypeName` property, which is set to reference the fully qualified proxy class. The rest of the implementation is very similar to the previous examples.

Summary

As this chapter has shown, the introduction of the `ObjectDataSource` control makes invoking the middle-tier method an almost trivial task. In this chapter, you have understood the basics of invoking a middle tier from the `ObjectDataSource` control. In addition to selecting records using the middle-tier methods, you have also learned the steps involved in updating and deleting data using the `Object DataSource` control.

This chapter has also demonstrated the steps involved in programmatically adding a `ObjectDataSource` control to the page and leveraging its `Select()` method to execute the select method. Caching is now automatically built into the `ObjectDataSource` control, meaning that you can easily configure and control data caching using the same declarative syntax.

7

ASP.NET 2.0 Site Navigation

Any web site you create has to provide features to allow users to move between the various pages on the site. This is not much of a task for a small, simple site, such as a personal site with four or five pages. As sites get more complex, however, any ad hoc approach is likely to cause frustration and errors. When a commercial site contains dozens or hundreds of pages in multiple layers, adding a new page or removing an old one should not require manual editing of links or menus on every other page.

With ASP.NET 1.x, the common approach for building this type of navigation is to sprinkle pages with hyperlinks. Hyperlinks are generally added to web pages by using include files or user controls. They can also be directly hard-coded onto a page so that they appear in the header or the sidebar of the page being viewed. The difficulties in working with navigation become worse when you move pages around or change page names. Sometimes developers are forced to go to each and every page in the application just to change some aspect of the navigation.

ASP.NET 2.0 tackles this problem with the introduction of a navigation system that makes it quite trivial to manage how end users work through the web sites you create. This new capability in ASP.NET is complex,but the great thing is that it can be as simple as you need it to be, or you can actually get in deep and control every aspect of how it works. The new site navigation system includes the capability to define your entire site in an XML file, which is called a *sitemap*. After you define a new sitemap, you can either programmatically or declaratively (using data source controls) work with it. This chapter takes a look at all these components in the new ASP.NET 2.0 navigation system.

Introduction to Site Navigation

As mentioned, ASP.NET 2.0 allows you to define the site navigation information in an external location and use that to drive your site navigation hierarchy. ASP.NET does not require a particular format for specifying the sitemap, although it does provide a default choice that uses an XML-formatted file known as Web.sitemap. In short, you can use ASP.NET 2.0's default XML-based method for specifying your web site's sitemap, or, with a bit of code, you can use your existing custom method or some other approach. This chapter will examine sitemaps based on the default XML-based sitemap, as well as a custom approach that uses data from an external database.

> **The details on how the sitemap is serialized can be customized because the site navigation builds on the ASP.NET 2.0 provider model concept. Through the provider model, you can customize the inner workings of a particular ASP.NET subsystem, such as the site navigation system, to suit the needs of your web site.**

In addition to providing a customizable means to specify site structure, ASP.NET 2.0 ships with a number of web controls that make displaying the sitemap as easy as dragging and dropping a control onto your ASP.NET page:

- `SiteMapPath`: Allows you to display a breadcrumb, showing the end user where he is relative to the site's structure. For example, when visiting the Novels section on Amazon, a breadcrumb would display something like: Home ⇨ Books ⇨ Novels.
- `TreeView`: Allows you to display the site's structure in a collapsible tree.
- `Menu`: Displays the site's structure using a menu.
- `SiteMapDataSource`: Creates a hierarchical data source that mirrors the structure of the sitemap. To display sitemap information in other web controls, such as the `TreeView` or `Menu`, or a `SiteMapPath`, the web controls do not query the sitemap directly; rather, they are bound to a `SiteMapDataSource` control, which handles reading in the sitemap structure.

When displaying site navigation, both the `TreeView` and `Menu` controls use the `SiteMapDataSource` control to read the contents of the sitemap. Underneath the covers, these controls call ASP.NET 2.0's site navigation API. Since the site navigation piece is implemented using the provider model, the controls are oblivious to the inner details of how the sitemap is serialized. Regardless of whether you use the default sitemap or roll your own custom sitemap logic, the navigation controls can be used to work against your sitemap of choice.

Implementing Site Navigation

As mentioned previously, the site navigation consists of two separate parts. First you need to define the site's logical structure, also called the sitemap. Creating a sitemap does not require any programming; in fact, a pencil and paper may be all you need. Once the sitemap is defined, the next step is implementing it. You can accomplish the second step either declaratively or programmatically. Figure 7-1 shows how the various components of the site navigation work together to produce the desired output.

As shown in Figure 7-1, you build a sitemap, place a `SiteMapDataSource` control onto the page, and bind a `Menu` or `TreeView` control to the `SiteMapDataSource`. The `SiteMapDataSource` uses the default sitemap provider (typically `XmlSiteMapProvider`) to read the sitemap, and then passes sitemap nodes to the `Menu` or `TreeView`, which renders the nodes into HTML. It is also possible for you to add a `SiteMapPath` control to the page to display the familiar breadcrumb element showing the path to the current page. The next section starts by defining the XML-based sitemap that will be used in the later examples.

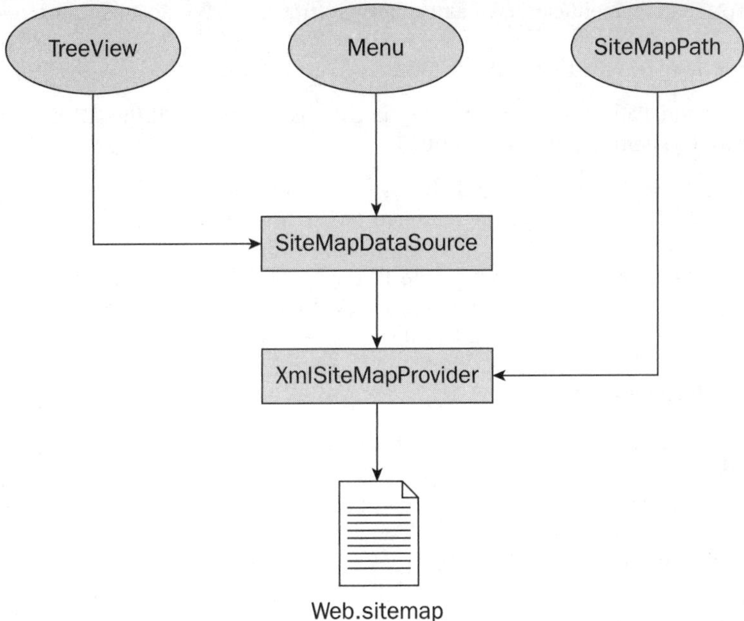

Figure 7-1

Defining the Sitemap

A sitemap is made up of a series of related `SiteMapNode` objects. The `SiteMapNode` objects are related in such a way as to form a hierarchy that has a single root node, which is the only node in the hierarchy that does not have a parent node. Each node in the hierarchy represents a logical section of the web site. Each section can have a title, URL, and description, which are exposed by the properties of the `SiteMapNode` class (`Title`, `Url`, and `Description`, respectively).

The hierarchy of `SiteMapNode` objects is how the sitemap is represented in memory when it is examined through ASP.NET 2.0's site navigation API. This sitemap, however, must be physically serialized in some manner, such as an XML file or in a database table. ASP.NET 2.0 provides a default implementation of serializing the sitemap using an XML-formatted file. To use this technique, you will need to create an XML file in your web site's root directory named `Web.sitemap` that has the following structure:

```
<?xml version="1.0" encoding="utf-8" ?>
<siteMap xmlns="http://schemas.microsoft.com/AspNet/SiteMap-File-1.0">
  <siteMapNode attributes>
    <siteMapNode attributes>
      <siteMapNode attributes>
        ...
      </siteMapNode>
      <siteMapNode attributes />
        ...
      <siteMapNode attributes />
    </siteMapNode>
  </siteMapNode>
</siteMap>
```

The <siteMapNode> element can have a number of attributes. The most common ones are:

- title: Specifies the title of the section.
- url: Optional attribute that specifies the URL of the section. If this attribute is provided, each URL in the sitemap must be unique.
- description: Optional attribute that specifies the optional description of the section that is used in the alt attribute of the rendered navigation controls.

Although the <siteMapNode> elements can be arbitrarily nested to any depth, the sitemap must contain a root <siteMapNode> element. That is, the <siteMap> node must have one and only one <siteMapNode> element child. Listing 7-1 shows the sitemap file for an e-commerce site.

Listing 7-1: Web.sitemap

```
<?xml version="1.0" encoding="utf-8" ?>
<siteMap xmlns="http://schemas.microsoft.com/AspNet/SiteMap-File-1.0" >
  <siteMapNode url="~/Default.aspx" title="Home">
    <siteMapNode url="~/Books/Default.aspx" title="Books">
      <siteMapNode url="~/Books/Novels.aspx" title="Novels" />
      <siteMapNode url="~/Books/History.aspx" title="History" />
      <siteMapNode url="~/Books/Romance.aspx" title="Romance" />
    </siteMapNode>
    <siteMapNode url="~/Electronics/Default.aspx" title="Electronics">
      <siteMapNode url="~/Electronics/Cameras.aspx" title="Camera" />
      <siteMapNode url="~/Electronics/Computers.aspx" title="Computer" />
    </siteMapNode>
    <siteMapNode url="~/DVDs/Default.aspx" title="DVDs">
      <siteMapNode url="~/DVDs/Horror.aspx" title="Horror" />
      <siteMapNode url="~/DVDs/Kids.aspx" title="Kids" />
    </siteMapNode>
    <siteMapNode url="~/Computers/Default.aspx" title="Computers">
      <siteMapNode url="~/Computers/Desktop.aspx" title="Desktop" />
      <siteMapNode url="~/Computers/Laptop.aspx" title="Laptop" />
    </siteMapNode>
  </siteMapNode>
</siteMap>
```

Once you have defined the sitemap, the next step is to use that from within an ASP.NET page.

Data Binding with the Sitemap

Binding a sitemap with the ASP.NET server controls is a very simple step and follows the data source model. For this reason, ASP.NET 2.0 introduces a new data source control named SiteMapDataSource that is specifically geared toward letting the page controls bind with the sitemap. Once you have placed a SiteMapDataSource control on the page, the only remaining task is to choose the controls you want to use to display the sitemap data. As an example, the ASP.NET page shown in Listing 7-2 shows the code required to display the site navigation using a TreeView control.

Listing 7-2: Data Binding with the Sitemap using SiteMapDataSource

```
<%@ Page Language="C#" %>
<html xmlns="http://www.w3.org/1999/xhtml" >
<head runat="server">
  <title>Displaying the navigation information in a TreeView</title>
</head>
<body>
  <form id="form1" runat="server">
    <div>
      <asp:SiteMapDataSource runat="Server" ID="SiteMapDataSource1" />
      <asp:TreeView DataSourceID="SiteMapDataSource1" runat="server"
        ID="tvwNavigation" ExpandImageUrl="Images/closed.gif"
        CollapseImageUrl="Images/open.gif">
      </asp:TreeView>
    </div>
  </form>
</body>
</html>
```

As with any other data source controls, you set the `DataSourceID` property of the `TreeView` control to the ID of the `SiteMapDataSource` control on the page. You also set the `ExpandImageUrl` and `CollapseImageUrl` properties of the `TreeView` to the `.gif` files that are placed in the Images folder. Requesting the page from a browser results in the output shown in Figure 7-2.

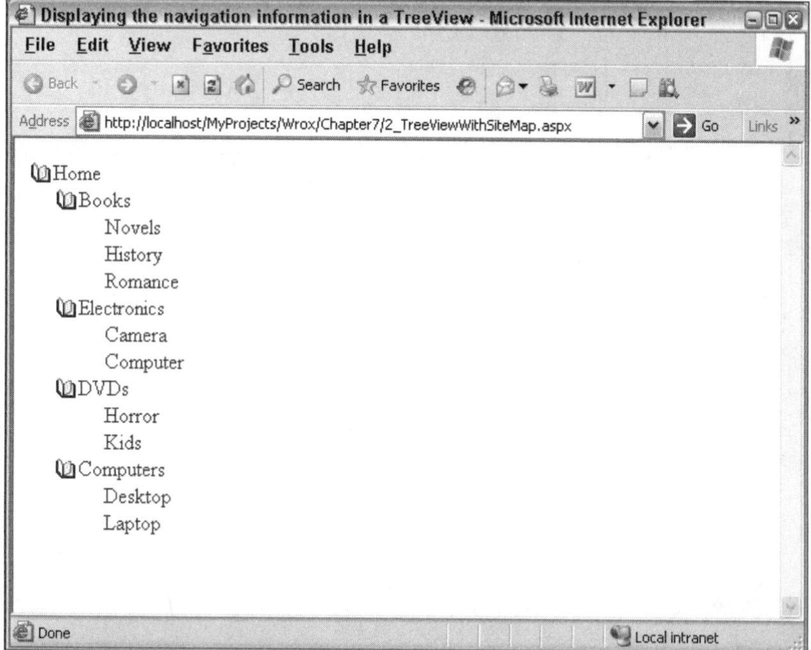

Figure 7-2

> **The `TreeView` control is a completely new control introduced with ASP.NET 2.0 that can be used in any situation in which you need to display hierarchical data. For example, you can use this control when displaying a navigation menu, displaying database records from database tables in a master/detail relation, displaying the contents of an XML document, or displaying files and folders from the file system. It is also possible for you to programmatically access the `TreeView` object model to dynamically create trees, populate nodes, set properties, and so on. The `TreeView` control consists of nodes, and there are three types of nodes that you can add to a `TreeView` control:**
>
> - `Root`: **A root node is a node that has no parent node. It has one or more child nodes**
> - `Parent`: **A node that has a parent node and one or more child nodes**
> - `Leaf`: **A node that has no child nodes**

Alternatively, you could use the fly out `Menu` control just as easily by replacing the `TreeView` control declaration with the following code:

```
<asp:Menu ID="mnuNavigation" runat="server" DataSourceID="SiteMapDataSource1" />
```

This produces the output shown in Figure 7-3.

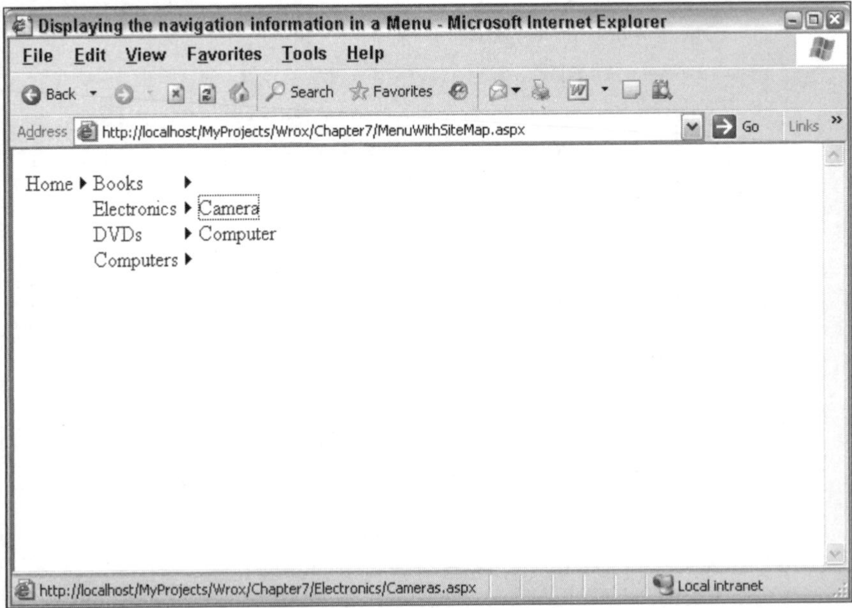

Figure 7-3

Note that the recommended practice is to define the site navigation controls, such as a `TreeView` *or* `Menu`*, in a master page so that they can be reused consistently in all the pages of the web site. Generally, you would define a basic structure in your master page that puts navigation controls on the left.*

You can do a lot more to customize the appearance of your navigation controls and the processing of your sitemap. You will consider these more advanced topics in the later sections of this chapter.

The following table provides a brief overview of the important properties of the `SiteMapDataSource` control.

Property	Description
`Provider`	Allows you to get or set the `SiteMapProvider` that is associated with the data source control
`ShowStartingNode`	Allows you to specify whether the starting node is retrieved and displayed
`SiteMapProvider`	Allows you to set or get the name of the `SiteMapProvider` that acts as the data source
`StartFromCurrentNode`	Allows you to specify if you want to retrieve the node tree relative to the current page
`StartingNodeOffset`	Allows you to set or get a positive or negative integer offset from the starting node that determines the root hierarchy exposed by the data source control
`StartingNodeUrl`	Allows you to specify a node that acts as a reference point for retrieving nodes from a hierarchical sitemap

Customizing the Appearance of the TreeView Control

The `TreeView` control comes with a number of prebuilt styles right out of the box. With a few lines of code, you can easily utilize these predefined styles to create sophisticated navigation systems. As an example, Listing 7-3 shows how to use some of the built-in styles of the `TreeView` control to create a rich-looking navigation system.

Listing 7-3: Using Styles to Customize the Appearance of the TreeView

```
<%@ Page Language="C#" %>
<html xmlns="http://www.w3.org/1999/xhtml" >
<head runat="server">
  <title>Customizing the TreeView using Styles</title>
</head>
<body>
  <form id="form1" runat="server">
    <div>
      <asp:SiteMapDataSource runat="Server" ID="SiteMapDataSource1" />
      <asp:TreeView ID="Treeview1" Runat="server" DataSourceID="SiteMapDataSource1"
        nodeindent="10" font-names="Verdana" font-size="8pt" forecolor="Black">
```

(continued)

Listing 7-3: *(continued)*

```
            <HoverNodeStyle BackColor="#CCCCCC" BorderColor="#888888"
              BorderStyle="Solid" BorderWidth="1px" Font-Underline="True">
            </HoverNodeStyle>
            <SelectedNodeStyle BackColor="White" VerticalPadding="1"
              BorderColor="#888888" BorderStyle="Solid" BorderWidth="1px"
              HorizontalPadding="3">
            </SelectedNodeStyle>
            <NodeStyle VerticalPadding="2" Font-Names="Verdana" Font-Size="8pt"
              NodeSpacing="1" HorizontalPadding="5" ForeColor="Black">
            </NodeStyle>
          </asp:TreeView>
        </div>
      </form>
    </body>
    </html>
```

As you can see, if you use these built-in styles, it is not too difficult to completely change the look and feel of the `TreeView` control. When this bit of code is run, you get the results shown in Figure 7-4.

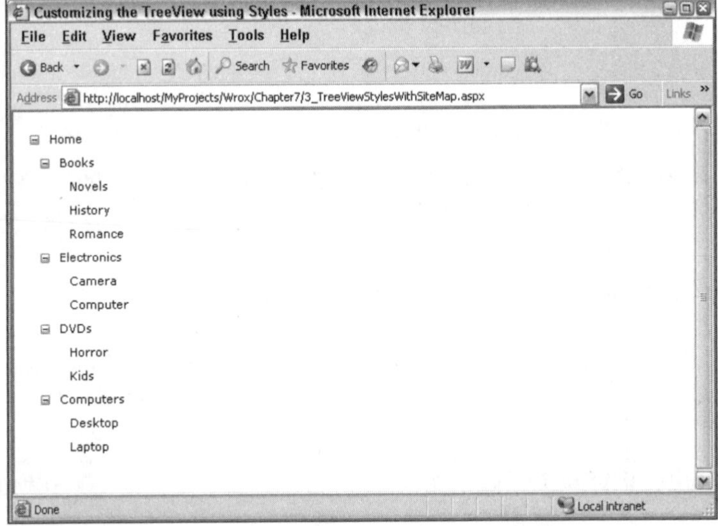

Figure 7-4

Implementing Breadcrumbs

As mentioned previously, ASP.NET actually defines three navigation controls: `TreeView`, `Menu`, and `SiteMapPath`. `SiteMapPath` provides breadcrumb navigation, meaning that it allows you to display the user's current location, thereby enabling the user to navigate back up the hierarchy to a higher level using links. The output of the `SiteMapPath` control is determined by three factors.

- The site's structure, as defined by the sitemap
- The page being visited
- The property values of the `SiteMapPath` control

When a page with a `SiteMapPath` control is visited, the `SiteMapPath` control attempts to map the page's URL to the `url` value of a sitemap node defined in the sitemap. If a match is found, the control walks up the structure to the root, emitting the following output: RootNode ⇨ ParentNode ⇨ . . . ⇨ ParentNode ⇨ CurrentNode. In this example, CurrentNode is the title of the sitemap node that maps to the URL of the current page request; the RootNode and ParentNodes are rendered as hyperlinks if the sitemap node has a URL value defined in the sitemap. A `SiteMapPath` control on the History Books page (`Books/History.aspx`) would render as Home ⇨ Books ⇨ History, with Home and Books rendered as links back to `Default.aspx` and `Books/Default.aspx`, respectively.

> **The `SiteMapPath` control is useful both for an at-a-glance view that provides the current position and for a way to move up the hierarchy. However, you always need to combine it with other navigation controls that let the user move down the sitemap hierarchy.**

Figure 7-5 shows an example with a `SiteMapPath` control when the user is on the `Novels.aspx` page. Using the `SiteMapPath` control, the user can return to the `Books.aspx` page or the `Default.aspx` page.

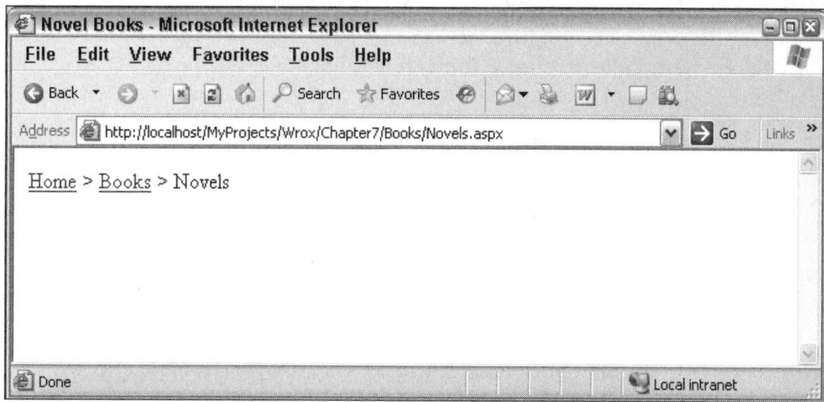

Figure 7-5

Here is how you define the `SiteMapPath` control:

```
<asp:SiteMapPath ID="SiteMapPath1" runat="server" />
```

Clearly, the output of the `SiteMapPath` is dependent upon both the sitemap itself and the page being visited. The `SiteMapPath` control's output can also be customized through the control's properties. The `SiteMapPath` control is also thoroughly customizable. The following table lists some of the most commonly configured appearance-related properties of `SiteMapPath`.

Property	Description
`ShowToolTips`	Set this to `false` if you don't want the description text to appear when the user hovers over a part of the sitemap path.
`ParentLevelsDisplayed`	Sets the maximum number of parent levels that will be shown at once. By default, this setting is `-1`, which means all levels will be shown.
`RenderCurrentNodeAsLink`	If `true`, the portion of the page that indicates the current page is turned into a clickable link. By default, this is `false` because the user is already at the current page.
`PathDirection`	You can set this property to either `RootToCurrent` (the default) or `CurrentToRoot` (which reverses the order of levels in the path).
`PathSeparator`	Indicates the characters that will be placed between each level in the path. The default is the greater-than (>) symbol. Another common path separator is the colon (:).

There are also style properties for setting `BackColor`, `Font`, `ForeColor`, and so on for various pieces of the `SiteMapPath` control.

Customizing the Rendered Output with Templates

For even more control, you can configure the `SiteMapPath` control with styles or even redefine the controls and HTML with templates, as shown in the following table.

Style	Template	Description
`NodeStyle`	`NodeTemplate`	All parts of the page except the root and current node.
`CurrentNodeStyle`	`CurrentNodeTemplate`	The node representing the current page.
`RootNodeStyle`	`RootNodeTemplate`	The node representing the root. If the root node is the same as current node, the current node template or styles are used.
`PathSeparatorStyle`	`PathSeparatorTemplate`	The separator between each node.

The four templates of the `SiteMapPath` allow for the rendered output to be further customized. Templates allow for a mix of static HTML markup, web controls, and data-binding syntax; if you have used the `DataList` or `Repeater` controls before, then you are already familiar with templates. For example, the following `SiteMapPath` uses an arrow image as a separator and a fixed string of bold text for the root node. The final part of the path, which represents the current page, is shown in bold:

```
<asp:SiteMapPath ID="SiteMapPath1" runat="server">
  <PathSeparatorTemplate>
    <asp:Image ID="Image1" ImageUrl="~/images/arrow.jpg"
      runat="server" GenerateEmptyAlternateText="True" />
```

```
    </PathSeparatorTemplate>
    <RootNodeTemplate>
      <b>Root</b>
    </RootNodeTemplate>
    <CurrentNodeTemplate>
      <b><asp:Label ID="Label1" runat="server" Text='<%# Eval("title") %>'>
      </asp:Label></b>
    </CurrentNodeTemplate>
  </asp:SiteMapPath>
```

Notice how the `CurrentNodeTemplate` uses a data-binding expression to bind to the title property of the current node. You can also get the `url` and `description` attributes that you declared in the sitemap file in the same way.

Using Templates for Event Processing

By default, the `SiteMapPath` renders the root and parent nodes as regular hyperlinks so that when a user clicks the link, he or she is immediately taken back up the control hierarchy. However, you may want to do some server-side processing before sending the user on their way up. For example, you might want to record where the user is going, or automatically save any changes he or she made on the page. Such functionality can be accomplished by using a template and having the node rendered as a `LinkButton`.

For example, if you want the `SiteMapPath` control's root node to be rendered as a `LinkButton`, you could add a `<RootNodeTemplate>` to the `SiteMapPath` control with the following markup:

```
  <asp:SiteMapPath ID="SiteMapPath1" runat="server">
    <RootNodeTemplate>
      <asp:LinkButton ID="LinkButton1" runat="server" Text='<%# Eval("title") %>'
        CommandArgument='<%# Eval("url") %>' OnCommand="LinkButton1_Command">
      </asp:LinkButton>
    </RootNodeTemplate>
  </asp:SiteMapPath>
```

This markup adds a `LinkButton` control to the `SiteMapPath` control and sets its `Text` property to the corresponding `SiteMapNode` element's `Title` property. When the `LinkButton` is clicked, a postback happens and the control's `Command` event fires, triggering the `LinkButton1_Command` event handler. The `Url` property of the `SiteMapNode` is passed to this event handler through the `CommandArgument` property. In the event handler, you could do the required server-side processing and then send the user on to the page he or she requested with the `Response.Redirect` call.

Programmatic Navigation

When it comes to using sitemaps, you are not limited to declarative code binding; you can also use the site navigation-related classes programmatically to display navigation hierarchies. You can use programmatic navigation specifically in these two scenarios:

- **To change the display of the page:** For example, you can retrieve the current node information and use that to configure details such as the page heading and title.
- **To implement different navigation logic:** For example, you might want to display just a portion of the full list of child nodes for the current page in a newsreader, or you might want to create previous/next navigation buttons.

The sitemap API is remarkably straightforward. To use it, you need to work with two classes from the `System.Web` namespace. The starting point is the `SiteMap` class, which provides the following static properties.

Property	Description
`CurrentNode`	Retrieves a `SiteMapNode` object for the current page.
`RootNode`	Retrieves a `SiteMapNode` object that starts from the root node and the rest of the site's navigation structure.
`Provider`	Retrieves the default `SiteMapProvider` for the current sitemap.
`Providers`	Retrieves a collection of available, named `SiteMapProvider` objects.

The `SiteMap` class is an in-memory representation of the site's navigation structure. This is a great class for programmatically working around the hierarchical structure of your site. Both the `CurrentNode` and `RootNode` properties of the `SiteMap` class return a `SiteMapNode` object. Using the `SiteMapNode`, you can retrieve information from the sitemap, including the title, description, and URL values. You can branch out to consider related nodes using the navigational properties in the following table.

Property	Description
`ParentNode`	Returns the node one level up in the navigation hierarchy, which contains the current node. On the root node, this returns a null reference.
`ChildNodes`	Provides a collection of all the child nodes. Before calling this property, make sure to check the `HasChildNodes` property to determine if there are child nodes.
`PreviousSibling`	Returns the previous node that's at the same level (or a null reference if no such node exists).
`NextSibling`	Returns the next node that's at the same level (or a null reference if no such node exists).

Note that you can also search for nodes using the methods of the current `SiteMapProvider` object, which is available through the `SiteMap.Provider` static property. For example, the `SiteMap.Provider.FindSiteMapNode()` method allows you to search for a node by its URL.

To see this in action, consider the following code, which configures two labels on a page to show the heading and description information retrieved from the current node:

```
protected void Page_Load(object sender, EventArgs e)
{
  lblHeader.Text = SiteMap.CurrentNode.Title;
  lblDescription.Text = SiteMap.CurrentNode.Description;
}
```

The next example is a little more ambitious. It implements the previous/next links, which allow the user to traverse an entire set of subnodes. The code checks for the existence of sibling nodes, and if there are no nodes in the required position, it simply hides the links.

```
protected void Page_Load(object sender, EventArgs e)
{
  if (SiteMap.CurrentNode.NextSibling != null)
  {
    lnkNext.NavigateUrl = SiteMap.CurrentNode.NextSibling.Url;
    lnkNext.Visible = true;
  }
  else
  {
    lnkNext.Visible = false;
  }
}
```

Binding to Other Controls

The `TreeView` and `MenuView` are two navigation controls that show hierarchical navigation information. However, you are not limited to these two controls — you can also use any ASP.NET control that supports data binding, from the `ListBox` to the `GridView`. For example, you can bind the navigation information to a template in a rich data control and use a data-binding expression to extract the title, description, and URL information. Listing 7-4 provides an example with a `GridView`.

Listing 7-4: Binding a GridView Control with SiteMapDataSource

```
<%@ Page Language="C#" %>
<html xmlns="http://www.w3.org/1999/xhtml">
<head runat="server">
  <title>Binding a GridView with the SiteMapDataSource control</title>
</head>
<body>
  <form id="form1" runat="server">
    <div>
      <asp:SiteMapDataSource runat="Server" ID="SiteMapDataSource1" />
      <asp:GridView ID="gridNavigationLinks" runat="server"
        DataSourceID="SiteMapDataSource1" AutoGenerateColumns="false"
        ShowHeader="False" BackColor="Linen" CellPadding="5">
        <Columns>
          <asp:TemplateField>
            <ItemTemplate>
              <a href='<%# Eval("Url") %>'><%# Eval("Title") %></a>
              <br/>
              <%# Eval("Description") %>
            </ItemTemplate>
          </asp:TemplateField>
        </Columns>
      </asp:GridView>
    </div>
  </form>
</body>
</html>
```

The only limitation in this example is that it shows links nested underneath the current page. It does not provide links to travel back up. You would need to add other controls to provide this functionality. You can use the `SiteMapPath` control along with the `GridView`, or you can use the SiteMap API. For example, you can use a `LinkButton` that, when clicked, runs this code to go up one level in the hierarchy:

```
protected void cmdGoUp_Click(object sender, EventArgs e)
{
  Response.Redirect(SiteMap.CurrentNode.ParentNode.Url);
}
```

Unfortunately, you have no way to bind to nodes further down the hierarchy, because the `SiteMapDataSource` control does not support the XPath syntax. However, you can embed a nested control and bind it programmatically.

Creating Custom Attributes for a Sitemap

In the sitemaps you have seen so far, the only information provided for a node is the title, description, and URL. This is the bare minimum of information that you will want to use. However, the schema for the XML sitemap is open, which means that you are free to insert custom attributes with your own data.

You might want to insert additional node data for a number of reasons. This additional information might be descriptive information that you intend to display, or contextual information that describes how the link should work. For example, you could add attributes that specify a target frame or indicate that a link should be opened in a pop-up window. The only catch is that it is up to you to act on the information later. In other words, you need to configure your user interface so that it uses this extra information.

As an example, the following code shows a sitemap that uses a target attribute to indicate the frame where the link should be opened. This technique is useful if you are using frames-based navigation rather than a master page. In this example, one link is set with a target of `_blank` so that it will open in a new pop-up browser window:

```
<siteMap xmlns="http://schemas.microsoft.com/AspNet/SiteMap-File-1.0" >
  <siteMapNode title="Home" description="Root" url="~/Default.aspx">
    <siteMapNode title="Products" description="Products"
      url="~/Products.aspx" target="_blank" />
    ...
  </siteMapNode>
</siteMap>
```

Now in your code, you have several options. If you are using a template in your navigation control, you can bind directly to the new attribute. Here is an example with the `GridView` as the data-bound control:

```
<asp:GridView ID="gridNavigationLinks" runat="server"
  DataSourceID="SiteMapDataSource1" AutoGenerateColumns="false" BackColor="Linen">
  <Columns>
    <asp:TemplateField>
      <ItemTemplate>
        <a href='<%# Eval("Url") %>' target='<%# Eval("[target]") %>'>
          <%#Eval("Title") %>
        </a>
```

```
          <br />
          <%# Eval("Description") %>
        </ItemTemplate>
      </asp:TemplateField>
    </Columns>
  </asp:GridView>
```

The one trick in this example is that you need to use square brackets around the attribute name to indicate that the value is being looked up (by name) in the data item's indexer.

If your navigation control does not support templates, you will need to find another approach. Both the `TreeView` and `Menu` controls expose an event that fires when an individual item is bound (`TreeNodeDataBound` and `MenuItemDataBound`). You can then customize the current item. To apply the new target, use this code:

```
protected void tvwNavigationLinks_TreeNodeDataBound(object sender,
  TreeNodeEventArgs e)
{
  e.Node.Target = ((SiteMapNode)e.Node.DataItem)["target"];
}
```

Notice that you cannot retrieve the custom attribute from a strongly typed property. Instead, you retrieve it by name using the `SiteMapNode` indexer. Note that you can also create a custom `SiteMapProvider` that returns instances of a custom `SiteMapNode`-derived class. However, a significant amount of extra code is required, and as a result it is often not worth the trouble.

Creating a Custom Sitemap Provider

The built-in ASP.NET site navigation has a limitation in that it ships with one and only sitemap provider (`XmlSiteMapProvider`) that is included in the box with ASP.NET 2.0. This means that the sitemaps must be stored in XML files. So, if you need to store sitemaps in external storage such as a database, the default approach does not work. However, you can overcome this limitation by creating a custom sitemap provider and registering that as the default provider. Within the implementation of the custom sitemap provider, you can decide where to get the sitemap's data. You might choose to create a custom sitemap provider for several reasons:

- You need to store sitemap information in a different data source (such as a relational database).
- You need to store sitemap information with a different schema from the XML format expected by ASP.NET. This is most likely if you have an existing system in place for storing sitemaps.
- You need to generate a different sitemap depending on the current logged-on user, the query string parameters, and so on.
- You need to change one of the limitations in the `XmlSiteMapProvider` implementation. For example, maybe you want the ability to have nodes with duplicate URLs.

You have two choices when implementing a custom sitemap provider. All sitemap providers are derived from the abstract base class `SiteMapProvider` in the `System.Web` namespace. You can derive from this class to implement a new provider from scratch. However, if you want to keep the same logic but use a different data store, just derive from the `StaticSiteMapProvider` class instead. It gives you a basic implementation of many methods, including the logic for node storing and searching. For the purposes of this book, you will see a custom provider (derived from the `StaticSiteMapProvider` class) that lets you store sitemap information in a database. Figure 7-6 shows the architecture of the solution that uses the custom sitemap provider to store and retrieve sitemap information from a database.

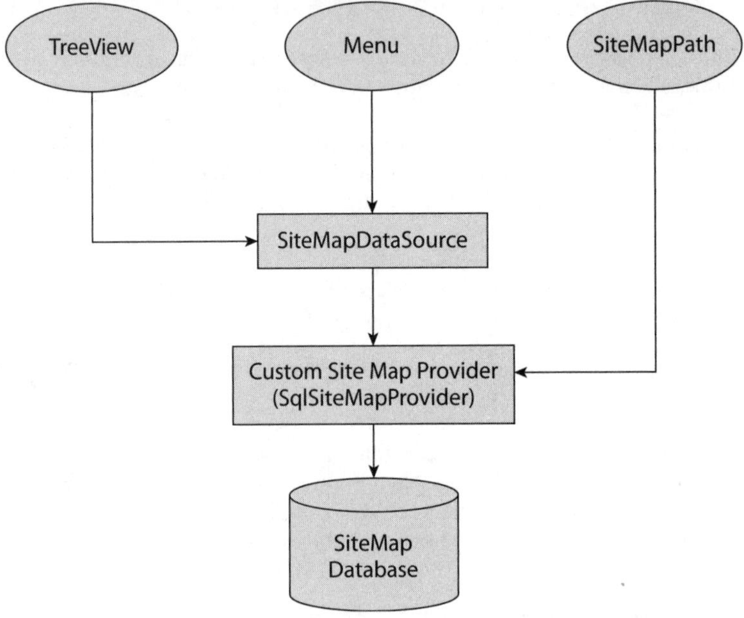

Figure 7-6

The next section starts by exploring the database required to store the sitemap information.

Storing Sitemap Information in a Database

In this example, all navigation links are stored in a single database table. Because databases do not lend themselves easily to hierarchical data, you need to be a little crafty. In this example, each navigation link is connected to a parent link in the same table, except for the root node. This means that although the navigational links are flattened into one table, you can recreate the correct structure by starting with the home page and then searching for the subset of rows at each level.

The following table shows the schema of the SiteMap table.

Column Name	Data Type	Length	AllowNull	Description
ID	`Int`	4	No	Represents the unique ID of the node
Title	`Varchar`	32	Yes	Represents the `title` attribute of the sitemap node
Description	`Varchar`	512	Yes	Represents the `description` attribute of the sitemap node

Column Name	Data Type	Length	AllowNull	Description
Url	Varchar	512	Yes	Represents the url attribute of the sitemap node
Roles	Varchar	512	Yes	Represents the roles that can see this node
Parent	Int	4	Yes	Represents the node ID of the parent node

For reasons of maintainability and abstraction, the sitemap provider will not directly access the SiteMap table. Instead it will invoke a stored procedure that returns the required data, providing some added flexibility and potentially allowing you to store your navigation information with a different schema, as long as you return a table with the expected column names from your stored procedure. For the purposes of this example, a stored procedure named `GetSiteMap` is declared as follows:

```
CREATE PROCEDURE [dbo].[GetSiteMap] AS
  SELECT [ID], [Title], [Description], [Url], [Roles], [Parent]
  FROM [SiteMap] ORDER BY [ID]
GO
```

Creating the SiteMap Provider

Because this sitemap provider does not change the underlying logic of sitemap navigation, you can derive from `StaticSiteMapProvider` instead of deriving from `SiteMapProvider` and re-implementing all the tracking and navigation behavior (which is a much more tedious task).

Here is the class declaration for the provider:

```
public class SqlSiteMapProvider : StaticSiteMapProvider
{ ... }
```

The first step is to override the `Initialize()` method to get all the information you need from the Web.config file. The `Initialize()` method gives you access to the configuration element that defines the sitemap provider.

In this example, your provider needs three pieces of information:

- The connection string for the database.
- The name of the stored procedure that returns the sitemap.
- The provider name for the database. This allows you to use provider agnostic coding, using which you can support SQL Server, Oracle, or another database equally easily, as long as there is a .NET provider factory installed.

You can configure your web site to use the custom provider (`SqlSiteMapProvider`) and supply the required three pieces of information using the `<siteMap>` section of the `Web.config` file as follows:

```
<siteMap enabled="true" defaultProvider="AspNetSqlSiteMapProvider">
  <providers>
    <add name="AspNetSqlSiteMapProvider" type="SqlSiteMapProvider"
      securityTrimmingEnabled="true"
      connectionStringName="SiteMapConnectionString"
      sqlCacheDependency="CommandNotification" />
  </providers>
</siteMap>
```

Now in your provider, you simply need to retrieve these three pieces of information and store them for later. Listing 7-5 shows the code of the `SqlSiteMapProvider` class.

Listing 7-5: Implementation of the SqlSiteMapProvider

```
using System;
using System.Web;
using System.Data.SqlClient;
using System.Collections.Specialized;
using System.Configuration;
using System.Web.Configuration;
using System.Collections.Generic;
using System.Configuration.Provider;
using System.Security.Permissions;
using System.Data.Common;
using System.Data;
using System.Web.Caching;

public class SqlSiteMapProvider : StaticSiteMapProvider
{
  private const string _cacheDependencyName = "SiteMapCacheDependency";
  private string _connectionString;
  private bool _dependencyRequested = false;
  private int _indexID, _indexTitle, _indexUrl, _indexDesc,
    _indexRoles, _indexParent;
  private Dictionary<int, SiteMapNode> _nodes =
    new Dictionary<int, SiteMapNode>(16);
  private readonly object _lock = new object();
  private SiteMapNode _root;

  public override void Initialize (string name, NameValueCollection config)
  {
    //Call the base class's Initialize method
    base.Initialize(name, config);
    string connectionStringName = config["connectionStringName"];
    _connectionString = WebConfigurationManager.ConnectionStrings
      [connectionStringName].ConnectionString;
    //Initialize SQL cache dependency info
    string dependency = config["sqlCacheDependency"];
    if (!String.IsNullOrEmpty(dependency))
    {
      if (String.Equals(dependency, "CommandNotification",
        StringComparison.InvariantCultureIgnoreCase))
      {
        SqlDependency.Start(_connectionString);
```

```
        _dependencyRequested = true;
      }
    }
  }

  public override SiteMapNode BuildSiteMap()
  {
    lock (_lock)
    {
      //Return immediately if this method has been called before
      if (_root != null)
        return _root;
      //Query the database for site map nodes
      SqlConnection connection = new SqlConnection(_connectionString);
      try
      {
        string storedProcedure = "GetSiteMap";
        SqlCommand command = new SqlCommand(storedProcedure, connection);
        command.CommandType = CommandType.StoredProcedure;
        //Create a SQL cache dependency if specified in the config
        SqlCacheDependency dependency = null;
        if (_dependencyRequested)
          dependency = new SqlCacheDependency(command);
        connection.Open();
        SqlDataReader reader = command.ExecuteReader();
        _indexID = reader.GetOrdinal("ID");
        _indexUrl = reader.GetOrdinal("Url");
        _indexTitle = reader.GetOrdinal("Title");
        _indexDesc = reader.GetOrdinal("Description");
        _indexRoles = reader.GetOrdinal("Roles");
        _indexParent = reader.GetOrdinal("Parent");
        if (reader.Read())
        {
          //Create the root SiteMapNode and add it to the site map
          _root = CreateSiteMapNodeFromDataReader(reader);
          AddNode(_root, null);
          //Build a tree of SiteMapNodes underneath the root node
          while (reader.Read())
          {
            //Create another site map node and add it to the site map
            SiteMapNode node = CreateSiteMapNodeFromDataReader(reader);
            AddNode(node, GetParentNodeFromDataReader(reader));
          }
          //Use the SQL cache dependency
          if (dependency != null)
          {
            HttpRuntime.Cache.Insert(_cacheDependencyName, new object(),
              dependency, Cache.NoAbsoluteExpiration, Cache.NoSlidingExpiration,
              CacheItemPriority.NotRemovable,
              new CacheItemRemovedCallback(OnSiteMapChanged));
          }
        }
      }
      finally
```

(continued)

Listing 7-5: *(continued)*

```
        {
          connection.Close();
        }
        //Return the root SiteMapNode
        return _root;
      }
    }

    protected override SiteMapNode GetRootNodeCore()
    {
      lock (_lock)
      {
        BuildSiteMap();
        return _root;
      }
    }

    private SiteMapNode CreateSiteMapNodeFromDataReader (DbDataReader reader)
    {
      if (reader.IsDBNull (_indexID))
        throw new ProviderException ("Invalid Node ID");
      //Get the node ID from the DataReader
      int id = reader.GetInt32 (_indexID);
      if (_nodes.ContainsKey(id))
        throw new ProviderException("Duplicate Node ID");
      //Get title, URL, description, and roles from the DataReader
      string title = reader.IsDBNull (_indexTitle) ? null : reader.GetString
        (_indexTitle).Trim ();
      string url = reader.IsDBNull (_indexUrl) ? null : reader.GetString
        (_indexUrl).Trim ();
      string description = reader.IsDBNull (_indexDesc) ? null : reader.GetString
        (_indexDesc).Trim ();
      string roles = reader.IsDBNull(_indexRoles) ? null :
        reader.GetString(_indexRoles).Trim();
      //If roles were specified, turn the list into a string array
      string[] rolelist = null;
      if (!String.IsNullOrEmpty(roles))
        rolelist = roles.Split(new char[] { ',', ';' }, 512);
      SiteMapNode node = new SiteMapNode(this, id.ToString(), url, title,
        description, rolelist, null, null, null);
      _nodes.Add(id, node);
      return node;
    }

    private SiteMapNode GetParentNodeFromDataReader(DbDataReader reader)
    {
      if (reader.IsDBNull (_indexParent))
        throw new ProviderException ("Missing parent ID");
      //Get the parent ID from the DataReader
      int pid = reader.GetInt32(_indexParent);
      if (!_nodes.ContainsKey(pid))
```

```
          throw new ProviderException("Invalid parent ID");
        //Return the parent SiteMapNode
        return _nodes[pid];
      }

      void OnSiteMapChanged(string key, object item, CacheItemRemovedReason reason)
      {
        lock (_lock)
        {
          if (key == _cacheDependencyName && reason ==
            CacheItemRemovedReason.DependencyChanged)
          {
            //Refresh the site map
            Clear();
            _nodes.Clear();
            _root = null;
          }
        }
      }
    }
```

As you can see, the `SqlSiteMapProvider` class is derived from the `StaticSiteMapProvider` class, which exposes the following methods that need to be overridden from the `SqlSiteMapProvider`:

- `BuildSiteMap()`
- `Initialize()`
- `GetRootNodeCode()`

The `Initialize()` method, which is present in all providers, is a special one that ASP.NET calls after loading the provider. ASP.NET passes the `Initialize()` method a `NameValueCollection` named `config` that contains all the configuration attributes (and their values) found in the configuration element that registered the provider. The `Initialize()` method's job is to apply configuration settings and do anything else required to initialize the provider. The overridden `Initialize()` method of the `SqlSiteMapProvider` performs the following tasks:

- Calls the base class's `Initialize()` method, which, among other things, processes the `securityTrimmingEnabled` configuration attribute, if present.
- Processes the `connectionStringName` and `sqlCacheDependency` configuration attributes, if present.

When you invoke the base class's `Initialize()` method, you supply the name and `config` collection as its arguments, as shown in the following code:

```
public override void Initialize (string name, NameValueCollection config)
{
  base.Initialize(name, config);
  string connectionStringName = config["connectionStringName"];
  _connectionString = WebConfigurationManager.ConnectionStrings
    [connectionStringName].ConnectionString;
```

The `sqlCacheDependency` attribute is the one that allows you to take advantage of `SqlSiteMapProvider` control's capability to refresh the sitemap if the underlying database changes. If the sitemap lives in a SQL Server 2005 database, you set `sqlCacheDependency` equal to `"CommandNotification"` instead. For the purposes of this example, the `sqlCacheDependency` is set to `"CommandNotification"`:

```
    //Initialize SQL cache dependency info
    string dependency = config["sqlCacheDependency"];
    if (!String.IsNullOrEmpty(dependency))
    {
      if (String.Equals(dependency, "CommandNotification",
        StringComparison.InvariantCultureIgnoreCase))
      {
        SqlDependency.Start(_connectionString);
        _dependencyRequested = true;
      }
    }
  }
```

If the `sqlCacheDependency` is set to `"CommandNotification"`, you then invoke the `Start()` method of the `SqlDependency` class to start the listener so that it begins monitoring for the dependency change notifications.

The real work that the provider does is in the `BuildSiteMap()` method, which constructs the `SiteMap Node` objects that make up the navigation tree. This method is called by ASP.NET sometime after the provider is loaded to build the sitemap, which is simply a collection of `SiteMapNode` objects linked together to form a tree. Each `SiteMapNode` represents one node in the sitemap and is distinguished by the following properties: `Title`, which specifies the text that a navigation control displays for the node; `Url`, which specifies the URL the user is sent to when the node is clicked; `Description`, which specifies the descriptive text that's displayed if the cursor hovers over the node; and `Roles`, which specifies the role or roles that are permitted to view the node if security trimming is enabled ("*" if anyone can view it). Multiple roles can be specified using commas or semicolons as separators. In the lifetime of an application, you will typically construct the `SiteMapNode` once and reuse it multiple times. To make that possible, the provider needs to store the sitemap in memory, and it is done using a private variable:

```
private SiteMapNode _root;
```

The root `SiteMapNode` contains the first level of nodes, which then contain the next level of nodes, and so on. Thus, the root node is the starting point for the whole navigation tree.

You override the `BuildSiteMap()` method to actually create the sitemap. The first step is to check if the sitemap has already been generated, and if not, to create it. Because multiple pages could share the same instance of the sitemap provider, it is a good idea to lock the object before you update any shared information (such as the in-memory navigation tree). Since all provider code outside the `Initialize()` method must be thread-safe, `SqlSiteMapProvider` wraps everything in `BuildSiteMap` in a `lock` statement in order to serialize concurrent thread accesses:

```
public override SiteMapNode BuildSiteMap()
{
  lock (_lock)
  {
    //Return immediately if this method has been called before
```

```
    if (_root != null)
      return _root;
```

Next, you need to create the SqlConnection and SqlCommand objects, and use them to execute the stored procedure that returns the navigation details from the SiteMap table:

```
  SqlConnection connection = new SqlConnection(_connectionString);
  try
  {
    string storedProcedure = "GetSiteMap";
    SqlCommand command = new SqlCommand(storedProcedure, connection);
    command.CommandType = CommandType.StoredProcedure;
```

In addition to querying the database and building the sitemap, BuildSiteMap() also creates the basic infrastructure that enables SqlSiteMapProvider to refresh the sitemap if the sitemap database changes. If the configuration element that registered the provider contains a sqlCacheDependency attribute with the value set to "CommandNotification" attribute, you then create a SQL Server 2005-compatible SqlCacheDependency object that wraps the SqlCommand used to query the sitemap database:

```
    //Create a SQL cache dependency if specified in the config
    SqlCacheDependency dependency = null;
    if (_dependencyRequested)
      dependency = new SqlCacheDependency(command);
```

Now, execute the stored procedure and get the results into a SqlDataReader object. The next step is to navigate the SqlDataReader object to create the SiteMapNode objects, beginning with the root node. Before that, you get the column index for each of the fields returned through the SqlDataReader into private variables so that you can use them for retrieving data from the SqlDataReader object later:

```
    connection.Open();
    SqlDataReader reader = command.ExecuteReader();
    _indexID = reader.GetOrdinal("ID");
    _indexUrl = reader.GetOrdinal("Url");
    _indexTitle = reader.GetOrdinal("Title");
    _indexDesc = reader.GetOrdinal("Description");
    _indexRoles = reader.GetOrdinal("Roles");
    _indexParent = reader.GetOrdinal("Parent");
```

You convert a specific row in the SqlDataReader to a sitemap node, using a helper function named CreateSiteMapNodeFromDataReader() that simply constructs a SiteMapNode object based on the data of the current row in the SqlDataReader:

```
    if (reader.Read())
    {
      //Create the root SiteMapNode and add it to the site map
      _root = CreateSiteMapNodeFromDataReader(reader);
```

Once you have the root SiteMapNode, you can then add that to the collection maintained by the StaticSiteMapProvider class by invoking the AddNode() method:

```
      AddNode(_root, null);
```

Once the root sitemap node is created and added, you need to do the same for the rest of the rows contained in the `SqlDataReader` object:

```
//Build a tree of SiteMapNodes underneath the root node
while (reader.Read())
{
  //Create another site map node and add it to the site map
   SiteMapNode node = CreateSiteMapNodeFromDataReader(reader);
   AddNode(node, GetParentNodeFromDataReader(reader));
 }
```

For the root node, obviously there is no parent node, but for the rest of the nodes, you retrieve the parent node using another helper function named the `GetParentNodeFromDataReader()` method that looks up the parent ID of the current node and returns the corresponding parent sitemap node.

Finally, the `BuildSiteMap()` then inserts a trivial object into the ASP.NET application cache, and creates a dependency between that object and the database by including the `SqlCacheDependency` in the call to `Cache.Insert()`.

```
//Use the SQL cache dependency
if (dependency != null)
{
  HttpRuntime.Cache.Insert(_cacheDependencyName, new object(), dependency,
    Cache.NoAbsoluteExpiration, Cache.NoSlidingExpiration,
    CacheItemPriority.NotRemovable,
    new CacheItemRemovedCallback(OnSiteMapChanged));
}
```

The final parameter to `Cache.Insert()` instructs ASP.NET to call the provider's `OnSiteMapChanged()` method if the `SqlCacheDependency` triggers a cache removal—that is, if the sitemap database changes. `OnSiteMapChanged()` clears out the old sitemap and calls `BuildSiteMap` to build a new one.

It may seem odd that `SqlSiteMapProvider` *uses the ASP.NET application cache when there is really nothing for it to cache. Note that the object it inserts into the cache is simply a marker that contains no meaningful data, but doing so enables* `SqlSiteMapProvider` *to capitalize on a key feature of ASP.NET 2.0's* `SqlCacheDependency` *object. Placing a marker object accompanied by a* `SqlCacheDependency` *in the cache and registering for cache removal callbacks is a convenient way to leverage the new features of* `SqlCacheDependency`*. If the underlying database changes, the marker object is removed from the cache, and the callback method is called and can take whatever action it deems appropriate—in this case, refreshing the sitemap.*

Finally, return the root sitemap node object to the caller:

```
return _root;
```

This completes the example. You can now request the same pages you created earlier, using the new sitemap provider (as configured in the `Web.config` file). The custom provider plugs in easily and neatly. The new information will flow through the custom provider and arrive in your pages without any indication that the underlying plumbing has changed.

You can deploy SqlSiteMapProvider by copying SqlSiteMapProvider.cs to your web site's App_Code directory. As mentioned previously, source code files deployed in the App_Code directory are automatically compiled and made available to all the ASP.NET pages. Once the provider is deployed, you need to register it and make it the default sitemap provider. To test this, create a simple ASP.NET page that leverages the SqlSiteMapProvider. Before that, modify your Web.config to look as shown in Listing 7-6.

Listing 7-6: Configuration Settings in the Web.config File

```
<?xml version="1.0"?>
<configuration>
  <connectionStrings>
    <add name="SiteMapConnectionString"
      connectionString="server=localhost;uid=sa;pwd=thiru;database=SiteMapDB;"
      providerName="System.Data.SqlClient" />
  </connectionStrings>
  <system.web>
    <siteMap enabled="true" defaultProvider="AspNetSqlSiteMapProvider">
      <providers>
        <add name="AspNetSqlSiteMapProvider" type="SqlSiteMapProvider"
          securityTrimmingEnabled="true"
          connectionStringName="SiteMapConnectionString"
          sqlCacheDependency="CommandNotification" />
      </providers>
    </siteMap>
    <caching>
      <sqlCacheDependency enabled="true" />
    </caching>
  </system.web>
</configuration>
```

Now that the required settings are added to the configuration file, create a simple ASP.NET page, as shown in Listing 7-7.

Listing 7-7: Displaying SQL Server Sitemap Information in an ASP.NET Page

```
<%@ Page Language="C#" %>
<html xmlns="http://www.w3.org/1999/xhtml" >
<head runat="server">
  <title>Loading Site Map Information from a SQL Server Database</title>
</head>
<body>
  <form id="form1" runat="server">
    <div>
      <asp:SiteMapDataSource ID="SiteMapDataSource1" runat="server" />
    </div>
    <asp:TreeView ID="tvwNavigationLinks" runat="server"
      DataSourceID="SiteMapDataSource1">
    </asp:TreeView>
  </form>
</body>
</html>
```

In a browser, navigate to the page described in Listing 7-7, and you will see the output shown in Figure 7-7.

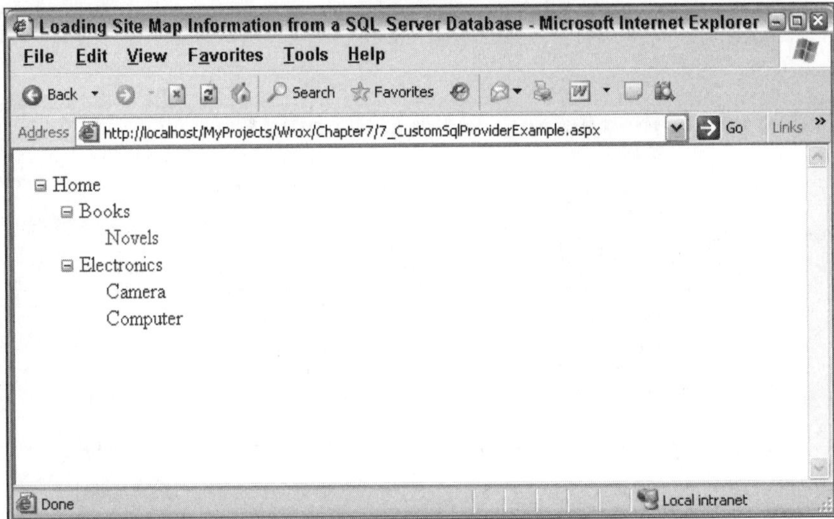

Figure 7-7

Now, go back to the SiteMap table in the SiteMapDB and modify the data using SQL Server Management Studio. If you refresh the page using the browser, you will notice that the `TreeView` displays the latest data from the database because of the automatic reloading of the sitemap that is enabled through the `SqlCacheDependency` object.

Using Multiple Sitemaps and Sitemap Providers

In some situations, you may want to have more than one sitemap and more than one sitemap provider. This flexibility is overkill for most web sites, but it can be very helpful in complex situations. For example, if different departments are responsible for different parts of the web site, each can create its own sitemap, and the various maps then can be linked together. If the different sitemaps are in different formats, then the ability to use two or more sitemap providers comes into play.

In the simplest scenario, you will use the default `XmlSiteMapProvider` with two or more sitemaps. Obviously, each sitemap has to be in the proper XML format. There is one parent sitemap, `Web.sitemap` in most cases, which links to one or more child sitemaps with a `<siteMapNode>` element, like this:

```
<siteMapNode siteMapFile="Childsitemap.sitemap" />
```

The end result, in terms of what the `SiteMap` object sees, is as if the content of the child sitemap were inserted into the parent sitemap at the indicated location. To use a custom sitemap provider for a child sitemap, you set the provider attribute of the `<siteMapNode>` to the name of the custom sitemap provider:

```
<siteMapNode provider="CustomProviderName" />
```

The above custom provider must also be included in `Web.config` in addition to the default `XmlSiteMapProvider`:

```
<siteMap defaultProvider="XmlSiteMapProvider">
  <providers>
    <add name="CustomProviderName" type="CustomProviderClass"
      siteMapFile = Childsitemap.sitemap />
  </providers>
</siteMap>
```

Configuring Site Navigation to Use Security Trimmings

By default, site navigation does not use security trimming. Regardless of what user is visiting the site, and regardless of the authorization rules defined, each user is shown all of the sections in the sitemap when viewing the sitemap data through a `TreeView` or a `Menu` web control. By turning on security trimmings, the site navigation system automatically limits the results based on the currently logged-on user and the authorization of the pages referenced by the `<siteMapNode>` elements in the sitemap.

> **The security trimming feature of the ASP.NET 2.0 site navigation enables you to ensure that only those sitemap nodes that the currently logged-on user has authorization to visit are available. That means the site's `TreeView` or `Menu` will contain just those sections accessible by the currently logged-on user.**

The site navigation settings can be configured through the `Web.config` file using the following pattern:

```
<siteMap defaultProvider="XmlSiteMapProvider" enabled="true">
  <providers>
    <add name="XmlSiteMapProvider" description="Default SiteMap provider."
      type="System.Web.XmlSiteMapProvider" siteMapFile="siteMapFileName"
       securityTrimmingEnabled="true" />
  </providers>
</siteMap>
```

As you can see from the previous snippet, the site navigation feature uses `XmlSiteMapProvider`, which obtains sitemap information from the XML-formatted sitemap file `Web.sitemap`. You can change what provider is used, or tweak the default provider's default settings, through the `Web.config` file. To customize the default provider's settings, simply add a new provider that uses the same type as the default provider (`System.Web.XmlSiteMapProvider`), customizing the settings as needed. The snippet of markup shown above illustrates customizing two of the `XmlSiteMapProvider`'s settings:

- ❑ The `siteMapFile` attribute specifies the filename of the sitemap file used by the provider. As mentioned previously, this value is `Web.sitemap` by default. You can customize the filename here, if you like. Regardless, it is recommended that you ensure that the sitemap filename ends with the `.sitemap` extension, since this extension is protected by the ASP.NET engine by default, thereby preventing web visitors from viewing the sitemap file.
- ❑ The `securityTrimmingEnabled` attribute indicates whether or not security trimming is used. To utilize security trimming, set this to `true`, as shown in the previous snippet.

That is all there is to enabling security with the site navigation system. With that single change, the site navigation system will be intelligent enough to return the appropriate sections, based on the currently logged-on user and the authorization settings defined for the URLs in the `<siteMapNode>` elements.

Summary

This chapter introduced the new navigation mechanics that ASP.NET 2.0 provides. At the core of the new navigation capabilities is the power to detail the navigation structure in an XML file, which can then be utilized by various navigation controls — such as the new `TreeView`, `Menu`, and `SiteMapPath` controls. The powerful functionality that the new navigation capabilities provide saves you a tremendous amount of coding time.

In addition to showing you the core infrastructure for navigation in ASP.NET 2.0, this chapter also described the new `TreeView` and `SiteMapPath` controls and how to use them throughout your applications. The great thing about these new controls is that, right out of the box, they can richly display your navigation hierarchy and allow the end user to work through the site easily. In addition, these controls are easily changeable, so you can go beyond the standard appearance and functionality that they provide.

This chapter also demonstrated the extensibility of the site navigation system by showing how to create a custom sitemap provider that uses SQL Server as the sitemap store. Finally, this chapter discussed the advanced concepts of site navigation, such as using multiple sitemaps and multiple providers for a web site and configuring security trimming with site navigation.

8

Displaying and Editing Data Using Templates

In the last few chapters, you saw how to use the data source controls to perform queries, both with and without the assistance of a custom data access class. Along the way, you used some of ASP.NET'stemplates, such as the templates supplied with a `GridView`. However, you have not delved into all the features of these templates. In this chapter, you will take a closer look at `GridView`, `DetailsView`, and `FormView`, and learn how to fine-tune formatting with templates and take control of features such as displaying, selection, and editing. Specifically, this chapter will cover:

- How to explicitly define columns using `GridView`
- How to format the `GridView`
- How to format fields in a `GridView` and apply styles
- How to select a row using a `GridView`
- How to leverage built-in templates supplied by the `GridView`
- How to perform editing and handle events in a template
- How to display summaries using a `GridView`'s footer
- How to work with `DetailsView` and `FormView`

ASP.NET 2.0 Templated Controls

ASP.NET 2.0 still provides the templated controls that were introduced with ASP.NET 1.x. These include the `DataGrid`, `DataList`, and `Repeater`. With ASP.NET 2.0, these controls should not be used except for backward-compatibility reasons.

- `DataGrid`: The `DataGrid` has been completely replaced by the `GridView`, which provides the same set of features (and more) and simplifies the coding mode.
- `DataList`: The `DataList` has been mostly replaced by the `GridView`, which provides a similar set of templates and a much simpler coding model. However, you can still use the `DataList` if you want to create a multicolumn table, where each cell is a separate record. `GridView` does not support this unusual design, because it forces every record to occupy a separate row.
- `Repeater`: The `Repeater` still plays the same role as a bare-bones template-based control. Although it does not provide many features or frills, you might use it to create customized data displays. The `Repeater` does not add any built-in elements, so you are not locked into a table-based format. However, getting the result you want takes a lot of work because the `Repeater` does not include higher-level features such as selection and editing.

The chapter focuses exclusively on the new ASP.NET 2.0 data controls: `GridView`, `DetailsView`, and `FormView`. If you are interested in using the older 1.x controls, please refer to the online documentation.

> **The `DataGrid` is still available in ASP.NET 2.0, and it now supports binding to a data source control. Although you cannot find it in the Toolbox in Visual Studio 2005, you can add it by right-clicking the Toolbox and selecting Choose Items. As a rule of thumb, the `DataGrid` should be used only for backward compatibility with existing ASP.NET web sites (where it still works quite well). When creating a new web site, use `GridView` instead.**

GridView

`GridView` is an extremely flexible grid control for showing data. It includes a wide range of hard-wired features, including selection, paging, and editing, and it is extensible through templates. The great advantage of the `GridView` over the `DataGrid` is its support for code-free scenarios. Using the `GridView`, you can accomplish many common tasks, such as paging and selection, without writing any code. With the `DataGrid`, you were forced to handle events to implement the same features.

Defining Columns

The `GridView` examples you have seen so far in the previous chapters have set the `AutoGenerateColumns` property to `true`. When this property is set, `GridView` uses reflection to examine that data object and finds all the fields of a record (if you are using `SqlDataSource` control) or properties of a custom object (if you are using `ObjectDataSource` control). It then creates a column for each one, in the order that it finds it.

This automatic column generation is good for creating quick test pages, but it does not give you the flexibility you will usually want. For example, if you want to hide columns, change their order, or configure some aspect of their display, such as the formatting or heading text, the automatic column generation is not sufficient. In all of these cases, you will need to set `AutoGenerateColumns` to `false` and define the columns yourself in the `<Columns>` section of the `GridView` control tag.

It is possible to have `AutoGenerateColumns` set to `true` and also define columns in the `<Columns>` section. In this case, the columns you explicitly defined are added before the auto-generated columns. You can use this technique to create a `GridView` with automatically generated bound columns and a *manually defined column with edit controls. However, for the most flexibility, you will usually want to explicitly define every column.*

Each column can be anyof several different types, as described in the following table. The order of your column tags determines the right-to-left order of columns in the `GridView`.

Column Type	Description
`BoundField`	Displays text from a field in the data source.
`ButtonField`	Displays a button for each item in the list.
`CheckBoxField`	Displays a checkbox for each item in the list. It is used automatically for true/false fields (in SQL Server, these are fields that use the bit data type).
`CommandField`	Provides selection or editing buttons.
`HyperlinkField`	Displays its contents (a field from the data source or static text) as a hyperlink.
`ImageField`	Displays image data from a binary field (providing it can be successfully interpreted as a supported image format).
`TemplateField`	Allows you to specify multiple fields, custom controls, and arbitrary HTML using a custom template. It gives you the highest degree of control but requires the most work.

The most basic column type is the `BoundField`, which binds to one field in the data object. For example, here is the definition for a single data-bound column that displays the ProductID field:

```
<asp:BoundField DataField="ProductID" HeaderText="ID" />
```

This achieves one improvement over the auto-generated column — the header text has been changed from ProductID to just ID. This approach has several advantages:

- You can easily fine-tune your column order, column headings, and other details by tweaking the properties of your column object.
- You can hide columns you do not want to show by removing the column tag. (However, do not overuse this technique, because it is better to cut down on the amount of data you are retrieving if you do not intend to display it). You can also hide columns programmatically. To hide a column, use the `Columns` collection for the `GridView`. For example, setting `GridView1.Columns[2].Visible` to `false` hides the third column. Hidden columns are left out of the rendered HTML altogether.
- Explicitly defined columns are faster than auto-generated columns. That is because auto-generated columns force the `GridView` to reflect on the data source at runtime.
- You can add extra columns to the mix for selecting, editing, and more.

Here is a complete example that shows `GridView` declaration with explicit columns:

Listing 8-1: Using Explicit Columns with GridView

```
<%@ Page Language="C#" %>
<html xmlns="http://www.w3.org/1999/xhtml" >
<head runat="server">
  <title>Using the BoundField for explicitly specifying Columns</title>
</head>
<body>
  <form id="form1" runat="server">
    <div>
      <asp:SqlDataSource ID="productsSource" runat="server"
        ProviderName="System.Data.SqlClient"
        ConnectionString="<%$ ConnectionStrings:AdventureWorks %>"
        SelectCommand="Select ProductID, Name, ProductNumber, DaysToManufacture
        from Production.Product">
      </asp:SqlDataSource>
      <asp:GridView runat="server" DataSourceID="productsSource"
        AutoGenerateColumns="false">
        <Columns>
          <asp:BoundField DataField="ProductID" HeaderText="ID" />
          <asp:BoundField DataField="Name" HeaderText="Name" />
          <asp:BoundField DataField="ProductNumber" HeaderText="Number" />
          <asp:BoundField DataField="DaysToManufacture"
            HeaderText="Days To Manufacture" />
        </Columns>
      </asp:GridView>
    </div>
  </form>
</body>
</html>
```

Here is the output produced by Listing 8-1 when viewed in a browser.

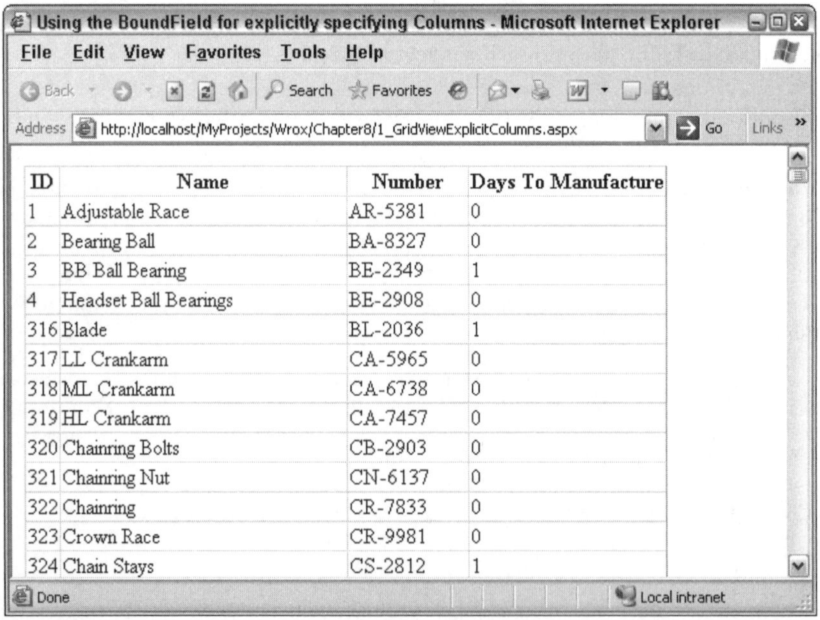
Using the BoundField for explicitly specifying Columns - Microsoft Internet Explorer
File Edit View Favorites Tools Help
Back Search Favorites
Address http://localhost/MyProjects/Wrox/Chapter8/1_GridViewExplicitColumns.aspx
Go Links
ID Name Number Days To Manufacture
1 Adjustable Race AR-5381 0
2 Bearing Ball BA-8327 0
3 BB Ball Bearing BE-2349 1
4 Headset Ball Bearings BE-2908 0
316 Blade BL-2036 1
317 LL Crankarm CA-5965 0
318 ML Crankarm CA-6738 0
319 HL Crankarm CA-7457 0
320 Chainring Bolts CB-2903 0
321 Chainring Nut CN-6137 0
322 Chainring CR-7833 0
323 Crown Race CR-9981 0
324 Chain Stays CS-2812 1
Done
Local intranet

Figure 8-1

When you explicitly declare a bound field, you have the opportunity to set other properties. The following table lists these properties.

Property	Description
`DataField`	The name of the field (for a row) or property (for an object) of the data item that you want to display in this column.
`DataFormatString`	A format string that formats the field. This is useful for getting the right representation of numbers and dates.
`ApplyFormatInEditMode`	If true, the format string will be used to format the value even when it appears in a text box in edit mode. The default is false, which means only the underlying normal will be used (1143.02 instead of $1,143.02).
`FooterText`, `HeaderText`, and `HeaderImageUrl`	Sets the text in the header and footer region of the grid, if this grid has a header (`ShowHeader` is `true`) and footer (`ShowFooter` is `true`). The header is most commonly used for a descriptive label such as the field name, while the footer can contain a dynamically calculated value such as a summary. To show an image in the header instead of text, set the `HeaderImageUrl` property.
`ReadOnly`	If true, the value for this column can't be changed in edit mode. No edit control will be provided. Primary key fields are often read-only.
`InsertVisible`	If false, the value for this column can't be set in insert mode. If you want a column value to be set programmatically or based on a default value defined in the database, you can use this feature.
`Visible`	If false, the column won't be visible in the page (and no HTML will be rendered for it). This property gives you a convenient way to programmatically hide or show specific columns, changing the overall view of the data.
`SortExpression`	An expression that can be appended to a query to perform a sort based on this column. This is always used in conjunction with sorting.
`HtmlEncode`	If true (the default), all text will be HTML encoded to prevent special characters from mangling the page. You could disable HTML encoding if you want to embed a working HTML tag (such as a hyperlink), but this approach isn't safe. It's always a better idea to use HTML encoding on all values and provide other functionality by reacting to `GridView` selection events.
`NullDisplayText`	The text that will be displayed for a null value. The default is an empty string, although you could change this to a hard-coded value, such as "not specified."
`ConvertEmptyStringToNull`	If true, before an edit is committed, all empty strings will be converted to null values.
`ControlStyle`, `HeaderStyle`, `FooterStyle`, and `ItemStyle`	Configures the appearance for just this column, overriding the styles for the row.

Now that you understand the underpinnings of `GridView`, you have still only started to explore its higher level features. In the following sections, you will tackle these topics:

- **Formatting:** How to format rows and data values
- **Selecting:** How to let users select a row in the `GridView` and respond accordingly
- **Templates:** How to take complete control of layout, formatting, and editing by defining templates

Formatting the GridView

Formatting consists of several related tasks. First, you want to ensure that dates, currencies, and other number values are presented in the appropriate way. You handle this job with the `DataFormatString` property. Next, you will want to apply the perfect mix of colors, fonts, borders, and alignment options to each aspect of the grid, from headers to data items. `GridView` supports these features through styles. Finally, you can intercept events, examine row data, and apply formatting to specific data points programmatically. In the following sections, you will consider each of these techniques.

The `GridView` itself also exposes several formatting properties that are self-explanatory and are not covered here. These include `GridLines` (for adding or hiding table borders), `CellPadding` and `CellSpacing` (for controlling the overall spacing between cells), and `Caption` and `CaptionAlign` (for adding a title to the top of the grid).

> **To create a `GridView` that scrolls inside a web page, just place the `GridView` inside a `Panel` control, set the appropriate size for the panel, and set the `Panel.Scrollbars` to `Auto`, `Vertical`, or `Both`.**

Formatting Fields

Each BoundField column provides a `DataFormatString` property that you can use to configure the appearance of numbers and dates using a format string. Format strings are generally made up of a placeholder and format indicator, which are wrapped inside curly brackets. A typical format string looks something like this:

```
{0:C}
```

In this case, the `0` represents the value that will be formatted, and the letter indicates a predetermined format style. In this case, `C` means currency format, which formats a number as a dollar figure (so 3400.34 becomes $3,400.34). Here is a column that uses this format string:

```
<asp:BoundField DataField="Price" HeaderText="Price" DataFormatString="{0:C}" />
```

The following table shows some of the other formatting options for numeric values.

Type	Format String	Example
Currency	`{0:C}`	$7,274.50 Brackets indicate negative values: ($1,234.50) Currency sign is locale-specific: (?1,234.50)
Scientific (Exponential)	`{0:E}`	1.234.50E+004
Percentage	`{0:P}`	45.6%
Fixed Decimal	`{0:F?}`	Depends on the number of decimal places you set. `{0:F3}` would be 123.400. `{0:F0}` would be 123

You can find other examples in the MSDN Help. For date or time values, there is also an extensive list. For example, if you want to write the `BirthDate` value in the format month/day/year (as in 12/01/05), you use the following column:

```
<asp:BoundField DataField="BirthDate" HeaderText="Birth Date"
  DataFormatString="{0:MM/dd/yy}" />
```

The next table shows some more examples.

Type	Format String	Example
Short Date	`{0:d}`	M/d/yyyy (for example: 10/30/2005)
Long Date	`{0:D}`	dddd, MMMM dd, yyyy (for example: Monday, January 30, 2005)
Long Date and Short Time	`{0:f}`	dddd, MMMM dd, yyyy HH:mm aa (for example: Monday, January 30, 2005 10:00 AM)
Long Date and Long Time	`{0:F}`	dddd, MMMM dd, yyyy HH:mm:ss aa (for example: Monday, January 30, 2005 10:00:23 AM)
ISO Sortable Standard	`{0:s}`	yyyy-MM-dd HH:mm:ss (for example: 2005-01-30 10:00:23)
Month and Day	`{0:M}`	MMMM dd (for example: January 30)
General	`{0:G}`	M/d/yyyy HH:mm:ss aa (depends on locale-specific settings) (for example: 10/30/2002 10:00:23 AM)

The format characters are not specific to `GridView`. You can use them with other controls, with data-bound expressions in templates, and as parameters for many methods. For example, the `Decimal` and `DateTime` types expose their own `ToString()` methods that accept a format string, allowing you to format values manually.

Styles

The GridView exposes a rich formatting model that is based on styles. Altogether, you can set eight GridView styles, described as follows.

Style	Description
HeaderStyle	Configures the appearance of the header row that contains column titles, if you've chosen to show it (if ShowHeader is true).
RowStyle	Configures the appearance of every data row.
AlternatingRowStyle	If set, applies additional formatting to every other row. This formatting acts in addition to the RowStyle formatting. For example, if you set a font using RowStyle, it is also applied to alternating rows, unless you explicitly set a different font through the AlternatingRowStyle.
SelectedRowStyle	Configures the appearance of the row that's currently selected. This formatting acts in addition to the RowStyle formatting.
EditRowStyle	Configures the appearance of the row that's in edit mode. This formatting acts in addition to the RowStyle formatting.
EmptyDataRowStyle	Configures the style that's used for the single empty row in the special case where the bound data object contains no rows.
FooterStyle	Configures the appearance of the footer row at the bottom of the GridView, if you've chosen to show it (if ShowFooter is true).
PagerStyle	Configures the appearance of the row with the page links, if you've enabled paging (set AllowPaging to true).

Styles are not simple single-value properties. Instead, each style exposes a Style object that includes properties for choosing colors (ForeColor and BackColor), adding borders (BorderColor, BorderStyle, and BorderWidth), sizing the row (Height and Width), aligning the row (HorizontalAlign and VerticalAlign), and configuring the appearance of text (Font and Wrap). These style properties allow you to refine almost every aspect of an item's appearance. And if you don't want to hard-code all the appearance settings in the web page, you can set the CssClass property of the style object reference to a style sheet class that is defined in a linked style sheet.

Defining Styles

When setting style properties, you can use two similar syntaxes. First, you can use the object-walker syntax to indicate the extended style properties as tag attributes. Here is an example:

```
<asp:GridView runat="server" ID="gridProducts"
  ItemStyle-ForeColor="DarkBlue" ... />
  ...
</asp:GridView>
```

Alternatively, you can add nested tags, as shown here:

```
<asp:GridView runat="server" ID="gridProducts" ...>
  <ItemStyle ForeColor="DarkBlue" ... />
  ...
</asp:GridView>
```

These approaches are equivalent. However, you make one other decision when setting style properties. You can specify global style properties that affect every column in the grid (as in the previous examples), or you can define column-specific styles. To create a column-specific style, you need to add style attributes or a nested tag inside the appropriate column tag, as shown here:

```
<asp:GridView runat="server" ID="gridProducts" ...>
  <Columns>
    <asp:BoundField DataField="ProductID" HeaderText="ID" ItemStyle-Width="30px" />
    ...
  </Columns>
</asp:GridView>
```

Or equivalently, you can use a nested tag:

```
<asp:GridView runat="server" ID="gridProducts" ...>
  <Columns>
    <asp:BoundField DataField="ProductID" HeaderText="ID">
      <ItemStyle Width="30px">
    </asp:BoundField>
    ...
  </Columns>
</asp:GridView>
```

This technique is often used to define specific column widths. If you do not define a specific column width, ASP.NET makes each column just wide enough to fit the data it contains. If values range in size, the width is determined by the largest value or the width of the column header, whichever is larger. However, if the grid is wide enough, you might want to expand a column so that it doesn't appear to be crowded against the adjacent columns. In this case, you need to explicitly define a larger width.

Listing 8-2 shows the completely formatted `GridView` control along with the data source control.

Listing 8-2: Formatting GridView Using Styles

```
<%@ Page Language="C#" %>
<html xmlns="http://www.w3.org/1999/xhtml" >
<head runat="server">
  <title>Formatting GridView using Styles</title>
</head>
<body>
  <form id="form1" runat="server">
    <div>
      <asp:SqlDataSource ID="productsSource" runat="server"
        ProviderName="System.Data.SqlClient"
```

(continued)

Listing 8-2: *(continued)*

```
          ConnectionString="<%$ ConnectionStrings:AdventureWorks %>"
          SelectCommand="Select ProductID, Name, ProductNumber, DaysToManufacture,
          SellStartDate from Production.Product">
        </asp:SqlDataSource>
        <asp:GridView runat="server" ID="gridProducts" DataSourceID="productsSource"
          Font-Names="Verdana" Font-Size="X-Small" ForeColor="#333333"
          CellPadding="4" GridLines="None" AutoGenerateColumns="False">
          <HeaderStyle BackColor="#990000" Font-Bold="True" ForeColor="White" />
          <RowStyle BackColor="#FFFBD6" ForeColor="#333333" />
          <AlternatingRowStyle BackColor="White" />
          <Columns>
            <asp:BoundField DataField="ProductID" HeaderText="ID">
              <ItemStyle Font-Bold="True" BorderWidth="1" />
            </asp:BoundField>
            <asp:BoundField DataField="Name" HeaderText="Name">
              <ItemStyle Wrap="True" Width="200"/>
            </asp:BoundField>
            <asp:BoundField DataField="ProductNumber" HeaderText="Number">
              <ItemStyle BackColor="LightSteelBlue" />
            </asp:BoundField>
            <asp:BoundField DataField="DaysToManufacture"
              HeaderText="Days To Manufacture" />
            <asp:BoundField DataField="SellStartDate" HeaderText="Sell Start Date"
              DataFormatString="{0:MM/dd/yyyy}" />
          </Columns>
        </asp:GridView>
      </div>
    </form>
  </body>
  </html>
```

This example uses `GridView` properties to set the font and adjust the cell spacing and cell gridlines. It uses styles to bold headings and configure the background of rows and alternating rows. Additionally, column-specific style settings highlight the location information with a different background, bold the ID values, and explicitly size the Notes column. A `DataFormatString` is used to format all date values in the `SellStartDate` field. Figure 8-2 shows the final result.

Formatting Specific Values

The formatting you have learned so far is not that fine-grained. At its most specific, this formatting applies to a single column of values. But there might be times when you want to change the formatting for a specific row, or even just a single cell. To accomplish this, you can leverage the `GridView.RowCreated` event. This event is raised when a part of the grid (the header, footer, or pager, or a normal, alternate, or selected item) is being created. You can access the current row as a `GridViewRow` control. The `GridViewRow.DataItem` property provides the data object for the given row, and the `GridViewRow.Cells` collection allows you to retrieve the row content. You can use `GridViewRow` to change colors and alignment, add or remove child controls, and so on.

Figure 8-2

The following example handles the `RowCreated` event and sets the colors according to the following rules:

- The item's background color is set to pink and the foreground color is set to maroon if the days to manufacturecolumn value is 0.
- The item's background color is set to dark blue and the foreground color is set to light cyan if the days to manufacturecolumn value is 1.
- For other values of days to manufacture, the item is rendered with the background color light gray and the foreground color set to red.

Listing 8-3 discusses the code for the `RowCreated` event handler that implements these rules.

Listing 8-3: Programmatically Formatting a GridView

```
protected void gridProducts_RowCreated(object sender, GridViewRowEventArgs e)
{
  if (e.Row.RowType == DataControlRowType.DataRow)
  {
    // Get the DaysToManufacture for the item that's being created
```

(continued)

Listing 8-3: *(continued)*

```
        int daysToManufacture = (int)DataBinder.Eval(e.Row.DataItem,
          "DaysToManufacture");
        //Change the item's colors.
        if (daysToManufacture == 0)
        {
          e.Row.BackColor = System.Drawing.Color.LightPink;
          e.Row.ForeColor = System.Drawing.Color.Maroon;
        }
        else if (daysToManufacture == 1)
        {
          e.Row.BackColor = System.Drawing.Color.LightCyan;
          e.Row.ForeColor = System.Drawing.Color.DarkBlue;
        }
        else
        {
          e.Row.BackColor = System.Drawing.Color.LightGray;
          e.Row.ForeColor = System.Drawing.Color.Red;
        }
      }
    }
```

First, the code checks if the item being created is an item or an alternate item. If it is neither of these, this means that the item is another interface element, such as the pager, footer, or header, and the procedure does nothing. If the item is of the right type, the code extracts the `DaysToManufacture` field from the data-bound item and compares it to some hard-coded string values.

Figure 8-3 shows the resulting page.

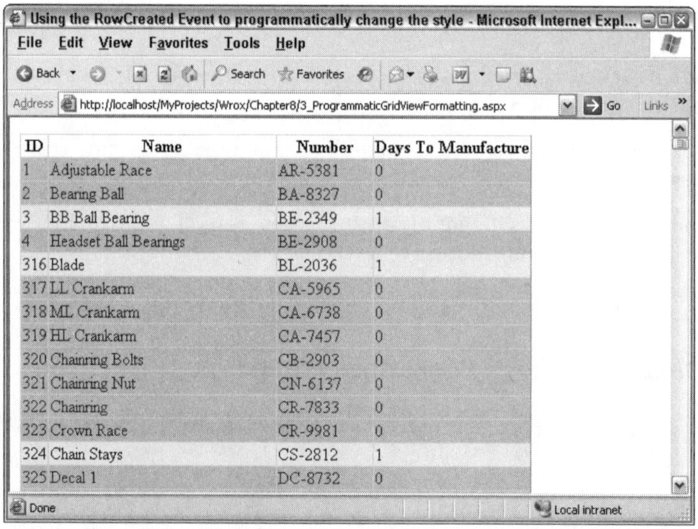

ID	Name	Number	Days To Manufacture
1	Adjustable Race	AR-5381	0
2	Bearing Ball	BA-8327	0
3	BB Ball Bearing	BE-2349	1
4	Headset Ball Bearings	BE-2908	0
316	Blade	BL-2036	1
317	LL Crankarm	CA-5965	0
318	ML Crankarm	CA-6738	0
319	HL Crankarm	CA-7457	0
320	Chainring Bolts	CB-2903	0
321	Chainring Nut	CN-6137	0
322	Chainring	CR-7833	0
323	Crown Race	CR-9981	0
324	Chain Stays	CS-2812	1
325	Decal 1	DC-8732	0

Figure 8-3

This is not the most useful example of using the `RowCreated` event, but it demonstrates how you can handle the event and read all the important information for the item. You could use much more imaginative formatting to change the way the pager's links are represented, add new buttons to the pager or header, render values that you want to highlight with special fonts and colors, create total and subtotal rows, and more.

> **This example uses the `DataBinder.Eval()` method to retrieve a piece of information from the data item using reflection. Alternatively, you could cast the `e.Row.DataItem` to the correct type (such as `ProductDetails` for the `ObjectDataSource`), `DataRowView` (for the `SqlDataSource` in `DataSet` mode), or `DbDataRecord` (for the `SqlDataSource` in `DataReader` mode). However, the `DataBinder.Eval()` approach works in all these scenarios (at the cost of being slightly slower).**

GridView Row Selection

Selecting a row means that the user can highlight or change the appearance of the row by clicking some sort of button or link. When the user clicks the button, not only will the row change its appearance, but also your code will have the opportunity to handle the event.

`GridView` provides built-in support for selection. You simply need to add a `CommandField` column with the `ShowSelect` property set to `true`. The `CommandField`can be rendered as a hyperlink, a button, or a fixed image. You choose the type using the `ButtonType` property. You can then specify the text through the `SelectText` property or specify the link to the image through the `SelectImageUrl` property.

Here is an example that displays a select button:

```
<asp:CommandField ShowSelectButton="True" ButtonType="Button"
  SelectText="Select" />
```

And here is an example that shows a small clickable icon:

```
<asp:CommandField ShowSelectButton="True" ButtonType="Image"
  SelectImageUrl="select.gif" />
```

When you click a select button, the page is posted back, and a series of steps unfolds. First, the `GridView.SelectedIndexChanging` event fires, which you can intercept to cancel the operation. Next, the `GridView.SelectedIndex` property is adjusted to point to the selected row. Finally, the `GridView.SelectedIndexChanged` event fires, which you can handle if you want to manually update other controls to reflect the new selection. When the page is rendered, the selected row is given the `SelectedRowStyle`.

Note that for the selection to work, you must configure the `SelectedRowStyle` so that selected rows look different from normal rows. Usually, selected rows will have a different `BackColor` property.

Using a Data Field as a Select Button

You do not need to create a new column to support row selection. Instead, you can turn an existing column into a link. This technique is commonly used to allow users to select rows in a table by the unique

ID value. To use this technique, remove the `CommandField` column and add a `ButtonField` column instead. Then, set the `DataTextField` to the name of the field you want to use:

```
<asp:ButtonField ButtonType="Button" DataTextField="ProductID" />
```

This field will be underlined and turned into a link that, when clicked, will post back the page and trigger the `GridView.RowCommand` event. You could handle this event, determine which row has been clicked, and programmatically set the `SelectedIndex` property. However, you can use an easier method. Instead, just configure the link to raise the `SelectedIndexChanged` event by specifying a `CommandName` with the text `Select`, as shown here:

```
<asp:ButtonField CommandName="Select" ButtonType="Button"
  DataTextField="ProductID" />
```

Now, clicking the data field automatically selects the record.

GridView Templates

So far, the examples have used the `GridView` control to show data using separate bound columns for each field. If you want to place multiple values in the same cell, or if you want to have the unlimited ability to customize the content in a cell by adding HTML tags and server controls, you need to use a `TemplateField`.

The `TemplateField` allows you to define a completely customized template for a column. Inside the template you can add control tags, arbitrary HTML elements, and data-binding expressions. You have complete freedom to arrange everything the way you want.

For example, imagine that you want to create a column that combines the first name and last name fields. To accomplish this trick, you can construct an `ItemTemplate` like this:

```
<asp:TemplateField HeaderText="Name">
  <ItemTemplate>
    <%# Eval("FirstName") %><%# Eval("LastName") %>
  </ItemTemplate>
</asp:TemplateField>
```

Now when you bind the `GridView`, it fetches the data from the data source and walks through the collection of items. It processes the `ItemTemplate` for each item, evaluates the data-binding expressions, and adds the rendered HTML to the table. This template is quite simple — it simply defines two data-binding expressions. When evaluated, these expressions are converted to ordinary text.

If you attempt to bind a field that is not present in your result set, you will receive a runtime error. If you retrieve additional fields that are never bound to any template, no problem will occur.

You will notice that these expressions use `Eval()`, which is a static method of the `System.Web.UI.DataBinder` class. The `Eval()` method automatically retrieves the data item that is bound to the current row, uses reflection to find the matching field (for a row) or property (for a custom object), and retrieves the value. This process of reflection adds a little bit of extra work. However, this overhead is unlikely to add much time to the processing of a request. Without the `Eval()` method, you would need to access the data object through the `Container.DataItem` property and use typecasting code like this:

```
<%# ((ProductDetails)Container.DataItem)["ProductID"] %>
```

The problem with this approach is that you need to know the exact type of data object. For example, the data-binding expression shown previously assumes that you are binding to an array of `ProductDetails` objects through the `ObjectDataSource`. If you switch to the `SqlDataSource`, or if you rename the `ProductDetails` class, your page will break. On the other hand, if you use the `Eval()` method, your data-binding expressions will keep working as long as the data object has a property with the given name. In other words, using the `Eval()` method allows you to create pages that are loosely bound to your data access layer.

> **Note that when binding to a `SqlDataSource` in `DataSet` mode, the data item is a `DataRowView`. When binding to a `SqlDataSource` in `DataReader` mode, the data item is a `DbDataRecord`.**

The `Eval()` method also adds the extremely useful ability to format data fields on the fly. To use this feature, you must use the overloaded version of the `Eval()` method that accepts an additional format string parameter. Here is an example:

```
<%# Eval("SellStartDate", "{0:MM/dd/yy}") %>
```

You can use any of the numeric format strings or time and date format strings defined previously with the `Eval()` *method.*

You are free to mix templated columns with other column types. Or, you could get rid of every other column and put all the information from the product table into one formatted template, as shown in Listing 8-4.

Listing 8-4: Using a Templated Column with GridView

```
<%@ Page Language="C#" %>
<html xmlns="http://www.w3.org/1999/xhtml" >
<head runat="server">
  <title>Using Templated Columns with GridView</title>
</head>
<body>
  <form id="form1" runat="server">
    <div>
      <asp:SqlDataSource ID="productsSource" runat="server"
        ProviderName="System.Data.SqlClient"
        ConnectionString="<%$ ConnectionStrings:AdventureWorks %>"
        SelectCommand="Select ProductID, Name, ProductNumber, DaysToManufacture,
        SellStartDate, ReorderPoint from Production.Product">
      </asp:SqlDataSource>
      <asp:GridView ID="gridProducts" runat="server" DataSourceID="productsSource"
        AutoGenerateColumns="False">
        <Columns>
          <asp:TemplateField HeaderText="Employees">
            <ItemTemplate>
              <b><%# Eval("ProductID") %> - <%# Eval("Name") %></b>
              <hr />
              <small><i>
```

(continued)

Listing 8-4: *(continued)*

```
                    Product Number: <%# Eval("ProductNumber") %><br />
                    Days to manufacture:<%# Eval("DaysToManufacture") %> <br />
                    Start Date: <%# Eval("SellStartDate", "{0:MM/dd/yy}") %><br />
                    </i><br/><br/>
                    Reorder Point:<%# Eval("ReorderPoint") %>
                  </small>
                </ItemTemplate>
              </asp:TemplateField>
            </Columns>
          </asp:GridView>
        </div>
      </form>
    </body>
    </html>
```

Figure 8-4 shows the result.

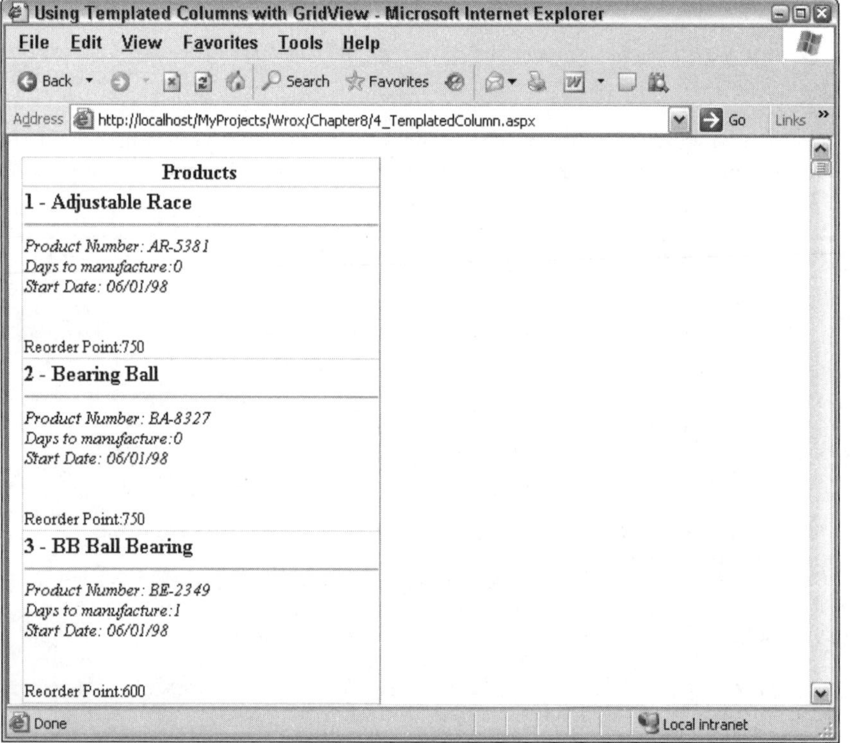

Figure 8-4

Using Multiple Templates

The previous example used a single template to configure the appearance of data items. However, the `ItemTemplate` is not the only template that the `GridView` provides. In fact, the `GridView` allows you to configure various aspects of its appearance with a number of templates. Inside every template column, you can use the templates listed as follows.

Mode	Description
`HeaderTemplate`	Determines the appearance and content of the header cell
`FooterTemplate`	Determines the appearance and content of the footer cell
`ItemTemplate`	Determines the appearance and content of each data cell (if you are not using the `AlternatingItemTemplate`) or every odd numbered data cell (if you are using `AlternatingItemTemplate`)
`AlternatingItem Template`	Used in conjunction with the `ItemTemplate` to format even-numbered and odd-numbered rows differently
`EditItemTemplate`	Determines the appearance and controls used in edit mode

Out of the templates listed in this table, the `EditItemTemplate` is one of the most useful, because it gives you the ability to control the editing experience for the field. If you do not use templated fields, you are limited to ordinary text boxes, and you will not have any validation. The `GridView` also defines two templates that you can use outside of any column. These are the `PagerTemplate`, which lets you customize the appearance of pager controls, and the `EmptyDataTemplate`, which lets you set the content that should appear if the `GridView` is bound to an empty data object.

Binding to a Method

One of the benefits of templates is that they allow you to use data-binding expressions that extend the ways you can format and present bound data. One key technique that recurs in many scenarios is using a method in your page class to process a field value. This removes the limitations of simple data binding and lets you incorporate dynamic information and conditional logic.

For example, you might create a column where you want to display an icon next to each row. However, you do not want to use a static icon — instead, you want to choose the best image based on the data in the row. Figure 8-5 shows an example where a warning indicates when the reorder point is less than 100 and a check mark image indicates when the reorder point is greater than 100.

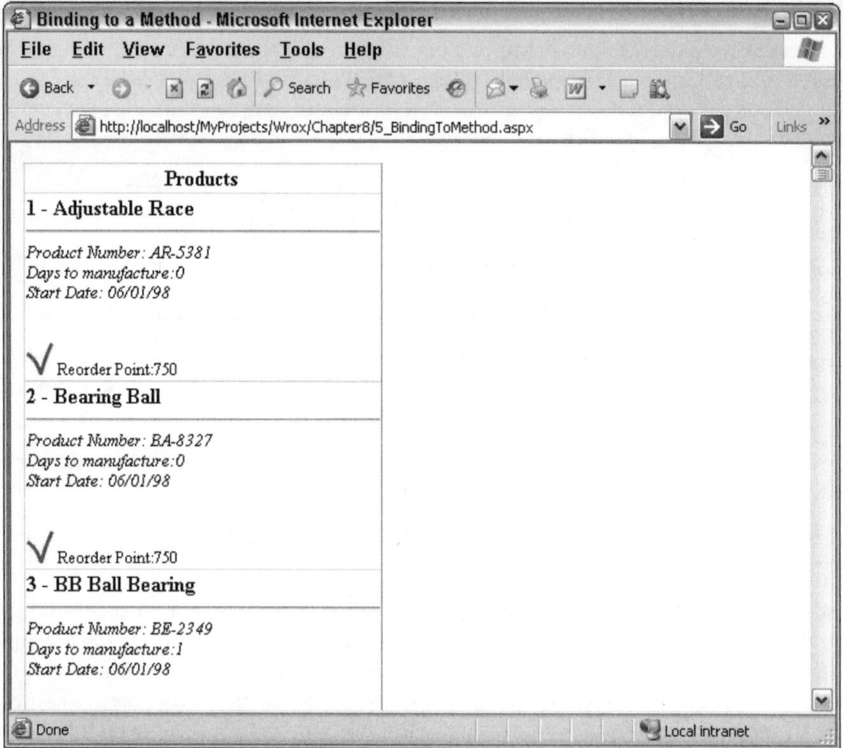

Figure 8-5

The complete code is shown in Listing 8-5.

Listing 8-5: Binding to a Method Using Templates

```
<%@ Page Language="C#" %>
<html xmlns="http://www.w3.org/1999/xhtml" >
<head runat="server">
  <title>Binding to a Method</title>
  <script runat="Server">
    protected string GetImageName(object dataItem)
    {
      int reorderPoint = Int32.Parse(DataBinder.Eval(dataItem,
        "ReorderPoint").ToString());
      if (reorderPoint < 100 )
        return "Warning.bmp";
      else
        return "Check.bmp";
    }
  </script>
</head>
```

```
<body>
  <form id="form1" runat="server">
    <div>
      <asp:SqlDataSource ID="productsSource" runat="server"
        ProviderName="System.Data.SqlClient"
        ConnectionString="<%$ ConnectionStrings:AdventureWorks %>"
        SelectCommand="Select ProductID, Name, ProductNumber, DaysToManufacture,
        SellStartDate, ReorderPoint from Production.Product">
      </asp:SqlDataSource>
      <asp:GridView ID="gridProducts" runat="server" DataSourceID="productsSource"
        AutoGenerateColumns="False">
        <Columns>
          <asp:TemplateField HeaderText="Products">
            <ItemTemplate>
              <b><%# Eval("ProductID") %> -<%# Eval("Name") %></br>
              <hr />
              <small><i>
                Product Number: <%# Eval("ProductNumber") %><br />
                Days to manufacture:<%# Eval("DaysToManufacture") %> <br />
                Start Date: <%# Eval("SellStartDate", "{0:MM/dd/yy}") %><br />
                </i><br/><br/>
                <img src='Images/<%# GetImageName(Container.DataItem) %>' />
                Reorder Point:<%# Eval("ReorderPoint") %>
              </small>
            </ItemTemplate>
          </asp:TemplateField>
        </Columns>
      </asp:GridView>
    </div>
  </form>
</body>
</html>
```

The line of code that is of interest is the line below, where you get the name of the image from the `GetImageName()` method.

```
<img src='Images/<%# GetImageName(Container.DataItem) %>' />
```

This technique turns up in many scenarios. For example, you could use it to adjust prices to take into consideration the current demand. Or, you could use it to translate a numeric code into a more meaningful piece of text. You might even want to create completely calculated columns — for example, use the `DateOfBirth` field to calculate a value for an Age column.

> **Note that if you use data-binding expressions to bind to methods, you can no longer use callbacks to optimize the `GridView` refresh process. To prevent an error, make sure that you do not set `GridView.EnableSortingAndPagingCallbacks` to `true`. If you do not want to sacrifice the callback features, you can get similar functionality by modifying the item when it first appears using the `GridView.ItemCreated` event.**

Handling Events in a Template

In some cases, you might need to handle events that are raised by the controls you add to a templated column. For example, imagine that you changed the previous example so that instead of showing a static status icon, it created a clickable image link through the `ImageButton` control. This is easy enough to accomplish:

```
<asp:TemplateField HeaderText="Products">
  <ItemTemplate>
    -------
    -------
    <asp:ImageButton ID="ImageButton1" runat="server"
      ImageUrl='<%# GetImageName(Container.DataItem) %>' />
    ---------
  </ItemTemplate>
</asp:TemplateField>
```

The problem is that if you add a control to a template, the `GridView` creates multiple copies of that control, one for each data item. When the `ImageButton` is clicked, you need a way to determine which image was clicked and which row it belongs to.

The way to resolve this problem is to use an event from the `GridView`, not the contained button. The `RowCommand` event serves this purpose, because it fires whenever any button is clicked in any template. This process, in which a control event in a template is turned into an event in the containing control, is called event bubbling.

Of course, you still need a way to pass information to the `RowCommand` event to identify the row where the action took place. The secret lies in two string properties of all button controls: `CommandName` and `CommandArgument`. `CommandName` sets a descriptive name you can use to distinguish clicks on your `ImageButton` from clicks on other button controls in the `GridView`. The `CommandArgument` supplies a piece of row-specific data you can use to identify the row that was clicked. You can supply this information using a data-binding expression.

Here is the revised `ImageButton` tag:

```
<asp:TemplateField HeaderText="Products">
  <ItemTemplate>
    ----
    ----
    <asp:ImageButton ID="ImageButton1" runat="server"
      ImageUrl='<%# GetImageName(Container.DataItem) %>'
      CommandName="ImageClick" CommandArgument='<%# Eval("ProductID") %>' />
  </ItemTemplate>
</asp:TemplateField>
```

And here is the code you need to respond when an `ImageButton` is clicked:

```
protected void gridProducts_RowCommand(object sender, GridViewCommandEventArgs e)
{
  if (e.CommandName == "ImageClick")
    lblMessage.Text = "You clicked product #" + e.CommandArgument;
}
```

This example simply displays the `ProductID` in a label named `lblMessage`.

Remember, you can simplify your life using the `GridView` control's built-in selection support. Just set the `CommandName` to `Select` and handle the `SelectIndexChanged` event, as described in the section "Using a Data Field as a Select Button" earlier in this chapter. Although this approach gives you easy access to the clicked row, it will not help you if you want to provide multiple buttons that perform different tasks.

Editing with a Template

One of the best reasons to use a template is to provide a better editing experience. In the previous chapter, you saw how `GridView` provides automatic editing capabilities — all you need to do is switch a row into edit mode by setting the `GridView.EditItemIndex` property. The easiest way to make this possible is to add a `CommandField` column with the `ShowEditButton` set to `true`. Then, the user simply needs to click a link in the appropriate row to begin editing it. At this point, every label in every column is replaced by a text box (unless the field is read-only).

The standard editing support has several limitations:

- It is not always appropriate to edit values using a text box: Certain types of data are best handled with other controls (such as drop-down lists), large fields need multiline text boxes, and so on.
- You get no validation — it would be nice to restrict the editing possibilities so that currency figures can't be entered as negative numbers, and so on. You can do that by adding validator controls to an `EditItemTemplate`.
- It is often ugly — a row of text boxes across a grid takes up too much space and rarely seems professional.

In a templated column, you do not have these issues. Instead, you explicitly define the edit controls and their layout using the `EditItemTemplate`. This can be a somewhat laborious process.

Listing 8-6 shows an example of an edit template that allows editing of a single field called the `ReorderPoint`.

Listing 8-6: Using EditItemTemplate to Edit the GridView Contents

```
<%@ Page Language="C#" %>
<html xmlns="http://www.w3.org/1999/xhtml" >
<head runat="server">
  <title>Editing Data using Templated Columns</title>
</head>
<body>
  <form id="form1" runat="server">
    <div>
      <asp:SqlDataSource ID="productsSource" runat="server"
        ProviderName="System.Data.SqlClient"
        ConnectionString="<%$ ConnectionStrings:AdventureWorks %>"
        SelectCommand="Select ProductID, Name, ProductNumber, DaysToManufacture,
        SellStartDate, ReorderPoint from Production.Product"
```

(continued)

Listing 8-6: *(continued)*

```
          UpdateCommand="Update Production.Product Set ReorderPoint = @ReorderPoint
          Where ProductID = @ProductID">
        </asp:SqlDataSource>
        <asp:GridView ID="gridProducts" runat="server" DataSourceID="productsSource"
          AutoGenerateColumns="False" DataKeyNames="ProductID">
          <Columns>
            <asp:CommandField ShowEditButton="true" />
            <asp:TemplateField HeaderText="Products">
              <ItemTemplate>
                <b><%# Eval("ProductID") %> -<%# Eval("Name") %> </b>><hr/>
                <small><i>
                  Product Number: <%# Eval("ProductNumber") %><br /></i>
                  Reorder Point:<%# Eval("ReorderPoint") %><br />
                </small>
              </ItemTemplate>
              <EditItemTemplate>
                <b><%# Eval("ProductID") %> -<%# Eval("Name") %></b><hr/>
                <small><i>
                  Product Number: <%# Eval("ProductNumber") %><br /></i>
                  Reorder Point:<asp:TextBox Text='<%# Bind("ReorderPoint") %>'
                    runat="server" id="textBox" Width="100px" />
                </small>
              </EditItemTemplate>
            </asp:TemplateField>
          </Columns>
        </asp:GridView>
      </div>
    </form>
  </body>
  </html>
```

When binding an editable value to a control, you must use the `Bind()` method in your data-binding expression instead of the ordinary `Eval()` method. Only the `Bind()` method creates the two-way link, ensuring that updated values will be sent back to the server.

Another important fact to keep in mind is that when the `GridView` commits an update, it will submit only the bound, editable parameters. In the previous example, this means the `GridView` will pass back a single `@ReorderPoint` parameter for the `ReorderPoint` field. This is important, because when you write your parameterized update command (if you are using `SqlDataSource`), you must use only one parameter, as shown here:

```
UpdateCommand="UPDATE Production.Product SET ReorderPoint=@ReorderPoint WHERE
ProductID=@ProductID"
```

Similarly, if you are using `ObjectDataSource`, you must make sure that your update method takes only one parameter, named `ReorderPoint`.

Figure 8-6 shows the row in edit mode.

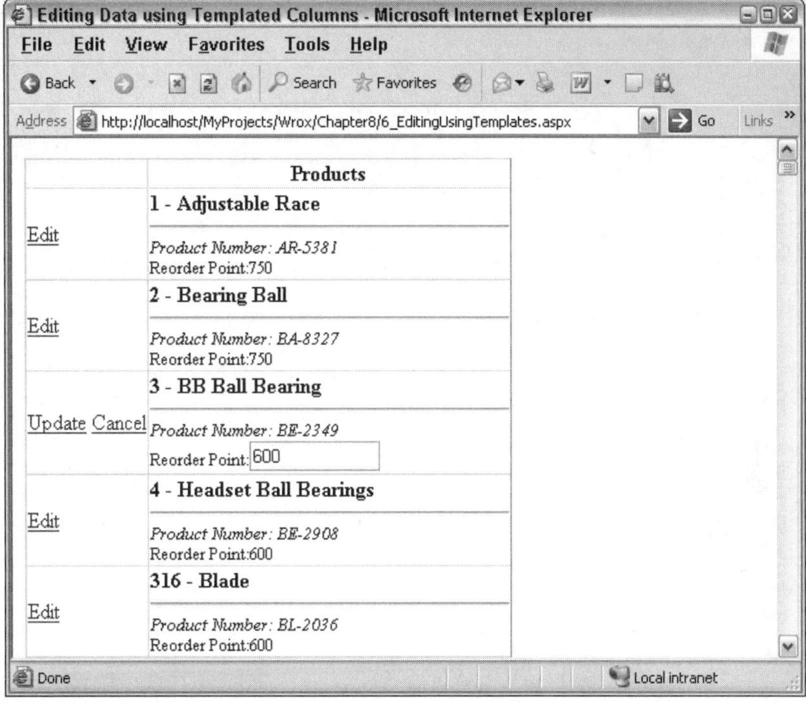

Figure 8-6

Editing with Advanced Controls

Template-based editing really shines if you need to bind to more interesting controls, such as lists. For example, you could change the previous example to add the `ProductSubCategoryID` column to the template and make it editable through a drop-down list. Listing 8-7 shows the complete code you need.

Listing 8-7: Using a DropDownList Control within the Template

```
<%@ Page Language="C#" %>
<%@ Import Namespace="System.Data" %>
<%@ Import Namespace="System.Data.SqlClient" %>
<%@ Import Namespace="System.Web.Configuration" %>
<html xmlns="http://www.w3.org/1999/xhtml" >
<head runat="server">
  <title>Advanced Editing using Templated Columns</title>
  <script runat="server">
    void Page_Load(object sender, EventArgs e)
    {
      if (!Page.IsPostBack)
        Page.DataBind();
    }

    private DataTable _categoriesTable;
```

(continued)

Listing 8-7: *(continued)*

```
    public DataView Categories
    {
      get
      {
        if (_categoriesTable == null)
        {
          _categoriesTable = new DataTable();
          string connectionString = WebConfigurationManager.ConnectionStrings
            ["AdventureWorks"].ConnectionString;
          using (SqlConnection connection = new SqlConnection(connectionString))
          {
            string sql = "Select IsNull(ProductSubcategoryID, -1) as " +
              "ProductSubCategoryID, Name from Production.ProductSubcategory";
            SqlDataAdapter adapter = new SqlDataAdapter(sql, connection);
            adapter.Fill(_categoriesTable);
          }
        }
        return _categoriesTable.DefaultView;
      }
    }

    public int GetSelectedCategory(int productSubCategoryID)
    {
      Categories.Sort = "ProductSubcategoryID";
      int index = Categories.Find(productSubCategoryID.ToString());
      //Add 1 to the index since the rows start from -1
      return index + 1;
    }

    protected void gridProducts_RowUpdating(object sender,
      GridViewUpdateEventArgs e)
    {
      //Get the reference to the list control
      DropDownList ddlCategories = (DropDownList)(gridProducts.Rows[e.RowIndex].
        FindControl("ddlCategories"));
      e.NewValues.Add("ProductSubcategoryID", ddlCategories.SelectedItem.Value);
    }
  </script>
</head>
<body>
  <form id="form1" runat="server">
    <div>
      <asp:SqlDataSource ID="productsSource" runat="server"
        ProviderName="System.Data.SqlClient"
        ConnectionString="<%$ ConnectionStrings:AdventureWorks %>"
        SelectCommand="Select ProductID, Name, ProductNumber, DaysToManufacture,
        IsNull(ProductSubcategoryID, -1) As ProductSubcategoryID, SellStartDate,
        ReorderPoint from Production.Product" UpdateCommand="Update
        Production.Product Set ProductSubcategoryID = @ProductSubcategoryID,
        ReorderPoint = @ReorderPoint Where ProductID = @ProductID">
      </asp:SqlDataSource>
      <asp:GridView ID="gridProducts" runat="server" DataSourceID="productsSource"
```

```
            AutoGenerateColumns="False" DataKeyNames="ProductID"
            OnRowUpdating="gridProducts_RowUpdating">
            <Columns>
              <asp:CommandField ShowEditButton="true" />
              <asp:TemplateField HeaderText="Products">
                <ItemTemplate>
                  <b><%# Eval("ProductID") %> - <%# Eval("Name") %> </b>
                  <hr/>Product Category: <%# Eval("ProductSubcategoryID")%> <hr />
                  <small><i>Product Number: <%# Eval("ProductNumber") %><br /></i>
                    Reorder Point:<%# Eval("ReorderPoint") %><br />
                  </small>
                </ItemTemplate>
                <EditItemTemplate>
                  <b><%# Eval("ProductID") %> -<%# Eval("Name") %></b><hr/>
                  Produt Category:
                  <asp:DropDownList runat="server" ID="ddlCategories"
                    AppendDataBoundItems="true" SelectedIndex=
                    '<%# GetSelectedCategory((int)Eval("ProductSubcategoryID")) %>'
                    DataSource='<%# Categories %>'
                    DataValueField="ProductSubcategoryID" DataTextField="Name" >
                    <asp:ListItem Value="-1" Text="Select" />
                  </asp:DropDownList>
                  <hr /><hr />
                  <small><i>Product Number: <%# Eval("ProductNumber") %><br /></i>
                    Reorder Point:<asp:TextBox Text='<%# Bind("ReorderPoint") %>'
                      runat="server" id="textBox" Width="100px" />
                  </small>
                </EditItemTemplate>
              </asp:TemplateField>
            </Columns>
          </asp:GridView>
        </div>
      </form>
    </body>
    </html>
```

In the above code, focus on the `EditItemTemplate`, since a lot is happening there.

The `EditItemTemplate` allows the user to pick a category from a selected list of categories. This category list is populated using `DropDownList.DataSource` with a data-binding expression that retrieves the categories from the `ProductSubcategory` table. This is accomplished by the property named `Categories` that returns the list of categories from the database.

Here is the definition for the `Categories` property in the ASP.NET page:

```
public DataView Categories
{
  get
  {
    -----
    return _categoriesTable.DefaultView;
  }
}
```

After retrieving the categories from the table, the `Categories` finally returns with an object of type `DataView`.

This step ensures that the drop-down list is populated, but it does not solve the related problem of making sure that the right category is selected in the list for the current value. The best approach here is to bind `SelectedIndex` to a custom method that takes the current category ID and returns the index of that value. In this example, the `GetSelectedCategory()` method performs this task. It takes a `productSubCategoryID` as input and returns the index of the respective value in the `DataView` returned by the `Categories` property:

```
public int GetSelectedCategory(int productSubCategoryID)
{
  Categories.Sort = "ProductSubcategoryID";
  int index = Categories.Find(productSubCategoryID.ToString());
  //Add 1 because there is a default item in the list box
  return index + 1;
}
```

This code searches the `DataView` using the static `DataView.Find()` method. Note that you must explicitly set the `DataView.Sort` property to the primary key on which you want to search the `DataView`. The return value of `GetSelectedCategory()` is directly assigned to the `SelectedIndex` property of the drop-down list.

```
<asp:DropDownList runat="server" ID="ddlCategories" AppendDataBoundItems="true"
  SelectedIndex='<%# GetSelectedCategory((int)Eval("ProductSubcategoryID")) %>'
  DataSource='<%# Categories %>' DataValueField="ProductSubcategoryID"
  DataTextField="Name">
  <asp:ListItem Value="-1" Text="Select" />
</asp:DropDownList>
```

Note that the drop-down list control also has a default value set. Because of the default value, you must set to the `AppendDataBoundItems` property to `true` so that the values from the data-binding operation can be appended to the default value. Figure 8-7 shows the drop-down list in action during editing.

Unfortunately, this still does not complete the example. Now, you have a list box that is populated in edit mode, with the correct item automatically selected. However, if you change the selection, the value is not sent back to the data source. In this example, you could tackle the problem by using the `Bind()` method with the `SelectedValue` property, because the text in the control exactly corresponds to the text you want to commit to the record. However, sometimes life is not as easy, because you need to translate the value into a different database representation. In this situation, the only option is to handle the `RowUpdating` event, find the list control in the current row, and extract the text. You can then dynamically add the extra parameter, as shown here:

```
protected void gridProducts_RowUpdating(object sender, GridViewUpdateEventArgs e)
{
  //Get the reference to the list control
  DropDownList ddlCategories =
    (DropDownList)(gridProducts.Rows[e.RowIndex].FindControl("ddlCategories"));
  e.NewValues.Add("ProductSubcategoryID", ddlCategories.SelectedItem.Value);
}
```

This will now successfully update both the `ReorderPoint` field and the `ProductSubcategoryID` fields. As you can see, editable templates give you a great deal of power, but they often are not quick to code. As an exercise, you can also add the validator controls to the above example to make `EditItemTemplate` more interesting.

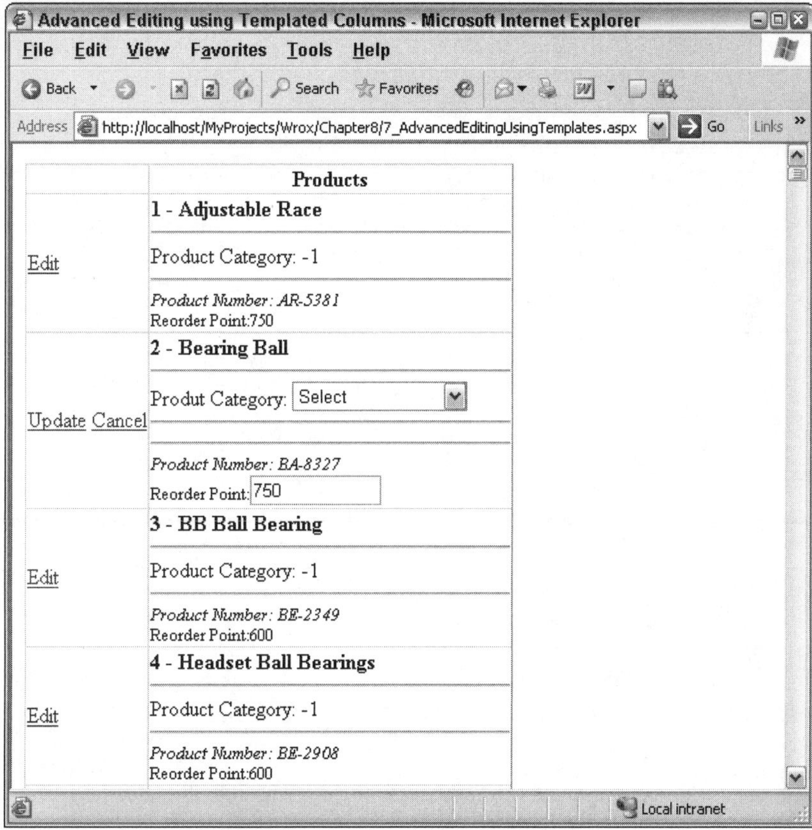

Figure 8-7

Editing without a Command Column

So far, all the examples you have seen have used a `CommandField` that automatically generates edit controls. However, now that you have made the transition over to a template-based approach, it is worth considering how you can add your own edit controls.

It is actually quite easy. All you need to do is add a button control to the item template and set the `CommandName` to `Edit` (see Listing 8-8). This automatically triggers the editing process, which fires the appropriate events and switches the row into edit mode.

Listing 8-8: Editing without a CommandField Template

```
<%@ Page Language="C#" %>
<html xmlns="http://www.w3.org/1999/xhtml" >
<head runat="server">
  <title>Editing Data without a CommandField Template</title>
</head>
<body>
  <form id="form1" runat="server">
    <div>
      <asp:SqlDataSource ID="productsSource" runat="server"
        ProviderName="System.Data.SqlClient"
        ConnectionString="<%$ ConnectionStrings:AdventureWorks %>"
        SelectCommand="Select ProductID, Name, ProductNumber, DaysToManufacture,
        SellStartDate, ReorderPoint from Production.Product"
        UpdateCommand="Update Production.Product Set ReorderPoint = @ReorderPoint
        Where ProductID = @ProductID">
      </asp:SqlDataSource>
      <asp:GridView ID="gridProducts" runat="server" DataSourceID="productsSource"
        AutoGenerateColumns="False" DataKeyNames="ProductID">
        <Columns>
          <asp:TemplateField HeaderText="Products">
            <ItemTemplate>
              <b><%# Eval("ProductID") %> -<%# Eval("Name") %></b><hr />
              <small><i>Product Number: <%# Eval("ProductNumber") %><br /></i>
                Reorder Point:<%# Eval("ReorderPoint") %><br />
                <asp:LinkButton runat="server" Text="Edit" CommandName="Edit"
                  ID="lnkEdit" />
              </small>
            </ItemTemplate>
            <EditItemTemplate>
              <b><%# Eval("ProductID") %> -<%# Eval("Name") %></b><hr />
              <small><i>Product Number: <%# Eval("ProductNumber") %><br /></i>
                Reorder Point:<asp:TextBox Text='<%# Bind("ReorderPoint") %>'
                  runat="server" id="textBox" Width="100px" />
                <asp:LinkButton runat="server" Text="Update"
                  CommandName="Update" ID="lnkUpdate" />
                <asp:LinkButton runat="server" Text="Cancel"
                  CommandName="Cancel" ID="lnkCancel" />
              </small>
            </EditItemTemplate>
          </asp:TemplateField>
        </Columns>
      </asp:GridView>
    </div>
  </form>
</body>
</html>
```

As shown in Listing 8-8, you add two more buttons with a `CommandName` of `Update` and `Cancel`, respectively, in the `EditItemTemplate`.

As long as you use these names, the `GridView` editing events will fire and the data source controls will react in the same way as if you were using the automatically generated editing controls. Figure 8-8 shows the custom edit buttons.

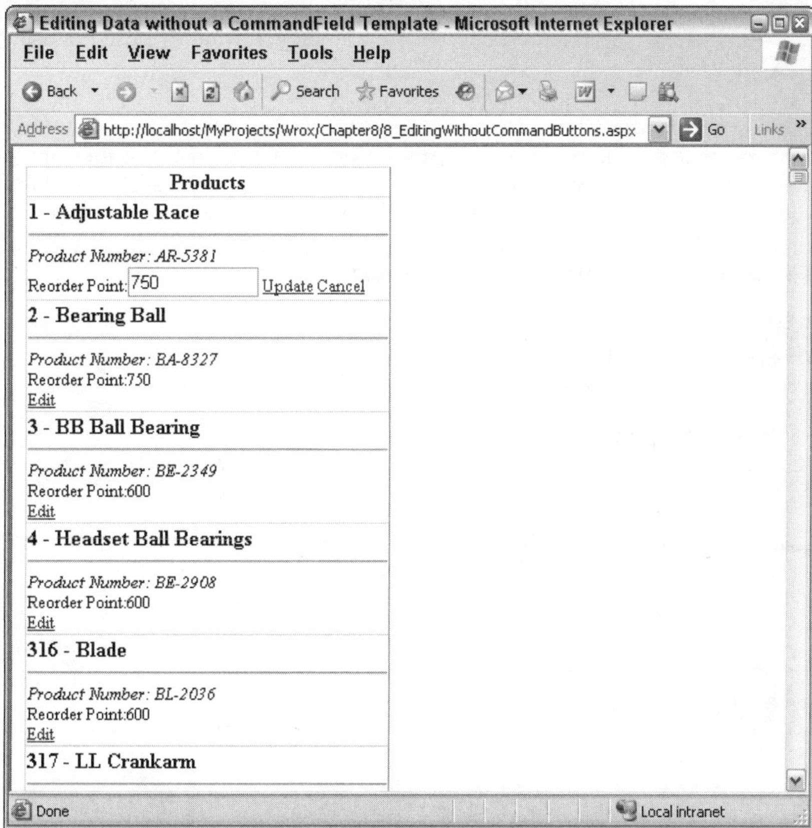

Figure 8-8

Displaying Summaries in the GridView Using a Footer

Although the prime purpose of a `GridView` is to show a set of records, you can also add some more interesting information, such as summary data. The first step is to add the footer row by setting the `GridView.ShowFooter` property to `true`. This displays a shaded footer row (which you can customize freely), but it does not show any data. To take care of that task, you need insert the content into the `GridView.FooterRow`.

For example, imagine that you are dealing with a list of products. A simple summary row could display the summary for the numbers of days (0, 1, 2, or 3) it takes to manufacture the products.

The first step is to decide when to calculate this information. If you are using manual binding, you could retrieve the data object and use it to perform your calculations before binding it to the `GridView`. However, if you are using declarative binding, you need another technique. You have two basic options — you can retrieve the data from the data object during the binding operation, or you can retrieve it from the grid itself after the grid has been bound. The following example uses the former approach, because it gives you the freedom to use the same calculation code no matter what data source was used to populate the control. It also gives you the ability to total just the records that are displayed on the current page, if you have enabled paging. The disadvantage is that your code is tightly bound to the `GridView`, because you need to pull out the information you want by position, using hard-coded column index numbers.

The basic strategy is to react to the `GridView.RowDataBound` event. This occurs immediately after each row in the `GridView` is populated with data. At this point, you cannot access the data source any longer, but you can navigate through the `GridView` as a collection of rows and cells. Once this total is calculated, it is inserted into the footer row. Listing 8-9 shows the complete code.

Listing 8-9: Displaying Summaries in a Footer

```
<%@ Page Language="C#" %>
<html xmlns="http://www.w3.org/1999/xhtml" >
<head id="Head1" runat="server">
  <title>Displaying Summary Data in Footer using GridView</title>
  <script runat="server">
    int zeroDaysToManufacture, oneDayToManufacture, twoDaysToManufacture,
      threeDaysToManufacture  = 0;

    protected void gridProducts_RowDataBound(object sender, GridViewRowEventArgs e)
    {
      if (e.Row.RowType == DataControlRowType.DataRow)
      {
        //Add the UnitPrice and QuantityTotal to the running total variables
        int daysToManufacture = Convert.ToInt32(DataBinder.Eval(e.Row.DataItem,
          "DaysToManufacture"));
        switch (daysToManufacture)
        {
          case 0:{zeroDaysToManufacture++;break;}
          case 1:{oneDayToManufacture++;break;}
          case 2:{twoDaysToManufacture++;break;}
          case 3:{threeDaysToManufacture++;break;}
        }
      }
      else if (e.Row.RowType == DataControlRowType.Footer)
      {
        e.Row.Cells[0].Text = "0 Days  - " + zeroDaysToManufacture.ToString();
        e.Row.Cells[1].Text = "1 Days  - " + oneDayToManufacture.ToString();
        e.Row.Cells[2].Text = "2 Days  - " + twoDaysToManufacture.ToString();
        e.Row.Cells[3].Text = "3 Days  - " + threeDaysToManufacture.ToString();
        e.Row.Font.Bold = true;
        e.Row.BackColor = System.Drawing.Color.BlueViolet;
        e.Row.ForeColor = System.Drawing.Color.White;
      }
    }
  </script>
</head>
<body>
  <form id="form1" runat="server">
```

```
        <div>
          <asp:SqlDataSource ID="productsSource" runat="server"
            ProviderName="System.Data.SqlClient"
            ConnectionString="<%$ ConnectionStrings:AdventureWorks %>"
            SelectCommand="Select ProductID, Name, ProductNumber, DaysToManufacture
            from Production.Product">
          </asp:SqlDataSource>
          <asp:GridView  runat="server" ID="gridProducts" DataSourceID="productsSource"
            AutoGenerateColumns="false" ShowFooter="true"
            OnRowDataBound="gridProducts_RowDataBound">
            <Columns>
              <asp:BoundField DataField="ProductID" HeaderText="ID" />
              <asp:BoundField DataField="Name" HeaderText="Name" />
              <asp:BoundField DataField="ProductNumber" HeaderText="Number" />
              <asp:BoundField DataField="DaysToManufacture" HeaderText="Days To
                Manufacture" />
            </Columns>
          </asp:GridView>
        </div>
      </form>
    </body>
    </html>
```

In the `RowDataBound` event, you check to see if the current row is a footer row using the `DataRow ControlType` enumeration. Figure 8-9 shows the output of the page.

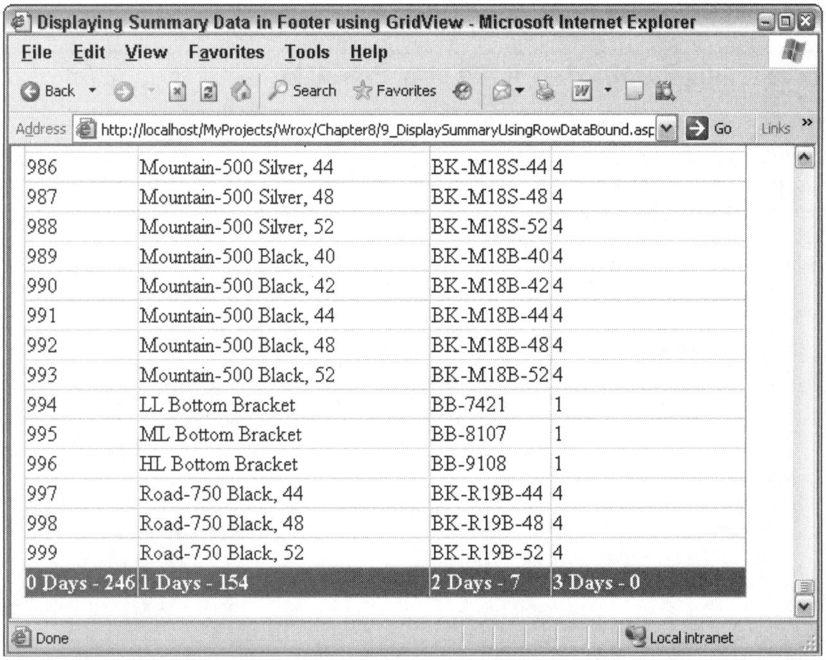

Displaying Summary Data in Footer using GridView - Microsoft Internet Explorer

File Edit View Favorites Tools Help

Address http://localhost/MyProjects/Wrox/Chapter8/9_DisplaySummaryUsingRowDataBound.asp

986	Mountain-500 Silver, 44	BK-M18S-44	4
987	Mountain-500 Silver, 48	BK-M18S-48	4
988	Mountain-500 Silver, 52	BK-M18S-52	4
989	Mountain-500 Black, 40	BK-M18B-40	4
990	Mountain-500 Black, 42	BK-M18B-42	4
991	Mountain-500 Black, 44	BK-M18B-44	4
992	Mountain-500 Black, 48	BK-M18B-48	4
993	Mountain-500 Black, 52	BK-M18B-52	4
994	LL Bottom Bracket	BB-7421	1
995	ML Bottom Bracket	BB-8107	1
996	HL Bottom Bracket	BB-9108	1
997	Road-750 Black, 44	BK-R19B-44	4
998	Road-750 Black, 48	BK-R19B-48	4
999	Road-750 Black, 52	BK-R19B-52	4
0 Days - 246	1 Days - 154	2 Days - 7	3 Days - 0

Done　Local intranet

Figure 8-9

DetailsView and FormView

`GridView` excels at showing a dense table with multiple rows of information. However, sometimes you want to provide a detailed look at a single record. Although you could work out a solution using a template column in a `GridView`, ASP.NET also includes two controls that are tailored for this purpose: `DetailsView` and `FormView`. Both show a single record at a time but can include optional pager buttons that let you step through a series of records (showing one per page). The difference between the `DetailsView` and the `FormView` is their support for templates. The `DetailsView` is built out of field objects, in the same way that the `GridView` is built out of column objects. On the other hand, the `FormView` is based on templates that work in the same way as a `GridView` templated column, which requires a little more work but gives you much more flexibility.

Note that once you understand the features of `GridView`*, you can get up to speed with* `DetailsView` *and* `FormView` *quite quickly. That is because both* `DetailsView` *and* `FormView` *borrow a portion of the* `GridView` *model.*

DetailsView

As mentioned previously, `DetailsView` is designed to display a single record at a time. It places each piece of information (be it a field or a property) in a separate row of a table. `DetailsView` can also bind to a collection of items. In this case, it shows the first item in the group. It also allows you to move from one record to the next using paging controls, if you have set the `AllowPaging` property to `true`. You can configure the paging controls using the `PagingStyle` and `PagingSettings` properties in the same way as you tweak the pager for the `GridView`. The only difference is that there is no support for custom paging, which means that the full data source object is always retrieved. Listing 8-10 shows a simple `DetailsView` control in action.

Listing 8-10: Using DetailsView to Display Products

```
<%@ Page Language="C#" %>
<html xmlns="http://www.w3.org/1999/xhtml" >
<head runat="server">
  <title>Using DetailsView to display Products</title>
</head>
<body>
  <form id="form1" runat="server">
    <div>
      <asp:SqlDataSource ID="productsSource" runat="server"
        ProviderName="System.Data.SqlClient"
        ConnectionString="<%$ ConnectionStrings:AdventureWorks %>"
        SelectCommand="Select ProductID, Name, ProductNumber, DaysToManufacture
        from Production.Product">
      </asp:SqlDataSource>
      <asp:DetailsView HeaderStyle-Font-Bold="true" HeaderText="Products"
        runat="server" ID="gridProducts" DataSourceID="productsSource"
        AllowPaging="true"/>
    </div>
  </form>
</body>
</html>
```

Figure 8-10 shows `DetailsView` when it is bound to a set of products records, with all the details of the products.

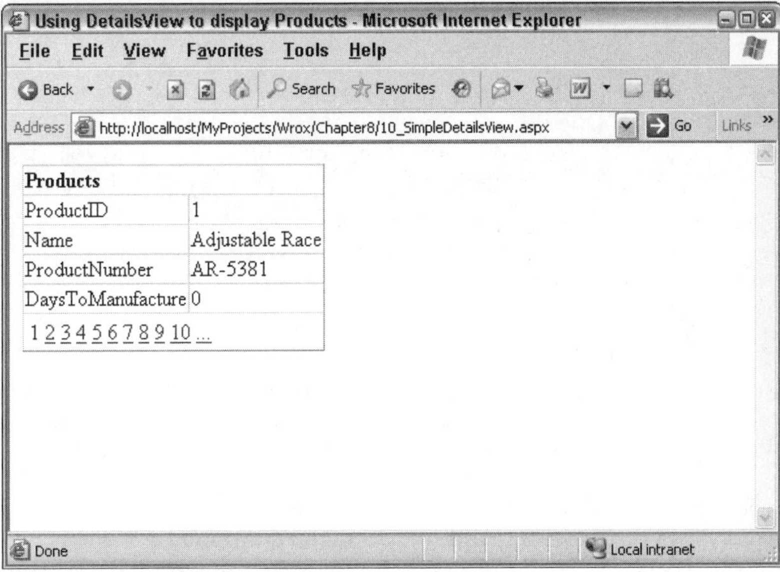

Figure 8-10

As you can see from Figure 8-10, paging is enabled for `DetailsView`. It is tempting to use the `DetailsView` pager controls to make a handy record browser. Unfortunately, this approach can be quite inefficient. First, a separate postback is required each time the user moves from one record to another (whereas a grid control can show multiple records at once). But the real drawback is that each time the page is posted back, the full set of records is retrieved, even though only a single record is shown. If you choose to implement a record browser page with `DetailsView`, at a bare minimum you must enable caching to reduce the database work.

Often, a better choice is to create your own pager controls using a subset of the full data. For example, you could create a drop-down list and bind this to a data source that queries just the product names. Then, when a name is selected from the list, you could retrieve the full details for just that record using another data source. Of course, several metrics can determine which approach is best, including the size of the full record (how much bigger it is than just the first and last name), the usage patterns (whether the average user browses to just one or two records or needs to see them all), and how many records there are in total.

Defining Fields

`DetailsView` uses reflection to generate the fields it shows. That means it examines the data object and creates a separate field for each field (in a row) or property (in a custom object), just like `GridView`. You can disable this automatic field generation by setting `AutoGenerateRows` to `false`. It is then up to you to declare the field objects.

Interestingly, you use the same field object to build a `DetailsView` as you used to design a `GridView`. For example, fields from the data item are represented with the `BoundField` tag, buttons can be created with the `ButtonField`, and so on. For the full list, refer to the first table in this chapter. The only `GridView` column type that `DetailsView` does not support is `TemplateField`.

Following is a portion of the ASP.NET page that shows field declarations for a DetailsView:

```
<asp:DetailsView HeaderStyle-Font-Bold="true" HeaderText="Products" runat="server"
  ID="gridProducts" DataSourceID="productsSource" AllowPaging="true"
  AutoGenerateRows="false">
  <Fields>
    <asp:BoundField DataField="ProductID" HeaderText="ProductID" />
    <asp:BoundField DataField="Name" HeaderText="Name" />
    <asp:BoundField DataField="ProductNumber" HeaderText="Product Number" />
    <asp:BoundField DataField="DaysToManufacture"
      HeaderText="Days To Manufacture"/>
  </Fields>
</asp:DetailsView>
```

You can use the BoundField tag to set properties such as header text, formatting string, editing behavior, and so on. In addition, you can use a certain property with a BoundField that has no effect in a GridView. When it is false, the header text is left out of the row, and the field data takes up both cells.

The field model is not the only part of the GridView that the DetailsView control adopts. It also uses a similar set of styles, a similar set of events, and a similar editing model. The only difference is that instead of creating a dedicated column for editing controls, you simply set Boolean properties such as AutoGenerateDeleteButton, AutoGenerateEditButton, and AutoGenerateInsertButton. The links for these tasks are added to the bottom of the DetailsView. When you add or edit a record, DetailsView always uses standard text box controls such as GridView. For more editing flexibility, you will want to use the FormView control.

FormView

DetailsView supports every type of GridView column except for templated columns. If you need the ultimate flexibility of templates, FormView provides a template-only control for displaying and editing a single record. The beauty of the FormView template model is that it matches the model of the TemplateField in the GridView quite closely. This means you have the following templates to work with: ItemTemplate, EditItemTemplate, InsertItemTemplate, FooterTemplate, HeaderTemplate, EmptyDataTemplate, and PagerTemplate.

This means you can take the exact template content you put in a TemplateField in a GridView and place it inside the FormView. Here is an example based on the previous templated GridView:

```
<asp:FormView AllowPaging="true" ID="gridProducts" runat="server"
  DataSourceID="productsSource">
  <ItemTemplate>
    <b><%# Eval("ProductID") %> -<%# Eval("Name") %></b><hr />
    <small><i>Product Number: <%# Eval("ProductNumber") %><br />
      Days to manufacture:<%# Eval("DaysToManufacture") %> <br />
      Start Date: <%# Eval("SellStartDate", "{0:MM/dd/yy}") %><br /></i><br/><br/>
      Reorder Point:<%# Eval("ReorderPoint") %>
    </small>
  </ItemTemplate>
</asp:FormView>
```

Figure 8-11 shows the result.

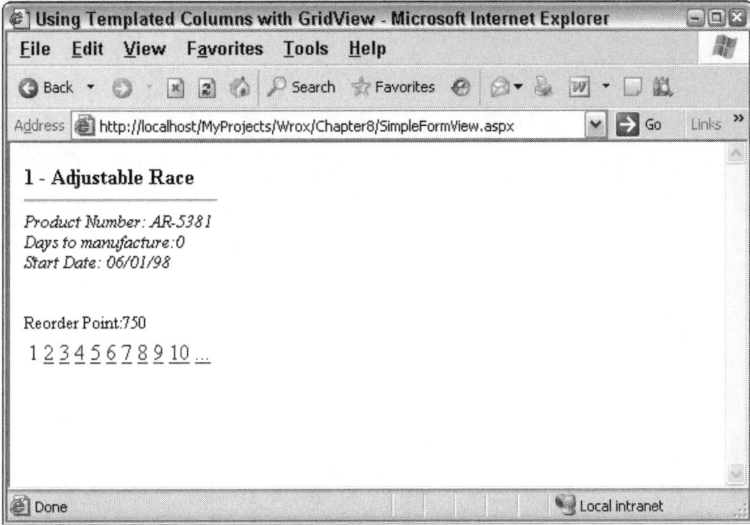

Figure 8-11

If you want to support editing, you need to add button controls that trigger the Edit and Update processes, which is very similar to editing with a `GridView` control.

Summary

This chapter introduced you to the editing, formatting, and displaying and selection features of `GridView` control. You took an exhaustive tour of the `GridView` and explored those of its features that are critical to creating rich data-bound pages. To that end, you looked at the formatting features of `GridView` and the extensibility of the built-in templates supplied with `GridView`. You also considered the steps involved in creating summary information in the footer. Next, you also learned about the steps involved in editing and updating the `GridView` data by considering the event-handling features of `GridView`. Finally, the chapter wrapped up by explaining `DetailsView` and `FormView` and their similarities to `GridView`.

Now that you have a complete understanding of the use of templates in `GridView`, the next chapter goes into two of the most important features of `GridView`, namely sorting and paging.

9

GridView Sorting and Paging

Paging and sorting in the `GridView` control represents the archetype of the advances in ASP.NET version 2.0. From the feedback Microsoft got from the developers after using ASP.NET 1.x, Microsoft knew that it had to implement a whole bunch of new features that everyone wants to utilize. With the release of ASP.NET 2.0, the ASP.NET team wrapped up the hundreds of lines of code necessary and exposed them as simple check boxes. One such feature that was in huge demand is paging and sorting. Now with ASP.NET 2.0, you can add paging or sorting to a table. This chapter will discuss the basics of sorting and paging, then cover some embellishments that solve common real-world problems. Specifically, this chapter will cover:

- How to perform codeless sorting
- How to retrieve sorted data from the database
- How to perform sorting using the middle-tier object
- How to handle events during sorting
- How to display sort direction using visual clues
- How to perform codeless paging
- How to perform paging in the middle tier
- How to customize page templates
- How to perform efficient sorting and paging using callbacks

The next section starts with an overview of the sorting and paging support provided by the `GridView` control.

Sorting and Paging

Paging is the ability to display only portions of the records at one time in a `GridView`; for example, just the first 10 products. It is a navigation tool of some sort that allows the viewer to switch to seeing other sets of products. *Paging* gives the page designer the opportunity to reduce information overload for the user, but at the loss of comprehensiveness of the data. Note that this paging is not concerned with switching between full web (`.aspx`) pages in a web site. That is a job for the site navigation features.

Sorting is the ability to change the order that records are listed in a `GridView`. With sorting enabled, a user can find a given record more easily and make associations between similar records (such as all employees from one state). These techniques are very flexible in ASP.NET 2.0, so this chapter will start with some basic scenarios, and then you'll study the enhancements and potential conflicts between sorting and paging.

As you can see from the brief description, sorting and paging go hand in hand and are closely related in a number of ways. For example, whenever the page index changes, it will have some impact to the way the data is sorted, and similarly, whenever the sorting column is changed, it will have a certain impact on the way the paging works. Before the examples related to sorting and paging, the following table discusses the key properties of `GridView` that are related to these topics.

Property	Description
`AllowSorting`	Indicates whether the `GridView` supports paging.
`AllowPaging`	Indicates whether the control supports sorting.
`EnableSortingAndPagingCallbacks`	Indicates whether sorting and paging are accomplished using script callback functions. This is disabled by default.
`SortDirection`	Gets the direction of the column sort.
`SortExpression`	Gets the current sort expression.

The `SortDirection` and `SortExpression` properties specify the direction and the sort expression on the column that currently determines the order of the rows. Both properties are set by the built-in sorting mechanism of the control when users click the column header. The whole sorting engine is enabled and disabled through the `AllowSorting` property. The `EnableSortingAndPagingCallbacks` property toggles on and off the control's capability for using script callbacks to page and sort without doing roundtrips to the server and changing the entire page.

In addition to the above properties, `GridView` also exposes a number of events. The next table discusses those events fired by the `GridView` control that pertain to sorting and paging.

Event	Description
`PageIndexChanging`, `PageIndexChanged`	Both events occur when one of the pager buttons is clicked. They fire before and after the `GridView` control handles the paging operation, respectively.

Event	Description
SelectedIndexChanging, SelectedIndexChanged	Both events occur when a row's Select button is clicked. The two events occur before and after the GridView control handles the select operation, respectively.
Sorting, Sorted	Both events occur when the hyperlink to sort a column is clicked. They fire before and after the GridView control handles the sort operation, respectively.

Now that you have had a brief look at the sorting and paging properties and events of the GridView control, the next section discusses them in detail.

Sorting Data

Sorting is a delicate, nonlinear operation that normally takes a lot of resources when performed on the client. Generally, the best place to sort records is in the database environment, because of the optimized code you end up running most of the time. Remember this as the next few sections discussing the sorting support of the GridView and data source controls. As already discussed in Chapter 4, GridView itself does not implement the sorting algorithm; instead, it relies on the data source control (or the page, when bound to an enumerable object) to provide sorted data.

Codeless Data Sorting

To enable the GridView control's sorting capabilities, you set the AllowSorting property to true. When sorting is enabled, the GridView gains the ability to render the header text of columns as links. You can associate each column with a sorting expression by using the SortExpression property. A sorting expression is any comma-separated sequence of column names. Each column name can be enriched with an order qualifier such as DESC (indicating descending order) or ASC (indicating ascending order). The ASC qualifier is the default; if omitted, the column is sorted in ascending order. The code in Listing 9-1 sets up the GridView column for sorting on the DepartmentID and Name columns.

Listing 9-1: Simple Sorting with GridView and SqlDataSource Controls

```
<%@ Page Language="C#" %>
<html xmlns="http://www.w3.org/1999/xhtml" >
<head id="Head1" runat="server">
  <title>Simple Sorting using GridView</title>
</head>
<body>
  <form id="form1" runat="server">
    <div>
      <asp:GridView ID="deptView" AllowSorting="true" runat="server"
        AutoGenerateColumns="false" DataSourceID="deptSource">
        <Columns>
          <asp:BoundField HeaderText="Department ID"
            DataField="DepartmentID" SortExpression="DepartmentID" />
          <asp:BoundField HeaderText="Name" DataField="Name"
```

(continued)

Listing 9-1: *(continued)*

```
                SortExpression="Name"/>
            <asp:BoundField HeaderText="Group Name" DataField="GroupName" />
          </Columns>
        </asp:GridView>
        <asp:SqlDataSource ID="deptSource" Runat="server" SelectCommandType="Text"
          SelectCommand="Select DepartmentID, Name, GroupName, ModifiedDate from
          HumanResources.Department"
          ConnectionString="<%$ConnectionStrings:AdventureWorks%>">
        </asp:SqlDataSource>
      </div>
    </form>
  </body>
  </html>
```

As you can see, with virtually no code, you can get the sorting behavior from the `GridView` control. When properly configured, the `GridView` control's sorting infrastructure works without further intervention and in a bidirectional way — that is, if you click on a column sorted in descending order, it is sorted in ascending manner, and vice versa. You need to add some custom code only if you want to implement more advanced capabilities, such as showing a simple indicator in the header to indicate the direction.

As mentioned previously, the main snag with sorting with the `GridView` control is that it totally depends on how the underlying data source control implements it. When the `GridView` is bound to a `SqlDataSource` object, all you need to do is set the `AllowSorting` property to `true` and add the sort expression to the sortable columns. When the user clicks to sort, the grid asks the `SqlDataSource` control to return sorted data. Remember from previous chapters that the `SqlDataSource` control returns a `DataSet` by default. If this is the case, the control retrieves the data, builds a `DataView` out of it, and calls the `Sort()` method of the `DataView` object. This approach works fine, but it is not exactly the fastest way you have to sort. You might still find it to be a good fit for your application, but be aware that sorting is performed using the web server's memory. When combined with caching, performing both paging and sorting in memory is a feasible solution for shared and relatively small sets of records.

Figure 9-1 shows the output produced by the sortable `GridView` bound to a `SqlDataSource` control.

Retrieving Sorted Data from the Database

Now that you have seen an example of sorting data in-memory using `GridView`, you might be wondering if ASP.NET 2.0 provides support for getting presorted data from the database server. To accomplish this, you need to go through the following steps:

1. First, set the `DataSourceMode` property of the `SqlDataSource` control to `DataReader`. If you leave it set to `DataSet`, sorting will occur in memory.
2. The second step requires you to write a stored procedure to retrieve data. To get data sorted, you also set the `SortParameterName` property of the data source control to the name of the stored procedure parameter that indicates the sort expression.
3. Third, you need the stored procedure to build its command text dynamically to incorporate the proper `ORDER BY` clause.

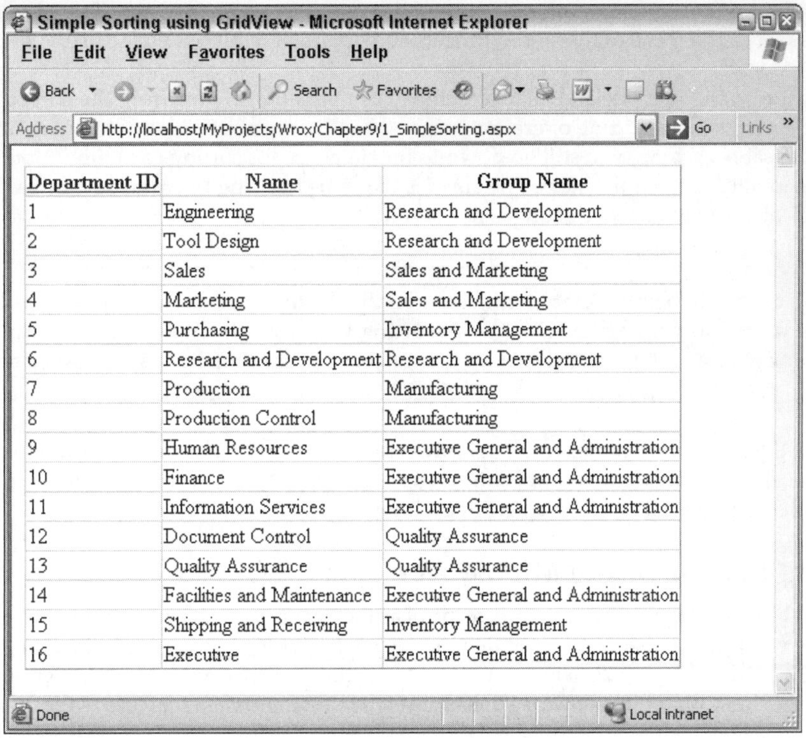

Simple Sorting using GridView - Microsoft Internet Explorer

File Edit View Favorites Tools Help

Address http://localhost/MyProjects/Wrox/Chapter9/1_SimpleSorting.aspx

Department ID	Name	Group Name
1	Engineering	Research and Development
2	Tool Design	Research and Development
3	Sales	Sales and Marketing
4	Marketing	Sales and Marketing
5	Purchasing	Inventory Management
6	Research and Development	Research and Development
7	Production	Manufacturing
8	Production Control	Manufacturing
9	Human Resources	Executive General and Administration
10	Finance	Executive General and Administration
11	Information Services	Executive General and Administration
12	Document Control	Quality Assurance
13	Quality Assurance	Quality Assurance
14	Facilities and Maintenance	Executive General and Administration
15	Shipping and Receiving	Inventory Management
16	Executive	Executive General and Administration

Done   Local intranet

Figure 9-1

Here is an example stored procedure that retrieves the sorted contents of the Department table in the AdventureWorks database, based on the supplied sort column.

```
CREATE PROCEDURE DeptSorted
  @SortColumn varchar(20)='DepartmentID' AS
  SET QUOTED_IDENTIFIER OFF
  IF @SortColumn = ''
    BEGIN
      SET @SortColumn = 'DepartmentID'
    END
    EXEC (
      'SELECT DepartmentID, Name, GroupName, ModifiedDate
       FROM HumanResources.Department ORDER BY ' + @SortColumn)
```

At this point, the `GridView` is ready to show sorted columns of data, and the burden of sorting has moved to the database server. Here is the modified `SqlDataSource` control declaration that leverages the `DeptSorted` stored procedure for sorting:

```
<asp:SqlDataSource ID="deptSource" Runat="server"
  SelectCommand="DeptSorted" SelectCommandType="storedProcedure"
  DataSourceMode="DataReader" SortParameterName="SortColumn"
  ConnectionString="<%$ConnectionStrings:AdventureWorks%>">
</asp:SqlDataSource>
```

Notice the use of the `SortParameterName` and `DataSourceMode` properties. The `SortParameterName` property is set to the name of the stored procedure parameter, which is `SortColumn` in this case.

If you use the `DataSet` mode and enable caching, you initially get data from the database, sorted as expected, but successive sorting operations are resolved in memory. Finally, if you use the `DataSet` mode and disable caching, you still go down to the database for sorting each time. Note that this option is mentioned only for completeness. The effect is the same as using `DataReader`, but a data reader is a more efficient approach when caching is not required.

It is essential to know that sorting data on the database, as shown here, is incompatible with caching. Using caching with sorting will result in an exception being thrown. As a result, you go back to the database every time the user clicks to sort.

In general, the availability of the `SortParameterName` property opens up a world of possibility for sorting the contents of other data-bound controls (for example, `Repeater` and custom controls) that mostly consume data and do not require paging or caching.

Performing Sorting in the Middle Tier

So far, you have used the `SqlDataSource` control as the data source control. You might be wondering how the sorting works if you use an `ObjectDataSource` control instead. In this case, the burden of sorting should be moved to the middle tier and exposed to the data source control by the programming interface of the bound business object. To showcase this, create a `Department` class that acts as the middle-tier object.

Listing 9-2: Performing Sorting in the Middle Tier

```
using System;
using System.Data;
using System.Data.SqlClient;
using System.Web.Configuration;

public class Department
{
  public Department(){}

  public DataTable GetDeptSorted(string sortColumn)
  {
    string connectionString = WebConfigurationManager.ConnectionStrings
      ["AdventureWorks"].ConnectionString;
    DataTable deptTable = new DataTable();
    using (SqlConnection connection = new SqlConnection(connectionString))
    {
      SqlDataAdapter adapter = new SqlDataAdapter();
      SqlCommand command = new SqlCommand("DeptSorted",connection);
      command.CommandType = CommandType.StoredProcedure;
      SqlParameter sortColumnParam = new SqlParameter("@SortColumn",
        SqlDbType.VarChar, 20);
      sortColumnParam.Value = sortColumn;
      command.Parameters.Add(sortColumnParam);
      adapter.SelectCommand = command;
      adapter.Fill(deptTable);
```

```
        }
        return deptTable;
    }
}
```

In Listing 9-2, the `GetDeptSorted()` method of the `Department` class simply invokes the stored procedure created in the previous example. This might not be the best approach ever devised, but it certainly fits the bill for having the burden of sorting moved down to the middle tier and from there to the database. At this point, you set the `SortParameterName` on the `ObjectDataSource` control to the sort control parameter that determines the sorting, which is `sortColumn` in this case:

```
<asp:ObjectDataSource ID="deptSource" Runat="server"
  SelectMethod="GetDeptSorted" TypeName="Department"
  SortParameterName="sortColumn"/>
```

The advantage of this approach is that you take full control of the sorting machinery, and you can decide how, where, and when to implement it. You might have to write some code in your middle tier for sorting, but you only write highly focused code. In fact, no infrastructural code is required, because ASP.NET provides the required plumbing to enable this.

Handling Events during Sorting

One more item worth mentioning about sorting on a `GridView` control is that you can intercept the sorting events and customize their behavior. For example, you can add another column to the sorting expression, or even cancel the sorting operation if required. To do this, you write a handler for the Sorting event. Listing 9-3 shows an example of how to accomplish this.

Listing 9-3: Handling Sorting Events and Customizing Sorting Behavior

```
<%@ Page Language="C#" %>
<script runat="server">
  void deptView_Sorting(object sender, GridViewSortEventArgs e)
  {
    if (e.SortExpression == "Name")
    {
      e.SortExpression = e.SortExpression + ", GroupName";
    }
  }
</script>
<html xmlns="http://www.w3.org/1999/xhtml" >
<head id="Head1" runat="server">
  <title>Handling Events during Sorting</title>
</head>
<body>
  <form id="form1" runat="server">
    <div>
      <asp:GridView ID="deptView" AllowSorting="true" runat="server"
        AutoGenerateColumns="false" DataSourceID="deptSource"
        OnSorting="deptView_Sorting">
        <Columns>
          <asp:BoundField HeaderText="Department ID"
            DataField="DepartmentID" SortExpression="DepartmentID" />
```

(continued)

Listing 9-3: *(continued)*

```
            <asp:BoundField HeaderText="Name" DataField="Name"
              SortExpression="Name" />
            <asp:BoundField HeaderText="Group Name" DataField="GroupName" />
          </Columns>
        </asp:GridView>
        <asp:SqlDataSource ID="deptSource" Runat="server" SelectCommandType="Text"
          SelectCommand="Select DepartmentID, Name, GroupName, ModifiedDate
          from HumanResources.Department"
          ConnectionString="<%$ConnectionStrings:AdventureWorks%>">
        </asp:SqlDataSource>
      </div>
    </form>
  </body>
  </html>
```

Listing 9-3 leverages the `Sorting` event of the `GridView` control to customize the sorting expression to also use the GroupName column whenever the user performs a sort based on the Name column.

> **To cancel the sorting operation, you need to set the `Cancel` property of the event argument data (that is of type `GridViewSortEventArgs`) to `true`.**

Figure 9-2 shows the output when the `GridView` is sorted on the Name column.

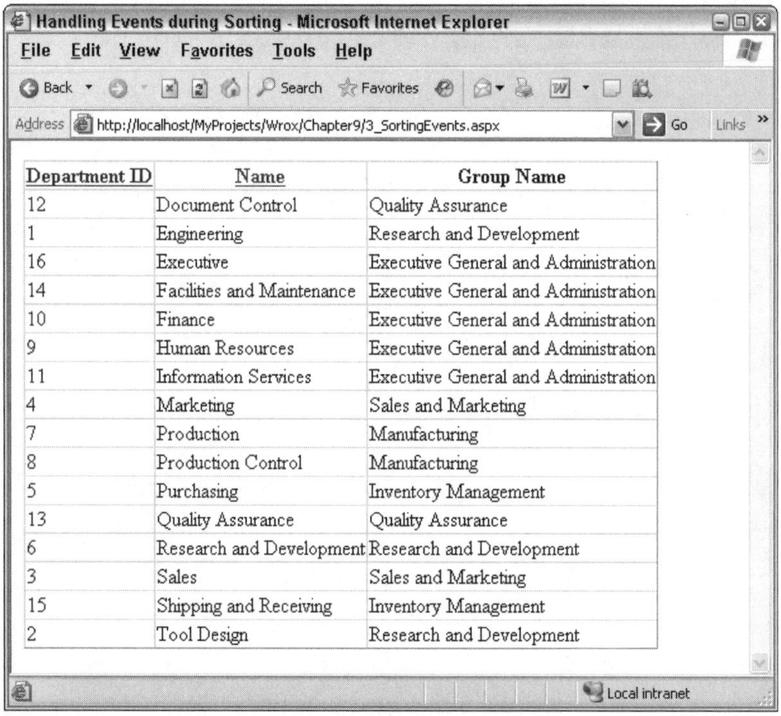

Handling Events during Sorting - Microsoft Internet Explorer

File Edit View Favorites Tools Help

Address http://localhost/MyProjects/Wrox/Chapter9/3_SortingEvents.aspx

Department ID	Name	Group Name
12	Document Control	Quality Assurance
1	Engineering	Research and Development
16	Executive	Executive General and Administration
14	Facilities and Maintenance	Executive General and Administration
10	Finance	Executive General and Administration
9	Human Resources	Executive General and Administration
11	Information Services	Executive General and Administration
4	Marketing	Sales and Marketing
7	Production	Manufacturing
8	Production Control	Manufacturing
5	Purchasing	Inventory Management
13	Quality Assurance	Quality Assurance
6	Research and Development	Research and Development
3	Sales	Sales and Marketing
15	Shipping and Receiving	Inventory Management
2	Tool Design	Research and Development

Local intranet

Figure 9-2

Displaying Sorting Direction

The `GridView` control doesn't automatically add any visual element to the output that indicates the direction of the sorting. This is one of the few cases in which some coding is needed to complete sorting. Listing 9-4 shows the code required to accomplish this.

Listing 9-4: Displaying the Sort Direction Using Images

```
<%@ Page Language="C#" %>
<script runat="server">
  void deptView_RowCreated(object sender, GridViewRowEventArgs e)
  {
    if (e.Row.RowType == DataControlRowType.Header)
    {
      string imageUrl = (deptView.SortDirection==SortDirection.Ascending ?
        "Asc.gif" :"Desc.gif");
      //Find the column you sorted by
      for(int i=0; i<deptView.Columns.Count; i++)
      {
        string columnExpression = deptView.Columns[i].SortExpression;
        if (columnExpression != "" && columnExpression == deptView.SortExpression)
        {
          Image img = new Image();
          img.ImageUrl =imageUrl;
          e.Row.Cells[i].Controls.Add(img);
        }
      }
    }
  }
</script>
<html xmlns="http://www.w3.org/1999/xhtml" >
<head id="Head1" runat="server">
  <title>Adding Indicators to display Sorting Direction</title>
</head>
<body>
  <form id="form1" runat="server">
    <div>
      <asp:GridView ID="deptView" AllowSorting="true" runat="server"
        AutoGenerateColumns="false" DataSourceID="deptSource"
        OnRowCreated="deptView_RowCreated">
        <Columns>
          <asp:BoundField HeaderText="Department ID"
            DataField="DepartmentID" SortExpression="DepartmentID" />
          <asp:BoundField HeaderText="Name" DataField="Name"
            SortExpression="Name" />
          <asp:BoundField HeaderText="Group Name" DataField="GroupName" />
        </Columns>
      </asp:GridView>
      <asp:SqlDataSource ID="deptSource" Runat="server" SelectCommandType="Text"
        SelectCommand="Select DepartmentID, Name, GroupName, ModifiedDate
        from HumanResources.Department"
        ConnectionString="<%$ConnectionStrings:AdventureWorks%>">
```

(continued)

Listing 9-4: *(continued)*

```
        </asp:SqlDataSource>
      </div>
    </form>
  </body>
  </html>
```

The idea is that you write a handler for the `RowCreated` event and look for the moment when the header is created. Next, you create a new `Image` control that represents the sorting direction and add that to the appropriate cell in the `GridView`.

You must add this image alongside the header text of the clicked column. The index of the column can be stored to the view state during the `Sorting` event. Alternately, it can simply be retrieved, comparing the current sort expression (represented by the `SortExpression` property of the `GridView`) to the sort expression of the column. Once you know the index of the column, you retrieve the corresponding table cells and add the image.

The results are shown in Figure 9-3.

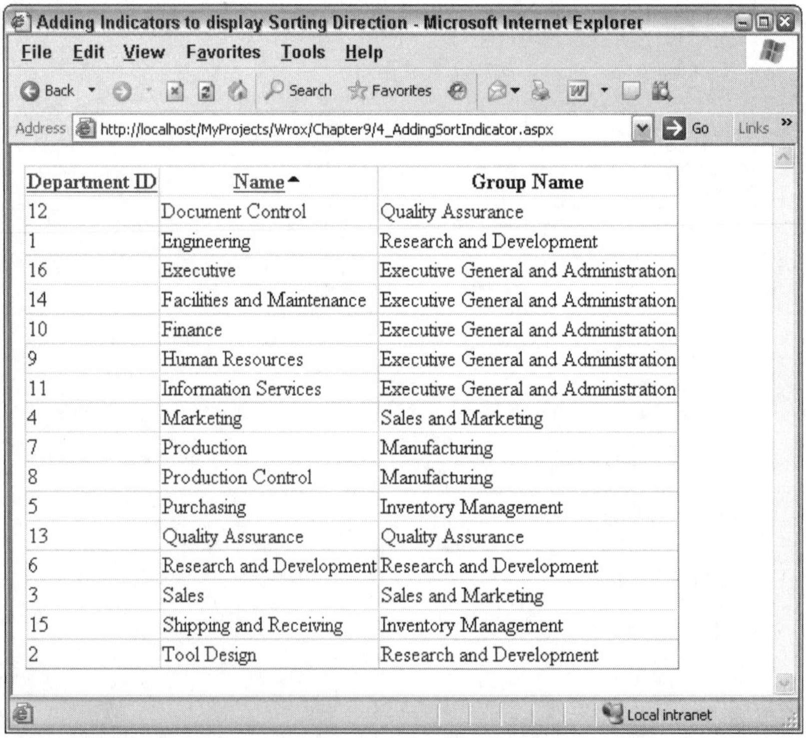

Adding Indicators to display Sorting Direction - Microsoft Internet Explorer

File Edit View Favorites Tools Help

Address http://localhost/MyProjects/Wrox/Chapter9/4_AddingSortIndicator.aspx

Department ID	Name ▲	Group Name
12	Document Control	Quality Assurance
1	Engineering	Research and Development
16	Executive	Executive General and Administration
14	Facilities and Maintenance	Executive General and Administration
10	Finance	Executive General and Administration
9	Human Resources	Executive General and Administration
11	Information Services	Executive General and Administration
4	Marketing	Sales and Marketing
7	Production	Manufacturing
8	Production Control	Manufacturing
5	Purchasing	Inventory Management
13	Quality Assurance	Quality Assurance
6	Research and Development	Research and Development
3	Sales	Sales and Marketing
15	Shipping and Receiving	Inventory Management
2	Tool Design	Research and Development

Local intranet

Figure 9-3

Notice the output in Figure 9-3 is sorted by the Name column in ascending order, and the black triangle right next to the Name column header text clearly reflects that.

Paging Data

`GridView` is designed to take advantage of specific capabilities of the underlying data source control. In this way, the `GridView` control can handle common operations on data such as sorting, paging, updating, and deleting. In general, not all data source components support all possible and feasible data operations. Data source components expose Boolean properties (such as the `CanSort` property) to signal whether they can perform a given operation.

> **If a `GridView` control is bound to its data source through the `DataSource` property — that is, it does not leverage data source controls — its overall behavior (as far as paging and other operations are concerned) is nearly identical to that of the `DataGrid` control. In this case, the `GridView` fires events and expects the binding code in the page to provide instructions and fresh data.**

To some extent, the `GridView` makes transparent for the page developer the implementation of commonly required features such as sorting and paging. In most cases, you need only a fraction of the code you need with the `DataGrid`. In some cases, no code at all is required. However, also keep in mind that the less code you write, the more you rely on the existing infrastructure to get things done. In doing so, you let the system make important decisions on your behalf. Paging and sorting are key operations in web applications. You can still accept what the `GridView` does by default, but if you get to know exactly what happens under the hood, you have a better chance of diagnosing and fixing in a timely manner any performance problems that show up in the lifetime of the application.

Codeless Data Paging

The ability to scroll a potentially large set of data is an important but challenging feature of modern, distributed applications. An effective paging mechanism allows customers to interact with a database without holding resources. To enable paging on a `GridView` control, all you do is set the `AllowPaging` property to `true`. When the `AllowPaging` property is set to `true`, the `GridView` displays a pager bar and can react to the user's pager button clicks.

When a user clicks to see a new page, the page posts back, but the `GridView` traps the event and handles it internally. This marks a major difference between `GridView` and the `DataGrid` and programming model you might know from ASP.NET 1.x. With the `GridView`, there is no need to write a handler for the `PageIndexChanged` event. The event is still exposed (and partnered with `PageIndexChanging`), but you should handle it only to perform extra actions. The `GridView` knows how to retrieve and display the requested new page. For example, consider the following control declaration:

```
<asp:GridView ID="deptView" runat="server"
  DataSourceID="deptSource" AllowPaging="true" />
```

The `deptSource` control bound to the `GridView` is immediately pageable. As in Figure 9-4, the control displays a pager with a few predefined links and automatically selects the correct subset of rows that fit in the selected page.

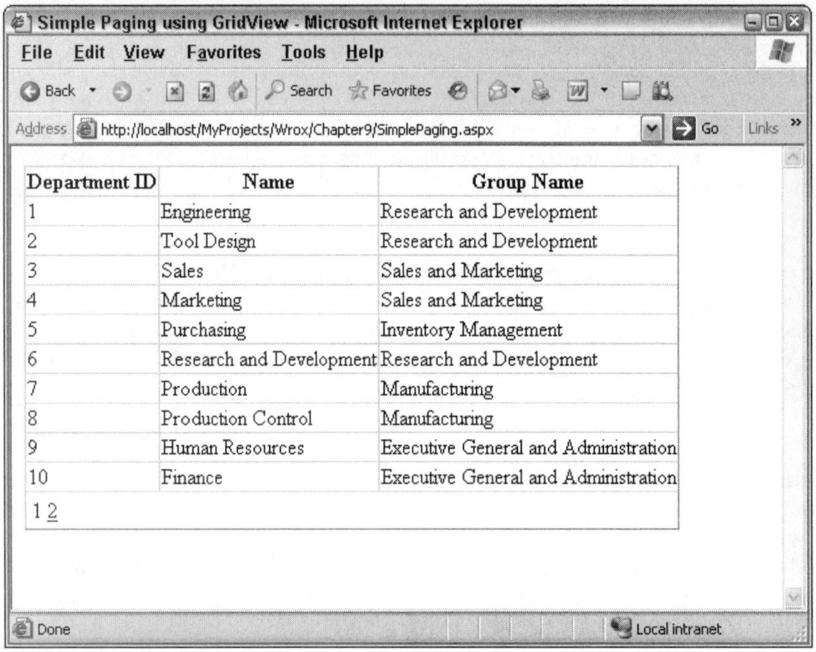
Simple Paging using GridView - Microsoft Internet Explorer
File Edit View Favorites Tools Help
Back
Search
Favorites
Address
http://localhost/MyProjects/Wrox/Chapter9/SimplePaging.aspx
Go
Links
Department ID
Name
Group Name
1 Engineering Research and Development
2 Tool Design Research and Development
3 Sales Sales and Marketing
4 Marketing Sales and Marketing
5 Purchasing Inventory Management
6 Research and Development Research and Development
7 Production Manufacturing
8 Production Control Manufacturing
9 Human Resources Executive General and Administration
10 Finance Executive General and Administration
1 2
Done
Local intranet

Figure 9-4

The default user interface you get with the `GridView` does not include the page number. Adding a page number label is as easy as writing a handler for the `PageIndexChanged` event:

```
void deptView_PageIndexChanged(object sender, EventArgs e)
{
  lblCurrentPage.Text = (deptView.PageIndex + 1).ToString();
}
```

Once again, note that the `PageIndexChanged` handler is not involved with data binding or page selection, as it is with `DataGrid` controls. If you do not need any post-paging operation, you can completely omit it altogether.

How Paging Works

The `GridView` control does not really know how to get a new page. It simply asks the bound data source control to return the rows that fit in the specified page. Paging is ultimately up to the data source control. When a grid is bound to a `SqlDataSource` control, paging requires that the whole data source be bound to the control. When a `GridView` is bound to an `ObjectDataSource` control, paging depends on the capabilities of the middle-tier object you are connecting to.

When using a `SqlDataSource` control, it is mandatory that you set `DataSourceMode` to `DataSet` (the default setting). This means that the whole dataset is retrieved, and only the few records that fit in the current page size are displayed. In an extreme scenario, you might end up downloading 1000 records for each postback to show only 10. Things go much better if you enable caching on `SqlDataSource` by setting EnableCaching to true. In this case, the whole data set is downloaded only once and stored in the ASP.NET cache for the specified duration. As long as the data stays cached, any page is displayed almost for free. However, a potentially large chunk of data is stored in memory. This option is therefore recommended only for relatively small sets of records shared by all users.

If you want to page records at the database level, the best that you can do is code the desired behavior in a stored procedure and bind the stored procedure to the SelectCommand *property of the* SqlDataSource *control. In this case, turn caching off.*

Performing Paging in the Middle Tier

As you saw in the previous section, the SqlDataSource control supports paging where you do not need to do anything except set the AllowPaging property to true. With ObjectDataSource control, you have to do some extra work, such as adding two arguments to your select method: one for the value of the current page index selected from the paging navigation, and another argument for the maximum number of rows that should be displayed on each page.

Note that the extra work is required only when you return a custom object from your middle tier. However, if your SelectMethod *returns a* DataSet*, the extra work is not required and paging works just fine out of the box.*

In addition to adding the above two arguments to the Select method, you also need to set the Select CountMethod property of the ObjectDataSource control to a method that returns the total number of output rows. Listing 9-5 shows the Department class with the select method (named GetDepartments) and the select count method (named GetNumberOfDepartments).

Listing 9-5: Methods of the Department Class That Enable Paging

```
using System;
using System.Collections.Generic;
using System.Data;
using System.Data.SqlClient;
using System.Web.Configuration;

public class Department
{
  public Department()
  {
  }

  public IList<DepartmentInfo> GetDepartments(int startIndex, int numRows)
  {
    string connectionString = WebConfigurationManager.ConnectionStrings
      ["AdventureWorks"].ConnectionString;
    IList<DepartmentInfo> deptCollection = new List<DepartmentInfo>();
    using (SqlConnection connection = new SqlConnection(connectionString))
    {
      string sql = "GetPagedDepartments";
      SqlCommand command = new SqlCommand(sql, connection);
      command.CommandType = CommandType.StoredProcedure;
```

(continued)

Listing 9-5: *(continued)*

```
        SqlParameter startIndexParameter = new
          SqlParameter("@StartRowIndex",SqlDbType.Int);
        startIndexParameter.Direction = ParameterDirection.Input;
        startIndexParameter.Value = startIndex;
        command.Parameters.Add(startIndexParameter);
        SqlParameter numRowsParameter = new SqlParameter("@NumRows", SqlDbType.Int);
        numRowsParameter.Direction = ParameterDirection.Input;
        numRowsParameter.Value = numRows;
        command.Parameters.Add(numRowsParameter);
        connection.Open();
        SqlDataReader reader = command.ExecuteReader
          (CommandBehavior.CloseConnection);
        while (reader.Read())
        {
          DepartmentInfo dept = new DepartmentInfo();
          dept.DepartmentID = Convert.ToInt32(reader["DepartmentID"]);
          dept.Name = reader["Name"].ToString();
          dept.GroupName = reader["GroupName"].ToString();
          dept.ModifiedDate = Convert.ToDateTime(reader["ModifiedDate"].ToString());
          deptCollection.Add(dept);
        }
      }
      return deptCollection;
    }

    public int GetNumberOfDepartments()
    {
      string connectionString = WebConfigurationManager.ConnectionStrings
        ["AdventureWorks"].ConnectionString;
      int count;
      using (SqlConnection connection = new SqlConnection(connectionString))
      {
        string sql = "GetNumberOfDepartments";
        SqlCommand command = new SqlCommand(sql, connection);
        command.CommandType = CommandType.StoredProcedure;
        connection.Open();
        count = (int) command.ExecuteScalar();
      }
      return count;
    }
  }
```

When the `GetDepartments()` method is executed by the `ObjectDataSource` control, the current selected index of the page will be passed as a value to the `startIndex` argument, and the number of rows per page will be passed to the `maxRows` argument. By using the values from those arguments, you return a list with only the item that should be displayed for the selected page. You should only return a list with the number of items equal to the `maxRows` argument. Inside the `GetDepartments()` method, you invoke a stored procedure named `GetPagedDepartments` that is declared as follows:

```
CREATE PROC [dbo].[GetPagedDepartments]
  @StartRowIndex int,
  @NumRows int
AS
  BEGIN
    WITH DeptEntries AS (
      SELECT ROW_NUMBER() OVER (ORDER BY DepartmentID ASC) AS Row, DepartmentID,
        Name, GroupName, ModifiedDate FROM HumanResources.Department)
    SELECT DepartmentID, Name, GroupName, ModifiedDate FROM DeptEntries
    Where Row BETWEEN @StartRowIndex AND @StartRowIndex + @NumRows
  END
```

The `GetPagedDepartments` stored procedure uses the SQL Server 2005 `ROW_NUMBER` function to identify the right set of records to return during a particular stage of paging. This is accomplished using the `ROW_NUMBER` function in conjunction with the `StartRow` and NumRows parameters.

SQL Server 2005 has a `ROW_NUMBER` function that can help with paging records for your database applications. The `ROW_NUMBER` function returns a sequential number, starting at 1, for each row returned in a result set. For example, if you want the first page of 10 records from a log file sorted by `Date DESC`, you can use the `ROW_NUMBER` function as follows:

```
SELECT  Description, Date FROM    (SELECT  ROW_NUMBER() OVER
  (ORDER BY Date DESC) AS Row, Description, Date FROM LOG)
  AS LogWithRowNumbers WHERE  Row >= 1 AND Row <= 10
```

Note that the `ROW_NUMBER` is only available in SQL Server 2005, but it provides an intuitive approach to enabling paging when compared to the previous paging implementations with SQL Server 2000, which involved using temp tables and a bunch of stored procedures.

The `DepartmentInfo` class used in Listing 9-5 just contains public properties such as `DepartmentID`, `Name`, `GroupName`, and `ModifiedDate`. Now that you have created the middle-tier class, the next step is to use it with the `ObjectDataSource` control. Listing 9-6 provides the ASP.NET page code.

Listing 9-6: Paging with the ObjectDataSource Control

```
<%@ Page Language="C#" %>
<html xmlns="http://www.w3.org/1999/xhtml" >
<head id="Head1" runat="server">
  <title>Paging using ObjectDataSource Control</title>
</head>
<body>
  <form id="form1" runat="server">
    <div>
      <asp:GridView ID="departmentsView" runat="server" DataSourceID="deptSource"
        AutoGenerateColumns="False" HeaderStyle-HorizontalAlign="Center"
        HeaderStyle-Font-Bold="True" HeaderStyle-BackColor="blue"
```

(continued)

Listing 9-6: *(continued)*

```
            HeaderStyle-ForeColor="White" AllowPaging="True" PageSize="5">
            <Columns>
              <asp:BoundField ReadOnly="True" HeaderText="DepartmentID"
                DataField="DepartmentID" />
              <asp:BoundField HeaderText="Name" DataField="Name" />
              <asp:BoundField HeaderText="GroupName" DataField="GroupName" />
              <asp:BoundField HeaderText="ModifiedDate" DataField="ModifiedDate" />
            </Columns>
          </asp:GridView>
          <asp:ObjectDataSource EnablePaging="True"
            SelectCountMethod="GetNumberOfDepartments"
            StartRowIndexParameterName="startIndex" MaximumRowsParameterName="numRows"
            ID="deptSource" runat="server" TypeName="Department"
            SelectMethod="GetDepartments">
          </asp:ObjectDataSource>
        </div>
      </form>
    </body>
    </html>
```

Remember from Listing 9-5 that the `GetDepartments()` methods accepts two arguments: `startIndex` and `maxRows`. The `ObjectDataSource` will not automatically know that your `startIndex` or `maxRows` argument is the argument that it should use to pass the paging information to your `select` method. You have to tell the `ObjectDataSource` which arguments it should use. You do that by using the `StartRowIndexParameterName` and `MaximumRowsParameterName` properties of the `ObjectDataSource`:

```
<asp:ObjectDataSource EnablePaging=true StartRowIndexParameterName="startIndex"
  MaximumRowsParameterName="maxRows" ID="deptSource" runat="server"
  TypeName="Department" SelectMethod="GetDepartments"
  SelectCountMethod="GetNumberOfDepartments" ...>
</asp:ObjectDataSource>
```

You also need to turn on the paging for the `ObjectDataSource` control. For this purpose, set the `EnablePaging` property of the `ObjectDataSource` to `true`. There is one thing more you need to do before the paging could work properly. You must specify a method that will return the total number of items of your `select` method (not the number of items on each page, the total number of items that should have been returned if the paging was not used). If you do not do that, the number of items the data control will get from your `select` method will be the number of rows that should be displayed on each page. If you set the page size to 10, the select method will probably return 10 items that should be bound to your data control. You can use the `SelectCountMethod` property to specify the method that will return the total number of items that your select method will return from your data source. With all these properties set, navigate to the page using a browser and you should see output similar to that in Figure 9-5.

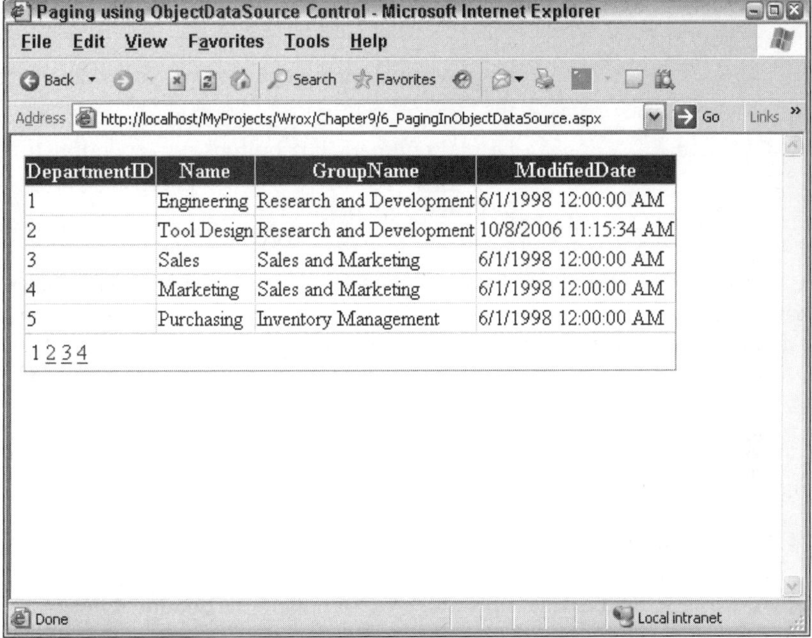

Figure 9-5

> **In the preceding code, you explicitly specify only the parameters whose contents are necessary for the method to work. The two paging-related parameters are left for the `GridView` to set. The page size parameter is automatically bound to the `PageSize` property of the `GridView`.**

Configuring the Pager

When the `AllowPaging` property is set to `true`, the grid displays a pager bar. You can control the characteristics of the pager, to a large extent, through the `<PagerSettings>` and `<PagerStyle>` tags or their equivalent properties. The pager of the `GridView` control also supports first and last page buttons and lets you assign an image to each button. The pager can work in either of two modes — displaying explicit page numbers, or providing a relative navigation system. In the former case, the pager contains numeric links, one representing a page index. In the latter case, buttons are present to navigate to the next or previous page and even to the first or last page. The `Mode` property rules the user interface of the pager. Available modes are listed in the following table.

Mode	Description
`NextPrevious`	Displays Next and Previous buttons to access the next and previous pages of the `GridView`.
`NextPreviousFirstLast`	Displays Next and Previous buttons, plus First and Last buttons to directly access first and last pages of the `GridView`.

Table continued on following page

Mode	Description
`Numeric`	Displays numeric link buttons corresponding to the pages of the `GridView`.
`NumericFirstLast`	Displays numeric link buttons corresponding to the pages of the grid, plus First and Last buttons to directly access first and last pages of the `GridView`.

In addition to the above modes, the `PagerSettings` class also exposes a whole bunch of ad hoc pairs of properties — `xxxPageText` and `xxxPageImageUrl`. These properties let you set the labels for these buttons as desired. The `xxx` stands for any of the following: `First`, `Last`, `Next`, or `Previous`.

Depending on the size of the `GridView`, the first and last rows in a grid might not necessarily fit in the screen real estate. To make it easier for users to page regardless of the scrollbar's position, you can enable top and bottom pagers for a grid. You do this by setting the `Position` attribute on the `<PagerSettings>` element:

```
<PagerSettings Position="TopAndBottom" />
```

Other options are to display the pager only at the top or only at the bottom of the grid.

The pager of the `GridView` control can be entirely replaced with a new one, in case of need. You do this by adding the `<PagerTemplate>` element to the control's declaration. Listing 9-7 provides an example.

Listing 9-7: Using Custom PagerTemplate

```
<%@ Page Language="C#" %>
<script runat="server">
  void deptView_RowCommand(object sender, GridViewCommandEventArgs e)
  {
    switch (e.CommandName)
    {
      case "Last":
        {deptView.PageIndex = deptView.PageCount - 1; break; }
      case "First":
        {deptView.PageIndex = 0; break;}
      case "Next":
        {deptView.PageIndex ++; break;}
      case "Prev":
        {deptView.PageIndex --;break;}
    }
  }
</script>
<html xmlns="http://www.w3.org/1999/xhtml" >
<head id="Head1" runat="server">
  <title>Customizing Paging using PagerTemplate</title>
</head>
<body>
  <form id="form1" runat="server">
    <div>
      <asp:GridView ID="deptView" AllowPaging="true" runat="server"
        AutoGenerateColumns="false" DataSourceID="deptSource"
```

```
          OnRowCommand="deptView_RowCommand">
          <Columns>
            <asp:BoundField HeaderText="Department ID"
              DataField="DepartmentID" SortExpression="DepartmentID" />
            <asp:BoundField HeaderText="Name" DataField="Name"
              SortExpression="Name"/>
            <asp:BoundField HeaderText="Group Name" DataField="GroupName" />
          </Columns>
          <PagerTemplate>
            <asp:Button ID="btnFirst" runat="server" commandname="First"
              Text="First" />
            <asp:Button ID="btnPrev" runat="server" commandname="Prev" Text="<<" />
            <asp:Button ID="btnNext" runat="server" commandname="Next" Text=">>" />
            <asp:Button ID="btnLast" runat="server" commandname="Last" Text="Last" />
          </PagerTemplate>
        </asp:GridView>
        <asp:SqlDataSource ID="deptSource" Runat="server" SelectCommandType="Text"
          SelectCommand="Select DepartmentID, Name, GroupName, ModifiedDate
          from HumanResources.Department"
          ConnectionString="<%$ConnectionStrings:AdventureWorks%>">
        </asp:SqlDataSource>
        <asp:Label runat="Server" ID="lblCurrentPage" />
      </div>
    </form>
  </body>
  </html>
```

The key thing in Listing 9-7 is the addition of the `RowCommand` event of `GridView` that allows you to capture command button clicks. In that event, you set the page index explicitly. Figure 9-6 shows the output produced by the pageable `GridView` with a custom pager.

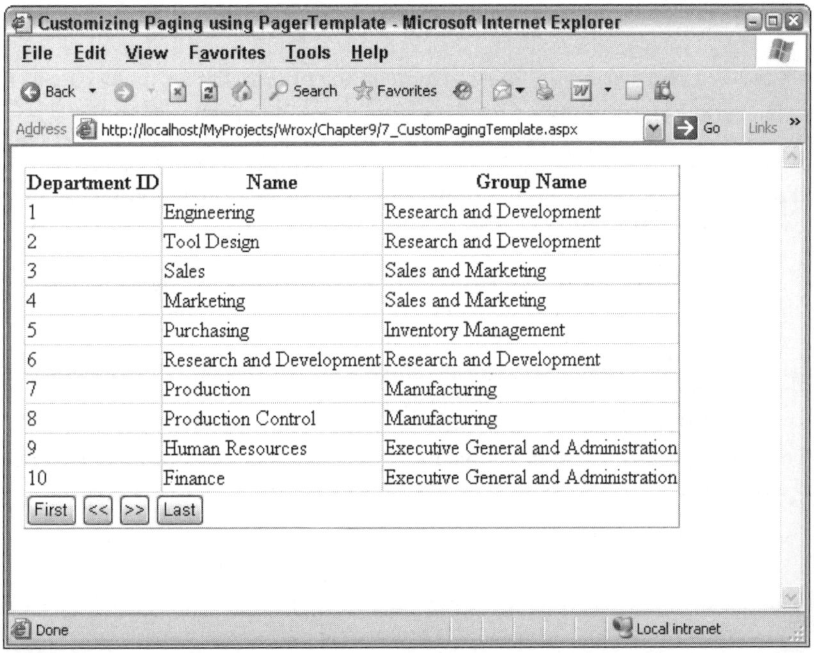

Department ID	Name	Group Name
1	Engineering	Research and Development
2	Tool Design	Research and Development
3	Sales	Sales and Marketing
4	Marketing	Sales and Marketing
5	Purchasing	Inventory Management
6	Research and Development	Research and Development
7	Production	Manufacturing
8	Production Control	Manufacturing
9	Human Resources	Executive General and Administration
10	Finance	Executive General and Administration

First << >> Last

Customizing Paging using PagerTemplate - Microsoft Internet Explorer
File Edit View Favorites Tools Help
Back Search Favorites
Address http://localhost/MyProjects/Wrox/Chapter9/7_CustomPagingTemplate.aspx Go Links
Done Local intranet

Figure 9-6

As you can see, this code is quite simple and should be fleshed out a little bit, at least to make it capable of disabling buttons when the first or last index is reached.

Efficient Paging and Sorting Using Callbacks

Both sorting and paging operations require a postback with subsequent full refresh of the page. In most cases, this is a heavy operation, because the page usually contains lots of graphics. To provide the user with a better experience, it would be nice if the `GridView` could go down to the web server, grab the new set of records, and update only a portion of the interface. In fact, the `GridView` control is capable of offering this feature. All that you have to do is turn on the Boolean property `EnableSortingAndPagingCallbacks`. As mentioned, the feature relies on the services of the ASP.NET script callback engine, which is also designed to work with non–Internet Explorer browsers, including Firefox, Netscape 6.x, and the latest Opera browser. Consider this code:

```
<asp:GridView ID="deptView" AllowSorting="true" AllowPaging="true"
  runat="server" AutoGenerateColumns="false" DataSourceID="deptSource"
  EnableSortingAndPagingCallbacks="true">
  <Columns>
    <asp:BoundField HeaderText="Department ID" DataField="DepartmentID"
      SortExpression="DepartmentID" />
    <asp:BoundField HeaderText="Name" DataField="Name" SortExpression="Name" />
    <asp:BoundField HeaderText="Group Name" DataField="GroupName" />
  </Columns>
</asp:GridView>
```

Notice the use of the `AllowSorting`, `AllowPaging`, and `EnableSortingAndPagingCallbacks` properties.

Summary

This chapter covered two capabilities that are high on the priority list for many clients: the abilities to sort and page within a table. Although it is powerful, the code is prewritten in the `GridView`, and our task as designers is very simple. To sort, you must turn on sorting and show headers in the `GridView` object. Within each tag you need a header text and a sort expression. Optionally, you can set the appearance for all the headers (using the header row style of the `GridView`) or you can set the appearance of just one header (using the column's header style property).

To add paging to a `GridView`, at a minimum set the `AllowPaging` to true within the `GridView`. This simple setting enables the paging behavior and creates a Pager cell at the bottom of the `GridView`. You can apply a style to the Pager using the `PagerStyle`, like any other row style. You can use the pager mode to determine which items of page navigation are available, including numeric, next, previous, first and last. These options can be presented to the user as ASCII arrows (default), literal text, or images.

With this background on sorting and paging, the next chapter looks at the advanced features of data source and data-bound controls.

10

Advanced Data Source and Data Bound Controls

As discussed in the previous chapters, Microsoft has expanded the concept of data binding to make it even easier to understand and use with ASP.NET 2.0. This is accomplished primarily through the introduction of a new layer of data abstraction called data source controls. The previous chapters have explored the basics of these data source controls, as well as data bound controls. Now that you have had a background on these, this chapter shifts gears and moves into the advanced features of these controls. Specifically, this chapter will cover:

- How to generate a master/detail display
- How to display a parent/child view in a single `GridView`
- How to display the selected rows in a `GridView`
- How to display images from database using an `HttpHandler`
- How to create custom templates for use within a `GridView`
- How to use themes with data bound controls
- How to perform two-way data binding with the `FormView` control
- How to extend the `GridView` control

Advanced Controls

In the last few chapters, you have understood the use of various data source and data bound controls supplied with ASP.NET 2.0. With that background, this chapter shifts focus from the how-to aspects of these controls to more advanced concepts of these controls. In the following sections, you will consider the advanced features of `GridView` such as displaying master/detail capability, displaying images in a `GridView`, and creating custom templates. You will also learn how themes can be used in conjunction with data bound controls for providing consistent look and feel for the entire web site. Finally, you will also learn more about the `FormView` control. The next section starts with an examination of the master/details display using a `GridView`.

Master/Detail Display

By pairing a `GridView` control with a `DetailsView` control, you can display a set of master and detail records from a data source. A master list of records is presented in the `GridView`. Each record is accompanied by a link or a button for selecting that row. On the basis of this selection, the `DetailsView` displays data fields associated with this same record. This section discusses an example master/detail display for the Product table in the AdventureWorks database. Clicking a Select link in the `GridView` retrieves and displays fields for the selected record in the `DetailsView`.

The `GridView` and `DetailsView` controls are linked separately to the same data source through their respective `SqlDataSource` controls. Special properties of these controls associate the record chosen from the `GridView` with the record displayed in the `DetailsView`. Listing 10-1 shows the complete code required to generate the master/detail display.

Listing 10-1: Generating Master/Detail Display

```
<%@ Page Language="C#" %>
<html xmlns="http://www.w3.org/1999/xhtml" >
<head id="Head1" runat="server">
  <title>Master Detail using GridView and DetailsView</title>
</head>
<body>
  <form id="form1" runat="server">
    <div>
      <asp:GridView ID="productsView" DataKeyNames="ProductID" runat="server"
        Style="float:left" Width="320" Caption="Products"
        AutoGenerateColumns="false" DataSourceID="productsSource"
        AutoGenerateSelectButton="True" SelectedIndex="0"
        SelectedRowStyle-BackColor="LightBlue" HeaderStyle-BackColor="Blue"
        HeaderStyle-ForeColor="White">
        <Columns>
          <asp:BoundField DataField="Name" HeaderText="Product Name"/>
          <asp:BoundField DataField="ProductNumber" HeaderText="Product Number"/>
        </Columns>
      </asp:GridView>
      <asp:SqlDataSource ID="productsSource" Runat="server"
        SelectCommandType="Text" SelectCommand="Select ProductID, Name,
        ProductNumber, ListPrice from Production.Product"
        ConnectionString="<%$ConnectionStrings:AdventureWorks%>">
      </asp:SqlDataSource>
      <asp:DetailsView id="productDetailView" DataSourceID="productDetailSource"
        Runat="Server" AutoGenerateRows="False" GridLines="None"
        Caption="Product Details" CaptionAlign="Left" BorderStyle="Ridge"
        HeaderText="Products Item" HeaderStyle-Font-Bold="True"
        HeaderStyle-HorizontalAlign="Center" HeaderStyle-BackColor="Lightblue"
        RowStyle-VerticalAlign="Top">
        <Fields>
          <asp:BoundField DataField="Name" HeaderText="Product Name" />
```

```
          <asp:BoundField DataField="ProductNumber" HeaderText="Product Number" />
          <asp:BoundField DataField="ListPrice" HeaderText="List Price"
            DataFormatString="{0:C}"/>
          <asp:BoundField DataField="Color" HeaderText="Color" />
          <asp:BoundField DataField="StandardCost" HeaderText="Standard Cost"
            DataFormatString="{0:C}"/>
          <asp:BoundField DataField="SellStartDate" HeaderText="Sell Start Date"
            DataFormatString="{0:d}"/>
        </Fields>
      </asp:DetailsView>
      <asp:SqlDataSource ID="productDetailSource" Runat="server"
        SelectCommandType="Text" SelectCommand="Select Name, ProductNumber,
        ListPrice, Color, StandardCost, SellStartDate from Production.Product
        Where ProductID = @ProductID"
        ConnectionString="<%$ConnectionStrings:AdventureWorks%>">
        <SelectParameters>
          <asp:ControlParameter Name="ProductID" ControlID="productsView"
            PropertyName="SelectedValue"/>
        </SelectParameters>
      </asp:SqlDataSource>
    </div>
  </form>
</body>
</html>
```

As you can see from Listing 10-1, the `GridView`, which displays a set of master records, exposes three additional properties, which are `AutoGenerateSelectButton`, `DataKeyNames`, and `SelectedIndex`.

- The `AutoGenerateSelectButton` property enables you to produce a column of Select link buttons (displayed as text links) for selecting individual rows of the `GridView`.
- The `DataKeyNames` property identifies a data field in the data source whose values are associated with the link buttons and that are used to retrieve matching records for displaying in the `DetailsView`.
- The `SelectedIndex` property of the `GridView` identifies a row that is selected by clicking the Select button. When the `GridView` is initially displayed, the `DetailsView` displays the first record from the `GridView`. To accomplish this, the `SelectedIndex` property is initially set to point to this first row (`row index = 0`) so that it will be highlighted when the `GridView` is first displayed.

> **Normally, the `DataKeyNames` value is the unique record key field in the data source. However, you can also use a combination of fields, separated by commas, as the unique identifier. It is important to remember that a clicked link supplies the `GridView` control's `SelectedValue` property, which is needed for locating the matching record for the `DetailsView`.**

A separate `SqlDataSource` is associated with the `DetailsView`. It uses slightly different SQL as part of the `SelectCommand` property to link to the AdventureWorks database. Also, it requires additional properties and controls in order to display details for the record selected from the `GridView`. To retrieve the record matching the one selected in the `GridView`, the `SqlDataSource` for the `DetailsView` must issue a `SelectCommand`. In this example, the matching record is one with a `ProductID` value matching the `ProductID` selected in the `GridView`. To retrieve the value from the `GridView` and use it as a parameter to the select query, you specify a parameterized command for the `SelectCommand` property:

```
SelectCommand="Select Name, ProductNumber, ListPrice, Color, StandardCost,
SellStartDate from Production.Product Where ProductID = @ProductID"
```

The value of the `ProductID` parameter comes from a source identified in an `<asp:ControlParameter>` control coded inside a `<SelectParameters>` tag enclosed in the `SqlDataSource`:

```
<asp:SqlDataSource ......>
  <SelectParameters>
    <asp:ControlParameter Name="ProductID" ControlID="productsView"
      PropertyName="SelectedValue"/>
  </SelectParameters>
</asp:SqlDataSource>
```

By associating the selected `ProductID` from the `GridView` (through the `SelectedValue` property) to the value for the `@ProductID` parameter, you can execute the query with the right parameters. Figure 10-1 shows the output produced by the page when it is navigated to from a browser.

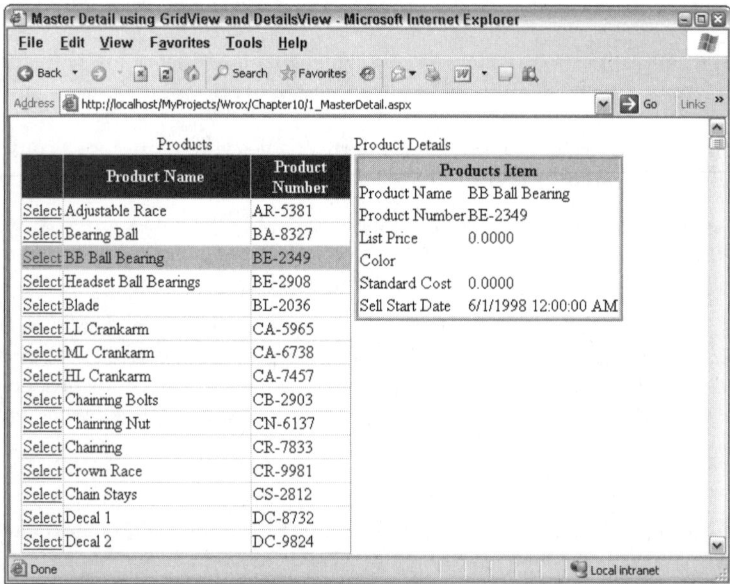

Figure 10-1

Displaying Parent/Child View in a Single GridView

In the previous section, you saw a master/detail page that used a combination of `GridView` and `DetailsView`. This gives you the flexibility to show the child records for just the currently selected parent record. However, sometimes you want to create a parent/child report that shows all the records from the child table, organized by parent. For example, you could use this to create a complete list of products organized by category. The next example demonstrates how you show a complete, subgrouped product list in a single grid.

The basic technique is to create a `GridView` for the parent table that contains an embedded `GridView` for each row. These child `GridView` controls are inserted into the parent `GridView` using a `TemplateField`. The only trick is that you cannot bind the child `GridView` controls at the same time that you bind the parent `GridView`, because the parent rows have not been created yet. Instead, you need to wait for the `GridView.RowDataBound` event to fire in the parent. The code required to achieve this output is shown in Listing 10-2.

Listing 10-2: Parent/Child Display Using Embedded GridView

```
<%@ Page Language="C#" %>
<script runat="server">
  void categoryView_RowDataBound(object sender, GridViewRowEventArgs e)
  {
    if (e.Row.RowType == DataControlRowType.DataRow)
    {
      //Retrieve the GridView control in the second column
      GridView productView = (GridView)e.Row.Cells[1].Controls[1];
      //Set the CategoryID parameter to return the products for current category
      string categoryID =
        categoryView.DataKeys[e.Row.DataItemIndex].Value.ToString();
      productSource.SelectParameters[0].DefaultValue = categoryID ;
      productView.DataSource =
        productSource.Select(DataSourceSelectArguments.Empty);
      productView.DataBind();
    }
  }
</script>
<html xmlns="http://www.w3.org/1999/xhtml" >
<head id="Head1" runat="server">
  <title>Embedding Child GridView within a Parent GridView</title>
</head>
<body>
  <form id="form1" runat="server">
    <div>
      <asp:GridView ID="categoryView" DataKeyNames="ProductSubcategoryID"
        runat="server" AutoGenerateColumns="false" DataSourceID="categorySource"
        OnRowDataBound="categoryView_RowDataBound" HeaderStyle-BackColor="blue"
        HeaderStyle-ForeColor="White">
        <Columns>
          <asp:TemplateField HeaderText="Category">
            <ItemStyle VerticalAlign="Top" Width="20%"/>
            <ItemTemplate>
              <br/><b><%# Eval("ProductSubcategoryID") %></b>
              <br/><br/><%# Eval("Name") %><br/>
            </ItemTemplate>
          </asp:TemplateField>
          <asp:TemplateField HeaderText="Products">
```

(continued)

Listing 10-2: *(continued)*

```
            <ItemStyle VerticalAlign="Top"/>
            <ItemTemplate>
              <asp:GridView AutoGenerateColumns="false" ID="productView"
                runat="server">
                <Columns>
                  <asp:BoundField DataField="Name" HeaderText="Product Name"/>
                  <asp:BoundField DataField="ProductNumber"
                    HeaderText="Product Number"/>
                  <asp:BoundField DataField="ListPrice" HeaderText="List Price"
                    DataFormatString="{0:C}"/>
                </Columns>
              </asp:GridView>
            </ItemTemplate>
          </asp:TemplateField>
        </Columns>
      </asp:GridView>
      <asp:SqlDataSource ID="categorySource" Runat="server"
        SelectCommandType="Text" SelectCommand="Select ProductSubcategoryID, Name
        from Production.ProductSubcategory"
        ConnectionString="<%$ConnectionStrings:AdventureWorks%>">
      </asp:SqlDataSource>
      <asp:SqlDataSource ID="productSource" Runat="server" SelectCommandType="Text"
        SelectCommand="Select Name, ProductNumber, ListPrice from
        Production.Product Where ProductSubcategoryID = @ProductSubcategoryID"
        ConnectionString="<%$ConnectionStrings:AdventureWorks%>">
        <SelectParameters>
          <asp:Parameter Name="ProductSubcategoryID" Type="String" />
        </SelectParameters>
      </asp:SqlDataSource>
    </div>
  </form>
</body>
</html>
```

In this example, the parent `GridView` defines two columns, both of which are the `TemplateField` type. The first column combines the category ID and category name:

```
<asp:TemplateField HeaderText="Category">
  <ItemStyle VerticalAlign="Top" Width="20%"/>
  <ItemTemplate>
    <br/><b><%# Eval("ProductSubcategoryID") %></b>
    <br/><br/><%# Eval("Name") %><br/>
  </ItemTemplate>
</asp:TemplateField>
```

The second column contains an embedded `GridView` of products, with two bound columns:

```
<asp:TemplateField HeaderText="Products">
  <ItemStyle VerticalAlign="Top"/>
  <ItemTemplate>
```

```
        <asp:GridView AutoGenerateColumns="false" ID="productView" runat="server">
          <Columns>
            <asp:BoundField DataField="Name" HeaderText="Product Name"/>
            <asp:BoundField DataField="ProductNumber" HeaderText="Product Number"/>
            <asp:BoundField DataField="ListPrice" HeaderText="List Price"
              DataFormatString="{0:C}"/>
          </Columns>
        </asp:GridView>
      </ItemTemplate>
    </asp:TemplateField>
```

Now, all you need to do is create two data sources, one for retrieving the list of categories and the other for retrieving all products in a specified category. The first query fills the parent `GridView`, and the second query is called multiple times to fill the child `GridView`.

You can bind the first grid directly to the data source, as shown here:

```
<asp:GridView id="categoryView" runat="server" DataKeyNames="ProductSubcategoryID"
  DataSourceID="categorySource" OnRowDataBound="categoryView_RowDataBound" ... >
```

This part of the code is typical. The trick is to bind the child `GridView` controls. If you leave out this step, the child `GridView` controls will not appear.

To bind the child `GridView` controls, you need to react to the `GridView.RowDataBound` event, which fires every time a row is generated and bound to the parent `GridView`. At this point, you can retrieve the child `GridView` control from the second column and bind it to the product information by programmatically calling the `Select()` method of the data source. To ensure that you show only the products in the current category, you must also retrieve the `CategoryID` field for the current item and pass it as a parameter. Here is the code you need:

```
void categoryView_RowDataBound(object sender, GridViewRowEventArgs e)
{
  if (e.Row.RowType == DataControlRowType.DataRow)
  {
    //Retrieve the GridView control in the second column
    GridView productView = (GridView)e.Row.Cells[1].Controls[1];
    //Set the CategoryID parameter to return the products for the current category
    string categoryID= categoryView.DataKeys[e.Row.DataItemIndex].Value.ToString();
    productSource.SelectParameters[0].DefaultValue = categoryID ;
    productView.DataSource = productSource.Select(DataSourceSelectArguments.Empty);
    productView.DataBind();
  }
}
```

Figure 10-2 shows the resulting output.

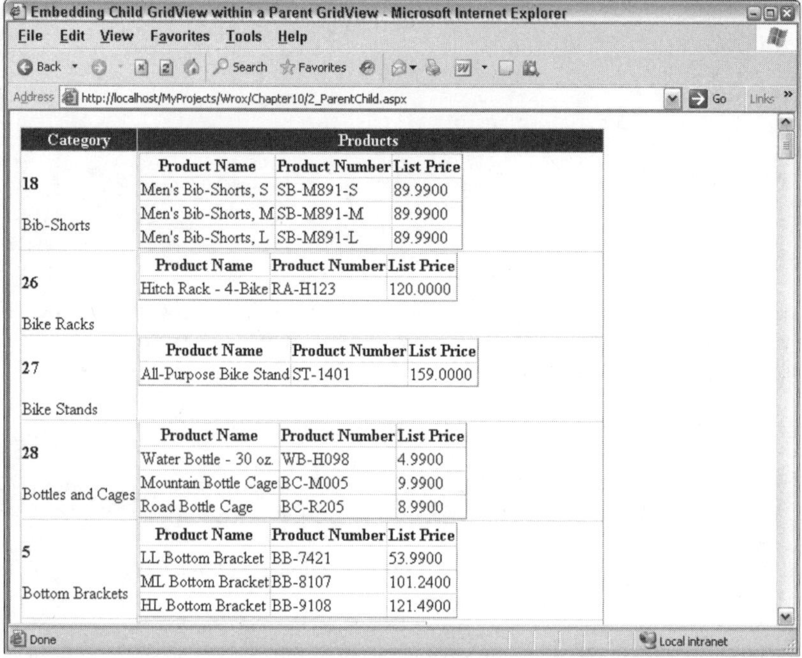

Figure 10-2

Multiple Selections in GridView

As explained in the previous chapters, `GridView` provides built-in support for single-row selection. It is also possible for you to extend the single-row selection to multiple rows by using a few lines of code. However, when you select multiple rows, it would be nice if you could change the background color of the selected row so that you could easily identify all the selected rows. To implement this, you need to be able to inject a client-side script for each of the rows displayed through the `GridView`. The correct place to do this is the `GridView.RowDataBound` event. Before viewing the required code, take a look at Listing 10-3, which shows how to accomplish this.

Listing 10-3: Displaying Visual Indicators for Selected Rows in a GridView

```
<%@ Page Language="C#" %>
<script runat="server">
  void categoryView_RowDataBound(object sender, GridViewRowEventArgs e)
  {
    if (e.Row.RowType == DataControlRowType.DataRow)
    {
      CheckBox chkBox = (CheckBox)e.Row.FindControl("chkSelect");
      string script = " function HighlightSelected(selectedCheckbox, RowState){ " +
        "if (selectedCheckbox.checked) selectedCheckbox." +
        "parentElement.parentElement.style.backgroundColor='#FFAA63';"+
        "else { if (RowState=='0') selectedCheckbox.parentElement."+
        "parentElement.style.backgroundColor='white'; "+
        "else selectedCheckbox.parentElement.parentElement."+
```

```
        "style.backgroundColor='#D6E3F7'; } }";
      Page.ClientScript.RegisterStartupScript(this.GetType(),
        "RowDataBoundScript", script, true);
      chkBox.Attributes.Add("onclick", "HighlightSelected(this,'" +
        Convert.ToString(e.Row.RowState) + "' );") ;
    }
  }
</script>
<html xmlns="http://www.w3.org/1999/xhtml" >
<head runat="server">
  <title>Differentiating Selected Rows in a GridView control</title>
</head>
<body>
  <form id="form1" runat="server">
    <div>
      <asp:SqlDataSource ID="categorySource" runat="server"
        ProviderName="System.Data.SqlClient"
        ConnectionString="<%$ ConnectionStrings:AdventureWorks %>"
        SelectCommand="Select ProductSubcategoryID, Name from
        Production.ProductSubcategory order by ProductSubcategoryID">
      </asp:SqlDataSource>
      <asp:GridView ID="categoryView" runat="server" DataSourceID="categorySource"
        AutoGenerateColumns="false" OnRowDataBound="categoryView_RowDataBound"
        HeaderStyle-HorizontalAlign="Center"  HeaderStyle-Font-Bold="True"
        HeaderStyle-BackColor="blue" HeaderStyle-ForeColor="White"
        AllowPaging="true">
        <RowStyle BackColor="White" ForeColor="#333333" />
        <Columns>
          <asp:TemplateField HeaderText="Select">
            <ItemTemplate>
              <asp:CheckBox ID="chkSelect" runat="server"/>
              <asp:Label ID="lblCategoryID" runat="server"
                Text='<%# Eval("ProductSubcategoryID") %>'
                Visible="false"></asp:Label>
            </ItemTemplate>
          </asp:TemplateField>
          <asp:TemplateField HeaderText="Category ID">
            <ItemTemplate>
              <br/><b><%# Eval("ProductSubcategoryID") %></b></br>
            </ItemTemplate>
          </asp:TemplateField>
          <asp:TemplateField HeaderText="Name">
            <ItemStyle VerticalAlign="Top"/>
            <ItemTemplate>
              <br/><br/><b><%# Eval("Name") %></b><br/>
            </ItemTemplate>
          </asp:TemplateField>
        </Columns>
      </asp:GridView>
    </div>
  </form>
</body>
</html>
```

The key in Listing 10-3 is the `RowDataBound` event handler, where you inject a block of code that does the job of highlighting the rows in the `GridView` whenever a row is selected. To inject this block of code, you use the `RegisterStartupScript()` method of the `ClientScriptManager` object:

```
Page.ClientScript.RegisterStartupScript(this.GetType(),
  "RowDataBoundScript", script, true);
```

After inserting the code, you associate that with the JavaScript `onclick()` event of the check box:

```
chkBox.Attributes.Add("onclick", "HighlightSelected(this,'" +
  Convert.ToString(e.Row.RowState) + "' );") ;
```

If you navigate to the page in a browser, you should see an output similar to that in Figure 10-3.

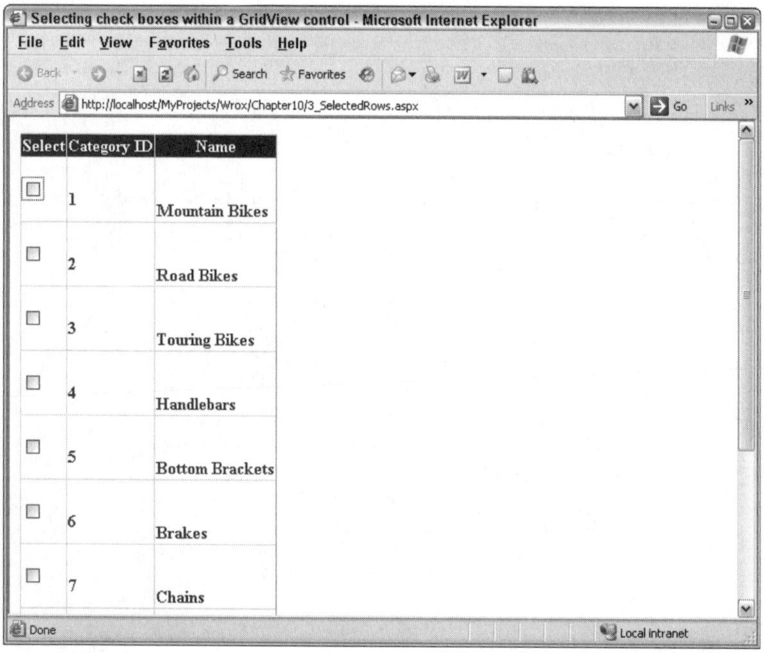

Select	Category ID	Name
☐	1	Mountain Bikes
☐	2	Road Bikes
☐	3	Touring Bikes
☐	4	Handlebars
☐	5	Bottom Brackets
☐	6	Brakes
☐	7	Chains

Figure 10-3

If you select a couple of rows in the `GridView`, you will see the background color of the selected rows changing to a different color, as shown in Figure 10-4.

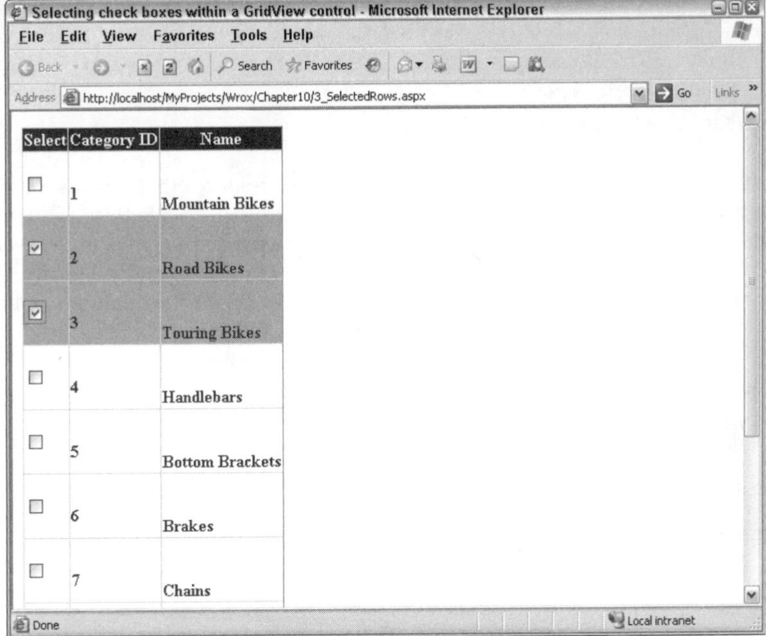

Figure 10-4

Displaying Images from a Database

So far, the examples in this chapter have focused on retrieving text, numeric, and date information from the databases. However, databases often have the additional challenge of storing binary data such as pictures. For example, you might have a Product table that contains pictures of each item in a binary field. Retrieving this data in an ASP.NET web page is fairly easy, but displaying it is not as simple. The basic problem is that in order to show an image in an HTML page, you need to add an image tag that links to a separate image file through the src attribute. For example:

```
<img src="Image.gif" />
```

Unfortunately, this approach will not work if you need to show image data dynamically. Although you can set the `src` attribute in code, you have no way to set the image content programmatically. You could first save the data to an image file on the web server's hard drive, but that approach would be dramatically slower, wastes space, and raises the possibility of concurrency errors if multiple requests are being served at the same time and they are all trying to write the same file.

You can solve this problem in two ways. One approach is to store all your images in separate files. Then your database record simply needs to store the filename, and you can bind the filename to a server-side image. This is a perfectly reasonable solution, but it does not help in situations where you want to store images in the database so that you can take advantage of the abilities of the RDBMS to cache data, log usage, and back up everything.

As a rule of thumb, storing images in a database works well as long as the images are not enormous (for example, more than 50 MB) and do not need to be frequently edited by other applications.

In these situations, the solution is to use a separate ASP.NET resource that returns the binary data directly. You can then use this binary data in other web pages in controls. To tackle this task, you also need to step outside the data binding and write custom ADO.NET code. For the purposes of this example, you will retrieve the images for each of the products stored in the Product table of the AdventureWorks and display them along with product details. These images are stored in the ProductPhoto table, with another table named ProductProductPhoto connecting the Product and ProductPhoto tables. The ASP.NET page used in this example will retrieve the product image along with the product details and display it using a `GridView` control. Here are the steps required to accomplish this:

1. Creating an `HttpHandler` that performs image retrieval
2. Registering the `HttpHandler` with the `Web.config` file
3. Using the `HttpHandler` to retrieve images from within the `GridView`

The following sections will discuss each of these steps in detail.

Creating an HttpHandler

ASP.NET provides a low-level request/response API, in the form of HTTP handlers, that enables you to customize the way incoming HTTP requests are handled and serviced. To accomplish this, you author a class that implements the `System.Web.IHttpHandler` interface, and implement the methods of the `IHttpHandler` interface.

Handlers are often useful when the services provided by the high-level page framework abstraction are not sufficient for processing the HTTP request. Common uses of handlers include filters and CGI-like applications, especially those that return binary data. Each incoming HTTP request received by ASP.NET is ultimately processed by a specific instance of a class that implements `IHttpHandler`.

As mentioned before, all `HttpHandlers` must implement the `IHttpHandler` interface. Some built-in classes such as `HttpApplication` and `Page` already implement the `IHttpHandler` interface. The `IHttpHandler` interface is extremely simple. The interface consists of a read-only property named `IsReusable`, which returns a Boolean value (typically true) indicating whether another request can use the `IHttpHandler` instance, and a `ProcessRequest()` method, which takes a parameter of type `HttpContext` and performs the job of handling the extension.

```
bool IsReusable {get;}
void ProcessRequest(HttpContext context);
```

Through the `HttpContext` object supplied to the `ProcessRequest()` method, you can obtain reference to `Request` and `Response` objects.

Now that you have had a look at the basics of the `HttpHandler`, you can create an `HttpHandler` named `ImageHandler` (represented by `ImageHandler.ashx`) that can retrieve the images from the ProductPhoto table. The implementation of `ImageHandler` is shown in Listing 10-4.

Listing 10-4: HttpHandler for Retrieving Images

```
using System;
using System.Data;
using System.Data.SqlClient;
using System.Web;
using System.Web.Configuration;

public class ImageHandler : IHttpHandler
{
  public void ProcessRequest(HttpContext context)
  {
    string connectionString = WebConfigurationManager.ConnectionStrings
      ["AdventureWorks"].ConnectionString;
    //Get the ID for this request
    string photoID = context.Request.QueryString["PhotoID"];
    if (photoID == null)
      throw new ApplicationException("Must specify ID");
    //Create a parameterized command for this record
    SqlConnection connection = new SqlConnection(connectionString);
    string sql = "SELECT ThumbNailPhoto FROM Production.ProductPhoto " +
      "WHERE ProductPhotoID=@ProductPhotoID";
    SqlCommand command = new SqlCommand(sql, connection);
    command.Parameters.AddWithValue("@ProductPhotoID", photoID);
    try
    {
      connection.Open();
      SqlDataReader reader=command.ExecuteReader(CommandBehavior.SequentialAccess);
      if (reader.Read())
      {
        //Specify Size of the buffer, the buffer, # of bytes read, starting index
        int bufferSize = 100;
        byte[] bytes = new byte[bufferSize];
        long bytesRead;
        long readFrom = 0;
        //Read the field 100 bytes at a time
        do
        {
          bytesRead = reader.GetBytes(0, readFrom, bytes, 0, bufferSize);
          context.Response.BinaryWrite(bytes);
          readFrom += bufferSize;
         } while (bytesRead == bufferSize);
       }
       reader.Close();
     }
     finally
     {
       connection.Close();
     }
   }
    public bool IsReusable
    {
        get { return true; }
    }
}
```

The `ProcessRequest()` method is where the majority of the code lies. It starts off by retrieving the PhotoID column from the query string. It then uses that value to execute a SQL query against the ProductPhoto table, returning the ThumbNailPhoto column value represented by the photo ID.

When it comes to processing the results of the query, the ThumbNailPhoto column from the ProductPhoto table is read piece by piece and then written to output stream, using `Response.BinaryWrite()`, in chunks. To be able to do this, you need to inform the `SqlDataReader` object to use the sequential access feature that supports this design. To use sequential access, you simply need to supply the `CommandBehavior.SequentialAccess` value to the `SqlCommand.ExecuteReader()` method. Then you can move through the row one block at a time, using the `SqlDataReader.GetBytes()` method.

When using sequential access, you need to keep a couple of limitations in mind. First, you must read the data as a forward-only stream. Once you have read a block of data, you automatically move ahead in the stream, and you cannot go backward. Second, you must read the fields in the same order that they are returned by your query. For example, if your query returns three columns, the third of which is a binary field, you must return the values of the first and second fields before accessing the binary data in the third field. If you access the third field first, you will not be able to access the first two fields.

The `GetBytes()` method returns a value that indicates the number of bytes retrieved. If you need to determine the total number of bytes in the field, you simply need to pass a null reference instead of a buffer when you call the `GetBytes()` method.

Registering the Handler

Now that you have created the handler, the next step is to register the handler in the `Web.config` file. Before doing that, you need to place the compiled assembly (that contains the `ImageHandler` class) in the `\bin` directory of the web site. After placing the assembly in the `\bin` directory, register the handler in the `<httpHandlers>` section of the `Web.config` file as follows:

```
<system.web>
  <httpHandlers>
    <add verb="GET" path="ImageHandler.ashx" type="ImageHandler" />
  </httpHandlers>
  ----
</system.web>
```

That is all there is to registering the assembly in the `Web.config` file. With the above registration in place, all HTTP `GET` requests for `ImageHandler.ashx` will be routed to an instance of the `ImageHandler` class.

Using the HttpHandler

Now that you have the `HttpHandler` created and registered, you are ready to leverage it from an ASP.NET page to display images. The ASP.NET page is shown in Listing 10-5.

Listing 10-5: Using the ImageHandler from an ASP.NET Page

```
<%@ Page Language="C#" %>
<html xmlns="http://www.w3.org/1999/xhtml" >
<head id="Head1" runat="server">
  <title>Displaying Images using GridView</title>
</head>
<body>
  <form id="form1" runat="server">
    <div>
      <asp:GridView ID="categoryView" runat="server"
        AutoGenerateColumns="false" DataSourceID="categorySource"
        HeaderStyle-BackColor="blue" HeaderStyle-ForeColor="White">
        <Columns>
          <asp:TemplateField HeaderText="Category">
            <ItemStyle VerticalAlign="Top" Width="20%"/>
            <ItemTemplate>
              <table border='1'><tr><td>
                <img src='ImageHandler.ashx?PhotoID=<%# Eval("ProductPhotoID")%>'/>
                </td></tr>
              </table>
              <b><%# Eval("ProductID") %></b><br/>
              <%# Eval("Name") %><br/><br/>
            </ItemTemplate>
          </asp:TemplateField>
        </Columns>
      </asp:GridView>
      <asp:SqlDataSource ID="categorySource" Runat="server"
        SelectCommandType="Text" SelectCommand="Select A.ProductID As ProductID,
        A.Name As Name, B.ProductPhotoID As ProductPhotoID From Production.Product
        A Inner Join Production.ProductProductPhoto B On A.ProductID = B.ProductID"
        ConnectionString="<%$ConnectionStrings:AdventureWorks%>">
      </asp:SqlDataSource>
    </div>
  </form>
</body>
</html>
```

The line of code that invokes the image handler to retrieve the corresponding image for the supplied product ID is embedded within the `ItemTemplate` of the `GridView` control:

```
<img src='ImageHandler.ashx?PhotoID=<%# Eval("ProductPhotoID")%>'/>
```

As you can see from this code, the `PhotoID` is passed to the image handler in the form of a query string. Figure 10-5 shows the output generated by the page.

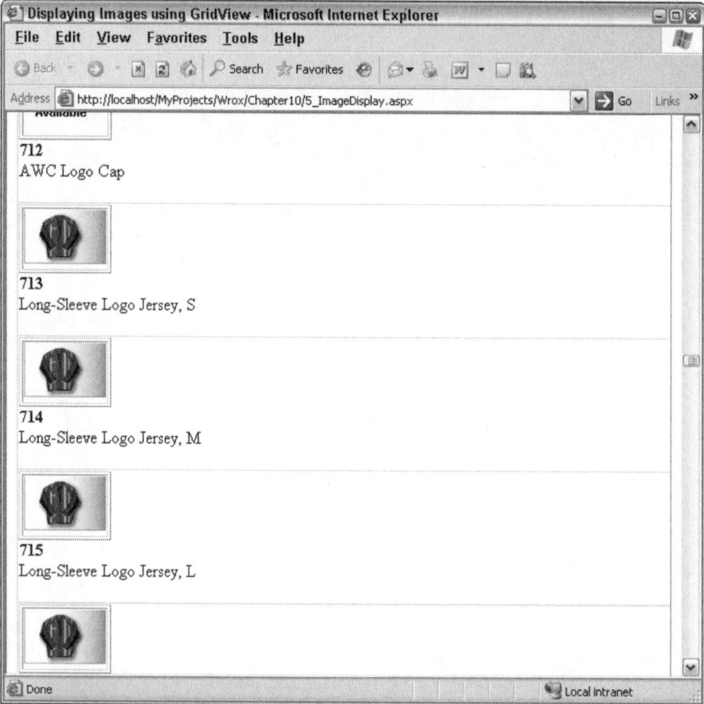

Figure 10-5

This current HttpHandler approach works well if you want to build a detail page with information about a single record. For example, you could show a list of products and then display the image for the appropriate product when the user makes a selection. However, this solution is not as efficient if you want to show image data for every product at once, for example in a list control. The approach still works, but it will be inefficient because it uses a separate request to the HttpHandler (and hence a separate database connection) to retrieve each image. You can solve this problem by creating an HttpHandler that checks for image data in the cache before retrieving it from the database. Before you bind the GridView, you would then perform a query that returns all the records with their image data and load each image into the cache.

Creating Custom Templates for GridView

When working with templated controls, you might not know until runtime what templates you need or what text or controls the template should contain. In that case, you can create the templates dynamically in code. You can create templates in code for all controls that use templates: the DataList, Repeater, GridView, FormView, DetailsView, and others. For the GridView control, you use templates to define columns, instead of the row layout templates as for the other controls. This section will examine the application of custom templates using GridView control.

A GridView template is a class that implements the ITemplate interface. It defines the controls that will be displayed on the GridView in a column and how they will bind to data, and can have special-case code to handle headers and footers. For the purposes of this chapter, a simplified example of building a

GridView from scratch, using a template that aids in formatting the contents of the GridView, will be discussed. Although this example is simple, you could easily extend this to cover much more complex situations. The next section starts by discussing the implementation of the custom template class.

Creating the Custom Template Class

The custom template class (named CustomGridViewTemplate) holds the code that will do the actual heavy lifting of putting controls in the GridView, as well as formatting them and binding them to data. Since the CustomGridViewTemplate class implements the ITemplate interface, it provides the implementation for the InstantiateIn() method, wherein you define the behavior for populating the GridView control with child controls. Listing 10-6 shows the complete code of this class.

Listing 10-6: Formatting the GridView Using Custom Templates

```
using System;
using System.Web.UI;
using System.Web.UI.WebControls;
using System.Web.UI.WebControls.WebParts;
using System.Web.UI.HtmlControls;

public class CustomGridViewTemplate : ITemplate
{
  private DataControlRowType _templateType;
  private string _columnName;
  private string _dataType;

  public CustomGridViewTemplate(DataControlRowType templateType,
    string columnName, string dataType)
  {
    _templateType = templateType;
    _columnName = columnName;
    _dataType = dataType;
  }

  public void InstantiateIn(System.Web.UI.Control container)
  {
    switch (_templateType)
    {
      case DataControlRowType.Header:
        //Build the header for this column
        Literal literal = new Literal();
        literal.Text = "<b><i><u>" + _columnName + "</u></i></b>";
        container.Controls.Add(literal);
        break;
      case DataControlRowType.DataRow:
        //Build one row in this column
        Label label = new Label();
        switch (_dataType)
        {
          case "DateTime":
            label.ForeColor = System.Drawing.Color.Blue;
            break;
```

(continued)

Listing 10-6: *(continued)*

```
            case "Double":
              label.ForeColor= System.Drawing.Color.Violet;
              break;
            case "Int32":
              label.ForeColor= System.Drawing.Color.Green;;
              break;
            case "String":
              label.ForeColor= System.Drawing.Color.Brown;
              break;
            default:
              label.ForeColor= System.Drawing.Color.Green;
              break;
          }
          //Register an event handler to perform the data binding
          label.DataBinding += new EventHandler(this.label_DataBinding);
          container.Controls.Add(label);
          break;
        default:
          break;
      }
    }

    private void label_DataBinding(Object sender, EventArgs e)
    {
      //Get the control that raised this event
      Label label = (Label)sender;
      //Get the containing row
      GridViewRow row = (GridViewRow)label.NamingContainer;
      //Get the raw data value and format it
      string rawValue = DataBinder.Eval(row.DataItem, _columnName).ToString();
      switch (_dataType)
      {
        case "DateTime":
          label.Text = String.Format("{0:d}", DateTime.Parse(rawValue));
          break;
        case "Double":
          label.Text = String.Format("{0:###,###,##0.00}", Double.Parse(rawValue));
          break;
        default:
          label.Text = rawValue;
          break;
      }
    }
  }
```

As you can see, the code in Listing 10-6 starts off with some private member variables and a constructor to set them. The key method is `InstantiateIn()`, where the majority of the work occurs.

The `InstantiateIn()` method is called whenever an instance of this template is instantiated. If you think of a template as corresponding to a column in the `GridView`, this happens every time a header, cell, or footer of the `GridView` is created for that column. You can inspect the `_templateType` member to figure out which of these is the case. Here, you want to create whatever control or controls you need to display the data. You are not limited to a single control, although this example uses only one label for display. This method also sets up for data binding by registering an event handler:

```
//Register an event handler to perform the data binding
label.DataBinding += new EventHandler(this.label_DataBinding);
```

As you would expect, the data-binding event handler is called when data is bound to the `GridView`. Inside the data-binding event handler, you get a reference to the container for the control and format the data.

Using the Template

If you place the `CustomGridViewTemplate` class inside the `App_Code` directory, it is automatically made available to all the ASP.NET pages in a web site. Listing 10-7 shows how to use the `CustomGrid ViewTemplate` with a `GridView` control.

Listing 10-7: Using Custom Templates inside a GridView

```
<%@ Page Language="C#" %>
<%@ Import Namespace="System.Data" %>
<%@ Import Namespace="System.Data.SqlClient" %>
<%@ Import Namespace="System.Web.Configuration" %>
<script runat="server">
  void Page_Load(object sender, EventArgs e)
  {
    string connectionString = WebConfigurationManager.ConnectionStrings
      ["AdventureWorks"].ConnectionString;
    DataTable deptTable = new DataTable();
    using (SqlConnection connection = new SqlConnection(connectionString))
    {
      string sql = "SELECT DepartmentID, Name, GroupName, ModifiedDate" +
        " FROM HumanResources.Department";
      SqlCommand command = new SqlCommand(sql);
      command.CommandType = CommandType.Text;
      command.Connection = connection;
      SqlDataAdapter adapter = new SqlDataAdapter();
      adapter.SelectCommand = command;
      adapter.Fill(deptTable);
    }
    //Clear any existing columns
    deptView.Columns.Clear();
    //Walk the DataTable and add columns to the GridView
    for (int i = 0; i < deptTable.Columns.Count; i++)
    {
      TemplateField templateField = new TemplateField();
      //Create the data rows
      templateField.ItemTemplate = new CustomGridViewTemplate
        (DataControlRowType.DataRow,
      deptTable.Columns[i].ColumnName,
      deptTable.Columns[i].DataType.Name);
      //Create the header
```

(continued)

Listing 10-7: *(continued)*

```
        templateField.HeaderTemplate = new CustomGridViewTemplate
          (DataControlRowType.Header, deptTable.Columns[i].ColumnName,
          deptTable.Columns[i].DataType.Name);
        //Add to the GridView
        deptView.Columns.Add(templateField);
      }
      //Bind and display the data
      deptView.DataSource = deptTable;
      deptView.DataBind();
    }
  </script>
  <html xmlns="http://www.w3.org/1999/xhtml" >
  <head runat="server">
    <title>Using Custom Templates with GridView</title>
  </head>
  <body>
    <form id="form1" runat="server">
      <div>
        <asp:GridView ID="deptView" Runat="server" AutoGenerateColumns="False">
          <Columns>
            <asp:BoundField HeaderText="Department ID"  DataField="DepartmentID"/>
            <asp:BoundField HeaderText="Name" DataField="Name"/>
            <asp:BoundField HeaderText="Group Name" DataField="GroupName"/>
            <asp:BoundField HeaderText="ModifiedDate" DataField="ModifiedDate"/>
          </Columns>
        </asp:GridView>
      </div>
    </form>
  </body>
  </html>
```

The only tricky part in Listing 10-7 is the place where you hook the template class up to the `GridView`. This is accomplished by creating a new `TemplateField` object and associating the `TemplateField` with the `CustomGridViewTemplate` for the `ItemTemplate` and `HeaderTemplate`. Note that you can use the same technique to set the other templates, such as the `AlternatingItemTemplate` and `FooterTemplate`.

Figure 10-6 shows the ASP.NET page in action.

Using Themes with Data Bound Controls

Building a professional web site involves much more than designing individual web pages. You also need the tools to integrate your web pages into a complete, unified web site. One of those important tools is a new feature introduced with ASP.NET 2.0 called themes. Themes let you define the formatting details for various controls and seamlessly reuse these formats in multiple pages. Themes make it much easier to standardize your web site's look and feel and tweak it later. Once a theme is in place, you can give your entire web site a facelift just by changing the theme definition.

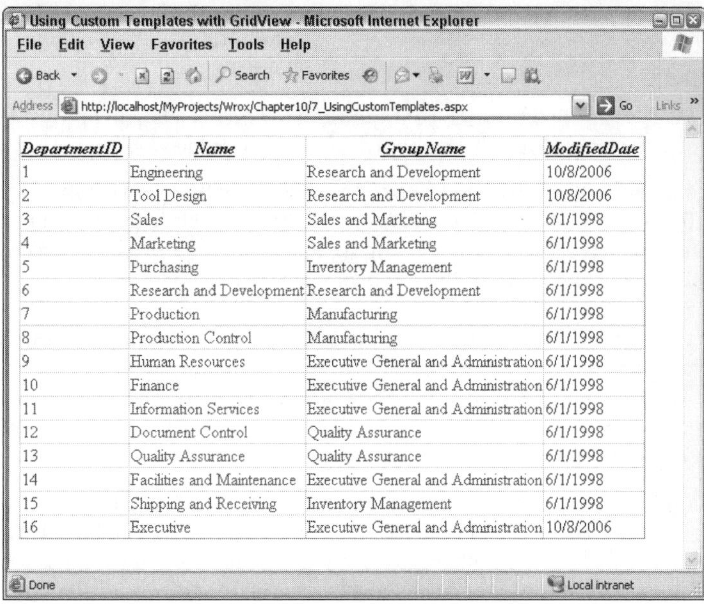

DepartmentID	Name	GroupName	ModifiedDate
1	Engineering	Research and Development	10/8/2006
2	Tool Design	Research and Development	10/8/2006
3	Sales	Sales and Marketing	6/1/1998
4	Marketing	Sales and Marketing	6/1/1998
5	Purchasing	Inventory Management	6/1/1998
6	Research and Development	Research and Development	6/1/1998
7	Production	Manufacturing	6/1/1998
8	Production Control	Manufacturing	6/1/1998
9	Human Resources	Executive General and Administration	6/1/1998
10	Finance	Executive General and Administration	6/1/1998
11	Information Services	Executive General and Administration	6/1/1998
12	Document Control	Quality Assurance	6/1/1998
13	Quality Assurance	Quality Assurance	6/1/1998
14	Facilities and Maintenance	Executive General and Administration	6/1/1998
15	Shipping and Receiving	Inventory Management	6/1/1998
16	Executive	Executive General and Administration	10/8/2006

Figure 10-6

Why Do You Need Themes?

One of the most common ways to apply standardized formatting is to use Cascading Style Sheets (CSS). CSS provides a cross-platform solution for formatting web pages that works in conjunction with HTML 4 and is supported by virtually all modern browsers.

With the inherent advantages of CSS styles, you might wonder why developers need anything more. The problem is that CSS rules are limited to a fixed set of style attributes. They allow you to reuse specific formatting details (fonts, borders, foreground and background colors, and so on), but they obviously cannot control other aspects of ASP.NET controls. For example, the `CheckBoxList` control includes properties that control how it organizes items into rows and columns. Although these properties affect the visual appearance of the control, they are outside the scope of CSS, so you need to set them by hand. Additionally, you might want to define part of the behavior of the control along with the formatting. For example, you might want to standardize the selection mode of a `Calendar` control or the wrapping in a `TextBox`. This obviously is not possible through CSS.

Themes fill this gap by allowing you to define a set of style attributes that you can apply to controls in multiple pages. However, unlike CSS, themes are not implemented by the browser. Instead, they are a native ASP.NET solution that is implemented on the server. Although themes do not replace styles, they have some features that CSS cannot provide. Here are the key differences:

- Themes are control-based, not HTML-based. As a result, themes allow you to define and reuse almost any control property. For example, themes allow you to specify a set of common node pictures and use them in numerous `TreeView` controls, or to define a set of templates for multiple `GridView` controls. CSS is limited to style attributes that apply directly to HTML.

- Themes are applied on the server. When a theme is applied to a page, the final styled page is sent to the user. When a style sheet is used, the browser receives both the page and the style information and then combines them on the client side.
- Themes can be applied through configuration files. This lets you apply a theme to an entire folder or your whole Web site without modifying a single web page.
- Themes do not cascade in the same way as CSS. Essentially, if you specify a property in a theme and in the individual control, the value in the theme overwrites the property in the control. However, you have the choice of changing this behavior and giving precedence to the properties in the page, which makes themes behave more like style sheets.

It would be overstating it to say that themes replace CSS. Instead, themes represent a higher-level model. To implement your formatting properties, ASP.NET will frequently render inline style rules. In addition, it is definitely possible to use your existing CSS styles in conjunction with themes.

Theme Folders and Skins

All themes are application-specific. To use a theme in a web site, you need to create a folder that defines it. You need to place this folder in a special folder named `App_Themes`, which must be inside the top-level directory for your web site. In other words, a web site named ShoppingAssistant might have a MasterTheme theme in the `ShoppingAssistant\App_Themes\MasterTheme` folder.

> **A web site can contain definitions for multiple themes, as long as each theme is in a separate folder. However, only one theme can be active on a given page at a time.**

To actually make your theme accomplish something, you need to create at least one skin file in the theme folder. A skin file is a text file with the .skinextension. ASP.NET never serves skin files directly — instead, they are used behind the scenes to define a theme.

A skin file is essentially a list of control tags — with a twist. The control tags in a skin file do not need to completely define the control. Instead, they need to set only the properties you want to standardize. For example, if you are trying to apply a consistent color scheme, you might be interested in setting properties such as `ForeColor` and `BackColor` only. When you add a control tag for the `ListBox` control, it might look like this:

```
<asp:ListBox runat="server" ForeColor="White" BackColor="Orange"/>
```

The `runat="server"` portion is always required. Everything else is optional. The `id` attribute is not allowed in a theme, because it is required to uniquely identify each control.

It is up to you whether you create multiple skin files or place all your control tags in a single skin file. Both approaches are equivalent, because ASP.NET treats all the skin files in a theme directory as part of the same theme definition. Often, it makes sense to separate the control tags for complex controls (such as the data controls) into separate skin files.

ASP.NET also supports global themes. These are themes you place in the `[WinDir]\Microsoft.Net\Framework\[Version]\Themes` *folder. However, it is recommended that you use local themes, even if you want to create more than one web site that has the same theme. Using local themes makes it easier to deploy your web site, and it gives you the flexibility of introducing site-specific differences in the future. If you have a local theme with the same name as a global theme, the local theme takes precedence, and the global theme is ignored. The themes are not merged together.*

Applying a Simple Theme

To add a theme to your project, create a subfolder under the `App_Themes` folder with the name of your theme, which is `CommonTheme` in this case. To that folder, add a file called `GridViewControl.skin` and modify it to look as shown in Listing 10-8.

Listing 10-8: GridViewControl.skin File

```
<asp:GridView runat="server" BackColor="White" BorderColor="#CC9966"
  BorderStyle="None" BorderWidth="1px" CellPadding="4">
  <FooterStyle BackColor="#FFFFCC" ForeColor="#330099" />
  <RowStyle BackColor="White" ForeColor="#330099" />
  <SelectedRowStyle BackColor="#FFCC66" Font-Bold="True" ForeColor="#663399" />
  <PagerStyle BackColor="#FFFFCC" ForeColor="#330099" HorizontalAlign="Center" />
  <HeaderStyle BackColor="#990000" Font-Bold="True" ForeColor="#FFFFCC" />
</asp:GridView>
```

To apply the above theme in a web page, you need to set the `Theme` attribute of the `Page` directive to the folder name for your theme. (ASP.NET will automatically scan all the skin files in that theme.)

```
<%@ Page Language="C#" Theme="CommonTheme" %>
```

When you apply a theme to a page, ASP.NET considers each control on your web page and checks your skin files to see if they define any properties for that control. If ASP.NET finds a matching tag in the skin file, the information from the skin file overrides the current properties of the control.

Figure 10-7 shows the result of applying the `CommonTheme` to a simple page that includes the `GridView` control.

Applying Themes through a Configuration File

Using the `Page` directive, you can bind a theme to a single page. However, there are times when you might want to roll out the themes for the entire web site. The cleanest way to apply this theme is to configure the `<pages>` element in the Web.config file for your application, as shown here:

```
<configuration>
  <system.web>
    <pages theme="CommonTheme" />
    -----
  </system.web>
</configuration>
```

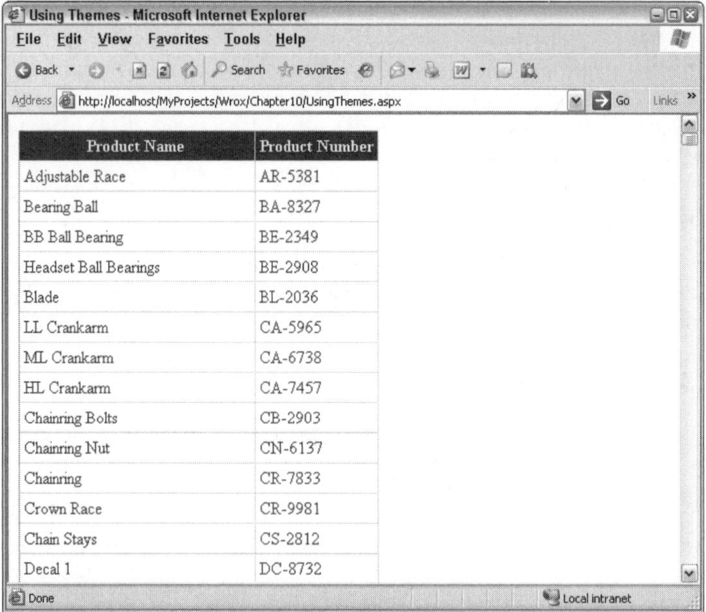

Figure 10-7

When you specify a theme in the `Web.config` file, the theme you specify will be applied throughout all the pages in your web site, provided these pages do not have their own theme settings. If a page specifies the `Theme` attribute, the page setting will take precedence over the `Web.config` setting.

Using this technique, it is just as easy to apply a theme to part of a web site. For example, you can create a separate `Web.config` file for each subfolder and use the `<pages>` setting to configure different themes.

Data Binding with the FormView Control

The last few sections in this chapter and previous chapters have discussed some of the advanced features of `GridView` and `DetailsView` controls. Similar to the `DetailsView` control, there is also the `FormView` control, which can be considered as the templated version of the `DetailsView`. The `FormView` control renders one record at a time, picked from the associated data source and that, optionally, provides paging buttons to navigate between records. Unlike the `DetailsView` control, `FormView` does not use data control fields and requires the user to define the rendering of each item by using templates. The `FormView` can support any basic operation its data source provides.

Note that `FormView` requires you to define everything through templates, and not just the things you want to change. `FormView` has no built-in rendering engine and is limited to printing out the user-defined templates.

The `FormView` control exposes many of the properties that you have seen already for the `DetailsView` control. Only the templates and related styles mark the difference between `FormView` and `DetailsView`.

Templates Supported by FormView

The output of the `FormView` control is exclusively based on templates. This means that you always need to specify the item template at a very minimum. The following table shows the list of supported templates.

Template	Description
`EditItemTemplate`	The template to use when an existing record is being updated
`InsertItemTemplate`	The template to use when a new record is being created
`ItemTemplate`	The template to use when an existing record is rendered for viewing only

You use the `ItemTemplate` to define the control's layout when in read-only view mode. You use `EditItemTemplate` to edit the contents of the current record, and you use `InsertItemTemplate` to add a new record. In addition to these templates, the control features the same set of templates offered by the `DetailsView`—that is, `HeaderTemplate`, `FooterTemplate`, and the other templates.

Operations Supported by FormView

Because the user interface of the control is largely defined by the page author, you cannot expect a `FormView` control to understand the click on a particular button and act accordingly. For this reason, the `FormView` control exposes a few publicly callable methods to trigger common actions, such as those listed in the following table.

Method	Description
`ChangeMode`	Changes the working mode of the control from the current to any of the modes defined in the `FormViewMode` type—ReadOnly, Edit, or Insert.
`DeleteItem`	Deletes the current record in the `FormView` control from the data source.
`InsertItem`	Inserts the current record in the data source. The `FormView` control must be in insert mode when this method is called; otherwise, an exception is thrown.
`UpdateItem`	Updates the current record in the data source. The `FormView` control must be in edit mode when this method is called; otherwise, an exception is thrown.

Both `InsertItem` and `UpdateItem` require a Boolean indicating whether input validation should be performed. In this context, performing validation simply means that any validator controls you might have in the template will be called. If no validators are found, no other form of validation occurs. The `InsertItem` and `UpdateItem` methods are designed to start a basic operation from within controls in any of the supported templates. You do not have to pass the record to insert, the values to update, or the key of the record to delete. The `FormView` control knows how to retrieve that information internally, in much the same way the `DetailsView` does.

The `DeleteItem`, `InsertItem`, and `UpdateItem` methods let you define your own delete, insert, and edit user interface and attach it to the standard data-binding model of ASP.NET controls. In the `DetailsView` control, this association is implicit because the user interface is relatively static and fixed. In the case of `FormView`, the same association must be explicitly defined in light of the totally customizable user interface.

Binding Data to a FormView Control

Now that you have had an overview of the templates and operations supported by the `FormView` control, this section shows how to use templates to configure and run a `FormView` control in an ASP.NET web page. As mentioned before, all templates must contain everything needed to accomplish tasks, including user interface elements and command buttons.

The final output of the `FormView` *control takes the form of an HTML table with a header and footer row, plus an optional row for the pager. Just like* `DetailsView`*, the* `FormView` *control provides templates for the header and footer. But it differs from* `DetailsView` *in that it does not provide simpler and handy text properties, such as* `HeaderText` *and* `FooterText`.

The following code snippet shows the typical layout of the code you write to embed a `FormView` in your pages:

```
<asp:FormView ID="deptView" runat="server" DataSourceID="deptSource"......>
  <ItemTemplate>...</ItemTemplate>
  <EditItemTemplate>...</EditItemTemplate>
  <InsertItemTemplate>...</InsertItemTemplate>
</asp:FormView>
```

Listing 10-9 shows the complete ASP.NET page that includes a `FormView` control to display department information from the AdventureWorks database.

Listing 10-9: Data Binding Using FormView Control

```
<%@ Page Language="C#" %>
<html xmlns="http://www.w3.org/1999/xhtml" >
<head id="Head1" runat="server">
  <title>Data Binding with FormView Control</title>
</head>
<body>
  <form id="form1" runat="server">
    <div>
      <asp:FormView runat="server" id="deptView" DataKeyNames="DepartmentID"
        DataSourceID="deptSource" AllowPaging="true">
        <ItemTemplate>
          <table style="border:solid 1px black;" width="100%">
            <tr>
              <td bgcolor="yellow" width="50px" align="center">
                <b><%# Eval("DepartmentID") %></b>
              </td>
            </tr>
            <tr>
              <td bgcolor="lightyellow" >
                <b><%# Eval("Name") %></b>
              </td>
            </tr>
```

```
            <tr>
              <td bgcolor="lightblue" >
                <b><%# Eval("GroupName") %></b>
              </td>
            </tr>
            <tr>
              <td bgcolor="lightcyan" >
                <b><%# Eval("ModifiedDate") %></b>
              </td>
            </tr>
          </table>
          <br/>
          <asp:Button ID="btnEdit" runat="server" CommandName="Edit" Text="Edit" />
        </ItemTemplate>
      </asp:FormView>
      <asp:SqlDataSource ID="deptSource" Runat="server" SelectCommandType="Text"
        SelectCommand="Select DepartmentID, Name, GroupName, ModifiedDate from
        HumanResources.Department"
        ConnectionString="<%$ConnectionStrings:AdventureWorks%>">
      </asp:SqlDataSource>
    </div>
  </form>
</body>
</html>
```

All the markup you place in the `ItemTemplate` is rendered in a table cell. As mentioned, the overall layout of the `FormView` is a table. The Edit button is added using a classic `<asp:Button>` button with the Edit command name. The command name will cause the `FormView` to automatically switch from the read-only mode to edit mode and display using the edit item template, if any is defined. You can use any button control with whatever command name and caption you like. If it does not change the mode automatically, you can call `ChangeMode` and the other methods supported by the `FormView` control.

Figure 10-8 shows the generated output.

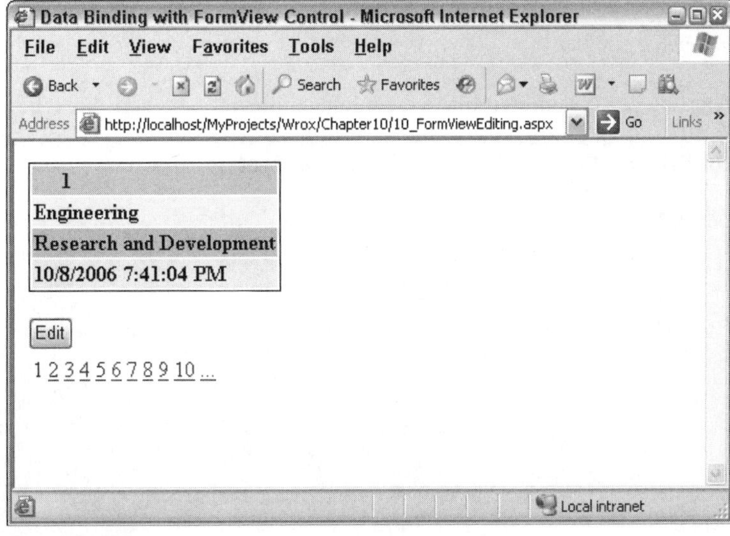

Figure 10-8

In Listing 10-9, the `Eval` function allows you to insert data. The `Eval` function exists in two forms that are functionally equivalent, as one of them is implemented in terms of the other. The first form you can use is the following:

```
<%# DataBinder.Eval(Container.DataItem, "DepartmentID")%>
```

The static function `Eval` on the `DataBinder` class uses reflection to parse and evaluate a data-binding expression against an object at runtime. With the release of ASP.NET 2.0, there is now a compact version of the `Eval` function (as shown in Listing 10-9) that allows you to specify the data-binding expression as an input argument. As you would expect, this newly released `Eval` function ends up calling into the `DataBinder.Eval` function.

> **The `Eval` function is useful only in read-only, one-way data-binding scenarios. For implementing real two-way data binding, an extension to `Eval` is required. This extension is the `Bind` function, which will be discussed in the next section.**

Editing Data Using the FormView Control

To edit bound records, you define an ad hoc edit template through the `EditItemTemplate` property. You can place on the form any combination of input controls, including validators. You are not limited to using text boxes and can use any type of controls to build the user interface. To retrieve values for updating the bound record, you use the newly introduced `Bind` function.

As an example, the following code snippet shows a sample `TextBox` control bound to the `Name` property of the data source. This is the key difference between the `Item` and `EditItem` templates.

```
<asp:TextBox runat="server" Text='<%# Bind("Name") %>' />
```

The `Bind` function stores the value of the bound control property into a collection of values that the `FormView` control automatically retrieves and uses to compose the parameter list of the edit command. The argument passed to `Bind` must match the name of a parameter in the update command or method, or one of the properties on the type used as an argument to the update method. An exception is raised if no parameter match is found.

Listing 10-10 shows a sample edit template. It contains quite a few standard text boxes.

Listing 10-10: Editing Data Using FormView Control

```
<EditItemTemplate>
  <table style="border:solid 1px black;" width="100%">
    <tr>
      <td bgcolor="yellow" align="center">
        <b><%# Eval("DepartmentID") %></b>
      </td>
    </tr>
  </table>
  <table style="font-family:Verdana;font-size:8pt;">
    <tr>
      <td><b>Department Name</b></td>
      <td><asp:textbox ID="txtName" runat="server" text='<%# Bind("Name")%>'/></td>
```

```
      </tr>
      <tr>
        <td><b>Group Name</b></td>
        <td><asp:textbox ID="txtGroupName" runat="server"
          text='<%# Bind("GroupName")%>' /></td>
      </tr>
      <tr>
        <td><b>Group ModifiedDate</b></td>
        <td><asp:textbox ID="Textbox1" runat="server"
          text='<%# Bind("ModifiedDate") %>' /></td>
      </tr>
    </table><br />
    <asp:Button ID="btnUpdate" runat="server" CommandName="Update" Text="Update" />
    <asp:Button ID="btnCancel" runat="server" CommandName="Cancel" Text="Cancel" />
  </EditItemTemplate>
```

Bear in mind that the edit template must contain buttons to save changes. These are ordinary buttons with specific command names — Update to save and Cancel to abort. Buttons trigger update commands whose details are stored in the associated data source object. You can choose any text for the captions as long as you do not change the command names. If you want to modify the command names, you need to handle the `ItemCommand` event on the `FormView` and call the `UpdateItem` method in response.

> **You use `Eval` to populate control properties not involved in the update process. Wherever you need two-way data binding (meaning both read and write capabilities), you use the `Bind` function instead of `Eval`, with the same syntax. For text boxes, you bind the `Text` property, and for drop-down lists, you typically bind the `SelectedValue` property.**

Figure 10-9 demonstrates the output of the preceding code when running in edit mode.

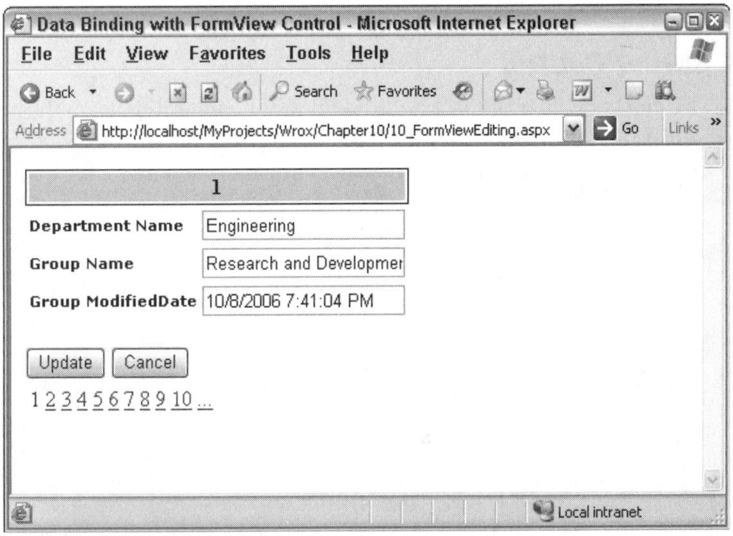

Figure 10-9

In addition to specifying the Update and Cancel buttons in the `EditItemTemplate`, you also need to set the `DataKeyNames` property of `FormView` to identify the key field. For deleting a record, just add a button with the `Delete` command name and configure the underlying data source control.

Inserting a New Record Using FormView Control

The `InsertItemTemplate` property allows you to define the input layout when a new record is being added. To avoid confusion, an insert template should not be much different from an edit template. At the same time, you should be aware that edit and insert are distinct operations with different requirements. For example, an insert template should provide default values to controls wherever that is acceptable, and it should display neutral or null values elsewhere.

To start an insert operation, you also need a button with a command name of `New`. Clicking on this button will force the `FormView` control to change mode to `Insert` and render the contents defined for the insert template. The insert template should also provide a couple of Update/Cancel buttons with the same command names discussed for edit operations.

Extending the GridView Control

Although the `GridView` control provides a number of features for data binding, there are times when you might want to extend it to support additional features. Extending a `GridView` is very simple, and it just requires you to follow these steps:

- Create a new server control that derives from the `GridView` class
- Compile the server control assembly and place that in the `/bin` directory of the web site
- Register the server control using the `Register` directive in the page
- Reference the server control in the page and set its properties

The next section starts by exploring the steps required to create the server control that extends the `GridView`.

Creating the Server Control

As mentioned, you can easily extend the `GridView` control by inheriting from the built-in `GridView` class. Listing 10-11 shows the implementation of the server control.

Listing 10-11: Custom Server Control that Extends the GridView Class

```
using System;
using System.Web;
using System.Web.UI;
using System.Web.UI.WebControls;

namespace CustomControls
{
  public class CustomGridView : GridView
  {
    int footerRowIndex = -1;
```

```
    //No of footer rows to be displayed
    int noOfExtraFooters = 1;

    public int ExtraFooterRows
    {
      get { return this.noOfExtraFooters; }
      set { this.noOfExtraFooters = value; }
    }

    protected override void OnRowCreated(GridViewRowEventArgs e)
    {
      base.OnRowCreated(e);
      if (e.Row.RowType != DataControlRowType.Footer)
      {
        //Increment the counter till we reach the footer row
        ++footerRowIndex;
      }
    }

    protected override void OnPreRender(EventArgs e)
    {
      base.OnPreRender(e);
      Table tbl = this.FooterRow.Parent as Table;
      if (tbl != null)
      {
        //Since we want to add another footer row, add 1
        CreateFooterRow(tbl, footerRowIndex + 1);
      }
    }

    private void CreateFooterRow(Table tbl, int index)
    {
      for (int i = 0; i < this.ExtraFooterRows; i++)
      {
        //Create a new Grid view row
        GridViewRow row = new GridViewRow(-1, -1, DataControlRowType.Footer,
          DataControlRowState.Normal);
        tbl.Rows.AddAt(index,row);
        TableCell cell = new TableCell();
        cell.Controls.Add(new LiteralControl("Footer Row "+ i));
        row.Cells.Add(cell);
        row.ID = "Dynamically Generated Row" + i;
      }
    }
  }
}
```

Every row in the `Grid` collection has a type associated with it. You can identify whether the current row is a Footer, Header, Pager, and so forth by using the `DataControlRowType` enumeration. You perform this check within the `OnRowCreated` event. To add the extra footer rows specified by the user, you override the `OnPreRender` event.

Using the Server Control

Once the custom control outlined in Listing 10-11 is compiled, all you need to do is to register the control with the page on which it will be used, place the control on the page, and set its new properties. Listing 10-12 shows an example of ASP.NET that leverages the `CustomGridView` control.

Listing 10-12: Using the CustomGridView Control

```
<%@ Page Language="C#" %>
<%@ Register TagPrefix="wrox" Namespace="CustomControls"
  Assembly="CustomControls"%>
<html xmlns="http://www.w3.org/1999/xhtml" >
<head id="Head1" runat="server">
  <title>Using the Custom GridView Control</title>
</head>
<body>
  <form id="form1" runat="server">
    <div>
      <wrox:CustomGridView ExtraFooterRows="2" ID="deptView"
        DataKeyNames="DepartmentID" runat="server"
        AutoGenerateColumns="false" DataSourceID="deptSource">
        <Columns>
          <asp:BoundField DataField="DepartmentID" HeaderText="Department ID"/>
          <asp:BoundField DataField="Name" HeaderText="Name"/>
        </Columns>
      </wrox:CustomGridView>
      <asp:SqlDataSource ID="deptSource" Runat="server" SelectCommandType="Text"
        SelectCommand="Select DepartmentID, Name, GroupName from
        HumanResources.Department"
        ConnectionString="<%$ConnectionStrings:AdventureWorks%>">
      </asp:SqlDataSource>
    </div>
  </form>
</body>
</html>
```

The first step in consuming the custom control is to register the control at the top of the page using the `Register` directive. Since the `CustomGridView` control is defined inside the `CustomControls` namespace, you set that value as part of the `Register` directive:

```
<%@ Register TagPrefix="wrox" Namespace="CustomControls"
  Assembly="CustomControls"%>
```

As you can see from the declaration, the custom `GridView` control specifies a new property named `ExtraFooterRows` that allows you to set the additional number of footer rows that you want to display through the `GridView` control:

```
<wrox:CustomGridView ExtraFooterRows="2" ID="deptView"....>
  <Columns>......</Columns>
</wrox:CustomGridView>
```

Now if you navigate to the page from within a browser, you should see an output similar to that in Figure 10-10.

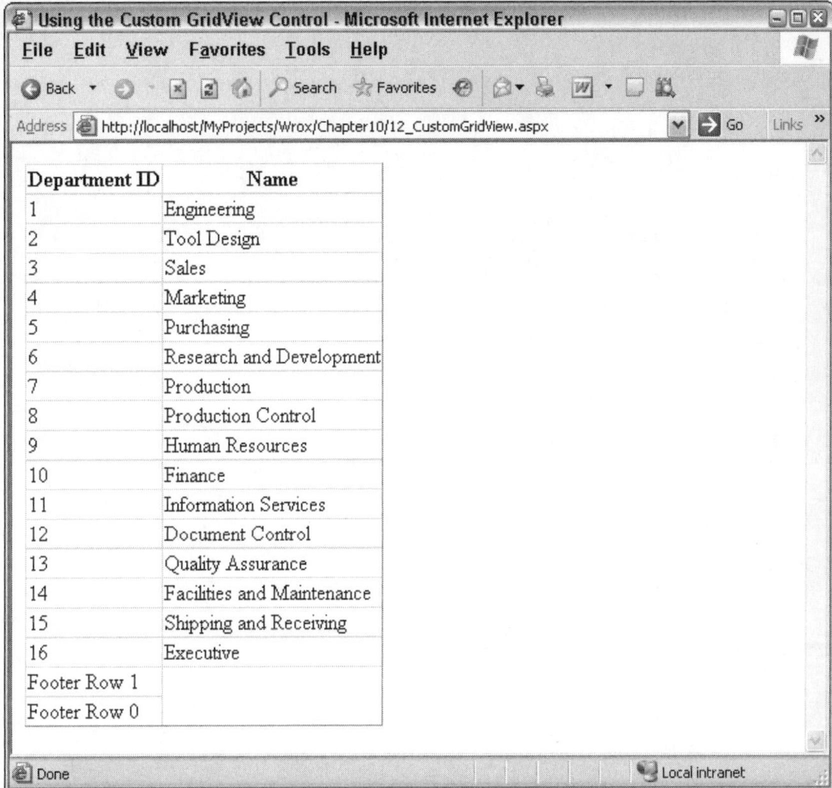

Figure 10-10

Summary

This chapter introduced you to the advanced features of the data bound controls. In addition, you also took an exhaustive look at the `FormView` control and explored its features, which are critical to creating rich data-bound pages. As you can see, these advanced features of data controls can go a long way toward increasing the usefulness of the data bound controls. Exploiting this abundance of features to build rich web-based applications is simple and straightforward, thanks to the extensibility features built into these controls.

So far, you have seen the use of data source controls and data bound controls in an ASP.NET page. The next chapter switches gears and discusses the transaction features of ADO.NET 2.0 and how they can be leveraged from within ASP.NET.

11

Transactions

Virtually all business applications require some level of transaction support. You can largely maintain data integrity in a static view by using the rules of schema that a relational database provides. In dynamic processes, however, a transaction can guarantee that all or none of the changes applied during the process are persisted when the process is complete. ACID properties (atomicity, consistency, isolation, and durability) are the cornerstone of any transaction infrastructure. Generally, transactions are related to database interactions, and it is common to think of work done with a database whenever you are considering transactions. Transactional behavior can be supplied for any resource, however, be it an in-memory hash table, a file on the disk, or an XML document. One of the design goals of the transactional engine built into version 2.0 of the .NET Framework is to make creating these resource managers much easier for any type of resource you want to participate in a transaction. This chapter will provide an overview of transactions and then go on to discuss the transaction features of .NET 1.x and 2.0 versions. Specifically, this chapter will cover:

- The different types of transactions
- How .NET 1.x transactions work in connected and disconnected mode
- How to manage transactions in .NET 1.x using `Transaction`
- How to manage distributed transactions using Enterprise Services
- How to leverage transactions without using Serviced Components
- How to use the classes contained in the `System.Transactions` namespace
- How to create implicit transactions using the `TransactionScope` class
- How to create promotable transactions
- How to configure transaction settings using `TransactionOptions`
- How to create explicit transactions
- How to handle transaction events
- Interoperability between `System.EnterpriseServices` and `System.Transactions`

Overview of Transactions

To understand the transaction support offered by .NET, it is important for you to have an overall understanding of transactions. Transactions ensure that data-oriented resources are not permanently updated unless all operations are completed successfully. A transaction is defined by a unit of operations that either all succeed or all fail. If all operations are completed successfully inside a transaction, the transaction is committed, and the updated data is written permanently. If one operation fails, however, a rollback is done; as a result, the data exists as it was before the transaction started. Suppose that you need to transfer $100 from account A to account B. This operation involves two steps:

1. $100 should be deducted from account A.
2. $100 should be added to account B.

Say that you successfully completed step 1, but due to some error, step 2 failed. If you do not undo step 1, then the entire operation will be faulty. Transactions help to avoid this. Operations in the same transaction will only make changes to the database if all the steps are successful. So in this example, if step 2 fails, then the changes made by step 1 will not be committed to the database.

Transactions usually follow certain guidelines known as the ACID properties, which ensure that even complex transactions will be self-contained and reliable.

ACID Properties

To pass the ACID test, a transaction must be atomic, consistent, isolated, and durable. While this acronym is easy to remember, the meaning of each word is not obvious. Here is a brief explanation:

- **Atomicity**: Atomicity ensures that either all updates occur or none at all. Because of the atomicity guaranteed by transactions, you do not have to write code to handle the situation where one update was successful, and another was not.
- **Consistency:** Consistency means that the result of a transaction leaves the system in a consistent state. Before the transaction is started, the data is in a valid state, as it is after the transaction is finished. The consistency property also ensures that the transaction must leave the database in a consistent state; so if one part of the transaction fails, all other parts must be undone.
- **Isolation:** Multiple users can access the same database simultaneously. With isolation, it is ensured that it is not possible outside of a transaction to see data that is being changed inside a transaction before the transaction is committed. It is not possible to access some in-between state that might never happen if the transaction is aborted.
- **Durability:** Durability means that a consistent state is guaranteed even in case of a system crash. If the database system crashes, it must be guaranteed that transactions that have been committed are really written to the database.

Database Transactions

Transactions are frequently used in many business applications because they lend robustness and predictability to a system. Typically, when you develop a software system, some data source is used to store the data. In order to apply the concept of transactions in such software systems, the data source must support transactions. Modern databases, such as Microsoft SQL Server 2005 and Oracle 9i, provide strong support for transactions. For instance, SQL Server 2005 provides support for T-SQL statements such as `BEGIN TRANSACTION`, `SAVE TRANSACTION`, `COMMIT TRANSACTION`, and `ROLLBACK TRANSACTION`.

Data access APIs, such as ODBC, OLE DB, and ADO.NET, enable developers to use transactions in their applications. Typically, RDBMSs and data access APIs provide transaction support as long as you are working with a single database. In many large applications where more than one database is involved, you may need to use the Microsoft Distributed Transaction Coordinator (MSDTC).

COM+, one of the popular middleware products, also uses MSDTC internally to facilitate multi-database transactions, or even transactions between different transaction-aware entities, commonly referred to as resource managers. It should be noted that .NET 1.1 provides access to COM+ functionality via the `System.EnterpriseServices` namespace, and in .NET 2.0 you can use the `System.Transactions` namespace to control distributed transactions as a better alternative to `System.EnterpriseServices`.

Types of Transactions

Transactions can be split into local and distributed categories.

- **Local transaction:** Uses a transaction-aware data resource (for example, SQL Server) and has the scope of a single transaction. When a single database holds all of the data involved in a transaction, it can enforce the ACID rules on its own. This means that on a single database server, such as SQL Server, you can even use local transactions across databases, as long as you are using the same connection.
- **Distributed transaction:** Spanning multiple transaction-aware data resources, distributed transactions may need to read messages from a Message Queue Server, retrieve data from a SQL Server database, and write to other databases.

Many software packages (such as MSDTC) are available to assist with programming distributed transactions, which help ensure integrity by controlling commit and rollback behavior across all data resources, using mechanisms such as a two-phase commit and rollback. MSDTC can only be used with applications that have compatible interfaces for transaction management. MSMQ, SQL Server, Oracle, Sybase, and several others are such applications (referred to as resource managers) that are currently available.

Two-Phase Commits

In a distributed transaction scenario, various resource managers need to implement a reliable commit protocol, the most common implementation of which is known as a *two-phase commit*. In a two-phase commit, the actual commit for the work is split into two phases:

- The first phase involves preparing the changes required for the commit. At this point, the RM communicates to the transaction coordinator that it has its changes prepared and ready to be committed, but not actually committed yet.
- Once all the resource managers give the green flag to the transaction coordinator, the transaction coordinator then lets everyone know that it is okay to go ahead and commit their changes.

In a two-phase commit, a single database or a number of databases can participate in a distributed transaction. In fact, anything that has the ability to enlist itself in an MSDTC transaction can enlist itself in a distributed transaction managed by the MSDTC. For instance, MSMQ can enlist in a transaction that has two other `SqlConnection` objects that connect to two different databases. This brief overview of two-phase commit is obviously oversimplified, and an in-depth discussion of two-phase commits is beyond the scope of this book. Now that you have had an overview of the transactions, you will be able to understand the support provided by .NET 1.x for transaction processing.

Transactions in .NET 1.x

ADO.NET 1.x provides strong support for database transactions. ADO.NET in itself supports single database transactions, which are tracked on a per-connection basis. The transaction functionality is provided with the connection object of ADO.NET. The ADO.NET connection object is used simply to start a transaction. The commit or rollback of the transaction is taken care of by a dedicated object, which is an implementation of the `Transaction` class. This enables you to associate different command objects with a single transaction object, so that those commands participate in the same transaction.

ADO.NET provides connected as well as disconnected data access and provides support for transactions in both of these modes. In connected mode, the typical sequence of operations in a transaction will be as follows:

1. Open a database connection.
2. Begin a transaction.
3. Fire queries directly against the connection via the `command` object.
4. Commit or roll back the transaction.
5. Close the connection.

Figure 11-1 shows how transactions are handled in connected mode.

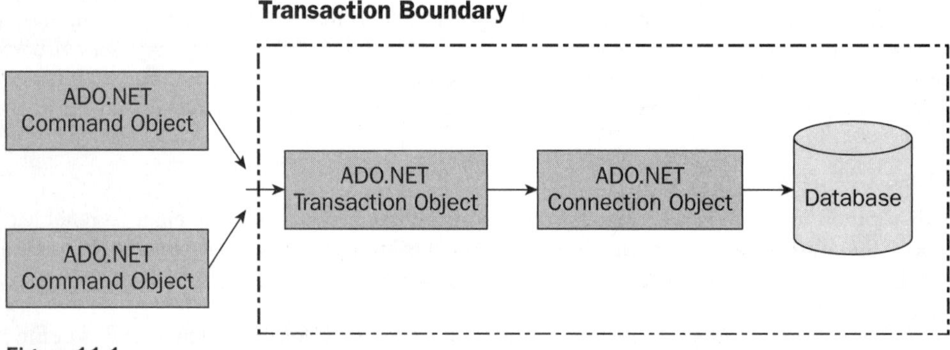

Figure 11-1

In disconnected mode, generally, data is fetched first (usually one or more tables) into a `DataSet` object, the connection with the data source is closed, the data is manipulated as required, and then the data is updated back into the database. In this mode, the typical sequence of operations will be as follows:

1. Open a database connection.
2. Fetch the required data in a `DataSet` object.
3. Close the database connection.

4. Manipulate the data in the `DataSet` object.
5. Again, open a connection with the database.
6. Start a transaction.
7. Assign the transaction object to the relevant commands on the data adapter.
8. Update the database with changes from the `DataSet`.
9. Close the connection.

Figure 11-2 illustrates this sequence of events.

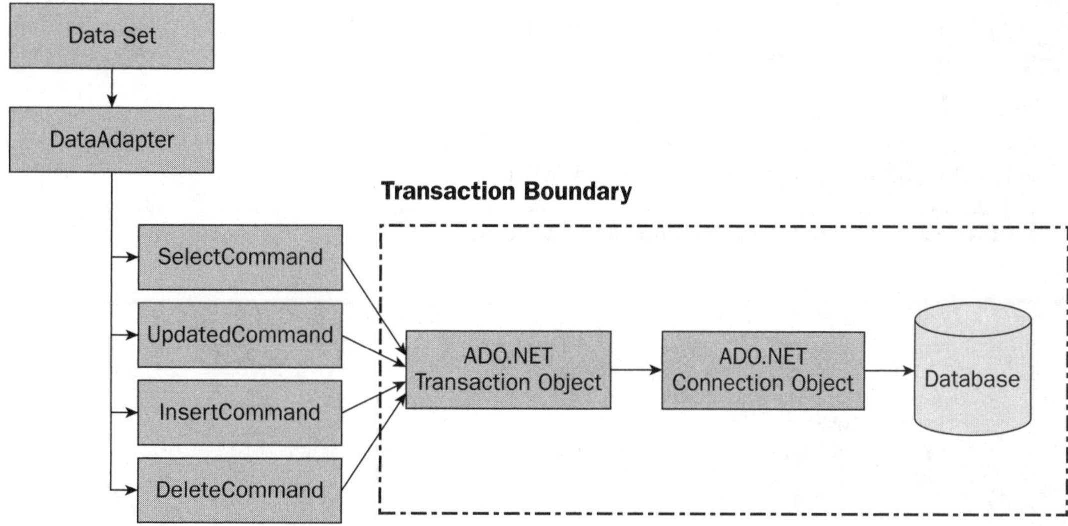

Figure 11-2

Implementing transactions in connected mode is relatively simple, because you have everything happening live; however, in disconnected mode, while updating the data back into the database, some care should be taken to account for concurrency issues. Also, depending on your architecture, it might be necessary to roll back any changes made to the `DataSet` that might have been done in a partially successful but rolled-back update.

Now that you understand the connected and disconnected transaction-processing architecture of ADO.NET, the following section will discuss the transaction class. It will also look at the commonly used methods of the transaction class and typical ways of using these methods.

Transaction Class

The .NET managed providers available in the .NET Framework, like `OleDb`, `SqlClient`, `OracleClient`, `ODBC`, and so on, all have their own implementations of the transaction class: the `OleDb` data provider has the `OleDbTransaction` class, which resides in the `System.Data.OleDb` namespace; the `ODBC` data provider has the `OdbcTransaction` class, which resides in the `System.Data.Odbc` namespace; and so on for the other providers (`SqlTransaction` class and `OracleTransaction` class).

All of these classes implement the IDbTransaction interface from the System.Data namespace. Most of the properties and methods of these classes are identical; however, each has some specific methods of its own, which will be discussed in the next section.

Methods of the Transaction Class

The transaction classes have two methods that will be used frequently:

- Commit: This method identifies a transaction as successful. Once you call this method, all the pending changes are written permanently to the underlying database once this method returns without an error. The exact implementation depends on the data provider, but typically this translates to executing a COMMIT on the underlying database.
- Rollback: This method marks a transaction as unsuccessful, and pending changes are discarded. The database state remains unchanged.

Typically, both of these methods are used together. The command object has a Transaction property that you must set in order to execute your command within a transaction. Listing 11-1 shows an example of how to explicitly start and manage the transaction.

Listing 11-1: Explicit Transaction Management in .NET 1.x

```
string connectionString = "...";
IDbConnection connection = new SqlConnection(connectionString);
connection.Open();
IDbCommand command = new SqlCommand();
command.Connection = connection;
IDbTransaction transaction;
transaction = connection.BeginTransaction(); //Enlisting database
command.Transaction = transaction;
try
{
  /* Interact with database here, then commit the transaction */
  transaction.Commit();
}
catch
{
  transaction.Rollback(); //Abort transaction
}
finally
{
  connection.Close();
}
```

You obtain an object representing the underlying database transaction by calling SqlConnection.Begin Transaction(). BeginTransaction() returns an implementation of the interface IDbTransaction used to manage the transaction. If all updates or other changes made to the database are consistent, you finally call Commit() on the transaction object. If any error occurred, you abort the transaction by calling Rollback().

While this explicit programming model is straightforward, requiring nothing of the class performing the transaction, it is most suitable for a single object or ASP.NET page interacting with a single database, as shown in Figure 11-3.

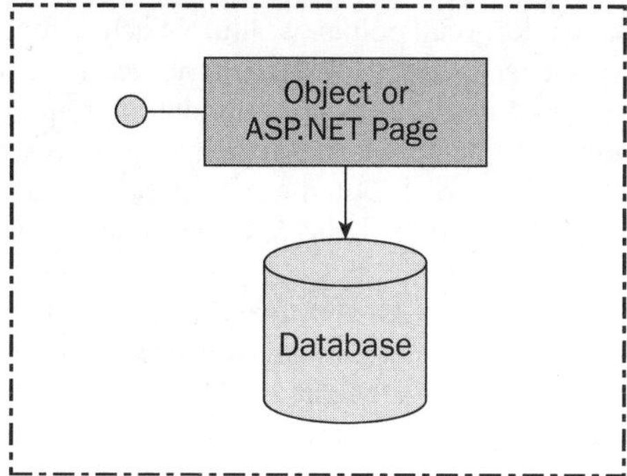

Figure 11-3

The scenario discussed in Figure 11-3 is simple in that it does not require coordination across multiple resources, since you are only communicating with a single database through a single object. However, if you extend this model to have multiple objects (shown in Figure 11-4) communicating with multiple resources to complete a transaction (without sacrificing transactional integrity), it becomes very complex. One possible solution is to couple the objects by adding logic for the transaction coordination, but such an approach is very fragile and would not withstand even minor changes to the business flow or the number of participating objects. In addition, the objects in Figure 11-4 could have been developed by different vendors, which would preclude any such coordination.

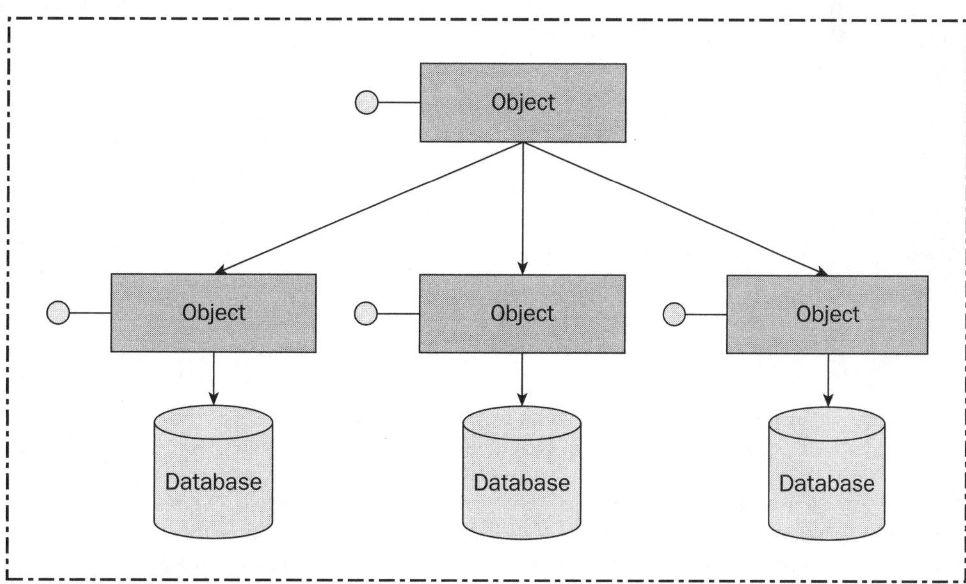

Figure 11-4

As you can see, the situation gets significantly more complex when multiple resources are involved. On top of the challenges involving multiple objects in a single transaction, the introduction of multiple resources actually introduces just as many additional points of failure. Each of the resources could fail committing its part of the transaction. This type of scenario is called a distributed transaction. A distributed transaction contains two or more independent parties or objects (often in different execution contexts), or two or more transactional resources, or both multiple objects and multiple resources. It is impractical to try to explicitly manage all the potential error cases of a distributed transaction. For a distributed transaction, you need to rely on the two-phase commit protocol and a dedicated transaction manager.

In Windows, the Distributed Transaction Coordinator (DTC) system service manages such transactions across components, processes, and machines using a protocol called OLE Transactions (OleTx). While it is possible to program directly against the DTC, in .NET 1.x the most common and easy way to utilize DTC transactions is to use the Enterprise Services available in the `System.EnterpriseServices` namespace. The next section discusses the use of Enterprise Services transactions.

Distributed Transactions Using Enterprise Services

.NET Enterprise Services (also referred to as COM+ Services) offer a declarative programming model: any class that derives from the abstract class `ServicedComponent` can use the `Transaction` attribute. The attribute ensures that when any method of the class is called, that method executes inside a transactional context. A context is the innermost execution scope of the serviced component. .NET intercepts calls coming into the context, and starts a transaction on behalf of the object. No explicit enlistment of resources is required. Obviously, this only works if the resource can automatically enlist in the transaction. Such resources are called transactional resource managers, and many of the popular commercial databases (including SQL Server, Oracle, DB2, etc.) and durable resources (such as Microsoft Message Queue) are resource managers. All the object has to do is inform .NET whether it should commit or abort the transaction. While it is possible to do so using the methods of the `ContextUtil` helper class, you can also accomplish that declaratively via the `AutoComplete` attribute. If no exception was thrown in the method, the `AutoComplete` attribute will commit the transaction, and if an exception occurred, the transaction will be aborted:

```
using System.EnterpriseServices;
[Transaction]
public class Product : ServicedComponent
{
  [AutoComplete]
  public void InsertProduct()
  {
    /*Interact with other serviced components and resource managers */
  }
}
```

Using the class attribute `[Transaction]`, you can specify whether objects of the class are aware of transactions, and whether transactions should be created automatically by the Enterprise Services runtime.

As you can see from the previous code, automatic transactions are very powerful in that you do not have to pass a transaction as an argument of a method; instead, a transaction flows automatically with the context. Using transaction attributes, you can specify whether a transaction is needed.

While the declarative model offers significant productivity benefits, it is not without flaws:

- Forcing inheritance from `ServicedComponent` occupies the precious place of a base class normally reserved for internal application modeling.
- Use of an Enterprise Services transaction always implies the use of a distributed DTC transaction, even when a single resource and a single object are involved. The two-phase commit protocol has its cost, both at the transaction manager level and at the resource level, since the resource has to keep logging its operations. The overhead could cause a degradation in performance compared with explicit transaction management.
- Implied with the use of Enterprise Services is the use of the COM+ hosting model, which many developers find intimidating.
- Enterprise services transactions are tightly coupled with Enterprise Services instance management strategies. All transactional objects are also just-in-time activated, and there are some issues when it comes to combining transactions with object pooling. While this coupling is important in a scalable application, for all other applications it forces a state-aware programming model that most developers have difficulty with.
- Enterprise services transactions are always thread-safe, meaning that there is no way for multiple threads to participate in the same transaction. While this greatly simplifies transaction management, especially in a multithreaded environment, in some edge cases it is a limitation.

In effect, .NET 1.x equates the use of a nondistributed transaction with explicit transaction management, and equates the use of a distributed transaction with that of a declarative transaction with Enterprise Services. There is no way of using a declarative transaction without using a DTC transaction, nor is there an easy way in managed code for explicit transaction management that utilizes the DTC. Choosing a programming model (explicit or declarative) invariably chooses a transaction manager as well, and vice versa.

Transactions without Serviced Components

Starting with Windows Server 2003 and Windows XP SP2, it is possible to create contexts with transactions without defining transactional attributes with serviced component classes. You can create transactional contexts with the `ServiceConfig`, the `ServiceDomain`, and the `Activity` classes (contained in the `System.EnterpriseServices` namespace). This is useful both with and without serviced components. With serviced components, this feature makes it possible that one method of a class uses a transaction, whereas another does not use it.

The code in Listing 11-2 demonstrates using transactions without serviced components. After reading the connection string from the configuration file, a new `ServiceConfig` object is created. With the `ServiceConfig` object, the context can be configured, and the transactional attributes can be set with the `Transaction` property of this class. The values that can be set with the `Transaction` property are of type `TransactionOption`. Here, `TransactionOption.Required` is used as the value for the `Transaction` property. In this example, you insert a category in the `ProductCategory` table and use the returned category ID value to insert a subcategory in the `ProductSubcategory` table.

Listing 11-2: Transactions without Serviced Components

```
<%@ Page Language="C#" %>
<%@ Import Namespace="System.Data" %>
<%@ Import Namespace="System.Data.SqlClient" %>
<%@ Import Namespace="System.EnterpriseServices" %>
```

(continued)

Listing 11-2: *(continued)*

```
<%@ Import Namespace="System.Web.Configuration" %>
<script runat="server">
  void btnSave_Click(object sender, EventArgs e)
  {
    int categoryID = 0;
    int subCategoryID =0;
    string connectionString = WebConfigurationManager.ConnectionStrings
      ["AdventureWorks"].ConnectionString;
    ServiceConfig config = new ServiceConfig();
    config.Transaction = TransactionOption.Required;
    //Begin transactional code
    ServiceDomain.Enter(config);
    //Insert the ProductCategory
    using (SqlConnection connection = new SqlConnection(connectionString))
    {
      categoryID = InsertCategory(connection);
    }
    //Insert the ProductSubCategory now under the same transaction
    using (SqlConnection connection = new SqlConnection(connectionString))
    {
      subCategoryID = InsertSubCategory(connection, categoryID);
    }
    lblResult.Text = "Category and Subcategory are written successfully---" +
      "  Category ID :" + categoryID.ToString() +
      "  Subcategory ID: " + subCategoryID.ToString();
    //End transactional code
    TransactionStatus status = ServiceDomain.Leave();
    Response.Write("Transaction Status : " + status.ToString());
  }

  int InsertCategory(SqlConnection connection)
  {
    string sql = "Insert into Production.ProductCategory(Name, rowguid," +
      " ModifiedDate) Values(@Name, @rowguid, @ModifiedDate);SELECT @@IDENTITY";
    //Opening the connection will enlist the connection in the transaction scope
    connection.Open();
    SqlCommand command = new SqlCommand(sql, connection);
    command.CommandType = CommandType.Text;
    SqlParameter nameParam = new SqlParameter("@Name", SqlDbType.NVarChar, 50);
    nameParam.Value = txtCategoryName.Text;
    command.Parameters.Add(nameParam);
    SqlParameter guidParam = new SqlParameter("@rowguid",
      SqlDbType.UniqueIdentifier);
    guidParam.Value = System.Guid.NewGuid();
    command.Parameters.Add(guidParam);
    SqlParameter modifieDateParam = new SqlParameter("@ModifiedDate",
      SqlDbType.DateTime);
    modifieDateParam.Value = System.DateTime.Now;
    command.Parameters.Add(modifieDateParam);
    int categoryID = Convert.ToInt32(command.ExecuteScalar());
    return categoryID;
```

```
  }

  int InsertSubCategory(SqlConnection connection,int categoryID)
  {
    string sql = "Insert into Production.ProductSubcategory(ProductCategoryID," +
      "Name, rowguid, ModifiedDate) Values(@ProductCategoryID, @Name, @rowguid," +
      "@ModifiedDate); SELECT @@IDENTITY";
    //Opening the connection will enlist the connection in the transaction scope
    connection.Open();
    SqlCommand command = new SqlCommand(sql, connection);
    command.CommandType = CommandType.Text;
    SqlParameter categoryIDParam = new SqlParameter("@ProductCategoryID",
      SqlDbType.Int);
    categoryIDParam.Value = categoryID;
    command.Parameters.Add(categoryIDParam);
    SqlParameter nameParam = new SqlParameter("@Name", SqlDbType.NVarChar, 50);
    nameParam.Value = txtSubCategoryName.Text;
    command.Parameters.Add(nameParam);
    SqlParameter guidParam = new SqlParameter("@rowguid",
      SqlDbType.UniqueIdentifier);
    guidParam.Value = System.Guid.NewGuid();
    command.Parameters.Add(guidParam);
    SqlParameter modifieDateParam = new SqlParameter("@ModifiedDate",
      SqlDbType.DateTime);
    modifieDateParam.Value = System.DateTime.Now;
    command.Parameters.Add(modifieDateParam);
    int subCategoryID = Convert.ToInt32( command.ExecuteScalar());
    return subCategoryID;
  }
</script>
<html xmlns="http://www.w3.org/1999/xhtml" >
<head id="Head1" runat="server">
  <title>Transactions using Enterprise Services</title>
</head>
<body>
  <form id="form1" runat="server">
    <div>
      <asp:Label ID="lblCategoryName" runat="server" Text="Category Name:"
        Width="179px"></asp:Label>
      <asp:TextBox ID="txtCategoryName" runat="server"/>
      <br/><br/><br/>
      <asp:Label ID="lblSubCategoryName" runat="server" Text="Subcategory Name"
        Width="177px"></asp:Label>
      <asp:TextBox ID="txtSubCategoryName" runat="server"/>
       <br/><br/>
      <asp:Button ID="btnSave" runat="server" Text="Save" Width="92px"
        OnClick="btnSave_Click"/>
      <br/><br/>
      <asp:Label ID="lblResult" runat="server" Font-Bold="true" Font-Size="Small"/>
    </div>
  </form>
</body>
</html>
```

As the name suggests, the `InsertCategory()` helper function contains the code required to insert a new category record into the `ProductCategory` table, and the `InsertSubCategory()` function performs the function of inserting a subcategory into the `ProductSubcategory` table, using the category ID returned from the `InsertCategory()` function. These methods are used in various examples throughout this chapter.

In Listing 11-2, the context is created as soon as you call `ServiceDomain.Enter()`, passing the context configuration information. The transaction is committed when the context is left with `ServiceDomain.Leave()`, which returns the status of the transaction as a value of the enumeration `TransactionStatus`. The possible values of `TransactionStatus` enumeration are listed in the following table.

Member	Description
`Aborted`	The transaction is aborted. Either the database returned an error or the method generated an exception, so the transaction is aborted.
`Aborting`	The transaction is in the process of being aborted.
`Committed`	The transaction committed successfully. Every member who was participating in the transaction voted the transaction by setting the consistent bit.
`LocallyOk`	The transaction is neither committed nor aborted. This status can be returned, if the context that is left is running inside another transactional context.
`NoTransaction`	The transaction did not have a context, so `NoTransaction` is returned.

> **The `ServiceDomain` class makes it possible for a .NET managed object to run in its own context. You can indicate that the object should run in its own context by using the `Enter()` and `Leave()` methods of the `ServiceDomain` class. The code that is enclosed within this block can use the functionalities exposed by `System.EnterpriseServices` namespace. It is also possible for you to nest the `Enter()` and `Leave()` methods. However, you need to ensure that for every `Enter()` method call, there is a corresponding `Leave()` method.**

Some examples of when it is helpful to use transactions without serviced components are:

- This can be helpful when using transactions with standalone applications.
- With ASP.NET web services that use serviced components, a root transactional context can be created without serviced component configuration.
- Services without components can also be useful within serviced components: for example, if the serviced component class has one method that requires a transaction and another method that doesn't require one.

Figure 11-5 shows the generated output.

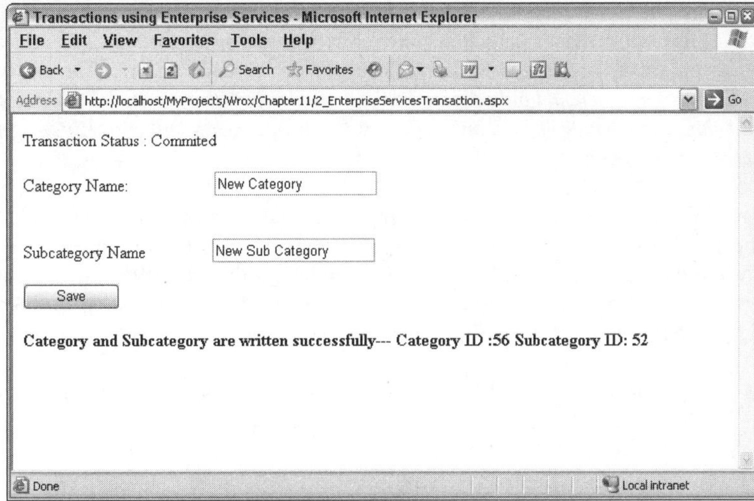

Figure 11-5

If you try running the sample application on Windows XP without SP2, you will get the exception `PlatformNotSupportedException`. *Services without components are only supported on Windows Server 2003 and Windows XP SP2.*

Transactions in .NET 2.0

The transaction management system in .NET 2.0 Framework sets out to address the problem of excessive overhead for dynamic composition of transactions by enlisting only the resource managers required for the type of transactional work being done. It also provides an infrastructure where you can roll in more volatile resources into the commit and rollback model of transactions. To address the problems just described with both the explicit and the declarative transactional programming models, the .NET Framework 2.0 introduces two new types of transaction managers and a management namespace. The two new transaction managers are:

- **Lightweight Transaction Manager (LTM):** The LTM is used to manage a transaction inside a single app domain that involves at most a single durable resource.
- **Distributed OleTx Transaction Manager:** This type of transaction manager manages transactions across the app domain boundaries (including across process and machine boundaries), or any transaction that involves more than one durable resource, even in the same app domain. The OleTx transaction manager relies on RPC for cross-machine calls, and it is equivalent to the DTC behavior with minor changes.

The LTM uses only intra-app domain calls and so is of higher performance than the OleTx Transaction Manger. Developers need not interact with these transaction managers directly. Instead, common infrastructure that defines interfaces, transaction factories, common behaviors, and helper classes is available in the `System.Transactions` namespace. The resources managed by the two transaction managers are called `System.Transactions` Resource Managers (RM). Similar to Enterprise Services, a `System.Transactions` Resource Manager is a resource that can automatically enlist in a transaction managed by the LTM or the OleTx transaction managers.

> *The main advantage of programming against a common transaction management namespace (*`System.Transactions`*) rather than a particular transaction manager is promotion. Transaction manager promotion is an innovative technique supported by* `System.Transactions`*. The idea behind promotion is simple: Developers should only decide on the desired programming model (either explicit or declarative transaction management), and* `System.Transactions` *will correctly assign the appropriate transaction manager.*

If a single object interacts with a single durable resource, it should only require the LTM and will obviously yield the best throughput and performance. If you provide the transaction to another object in another app domain on the same machine, or if you enlist another durable resource manager, the transaction will automatically be promoted for management by OleTx. Once promoted, the transaction remains managed in its elevated state till its completion.

Both the LTM and the OleTx transaction manager represent their transaction using a class called `Transaction`, defined in the `System.Transactions` namespace. The `Transaction` class is used to enlist resources in the transaction, to abort the transaction, to set the isolation level, to obtain the transaction status and ID, and to clone the transaction.

Lightweight Transaction Manager

The LTM is a very fast, very inexpensive resource manager for transactions occurring in a single application domain. It is the starting point of all transactions in the Framework, and it monitors the resources being touched by a transaction and enlists the services of more robust resource managers on an as-needed basis.

When the transactional work goes out-of-process (i.e., you start modifying database data), the LTM will automatically use a resource manager that supports the Promotable Single Phase Enlistment (PSPE) model of transaction management. This is a new transactional infrastructure that knows and understands the "pay as you go" mechanism of the LTM. If there is no PSPE manager available, the LTM enlists the DTC. And then, of course, the DTC is enlisted any time multiple remote data sources are modified. When the PSPE model can do the job, then your transactions will perform as well as an ADO.NET Transaction would in version 1.x. You might be questioning the need for PSPE model, when it provides the same performance as that of ADO.NET transactions. It is used so that the transaction is automatically promoted to the DTC when more than one database is touched.

> **In .NET Framework 2.0, you will automatically get a PSPE transaction when working with SQL Server 2005. If the transactional work touches another server or another database, it automatically uses the DTC. Volatile transactions automatically participate in the PSPE without invoking the DTC.**

Using the TransactionScope Class

As the name implies, the `TransactionScope` class is used to scope a code section with a transaction. Internally in its constructor, the `TransactionScope` object creates a transaction (Lightweight Transaction Manager by default in .NET 2.0), and assigns that to the `Current` property of the `Transaction` class. Since the `TransactionScope` is a disposable object, the transaction will end once the `Dispose()` method is called:

```
using(TransactionScope scope = new TransactionScope())
{
  /* Perform transactional work here */
  //No errors - commit transaction
  scope.Complete();
}
```

Listing 11-3 shows one way to create transactions with .NET 2.0. Creating and disposing of a `TransactionScope` object defines a transactional code block. With the constructor of the `TransactionScope` object and the `TransactionScopeOption` enumeration, you can define whether a new transaction is required or whether a transaction that already exists from the outer block should be used. The method `TransactionScope.Complete()` method indicates that all operations within the scope of the transaction have been successful. At the end of the `using` statement (where the `Dispose()` method is called), the transaction outcome of the block is defined. If the `Complete()` method was not called because an exception occurred, the transaction is aborted. If the scope of the transaction was successful, the transaction is committed if it is a root transaction. If the scope is not the root of the transaction, the outcome of the transaction is influenced.

Listing 11-3: Implicit Transactions Using TransactionScope

```
<%@ Page Language="C#" %>
<%@ Import Namespace="System.Data" %>
<%@ Import Namespace="System.Data.SqlClient" %>
<%@ Import Namespace="System.Transactions" %>
<%@ Import Namespace="System.Web.Configuration" %>
<script runat="server">
  void btnSave_Click(object sender, EventArgs e)
  {
    try
    {
      int categoryID;
      string connectionString = WebConfigurationManager.ConnectionStrings
        ["AdventureWorks"].ConnectionString;
      using (TransactionScope scope = new TransactionScope())
      {
        using (SqlConnection connection = new SqlConnection(connectionString))
        {
          categoryID = InsertCategory(connection);
        }
        //Commit the transaction
        scope.Complete();
      }
      lblResult.Text= "Category is written successfully*****Category ID= " +
        categoryID.ToString();
    }
    catch (Exception ex)
    {
      lblResult.Text= "Exception is : " + ex.Message;
    }
  }

  int InsertCategory(SqlConnection connection)
```

(continued)

Listing 11-3: *(continued)*

```
    {
      //Same as in InsertCategory method shown in Listing 11-2
    }
  </script>
  <html xmlns="http://www.w3.org/1999/xhtml" >
  <head runat="server">
    <title>Implicit Transactions using TransactionScope</title>
  </head>
  <body>
    <form id="form1" runat="server">
      <div>
        <asp:Label ID="lblCategoryName" runat="server" Text="Category Name:"
          Width="179px"></asp:Label>
        <asp:TextBox ID="txtCategoryName" runat="server"/> 
        <asp:Button ID="btnSave" runat="server" Text="Save" Width="92px"
          OnClick="btnSave_Click"/>
        <br/><br/>
        <asp:Label ID="lblResult" runat="server" Font-Bold="true" Font-Size="Small"/>
      </div>
    </form>
  </body>
  </html>
```

In Listing 11-3, the code that executes the insert SQL statement against the ProductCategory table in the AdventureWorks database is enclosed in a `TransactionScope` object `using` block. The `InsertCategory()` method is the one that performs the actual insertion of a new record into the ProductCategory table. After inserting the record, it also returns the identity value (category ID column) of the newly inserted record back to the caller. Once the code has successfully executed, you invoke the `Complete()` method of the `TransactionScope` object to signal the .NET Framework that the statement has been successfully committed, which will result in the transaction being committed to the database.

Here are some things `TransactionScope` does for you:

- Any statement(s) appearing within the brackets of the `using` statement will be executed within the scope of a transaction.
- Any connection created in this block will be enlisted in the transaction.
- If an error occurs within the using block, the transaction will automatically be rolled back.
- If the statement is executed successfully, then call `Complete()` on the transaction for your portion of the work.
- Every step of the call stack must call `Complete()` for the transaction to be committed.

The `TransactionScope` object has no way of knowing whether the transaction should commit or abort, yet the main objective of `TransactionScope` is to shield the developers from the need to interact with the transaction directly. To address this, every `TransactionScope` object has a consistency bit, which is by default set to false. You can set the consistency bit to true by calling the `Complete()` method. Note that you can only call `Complete()` once. Subsequent calls to `Complete()` will raise an `InvalidOperation` exception, since it ensures that you cannot have transactional code after the call to `Complete()`.

If the transaction ends (due to calling `Dispose()` or garbage collection) and the consistency bit is set to false, the transaction will abort. For example, the following scope object will always roll back its transaction, because the consistency bit is never changed from its default value:

```
using(TransactionScope scope = new TransactionScope())
{
}
```

On the other hand, if you do call `Complete()` and the transaction ends with the consistency bit set to true as in Listing 11-3, the transaction will commit.

Advantages of the TransactionScope Class

The `TransactionScope` object offers clear advantages and benefits compared with the previous transaction programming of .NET 1.x. They are:

- The code inside the transactional scope is not only transactional, it is also promotable. The transaction starts with the LTM (Lightweight Transaction Manager), and `System.Transactions` will promote it as required, according to the nature of its interaction with the resources or remote objects.
- The scope is independent of the application object model, meaning that any piece of code can use the `TransactionScope` and thus become transactional. There is no need for a special base class or attributes.
- There is no need to enlist resources explicitly with the transaction. Any `System.Transactions` resource manager will detect the ambient transaction created by the scope and automatically enlist.
- It provides a simple and intuitive programming model, even for the more complex scenarios that involve transaction flow and nesting.

Promotable Transactions

As mentioned previously, the `System.Transactions` namespace can make the management of transactions quick and easy without the need to worry about the complexities associated with `Serviced Component`-based implementations. One of the greatest features of the lightweight transaction in `System.Transactions` is that it can automatically determine if it needs to promote a lightweight transaction to a distributed transaction that involves MSDTC. The lightweight transactions are also a faster alternative to using the DTC for local transactions.

This section will demonstrate how a fast, lightweight transaction covering a single SQL connection can be easily and automatically promoted to a full distributed transaction spanning perhaps multiple connections. This can all take place within a single transaction context (using `TransactionScope`), without inheriting from `ServicedComponent`.

To demonstrate this, this section will build on Listing 11-3 by adding the execution of another method named `InsertSubCategory()` that inserts a subcategory into the `ProductSubcategory` table. Both of these methods (`InsertCategory` and `InsertSubCategory`) are embedded within the same `TransactionScope` block.

Listing 11-4: Using Promotable Transactions

```
<%@ Page Language="C#" %>
<%@ Import Namespace="System.Data" %>
<%@ Import Namespace="System.Data.SqlClient" %>
<%@ Import Namespace="System.Transactions" %>
<%@ Import Namespace="System.Web.Configuration" %>
<script runat="server">
  void btnSave_Click(object sender, EventArgs e)
  {
    try
    {
      string connectionString = WebConfigurationManager.ConnectionStrings
        ["AdventureWorks"].ConnectionString;
      int categoryID, subCategoryID;
      using (TransactionScope scope = new TransactionScope())
      {
        //Insert the ProductCategory
       using (SqlConnection connection = new SqlConnection(connectionString))
       {
         categoryID = InsertCategory(connection);
       }
       //Insert the ProductSubCategory now under the same transaction
       using (SqlConnection connection = new SqlConnection(connectionString))
       {
         subCategoryID = InsertSubCategory(connection, categoryID);
       }
       //Commit the transaction
       scope.Complete();
     }
     lblResult.Text = "Category and Subcategory are written successfully---" +
       "  Category ID :" + categoryID.ToString() +
       "  Subcategory ID: " + subCategoryID.ToString();
     }
     catch (Exception ex)
     {
       lblResult.Text = "Exception is : " + ex.Message;
     }
  }

  int InsertCategory(SqlConnection connection)
  {
    //Same as in InsertCategory method shown in Listing 11-2
  }

  int InsertSubCategory(SqlConnection connection,int categoryID)
  {
    //Same as in InsertSubCategory method shown in Listing 11-2
  }
</script>
<html xmlns="http://www.w3.org/1999/xhtml" >
<head runat="server">
  <title>Implicit Distributed Transactions using TransactionScope</title>
```

```
</head>
<body>
  <form id="form1" runat="server">
    <div>
      <asp:Label ID="lblCategoryName" runat="server" Text="Category Name:"
        Width="179px"></asp:Label>
      <asp:TextBox ID="txtCategoryName" runat="server"/>
      <br/><br/><br/>
      <asp:Label ID="lblSubCategoryName" runat="server" Text="Subcategory Name"
        Width="177px"></asp:Label>
      <asp:TextBox ID="txtSubCategoryName" runat="server"/>
       <br/><br/>
      <asp:Button ID="btnSave" runat="server" Text="Save" Width="92px"
        OnClick="btnSave_Click"/>
      <br/><br/>
      <asp:Label ID="lblResult" runat="server" Font-Bold="true" Font-Size="Small"/>
    </div>
  </form>
</body>
</html>
</html>
```

When the connection to the first database is opened, the transaction is created as a lightweight transaction. However, when you open the second `SqlConnection`, the transaction is automatically promoted to a distributed transaction. Note that this promotion from a lightweight to a distributed transaction happens only with SQL Server 2005.

Configuring Transaction Settings Using TransactionOptions

Listing 11-3 utilized the `TransactionScope` object with the default constructor, and because of this, the default isolation level and the timeout values are used. The default value for the transaction isolation level is `System.Transactions.IsolationLevel.Serializable`, and for the timeout it is 60 seconds. There are times when you might want to override these values with your own values so that you have a finer level of control over these settings. The `TransactionScope` object provides a number of overloaded constructors that allow you to supply these values. Listing 11-5 shows you an example of how to accomplish this.

Listing 11-5: Using TransactionOptions to Configure Transaction Settings

```
<%@ Page Language="C#" %>
<%@ Import Namespace="System.Data" %>
<%@ Import Namespace="System.Data.SqlClient" %>
<%@ Import Namespace="System.Transactions" %>
<%@ Import Namespace="System.Web.Configuration" %>
<script runat="server">
  void btnSave_Click(object sender, EventArgs e)
  {
    try
    {
      int categoryID;
      string connectionString = WebConfigurationManager.ConnectionStrings
```

(continued)

Listing 11-5: *(continued)*

```
          ["AdventureWorks"].ConnectionString;
        TransactionOptions transactionOption = new TransactionOptions();
        transactionOption.IsolationLevel =
          System.Transactions.IsolationLevel.ReadCommitted;
        //Set the transaction timeout to 60 seconds
        transactionOption.Timeout = new TimeSpan(0, 0, 60);
        using (TransactionScope scope = new
          TransactionScope(TransactionScopeOption.Required, transactionOption))
        {
          using (SqlConnection connection = new SqlConnection(connectionString))
          {
            categoryID = InsertCategory(connection);
          }
          //Commit the transaction
          scope.Complete();
        }
        lblResult.Text= "Category is written successfully*****Category ID= " +
          categoryID.ToString();
      }
      catch (Exception ex)
      {
        lblResult.Text= "Exception is : " + ex.Message;
      }
    }

    int InsertCategory(SqlConnection connection)
    {
      //Same as in InsertCategory method shown in Listing 11-2
    }
  </script>
  <html xmlns="http://www.w3.org/1999/xhtml" >
  <head runat="server">
    <title>Configuring Settings with TransactionScope</title>
  </head>
  <body>
    <form id="form1" runat="server">
      <div>
        <asp:Label ID="lblCategoryName" runat="server" Text="Category Name:"
          Width="179px"></asp:Label>
        <asp:TextBox ID="txtCategoryName" runat="server"/> 
        <asp:Button ID="btnSave" runat="server" Text="Save" Width="92px"
          OnClick="btnSave_Click"/>
        <br/><br/>
        <asp:Label ID="lblResult" runat="server" Font-Bold="true" Font-Size="Small"/>
      </div>
    </form>
  </body>
  </html>
```

To set the isolation level and the transaction timeout period, create an instance of the `TransactionOptions` object, and set its `IsolationLevel` and `Timeout` properties to appropriate values. The next table discusses the members supported by the `TransactionIsolationLevel` enumeration.

Member	Description
`Any`	If you set the isolation level to `Any`, the same isolation level as the calling component is used. If the object is the root object, the isolation level is `Serializable`.
`ReadUncommitted`	With `ReadUncommitted`, only shared locks are used and exclusive locks are not honored. You should use this option only for read access, to generate some results that do not need to be actually up to the second.
`ReadCommitted`	With this option, shared locks are used while data is being read. After reading the data, the shared lock is released. Before the transaction is finished, the data can be changed.
`RepeatableRead`	If you set the option to `RepeatableRead`, locks are placed on all data that is used.
`Serializable`	The level `Serializable` has the best isolation. With this option, updates or inserts that belong to the range of the data that is used are not possible.

Then you supply the `TransactionOptions` object as an argument to the constructor of the `TransactionScope` object. In Listing 11-5, the constructor of the `TransactionScope` object also takes the `TransactionScopeOption` enumeration as an argument. The `TransactionScopeOption` enumeration can take in any of the values shown in the following table.

Member	Description
`Required`	If within a currently active transaction scope, this transaction scope will join it. Otherwise, it will create its own transaction scope.
`RequiresNew`	This transaction will create its own transaction scope.
`Suppress`	The current transaction context is suppressed when creating the scope. All operations within the scope are done without a transaction context.

Controlling Explicit Transactions

There are times when the default implicit automatic transaction capability of the `TransactionScope` object may not provide you with the finer level of control you need. In those cases, you may want to manually create a transaction and explicitly commit or roll back the transaction. Listing 11-6 shows the steps involved in creating an explicit transaction using the `CommittableTransaction` class.

Listing 11-6: Explicit Transactions Using CommittableTransaction

```
<%@ Page Language="C#" %>
<%@ Import Namespace="System.Data" %>
<%@ Import Namespace="System.Data.SqlClient" %>
<%@ Import Namespace="System.Transactions" %>
<%@ Import Namespace="System.Web.Configuration" %>
```

(continued)

Listing 11-6: *(continued)*

```
<script runat="server">
  void btnSave_Click(object sender, EventArgs e)
  {
    CommittableTransaction trans = new CommittableTransaction();
    try
    {
      string connectionString =  WebConfigurationManager.ConnectionStrings
        ["AdventureWorks"].ConnectionString;
      using (SqlConnection connection = new SqlConnection(connectionString))
      {
        string sql = "Insert into Production.ProductCategory(Name," +
          "rowguid, ModifiedDate) Values(@Name, @rowguid, @ModifiedDate)";
        //Opening the connection will enlist the connection in transaction scope
        connection.Open();
        SqlCommand command = new SqlCommand(sql, connection);
        command.CommandType = CommandType.Text;
        SqlParameter nameParam = new SqlParameter("@Name", SqlDbType.NVarChar, 50);
        nameParam.Value = txtCategoryName.Text;
        command.Parameters.Add(nameParam);
        SqlParameter guidParam = new SqlParameter("@rowguid",
          SqlDbType.UniqueIdentifier);
        guidParam.Value = System.Guid.NewGuid();
        command.Parameters.Add(guidParam);
        SqlParameter modifieDateParam = new SqlParameter("@ModifiedDate",
          SqlDbType.DateTime);
        modifieDateParam.Value = System.DateTime.Now;
        command.Parameters.Add(modifieDateParam);
        //Enlist the transaction in the scope of the current transaction
        connection.EnlistTransaction(trans);
        command.ExecuteNonQuery();
        //Commit the transaction if everything executed successfully
        trans.Commit();
      }
      lblResult.Text = "Category is written successfully";
    }
    catch (Exception ex)
    {
      //Rollback the transaction if there is an exception
      trans.Rollback();
      lblResult.Text = "Exception is : " + ex.Message;
    }
  }
</script>
<html xmlns="http://www.w3.org/1999/xhtml" >
<head runat="server">
  <title>Using Explicit Transactions using CommittableTransaction</title>
</head>
<body>
  <form id="form1" runat="server">
    <div>
      <asp:Label ID="lblCategoryName" runat="server" Text="Category Name:"
        Width="179px"></asp:Label>
```

```
            <asp:TextBox ID="txtCategoryName" runat="server"/> 
            <asp:Button ID="btnSave" runat="server" Text="Save" Width="92px"
              OnClick="btnSave_Click"/>
            <br/><br/>
            <asp:Label ID="lblResult" runat="server" Font-Bold="true" Font-Size="Small"/>
        </div>
    </form>
</body>
</html>
```

In this approach, you need to associate the `SqlConnection` object with the `CommittableTransaction` object by invoking the `EnlistTransaction()` method of the `SqlConnection` object, passing in the `CommittableTransaction` object as an argument. Once that is done, you can then explicitly commit or roll back the transactions through the call to the `Commit()` or `Rollback()` methods of the `Committable Transaction` object. As you can imagine, this manual approach is not recommended, and you might run the risk of not rolling back the transaction when different types of exceptions occur.

Automatic Transactions in ASP.NET

ASP.NET supports automatic transactions on systems by allowing you to insert a transaction directive in your ASP.NET page. Through this `Transaction` directive, you can instruct the page to participate in an existing transaction, begin a new transaction, or never participate in a transaction. The following table lists and describes the transaction values available in ASP.NET.

Value	Description
`Disabled`	Indicates that the transaction context is ignored by ASP.NET. This is the default transaction state.
`NotSupported`	Indicates that the page does not run within the scope of transactions. When a request is processed, its object context is created without a transaction, regardless of whether or not there is a transaction active.
`Supported`	Indicates that the page runs in the context of an existing transaction. If no transaction exists, the page runs without a transaction.
`Required`	The page runs in the context of an existing transaction. If no transaction exists, the page starts one.
`RequiresNew`	Indicates that the page requires a transaction, and a new transaction is started for each request.

You can indicate the level of transaction support on a page by placing the `Transaction` attribute in the `Page` directive in your code. For example, you can ensure that the page activities always execute in the scope of a transaction by inserting the following directive:

```
<%@ Page Transaction="Required" %>
```

If you omit the `Transaction` directive, transactions are disabled for the page. The static methods of the `System.EnterpriseServices.ContextUtil` class are used to commit or abort transactions in ASP.NET pages. These static methods are `SetComplete()` and `SetAbort()` (which correspond to the

Page events CommitTransaction() and AbortTransaction(), respectively). The following code shows the skeleton implementation for a page that has its Transaction attribute of the Page directive set to Required:

```
void Page_Load(object sender, System.EventArgs e)
{
AbortTransaction += new System.EventHandler(AbortTransactionEvent);
CommitTransaction += new System.EventHandler(CommitTransactionEvent);
try
{
    /*Place your transactional code here */
    ContextUtil.SetComplete();
}
catch(Exception)
{
    ContextUtil.SetAbort();
}
}

void AbortTransactionEvent(object sender,System.EventArgs e)
{
  /*Code for RollBack activity */
}

void CommitTransactionEvent(object sender,System.EventArgs e)
{
  /*Code for Commit Activity*/
}
```

In the CommitTransaction() and AbortTransaction() events, you write the required code to process the results of the transaction.

Transaction Events

The Transaction class provides a public event called TransactionCompleted, defined as follows:

```
public delegate void TransactionCompletedEventHandler(object sender,
  TransactionEventArgs e);
```

TransactionCompleted is raised after the transaction is completed (be it committed or aborted). The event is of the delegate type TransactionCompletedEventHandler, which takes two parameters: sender is the transaction that just completed, and e is of the type TransactionEventArgs, which also provides access to the same transaction:

```
public class TransactionEventArgs: EventArgs
{
public TransactionEventArgs();
  public Transaction Transaction{get;}
}
```

You can subscribe to the TransactionCompleted event to be notified when the transaction is completed, as shown in Listing 11-7.

Listing 11-7: Handling the TransactionCompleted Event

```
<%@ Page Language="C#" %>
<%@ Import Namespace="System.Data" %>
<%@ Import Namespace="System.Data.SqlClient" %>
<%@ Import Namespace="System.Transactions" %>
<%@ Import Namespace="System.Web.Configuration" %>
<script runat="server">
  void btnSave_Click(object sender, EventArgs e)
  {
    try
    {
      int categoryID;
      string connectionString = WebConfigurationManager.ConnectionStrings
        ["AdventureWorks"].ConnectionString;
      using (TransactionScope scope = new TransactionScope())
      {
        using (SqlConnection connection = new SqlConnection(connectionString))
        {
          Transaction trans = Transaction.Current;
          trans.TransactionCompleted += OnCompleted;
          categoryID = InsertCategory(connection);
        }
        //Commit the transaction
        scope.Complete();
      }
      lblResult.Text= "Category is written successfully*****Category ID= " +
        categoryID.ToString();
    }
    catch (Exception ex)
    {
      lblResult.Text= "Exception is : " + ex.Message;
    }
}

void OnCompleted(object sender, TransactionEventArgs e)
{
    Transaction transaction = e.Transaction;
    switch(transaction.TransactionInformation.Status)
    {
      case TransactionStatus.Aborted:
      {
        Response.Write("Transaction Aborted!");
        break;
      }
      case TransactionStatus.Committed:
      {
        Response.Write("Transaction Committed!");
        break;
      }
    }
}
```

(continued)

Listing 11-7: *(continued)*

```
int InsertCategory(SqlConnection connection)
{
    //Same as shown in previous examples
}
</script>
<html xmlns="http://www.w3.org/1999/xhtml" >
<head runat="server">
  <title>Handling Transaction Events</title>
</head>
<body>
  <form id="form1" runat="server">
    <div>
      <asp:Label ID="lblCategoryName" runat="server" Text="Category Name:"
        Width="179px"></asp:Label>
      <asp:TextBox ID="txtCategoryName" runat="server"/> 
      <asp:Button ID="btnSave" runat="server" Text="Save" Width="92px"
        OnClick="btnSave_Click"/>
      <br/><br/>
      <asp:Label ID="lblResult" runat="server" Font-Bold="true" Font-Size="Small"/>
    </div>
  </form>
</body>
</html>
```

While developers know when an LTM transaction starts (when the scope is constructed), your code may also want to know when that LTM transaction is promoted to a distributed OleTx transaction. The static class `TransactionManager` provides the event `TransactionStarted`, defined as follows:

```
public delegate void TransactionStartedEventHandler(object sender,
  TransactionEventArgs e);
```

The `DistributedTransactionStarted` event is raised whenever a distributed transaction starts. You can subscribe to both a distributed transaction's start and completion events, as shown in the following code:

```
public void DoWork()
{
TransactionManager.DistributedTransactionStarted += OnDistributedStarted;
using(TransactionScope scope = new TransactionScope())
{
    Transaction transaction = Transaction.Current;
    transaction.TransactionCompleted += OnCompleted;
    /* Perform transactional work here */
    scope.Complete();
}
}

void OnDistributedStarted(object sender,TransactionEventArgs e)
{...}

void OnCompleted(object sender,TransactionEventArgs e)
{...}
```

It is important to ensure that the work you do in the distributed transaction's start event handlers should be of short duration, because the distributed transaction will not start until all the event subscribers have been notified.

Interoperability between System.Transactions and System.EnterpriseServices

`System.Transactions` provides inherent support for .NET Enterprise Services, meaning that any serviced component can take advantage of the new transaction managers and transaction promotion, without you having to do anything special. The interesting questions are what happens when a transactional serviced component creates a `TransactionScope` object, or when a transactional scope creates serviced components? Since the Enterprise Services transaction programming model is coupled to the object life-cycle and state management, combining that with transactional scopes that are not even object-based may lead to some complicated side effects.

`System.Transactions` defines three levels of interoperability between itself and Enterprise Services: None, Automatic, and Full. The enum `EnterpriseServicesInteropOption` is defined as:

```
public enum EnterpriseServicesInteropOption
{
Automatic,
Full,
  None
}
```

The `TransactionScope` class provides constructors that accept `EnterpriseServicesInteropOption`. For example:

```
public TransactionScope(TransactionScopeOption scopeOption,
  TransactionOptions transactionOptions,
  EnterpriseServicesInteropOption interopOption);
```

`EnterpriseServicesInteropOption.None`, as the name implies, means that there is no interoperability between Enterprise Services contexts and transactional scopes. Such transactional scopes will completely ignore the transactional context or their creating client, and will use its own transaction. This transaction will be distinct from the Enterprise Services–managed transaction. As a result, you could have the transactional scope's transaction abort while the Enterprise Services transaction around it commits. The following code shows how to use the `TransactionScope` class within the scope of a serviced component:

```
Transaction]
public class MyComponent : ServicedComponent
{
  [AutoComplete]
public void DoWork()
{
    TransactionOptions options = new TransactionOptions();
    options.IsolationLevel = IsolationLevel.Serializable;
    options.Timeout = TransactionManager.DefaultTimeout;
    using(TransactionScope scope = new TransactionScope(
      TransactionScopeOption.Required, options,
```

```
        EnterpriseServicesInteropOption.None)
      {
        //No call to scope.Complete(), yet the COM+ transaction still can commit
      }
    }
  }
```

`EnterpriseServicesInteropOption.None` eliminates any side effects resulting from mixing Enterprise Services transactions and transactions, and therefore it is the safest option. It is also the default used by `TransactionScope` with all constructors that do not accept an `EnterpriseServicesInteropOption` value.

If you do want to combine Enterprise Services transactions with your `System.Transactions` transaction, you need to use either `EnterpriseServicesInteropOption.Automatic` or `EnterpriseServicesInteropOption.Full`. Both of these values rely on serviced domains and therefore require running with Windows XP Service Pack 2 or Windows 2003 Server. `EnterpriseServicesInteropOption.Full` will try to behave as much as possible as a serviced component would. If the `TransactionScope` object needs a transaction (either joining an existing transaction or creating a new one), `EnterpriseServicesInteropOption.Full` will create a new Enterprise Services transactional context, flow into it any existing Enterprise Services transaction (or create a new Enterprise Services transaction), and the `System.Transactions` transaction used will be the same transaction used by that Enterprise Services context. If the `TransactionScope` object does not require a transaction, the scope will be placed in the default Enterprise Services context.

When to Use Transactions

Although .NET 2.0 provides good support for transactions, it is not always necessary to use transactions. A more accurate statement, perhaps, could be that you should use transactions when you can, but not overuse them. Every time you use a transaction, you carry some overhead. Plus, transactions may involve some kind of locking of table rows. Thus, unnecessary use of transactions will cause performance penalties. As a rule of thumb, use a transaction only when your operation requires one. For example, if you are simply selecting records from a database, or firing a single query, then most of the time you will not need an explicit transaction because your statement is already wrapped in an implicit transaction. However, as mentioned previously, it is important to note that in multi-statement updates, transactions can actually make the operation faster, rather than slower. Also, if it comes down to a choice between a few milliseconds saved versus compromising your data sanctity, the right answer is to not worry about the milliseconds and keep your data clean.

This effect is even more pronounced when using distributed transactions involving MSDTC. Since true distributed transactions (involving more than one resource manager in different appdomains or durable resource managers) involve running the underlying transactions in `IsolationLevel.Serializable`, distributed transactions are typically extremely expensive and problematic.

As a matter of fact, in a database scenario or ADO.NET world, you should prefer to use distributed transactions only when you have a non-database entity, such as a resource manager that you wrote yourself enlisting itself in the transaction, or when you cannot wrap the multi-database transaction inside the database using SQL. For instance, in many scenarios, you can get away with using linked tables or linked servers. If you do have non-database resource managers involved, or you cannot get away with wrapping up distributed transactions inside the database itself, then you could apply sanctity checks at the end of a transaction, so incorrectly committed transactions can be recovered to protect the transactional integrity. The key thing is to note the limit the scope of your transaction to as little as possible.

Transactions and Performance

Always keep in mind that a lengthy transaction that performs data modification to many different tables can effectively block the work of all other users in the system. This may cause serious performance problems. While implementing a transaction, the following practices can be followed to achieve acceptable results:

- Keep transactions as short as possible.
- Avoid returning data with a `SELECT` in the middle of a transaction, unless your statements depend on the data returned.
- If you use the `SELECT` statement, select only the rows that are required, so as not to lock too many resources and to keep performance as good as possible. If your architecture permits you to do so, simply move the `SELECTs` out of the transaction.
- Try to write transactions completely in either T-SQL or the API. Mixing and matching will only cause confusion. Also, try and give preference to wrap transactions from the client using the API rather than T-SQL. There could be instances where you may need to wrap a transaction completely within T-SQL; if that is what you need, it is perfectly acceptable. What you want to avoid is beginning a transaction using `SqlTransaction` and rolling back or committing from within the stored procedure, or the other way around.
- Avoid transactions that combine multiple, independent batches of work. Put such batches in individual transactions.
- Avoid large updates if at all possible. Of course, this does not mean that you should give up transactional robustness to avoid a large update. However, it is important to ensure that you do not unnecessarily increase the size of your transaction, because doing so will lock more resources.

One point to note is the default behavior of transactions. By default, if you do not explicitly commit the transaction, then the transaction is rolled back. Even though default behavior allows the rolling back of a transaction, it is always a good programming practice to explicitly roll back a method. This will not only release any locks from data, but also make code much more readable and less error-prone.

Summary

This chapter covered the transaction features offered by ADO.NET, as well as the Enterprise Services. Instead of doing transactions programmatically, you can task transactions automatically by applying the attribute `[Transaction]` to specify transactional requirements. The transactional options `Required`, `RequiresNew`, `Supported`, `NotSupported`, and `Disabled` influence the Enterprise Services interception code so that a new transaction is created, an existing transaction is used, or no transaction is used at all. Windows Server 2003 also offers the new feature named services without components, which allows you to leverage the transaction features of `System.EnterpriseServices` without deriving from the `ServicedComponent` class.

Transaction processing is dramatically revamped in the .NET Framework 2.0. A new lightweight transaction management system has been added to the Framework, and an easy infrastructure for participating in these transactions has been exposed. Transactions use only the resources they need for the work that they are doing. This means that instead of using the DTC for every transaction from the start, transactions are smart enough to realize when they need the services of distributed transaction management, and enlist the DTC only then. Finally, you need to be mindful of the way you use transactions, as excessive use of transactions can result in negative impact to performance.

So far in this book, you have seen a number of ASP.NET 2.0 features, including the data controls, transactions, and so on. The next chapter discusses how all of these features can be used in a real-world web site thorough a case study.

12

Case Study: Creating an Online Rental Reservation System Using N-Tier Architecture with ASP.NET 2.0 and SQL Server 2005

So far in this book, you have learned about the various data source controls such as `XmlDataSource`, `ObjectDataSource`, and so on, and their features, XML data display, and XML support in SQL Server 2005. This chapter will focus on incorporating these features into a real-world web site. This case study will not only discuss the application of these features in a web site, but also demonstrate the best practices for using these features. Toward this end, this chapter will discuss and showcase the following features:

- How to design and develop an n-tier web site using the XML features of ASP.NET 2.0 and SQL Server 2005. To support this design, this chapter will discuss how to encapsulate the data access logic in the form of reusable components.
- How to work with SQL Server 2005 XML data type column by persisting data in it using ADO.NET.
- How to utilize the XSD schemas to validate XML data using .NET Framework 2.0 XML support.
- How to implement data binding using the `ObjectDataSource` control.
- How to transform the XML data into HTML using the XSLT features of .NET 2.0.
- How to display the XML data using an `XmlDataSource` control with a `GridView` control.

- How to read and write XML data using `XmlReader` and `XmlWriter` classes.
- How to create a consistent site design using master pages in ASP.NET 2.0.

Overview of the Case Study

For this case study, you will consider an online rental car reservation system. This system provides the basic features of an online reservation system. Some of the features include searching for rental cars based on specific search criteria and reserving cars. It also provides for the users to have membership in the site by registering themselves with the site.

Architecture of System

Figure 12-1 illustrates the proposed architecture of the online reservation system.

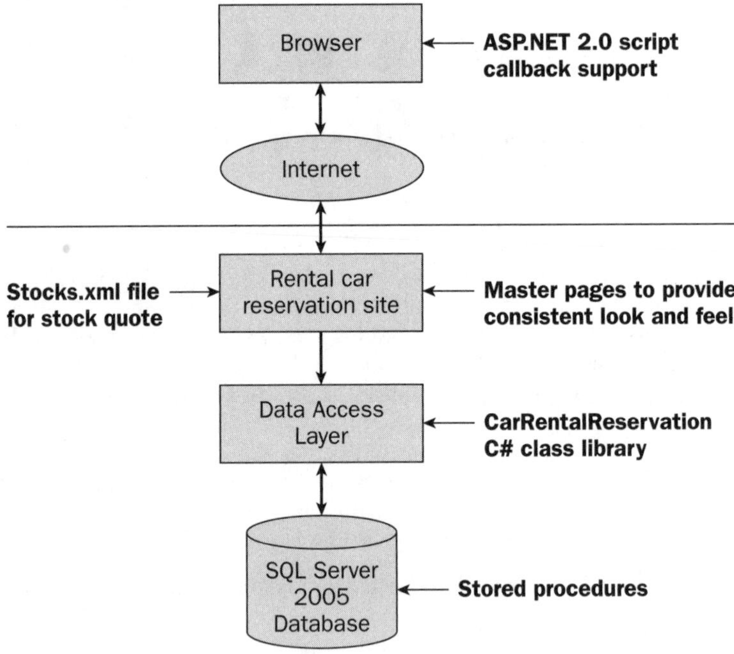

Figure 12-1

As shown in Figure 12-1, the web site primarily depends on the middle-tier .NET component (`CarRentalReservation`) for all of its functionalities. When the user comes to the site and performs operations such as searching for rental cars, the web site invokes the methods of the .NET component to carry out those tasks. Before looking at the implementation of the architecture, it is important to examine the business processes supported by the web site.

Business Processes

Although the scope of the case study is to show how to create an n-tier web site using ASP.NET 2.0 and SQL Server 2005, it is imperative that you review the business processes before choosing the best approach. The business processes that the online reservation system is going to have to enable are as follows:

- **Login process:** The login system allows the users to identify themselves to the system. The user must provide a valid user ID and a valid password to be able to log on to the system. Once logged in, the user can carry out tasks such as searching for cars and making reservations.
- **New user registration process:** If you are a new user, you will have the opportunity to become a member of the site by filling out the online forms and selecting the desired preferences. In this step, the user is asked to create a unique user ID, which is used to identify the user in the system. The user is also required to choose a password of his choice to protect his membership and prevent someone else from using his account. And the user also can fill out relevant details like name, address, and so on. Once the user enters all the details, the user's profile is stored in the database for later retrieval.
- **Search cars process:** As the name suggests, this process allows the user to search for cars.
- **Book reservations process:** In this process, the user can book the cars for a specific date.
- **Logout process:** Allows the user to log out of the site, thereby terminating the session.

Limitations

This case study is not aimed at demonstrating how to build and deploy a real-world online reservation system. The intended purpose is to show how to tie different XML features of ASP.NET together. For that reason, many issues are not addressed in this example, including:

- **Security:** Security is not taken into regard in the implementation of the web services in this example.
- **Payment:** Obviously, in this example no real bookings are made and none of the issues concerned with payment are handled.

Implementation

Now that you understand the business processes involved, the following sections examine the individual building blocks that are required to implement this solution. For the purposes of this example, the discussion of the remaining part of the case study is split into the following sections:

- Database design
- Implementation of .NET component (`CarRentalReservation`)
- Implementation of web site

To start with, consider the database design that is required to support the web site.

Database Design

The database used in this case study, called RentalCarReservation, will have the minimum number of tables required to implement this solution. The RentalCarReservation database consists of six tables. The entity relationship diagram for the database is shown in Figure 12-2.

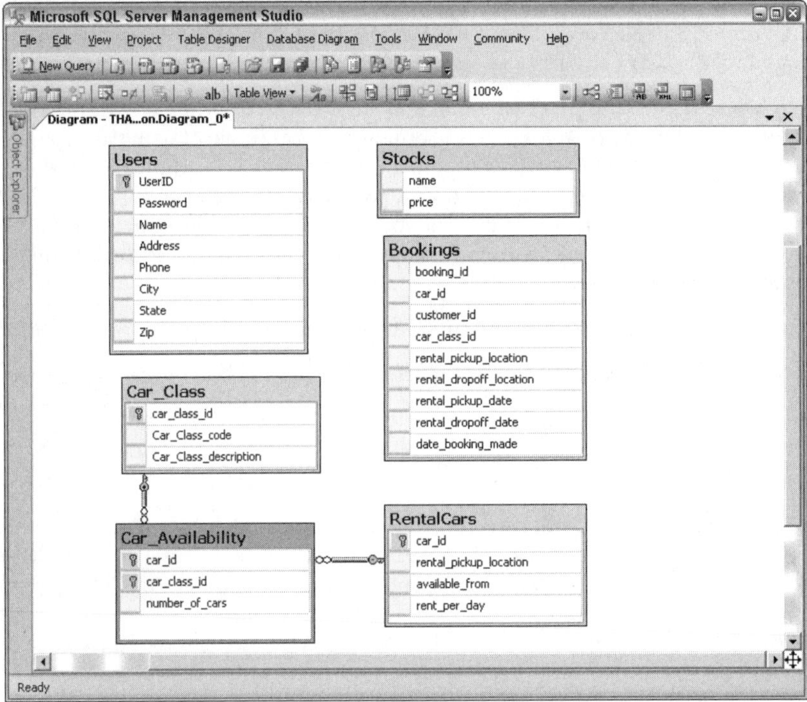

Figure 12-2

The structure of these tables is shown as follows, starting with the RentalCars table.

Name	Data Type	Length	AllowNull	Description
`car_id`	`int`	4	No	Represents the car ID
`rental_pickup_location`	`varchar`	50	No	Rental car pickup location
`available_from`	`datetime`	8	No	Rental car available date
`rent_per_day`	`money`	8	No	Rental price per day

The Car_Class table is defined as follows.

Name	Data Type	Length	AllowNull	Description
car_class_id	int	4	No	Represents the car class ID
car_class_code class codes	char	1	No	Represents the different car
car_class_ description	varchar	50	No	Provides a description of the car class

The stored procedure named `GetCarClassCodes` simply returns all the car class codes contained in the `Car_Class` table:

```
create procedure GetCarClassCodes
  as
begin
  set nocount on
  select car_class_id, Car_Class_description from Car_Class
end
GO
```

The stored procedure named `SearchRentalCar` is used to used to search for cars based on the following parameters: rental pickup location, pickup date, and the type of car class:

```
CREATE procedure dbo.SearchRentalCar
  @rentalPickupLocation varchar(50)
  ,@pickupDate datetime
  ,@carClassID int
as
begin
  set nocount on
  select RC.*,CC.car_class_id from RentalCars RC inner join
  Car_Availability CA on CA.car_id = RC.car_id
  inner join Car_Class CC
  on CC.car_class_id = CA.car_class_id
  where RC.rental_pickup_location = @rentalPickupLocation
  and RC.available_from < @pickupDate and CC.car_class_id = @carClassID
  and CA.number_of_cars > 0
end
GO
```

The following table describes the structure of the Car_Availability table.

Name	Data Type	Length	AllowNull	Description
car_id	int	4	No	Represents the car ID
car_class_id	int	4	No	Represents the car class ID
number_of_cars	int	4	No	Number of cars available in a particular category

The Bookings table is defined as follows.

Name	Data Type	Length	AllowNull	Description
booking_id	int	4	No	Identity column that represents the booking ID
car_id	int	4	No	Represents the car ID
customer_id	varchar	20	No	Specifies the customer ID
car_class_id	int	4	No	Specifies the car class ID
rental_pickup_location	varchar	50	No	Specifies the car pickup location
rental_dropoff_location	varchar	50	No	Specifies the car drop-off location
rental_pickup_date	datetime	8	No	Specifies the car pickup date
rental_dropoff_date	datetime	8	No	Specifies the car drop-off date
date_booking_made	datetime	8	No	Specifies the date of booking, and it has the default value set to `getdate()`

To create a new booking in the Bookings table, a stored procedure named `AddBooking` is utilized:

```
CREATE procedure dbo.AddBooking
  @carID int
  ,@customerID varchar(20)
  ,@carClassID int
  ,@rentalPickupLocation varchar(50)
  ,@rentalDropOffLocation varchar(50)
  ,@pickupDate datetime
  ,@dropoffDate datetime
  ,@bookingID int output
as
begin
  set nocount on
  insert into Bookings
  (car_id,customer_id,car_class_id,rental_pickup_location,
   rental_dropoff_location,rental_pickup_date,rental_dropoff_date)
  values (@carID,@customerID,@carClassID,@rentalPickupLocation,
  @rentalDropOffLocation,@pickupDate,@dropoffDate)
  select @bookingID = @@identity
end
GO
```

The definition of Stocks table looks as follows.

Name	Data Type	Length	AllowNull	Description
`name`	`char`	4	No	Represents the company symbol
`price`	`varchar`	10	No	Represents the stock price

The stored procedure `GetStockQuote` retrieves the stock quote based on the supplied symbol:

```
Create procedure GetStockQuote
  @Name char(4)
as
begin
  set nocount on
  select * from Stocks where Name = @Name FOR XML AUTO
end
```

The Users table that is meant for storing the details of the logged-on users is shown in the following table.

Name	Data Type	Length	AllowNull	Description
`UserID`	`varchar`	20	No	Represents the user ID
`Password`	`varchar`	10	No	Represents the password assigned to a user
`Name`	`varchar`	128	No	Represents the name of the logged-on user
`Address`	`varchar`	128	Yes	Represents the address of the user
`Phone`	`xml`	N/A	Yes	Typed XML column that represents the phone numbers in XML format
`City`	`varchar`	50	Yes	Represents the city
`State`	`char`	2	Yes	Represents the state
`Zip`	`char`	9	Yes	Represents the ZIP Code

As you can see from the previous table, the Phone column is a typed column that has an XML schema named `PhoneSchema` associated with it. The DDL for creating the schema used by this column is:

```
CREATE XML Schema collection PhoneSchema as
  N'<xs:schema attributeFormDefault="unqualified"
  elementFormDefault="qualified" xmlns:xs="http://www.w3.org/2001/XMLSchema">
  <xs:element name="phone">
    <xs:complexType>
      <xs:sequence>
```

```
        <xs:element name="homePhone" type="xs:string" />
        <xs:element name="cellPhone" type="xs:string" />
        <xs:element name="officePhone" type="xs:string" />
      </xs:sequence>
    </xs:complexType>
  </xs:element>
</xs:schema>'
GO
```

Once the schema is created, you can associate the schema with the Phone column by using the `Alter table` statement:

```
Alter table Users Alter Column Phone XML(PhoneSchema)
```

To insert rows into the Users table, use the `AddUser` stored procedure:

```
CREATE Procedure AddUser
  (@UserID char(20), @Password char(10), @Name varchar(128),
   @Address varchar(128), @Phone xml, @City varchar(50),
   @State char(2), @Zip char(5))
As
begin
 insert into Users(UserID,Password,Name,Address,Phone, City,State,Zip)
 values(@UserID,@Password,@Name,@Address,@Phone,@City,@State,@Zip)
End
```

In addition to storing the user details, you also need a way to verify the credentials of a user who is trying to log onto the site. To this end, the `IsValidUserLogin` is used:

```
CREATE procedure IsValidUserLogIn
  @UserID varchar(20)
  ,@Password varchar(10)
  ,@RetValue int OUTPUT
as
begin
  select * from Users where UserID = @UserID and Password = @Password
if @@Rowcount < 1
    select @RetValue = -1
else
    select @RetValue = 1
end
```

Now that you have implemented the stored procedures, the next step is to implement the middle-tier component that will consume the stored procedures.

Implementation of CarRentalReservation Component

In this section, you will understandthe implementation of the C# class library `CarRentalReservation`. This component contains all the necessary classes and methods that provide the core functionalities for the online reservations system. To start, create a new Visual C# class library project named `CarRentalReservation` using Visual Studio 2005. Once the project is created, change the name of the default class from `Class1` to `UserDetail`. The `UserDetail` class simply acts as a container for holding user-related data, and its implementation is shown in Listing 12-1.

Listing 12-1: Declaration of the UserDetail Class

```
using System;
namespace CarRentalReservation
{
[Serializable]
public class UserDetail
{
    protected string userID;
    protected string passWord;
    protected string name;
    protected string address;
    protected string phone;
    protected string city;
    protected string state;
    protected string zip;

    public string UserID
    {
      get{return userID;}
      set{userID = value;}
    }
    public string PassWord
    {
      get{return passWord;}
      set{passWord = value;}
    }
    public string Name
    {
      get{return name;}
      set{name = value;}
    }
    public string Address
    {
      get{return address;}
      set{address = value;}
    }
    public string Phone
    {
      get{return phone;}
      set{phone = value;}
    }
    public string City
    {
      get{return city;}
      set{city = value;}
    }
    public string State
    {
      get{return state;}
```

(continued)

Listing 12-1: *(continued)*

```
        set{state = value;}
      }
      public string Zip
      {
        get{return zip;}
        set{zip = value;}
      }
    }
  }
```

As you can see from the code in Listing 12-1, the `UserDetail` class simply exposes a bunch of properties that act as the container for user-related data.

Implementation of Data Access Layer Methods

So far, you have seen the container class for holding user-related data. That is only part of the story, and you need a data access layer class for persisting that data and retrieving that data from the Users table. This is where the `UserDB` class comes into play. Implementation of the `UserDB` class is illustrated in Listing 12-2.

Listing 12-2: Implementation of the UserDB Class

```
using System;
using System.Collections.Generic;
using System.Data;
using System.Data.SqlClient;
using System.Data.SqlTypes;
using System.Text;
using System.Xml;
namespace CarRentalReservation
{
  public class UserDB
  {
    public bool IsValidUserLogIn(string userName, string passWord)
    {
      try
      {
        using (SqlConnection connection = new SqlConnection())
        {
          string connectionString =
            System.Web.Configuration.WebConfigurationManager.
            ConnectionStrings["rentalCarReservation"].ConnectionString;
          connection.ConnectionString = connectionString;
          connection.Open();
          SqlCommand command = new SqlCommand("IsValidUserLogIn", connection);
          command.CommandType = CommandType.StoredProcedure;
          SqlParameter paramUserName = new SqlParameter("@UserID",
            SqlDbType.VarChar, 20);
          paramUserName.Value = userName;
          command.Parameters.Add(paramUserName);
          SqlParameter paramPassWord = new SqlParameter("@Password",
```

```
          SqlDbType.VarChar, 10);
        paramPassWord.Value = passWord;
        command.Parameters.Add(paramPassWord);
        SqlParameter paramRetValue = new SqlParameter("@RetValue",
          SqlDbType.Int, 4);
        paramRetValue.Direction = ParameterDirection.Output;
        command.Parameters.Add(paramRetValue);
        command.ExecuteNonQuery();
        //Obtain the return value of the stored procedure into a variable
        int retValue = (int)paramRetValue.Value;
        if (retValue == -1)
        {
          throw new InvalidCredentialsException("Invalid Login");
        }
        else
        {
          return true;
        }
      }
    }
    catch (Exception ex)
    {
      throw ex;
    }
  }

  public bool AddUserInfo(UserDetail user)
  {
    try
    {
      using (SqlConnection connection = new SqlConnection())
      {
        string connectionString =
          System.Web.Configuration.WebConfigurationManager.
          ConnectionStrings["rentalCarReservation"].ConnectionString;
        connection.ConnectionString = connectionString;
        connection.Open();
        SqlCommand command = new SqlCommand("AddUser", connection);
        command.CommandType = CommandType.StoredProcedure;
        SqlParameter paramUserName = new SqlParameter("@UserID",
          SqlDbType.VarChar, 20);
        paramUserName.Value = user.UserID;
        command.Parameters.Add(paramUserName);
        SqlParameter paramPassWord = new SqlParameter("@Password",
          SqlDbType.VarChar, 10);
        paramPassWord.Value = user.PassWord;
        command.Parameters.Add(paramPassWord);
        SqlParameter paramName = new SqlParameter("@Name",
          SqlDbType.VarChar, 128);
        paramName.Value = user.Name;
        command.Parameters.Add(paramName);
        SqlParameter paramAddress = new SqlParameter("@Address",
```

(continued)

Listing 12-2: *(continued)*

```
              SqlDbType.VarChar, 128);
            paramAddress.Value = user.Address;
            command.Parameters.Add(paramAddress);
            SqlParameter paramPhone = new SqlParameter("@Phone", SqlDbType.Xml);
            paramPhone.Value = new SqlXml(new XmlTextReader(user.Phone,
              XmlNodeType.Document, null));
            command.Parameters.Add(paramPhone);
            SqlParameter paramCity = new SqlParameter("@City",
              SqlDbType.VarChar, 50);
            paramCity.Value = user.City;
            command.Parameters.Add(paramCity);
            SqlParameter paramState = new SqlParameter("@State",
              SqlDbType.Char, 2);
            paramState.Value = user.State;
            command.Parameters.Add(paramState);
            SqlParameter paramZip = new SqlParameter("@Zip", SqlDbType.Char, 5);
            paramZip.Value = user.Zip;
            command.Parameters.Add(paramZip);
            command.ExecuteNonQuery();
            return true;
          }
        }
        catch (Exception ex)
        {
          throw ex;
        }
      }
    }
  }
```

The `UserDB` class contains two methods: `IsValidUserLogIn()` and `AddUserInfo()`.The `IsValidUserLogIn()` method authenticates a customer's username and password against the RentalCar Reservation database. Under the hood, `IsValidUserLogIn()` method invokes the stored procedure `IsValidUserLogIn`. The `IsValidUserLogIn` stored procedure returns `1` if a record with the specified username and password is found; otherwise, it returns `-1`. Depending on the value returned by the stored procedure, the `IsValidUserLogIn` method either returns true or raises an exception of type `InvalidCredentialsException`. The declaration of the `InvalidCredentialsException` is as follows:

```
public class InvalidCredentialsException : Exception
{
  public InvalidCredentialsException(string exceptionMessage) :
    base(exceptionMessage)
  {}
}
```

User-defined exceptions allow you to notify the clients when a particular business logic violation occurs or when a specific condition is reached. They also allow you to implement custom exception-processing mechanisms such as logging errors to the event log, sending emails to an administrator, and so on.

The `AddUserInfo()` method persists the details of the user in the Users table. It takes the `UserDetail` object as an argument, parses its contents, executes a stored procedure, and returns true or false depending on the result of its execution. Note how the phone column (which is of type XML) is added to the `Parameters` collection of the `SqlCommand` object:

```
SqlParameter paramPhone = new SqlParameter("@Phone", SqlDbType.Xml);
paramPhone.Value = new SqlXml(new XmlTextReader(user.Phone,
  XmlNodeType.Document, null));
command.Parameters.Add(paramPhone);
```

You specify the type of the column as XML by passing in the enumeration `SqlDbType.Xml` to the second parameter of the `SqlParameter` object's constructor. You then assign an object of type `System.Data.SqlTypes.SqlXml` to the `Value` property of the `SqlParameter` object. Now that you have had a look at the `UserDB` class, you can focus on the `RentalDB` class, which is specifically focused on searching for cars and making reservations.

Implementation of RentalDB Class

One of the methods exposed by the `RentalDB` class is `SearchRentalCar()`, which allows you to search for cars based on a specific set of search criteria. Listing 12-3 shows the code of the `RentalDB` class.

Listing 12-3: Implementation of the RentalDB Class

```
using System;
using System.Data;
using System.Data.SqlClient;
namespace CarRentalReservation
{
  public class RentalDB
  {
    public DataSet SearchRentalCar(string rentalPickupLocation,
      DateTime pickupDate, int carClassID)
    {
      try
      {
        using (SqlConnection connection = new SqlConnection())
        {
          string connectionString = System.Web.Configuration.
            WebConfigurationManager.ConnectionStrings
            ["rentalCarReservation"].ConnectionString;
          connection.ConnectionString = connectionString;
          DataSet car = new DataSet("Cars");
          SqlDataAdapter adapter = new SqlDataAdapter("SearchRentalCar",
            connection);
          adapter.SelectCommand.CommandType = CommandType.StoredProcedure;
          SqlParameter paramRentalPickupLocation = new
            SqlParameter("@rentalPickupLocation", SqlDbType.VarChar, 50);
          paramRentalPickupLocation.Value = rentalPickupLocation;
          adapter.SelectCommand.Parameters.Add(paramRentalPickupLocation);
          SqlParameter paramPickupDate = new SqlParameter("@pickupDate",
            SqlDbType.DateTime);
          paramPickupDate .Value = pickupDate;
```

(continued)

Listing 12-3: *(continued)*

```
            adapter.SelectCommand.Parameters.Add(paramPickupDate );
            SqlParameter paramCarClassID = new SqlParameter("@carClassID",
              SqlDbType.Int);
            paramCarClassID.Value = carClassID;
            adapter.SelectCommand.Parameters.Add(paramCarClassID);
            adapter.Fill(car, "Car");
            return car;
          }
        }
        catch (Exception ex)
        {
          throw ex;
        }
      }

      public int AddBooking(int carID, string customerID, int carClassID,
        string rentalPickupLocation, string rentalDropoffLocation,
        DateTime pickupDate, DateTime dropoffDate)
      {
        try
        {
          using (SqlConnection connection = new SqlConnection())
          {
            string connectionString = System.Web.Configuration.
              WebConfigurationManager.ConnectionStrings
              ["rentalCarReservation"].ConnectionString;
            connection.ConnectionString = connectionString;
            connection.Open();
            SqlCommand command = new SqlCommand("AddBooking", connection);
            command.CommandType = CommandType.StoredProcedure;
            SqlParameter paramCarID = new SqlParameter("@carID", SqlDbType.Int);
            paramCarID.Value = carID;
            command.Parameters.Add(paramCarID);
            SqlParameter paramCustomerID = new SqlParameter("@customerID",
              SqlDbType.VarChar, 20);
            paramCustomerID.Value = customerID;
            command.Parameters.Add(paramCustomerID);
            SqlParameter paramCarClassID = new SqlParameter("@carClassID",
              SqlDbType.Int);
            paramCarClassID.Value = carClassID;
            command.Parameters.Add(paramCarClassID);
            SqlParameter paramRentalPickupLocation = new
              SqlParameter("@rentalPickupLocation", SqlDbType.VarChar, 50);
            paramRentalPickupLocation.Value = rentalPickupLocation;
            command.Parameters.Add(paramRentalPickupLocation);
            SqlParameter paramRentalDropoffLocation = new
              SqlParameter("@rentalDropOffLocation", SqlDbType.VarChar, 50);
            paramRentalDropoffLocation.Value = rentalDropoffLocation;
            command.Parameters.Add(paramRentalDropoffLocation);
            SqlParameter paramPickupDate = new SqlParameter("@pickupDate",
              SqlDbType.DateTime);
```

```
            paramPickupDate .Value = pickupDate;
            command.Parameters.Add(paramPickupDate);
            SqlParameter paramDropoffDate = new SqlParameter("@dropoffDate",
              SqlDbType.DateTime);
            paramDropoffDate.Value = dropoffDate;
            command.Parameters.Add(paramDropoffDate);
            SqlParameter paramBookingID = new SqlParameter("@bookingID",
              SqlDbType.Int);
          //Indicate that the Booking ID parameter is an Output parameter
          paramBookingID.Direction = ParameterDirection.Output;
          command.Parameters.Add(paramBookingID);
          command.ExecuteNonQuery();
          int bookingID = Convert.ToInt32(command.Parameters["@bookingID"].Value);
          return bookingID;
        }
      }
      catch (Exception ex)
      {
        throw ex;
      }
    }

    public DataTable GetCarClassCodes()
    {
      try
      {
        using (SqlConnection connection = new SqlConnection())
        {
          string connectionString = System.Web.Configuration.
            WebConfigurationManager.ConnectionStrings
            ["rentalCarReservation"].ConnectionString;
          connection.ConnectionString = connectionString;
          DataTable car = new DataTable("CarClassCodes");
          SqlDataAdapter adapter = new SqlDataAdapter("GetCarClassCodes",
            connection);
          adapter.SelectCommand.CommandType = CommandType.StoredProcedure;
          adapter.Fill(car);
          return car;
        }
      }
      catch (Exception ex)
      {
        throw ex;
      }
    }
  }
}
```

In addition to the `SearchRentalCar()` method, the `RentalDB` class also contains two methods: one named `AddBooking()`, which persists the details of the reservation in the database, and `GetCarClassCodes()`, which returns all the car class codes contained in the Car_Class table. For reasons of brevity, implementation of these methods will not be discussed in detail. However, you can download the complete code of the case study from `www.wrox.com`.

Implementation of the StockDB Class

As the name suggests, the StockDB class provides methods specifically for working with the Stocks table. It exposes a method named GetStockQuote(), which returns the stock quote based on the supplied symbol. Listing 12-4 illustrates the code of the StockDB class.

Listing 12-4: Implementation of the StockDB Class

```
using System;
using System.Data;
using System.Data.SqlClient;
using System.Xml;
namespace CarRentalReservation
{
  public class StockDB
  {
    public XmlDocument GetStockQuote(string name)
    {
      try
      {
        using (SqlConnection connection = new SqlConnection())
        {
          string connectionString =
            System.Web.Configuration.WebConfigurationManager.
            ConnectionStrings["rentalCarReservation"].ConnectionString;
          connection.ConnectionString = connectionString;
          connection.Open();
          SqlCommand command = connection.CreateCommand();
          command.CommandText = "GetStockQuote";
          command.CommandType = CommandType.StoredProcedure;
          SqlParameter paramName = new SqlParameter("@Name",
            SqlDbType.Char, 4);
          paramName.Value = name;
          command.Parameters.Add(paramName);
          XmlReader reader = command.ExecuteXmlReader();
          XmlDocument doc = new XmlDocument();
          //Load the XmlReader to an XmlDocument object
          doc.Load(reader);
          return doc;
        }
      }
      catch (Exception ex)
      {
        throw ex;
      }
    }
  }
}
```

The GetStockQuote() method simply retrieves the stock quote by executing a stored procedure named GetStockQuote that accepts the stock ticker company as an argument and returns the XML output in the form of an XmlReader object. This XmlReader object is then loaded into an XmlDocument object and then finally returned to the caller.

Implementation of the Web Site

This section will focus on the implementation of the ASP.NET web site. I will discuss the code of the web site by describing the different processes involved. Before getting into that discussion, the following sections go over the code of the master page that will be used throughout the web site.

A Look at Master Pages

A professional web site will have a standardized look across all pages. For example, one of the commonly used layouts has its navigation menu on the left side of the page, a copyright on the bottom, and content in the middle. It can be difficult to maintain a standard look if you must duplicate the common logic and look and feel in every web page you build. In ASP.NET 2.0, master pages will make the job easier. You will need to write the common pieces only once in the master page. A master page can serve as a template for one or more web pages. Each ASPX web page only needs to define the content unique to itself, and this content will plug into specified areas of the master page layout.

A master page looks very similar to an ASPX file, except that a master page will have a `.master` *file extension instead of an* `.aspx` *extension, and uses an* `@ Master` *directive instead of an* `@ Page` *directive at the top. Master pages will define the* `<html>`, `<head>`, `<body>`, *and* `<form>`, *tags. A new control, the* `ContentPlaceHolder` *control, also appears in the master page. You can have one or more* `ContentPlaceHolder` *controls in a master page.* `ContentPlaceHolder` *controls are where you want the ASPX web pages to place their content. A web page associated with a master page is called a content page. A content page may only contain markup inside of content controls. If you try to place any markup or controls outside of the* `Content` *controls, you will receive a compiler error. Each* `Content` *control in a content page maps to exactly one of the* `ContentPlaceHolder` *controls in the master page.*

Listing 12-5 shows the code of the master page named `Common.master` that will be used in the online reservations web site.

Listing 12-5: Master Page That Provides a Consistent Look and Feel

```
<%@ Master Language="C#" %>
<%@ Import Namespace="System.IO" %>
<%@ Import Namespace="System.Xml" %>
<%@ Import Namespace="CarRentalReservation" %>
<script runat="server">
  void Page_Load(object sender, EventArgs e)
  {
    string path = Server.MapPath("App_Data/Stocks.xml");
    if (!File.Exists(path))
    {
      //Create the XML file for the first time
      CreateXmlFile(path);
    }
    else
    {
      //Check to make sure that the file is not more than 20 minutes old
      TimeSpan elapsedTimespan =
        DateTime.Now.Subtract(File.GetLastWriteTime(path));
```

(continued)

Listing 12-5: *(continued)*

```
      if (elapsedTimespan.Minutes > 20)
      //Refresh the contents of the XML file
      CreateXmlFile(path);
    }
  }

  void CreateXmlFile(string path)
  {
    StockDB stock = new StockDB();
    XmlDocument doc = stock.GetStockQuote("RCRS");
    doc.Save(path);
  }
</script>
<html xmlns="http://www.w3.org/1999/xhtml" >
<head runat="server">
  <title>Master Page</title>
</head>
<body>
  <form id="form1" runat="server">
    <div>
      <asp:Table id="tblTop" BackColor="DarkSeaGreen" runat="server" Width="819px"
        Height="108px" ForeColor="blue">
        <asp:TableRow runat="server">
          <asp:TableCell ColumnSpan="2" runat="server">
            <img src="Images/crrs_logo.gif">
          </asp:TableCell>
        </asp:TableRow>
        <asp:TableRow  runat="server" HorizontalAlign="Center">
          <asp:TableCell  runat="server" ColumnSpan="2">
            <asp:Label id="Label1" runat="server" ForeColor="White"
              Font-Size="medium">Online Reservation System
            </asp:Label>
          </asp:TableCell>
        </asp:TableRow>
      <asp:TableRow  runat="server" HorizontalAlign="Center">
        <asp:TableCell  runat="server" ColumnSpan="2" ForeColor="White">
          <asp:XmlDataSource runat="server" DataFile="~/App_Data/Stocks.xml"
            ID="XmlDataSource1" XPath="Stocks" />
          <asp:GridView BorderWidth=0 BorderStyle=Ridge Font-Bold="true"
            Font-Size=Small ShowHeader=false runat="server" ID="stockoutput"
            AutoGenerateColumns="false" DataSourceID="XmlDataSource1">
            <Columns>
              <asp:HyperLinkField Text="RCRS:"
                NavigateUrl="http://finance.yahoo.com/q?s=RCRS"/>
              <asp:BoundField HeaderText="Price" DataField="price"
                SortExpression="price"></asp:BoundField>
            </Columns>
          </asp:GridView>
        </asp:TableCell>
      </asp:TableRow>
      <asp:TableRow runat="server" HorizontalAlign="Right">
        <asp:TableCell runat="server" ColumnSpan="2">
```

```
          <asp:HyperLink runat="server" ForeColor="White" Text="Logout"
            NavigateUrl="Logout.aspx" />
        </asp:TableCell>
      </asp:TableRow>
    </asp:Table>
    <asp:contentplaceholder id="ContentPlaceHolder1" runat="server">
    </asp:contentplaceholder>
  </div>
</form>
</body>
</html>
```

The master page encapsulates the header information for all the pages of the web site. The header also contains the stock quote details displayed through a combination of an `XmlDataSource` control and a `GridView` control. The `XmlDataSource` control acts as the source of data for the `GridView` control that actually displays the stock quote:

```
<asp:XmlDataSource runat="server" DataFile="~/App_Data/Stocks.xml"
  ID="XmlDataSource1" XPath="Stocks" />
```

The `XmlDataSource` control utilizes a local XML file, `Stocks.xml`, as the source of XML data. The `Stocks.xml` file is very simple, and it just contains only one line of code:

```
<?xml version="1.0" ?>
<Stocks name="RCRS" price="45"/>
```

The contents of the `Stocks.xml` are updated periodically (specifically, only every 20 minutes) through the logic contained in the `Page_Load` event.

In the `Page_Load` event, you first check to see if an XML file named `Stocks.xml` file is available:

```
if (!File.Exists(path))
{
  //Create the XML file for the first time
  CreateXmlFile(path);
}
```

If the XML file is not available, `Page_Load` invokes a local method named `CreateXml()` to create the XML file by calling the `GetStockQuote()` method of the `StockDB` class:

```
void CreateXmlFile(string path)
{
  StockDB stock = new StockDB();
  XmlDocument doc = stock.GetStockQuote("RCRS");
  doc.Save(path);
}
```

The `XmlDocument` returned by the `GetStockQuote()` method is directly saved to the `Stocks.xml` file.

If the `Stocks.xml` file is available locally, the `Page_Load` method then checks to make sure that the file is not more than 20 minutes old. If the file is more than 20 minutes old, it invokes the `CreateXml()` method to refresh the contents of the XML file with the latest quote from the database:

```
else
{
  //Check to make sure that the file is not more than 20 minutes old
  TimeSpan elapsedTimespan = DateTime.Now.Subtract
    (File.GetLastWriteTime(path));
  if (elapsedTimespan.Minutes > 20)
    //Refresh the contents of the XML file
    CreateXmlFile(path);
}
```

Now that you have had a look at the master page, the following sections discuss the content pages that provide the core functionality. To start with, consider the login process.

Login Process

On the web site, the user must be logged in to perform tasks such as searching for cars and making the reservations. The login page will authenticate the customer's username and password against the Users table in the RentalCarReservation database. After validation, the user is redirected to the search cars page. If the user does not have a valid login, they can opt to create one by clicking the hyperlink New Users Click Here in the login page. Clicking this hyperlink takes the user to the registration page, where the user provides all the necessary details for completing the registration.

The login feature of the web site is implemented using a forms-based authentication mechanism. To enable forms-based authentication for the web site, add the following entry in the `Web.config` file directly under the `<system.web>` element:

```
<authentication mode="Forms">
  <forms name="CarRentalReservationAuth" loginUrl="Login.aspx" protection="All"
    path="/">
  </forms>
</authentication>
```

The `loginUrl` attribute in the `<forms>` element specifies the name of the login page that you want the users to be redirected to, any time they access a page or resource that does not allow anonymous access. For every web page that you want to secure using the forms-based authentication mechanism, you need to add an entry to the `Web.config` file. For example, to set the restrictions of authenticated user access for a page called `SearchCars.aspx`, set the following entry directly under the `<configuration>` element of the `Web.config` file:

```
<location path="SearchCars.aspx">  <system.web>
    <authorization>
 <deny users="?" />
    </authorization>
</system.web>
</location>
```

When a user attempts to access the `SearchCars.aspx` page, the ASP.NET forms-based security system will automatically redirect the user to the `Login.aspx` page, and will continue to prevent them from accessing the page until they have successfully validated their username and password credentials to the application. Similarly, you protect the other secured pages by using similar entries in the `Web.config` file.

The forms-based authentication technology depends on cookies to store the authentication information for the currently logged-in user. Once the user is authenticated, cookies are used to store and maintain session information, enabling the users to identify themselves to the web site.

Now that you have a general understanding of the forms-based authentication, you are ready to examine the `Login.aspx` page, described in Listing 12-6.

Listing 12-6: Implementation of the Login Page That Derives from the Master Page

```
<%@ Page Language="C#" MasterPageFile="~/Common.master" Title="Login Page" %>
<%@ Import Namespace="CarRentalReservation" %>
<script runat="server">
void btnLogin_Click(object sender, System.EventArgs e)
{
  try
  {
    UserDB user = new UserDB();
    if (user.IsValidUserLogIn(txtUserName.Text, txtPassword.Text) == true)
    {
      FormsAuthentication.SetAuthCookie(txtUserName.Text, true);
      Session["UserID"] = txtUserName.Text;
      Response.Redirect("SearchCars.aspx");
  }
  }
    catch (InvalidCredentialsException ex)
    {
      lblMessage.Visible = true;
      lblMessage.Text = ex.Message;
    }
  }
</script>
<asp:Content ID="Content1" ContentPlaceHolderID="ContentPlaceHolder1"
  Runat="Server">
  <table align=center>
    <tr>
      <td colspan=2 align=center>
        <asp:Label id="lblHeading" runat="server" ForeColor="Black" Height="27px"
          Width="154px" BackColor="Transparent" BorderStyle="Ridge"> Login
        </asp:Label>
      </td>
    </tr>
    <tr height="60">
      <td>
        <asp:Label id="lblUserName" tabIndex="5" runat="server" Height="19px"
          Width="131px" Font-Bold="True">User Name:</asp:Label>
      </td>
      <td>
        <asp:TextBox id="txtUserName" tabIndex="1" runat="server"></asp:TextBox>
```

(continued)

Listing 12-6: *(continued)*

```
        <asp:RequiredFieldValidator id="RequiredFieldValidator1" tabIndex="10"
          runat="server" ControlToValidate="txtUserName" ErrorMessage="*"
          Enabled="True"></asp:RequiredFieldValidator>
      </td>
    </tr>
    <tr height="40">
      <td>
        <asp:Label id="lblPassWord" tabIndex="6" runat="server" Height="19px"
          Width="121px" Font-Bold="True">Password:</asp:Label>
      </td>
      <td>
        <asp:TextBox TextMode="Password" id="txtPassword" tabIndex="2"
          runat="server"></asp:TextBox>
        <asp:RequiredFieldValidator id="RequiredFieldValidator2" tabIndex="11"
          runat="server" ControlToValidate="txtPassword" ErrorMessage="*"
          Enabled="True"></asp:RequiredFieldValidator>
      </td>
    </tr>
    <tr height="40">
      <td colspan=2 align=center>
        <asp:Label id="lblMessage" tabIndex="8" runat="server" Height="19px"
          Width="203px" Visible="False"></asp:Label>
      </td>
    </tr>
    <tr height="40">
      <td colspan=2 align=center>
        <asp:Button id="btnLogin" OnClick="btnLogin_Click" tabIndex="3"
          runat="server" Height="29px" Width="105px" Text="Login">
        </asp:Button>
      </td>
    </tr>
    <tr height="40">
      <td colspan=2 align=center>
        <asp:HyperLink id="lnkUserRegistration" tabIndex="4" runat="server"
          Height="28px" Width="176px" Font-Bold="True"
          NavigateUrl="Registration.aspx">New Users Click here</asp:HyperLink>
      </td>
    </tr>
  </table>
</asp:Content>
```

Once the user enters the username and password and hits the Login button, you invoke the `IsValidUserLogIn()` method of the `UserDB` class to validate the user:

```
UserDB user = new UserDB();
if (user.IsValidUserLogIn(txtUserName.Text, txtPassword.Text) == true)
{
  FormsAuthentication.SetAuthCookie(txtUserName.Text, true);
  Session["UserID"] = txtUserName.Text;
  Response.Redirect("SearchCars.aspx");
}
```

If the login is successful, you invoke the `SetAuthCookie()` method to generate an authentication ticket for the authenticated username and password, and attach it to the cookies collection of the outgoing response. Once the cookie is generated, it is used to maintain information about the session information for every user that logs in to the site. You also store the logged-in user ID in a session variable for later use.

Whenever the exception `InvalidCredentialsException` occurs, you catch that in the `catch` block and display the exception message in the label control `lblMessage`:

```
catch (InvalidCredentialsException ex)
{
  lblMessage.Visible = true;
  lblMessage.Text = ex.Message;
}
```

Figure 12-3 shows the Login page in action.

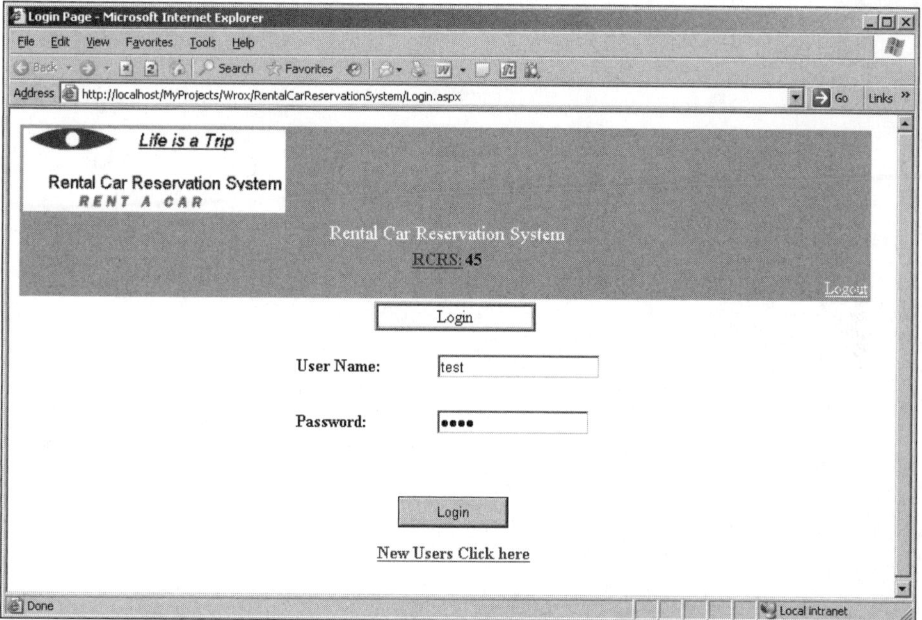

Figure 12-3

This case study utilized a custom user table (with an XML data-typed column for the Phone column) mainly to demonstrate the XML feature of SQL Server 2005. Because of this, it was necessary to create the plumbing code required to validate the user credentials against the custom table. However, with ASP.NET 2.0, you can utilize the membership store to store user details and also leverage the built-in security mechanisms to validate the user.

New User Registration Process

The registration page allows users wanting to take advantage of the online reservation system to register themselves as members. Implementation of the registration page is discussed in Listing 12-7.

Listing 12-7: New User Registration Page

```
<%@ Page Language="C#" MasterPageFile="~/Common.master" Title="New User
  Registration Page" %>
<%@ Import Namespace="System.Xml" %>
<%@ Import Namespace="CarRentalReservation" %>
<script runat="server">
  void btnSave_Click(object sender, EventArgs e)
  {
    UserDetail user = new UserDetail();
    user.UserID = txtUserName.Text;
    user.PassWord = txtPassWord.Text;
    user.Name = txtName.Text;
    user.Address = txtAddress.Text;
    string xml = CreateXml();
    user.Phone = xml;
    user.City = txtCity.Text;
    user.State = txtState.Text;
    user.Zip = txtZip.Text;
    UserDB userDB = new UserDB();
    userDB.AddUserInfo(user);
    //Redirect the user to the Confirmation page
    Server.Transfer("Confirmation.aspx");
  }

  string CreateXml()
  {
    System.Text.StringBuilder output = new System.Text.StringBuilder();
    XmlWriter writer = XmlWriter.Create(output);
    writer.WriteStartDocument(false);
    writer.WriteStartElement("phone");
    writer.WriteElementString("homePhone", txtHomePhone.Text);
    writer.WriteElementString("cellPhone", txtCellPhone.Text);
    writer.WriteElementString("officePhone", txtOfficePhone.Text);
    writer.WriteEndElement();
    writer.WriteEndDocument();
    writer.Flush();
    return output.ToString();
  }
</script>
<asp:Content ID="Content1" ContentPlaceHolderID="ContentPlaceHolder1"
Runat="Server">
  <table align=center>
    <tr>
      <td colspan=2 align=center>
        <asp:Label id="lblHeading" runat="server" ForeColor="Black"
          Height="27px" Width="154px" BackColor="Transparent"
          BorderStyle="Ridge"> New User Registration</asp:Label>
      </td>
    </tr>
    <tr height="32">
      <td>
        <asp:Label id="lblUserName" runat="server" Height="19px" Width="93px"
          Font-Bold="True">User Name:</asp:Label>
```

```
    </td>
    <td>
      <asp:TextBox id="txtUserName" tabIndex="1" runat="server"
        MaxLength="8"></asp:TextBox>
      <asp:RequiredFieldValidator id="RequiredFieldValidator1" runat="server"
        ControlToValidate="txtUserName" ErrorMessage="*">
      </asp:RequiredFieldValidator>
    </td>
  </tr>
  <tr height="32">
    <td>
      <asp:Label id="lblPassWord" runat="server" Height="19px" Width="93px"
        Font-Bold="True">Password:</asp:Label>
    </td>
    <td>
      <asp:TextBox id="txtPassWord" TextMode="Password" tabIndex="2"
        runat="server" MaxLength="8"></asp:TextBox>
      <asp:RequiredFieldValidator id="RequiredFieldValidator2" runat="server"
        ControlToValidate="txtPassWord" ErrorMessage="*">
      </asp:RequiredFieldValidator>
    </td>
  </tr>
  <tr height="32">
    <td>
      <asp:Label id="lblConfirmPassWord" runat="server" Height="24px"
        Width="103px" Font-Bold="True">Confirm Password:</asp:Label>
    </td>
    <td>
      <asp:TextBox id="txtConfirmPassword" TextMode="Password" tabIndex="3"
        runat="server" MaxLength="8"></asp:TextBox>
      <asp:RequiredFieldValidator id="RequiredFieldValidator3" runat="server"
         ControlToValidate="txtConfirmPassword" ErrorMessage="*">
      </asp:RequiredFieldValidator>
      <asp:CompareValidator id="CompareValidator1" style="Z-INDEX: 105; LEFT:
        648px; POSITION: absolute; TOP: 259px" runat="server" Height="20px"
        Width="203px" ControlToValidate="txtPassWord" ErrorMessage="Please
        enter same value for Password and Confirm Password"
        ControlToCompare="txtConfirmPassword"></asp:CompareValidator>
    </td>
  </tr>
  <tr height="32">
    <td>
      <asp:Label id="lblName" runat="server" Height="25px" Width="39px"
        Font-Bold="True">Name:</asp:Label>
    </td>
    <td>
      <asp:TextBox id="txtName" tabIndex="4" runat="server" MaxLength="50">
      </asp:TextBox>
      <asp:RequiredFieldValidator id="RequiredFieldValidator4" runat="server"
        ControlToValidate="txtName" ErrorMessage="*">
      </asp:RequiredFieldValidator>
    </td>
  </tr>
```

(continued)

Listing 12-7: *(continued)*

```
        <tr height="32">
          <td>
            <asp:Label id="lblAddress" runat="server" Height="25px" Width="62px"
              Font-Bold="True">Address:</asp:Label>
          </td>
          <td>
            <asp:TextBox id="txtAddress" tabIndex="5" runat="server"
              MaxLength="60"></asp:TextBox>
            <asp:RequiredFieldValidator id="RequiredFieldValidator5" runat="server"
              ControlToValidate="txtAddress" ErrorMessage="*">
            </asp:RequiredFieldValidator>
          </td>
        </tr>
        <tr height="32">
          <td>
            <asp:Label id="lblHomePhone" runat="server" Height="25px" Width="116px"
              Font-Bold="True">Home Phone:</asp:Label>
          </td>
          <td>
            <asp:TextBox id="txtHomePhone" tabIndex="5" runat="server"
              MaxLength="60"></asp:TextBox>
            <asp:RequiredFieldValidator id="RequiredFieldValidator9" runat="server"
              ControlToValidate="txtHomePhone" ErrorMessage="*">
            </asp:RequiredFieldValidator>
          </td>
        </tr>
        <tr height="32">
          <td>
            <asp:Label id="lblOfficePhone" runat="server" Height="25px"
              Width="126px" Font-Bold="True">Office Phone:</asp:Label>
          </td>
          <td>
            <asp:TextBox id="txtOfficePhone" tabIndex="5" runat="server"
              MaxLength="60"></asp:TextBox>
            <asp:RequiredFieldValidator id="RequiredFieldValidator10" runat="server"
              ControlToValidate="txtOfficePhone" ErrorMessage="*">
            </asp:RequiredFieldValidator>
          </td>
        </tr>
        <tr height="32">
          <td>
            <asp:Label id="lblCellPhone" runat="server" Height="25px" Width="136px"
              Font-Bold="True">Cell Phone:</asp:Label>
          </td>
          <td>
            <asp:TextBox id="txtCellPhone" tabIndex="5" runat="server"
              MaxLength="60"></asp:TextBox>
            <asp:RequiredFieldValidator id="RequiredFieldValidator11" runat="server"
              ControlToValidate="txtCellPhone" ErrorMessage="*">
            </asp:RequiredFieldValidator>
          </td>
        </tr>
```

```
    <tr height="32">
      <td>
        <asp:Label id="lblCity" runat="server" Height="25px" Width="44px"
          Font-Bold="True">City:</asp:Label>
      </td>
      <td>
        <asp:TextBox id="txtCity" tabIndex="6" runat="server"
          MaxLength="25"></asp:TextBox>
        <asp:RequiredFieldValidator id="RequiredFieldValidator6" runat="server"
          ControlToValidate="txtCity" ErrorMessage="*">
        </asp:RequiredFieldValidator>
      </td>
    </tr>
    <tr height="32">
      <td>
        <asp:Label id="lblState" runat="server" Height="20px" Width="52px"
          Font-Bold="True">State:</asp:Label>
      </td>
      <td>
        <asp:TextBox id="txtState" tabIndex="7" runat="server"
          MaxLength="2"></asp:TextBox>
        <asp:RequiredFieldValidator id="RequiredFieldValidator7" runat="server"
          ControlToValidate="txtState" ErrorMessage="*">
        </asp:RequiredFieldValidator>
      </td>
    </tr>
    <tr height="32">
      <td>
        <asp:Label id="lblZip" runat="server" Height="20px" Width="52px"
          Font-Bold="True">Zip:</asp:Label>
      </td>
      <td>
        <asp:TextBox id="txtZip" tabIndex="8" runat="server"
          MaxLength="9"></asp:TextBox>
        <asp:RequiredFieldValidator id="RequiredFieldValidator8" runat="server"
          ControlToValidate="txtZip" ErrorMessage="*">
        </asp:RequiredFieldValidator>
      </td>
    </tr>
    <tr height="32">
      <td colspan=2 align=center>
        <asp:Button id="btnSave" OnClick="btnSave_Click" tabIndex="9"
          runat="server" Height="24px" Width="100px" Text="Save Details">
        </asp:Button>
      </td>
    </tr>
  </table>
</asp:Content>
```

The registration page contains a number of input controls, and for each of the mandatory fields, server side validation controls are leveraged to validate their data. Once the user fills out all the mandatory fields and hits the Save Details button, you create an instance of the `UserDetail` object, populate the object with the information entered by the user, and then invoke the `AddUserInfo()` method of the

`UserDB` class. The population of the `UserDetail` object with the values from the form is a very simple exercise, except for the fact that you need to create an XML string for the `Phone` property of the `UserDetail` object:

```
string xml = CreateXml();
user.Phone = xml;
```

The creation of an XML structure for the phone details is accomplished through a helper method named `CreateXml()`, which simply creates an XML string dynamically using the methods of the `XmlWriter` object.

Figure 12-4 shows the registration page when requested from a browser.

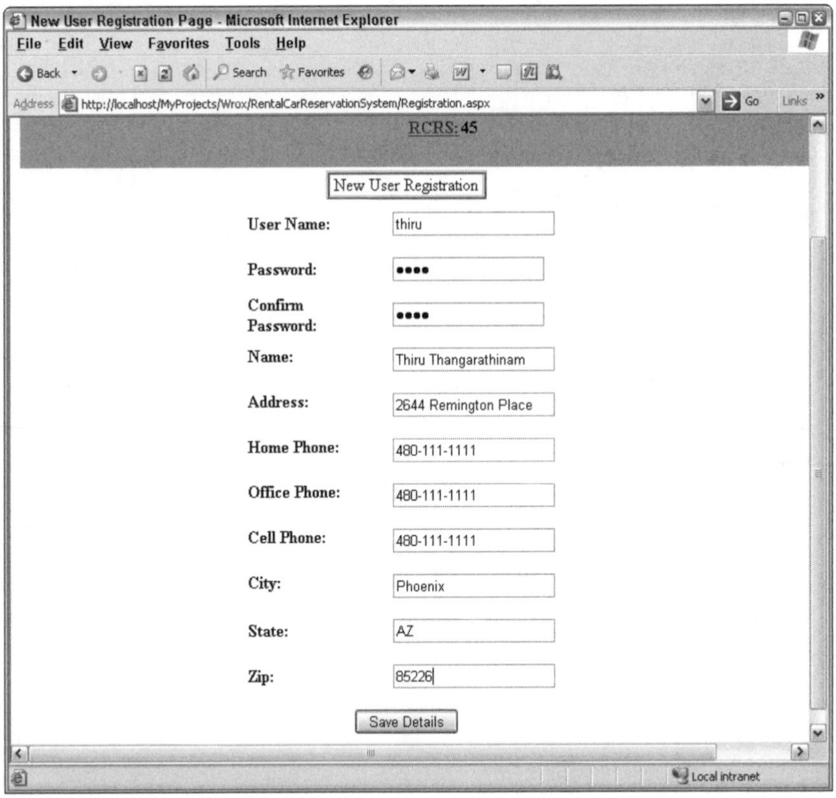

Figure 12-4

Once the registration is completed, the web site redirects the user to the `SearchCars.aspx` page through a call to the `Server.Transfer()` method.

Logout Process

All you need to do to log out of the site is click on the Logout hyperlink in the header. When you click on that link, you are redirected to the `Logout.aspx` page, as shown in Listing 12-8.

Listing 12-8: Implementation of Logout Functionality

```
<%@ Page Language="C#" MasterPageFile="~/Common.master" Title="Logout Page" %>
<%@ Import Namespace="CarRentalReservation" %>
<script runat="server">
  void Page_Load(object sender, System.EventArgs e)
  {
    FormsAuthentication.SignOut();
  }
</script>
<asp:Content ID="Content1" ContentPlaceHolderID="ContentPlaceHolder1"
  Runat="Server">
  <asp:Label id="lblMessage" style="Z-INDEX: 101; LEFT: 170px; POSITION: absolute;
    TOP: 200px" runat="server" Width="409px" Height="59px" Font-Size="Medium"
    Forecolor="Indigo">
    You have been logged out of the system. Thank you for using Online Reservation
    System
</asp:Label>
</asp:Content>
```

As Listing 12-8 shows, the logout implementation requires just one line of code. You simply call the `SignOut()` method of the `System.Web.Security.FormsAuthentication` class. That will clear all the cookies (used for authentication purposes) in the client machine, and the user will be automatically redirected to the Login page.

Search Cars Process

This involves searching for cars based on parameters such as rental pickup location, pickup date, and car class code. The Search page is an important page in that it showcases the various features of .NET 2.0. One of the important features of Search page is that it retrieves the search results from the server side without even posting back to the server. Figure 12-5 clearly outlines the flow of the page as it relates to the communication from the client side to the server side, as well as the different XML features used during those steps.

The features utilized in the search page are as follows:

- XSD validation of input XML search criteria
- Use of ASP.NET 2.0 script callback to asynchronously retrieve XML data from the client side without refreshing the browser
- How to retrieve data from the middle tier using the `ObjectDataSource` control
- Use of the XML features of the `DataSet` object to convert the `DataSet` object's contents into an XML representation
- Transformation of XML to HTML using XSL transformation

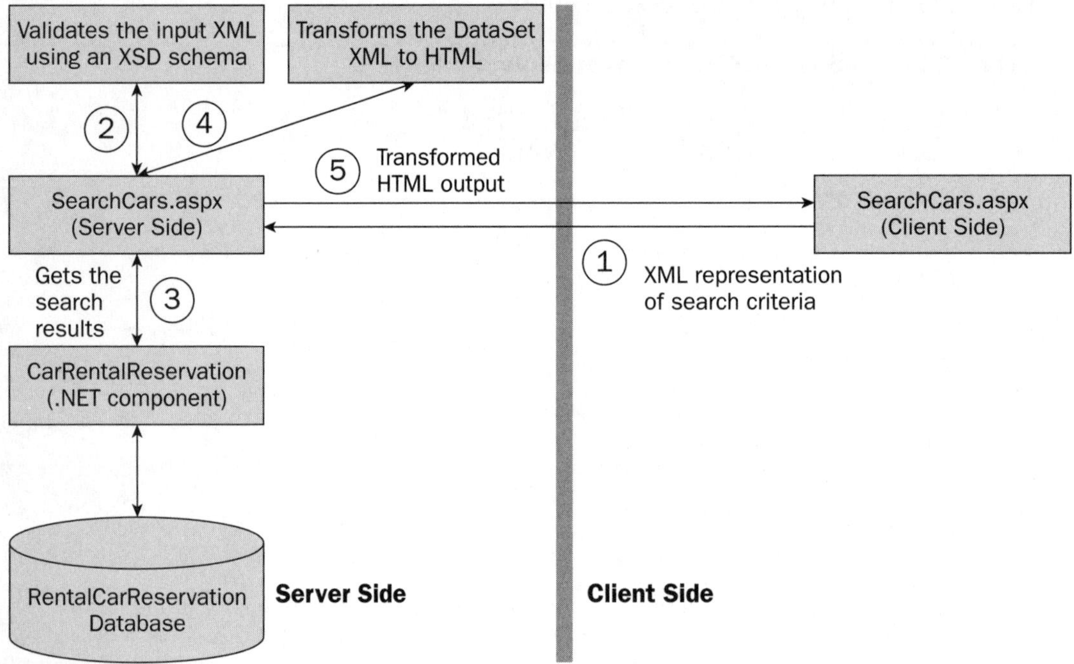

Figure 12-5

Listing 12-9 discusses the code of the `SearchCars.aspx` page.

Listing 12-9: Implementation of Search Functionality

```
<%@ Page Language="C#" MasterPageFile="~/Common.master"
  Title="Search Cars" %>
<%@ Import Namespace="System.Data" %>
<%@ Import Namespace="System.Data.SqlClient" %>
<%@ Import Namespace="System.IO" %>
<%@ Import Namespace="System.Xml" %>
<%@ Import Namespace="System.Xml.Schema" %>
<%@ Import Namespace="System.Xml.Xsl" %>
<%@ Import Namespace="CarRentalReservation" %>
<%@ implements interface="System.Web.UI.ICallbackEventHandler" %>
<script runat="server">
  private StringBuilder _builder = new StringBuilder();
  private string _callbackArg;
  void ICallbackEventHandler.RaiseCallbackEvent(string eventArgument)
  {
    _callbackArg = eventArgument;
  }

  string ICallbackEventHandler.GetCallbackResult()
  {
```

```
    try
    {
      return GetSearchResults(_callbackArg);
    }
    catch (Exception ex)
    {
      throw new ApplicationException("An Error has occurred during the " +
        "processing of your request. Error is :" + ex.Message);
    }
  }

  string GetSearchResults(string input)
  {
    XmlDocument inputDoc = new XmlDocument();
    if (IsInputXmlValid(input))
    {
      inputDoc.LoadXml(input);
      string pickupLocation = inputDoc.DocumentElement.SelectSingleNode
        ("pickupLocation").InnerText;
     string dropoffLocation = inputDoc.DocumentElement.SelectSingleNode
        ("dropoffLocation").InnerText;
     DateTime pickupDate = Convert.ToDateTime(inputDoc.DocumentElement.
        SelectSingleNode("pickupDate").InnerText);
     DateTime dropoffDate = Convert.ToDateTime(inputDoc.DocumentElement.
        SelectSingleNode("dropoffDate").InnerText);
     int carClassID = Convert.ToInt32(inputDoc.DocumentElement.
        SelectSingleNode("carClassCode").InnerText);
     //Assign the required variables to session for future use
     Session["CarClassID"] = carClassID;
     Session["PickupLocation"] = pickupLocation;
     Session["PickupDate"] = pickupDate;
     Session["DropoffLocation"] = dropoffLocation;
     Session["DropoffDate"] = dropoffDate;
     RentalDB carObj = new RentalDB();
     DataSet cars = carObj.SearchRentalCar(pickupLocation,
       pickupDate, carClassID);
     return TransformXmltoHtml(cars.GetXml());
   }
   else
   {
     throw new ApplicationException("Input XML is Invalid");
   }
 }

  string TransformXmltoHtml(string xml)
  {
    XmlDocument xmlDoc = new XmlDocument();
    xmlDoc.LoadXml(xml);
    string xslPath = Request.PhysicalApplicationPath +
      @"\App_Data\SearchOutput.xsl";
    XslCompiledTransform transform = new XslCompiledTransform();
    //Load the XSL stylsheet into the XslCompiledTransform object
    transform.Load(xslPath);
```

(continued)

Listing 12-9: *(continued)*

```
      StringWriter writer = new StringWriter();
      transform.Transform(xmlDoc, null, writer);
      return writer.ToString();
    }

    bool IsInputXmlValid(string xml)
    {
      TextReader textReader = new StringReader(xml);
      string xsdPath = Request.PhysicalApplicationPath +
        @"\App_Data\SearchInput.xsd";
      XmlReader reader = null;
      XmlReaderSettings settings = new XmlReaderSettings();
      settings.ValidationEventHandler += new
        ValidationEventHandler(this.ValidationEventHandler);
      settings.ValidationType = ValidationType.Schema;
      settings.Schemas.Add(null, XmlReader.Create(xsdPath));
      reader = XmlReader.Create(textReader, settings);
      while (reader.Read())
      {}
      bool success;
      if (_builder.ToString() == String.Empty)
        success = true;
      else
        success = false;
      return success;
    }

    void ValidationEventHandler(object sender, ValidationEventArgs args)
    {
      _builder.Append("Validation error: " + args.Message + "<br>");
    }

    public void Page_Load(object sender, EventArgs e)
    {
      if (!Request.Browser.SupportsCallback)
        throw new ApplicationException("Browser doesn't support callbacks.");
      string src = Page.ClientScript.GetCallbackEventReference(this, "arg",
        "DisplayResultsCallback","ctx", "DisplayErrorCallback", false);
      string mainSrc = @"function GetSearchDetailsUsingPostback(arg, ctx)
        { " + src + "; }";
      Page.ClientScript.RegisterClientScriptBlock(this.GetType(),
        "GetSearchDetailsUsingPostback", mainSrc, true);
    }
  </script>
  <asp:Content ID="Content1" ContentPlaceHolderID="ContentPlaceHolder1"
    Runat="Server">
  <script language="javascript">
    function GetSearchDetails()
    {
      var inputXML ="<input>" +
        "<pickupLocation>" + document.all.<%=lstPickupLocation.ClientID%>.value +
        "</pickupLocation>" + "<dropoffLocation>" +
```

```
        document.all.<%=lstDropoffLocation.ClientID%>.value + "</dropoffLocation>" +
        "<pickupDate>" + document.all.<%=txtPickupDate.ClientID%>.value +
        "</pickupDate>" + "<dropoffDate>" +
        document.all.<%=txtDropoffDate.ClientID%>.value + "</dropoffDate>" +
        "<carClassCode>" + document.all.<%=lstCarClassCode.ClientID%>.value +
        "</carClassCode>" + "</input>";
      GetSearchDetailsUsingPostback(inputXML, "Input");
    }

    function DisplayResultsCallback( result, context )
    {
      divSearchOutput.innerHTML = result;
    }

    function DisplayErrorCallback( error, context )
    {
      alert("Search Failed. " + error);
    }
  </script>
  <table align=center>
    <tr>
      <asp:XmlDataSource ID="CitiesSource" Runat="server"
        DataFile="~/App_Data/Cities.xml" XPath="cities/city">
      </asp:XmlDataSource>
      <td colspan=2 align=center>
        <asp:Label id="lblHeading" runat="server" ForeColor="Black" Height="27px"
          Width="154px" BackColor="Transparent" BorderStyle="Ridge"> Search for
          Cars</asp:Label>
      </td>
    </tr>
    <tr height="40">
      <td>
        <asp:Label id="lblPickupLocation" runat="server" Width="112px"
          Height="19px">Pickup Location:</asp:Label>
      </td>
      <td>
        <asp:DropDownList id="lstPickupLocation" runat="server" Width="176px"
          Height="22px" tabIndex="1" DataSourceID="CitiesSource" DataTextField="name"
          DataValueField="name"/>
      </td>
    </tr>
    <tr height="40">
      <td>
        <asp:Label id="lblDropoffLocation" runat="server" Width="112px"
          Height="19px">Dropoff Location:</asp:Label>
      </td>
      <td>
        <asp:DropDownList id="lstDropoffLocation" runat="server" Width="176px"
          Height="22px" tabIndex="2" DataSourceID="CitiesSource" DataTextField="name"
          DataValueField="name"/>
      </td>
    </tr>
    <tr height="40">
```

(continued)

Listing 12-9: *(continued)*

```
      <td>
        <asp:Label id="lblPickupDate" runat="server" Width="112px"
          Height="19px">Pickup Date:</asp:Label>
      </td>
      <td>
        <asp:TextBox id="txtPickupDate" runat="server" Width="169px"
          Height="26px" tabIndex="3"></asp:TextBox> 
      </td>
    </tr>
    <tr height="40">
      <td>
        <asp:Label id="lblDropoffDate" runat="server" Width="112px"
          Height="19px">Dropoff Date:</asp:Label>
      </td>
      <td>
        <asp:TextBox id="txtDropoffDate" runat="server" Width="169px"
          Height="26px" tabIndex="4"></asp:TextBox> 
      </td>
    </tr>
    <tr height="40">
      <td>
        <asp:Label id="lblCarClassCode" runat="server" Width="125px"
          Height="38px">Car Class Code:</asp:Label>
      </td>
      <td>
        <asp:DropDownList id="lstCarClassCode" runat="server" Width="176px"
          DataSourceID="carClassCodesSource" DataTextField="Car_Class_description"
          DataValueField="car_class_id" Height="38px" tabIndex="5"/>
        </asp:DropDownList>
        <asp:ObjectDataSource ID="carClassCodesSource" CacheDuration="3600"
          runat="Server" TypeName="CarRentalReservation.RentalDB"
          SelectMethod="GetCarClassCodes" />
      </td>
    </tr>
    <tr height="40">
      <td colspan=2 align=center>
        <input type="button" id="btnSearch" value="Search"
          onclick="GetSearchDetails()"/>
      </td>
    </tr>
  </table>
  <div id="divSearchOutput">
  </div>
  </asp:Content>
```

Note that the city's name is retrieved from an XML file named `Cities.xml`, using the `XmlDataSource` control as the data source control. The `Cities.xml` file is defined as follows:

```
<?xml version="1.0" encoding="utf-8" ?>
<cities>
  <city name="Phoenix"/>
  <city name="Los Angeles"/>
```

```
    <city name="Chicago"/>
    <city name="New York"/>
    <city name="SanFrancisco"/>
    <city name="Philadelphia"/>
    <city name="Seattle"/>
    <city name="Sacramento"/>
    <city name="San Jose"/>
    <city name="Washington"/>
  </cities>
```

The `Cities.xml` file acts as the data source for the `DropDownList` controls `lstPickupLocation` and `lstDropoffLocation`. In addition to the `XmlDataSource` control, there is also an `ObjectDataSource` control that retrieves all the car class codes from the database and makes them available for the `lstCar ClassCode DropDownList` control:

```
<asp:DropDownList id="lstCarClassCode" runat="server" Width="176px"
  DataSourceID="carClassCodesSource" DataTextField="Car_Class_description"
  DataValueField="car_class_id" Height="38px" tabIndex="5"/>
</asp:DropDownList>
<asp:ObjectDataSource ID="carClassCodesSource" CacheDuration="3600"
  runat="Server" TypeName="CarRentalReservation.RentalDB"
  SelectMethod="GetCarClassCodes" />
```

Since the car class codes are static data, the `ObjectDataSource` control also caches that data in memory for 60 minutes. This is specified through the `CacheDuration` property.

As you can see, the Search page is complex and utilizes a variety of features to provide the complete functionality. For reasons of brevity, the implementation of the Search page is discussed in the following sections.

ASP.NET 2.0 Script Callback

The script callback is the core feature that provides you with the ability to retrieve the search results returned by the server-side method call without refreshing the page. The Search page uses this feature to search for cars from the client side.

> **ASP.NET 2.0 script callback is a new feature introduced with ASP.NET 2.0 that enables you to invoke a remote function from the server side of a web page without refreshing the browser. This new feature builds on the foundation of the `XmlHttp` object library. Using the ASP.NET 2.0 script callback feature, you can emulate some of the behaviors of a traditional rich client application in a web-based application. It can be used to refresh individual controls, to validate controls, or even to process a form without having to post the whole page to the server.**

At the top of the page, you use the implements directive to implement the `ICallbackEventHandler` interface, which has two methods named `RaiseCallbackEvent()` and `GetCallbackResult()` that must be implemented to make the callback work.

```
<%@ implements interface="System.Web.UI.ICallbackEventHandler" %>
```

The signature of the `RaiseCallbackEvent()` method is as follows:

```
void ICallbackEventHandler.RaiseCallbackEvent(string eventArgument)
```

The `RaiseCallbackEvent` method takes an argument of type string. This argument allows you to pass values to the server side method. Inside the `RaiseCallbackEvent` method, you simply assign the supplied argument to a private variable for further processing:

```
_callbackArg = eventArgument;
```

After invoking the `RaiseCallbackEvent()` method, the ASP.NET runtime invokes the `GetCallbackResult()` method, wherein you can perform the actual server-side processing and render out the results back to the client application:

```
string ICallbackEventHandler.GetCallbackResult()
{
  try
  {
    return GetSearchResults(_callbackArg);
  }
  catch (Exception ex)
  {
    throw new ApplicationException("An Error has occurred during the " +
      "processing of your request. Error is :" + ex.Message);
  }
}
```

The `GetSearchResults()` method is the one that does the majority of the work. It starts out by invoking another method named `IsInputXmlValid()` to check the validity of the input XML (learn more about the `IsInputXmlValid()` method in the "XSD Validation" section):

```
if (IsInputXmlValid(input))
{
  inputDoc.LoadXml(input);
  string pickupLocation = inputDoc.DocumentElement.SelectSingleNode
    ("pickupLocation").InnerText;
  string dropoffLocation = inputDoc.DocumentElement.SelectSingleNode
    ("dropoffLocation").InnerText;
  DateTime pickupDate = Convert.ToDateTime(inputDoc.DocumentElement.
    SelectSingleNode("pickupDate").InnerText);
  DateTime dropoffDate = Convert.ToDateTime(inputDoc.DocumentElement.
    SelectSingleNode("dropoffDate").InnerText);
  int carClassID = Convert.ToInt32(inputDoc.DocumentElement.
    SelectSingleNode("carClassCode").InnerText);
  //Assign the required variables to session for future use
  Session["CarClassID"] = carClassID;
  Session["PickupLocation"] = pickupLocation;
  Session["PickupDate"] = pickupDate;
  Session["DropoffLocation"] = dropoffLocation;
  Session["DropoffDate"] = dropoffDate;
  RentalDB carObj = new RentalDB();
  DataSet cars = carObj.SearchRentalCar(pickupLocation,
    pickupDate, carClassID);
  return TransformXmltoHtml(cars.GetXml());
}
```

If the input XML is valid, you then parse the contents of the XML into local variables and pass them as arguments to the `SearchRentalCar()` method of the `RentalDB` class. The `SearchRentalCar()` method returns a `DataSet` object, which is then converted to an XML format and passed to a helper method named `TransformXmlToHtml()`. The `TransformXmlToHtml()` method is discussed in detail in the "Transforming XML to HTML" section. Finally, you also persist the required fields onto session variables for later use.

In addition to the implementing the `ICallbackEventHandler` interface on the server side, the ASP.NET 2.0 script callback also requires you to generate appropriate hooks on the client side to enable the server side method to be called. To this end, the `Page_Load` method uses the `Page.ClientScript.GetCallbackEventReference()` method:

```
string src = Page.ClientScript.GetCallbackEventReference(this, "arg",
  "DisplayResultsCallback","ctx", "DisplayErrorCallback", false);
```

The `GetCallbackEventReference()` method generates the client-side code that is required to initiate the asynchronous call to the server.

Then you embed the callback code inside a function by concatenating the generated code with a JavaScript function named `GetSearchDetailsUsingPostback`, using the following line of code:

```
string mainSrc = @"function GetSearchDetailsUsingPostback(arg, ctx)
  { " + src + "; }";
```

Finally, you register the client script block through the `Page.ClientScript.RegisterClientScriptBlock()` method call:

```
    Page.ClientScript.RegisterClientScriptBlock(this.GetType(),
      "GetSearchDetailsUsingPostback", mainSrc, true);
```

XML Formatted Search Criteria

Once the user has entered all the search details, you need a way to be able to pass in the search criteria to the server side. Since you can only send in a string value to the server side using the ASP.NET 2.0 script callback, you must create an XML string on the client side and send the XML string to the server. This is shown here:

```
function GetSearchDetails()
{
  var inputXML ="<input>" +
    "<pickupLocation>" + document.all.<%=lstPickupLocation.ClientID%>.value +
    "</pickupLocation>" + "<dropoffLocation>" +
    document.all.<%=lstDropoffLocation.ClientID%>.value + "</dropoffLocation>" +
    "<pickupDate>" + document.all.<%=txtPickupDate.ClientID%>.value +
    "</pickupDate>" + "<dropoffDate>" +
    document.all.<%=txtDropoffDate.ClientID%>.value + "</dropoffDate>" +
    "<carClassCode>" + document.all.<%=lstCarClassCode.ClientID%>.value +
    "</carClassCode>" + "</input>";
  GetSearchDetailsUsingPostback(inputXML, "Input");
}
```

Since all the input controls are placed inside `<asp:Content>` control, you need to utilize the `<Control_Name>.ClientID` property to reference them in the client side.

XSD Validation

As you have already seen, the client generates XML on the fly and sends that XML as an input to the `SearchRentalCar()` method. In a service-oriented world, you should never trust the input, especially when the input is coming directly from a browser. To ensure that the input XML is valid and does not contain malicious data, the server side validates the XML data using a helper method named `IsInputXmlValid()`. Before looking at the `IsInputXmlValid()` method, briefly review the XSD file that actually contains the schema.

Listing 12-10: XSD Schema Used for Validating Input XML Data

```
<?xml version="1.0" encoding="utf-8"?>
<xs:schema attributeFormDefault="unqualified" elementFormDefault="qualified"
  xmlns:xs="http://www.w3.org/2001/XMLSchema">
  <xs:element name="input">
    <xs:complexType>
      <xs:sequence>
        <xs:element name="pickupLocation" type="xs:string" />
        <xs:element name="dropoffLocation" type="xs:string" />
        <xs:element name="pickupDate" type="xs:string" />
        <xs:element name="dropoffDate" type="xs:string" />
        <xs:element name="carClassCode" type="xs:unsignedByte" />
      </xs:sequence>
    </xs:complexType>
 </xs:element>
</xs:schema>
```

Now that you have looked at the schema itself, it is time to examine the `IsInputXmlValid()` method.

The `IsInputXmlValid()` method starts out by loading the XML into a `StringReader` object:

```
TextReader textReader = new StringReader(xml);
```

Then it uses an `XmlReaderSettings` object to set the validation type and validation event handler, as well as the XSD schema used for validation:

```
string xsdPath = Request.PhysicalApplicationPath +
  @"\App_Data\SearchInput.xsd";
XmlReader reader = null;
XmlReaderSettings settings = new XmlReaderSettings();
settings.ValidationEventHandler += new
  ValidationEventHandler(this.ValidationEventHandler);
settings.ValidationType = ValidationType.Schema;
settings.Schemas.Add(null, XmlReader.Create(xsdPath));
reader = XmlReader.Create(textReader, settings);
```

Then the `Read()` method of the `XmlReader` object is invoked in a `While` loop so that the entire XML file can be read and validated. The `ValidationEventHandler()` method will be invoked whenever a validation error occurs. Inside this method, a `StringBuilder` object keeps appending the contents of the validation error message to itself:

```
while (reader.Read())
{}
bool success;
if (_builder.ToString() == String.Empty)
  success = true;
else
  success = false;
```

At the end of the method, you examine the `StringBuilder` object to verify if the validation is successful.

Transforming XML to HTML

Once you invoke the `SearchRentalCar()` method of the `RentalDB` class and have the results in the form of a `DataSet` object, there are two ways by which you can send them to the client:

- Send the `DataSet` contents in XML format and also send an XSL file, and let the client transform the XML into the required HTML format
- Convert the XML output of the `DataSet` to HTML using XSL transformation and send in the converted HTML

This example will consider the second approach and perform the XML-to-HTML transformation on the server side. Before looking at the code required for this, Listing 12-11 examines the code of the XSL file.

Listing 12-11: XSL File for Transforming the XML Search Result to HTML

```
<?xml version="1.0" ?>
<xsl:stylesheet version="1.0" xmlns:xsl="http://www.w3.org/1999/XSL/Transform"
  xmlns:ms="urn:schemas-microsoft-com:xslt"
  xmlns:dt="urn:schemas-microsoft-com:datatypes">
  <xsl:output method="html" />
  <xsl:template match="/">
    <table border="1" cellSpacing="1" cellPadding="1" align="center">
      <center>
        <tr bgcolor="#00AAAA" height="40">
          <td>Car ID</td>
          <td>Rental Pickup Location</td>
          <td>Available From</td>
          <td>Rent Per Day</td>
          <td>Car Class ID</td>
          <td>Book Tickets</td>
        </tr>
        <xsl:for-each select="/Cars/Car">
          <xsl:element name="tr">
            <xsl:attribute name="style">background-
              color:buttonface;</xsl:attribute>
            <xsl:attribute name="height">40</xsl:attribute>
            <xsl:element name="td">
              <xsl:value-of select="car_id" />
            </xsl:element>
            <xsl:element name="td">
              <xsl:attribute name="align">center</xsl:attribute>
```

(continued)

Listing 12-11: *(continued)*

```
                <xsl:value-of select="rental_pickup_location" />
              </xsl:element>
              <xsl:element name="td">
                <xsl:attribute name="align">center</xsl:attribute>
                <xsl:value-of select="ms:format-date(available_from,
                  'MMM dd, yyyy')" />
              </xsl:element>
              <xsl:element name="td">
                <xsl:attribute name="align">center</xsl:attribute>
                <xsl:value-of select='format-number(rent_per_day, "#.00")' />
              </xsl:element>
              <xsl:element name="td">
                <xsl:attribute name="align">center</xsl:attribute>
                <xsl:value-of select="car_class_id" />
              </xsl:element>
              <xsl:element name="td">
                <xsl:attribute name="align">center</xsl:attribute>
                <a><xsl:attribute name="href">BookReservation.aspx?CarID=
                  <xsl:value-of select="car_id" />
                 </xsl:attribute>Click here to make the reservation</a>
              </xsl:element>
            </xsl:element>
          </xsl:for-each>
        </center>
      </table>
  </xsl:template>
</xsl:stylesheet>
```

Now that you have had a look at the XSL file, turn your focus to the .NET code that actually performs the transformation. As mentioned previously, the transformation logic is embedded inside the `TransformXmlToHtml()` method:

```
string TransformXmltoHtml(string xml)
{
  XmlDocument xmlDoc = new XmlDocument();
  xmlDoc.LoadXml(xml);
  string xslPath = Request.PhysicalApplicationPath +
    @"\App_Data\SearchOutput.xsl";
  XslCompiledTransform transform = new XslCompiledTransform();
  //Load the XSL stylsheet into the XslCompiledTransform object
  transform.Load(xslPath);
  StringWriter writer = new StringWriter();
  transform.Transform(xmlDoc, null, writer);
  return writer.ToString();
}
```

The `XslCompiledTransform` class encapsulates the XSLT processor engine and does the actual transformation. The transformation is initiated through the call to the `Transform()` method. In this example, the output of the transformation is placed inside a `StringWriter` object.

When the user performs a search after entering all the search criteria, the page produces output similar to that in Figure 12-6.

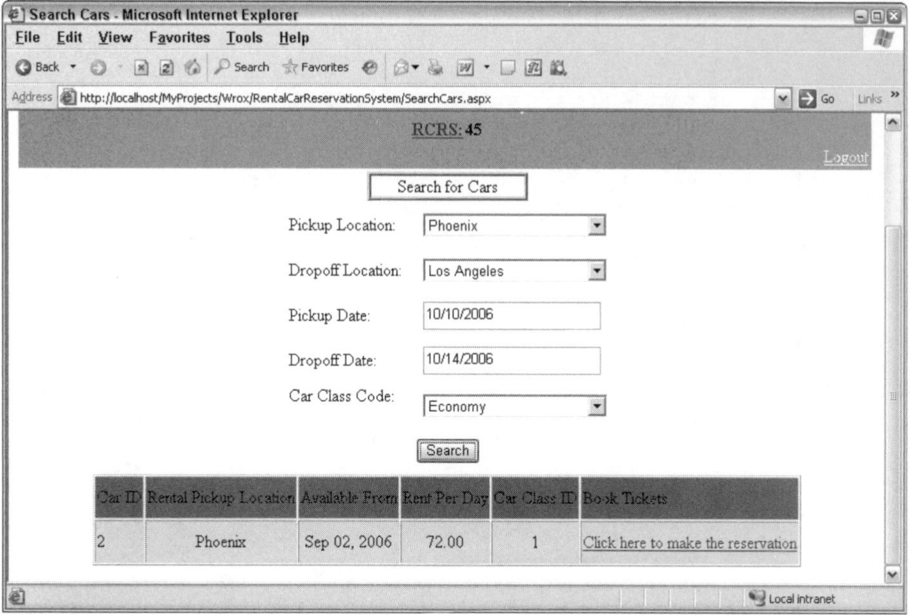

Figure 12-6

From the search output, the user can choose to book a particular car by following the hyperlink "Click here to make the reservation." This hyperlink transfers the user to the confirmation page, which is the topic of discussion in the next section.

Implementation of Confirmation Page

As mentioned previously, when the user clicks the link to make the reservation in the search results page, he is redirected to the `BookReservation.aspx` page. The code of the `BookReservation.aspx` page is shown in Listing 12-12.

Listing 12-12: Implementation of the Confirmation Page

```
<%@ Page Language="C#" MasterPageFile="~/Common.master"
Title="Confirmation Page" %>
<%@ Import Namespace="CarRentalReservation" %>
<script runat="server">
  void Page_Load(object sender, EventArgs e)
  {
    if (!Page.IsPostBack)
    {
      int carID = Convert.ToInt32(Request.QueryString["CarID"]);
      string customerID = Session["UserID"].ToString();
```

(continued)

Listing 12-12: *(continued)*

```
            int carClassID = Convert.ToInt32(Session["CarClassID"]);
            string pickupLocation = Session["PickupLocation"].ToString();
            DateTime pickupDate = Convert.ToDateTime(Session["PickupDate"]);
            string dropoffLocation = Session["DropoffLocation"].ToString();
            DateTime dropoffDate = Convert.ToDateTime(Session["DropoffDate"]);
            RentalDB car = new RentalDB();
            int bookingID = car.AddBooking(carID, customerID, carClassID,
              pickupLocation,dropoffLocation,pickupDate,dropoffDate);
            lblConfirmationNumber.Text = bookingID.ToString();
        }
    }
</script>
<asp:Content ID="Content1" ContentPlaceHolderID="ContentPlaceHolder1"
Runat="Server">
<asp:Label id="lblTitle" style="Z-INDEX: 100; LEFT: 262px; POSITION: absolute;
  TOP: 266px" runat="server" Width="225px" Height="46px" Font-Bold="True">
  Your ticket has been booked. Your confirmation number is :</asp:Label>
<asp:Label id="lblConfirmationNumber" style="Z-INDEX: 101; LEFT: 528px;
  POSITION: absolute; TOP: 268px" runat="server" Height="29px" Width="168px"
  Font-Bold="True"></asp:Label>
</asp:Content>
```

The `Page_Load` method retrieves the required parameters and simply sends them onto the `AddBooking()` method of the `RentalDB` class to save the booking. The `AddBooking()` method returns a confirmation number that is displayed in a label control.

Putting It All Together

Now that you've constructed the different parts of the application, you can test it by navigating to the Login page of our site. If you enter a valid user ID and password and click Login, you will be directed to the search cars page, where you are presented with a web form that allows you to search for rental cars. If you enter all the details and click Search, an asynchronous search is initiated through the script callback. The search results are then sent to the client side in the form of HTML. From the search results list, you can opt to make a reservation for a particular car by clicking the link "Click here to make the reservation." This will take you to the Confirmation page, where you are given the confirmation message and the booking number. If you are a new user and would like to create a new account, you can get to the New User page using the hyperlink in the Login page.

Summary

This case study has discussed the following features:

- How to work with a typed XML column in the SQL Server 2005 database
- How to validate XML data using XSD schemas
- How to transform XML to HTML using the XSLT support provided by the .NET Framework

- How to generate XML output from a `DataSet` object
- How to create rich ASP.NET web pages using the new script callback feature
- How to perform data binding with data source controls such as the `XmlDataSource` and `ObjectDataSource` controls
- How to cache the data returned from the middle-tier object through the `ObjectDataSource` control

With this knowledge in hand, you should be able to create a real-world web site that leverages the new features of ASP.NET 2.0 for creating scalable and maintainable web sites. As an exercise, you can also extend this case study to add more features, such as payment processing, integrating with external partners using web services, and so on.

Part III

ASP.NET and XML

13

Advanced ADO.NET for ASP.NET Data Display

The previous chapters were really focused on data retrieval and display from the data source controls' point of view. Although the data source controls provide a rich set of data retrieval and manipulation capabilities, there are times when you may have to work directly with ADO.NET for data retrieval purposes. One of the reasons for working with ADO.NET directly could be to overcome the limitations of data source controls. For example, if you want to take advantage of the ADO.NET 2.0 features such as MARS (Multiple Active Result Sets), asynchronous execution of commands, provider-independent data access code, and so on, you need to work directly with ADO.NET classes. This chapter will focus on these advanced features of ADO.NET 2.0 and show how they can be utilized from an ASP.NET page, enabling you to create high-performance web sites. Specifically, this chapter covers:

- Overview of the `DataSet` object
- How to programmatically create a `DataSet` object
- How to create and work with strongly typed `DataSets`
- How to serialize a `DataSet` using the binary format
- How to retrieve XML data from a `DataTable`
- How to associate a `DataReader` with a `DataTable`
- How to create provider-independent data access code
- How to asynchronously execute commands
- How to work with MARS (Multiple Active Result Set)
- How to work with an Enterprise Library data access block

The next section starts with an overview of the `DataSet` object before looking at examples.

The DataSet Object

As mentioned before, the `DataSet` object is central to supporting disconnected, distributed data scenarios with ADO.NET. The `DataSet` object is contained in the `System.Data` namespace. The `DataSet` object is a memory-resident representation of data that provides a consistent relational programming model regardless of the data source. The `DataSet` represents a complete set of data including related tables, constraints, and relationships among the tables; basically, it's like having a small relational database residing in memory.

> **Because the `DataSet` contains a lot of metadata, you need to be careful about how much data you try to store in it, since it will be consuming memory and that could have in a negative impact on performance.**

The methods and objects in a `DataSet` are consistent with those in the relational database model. The `DataSet` can also persist and reload its contents as XML and its schema as XSD. Since it is completely disconnected from any database connections, it is totally up to you to fill it with whatever data you need in memory.

DataSet Collections

The `DataSet` object exposes a number of collection objects, which are discussed in the next few sections.

DataTableCollection

An ADO.NET `DataSet` contains a collection of zero or more tables represented by `DataTable` objects. The `DataTableCollection` contains all of the `DataTable` objects in a `DataSet`. A `DataTable` is defined in the `System.Data` namespace and represents a single table of memory-resident data. It contains a collection of columns represented by the `DataColumnCollection`, which defines the schema and rows of the table. It also contains a collection of rows represented by the `DataRowCollection`, which contains the data in the table. Along with the current state, a `DataRow` retains its original state and tracks changes that occur to the data.

DataRelationCollection

A `DataSet` contains relationships in its `DataRelationCollection` object. A relationship (represented by the `DataRelation` object) associates rows in one `DataTable` with rows in another `DataTable`. The relationships in the `DataSet` can have constraints, which are represented by `UniqueConstraint` and `ForeignKeyConstraint` objects. It is analogous to a `JOIN` path that might exist between the primary and foreign key columns in a relational database. A `DataRelation` identifies matching columns in two tables of a `DataSet`.

Relationships enable you to see what links information within one table to another. The essential elements of a `DataRelation` are the name of the relationship, the two tables being related, and the related columns in each table. Relationships can be built with more than one column per table, with an array of `Data Column` objects for the key columns. When a relationship is added to the `DataRelationCollection`, it may optionally add `ForeignKeyConstraints` that disallow any changes that would invalidate the relationship.

ExtendedProperties

DataSet (as well as DataTable and DataColumn objects) has an ExtendedProperties property. ExtendedProperties is a PropertyCollection where a user can place customized information, such as the SELECT statement that was used to generate the result set, or a date/time stamp of when the data was generated. Since the ExtendedProperties contains customized information, this is a good place to store extra user-defined data about the DataSet (or DataTable or DataColumn), such as a time when the data should be refreshed. The ExtendedProperties collection is persisted with the schema information for the DataSet (as well as DataTable and DataColumn). The following code is an example of adding an Expiration property to a DataSet:

```
void Page_Load(object sender, EventArgs e)
{
  string connectionString = WebConfigurationManager.ConnectionStrings
    ["AdventureWorks"].ConnectionString;
  string sql = "SELECT * FROM Production.ProductCategory";
  SqlDataAdapter adapter = new SqlDataAdapter(sql, connectionString);
  DataSet categories = new DataSet();
  adapter.Fill(categories);
  //Add an extended property called "Expiration."
  categories.ExtendedProperties.Add("Expiration", DateTime.Now.AddDays(1));
  Response.Write(categories.ExtendedProperties["Expiration"].ToString());
}
```

This code starts out by filling a DataSet with the ProductCategory table from the AdventureWorks database. You then add a new extended property, called Expiration, and set its value to the current date and time plus one day. You then simply read it back and display it in the page using the Response.Write() statement. As you can see, it is very easy to add extended properties to DataSet objects. The same pattern also applies to DataTable and DataColumn objects.

Creating and Using DataSet Objects

As mentioned previously, the ADO.NET DataSet is a memory-resident representation of the data that provides a consistent relational programming model, regardless of the source of the data it contains. A DataSet represents a complete set of data, including the tables that contain, order, and constrain the data, as well as the relationships between the tables. The advantage to using a DataSet is that the data in a DataSet can come from multiple sources, and it is fairly easy to get the data from multiple sources into the DataSet. Also, you can define your own constraints between the data tables in a DataSet.

There are several methods of working with a DataSet, which can be applied independently or in combination. You can:

- Programmatically create DataTable, DataRelation, and Constraint objects within the DataSet and populate them with data
- Populate the DataSet or a DataTable from an existing RDBMS using a DataAdapter
- Load and persist a DataSet or DataTable using XML
- Load a DataSet from an XSD schema file
- Load a DataSet or a DataTable from a DataReader

Here is a typical usage scenario for a DataSet object:

1. A client makes a request to a web service.
2. Based on this request, the web service populates a DataSet from a database using a DataAdapter and returns the DataSet to the client.
3. The client then views the data and makes modifications.
4. When finished viewing and modifying the data, the client passes the modified DataSet back to the web service, which again uses a DataAdapter to reconcile the changes in the returned DataSet with the original data in the database.
5. The web service may then return a DataSet that reflects the current values in the database.
6. This is an optional step in which the client can then use the DataSet class's Merge method to merge the returned DataSet with the client's existing copy of the DataSet; the Merge method will accept successful changes and mark with an error any changes that failed.

The design of the ADO.NET DataSet makes this scenario fairly easy to implement. Since the DataSet is stateless, it can be safely passed between the server and the client without tying up server resources such as database connections. Although the DataSet is transmitted as XML, web services and ADO.NET automatically transform the XML representation of the data to and from a DataSet, creating a rich, yet simplified programming model. In addition, because the DataSet is transmitted as an XML stream, non-ADO.NET clients can consume the same web service as that consumed by ADO.NET clients.

Similarly, ADO.NET clients can interact easily with non-ADO.NET web services by sending any client DataSet to a web service as XML, and by consuming any XML returned as a DataSet from the web service. One thing to be careful of is the size of the data; if there are a large number of rows in the tables of your DataSet, then it will eat up a lot of bandwidth. Throughout this book, you have seen a number of examples wherein you created the schema of a DataSet object and populated it using a single call to the DbDataAdapter.Fill(). However, there are times when you might want to programmatically create a DataSet object so that it can be passed off to an external application for further processing. The next section explains the steps involved in programmatically creating a DataSet object.

Programmatically Creating DataSet Objects

You can programmatically create a DataSet object to use as a data structure in your programs. This could be quite useful if you have complex data that needs to be passed around to another object's method. For example, when creating a new customer, instead of passing 20 arguments about the new customer to a method, you could just pass the programmatically created DataSet object with all of the customer information to the object's method. Listing 13-1 shows the code for building an ADO.NET DataSet object that is composed of related tables.

Listing 13-1: Programmatically Creating a DataSet object

```
<%@ Page Language="C#" %>
<%@ Import Namespace="System.Data" %>

<script runat="server">
  void Page_Load(object sender, EventArgs e)
```

```
    {
      DataSet customerOrders = new DataSet("CustomerOrders");
      DataTable customers = customerOrders.Tables.Add("Customers");
      DataTable orders = customerOrders.Tables.Add("Orders");
      customers.Columns.Add("CustomerID", Type.GetType("System.Int32"));
      customers.Columns.Add("FirstName", Type.GetType("System.String"));
      customers.Columns.Add("LastName", Type.GetType("System.String"));
      customers.Columns.Add("Phone", Type.GetType("System.String"));
      customers.Columns.Add("Email", Type.GetType("System.String"));
      orders.Columns.Add("CustomerID", Type.GetType("System.Int32"));
      orders.Columns.Add("OrderID", Type.GetType("System.Int32"));
      orders.Columns.Add("OrderAmount", Type.GetType("System.Double"));
      orders.Columns.Add("OrderDate", Type.GetType("System.DateTime"));
      customerOrders.Relations.Add("Cust_Order_Rel",
        customerOrders.Tables["Customers"].Columns["CustomerID"],
        customerOrders.Tables["Orders"].Columns["CustomerID"]);
      DataRow row = customers.NewRow();
      row["CustomerID"] = 1;
      row["FirstName"] = "Thiru";
      row["LastName"] = "Thangarathinam";
      row["Phone"] = "329-3005";
      row["Email"] = "test@test.com";
      customers.Rows.Add(row);
      row = orders.NewRow();
      row["CustomerID"] = 1;
      row["OrderID"] = 22;
      row["OrderAmount"] = 0;
      row["OrderDate"] = "11/10/1997";
      orders.Rows.Add(row);
      Response.Write(Server.HtmlEncode(customerOrders.GetXml()));
    }
</script>
<html xmlns="http://www.w3.org/1999/xhtml" >
<head id="Head1" runat="server">
  <title>Programmatically creating a DataSet object</title>
</head>
<body>
  <form id="form1" runat="server">
    <div></div>
  </form>
</body>
</html>
```

Here is what the resulting XML of the `DataSet` looks like:

```
<CustomerOrders>
  <Customers>
    <CustomerID>1</CustomerID>
    <FirstName>Thiru</FirstName>
    <LastName>Thangarathinam</LastName>
    <Phone>329-3005</Phone>
    <Email>test@test.com</Email>
  </Customers>
```

```
    <Orders>
      <CustomerID>1</CustomerID>
      <OrderID>22</OrderID>
      <OrderAmount>0</OrderAmount>
      <OrderDate>1997-11-10T00:00:00.0000</OrderDate>
    </Orders>
  </CustomerOrders>
```

You start out by first defining a `DataSet` object named (`customerOrders`). You then create two tables, one for customers (Customers), and one for orders (Orders). You then define the columns of the tables. Notice how you call the `Add()` method of the `DataSet` object's `Tables` collection. You then define the columns of each of the tables and create a relation in the `DataSet` between the Customers table and the Orders table on the CustomerID column. Finally, you create instances of rows for the tables, add the data, and then append the rows to the `Rows` collection of the `DataTable` objects. If you create a `DataSet` object with no name, it will be given the default name of `NewDataSet`.

In this example, you simply displayed the XML representation of the `DataSet` on the ASP.NET page using the `DataSet.GetXml()` method. However, you can also data bind the above `DataSet` with a data bound control such as a `GridView`. For example, if you have a `GridView` named `gridResults` on the ASP.NET page and you want to display the data contained in the Customers `DataTable`, you can easily accomplish that by adding couple of lines of code:

```
gridResults.DataSource = customerOrders.Tables["Customers"];
gridResults.DataBind();
```

As you can see, performing data binding with a `DataSet` is the same whether you create the `DataSet` programmatically or through the execution of a SQL statement.

Strongly Typed DataSets

So far, you have looked at how to use the `DataSet` class provided by the `System.Data` namespace. You learned about the `Rows` collection and the `Columns` collection, and how to access individual rows and columns of data within the `DataSet`. For example, in a typical `DataSet`, you might access the name of a category like this:

```
DataRow row = categoriesDataSet.Tables["Categories"].Rows[0];
Response.Write(row["Name"]);
```

With strongly typed `DataSets`, you will be able to access your data in a much more programmer-friendly fashion:

```
Response.Write(categoriesDataSet.Categories[0].Name);
```

As you can see, the second method is much easier to understand and write. The functionality just described is made possible by a convention in the .NET Framework known as strongly typed `DataSets`. Strongly typed `DataSets` are classes that inherit from a `DataSet`, giving them a strongly typed nature based on an XSD structure you specify.

A typed `DataSet` *is not a built-in member of the .NET Framework. As you will discover, it is a generated class that inherits directly from the* `DataSet` *class, and allows properties and methods to be customized from an XML schema that you specify. This class also contains other classes for* `DataTable` *and* `DataRow` *objects that are enhanced in similar ways. As a result, you can create schemas and classes for data that are customized precisely for your data, enabling you to write data access code more efficiently. Do note, however, that even though your code will be up and running more quickly, you will also be burdened eventually with keeping the structures of your strongly typed* `DataSets` *up to date as your system changes.*

As you may have guessed by now, strongly typed `DataSets` require you to write XSD schemas. In fact, not every XSD schema qualifies to be a `DataSet`, so it may be argued that you need to know specifically what is allowed in an XML schema that controls what aspect of a `DataSet`. The good news, however, is that for a majority of your needs, Visual Studio makes it extremely easy to author strongly typed `DataSets`. So as you add a new `DataTable`, it creates and maintains an XSD schema underneath for you. In the case of strongly typed `DataSets`, an XML schema provides a rich definition of the data types, relationships, keys, and constraints within the data it describes. The next section provides you with a discussion on how to create strongly typed `DataSets`.

There are several ways to create strongly typed `DataSets`. This chapter will illustrate the creation of strongly typed `DataSets` in Visual Studio 2005.

Creating a Strongly Typed DataSet in Visual Studio 2005

As mentioned previously, strongly typed `DataSets` are merely generic `DataSets` that have their columns and tables defined in advance, so the compiler already knows what they will contain. Each version of Visual Studio has made the process of strongly typing a `DataSet` easier, and Visual Studio 2005 has lived up to this expectation by providing an easy-to-use interface for creating and managing strongly typed `DataSets`. In this example, you will use the Production.Product table in the AdventureWorks database to demonstrate this feature. Simply perform the following steps:

1. Open Visual Studio, and create a new ASP.NET web site.
2. In Solution Explorer, right-click to add a new item, and select `DataSet`. Give it the name `ProductDataSet.xsd`. Visual Studio will recommend placing the `DataSet` file inside the `App_Code` folder, which you should allow it to do for you.
3. The `ProductDataSet.xsd` will open in design mode, and the TableAdapter Configuration Wizard will be launched. For now, just click Cancel, because you will add tables by dragging them from the Server Explorer.
4. Locate the Server Explorer Toolbox, navigate to your SQL Server 2005 database, and the AdventureWorks database.
5. Drag the Production.Product table to your `DataSet` Designer window. The window should now resemble Figure 13-1.

As you can see from Figure 13-1, for each table that is added to the designer, Visual Studio creates a strongly typed `DataTable` (the name is based on the original table) and a `TableAdapter`. The `DataTable` has all of its columns already defined. The table adapter is the object you will use to fill the table. By default, you have a `Fill()` method that will find every row from that table.

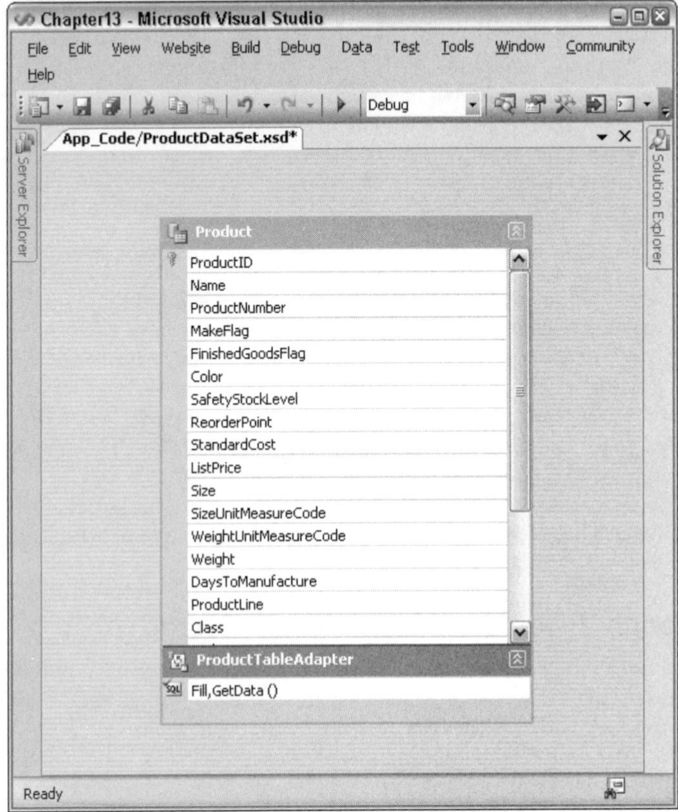

Figure 13-1

This strongly typed `DataSet`, as is, will return all of the records in the Product table. Since the Product table contains a lot of information, let us modify the default query to return only the products that belong to the supplied product category. To do this, right-click the ProductTableAdapter and select Add Query. Pick Use SQL statements and click the Next button. Then, choose SELECT, which returns rows, and click Next. Finally, enter the following query in the window (or use the Query Builder to accomplish the same task):

```
SELECT ProductID, Name, ProductNumber, MakeFlag  FROM Production.Product
Where ProductSubcategoryID = @ProductSubcategoryID
```

This SQL query is a simple `SELECT` query with an `@ProductSubcategoryID` parameter to narrow down the results. This will enable you to return the products that belong to the supplied category. Leaving the Fill a DataTable and Return a DataTable check boxes checked, click Finish. After adding this `SELECT` statement, your designer should now have an extra query added to the `ProductTableAdapter`, as shown in Figure 13-2.

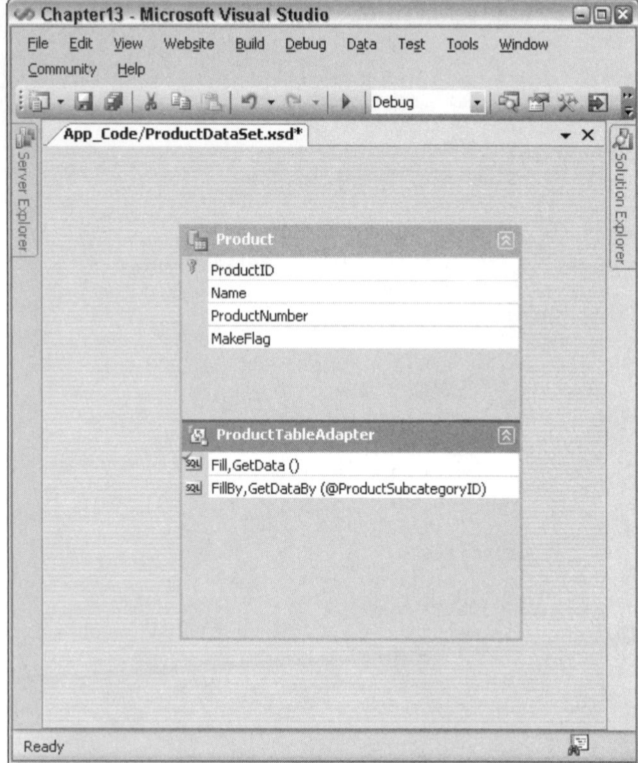

Figure 13-2

Note that you can also build strongly typed `DataSets` using a command-line utility called `xsd.exe`. To create the strongly typed `DataSet` based on the `Categories.xsd` schema, use the following command:

```
xsd /d /l:CS Categories.xsd
```

Now that you have created the strongly typed `DataSet`, the next step is to utilize it from an ASP.NET page.

Using the Strongly Typed DataSet in an ASP.NET Page

With the strongly typed `DataSet` created, you can easily display this data in an ASP.NET page with just a few lines of code. Listing 13-2 discusses the ASP.NET page that utilizes the `DataSet` created in the previous section.

Listing 13-2: Using a Strongly Typed DataSet

```
<%@ Page Language="C#" %>
<%@ Import Namespace="System.Data" %>

<script runat="server">
  void Page_Load(object sender, EventArgs e)
  {
    ProductDataSetTableAdapters.ProductTableAdapter adapter = new
      ProductDataSetTableAdapters.ProductTableAdapter();
    ProductDataSet.ProductDataTable table = adapter.GetDataBy(1);
    gridResults.DataSource = table;
    gridResults.DataBind();
  }
</script>
<html xmlns="http://www.w3.org/1999/xhtml" >
<head id="Head1" runat="server">
  <title>Using a Strongly Typed DataSet</title>
</head>
<body>
  <form id="form1" runat="server">
    <div>
      <asp:GridView HeaderStyle-BackColor="Control" HeaderStyle-ForeColor="Brown"
        RowStyle-BackColor="Snow" runat="Server" ID="gridResults">
      </asp:GridView>
    </div>
  </form>
</body>
</html>
```

This code is very simple. You create an instance of the `ProductTableAdapter`, which you will use to fill the `DataTable`. Notice that instead of declaring a generic `DataTable`, you declare an object of type `ProductDataTable`. To fill this `DataTable`, you call the `GetDataBy()` method and pass it a category ID. Figure 13-3 illustrates the result of the above code sample.

In addition to binding the results to the `GridView` through code, you could also use an `ObjectDataSource`, setting its `TypeName` property to `ProductDataSetTableAdapters.Product TableAdapter` and its `SelectMethod` to `GetDataBy()`.

> **Note that strongly typed `DataSets` are not just limited to read-only scenarios. You can easily use strongly typed `DataSets` for insert, update, and delete scenarios the same way you would do with untyped `DataSets`.**

There are additional methods to accomplish strong typing in your applications, outside of using strongly typed `DataSets`. For example, you can create custom classes that are more lightweight than `DataSets` and correspond exactly to your database.

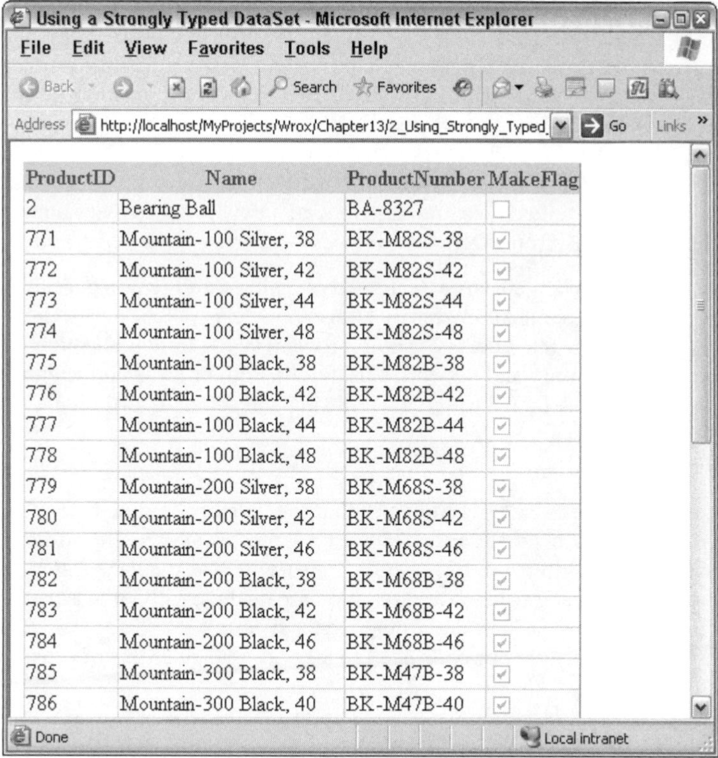

Figure 13-3

Key Considerations for Strongly Typed DataSets

So far, you have seen examples demonstrating how strongly typed `DataSets` make the jobs of creating and consuming `DataSets` far easier. Typed `DataSets` are easier to maintain, have strongly typed accessors, provide rigid data validation, and, because they can still be serialized, can be exposed as the return types of web service function calls.

It would be reasonable to ask, however, whether these things are any faster or slower than regular `DataSets`. Unfortunately, the answer is far from clear. You may already know that throwing exceptions incurs a slight overhead from the runtime, as does typecasting. All of the properties and functions in a strongly typed `DataSet` are wrapped in exception-handling calls, and a great many are wrapped in typecasting code. This leads some people to believe that they are slightly less efficient than standard `DataSets`. However, in any production application, you'll be wrapping your `DataSet` in exception-handling and typecasting code anyway, so the fact that the typed `DataSet` does this for you should be considered an advantage and not a performance drain.

Because of the inherent advantages of strongly typed `DataSets` and their role in making your code easier to develop and maintain, you should consider the feasibility of using strongly typed `DataSets` for your applications.

ADO.NET 2.0 Enhancements to the DataSet

One of the main areas of complaint developers had in ADO.NET 1.x was the performance of the `DataSet` and its `DataTable` children, in particular when there is a large amount of data in them. The performance hit comes in two different ways:

- The first way is the time it takes to actually load a `DataSet` with a lot of data. As the number of rows in a `DataTable` increases, the time to load a new row increases almost proportionally to the number of rows in the `DataTable`.
- The second way is when the large `DataSet` is serialized and remoted. A key feature of the `DataSet` is the fact that it automatically knows how to serialize itself, especially when you want to pass it between application tiers. The only problem is that the serialization is quite verbose and takes up a lot of memory and network bandwidth. Both of these performance problems are addressed in ADO.NET 2.0 through the indexing and serialization enhancements discussed below.

Indexing

The first improvement to the `DataSet` family was that the indexing engine for the `DataTable` has been completely rewritten, and it now scales much better for large `DataSets`. The addition of the new indexing engine results in faster basic inserts, updates, and deletes, which also means faster `Fill()` and `Merge()` operations. Just as in relational database design, if you are dealing with large `DataSets`, it really pays big dividends now if you add unique keys and foreign keys to your `DataTable`. The nice part, though, is that you do not have to change any of your code at all to take advantage of this new feature.

Serialization

The second improvement made to the `DataSet` family was adding new options to the way that the `DataSet` and `DataTable` are serialized. The main complaint about retrieving `DataSet` objects from web services and remoting calls was that they were way too verbose and took up too much network bandwidth. In ADO.NET 1.x, the `DataSet` serializes as XML, even when using the binary formatter. In ADO.NET 2.0, in addition to this behavior, you can also specify true binary serialization by setting the newly added `RemotingFormat` property to `SerializationFormat.Binary` rather than (the default) `SerializationFormat.XML`. Listing 13-3 shows an example of how to serialize the `DataSet` to binary representation and then deserialize it back to a `DataSet` using this new feature.

Listing 13-3: Serialization and Deserialization of DataSet Using the Binary Format

```
<%@ Page Language="C#"%>
<%@ Import Namespace="System.Data" %>
<%@ Import Namespace="System.Data.SqlClient" %>
<%@ Import Namespace="System.IO" %>
<%@ Import Namespace="System.Runtime.Serialization.Formatters.Binary" %>
<%@ Import Namespace="System.Web.Configuration" %>

<script runat="server">
  void Page_Load(object sender, System.EventArgs e)
  {
    DataSet categories = GetCategories();
    string fileName = Server.MapPath("App_Data/Categories.dat");
    using (FileStream stream = new FileStream(fileName, FileMode.Create))
    {
      categories.RemotingFormat = SerializationFormat.Binary;
```

```
      BinaryFormatter format = new BinaryFormatter();
      format.Serialize(stream, categories);
      stream.Flush();
    }
    Response.Write("File written successfully");
  }

  void btnReadFromFile_Click(object sender, EventArgs e)
  {
    string fileName = Server.MapPath("App_Data/Categories.dat");
    //Read the contents of the DataSet from the file
    using (FileStream stream = new FileStream(fileName, FileMode.Open))
    {
      BinaryFormatter format = new BinaryFormatter();
      DataSet categoriesFromFile = (DataSet) format.Deserialize(stream);
      gridCategories.DataSource = categoriesFromFile.Tables[0].DefaultView;
      gridCategories.DataBind();
    }
  }

  DataSet GetCategories()
  {
    string connString = WebConfigurationManager.ConnectionStrings
      ["AdventureWorks"].ConnectionString;
    string sql = "Select * from Production.ProductSubcategory";
    DataSet categories = new DataSet("Categories");
    using (SqlConnection connection = new SqlConnection(connString))
    {
      SqlDataAdapter adapter = new SqlDataAdapter(sql, connection);
      adapter.Fill(categories);
    }
    return categories;
  }
</script>
<html xmlns="http://www.w3.org/1999/xhtml" >
<head id="Head1" runat="server">
  <title>DataSet Serialization and Deserialization using Binary Format</title>
</head>
<body>
  <form id="form1" runat="server">
    <div>
      <asp:Button runat="Server" ID="btnReadFromFile"
        OnClick="btnReadFromFile_Click" Text="Read the Data from file" />
      <br />
      <asp:GridView id="gridCategories" runat="server" AutoGenerateColumns="False"
        CellPadding="4" HeaderStyle-BackColor="blue" HeaderStyle-ForeColor="White"
        HeaderStyle-HorizontalAlign="Center" HeaderStyle-Font-Bold="True">
        <Columns>
          <asp:BoundField HeaderText="Category ID"
            DataField="ProductSubcategoryID"/>
          <asp:BoundField HeaderText="Name" DataField="Name"
            ItemStyle-HorizontalAlign="Right" />
          <asp:BoundField HtmlEncode="false" DataFormatString="{0:d}"
            HeaderText="Last Modified Date" DataField="ModifiedDate" />
        </Columns>
```

(continued)

Listing 13-3: *(continued)*

```
        </asp:GridView>
      </div>
    </form>
  </body>
  </html>
```

This code starts out by calling the helper method `GetCategories()` to get a `DataSet` of the categories from the AdventureWorks database. Once you have the `DataSet` object, then you actually serialize the `DataSet` to binary format.

This code takes advantage of the `using` statement to wrap up creating and disposing of a `FileStream` instance that will hold serialized `DataSet` data. The next step is to set the `DataSet` object's `RemotingFormat` property to the `SerializationFormat.Binary` enumeration value. Once that is done, simply create a new `BinaryFormatter` instance, and then call its `Serialize()` method to serialize the `DataSet` into the `FileStream` instance. Then finish by showing a confirmation to the user that the data has been serialized.

In the `Click` event of the button, you read the contents of the serialized file using the `Deserialize()` method and display them using the `GridView` control. Figure 13-4 shows the output generated by the page when you click on the button.

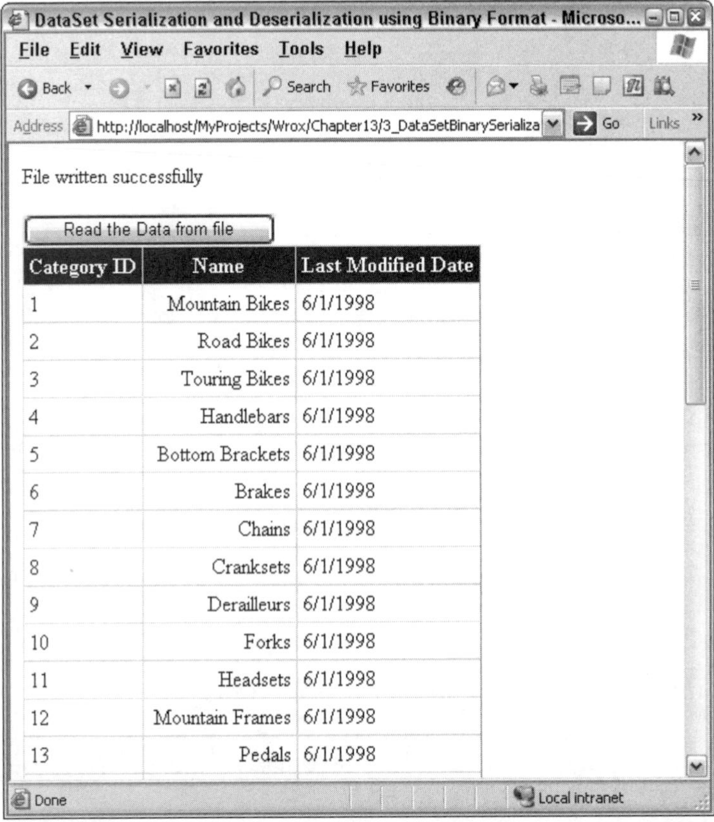

Figure 13-4

ADO.NET 2.0 DataTable

A DataSet is made up of a collection of tables, relationships, and constraints. In ADO.NET, DataTable objects are used to represent the tables in a DataSet. A DataTable represents one table of in-memory relational data. The data is local to the .NET application in which it resides, but can be populated from a data source such as SQL Server using a DataAdapter.

The DataTable class is a member of the System.Data namespace within the .NET Framework class library. You can create and use a DataTable independently or as a member of a DataSet, and DataTable objects can also be used by the other.NET Framework objects, including the DataView. You access the collection of tables in a DataSet through the DataSet object's Tables property. The schema, or structure, of a table is represented by columns and constraints. You define the schema of a DataTable using DataColumn objects, as well as ForeignKeyConstraint and UniqueConstraint objects. The columns in a table can map to columns in a data source, contain calculated values from expressions, automatically increment their values, or contain primary key values.

If you populate a DataTable from a database, it will inherit the constraints from the database, so you do not have to do all of that work manually. A DataTable must also have rows in which to contain and order the data. The DataRow class represents the actual data contained in the table. You use the DataRow and its properties and methods to retrieve, evaluate, and manipulate the data in a table. As you access and change the data within a row, the DataRow object maintains both its current and original state.

You can create parent/child relationships between tables within a database, as in SQL Server, using one or more related columns in the tables. You create a relationship between DataTable objects by using a DataRelation, which can then be used to return a row's related child or parent rows.

DataTable and XML

Now with ADO.NET 2.0, the DataTable is a first-class citizen and supports serialization along with other DataSet features. It is made possible by the fact that the DataTable class now implements the IXmlSerializable interface. In addition, the DataTable class now supports the ReadXml and WriteXml methods that could only be emulated in 1.x. The following table outlines the important XML-related methods supported by the DataTable class.

Method	Description
ReadXml	Reads XML and data into the DataTable from sources, such as a Stream, XmlWriter, or a TextWriter
ReadXmlSchema	Reads an XML schema into the DataTable from a variety of sources, such as a Stream, XmlWriter, or a TextWriter
WriteXml	Allows you to write the current contents of the DataTable to a File, Stream, TextWriter, or an XmlWriter object
WriteXmlSchema	Allows you to write the schema of the DataTable object

In addition to the rich XML support, the Merge method of the DataSet has now been added to the DataTable as well. In addition to the existing functionality of the DataSet class, some of the new features of the DataSet class have also been added to the DataTable class, namely the RemotingFormat property, the Load() method, and the GetDataReader() method.

Now that you have a general understanding of the XML-related methods of the `DataTable`, Listing 13-4 shows you a code example that exercises some of these methods.

Listing 13-4: Using the XML Features of DataTable for Data Binding

```
<%@ Page Language="C#"%>
<%@ Import Namespace="System.Data" %>
<%@ Import Namespace="System.Data.SqlClient" %>
<%@ Import Namespace="System.IO" %>
<%@ Import Namespace="System.Xml" %>
<%@ Import Namespace="System.Web.Configuration" %>

<script runat="server">
  void Page_Load(object sender, System.EventArgs e)
  {
    DataTable categoriesTable;
    string xmlFilePath = Server.MapPath("App_Data/Categories.xml");
    string xmlSchemaFilePath = Server.MapPath("App_Data/Categories.xsd");
    //Check if the file exists in the hard drive
    if (File.Exists(xmlFilePath))
    {
      categoriesTable = new DataTable();
      //Read the contents of the XML file into the DataTable
      categoriesTable.ReadXmlSchema(xmlSchemaFilePath);
      categoriesTable.ReadXml(xmlFilePath);
    }
    else
    {
      //Get the values from the database
      categoriesTable = GetCategories();
      //Write the contents of the DataTable to a local XML file
      categoriesTable.WriteXml(xmlFilePath);
      categoriesTable.WriteXmlSchema(xmlSchemaFilePath);
    }
    gridCategories.DataSource = categoriesTable.DefaultView;
    gridCategories.DataBind();
  }

  DataTable GetCategories()
  {
    string connString = WebConfigurationManager.ConnectionStrings
      ["AdventureWorks"].ConnectionString;
    string sql = "Select * from Production.ProductSubcategory";
    DataTable categoriesTable = new DataTable("Categories");
    using (SqlConnection connection = new SqlConnection(connString))
    {
      SqlDataAdapter adapter = new SqlDataAdapter(sql, connection);
      adapter.Fill(categoriesTable);
    }
    return categoriesTable;
  }
</script>
<html xmlns="http://www.w3.org/1999/xhtml" >
<head id="Head1" runat="server">
  <title>XML Features of DataTable</title>
```

```
</head>
<body>
  <form id="form1" runat="server">
    <div>
      <asp:GridView id="gridCategories" runat="server"
        AutoGenerateColumns="False" CellPadding="4"
        HeaderStyle-BackColor="blue" HeaderStyle-ForeColor="White"
        HeaderStyle-HorizontalAlign="Center" HeaderStyle-Font-Bold="True">
        <Columns>
          <asp:BoundField HeaderText="Category ID"
            DataField="ProductSubcategoryID" />
          <asp:BoundField HeaderText="Name" DataField="Name"
            ItemStyle-HorizontalAlign="Right" />
          <asp:BoundField HtmlEncode="false" DataFormatString="{0:d}"
            HeaderText="Last Modified Date" DataField="ModifiedDate" />
        </Columns>
      </asp:GridView>
    </div>
  </form>
</body>
</html>
```

To start with, Listing 13-4 checks to see the existence of the `Categories.xml` file. If the file is available, you read the XML file into the `DataTable` object by calling the `ReadXml()` method. Before doing that, you read the schema into the `DataTable` object using the `ReadXmlSchema()` method. If the file is not available, you invoke a helper method named `GetCategories()` that retrieves the categories information from the AdventureWorks database and returns the output in the form of a `DataTable` to the caller. Finally, you bind the `DataTable` to a `GridView` control on the page. You write the XML output of this `DataTable` along with its schema by invoking the `ReadXml()` and `ReadXmlSchema()` methods.

Associating a DataReader with a DataTable

Now with ADO.NET 2.0, you can load a `DataReader` or a `DataSet` object into a `DataTable` directly. A new method named `Load()` is available in `DataSet` and `DataTable`, using which you can load `DataReader` into `DataSet` or `DataTable`. Similarly, you can get a `DataReader` back from `DataSet` or `DataTable`.

The `DataTable` object now provides a new method named `CreateDataReader()` that returns a `DataTableReader` object corresponding to the data contained in the `DataTable`. This method, in addition to the `WriteXml()` method, enables you to easily switch between relational and hierarchical views of data when navigating through the data contained in the `DataTable`. Note that the `DataTableReader` is a new class introduced with .NET Framework 2.0, and this class provides forward-only read-only access to the data contained in the `DataTable`. The following code shows how to load XML data into a `DataTable` and then navigate through the contents of the `DataTable` using a `DataTableReader` object in a forward-only, read-only fashion:

```
DataTable table = new DataTable();
table.ReadXmlSchema(Server.MapPath("App_Data/Categories.xsd"));
table.ReadXml(Server.MapPath("App_Data/Categories.xml"));
DataTableReader reader = newTable.CreateDataReader();
while(reader.Read())
{
  //Do something with the DataTableReader contents
}
```

Provider-Independent Data Access Code

In ADO.NET 1.x, you could code either to the provider-specific classes, such as `SqlConnection`, or to the generic interfaces, such as `IDbConnection`. If a possibility existed that the database you were programming against would change during your project, or if you were creating a commercial package intended to support customers with different databases, then you had to use the generic interfaces. You can't call a constructor on an interface, so most generic programs included code that accomplished the task of obtaining the original `IDbConnection` by means of their own factory method, such as a `GetConnection()` method that would return a provider-specific instance of the `IDbConnection` interface.

ADO.NET 2.0 has a more elegant solution for getting the provider-specific connection. Each data provider registers a `ProviderFactory` class and a provider string in the .NET `machine.config` file. There is a base `ProviderFactory` class (`DbProviderFactory`) and a `System.Data.Common.ProviderFactories` class that can return a `DataTable` of information about different data providers registered in `machine.config`, and it can also return the correct `ProviderFactory` given the provider string (called `ProviderInvariantName`) or a `DataRow` from the `DataTable`. Instead of writing your own framework to build connections based on the name of the provider, ADO.NET 2.0 makes it much more straightforward, more flexible, and easier to solve this problem.

Provider Factory Class Hierarchy

ADO.NET 2.0 introduces a myriad of new base classes in the new `System.Data.Common` namespace. These classes are specifically focused on enabling the creation of provider-independent data access code. These base classes are abstract, meaning that they can't be instantiated directly. Figure 13-5 shows the factory class hierarchy that is used for creating provider-independent data access code.

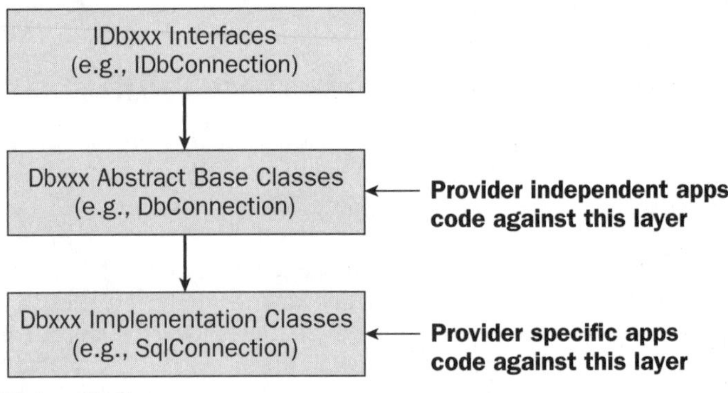

Figure 13-5

As you can see from Figure 13-5, at the top of the hierarchy is a set of interfaces like `IDbConnection`, `IDbCommand`, and `IDbDataAdapter`. Then there is a set of classes like `DbConnection`, `DbCommand`, and `DbDataAdapter` that inherit from the base interfaces. Next are the set of implementation classes like `SqlConnection`, `SqlCommand`, and `SqlDataAdapter` that inherit from the base abstract classes. The introduction of the abstract base classes with ADO.NET 2.0 provides you with the ability to write your data access code against this layer. If you are fairly certain the database is not going to change, then you can directly code against the implementation classes. But this approach does not give you any benefits in terms of performance improvements. However, with the introduction of abstract classes and the flexibility it offers, there is no reason to lock yourself into the implementation of a specific provider.

In addition to base classes, the `System.Data.Common` namespace also contains two important factory classes: `DbProviderFactories` and `DbProviderFactory`. The `DbProviderFactories` class provides a method named `GetFactoryClasses()` to enumerate the providers registered in your machine. In addition to that, the `DbProviderFactories` class also exposes a method named `GetFactory()` that returns reference to a `DbProviderFactory` implementation, which can then be used to create provider-specific implementations of connection and command objects. The methods of the `DbProviderFactory` class that return provider-specific instances of objects are shown in the following table.

Method	Description
`CreateCommand`	Returns a provider-specific instance of the `DbCommand` class that can be used to execute SQL statements and stored procedures
`CreateCommandBuilder`	Returns a provider-specific instance of the `DbCommandBuilder` class that you can use it to SQL statements for CRUD operations
`CreateConnection`	Returns a provider-specific instance of the `DbConnection` that you can use to connect to a specific data store
`CreateConnectionStringBuilder`	Returns an instance of the `DbConnectionString Builder` object that you can use to construct the connection string
`CreateDataAdapter`	Returns a provider-specific instance of the `DbDataAdapter` object that you can use to fill or update a `DataSet` or a `DataTable`
`CreateDataSourceEnumerator`	Returns an instance of a `DbDataSourceEnumerator` that you can use to examine the data sources available through the `DbProviderFactory` instance
`CreateParameter`	Returns a provider-specific instance of the `DbParameter` object that you can use to pass parameters in and out of SQL statements and stored procedures

Now that you have a general understanding of the important classes in the `System.Data.Common` namespace, let us look at an example wherein you create a generic query execution capability using the provider-independent approach.

Creating a Generic Query Execution Framework

In this section, you will understand the steps involved in creating a generic query execution framework using the `DbProviderFactories` class in conjunction with the `DbProviderFactory` class. In this example, you specify information such as the provider to use, server name, database name, and table name through the input text controls. That information is then used to execute the `select` query against the specified database. The key to this example is the ability to get reference to a provider-specific factory implementation (represented by the `DbProviderFactory` class) using the `DbProviderFactories` class. This is where the `GetFactory()` method of the `DbProviderFactories` class comes into play. This method has two overloads:

- `GetFactory(String)` accepts a provider invariant name, such as `"System.Data.SqlClient"`.
- `GetFactory(DataRow)` accepts a reference to a row in the `DataTable` returned by the `GetFactoryClasses()` method.

This example will utilize the `GetFactory()` method. Listing 13-5 shows the ASP.NET page.

Listing 13-5: Executing Dynamic Queries Using the Provider-Independent Approach

```
<%@ Page Language="C#"%>
<%@ Import Namespace="System.Web.Configuration" %>
<%@ Import Namespace="System.Data" %>
<%@ Import Namespace="System.Data.Common" %>

<script runat="server">
  void Page_Load(object source, EventArgs e)
  {
    if (!Page.IsPostBack)
    {
      DataTable table = DbProviderFactories.GetFactoryClasses();
      ddlProvider.DataSource = table;
      ddlProvider.DataTextField = "Name";
      ddlProvider.DataValueField = "InvariantName";
      ddlProvider.DataBind();
    }
  }

  void btnExecute_Click(object sender, EventArgs e)
  {
    string sql = "Select * from " + txtTableName.Text;
    ExecuteQuery(ddlProvider.SelectedItem.Value, sql);
  }

  void ExecuteQuery(string providerName, string sql)
  {
    DbProviderFactory factory = DbProviderFactories.GetFactory(providerName);
    string connectionString = CreateConnectionString
      (factory.CreateConnectionStringBuilder());
    using (DbConnection conn = factory.CreateConnection())
    {
      conn.ConnectionString = connectionString;
      using (DbDataAdapter adapter = factory.CreateDataAdapter())
      {
        adapter.SelectCommand = conn.CreateCommand();
        adapter.SelectCommand.CommandText = sql;
        DataTable table = new DataTable("Table");
        adapter.Fill(table);
        gridResults.DataSource = table;
        gridResults.DataBind();
      }
    }
  }
```

```
  string CreateConnectionString(DbConnectionStringBuilder builder)
  {
    builder.Add("Integrated Security", true);
    builder.Add("Initial Catalog", txtDatabaseName.Text);
    builder.Add("Data Source", txtServerName.Text);
    return builder.ConnectionString;
  }
</script>
<html xmlns="http://www.w3.org/1999/xhtml" >
<head id="Head1" runat="server">
  <title>Executing Dynamic Queries using Provider Independant Code</title>
</head>
<body>
  <form id="form1" runat="server">
    <div>
      <table>
        <tr>
          <td>Select Provider:</td>
          <td>
            <asp:DropDownList ID="ddlProvider" runat="server" Width="190px"/>
          </td>
        </tr>
        <tr>
          <td>Server Name:</td>
          <td><asp:TextBox ID="txtServerName" runat="server" Width="183px"/></td>
        </tr>
        <tr>
          <td>Database Name: </td>
          <td><asp:TextBox ID="txtDatabaseName" runat="server" Width="180px"/></td>
        </tr>
        <tr>
          <td>Table Name: </td>
          <td><asp:TextBox ID="txtTableName" runat="server" Width="176px"/></td>
        </tr>
        <tr>
          <td colspan="2">
            <asp:Button ID="btnExecute" runat="server" OnClick="btnExecute_Click"
              Text="Execute Query" />
          </td>
        </tr>
      </table>
      <asp:GridView HeaderStyle-BackColor="Control" HeaderStyle-ForeColor="Brown"
        RowStyle-BackColor="Snow" runat="Server" ID="gridResults">
      </asp:GridView>
    </div>
  </form>
</body>
</html>
```

The code starts by populating the `DropDownList ddlProvider` with the list of provider names from the `machine.config` file. The `DataTable` is returned by the `GetFactoryClasses()` method of the `DbProviderFactories` object:

```
DataTable table = DbProviderFactories.GetFactoryClasses();
ddlProvider.DataSource = table;
```

Next, you set the DataTextField and DataValueField properties of the DropDownList to appropriate columns in the DataTable object:

```
ddlProvider.DataTextField = "Name";
ddlProvider.DataValueField = "InvariantName";
ddlProvider.DataBind();
```

Then you also declare three text box controls to allow the users to enter a server name, database name, and table name, respectively. In addition to the text box controls, you also declare a button control named btnExecute. In the Click event of the button, you invoke a helper method named ExecuteQuery(), passing in the provider name and dynamic SQL statement as arguments:

```
string sql = "Select * from " + txtTableName.Text;
ExecuteQuery(ddlProvider.SelectedItem.Value, sql);
```

The ExecuteQuery() method starts by invoking the GetFactory() method of the DbProvider Factories class to retrieve the appropriate DbProviderFactory class based on the provider name:

```
DbProviderFactory factory = DbProviderFactories.GetFactory(providerName);
```

Once you have the DbProviderFactory object, you can then use that to create provider-specific instances of the DbConnectionStringBuilder, DbConnection, and DbDataAdapter objects using the CreateConnectionStringBuilder(), CreateConnection(), and CreateDataAdapter() methods, respectively.

Then you invoke the CreateConnectionStringBuilder() method of the DbProviderFactory class. You then pass in the DbConnectionStringBuilder object to the CreateConnectionString() helper function:

```
string connectionString =
  CreateConnectionString(factory.CreateConnectionStringBuilder());
```

Inside the CreateConnectionString() method, you add the connection string attributes to the DbConnectionStringBuilder object, using the Add() method. Finally, you return the complete connection string back to the caller:

```
string CreateConnectionString (DbConnectionStringBuilder builder)
{
  builder.Add("Integrated Security", true);
  builder.Add("Initial Catalog", txtDatabaseName.Text);
  builder.Add("Data Source", txtServerName.Text);
  return builder.ConnectionString;
}
```

Once you have the connection string from the CreateConnectionString() method, you then create the DbConnection object using the CreateConnection() method of the DbProviderFactory class. Similarly, you create the DbDataAdapter object through the DbProviderFactory.CreateDataAdapter() method. Once you have the DbConnection and DbDataAdapter objects, executing the actual query is very simple and straightforward. You simply set the CommandText property of the DbCommand object (returned by the SelectCommand property of the DbDataAdapter object) to the dynamically created SQL statement:

```
adapter.SelectCommand = conn.CreateCommand();
adapter.SelectCommand.CommandText = sql;
DataTable table = new DataTable("Table");
```

Here, you invoke the `Fill()` method of the `DbDataAdapter` object, passing in the `DataTable` as an argument:

```
adapter.Fill(table);
```

Finally, you data bind the `DataTable` object with the `GridView` named `gridResults`:

```
gridResults.DataSource = table;
gridResults.DataBind();
```

If you request the page from a browser and enter all the details, you will get an output similar to Figure 13-6.

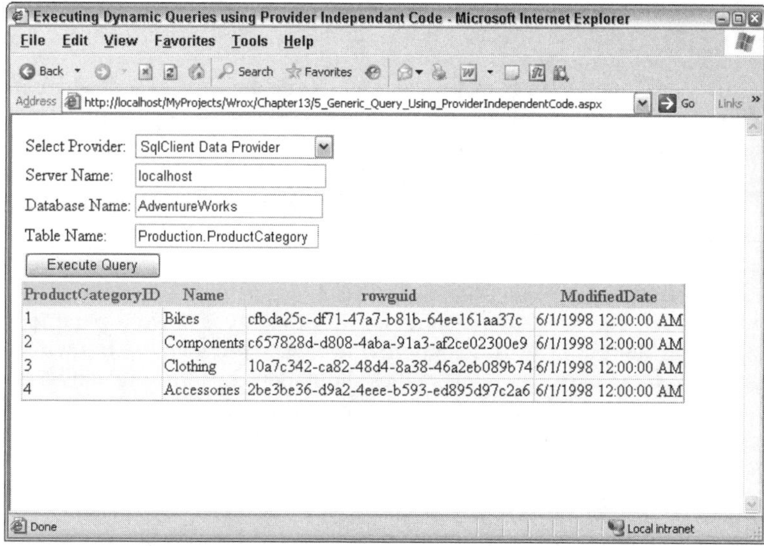

Figure 13-6

For reasons of brevity, the previous example did not include sufficient checks for validating the data entered by the user. Note that when you use dynamic SQL, you need to check the SQL statement for malicious SQL injection attacks. This means that you need to validate the user-entered data for malicious SQL statements.

Storing Connection Strings in Web.config

In the previous example, you created the connection string dynamically using the `DbConnectionStringBuilder` class. This approach will not work if you intend to store the connection string in the `Web.config` file. In that case, you store the provider invariant name in the `<connectionStrings>` element, in addition to storing the actual connection string:

```
<connectionStrings>
  <add name="AdventureWorks" connectionString="server=localhost;integrated
    security=true;database=AdventureWorks;" providerName="System.Data.SqlClient"/>
</connectionStrings>
```

You can retrieve the value of the `providerName` attribute from the code and use that as a foundation for creating database-independent code. To retrieve the `providerName` attribute value, you utilize the `ProviderName` property, as shown here:

```
string providerName = WebConfigurationManager.ConnectionStrings
  ["AdventureWorks"].ProviderName;
DbProviderFactory factory=DbProviderFactories.GetFactory(providerName);
```

Once you have the `DbProviderFactory` class, the rest of the steps are very similar to the previous example.

Key Considerations

As you can see, the new factory classes make it easier to write data access code independently of the database. Although you can use this approach to write almost completely generic code, it is important to understand that databases are not completely generic, meaning that you can never write data access logic and have it work seamlessly across different databases. Because of the inherent differences between the databases, each data provider may support some properties, methods, and events that are not supported by other data providers. For example, the way you pass in parameters to parameterized SQL statements or stored procedures completely varies, depending on the database you are connecting to. The `SqlClient` and the Microsoft implementation of `OracleClient` provider insist on named parameters; OLE DB and ODBC use positional parameters. Another difference is how the parameter markers (symbols like ? and @, :) are interpreted by different providers. Each provider has its own interpretation of the parameter markers. You can overcome some of these limitations by resorting to dynamic SQL statements. Although the use of dynamic SQL statements opens up room for SQL injection attacks, the dynamic SQL approach works in most of the cases as long as you thoroughly validate the SQL statement.

Executing Commands Asynchronously

In ADO.NET 2.0, additional support has been added to allow `SqlCommand` objects to execute their commands asynchronously. This can be a huge perceived performance gain in many applications, especially in Windows Forms applications. Using this new feature, you can now asynchronously execute commands against a SQL Server database without waiting for the command execution to finish. This feature can be very handy in situations where you are trying to execute long-running database commands from a client application, such as a Windows Forms application or an ASP.NET application. With this new feature, you can not only improve the overall performance of your application, but also make your application more responsive.

Synchronous versus Asynchronous Execution of Commands

Synchronous operations consist of component or function calls that operate in lockstep. A synchronous call blocks a process until the operation completes. Only then will the next line to be executed be invoked. Figure 13-7 details the steps involved in synchronously executing a command against the database.

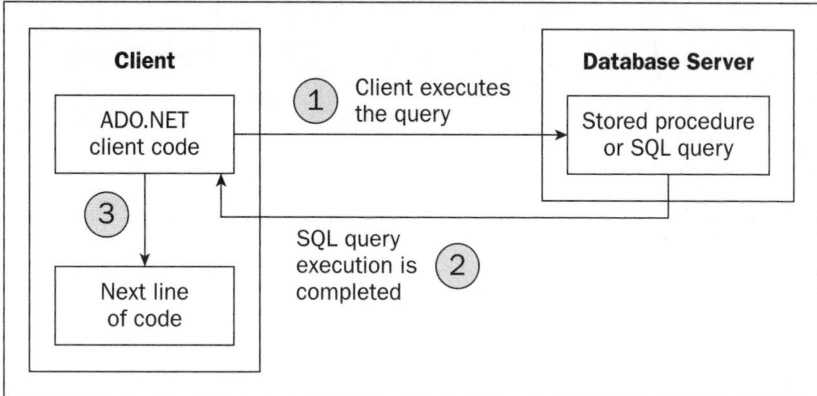

Figure 13-7

The following things are occurring in Figure 13-7:

- The client application starts by creating a `SqlCommand` object and initializing various properties of the `SqlCommand` object with the appropriate values.
- Then the client invokes any of the synchronous methods of the `SqlCommand`, such as `ExecuteNonQuery()`, `ExecuteReader()`, `ExecuteXmlReader()`, and so on, through the `SqlCommand` object.
- The client waits until the database server either completes the query execution or, if there is no response for a given period of time, the client times out, raising an error. Only after the method call returns is the client free to continue with its processing.

Now that you understand the steps involved in the synchronous execution of a command, look at the steps involved in asynchronous execution. Figure 13-8 shows the steps involved in asynchronously executing a command against the database.

The different steps in Figure 13-8 are:

- The client creates a `SqlCommand` object and initializes various properties of the `SqlCommand` object with the appropriate values. The client application also sets the `"Asynchronous Processing"` attribute in the connection string to `"true"`.
- Then the client invokes any of the asynchronous methods, such as `BeginExecuteNonQuery()`, `BeginExecuteReader()`, and `BeginExecuteXmlReader()`, through the `SqlCommand` object. Note that for this release of ADO.NET 2.0, these are the only asynchronous methods available for use.
- After the SQL command is invoked, the client code immediately moves on to the next line of code without waiting for a response from the database. This means that instead of waiting, the client code can perform some other operations while the database server is executing the query, resulting in better utilization of resources.

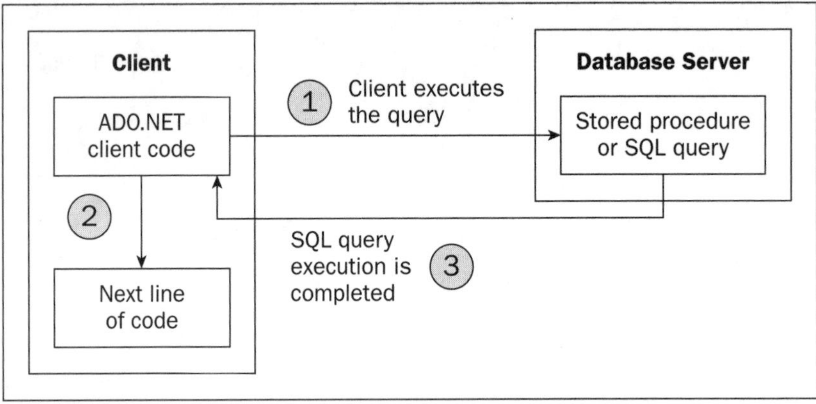

Figure 13-8

Now that you have an understanding of asynchronous execution in a general sense, the following sections discuss it in detail.

Overview of Asynchronous Command Execution

In .NET, to be able to invoke a method named `XXX` asynchronously, you need to ensure that the method has a `BeginXXX` and an `EndXXX` variation. The `BeginXXX` method initiates an asynchronous operation and returns immediately, returning a reference to an object that implements the `IAsyncResult` interface. After that, the client code will need to access that interface to monitor the progress of the asynchronous operation. Once the operation is complete, you then need to call the `EndXXX` method to obtain the result and clean up the resources that were utilized to support the asynchronous call.

There are four common ways to use `BeginXXX` and `EndXXX` to make asynchronous calls. In all cases, you invoke `BeginXXX` to initiate the call. After that, you can do one of the following:

- Do some work and then call `EndXXX`. If the asynchronous operation is not finished, `EndXXX` will block until it is completed.
- Using a `WaitHandle` obtained from the `IAsyncResult.AsyncWaitHandle`, call the `WaitOne()` method to block until the operation is completed. Then call `EndXXX`.
- Poll the returned `IAsynResult.IsCompleted` property to determine when the asynchronous operation has been completed. Then call `EndXXX`.
- Pass a delegate for a callback function that you supply (of type `IAsyncCallback`) to `BeginXXX`. When the asynchronous operation is completed, that callback function will be executed. Code in the callback function calls `EndXXX` to retrieve the result.

The `SqlCommand` object provides three different asynchronous call options, `BeginExecuteReader()`, `BeginExecuteNonQuery()`, and `BeginExecuteXmlReader()`. Each of these methods has a corresponding `EndXXX` method, that is, `EndExecuteReader()`, `EndExecuteNonQuery()`, and `EndExecuteXmlReader()`.

For the purposes of this chapter, I will demonstrate the steps involved in using the `BeginExecuteReader()` to execute a long-running query. This example will execute two different queries in parallel to retrieve the categories and database logs from AdventureWorks and AdventureWorksDW, respectively.

Listing 13-6: Asynchronously Executing a SQL Command

```
<%@ Page Language="C#"%>
<%@ Import Namespace="System.Data" %>
<%@ Import Namespace="System.Data.SqlClient" %>
<%@ Import Namespace="System.Threading"%>
<%@ Import Namespace="System.Web.Configuration" %>

<script runat="server">
  void Page_Load(object sender, System.EventArgs e)
  {
    string adventureWorksConnectionString = WebConfigurationManager.
      ConnectionStrings["AdventureWorks"].ConnectionString;
    string adventureWorksDWConnectionString  = WebConfigurationManager.
      ConnectionStrings["AdventureWorksDW"].ConnectionString;
    using (SqlConnection adventureWorksConnection = new
      SqlConnection(adventureWorksConnectionString))
    {
      using (SqlConnection adventureWorksDWConnection  = new
        SqlConnection(adventureWorksConnectionString))
      {
        //Execute the first query
        adventureWorksConnection.Open();
        string categorySql = "Select * from Production.ProductCategory";
        SqlCommand categoryCommand = new SqlCommand(categorySql,
          adventureWorksConnection);
        IAsyncResult arCategory = categoryCommand.BeginExecuteReader();
        //Execute the second query
        adventureWorksDWConnection.Open();
        string databaseLogSql = "Select * from dbo.DatabaseLog";
        SqlCommand databaseLogCommand = new SqlCommand(databaseLogSql,
          adventureWorksDWConnection);
        IAsyncResult arDatabaseLog = databaseLogCommand.BeginExecuteReader();
        /* Start some other processing
        End processing */
        //Now wait for each of the queries to return and display the results
        arCategory.AsyncWaitHandle.WaitOne();
        SqlDataReader categoryReader=categoryCommand.EndExecuteReader(arCategory);
        gridCategories.DataSource= categoryReader;
        gridCategories.DataBind();
        //Wait for the DatabaseLog Query to return
```

(continued)

Listing 13-6: *(continued)*

```
                arDatabaseLog.AsyncWaitHandle.WaitOne();
                SqlDataReader databaseLogReader =
                  databaseLogCommand.EndExecuteReader(arDatabaseLog);
                gridDatabaseLogs.DataSource = databaseLogReader;
                gridDatabaseLogs.DataBind();
            }
        }
    }
</script>
<html xmlns="http://www.w3.org/1999/xhtml" >
<head id="Head1" runat="server">
  <title>Asynchronously Executing a Command in ADO.NET</title>
</head>
<body>
  <form id="form1" runat="server">
    <div>
      Categories: (from AdventureWorks Database)<br />
      <asp:GridView id="gridCategories" runat="server"
        AutoGenerateColumns="False" CellPadding="4"
        HeaderStyle-BackColor="blue" HeaderStyle-ForeColor="White"
        HeaderStyle-HorizontalAlign="Center" HeaderStyle-Font-Bold="True">
        <Columns>
          <asp:BoundField HeaderText="Category ID" DataField="ProductCategoryID" />
          <asp:BoundField HeaderText="Name" DataField="Name"
            ItemStyle-HorizontalAlign="Right" />
          <asp:BoundField HtmlEncode="false" DataFormatString="{0:d}"
            HeaderText="Last Modified Date" DataField="ModifiedDate" />
        </Columns>
      </asp:GridView>
      <br />
      DatabaseLogs: from AdventureWorksDW Database): <br />
      <asp:GridView id="gridDatabaseLogs" runat="server"
        AutoGenerateColumns="False" CellPadding="4"
        HeaderStyle-BackColor="blue" HeaderStyle-ForeColor="White"
        HeaderStyle-HorizontalAlign="Center" HeaderStyle-Font-Bold="True">
        <Columns>
          <asp:BoundField HeaderText="ID" DataField="DatabaseLogID" />
          <asp:BoundField HeaderText="User Name" DataField="DatabaseUser"
            ItemStyle-HorizontalAlign="Right" />
          <asp:BoundField HeaderText="Schema" DataField="Schema" />
        </Columns>
      </asp:GridView>
    </div>
  </form>
</body>
</html>
```

In this example, you create two different `SqlConnection` objects that point to the AdventureWorks and AdventureWorksDW databases, respectively. Then the code invokes two different `BeginExecuteReader()` methods to fire off SQL `SELECT` queries against the ProductCategory table in the AdventureWorks database and the DatabaseLog table in the AdventureWorksDW database. After that, the code retrieves the results of the SQL query executions by calling the `EndExecuteReader()` methods and then displays the results in two `GridViews`. Note that the call to the `EndExecuteReader()` method will be a blocking call, meaning that if the query has not finished its execution, the code will be blocked until the execution of the query is complete. Figure 13-9 shows the resulting output.

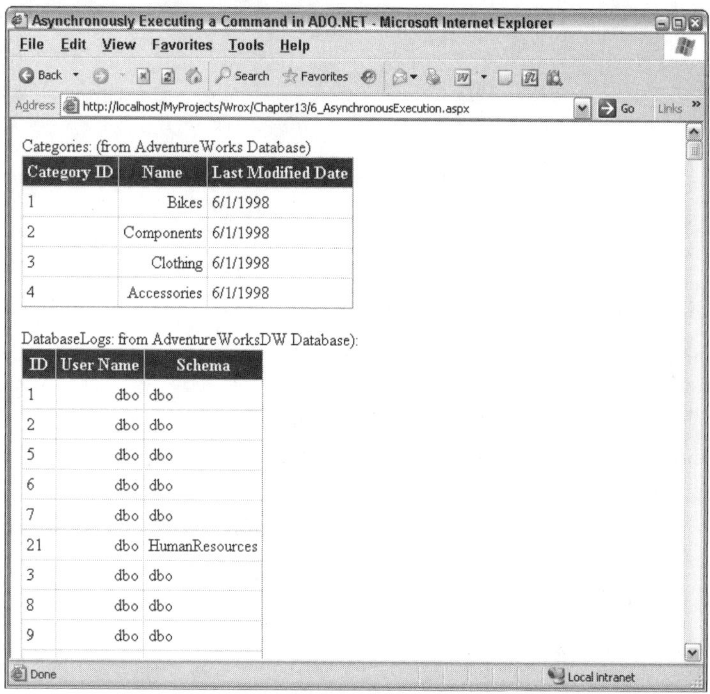

Category ID	Name	Last Modified Date
1	Bikes	6/1/1998
2	Components	6/1/1998
3	Clothing	6/1/1998
4	Accessories	6/1/1998

ID	User Name	Schema
1	dbo	dbo
2	dbo	dbo
5	dbo	dbo
6	dbo	dbo
7	dbo	dbo
21	dbo	HumanResources
3	dbo	dbo
8	dbo	dbo
9	dbo	dbo

Figure 13-9

> **Note that the connection strings defined in the `Web.config` file for AdventureWorks and AdventureWorksDW databases also have a new attribute named `Asynchronous Processing`, which is set to `true`. This must be set in order for ADO.NET 2.0 to make asynchronous calls to SQL Server.**

Multiple Active Result Sets (MARS)

You might have already seen the dreaded error message "There is already an open `DataReader` associated with this Connection which must be closed first" while using `DataReader` in your applications. MARS allows you to overcome this limitation by allowing you to open multiple `SqlDataReader` objects on a single connection. MARS allows an application to have more than one `SqlDataReader` open on a connection when each instance of `SqlDataReader` is started from a separate command. As you add each `SqlCommand` object, an additional session is added to the connection.

By default, MARS is available only on MARS-enabled hosts. SQL Server 2005 is the first SQL Server version to support MARS. However, note that MARS is not supported in SQL Server 2005 Express Edition. By default, MARS is enabled whenever you use the classes in the `System.Data.SqlClient` namespace to connect to SQL Server. However, you can also explicitly control this feature by using a keyword pair in your connection string. To MARS-enable your connections, set the `MultipleActiveResultSets` attribute in the connection string to true as follows:

```
<add name="AdventureWorks"
  connectionString="server=localhost;uid=user;pwd=word;database=AdventureWorks;
  MultipleActiveResultSets=true;"/>
```

Now that you have had an introduction to MARS, the following list helps you understand the steps involved in using MARS from ADO.NET 2.0:

1. Create a `SqlConnection` object and initialize it with the appropriate connection string.
2. Open the connection by using the `Open` method of the `SqlConnection` object.
3. Create individual `SqlCommand` objects with the required parameters to execute the query. While creating the `SqlCommand` objects, remember to associate the `SqlCommand` objects with the previously created `SqlConnection` object.
4. Once you have created the `SqlConnection` object, you can then invoke the `ExecuteReader()` method of the `SqlCommand` object to execute the queries.
5. Finally, close the `SqlConnection` object by executing the `Close()` method.

Listing 13-7 shows an example ASP.NET page that utilizes MARS.

Listing 13-7: Executing Multiple Queries Using MARS

```
<%@ Page Language="C#" %>
<%@ Import Namespace="System.Data" %>
<%@ Import Namespace="System.Data.SqlClient" %>
<%@ Import Namespace="System.Web.Configuration" %>

<script runat="server">
  void Page_Load(Object e, EventArgs sender)
  {
    string connectionString = WebConfigurationManager.ConnectionStrings
      ["AdventureWorks"].ConnectionString;
    int categoryID;
    SqlDataReader productReader = null;
    string categorySql = "SELECT ProductSubcategoryID, Name FROM " +
      " Production.ProductSubcategory";
    string productSQL = "SELECT ProductID, Name, ProductNumber FROM " +
      " Production.Product WHERE ProductSubcategoryID = @ProductSubcategoryID";
   using (SqlConnection connection = new SqlConnection(connectionString))
   {
     connection.Open();
     //Check if the SQL Server supports MARS
     if (connection.ServerVersion.StartsWith("09"))
```

```
    {
      SqlCommand categoryCommand = new SqlCommand(categorySql, connection);
      SqlCommand productCommand = new SqlCommand(productSQL, connection);
      productCommand.Parameters.Add("@ProductSubcategoryID", SqlDbType.Int);
      using (SqlDataReader categoryReader = categoryCommand.ExecuteReader())
      {
        while (categoryReader.Read())
        {
          categoryPlaceHolder.Controls.Add(new LiteralControl("<b>" +
            categoryReader["Name"] + "</b><br>"));
          categoryID = (int)categoryReader["ProductSubcategoryID"];
          productCommand.Parameters["@ProductSubcategoryID"].Value = categoryID;
          //Executing Multiple Commands using a single connection
          productReader = productCommand.ExecuteReader();
          using (productReader)
          {
            if (productReader.HasRows)
            {
              GridView productView = new GridView();
              productView.ID = "ProductView" + categoryID.ToString();
              productView.DataSource = productReader;
              productView.DataBind();
              productView.Visible = true;
              productView.ForeColor = System.Drawing.Color.Brown;
              productView.BackColor = System.Drawing.Color.Snow;
              categoryPlaceHolder.Controls.Add(productView);
            }
            else
              categoryPlaceHolder.Controls.Add(new LiteralControl
                ("No Products Found in this category<br>"));
          }
          categoryPlaceHolder.Controls.Add(new LiteralControl("<br>"));
        }
      }
    }
    else
      Response.Write("MARS is not supported in this version of SQL Server");
  }
 }
</script>
<html xmlns="http://www.w3.org/1999/xhtml" >
<head id="Head1" runat="server">
  <title>Executing Multiple Queries using MARS</title>
</head>
<body>
  <form id="form1" runat="server">
    <div>
      <asp:PlaceHolder ID="categoryPlaceHolder" Runat="Server"></asp:PlaceHolder>
    </div>
  </form>
</body>
</html>
```

You start by creating instances of the `SqlCommand` object and assigning them to `categoryCommand` and `productCommand` variables, respectively. Apart from that, you also add the `CategoryID` parameter to the `productCommand` variable. Then you execute the query contained in the `categoryCommand` object by invoking the `ExecuteReader()` method of the `categoryCommand` object. Then you capture the results of the SQL query execution in a `SqlDataReader` variable, and then loop through all the records in that `SqlDataReader` object.

After that, you add the category name to the `PlaceHolder` control through a `LiteralControl`. Then, for each category, you retrieve the products that belong to that category through the `ExecuteReader()` method of the `productCommand` object. If the `productReader` object contains any valid rows, you simply data bind that object with a dynamically created `GridView` control. While creating the `GridView` control, you also set various properties of the `GridView` control such as `Visible`, `BackColor`, and `ForeColor`. If the `productReader` object has no valid rows, you simply display the message "No products found in this category."

If you browse to the web page produced by Listing 13-7, you will see the output shown in Figure 13-10.

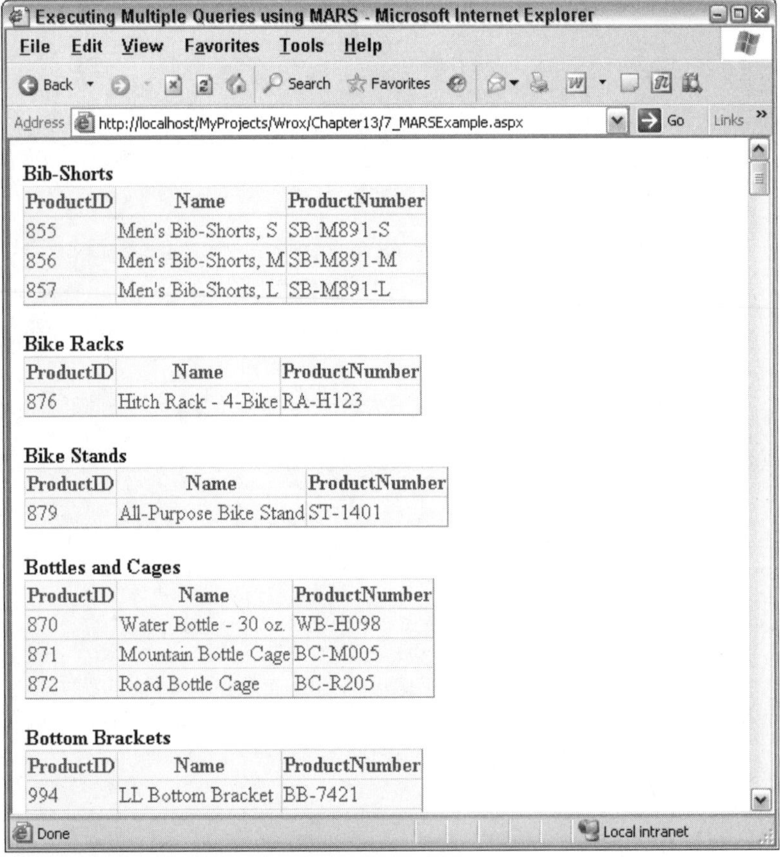

Figure 13-10

As mentioned previously, the key is to add `MultipleActiveResultSets=true` to your connection string. As in many chapters, this example uses a normal connection string, but to activate MARS in the application, the `MultipleActiveResultSets` keyword is used with a value of `True` passed to it.

In the previous example, you used two T-SQL statements to demonstrate MARS functionality, but in fact you are not limited to just inline T-SQL statements. The first command can use inline T-SQL, while the second command can use a stored procedure. The point is that regardless of the type of execution, multiple results can be returned via the same. It is even possible for each command to have more than one statement associated with it, returning multiple result sets per command.

The advantages of MARS are:

- MARS provides a lighterweight alternative to some applications that may have been using multiple connections to overcome lack-of-MARS limitations.
- A common use of MARS is to retrieve data through multiple `SqlDataReader` objects. Prior to MARS, only one command or result set could be active at one time on a connection, requiring the use of two or more connections to execute multiple queries. As you saw in the previous example, MARS enables this scenario by allowing you to execute multiple queries against the single connection. However, note that MARS does not enable parallel execution of queries; it only enables sequential execution of multiple queries.

> **Note that MARS does not support parallel execution of multiple commands against the database. Also, MARS is not designed to remove all need for multiple connections in an application. If your application needs true parallel execution of commands against a server, you should consider using multiple connections instead of MARS.**

Enterprise Library Data Access Block

So far in this book, you have invoked SQL queries and stored procedures directly from within the ASP.NET page using custom ADO.NET code. This involves writing code to connect to the database, open the database, execute SQL or stored procedures, retrieve the results back to the client applications, and close the connection. This is plumbing code that you will be forced to write in almost any application you develop and does not really add any value to the core business users. The only thing that might be different about this code in each application you develop is the SQL statement or name of the stored procedure, the parameters to the command, and the connection string. As long as you can parameterize these variables, you can abstract most of the plumbing code into reusable classes that can be leveraged across multiple applications. This is exactly what Microsoft has done in the form of Enterprise Library (known as EntLib) Data Access Block. In this section, you will come to understand how the EntLib data access block aids in communicating with the database.

What Is the Enterprise Data Access Block?

As mentioned previously, the data access block is geared towards addressing the most common tasks developers face when developing database applications. By providing a set of encapsulated methods, the data access block greatly simplifies the most common methods of accessing a database. Each method encapsulates the logic required to retrieve the data, and also manages the connection to the database. In addition, the data access block supplements the code in ADO.NET 2.0 by allowing you to write data access code that can work across different database types without ever having to change the code. These classes contain code that provides database-specific implementations for features such as parameter handling and cursors.

Moreover, the data access block also provides specific derived classes for SQL Server and Oracle databases. In addition, the `GenericDatabase` class allows you to use the application block with any configured ADO.NET 2.0 `DbProviderFactory` object. You can extend the application block by adding new database types that include database-specific features, or that provide a custom implementation of an existing database.

The data access block 2.0 is an evolution of the 1.0 version and is redesigned to take advantage of the new ADO.NET 2.0 features. You can download the EntLib data access block from: `www.microsoft.com/downloads`.

Steps Involved in Using the Data Access Block

To use the data access block, you need to go through the following steps:

1. Add references to the `Microsoft.Practices.EnterpriseLibrary.Common.dll` and `Microsoft.Practices.EnterpriseLibrary.Data.dll` assemblies from your solution. These assemblies are located in the `<Drive Name>:\Program Files\Microsoft Enterprise Library January 2006\bin` folder.
2. Add the necessary configuration entries to the `Web.config` or a custom configuration file. To this end, you add the following `<configSections>` element under the root `<configuration>` element:

```
<configSections>
  <section name="dataConfiguration"
    type="Microsoft.Practices.EnterpriseLibrary.Data.Configuration.
    DatabaseSettings, Microsoft.Practices.EnterpriseLibrary.Data" />
</configSections>
```

   - Then you also add the `<dataConfiguration>` element directly under the root `<configuration>` element as follows:

```
<dataConfiguration defaultDatabase="AdventureWorks"/>
```

   - As you can see from the previous line of code, the AdventureWorks database is marked as the default database, which is declared separately under the `<connectionStrings>` element:

```
<connectionStrings>
  <add name="AdventureWorks" providerName="System.Data.SqlClient"
   connectionString="server=localhost;database=AdventureWorks;UID=user;PWD=word;"/>
</connectionStrings>
```

3. Import the core namespace of the data access block, `Microsoft.Practices.EnterpriseLibrary.Data`, from within your code.
4. Start writing code against the classes in that namespace.

Database Object

Anytime you work with the data access block, the first class that you will have to deal with is the `Database` class. The `Database` class represents the database and provides methods for you to execute against the database. The `Database` object exposes the following methods that you can use to perform CRUD operations against the database.

Method	Description
`ExecuteDataSet`	Executes a SQL query or stored procedure and returns the results in the form of a `DataSet` object
`ExecuteNonQuery`	Executes a QL query or stored procedure and returns the number of records affected
`ExecuteReader`	Executes a SQL query or stored procedure and returns the results in the form of an `IDataReader` object
`ExecuteScalar`	Executes a SQL query or stored procedure and returns the first column of the first row in the result set
`LoadDataSet`	Executes a command and adds a new `DataTable` to the existing `DataSet`
`UpdateDataSet`	Synchronizes the `DataSet` contents with the database by executing appropriate `Insert`, `Update`, and `Delete` statements

Now that you have an understanding of the methods of the `Database` class, look at a simple example wherein you use the data access block to execute a SQL query that returns a `DbDataReader` object. The resultant `DbDataReader` object is then bound to a `GridView` control in the ASP.NET page. The complete ASP.NET page code is shown in Listing 13-8.

Listing 13-8: Executing a SQL Statement Using the EntLib Data Access Block

```
<%@ Page Language="C#" %>
<%@ Import Namespace="System.Data" %>
<%@ Import Namespace="System.Data.Common" %>
<%@ Import Namespace="Microsoft.Practices.EnterpriseLibrary.Data" %>

<script runat="server">
  void Page_Load(object sender, EventArgs e)
  {
    Database db = DatabaseFactory.CreateDatabase();
    string sqlCommand = "Select EmployeeID, NationalIDNumber," +
      "LoginID, Title from HumanResources.Employee ";
    DbCommand dbCommand = db.GetSqlStringCommand(sqlCommand);
    using (IDataReader reader = db.ExecuteReader(dbCommand))
    {
      gridEmployees.DataSource = reader;
      gridEmployees.DataBind();
    }
  }
</script>
```

(continued)

Listing 13-8: *(continued)*

```
<html xmlns="http://www.w3.org/1999/xhtml" >
<head id="Head1" runat="server">
  <title>Executing a SQL Select Statement using DbDataReader</title>
</head>
<body>
  <form id="form2" runat="server">
    <div>
      <asp:GridView HeaderStyle-BackColor="Control" HeaderStyle-ForeColor="Brown"
        RowStyle-BackColor="Snow" runat="Server" ID="gridEmployees">
      </asp:GridView>
    </div>
  </form>
</body>
</html>
```

To start with, you invoke the `CreateDatabase()` method of the `DatabaseFactory` class to obtain an instance of the `Database` object. As the name suggests, the `DatabaseFactory` is a class that contains factory methods for creating `Database` objects. Note that the `CreateDatabase()` method is overloaded and returns a default database when you invoke the parameter-less version of the `CreateDatabase()` method. To accomplish this, you set the `defaultDatabase` attribute to the appropriate database configuration key in the configuration file as follows:

```
<dataConfiguration defaultDatabase="AdventureWorksDB"/>
```

Once you have an instance of the `Database` object, you then invoke the `GetSqlStringCommand()` method to construct an instance of the ADO.NET 2.0 `DbCommand` object. After that, you execute the SQL through the `Database.ExecuteReader()` method, passing in the `DbCommand` as an argument. If you navigate to the page using a browser, you should see an output similar to that in Figure 13-11.

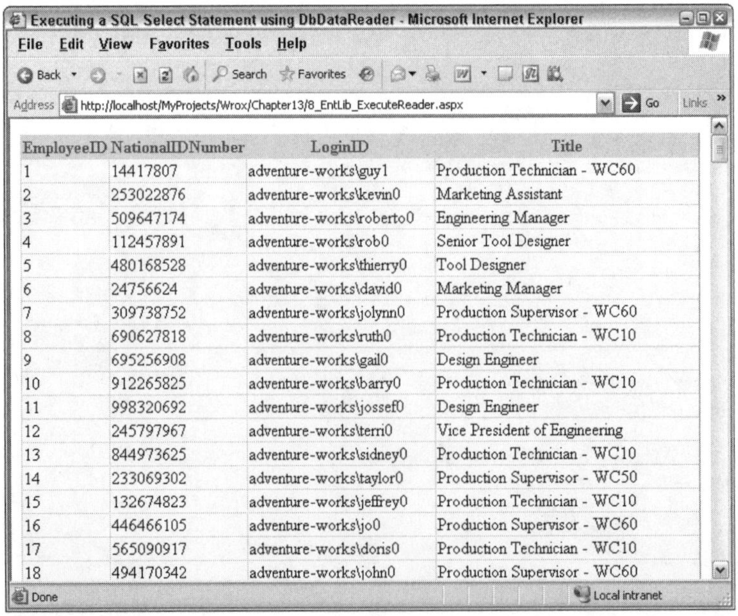

Executing a SQL Select Statement using DbDataReader - Microsoft Internet Explorer

Address: http://localhost/MyProjects/Wrox/Chapter13/8_EntLib_ExecuteReader.aspx

EmployeeID	NationalIDNumber	LoginID	Title
1	14417807	adventure-works\guy1	Production Technician - WC60
2	253022876	adventure-works\kevin0	Marketing Assistant
3	509647174	adventure-works\roberto0	Engineering Manager
4	112457891	adventure-works\rob0	Senior Tool Designer
5	480168528	adventure-works\thierry0	Tool Designer
6	24756624	adventure-works\david0	Marketing Manager
7	309738752	adventure-works\jolynn0	Production Supervisor - WC60
8	690627818	adventure-works\ruth0	Production Technician - WC10
9	695256908	adventure-works\gail0	Design Engineer
10	912265825	adventure-works\barry0	Production Technician - WC10
11	998320692	adventure-works\jossef0	Design Engineer
12	245797967	adventure-works\terri0	Vice President of Engineering
13	844973625	adventure-works\sidney0	Production Technician - WC10
14	233069302	adventure-works\taylor0	Production Supervisor - WC50
15	132674823	adventure-works\jeffrey0	Production Technician - WC10
16	446466105	adventure-works\jo0	Production Supervisor - WC60
17	565090917	adventure-works\doris0	Production Technician - WC10
18	494170342	adventure-works\john0	Production Supervisor - WC60

Figure 13-11

Figure 13-11 shows the output when the `DbDataReader` object returned by the `ExecuteReader()` method is bound to a `GridView` control.

In this example, you used the `Database.ExecuteReader()` *method to execute the SQL query and returned the results in the form of an* `IDataReader` *object. However, you could also have achieved the same results with the* `Database.ExecuteDataSet()` *method while returning the* `DataSet` *object to the ASP.NET page, which can then be bound to the* `GridView` *control.*

Executing a Stored Procedure Using the EntLib Data Access Block

There are times when you might want to execute a stored procedure instead of using inline SQL statements. Similarly to executing a SQL statement, the EntLib data access block also provides excellent support for executing stored procedures. This section looks at an example that executes a stored procedure using the data access block.

This example executes a stored procedure named `GetEmployeeDetails` that returns the details of an employee based on the supplied employee ID. Instead of returning the employee details as a `SqlDataReader` or `DataSet`, the stored procedure returns that single row of employee details as output parameters. The stored procedure is declared as follows:

```
Create Procedure GetEmployeeDetails
  @EmployeeID int,
  @NationalIDNumber nvarchar(15) OUTPUT,
  @LoginID nvarchar(256) OUTPUT,
  @Title nvarchar(50) OUTPUT
AS
  Select @NationalIDNumber = NationalIDNumber, @LoginID = LoginID,
  @Title = Title from HumanResources.Employee
  Where EmployeeID = @EmployeeID
GO
```

Now that the stored procedure is created, the next step is to invoke the stored procedure from the ASP.NET page. To accomplish this, you use the `ExecuteNonQuery()` method of the `Database` class. As part of the preparation of the `DbCommand`, you also need to add the input (`EmployeeID`) and output (`NationalIDNumber`, `LoginID`, `Title`) parameters to the `DbCommand` object.

Listing 13-9: Executing a Stored Procedure Using the EntLib Data Access Block

```
<%@ Page Language="C#" %>
<%@ Import Namespace="System.Data" %>
<%@ Import Namespace="System.Data.Common" %>
<%@ Import Namespace="Microsoft.Practices.EnterpriseLibrary.Data" %>
<script runat="server">
  void btnRetrieve_Click(object sender, EventArgs e)
  {
    Database db = DatabaseFactory.CreateDatabase();
    string storedProcedure = "GetEmployeeDetails";
    DbCommand command = db.GetSqlStringCommand(storedProcedure);
    command.CommandType = CommandType.StoredProcedure;
```

(continued)

Listing 13-9: *(continued)*

```
        db.AddInParameter(command, "EmployeeID", DbType.Int32,txtEmployeeID.Text);
        db.AddOutParameter(command, "NationalIDNumber", DbType.String, 15);
        db.AddOutParameter(command, "LoginID", DbType.String, 256);
        db.AddOutParameter(command, "Title", DbType.String, 50);
        db.ExecuteNonQuery(command);
        Response.Write("NationalID : " + db.GetParameterValue(command,
          "NationalIDNumber") + "<br>");
        Response.Write("Login ID : " + db.GetParameterValue(command, "LoginID") +
          "<br>");
        Response.Write("Title : " + db.GetParameterValue(command, "Title") + "<br>");
    }
</script>
<html xmlns="http://www.w3.org/1999/xhtml" >
<head id="Head1" runat="server">
  <title>Executing a Stored Procedure and retrieving the Output Parameter</title>
</head>
<body>
  <form id="form1" runat="server">
    <div>
      Employee ID: <asp:TextBox runat="server" ID="txtEmployeeID" />
      <asp:Button runat="server" ID="btnRetrieve"
        OnClick="btnRetrieve_Click" Text="Retrieve Employee" />
    </div>
  </form>
</body>
</html>
```

When the user enters the employee ID and clicks the button, you invoke the `GetEmployeeDetails` stored procedure after supplying the necessary parameters. Specifically, you add the input parameters using the `DbCommand.AddInParameter()` method, and the output parameters are added using the `DbCommand.AddOutParameter()` method of the `DbCommand` object. After executing the stored procedure, you simply retrieve the output parameter values by using the `GetParameterValue()` method of the `DbCommand` object, passing in the `DbCommand` object and the name of the output parameter as arguments. The output produced by the page for the employee ID of 1 is shown in Figure 13-12.

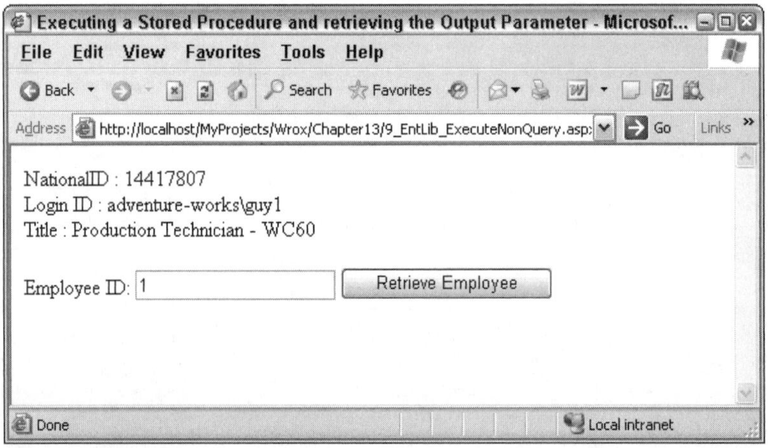

Executing a Stored Procedure and retrieving the Output Parameter - Microsof...
File Edit View Favorites Tools Help
Back Search Favorites
Address http://localhost/MyProjects/Wrox/Chapter13/9_EntLib_ExecuteNonQuery.asp: Go Links
NationalID : 14417807
Login ID : adventure-works\guy1
Title : Production Technician - WC60

Employee ID: 1 Retrieve Employee
Done Local intranet

Figure 13-12

Summary

In this chapter, you looked at various constituents of the `DataSet` object. You looked at `DataTables`, `DataRelations`, and so on, and came to understood the steps involved in programmatically creating a `DataSet` object. Then you learned the applicability of strongly typed `DataSets` and looked at many practical examples elucidating the creation and usage of a strongly typed `DataSet`.

Then you looked at the new XML features and the `DataReader` association features from the `DataTable` point of view. It was also noted that a lot of concepts mentioned for the `DataTable` are equally applicable to the `DataSet` object. This will become clearer as you subject the `DataSet` or `DataTable` to real-world scenarios that involve connecting to a data source.

After that you explored the new ADO.NET 2.0 features, such as MARS, the asynchronous execution of commands, and the provider-independent approach to creating data access code.

This chapter has also demonstrated the steps involved in programmatically adding a `ObjectDataSource` control to the page and leveraging its `Select()` method to execute the `select` method. You have also examined how the `ObjectDataSource` control can be used to implement custom paging. Caching is now automatically built into the `ObjectDataSource` control. This means that you can easily configure and control data caching using the same declarative syntax. Finally, you also explored the Enterprise Library data access block and learned about the steps involved in utilizing it to create highly efficient, error-free data access code.

14

Accessing Data from SQL Server 2005

In the previous chapter, you looked at the advanced features of ADO.NET, including the XML features of ADO.NET and also its interoperability with the `System.Xml` namespace. Specifically, you saw the interoperability features of `DataSet` objects and XML. You also saw how easy it is to convert both a `DataSet` and a `DataTable` to XML, and vice versa. You also saw how XSD schemas, which are XML, dictate the structure and data validity of a strongly typed `DataSet`. With that background, this chapter will shift gears and move on to focus on the features of SQL Server 2005. In particular, this chapter will present concepts specific to SQL Server 2005 by focusing on the CLR integration and XML-specific features of SQL Server 2005. This chapter also looks into the new `XML` data type in SQL Server 2005 and shows how you can use that to build better architected applications. Specifically, this chapter covers:

- CLR integration features in SQL Server 2005
- How to create stored procedures in managed code
- Pros and cons of using managed code in SQL Server
- New `FOR XML` query features in SQL Server 2005
- How to execute `FOR XML` queries from ADO.NET
- How to asynchronously execute `FOR XML` queries
- The `XML` data type and how to work with `XML` data-typed columns from ADO.NET
- Differences between typed versus untyped XML columns
- How to associate schemas with an XML column
- Methods supported by the XML data type and how to work with them
- How to retrieve the XML data-typed column as a `String` or a `SqlXml` object

- How to pass parameters to an `XML` data-typed column
- How to retrieve XML from the client-side browser using ASP.NET 2.0 script callback

The next section starts with an overview of the SQL Server 2005 features, before looking at examples.

Introduction to SQL Server 2005

SQL Server 2005 is a major advancement over SQL Server 2000. SQL Server 2005 brings with it a vast array of new features, graphical user interfaces (GUIs), and management tools, some of which are discussed in this book. The following list should give you a brief taste:

- The ability to host the .NET Framework common language runtime (CLR) in the database, so you can now program assemblies in Visual Basic 2005 and C# in the database. This may have interesting consequences for the SQL Server database programmer, who previously was limited to SQL and T-SQL, and it will have dramatic implications for the way that applications may be architected.
- Deep support for XML, via a full-fledged `XML` data type that carries all the capabilities of relational data types. You can enter an XML document into your database, have it validated, and extract just part of the document. This means that you can marry semistructured data with relational data, storing them in the same place and treating them in the same way. Additionally, server-side support is provided for XML Query (XQuery) and XML Schema Definition language (XSD) standards.
- A completely revamped GUI management tool called SQL Server Management Studio (SSMS), which provides a single, integrated environment to meet most management/administration requirements.
- A reporting framework (SQL Server Reporting Services, or SSRS) as an integral part of the database.
- A new application framework, the Service Broker, for asynchronous message delivery.
- Vastly improved and expanded SQL Server Integration Services (SSIS; formerly Data Transformation Services), a tool for extracting, transforming, and loading data (again, a feature that is a costly add-on with other relational database management systems).

The latter three are excellent examples of features that SQL Server provides as an integral part of the product, rather than as (extra-cost) add-ons. In this chapter, you will understand the CLR integration features and the XML features of SQL Server 2005. You will also see the steps involved in interacting with the SQL Server 2005 database for leveraging these two features from within ADO.NET.

CLR in SQL Server 2005

With the integration of the Common Language Runtime (CLR) in SQL Server 2005, a means of providing access to the rich programming model of the .NET Framework functionality from within a SQL Server instance was necessary. To accomplish this, the concept of assemblies is introduced in SQL Server 2005.

Assemblies are .NET-compiled and -hosted DLL files used by SQL Server to deploy objects such as stored procedures, user-defined types, triggers, and user-defined functions that are typically written in T-SQL, but that can now be created and written using a number of managed code languages such as VB.NET or C#.

This new addition to SQL Server 2005 also provides the capability to access the very improved programming model of the .NET Framework from within database objects such as stored procedures, functions, and types. There have been many enhancements to version 2.0 of the .NET Framework, and many of these new improvements have now been made available via integration with the CLR.

This section discusses the topic of assemblies as they pertain to SQL Server 2005, covering the CLR integration features of SQL Server 2005 that can be used to create database objects in managed code.

Managed Assemblies in SQL Server 2005

Prior to SQL Server 2005, an assembly was known as, and really still is, a unit of code compiled into a `.dll` or `.exe` file, also known as managed code. This terminology and functionality still exists with the .NET Framework. However, with SQL Server 2005, the term of assembly just got a little fuzzier.

In the realm of SQL Server, an assembly is an object that references a physical assembly `.dll` file. The managed code is a `.dll` file that is created using the .NET Framework CLR and accessible to other managed code, and more specifically, from within SQL Server. Each piece of managed code contains a couple of pieces of important information. The first is the metadata that describes the assembly, such as the methods and properties of the assembly, and the version number of the assembly. The second piece of information is the actual managed code, the methods and properties that make up the assembly.

> **The managed code is usually the code written in one of several high-level programming languages such as C# or Visual Basic .NET, which share class libraries and are compiled into an Intermediate Language (IL).**

The managed code within an assembly runs the functionality of SQL Server objects such as stored procedures, UDTs, CLR functions, and CLR triggers. More importantly, an assembly itself controls the permission level at which the managed code can access internal and external resources.

When an assembly is created in SQL Server via the `CREATE ASSEMBLY` statement, the `.dll` file is physically loaded into SQL Server so that it can be referenced and used by the SQL Server engine. Two tables exist in SQL Server 2005 that show the created assemblies. Those tables are called sys.assemblies and sys.assembly_files. At any time during the examples in this chapter, feel free to query those two tables to look at the information stored.

Enabling CLR Integration

Before you can start utilizing assemblies in SQL Server 2005, you need to tell SQL Server that it is okay to start talking to the CLR inside SQL Server. By default, CLR integration is turned off and needs to be enabled to be able to access .NET objects from within SQL Server.

To enable CLR integration, run the following code in a query window in SQL Server Management Studio:

```
EXEC sp_configure 'clr enabled', 1
GO
RECONFIGURE
GO
```

To enable CLR integration, you must have `ALTER SETTINGS` server-level permissions. These permissions are implicitly held by members of the sysadmin and serveradmin server roles.

The other method of enabling CLR integration is to turn it on via the SQL Server Surface Area Configuration tool. To get to this tool, select the SQL Server Surface Area Configuration menu from the Microsoft SQL Server 2005 ➪ Configuration Tools menu. To configure CLR integration, click the Surface Area Configuration for Features option at the bottom of the dialog. In the resultant dialog box, select CLR Integration on the left under Database Engine, and then check the Enable CLR Integration box on the right. Click OK to enable the option and close the form. You are now ready to go.

Creating Stored Procedures in Managed Code

This first example is an easy one, to help you get your feet wet in understanding how assemblies work with SQL Server 2005. To begin, create a directory called Chapter14 in the `C:\Projects\Wrox` directory. Open your favorite text editor, enter the following code, and save it as HelloWorldStoredProcedures.cs:

```
using System;
using System.Data;
using Microsoft.SqlServer.Server;
using System.Data.SqlTypes;
public class HelloWorldStoredProcedures
{
  public static void HelloWorld()
  {
    SqlContext.Pipe.Send("Hello World");
  }
}
```

In the `HelloWorld()` method, you get reference to the `SqlPipe` object by invoking the `Pipe` property of the `SqlContext` class. Once you have reference to the `SqlPipe` object, you can then return tabular results and messages to the client. This is accomplished using the `Send()` method of the `SqlPipe` class. The `SqlPipe` object is very similar to the `Response` object in ASP.NET. By calling the various overloads of the `Send()` method, you can transmit data through the pipe to the calling application. Various overloads of the `Send()` method are:

- `Send(SqlDataReader)`: Allows you to send the tabular results in the form of a `SqlDataReader` object
- `Send(SqlDataRecord)` : Allows you to send the results in the form of a `SqlDataRecord` object
- `Send(String)`: Using this method, you can send messages to the calling application

Once the class is created, the next step is where you create the managed code. To accomplish this, open the command prompt from Start ➪ All Programs ➪ Microsoft .NET Framework SDK v2.0 ➪ SDK Command Prompt.

At the command prompt, navigate to `C:\Projects\Wrox\Chapter14`, and execute the following:

```
CSC /target:library C:\Projects\Wrox\Chapter14\HelloWorldStoredProcedures.cs
```

Now you should see a new file called `HelloWorldStoredProcedures.dll` in the `C:\Projects\Wrox\Chapter14` directory.

The next step is to register the assembly with the SQL Server. Open a query window in the SQL Server Management Studio, making sure that the AdventureWorks database is selected, and execute the following T-SQL statement:

```
CREATE ASSEMBLY HelloWorld
FROM 'C:\Projects\Wrox\Chapter14\HelloWorldStoredProcedures.dll'
WITH PERMISSION_SET = SAFE
```

The `CREATE ASSEMBLY` statement loads the compiled `.dll` into SQL Server, and it can now be referenced from within SQL Server. Multiple copies, or versions, of the assembly can be stored in SQL Server with the same filename, as long as each `.dll` has a different file version number.

One thing to notice about this `CREATE ASSEMBLY` statement is the `WITH PERMISSION_SET` clause at the end. This clause specifies the access permissions that are given to the assembly when it is used and accessed by SQL Server. The available values for this clause are:

- `SAFE`: This is the default level and most restrictive. This means that your code does not need any external resources, and the operation is wholly controlled inside SQL Server. Safe code can access data from the local SQL Server databases, or perform computations and process business logic that does not involve accessing resources outside the local databases. A good example of this is factorial calculation. Factorial calculation only needs an input of type integer, and then it returns another integer. To calculate a factorial, you do not need to open a file on the disk.
- `EXTERNAL_ACCESS`: This level signifies that certain external resources such as files, networks, web services, environmental variables, and the registry are accessible. Thus, if your code intends to write out some results to a file on the disk, you would need to register that code inside SQL Server under the `EXTERNAL_ACCESS` security category.
- `UNSAFE`: This level, which you should try very hard to avoid, specifies that your code is allowed to do anything. In other words, you are requesting to be free of any granular level control, and thus giving it the same permissions as an extended stored procedure. Even though you get the same rights and permissions as with an extended stored procedure, the CLR still gives you certain benefits. However, there could be a hole in your logic that a hacker could abuse and gain access to crucial parts of your system with. Thus, you should avoid running `UNSAFE` code inside SQL Server.

The code in this example creates an assembly called `HelloWorld` using the `HelloWorldStoredProcedures.dll` and sets the permission to `SAFE`.

With the assembly created, the next step is to create a simple T-SQL stored procedure that will use the assembly. The following DDL statement creates the entry point for the assembly:

```
CREATE PROCEDURE HelloWorld
AS
EXTERNAL NAME HelloWorld.HelloWorldStoredProcedures.HelloWorld
```

Before you execute the stored procedure, take a look at the `EXTERNAL NAME` syntax of the `CREATE PROCEDURE` statement. This specifies the method of the .NET assembly. The format of the syntax is:

```
Assembly_name.Class_name.Method_name
```

Using the previous example, the assembly name comes from the `CREATE ASSEMBLY` statement, which in this case is `HelloWorld`. The second part is the class name, which comes from the code in the `HelloWorldStoredProcedures.cs` file. The third part is the method name, which also comes from the `HelloWorldStoredProcedures.cs`, which in this example is `HelloWorld`.

Putting these pieces of information together in the `EXTERNAL NAME` clause tells the stored procedure what to execute when the stored procedure is executed.

At this point, you are ready to test the assembly and get data back. To test this example, run the stored procedure by executing the following statement:

```
EXEC HelloWorld
```

Figure 14-1 shows the output produced when running the `EXEC` statement.

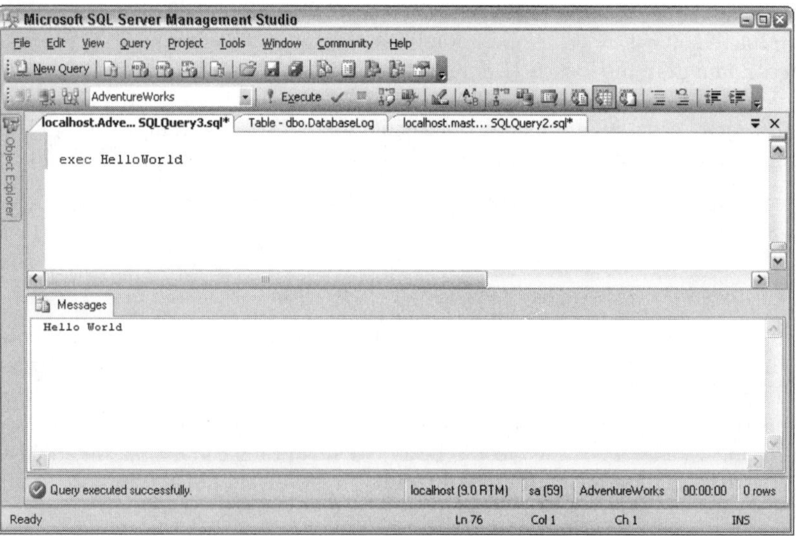

Figure 14-1

While this example is quite simple, it does show the basic steps for creating and deploying assemblies. The next example builds on this code and demonstrates more complex functionality that involves accessing SQL Server data.

You must be thinking, "There has to be an easier way to build and deploy these assemblies." Well, actually, there is. However, the reason these exercises have you building and deploying these assemblies manually is so that you understand what is happening behind the scenes when these assemblies are created. The next section shows how easy it is to create the CLR stored procedures using Visual Studio 2005 Professional Edition.

Creating a Complex CLR Stored Procedure

In this next example, you will create a stored procedure that returns data from the Production.Product table from the AdventureWorks database. To start with, create a new project named SqlServerDataAccess in Visual Studio 2005 by selecting the File ➪ New Project menu and then selecting the SQL Server Project as the Project Template after selecting Visual C# ➪ Database in the left navigation menu. If you hit OK in the project creation dialog box, you will be asked to add the database reference. Add reference to the AdventureWorks database using the Add New Reference option if the AdventureWorks reference is not already available. This is shown in Figure 14-2.

Figure 14-2

You will then be prompted if you want to enable SQL/CLR debugging for this connection, as shown in Figure 14-3.

Click Yes in Figure 14-3 if you want to be able to debug the CLR stored procedure. Once the project is created, select Project ➪ Add Stored Procedure from the menu and specify the name of the class as `GetProducts.cs`. Once the class is created, modify its code to look as shown in Listing 14-1.

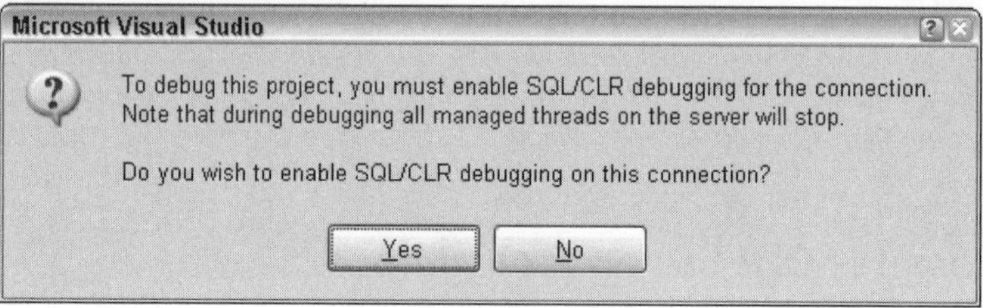

Figure 14-3

Listing 14-1: Returning a Tabular Result Set from a CLR Stored Procedure

```
using System;
using System.Data;
using System.Data.SqlClient;
using System.Data.SqlTypes;
using Microsoft.SqlServer.Server;

public partial class StoredProcedures
{
  [Microsoft.SqlServer.Server.SqlProcedure]
  public static void GetProducts(int categoryID)
  {
    SqlConnection connection = new SqlConnection("context connection = True");
    connection.Open();
    SqlCommand command = new SqlCommand("SELECT ProductID, Name FROM " +
      "Production.Product WHERE ProductSubcategoryID = " + categoryID.ToString(),
      connection);
    SqlDataReader reader = command.ExecuteReader();
    SqlContext.Pipe.Send(reader);
  }
};
```

This code in this assembly creates a connection to the database and executes a T-SQL statement, returning the ProductID and Name columns for all the records in the Product table that belong to the supplied category ID. Note that the context connection shown in Listing 14-1 allows you to execute SQL statements in the same context (in-process) that the CLR code was invoked. To enable the context connection, you specify the connection string as `"context connection=True"`.

> **The `in-proc` provider is optimized for working with data inside the SQL Server process. Using the classes and methods of the in-process managed provider, you can easily submit queries to the database, execute DML and DDL statements, and return result sets and messages to client applications. The `Microsoft.SqlServer.Server` namespace groups the types that make up the `in-proc` provider. This namespace shares many similarities and interfaces with ADO.NET's `SqlClient` namespace, which is used by developers for accessing SQL Server data from managed-client and middle-tier applications. Because of this similarity, you can easily migrate code from client applications to server libraries and back again.**

There are two important classes in the `Microsoft.SqlServer.Server` namespace that are specific to the `in-proc` provider:

- `SqlContext`: This class encapsulates the other extensions. In addition, it provides the transaction and database connection, which are part of the environment in which the routine executes.
- `SqlPipe`: This class enables routines to send tabular results and messages to the client. This class is conceptually similar to the `Response` class found in ASP.NET, in that it can be used to send messages to the callers.

Now that you have created the stored procedure, build it using the Build ➪ Build SqlServerDataAccess menu option. Once the project is built, the next step is to deploy the stored procedure to the SQL Server. Unlike the previous example, wherein you had to go through a number of steps to deploy the stored procedure, Visual Studio 2005 allows you to deploy the stored procedure with the click of a button. To accomplish this, select Build ➪ Deploy SqlServerDataAccess from the menu. That's all there is to deploying a CLR stored procedure using Visual Studio 2005.

Now you are ready to test this stored procedure by executing it. For the purposes of this example, test this stored procedure by creating a simple ASP.NET page, as shown in Listing 14-2.

Listing 14-2: Executing a CLR Stored Procedure from an ASP.NET Page

```
<%@ Page Language="C#" %>
<html xmlns="http://www.w3.org/1999/xhtml" >
<head id="Head1" runat="server">
  <title>Retrieving Data from a CLR Stored Procedure</title>
</head>
<body>
  <form id="form1" runat="server">
    <div>
      Enter Category ID: <asp:TextBox runat="server" ID="txtCategoryID" />
      <asp:Button runat="server" ID="btnRetrieve" Text="Retrieve Products" /><br/>
      <asp:GridView ID="productsView" runat="server" AutoGenerateColumns="false"
        DataSourceID="productSource">
        <Columns>
          <asp:BoundField HeaderText="Product ID" DataField="ProductID" />
          <asp:BoundField HeaderText="Name" DataField="Name"/>
        </Columns>
      </asp:GridView>
      <asp:SqlDataSource ID="productSource" Runat="server"
        SelectCommand="GetProducts" SelectCommandType="StoredProcedure"
        ConnectionString="<%$ConnectionStrings:AdventureWorks%>">
        <SelectParameters>
          <asp:ControlParameter DefaultValue="1" Name="categoryID"
            ControlID="txtCategoryID" PropertyName="Text" />
        </SelectParameters>
      </asp:SqlDataSource>
    </div>
  </form>
</body>
</html>
```

In Listing 14-2, you display the products that belong to the supplied category ID in the `GridView` control. By default, you display the products that belong to the category that is identified by category ID 1. Figure 14-4 illustrates the output produced by the page.

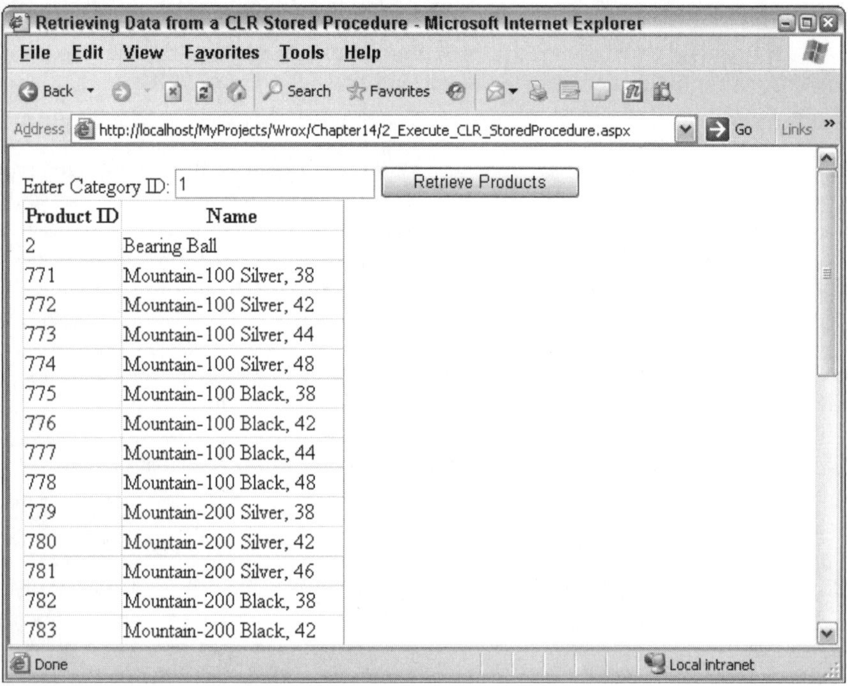

Figure 14-4

As you can see from this example, invoking a CLR stored procedure is not any different from invoking a T-SQL stored procedure. It follows exactly the same steps without any change. Your results should show the Name and ProductNumber columns for all the records from the Production.Product table.

In this example, the Name and ProductNumber columns are returned for all the rows because the query does not specify a specific ProductID to return a single row. Thus, all the rows are returned.

T-SQL versus Managed Code in SQL Server

It is quite tempting to think that you can get rid of your business layer and write all your code using a managed language inside SQL Server. However, it is important to keep in mind that the SQLCLR is not a replacement for the business layer. Thus, just because you can write C# or VB.NET code inside SQL Server, do not expect to use SQL Server as the application server that hosts all your .NET code. The SQLCLR is there for the specific purpose of working inside the database, where T-SQL might not be the right choice.

> **Note that you should use SQLCLR as an alternative for logic that cannot be expressed declaratively in T-SQL — not as a replacement for the business layer logic. So as a rule of thumb, you should try solving your problem using T-SQL first.**

T-SQL is better for set-based operations, such as tabular data, whereas SQLCLR is better for procedural code and recursive operations. However, which truly performs better than the other is dictated by many other factors. A good comparison of T-SQL versus SQLCLR can be summarized using the three cardinal rules:

- Set-based operations work better in T-SQL.
- Procedural and recursive code works better in SQLCLR.
- These two rules can be affected by a number of factors involved, such as compiled CLR code versus interpreted T-SQL code, the overhead of loading CLR in SQL Server, data access needs during processing, the library of helper functions, and so forth.

There are various reasons for this, and many of them stem from the fact that CLR inside the database operates under a different set of restrictions than it does on your Windows machine. The CLR on your Windows machine is run by the operating system, which works differently than it does when that same CLR runs inside SQL Server. The main difference is that SQL Server takes the responsibility and manages thread scheduling, synchronization, locking, and memory allocation.

Another important difference between the CLR on a Windows machine and the CLR inside SQL Server is the bootstrap mechanism that is used to load the CLR. SQL Server 2005 does not load the CLR unless it needs to. This is because SQL Server follows the principle of conserving memory and lazily loading any resource that it might need. By not loading the CLR unless it needs to, it saves a few megabytes of memory that the CLR would otherwise have occupied. Thus, if you have one minor piece of your code that uses the CLR, you are loading the CLR and, in turn, affecting any other operation on that particular computer.

Having delegated such responsibilities to the host (SQL Server) instead brings up interesting challenges. Essentially, what this means is that individual operations running inside SQL Server can now decide to be rogue and potentially be a security threat, or bring down the server. Therefore, it becomes critical that when taking advantage of the freedom of hosting the CLR and its various operations, the SQL Server application also takes on the responsibility of doing it correctly in such a manner that individual applications should not inadvertently or surreptitiously harm the server in any manner.

SQL Server enforces this by giving you a granular level of control over the set of operations your .NET code can perform inside SQL Server. This mechanism is built on top of the Code Access Security (CAS) that is a part of the CLR. The developers at Microsoft took a long and hard look at every single class in the .NET Framework, and classified them into three categories (`SAFE`, `EXTERNAL_ACCESS`, and `UNSAFE`) that you already looked at in the previous section. In other words, you need to tell SQL Server that your code falls into one of three categories based upon the specific operations it intends to do. If your code tries doing something other than what you had initially specified, SQL Server will block it from doing so.

New XML Features in SQL Server 2005

Since SQL Server 2000 lets you store XML on the server by storing the XML text in a BLOB field, you can't really work with or reference the XML on the server in its native format. To work with the XML in SQL Server 2000, you have to extract it to an application layer, and then use a standard XML parser or Document Object Model (DOM) — a programming object for handling XML documents — to work with the data.

The SQL Server 2005 XML data type removes this limitation because it is implemented as a first-class native data type. The new data type lets the SQL Server engine understand XML data in the same way that it understands integer or string data. The XML data type lets you create tables that store only XML or store both XML and relational data. This flexibility lets you make the best use of the relational model for structured data and enhance that data with XML's semistructured data. When you store XML values natively in an XML data type column, you have two options:

- **Typed Column:** XML data stored in this kind of column is validated using a collection of XML schemas.
- **Untyped Column:** In this kind of column, you can insert any kind of XML data as long as the XML is well formed.

> **To help you get the most out of this combination of semi-structured and relational data, the native SQL Server 2005 XML data type supports several built-in methods that let you query and modify the XML data. These methods accept XQuery, an emerging World Wide Web Consortium (W3C) standard language, and include the navigational language XPath 2.0 along with a language for modifying XML data. You can combine query calls to the XML data type methods with standard T-SQL to create queries that return both relational and XML data.**

In addition to the `XML` data type, `FOR XML` and `OpenXML` features have also been extended in SQL Server 2005. These features combined with the support for XQuery, SQL Server 2005 provide a powerful platform for developing rich applications for semistructured and unstructured data management. With all the added functionality, the users have more design choices for their data storage and application development. To start with, the next section examines the `FOR XML` feature in SQL Server 2005.

FOR XML in SQL Server 2005

SQL Server 2000 introduced the `FOR XML` clause to the `SELECT` statement, and the `FOR XML` clause provided the ability to aggregate the relational rowset returned by the `SELECT` statement into XML. `FOR XML` on the server supports three modes, shown below, and these modes provide different transformation semantics:

- **RAW:** The RAW mode generates single elements, which are named row, for each row returned.
- **AUTO:** This mode infers a simple, one element name-per-level hierarchy based on the lineage information and the order of the data in a `SELECT` statement.
- **EXPLICIT:** This mode requires a specific rowset format that can be mapped into almost any XML shape, while still being formulated by a single SQL query.

All three modes are designed to generate the XML in a streamable way in order to be able to produce large documents efficiently. Although the EXPLICIT mode format is highly successful in achieving its goals, the SQL expression required to generate the rowset format is quite complex. Now with SQL Server 2005, the complexities associated with `FOR XML` modes have been simplified to a great extent. In addition to that, the `FOR XML` queries have also been integrated with the `XML` data type.

If you execute an XML query of any type (for example, `SELECT * FROM HumanResources.Employee FOR XML AUTO`*), you will notice that the results shown in SQL Server Management Studio look very similar to the XML results in SQL Server 2000 Query Analyzer, except for the difference that the results are underlined now, meaning that you can click them now. Clicking on the results will result in a nice XML view for you to look at your XML results.*

The next few sections will provide an overview of the new extensions added to `FOR XML` clause in SQL Server 2005.

Integration with XML Data Type

With the introduction of the `XML` data type, the `FOR XML` clause now provides the ability to generate an instance of XML directly using the new `TYPE` directive. For example, the following query returns the `Employee` elements as an `XML` data type instance, instead of the `nvarchar(max)` instance that would have been the case without the `TYPE` directive:

```
SELECT * FROM HumanResources.Employee as Employee FOR XML AUTO, TYPE
```

This result is guaranteed to conform to the well-formedness constraints provided by the `XML` data type. Since the result is an `XML` data type instance, you can also use XQuery expressions to query and reshape the result. For example, the following expression retrieves the employee title into a new element:

```
SELECT (SELECT * FROM HumanResources.Employee as Employee
FOR XML AUTO, TYPE).query(
'<Output>{
    for $c in /Employee
     return <Employee name="{data($c/@Title)}"/>
  }</Output>')
```

The previous query will produce the following output:

```
<Output>
  <Employee name="Production Technician - WC60" />
  <Employee name="Marketing Assistant" />
  <Employee name="Engineering Manager" />
  ------
  ------
</Output>
```

Assigning FOR XML Results

Since `FOR XML` queries now return assignable values, the result of a `FOR XML` query can be assigned to an `XML` variable, or inserted into an XML column:

```
/* Assign the output of FOR XML to a variable */
DECLARE @Employee XML;
SET @Employee = (SELECT * FROM HumanResources.Employee FOR XML AUTO, TYPE)
CREATE TABLE Employee_New (EmployeeID int, XmlData XML)
/* Assign the output of FOR XML to a column*/
INSERT INTO Employee_New SELECT 1, @Employee
```

In these statements, you retrieve the results of the `FOR XML` query into an `XML` data-typed variable, and utilize that variable to insert values into a table named Employee_New.

Executing FOR XML Queries from ADO.NET

To return an XML stream directly from SQL Server through the `FOR XML` query, you need to leverage the `ExecuteXmlReader()` method of the `SqlCommand` object. The `ExecuteXmlReader()` method returns an `XmlReader` object populated with the results of the query specified for a `SqlCommand`. Listing 14-3 shows you an example of `ExecuteXmlReader()` in action by querying the DatabaseLog table in the AdventureWorks database.

Listing 14-3: Executing a FOR XML Query Using the ExecuteXmlReader Method

```
<%@ Page Language="C#" ValidateRequest="false" %>
<%@ Import Namespace="System.Data" %>
<%@ Import Namespace="System.Data.SqlClient" %>
<%@ Import Namespace="System.Data.Sql" %>
<%@ Import Namespace="System.Xml" %>
<%@ Import Namespace="System.Web.Configuration" %>
<%@ Import Namespace="System.Data.SqlTypes" %>
<script runat="server">
  void btnReadXml_Click(object sender, EventArgs e)
  {
    int ID = Convert.ToInt32(txtID.Text);
    //Get the connection string from the web.config file
    string connectionString = WebConfigurationManager.ConnectionStrings
      ["AdventureWorks"].ConnectionString;
    using (SqlConnection connection = new SqlConnection(connectionString))
    {
      System.Text.StringBuilder builder = new System.Text.StringBuilder();
      connection.Open();
      SqlCommand command = connection.CreateCommand();
      command.CommandText = "SELECT DatabaseLogID, XmlEvent FROM " +
        " DatabaseLog WHERE DatabaseLogID = " + ID.ToString() +
        " FOR XML AUTO, ROOT('DatabaseLogs'), ELEMENTS";
      XmlReader reader = command.ExecuteXmlReader();
      XmlDocument doc = new XmlDocument();
      //Load the XmlReader to an XmlDocument object
      doc.Load(reader);
      builder.Append("<b>Complete XML :</b>" +
        Server.HtmlEncode(doc.OuterXml) + "<br><br>");
      //Retrieve the DatabaseLogID and XmlEvent column values
      string idValue = doc.DocumentElement.SelectSingleNode
        ("DatabaseLog/DatabaseLogID").InnerText;
      builder.Append("<b>id :</b>" + Server.HtmlEncode(idValue) + "<br><br>");
      string xmlEventValue = doc.DocumentElement.SelectSingleNode
        ("DatabaseLog/XmlEvent").OuterXml;
      builder.Append("<b>XmlEvent :</b>" + Server.HtmlEncode(xmlEventValue) +
        "<br>");
      output.Text = builder.ToString();
    }
  }
</script>
<html xmlns="http://www.w3.org/1999/xhtml" >
<head id="Head1" runat="server">
  <title>Executing a FOR XML Query from ADO.NET</title>
</head>
```

```
<body>
  <form id="form1" runat="server">
    <div>
      <asp:Label ID="lblID" Runat="server" Text="Enter ID:"></asp:Label>
      <asp:TextBox ID="txtID" Runat="server"></asp:TextBox>
      <asp:Button ID="btnReadXml" Runat="server" Text="Read Xml"
        Width="118px" Height="30px" OnClick="btnReadXml_Click" />
      <br/><br/><br/>
      <asp:Literal runat="server" ID="output" />
    </div>
  </form>
</body>
</html>
```

Listing 14-3 starts by opening the connection to the database passing in the connection string as an argument:

```
using (SqlConnection connection = new SqlConnection(connectionString))
```

After that, you create an instance of the `SqlCommand` object and set its properties:

```
SqlCommand command = connection.CreateCommand();
command.CommandText = "SELECT DatabaseLogID, XmlEvent FROM " +
  " DatabaseLog WHERE DatabaseLogID = " + ID.ToString() +
  " FOR XML AUTO, ROOT('DatabaseLogs'), ELEMENTS";
```

Now you execute the actual query by calling the `ExecuteXmlReader()` method on the `SqlCommand` object:

```
XmlReader reader = command.ExecuteXmlReader();
```

Then you load the `XmlReader` object onto an `XmlDocument` for further processing:

```
XmlDocument doc = new XmlDocument();
//Load the XmlReader to an XmlDocument object
doc.Load(reader);
```

Once the XML is loaded into an `XmlDocument`, then the Complete XML, DatabaseLogID, and XmlEvent column values are displayed in a sequence. Figure 14-5 shows the resultant output.

In Figure 14-5, the first line displays the entire XML output produced by the `FOR XML` query, and the second and third lines display the values of the DatabaseLogID and XmlEvent columns, respectively. Since the XmlEvent column is an `XML` data-typed column, you see the XML output directly being displayed by the XmlEvent column.

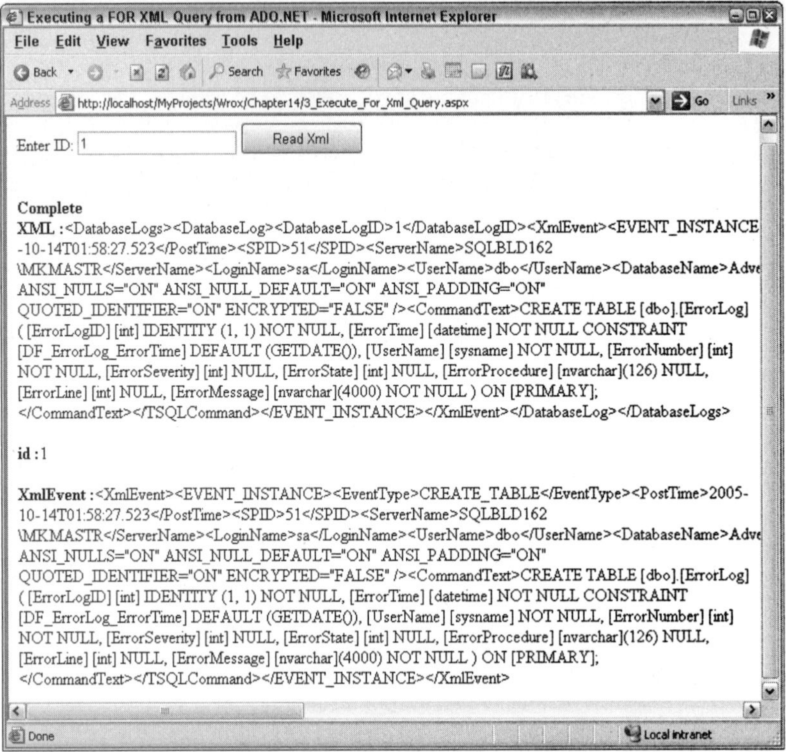

Figure 14-5

Asynchronous Execution of FOR XML Query

In the previous section, you saw how to synchronously execute a `FOR XML` query using the `ExecuteXml Reader()` method. Although this approach works, there are times when you might want to execute the query asynchronously for scalability and throughput reasons. Fortunately, ADO.NET 2.0 comes shipped with a new feature that provides for asynchronous execution of SQL commands. Using this new feature, you can now asynchronously execute commands against a SQL Server database without waiting for the command execution to finish. This feature can be very handy in situations where you execute long-running database commands from a client application, such as a Windows Forms application or an ASP.NET application. By doing this, you improve the overall performance and responsiveness of your application. The next section will explore the execution of a `FOR XML` query using the asynchronous features of ADO.NET 2.0.

Steps Involved in Asynchronous Execution of FOR XML Queries

Chapter 13 outlined the differences between synchronous and asynchronous execution of commands in the context of retrieving a `SqlDataReader` object. This chapter will focus on the asynchronous execution of an `ExecuteXmlReader()` method that returns an `XmlReader` object.

As mentioned in Chapter 13, the asynchronous execution requires that the corresponding method has both `BeginXXX` and `EndXXX` variations. The `BeginXXX` method initiates an asynchronous operation and returns immediately, returning a reference to an object that implements the `IAsyncResult` interface. Your client code will need to access that interface to monitor the progress of the asynchronous operation. When the asynchronous operation is completed, you call the `EndXXX` method to obtain the result and clean up any supporting resources that were utilized to support the asynchronous call.

There are four common ways to use `BeginXXX` and `EndXXX` to make asynchronous calls. In all cases, you invoke `BeginXXX` to initiate the call. After that, you can do one of the following:

- Do some work and then call `EndXXX`. If the asynchronous operation is not finished, `EndXXX` will block until it is completed.
- Using a `WaitHandle` obtained from the `IAsyncResult.AsyncWaitHandle` property, call the `WaitOne()` method to block until the operation completes. Then call `EndXXX`.
- Poll the `IAsynResult.IsCompleted` property to determine when the asynchronous operation has been completed. Then call `EndXXX`.
- Pass a delegate for a callback function that you supply (of type `IAsyncCallback`) to `BeginXXX`. That callback function will execute when the asynchronous operation is completed. Code in the callback function calls `EndXXX` to retrieve the result.

Listing 14-4 will demonstrate the use of `WaitHandle` to retrieve the results of the asynchronous query execution.

Listing 14-4: Asynchronously Executing the FOR XML Query

```
<%@ Page Language="C#" ValidateRequest="false" %>
<%@ Import Namespace="System.Data" %>
<%@ Import Namespace="System.Data.SqlClient" %>
<%@ Import Namespace="System.Threading" %>
<%@ Import Namespace="System.Xml" %>
<%@ Import Namespace="System.Web.Configuration" %>
<%@ Import Namespace="System.Data.SqlTypes" %>
<script runat="server">
  void btnRetrieve_Click(object sender, EventArgs e)
  {
    int ID = Convert.ToInt32(txtID.Text);
    string connectionString = WebConfigurationManager.ConnectionStrings
      ["AdventureWorks"].ConnectionString;
    using (SqlConnection connection = new SqlConnection(connectionString))
    {
      connection.Open();
      SqlCommand command = connection.CreateCommand();
      command.CommandText = "SELECT DatabaseLogID, XmlEvent " +
        "FROM DatabaseLog WHERE DatabaseLogID = " +  ID.ToString() +
        " FOR XML AUTO, ROOT('DatabaseLogs'), ELEMENTS";
      IAsyncResult asyncResult = command.BeginExecuteXmlReader();
      //Do some other processing here
      asyncResult.AsyncWaitHandle.WaitOne();
      XmlReader reader = command.EndExecuteXmlReader(asyncResult);
      XmlDocument doc = new XmlDocument();
```

(continued)

Listing 14-4: *(continued)*

```
            //Load the XmlReader to an XmlDocument object
            doc.Load(reader);
            output.Text = "XML : " + Server.HtmlEncode(doc.OuterXml);
        }
    }
</script>
<html xmlns="http://www.w3.org/1999/xhtml" >
<head id="Head1" runat="server">
  <title>
    Asynchronously executing a FOR XML Query using ExecuteXmlReader
  </title>
</head>
<body>
  <form id="form1" runat="server">
    <div>
      <asp:Label ID="lblID" Runat="server" Text="Enter ID:"></asp:Label>
      <asp:TextBox ID="txtID" Runat="server"></asp:TextBox>
      <asp:Button ID="btnRetrieve" Runat="server" Text="Retrieve Xml"
        OnClick="btnRetrieve_Click" />
      <br/><br/><br/>
      <asp:Literal runat="server" ID="output" />
    </div>
  </form>
</body>
</html>
```

Note that the connection string used in the `Web.config` file has a new attribute named `Asynchronous Processing`, which is set to `true`:

```
<connectionStrings>
  <add name="AdventureWorks" connectionString="server=localhost;
    database=AdventureWorks;uid=sa;pwd=thiru;Asynchronous Processing=true;"/>
</connectionStrings>
```

In Listing 14-4, you create instances of `SqlConnection` and `SqlCommand` objects and set their properties to appropriate values. After that, you invoke the `BeginExecuteXmlReader()` method of the `SqlCommand` objects and assign the returned `IAsyncResult` object to a local variable for later use:

```
IAsyncResult asyncResult = command.BeginExecuteXmlReader();
```

Next, you call the `WaitOne()` method of the `WaitHandle` object to wait for the query execution to finish. Note that before you invoke the `WaitOne()` method, you are free to do other processing.

```
//Do some other processing here
asyncResult.AsyncWaitHandle.WaitOne();
```

Note that the `WaitOne()` method is a blocking call, meaning that it will not return till the query execution is complete. Finally, you retrieve the results of the query by calling the `EndExecuteXmlReader()` method, passing in the `IAsyncResult` object as an argument:

```
XmlReader reader = command.EndExecuteXmlReader(asyncResult);
```

Next, you load the returned `XmlReader` into an `XmlDocument` object and display the output:

```
XmlDocument doc = new XmlDocument();
//Load the XmlReader to an XmlDocument object
doc.Load(reader);
output.Text = "XML : " + Server.HtmlEncode(doc.OuterXml);
```

The output produced by the above page is shown in Figure 14-6.

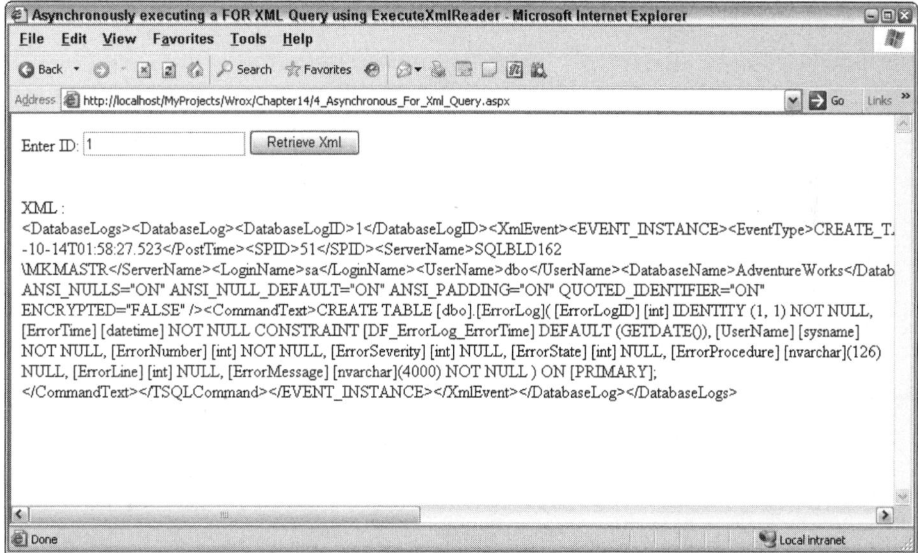

Figure 14-6

> **Listing 14-4 uses the `WaitHandle` object's `WaitOne()` method to wait for the command execution to complete. The `WaitHandle` class also contains other static methods such as `WaitAll()` and `WaitAny()`. These static methods take arrays of `WaitHandle` objects as parameters, and return either when all the calls have been completed or as soon as any of the calls has completed, depending on the method that you call. For example, if you are making three separate command execution calls, you can call each asynchronously; place the `WaitHandle` for each in an array, then call the `WaitAll` method until they are finished. Doing that lets all three commands execute at the same time. It is also important to note that the `WaitOne()`, `WaitAll()`, and `WaitAny()` methods optionally accept a timeout parameter value. Using the timeout option, you can specify the amount of time that you want to wait for a command to return. If the methods time out, they will return a value of `False`.**

XML Data Type in SQL Server 2005

The SQL Server 2005 `XML` data type implements the ISO SQL-2003 standard `XML` data type. In an `XML` data-typed column, you can store both well-formed XML 1.0 documents and XML content fragments with text nodes. Moreover, you can also store an arbitrary number of top-level elements in an untyped XML column. At the time of inserting the XML data, the system checks for the well-formedness of the data and rejects data that is not well-formed in the extended sense. The extent of the server-side validation depends on if an XSD schema is associated with the `XML` data type column. Before looking at the XSD schemas and their role in an XML column, you need to understand the reasons for storing native XML data in an `XML` data type column. Storing XML data in an `XML` data type column can be extremely useful in following situations:

- By storing XML data in the SQL Server, you have a straightforward way of storing your XML data at the server, while preserving document order and document structure.
- When you want the ability to query and modify your XML data.
- When you want to exchange data with external systems without performing a lot of transformations.
- When you have XML documents with a wide range of structures, or XML documents conforming to different or complex schemas that are too hard to map to relational structures.

> **SQL Server 2005 stores XML data as Unicode (UTF-16). XML data retrieved from the server comes out in UTF-16 encoding as well. If you want a different encoding, you need to perform the necessary conversion after retrieving the data either by casting or on the mid-tier. For example, you may cast your XML data to varchar type on the server, in which case the database engine serializes the XML with an encoding determined by the collation of the varchar.**

Typed versus Untyped XML Columns

For more structure or validation of XML data, SQL Server lets you associate schema with a particular XML column. This column is named typed XML column. If an XML schema is associated with an XML column, the schema validates the XML data at the time of inserting the XML data into the field. SQL Server 2005 supports many schemas grouped together in a schema collection, which lets you apply different schemas to an XML column. The server will validate all incoming XML against all the schemas. If the XML is valid for any of the collection's schemas, it can be stored in the XML field. The following table summarizes the differences between a typed XML column and an untyped XML column.

Characteristics	Untyped Column	Typed Column
Presence of schema	No schema to validate your XML data.	The typed column is associated with an XML schema.
Validation location	Since there is no schema on the server side, XML validation needs to be performed on the client side.	Validation is automatically performed on the server at the time of inserting the XML data.

Characteristics	Untyped Column	Typed Column
Query optimization	Not possible because of lack of type information.	Allows you to take advantage of storage and query optimizations based on type information.
Constraint for one top-level element	Not possible.	You can constrain a typed column to allow only one top-level element, using the optional `DOCUMENT` keyword.

In addition to typing an XML column, you can use relational (column or row) constraints on typed or untyped `XML` data type columns.

Untyped XML Columns

Untyped XML is useful when the schema is not known prior, so that a mapping-based solution is not possible. It is also useful when the schema is known but mapping to relational data model is very complex and hard to maintain, or multiple schemas exist and are late bound to the data based on external requirements. The following statement creates a table called Customer in the AdventureWorks with an integer primary key ID and an untyped XML column XmlData:

```
Use AdventureWorks
CREATE TABLE Customer(ID int primary key, XmlData xml)
```

The Customer table that is created in the AdventureWorks database will be used throughout this chapter. To insert values into the above table, use the following T-SQL statement.

```
INSERT INTO Customer values(2, '<customer id="2"><name>Joe</name></customer>')
```

Note that you can also create a table with more than one XML or relational column with or without a primary key.

Typed XML Columns

If you have XML schemas in an XML schema collection describing your XML data, you can associate the XML schema collection with the XML column to yield typed XML. The XML schemas are used to validate the data, perform more precise type checks than untyped XML during compilation of query and data modification statements, and optimize storage and query processing.

XML Schema Collections

As mentioned before, support for typed XML columns is enabled by using XML schema collections in SQL Server. XML schema collections are defined like any other SQL Server object, and they are stored in SQL Server. An XML schema collection is created using a `CREATE XML SCHEMA COLLECTION` T-SQL statement by providing one or more XML schemas. More XML schema components can be added to an existing XML schema, and more schemas can be added to an XML schema collection using `ALTER XML`

SCHEMA COLLECTION syntax. XML schema collections can be secured like any SQL object using SQL Server 2005's security model. The syntax for the T-SQL DDL CREATE XML SCHEMA COLLECTION statement is:

```
CREATE XML SCHEMA COLLECTION <Schema_Name>
AS
  -- Specify the schema contents here
GO
```

For example, to create a schema named CustomerSchema, use the following command:

```
Create xml schema collection CustomerSchema as
  N'<xs:schema xmlns:xs="http://www.w3.org/2001/XMLSchema"
  xmlns:company="http://www.wrox.com/books"
  targetNamespace="http://www.wrox.com/books"
  elementFormDefault="qualified">
  <xs:element name="customer">
    <xs:complexType>
      <xs:all>
        <xs:element name="name" type="xs:string" />
      </xs:all>
      <xs:attribute name="id" type="xs:int" />
    </xs:complexType>
  </xs:element>
</xs:schema>'
```

In addition to using the XML schema collection to type XML columns, you can also leverage that to type XML variables and parameters.

Associating Schemas with an XML Column

Once the CustomerSchema is created, you can then easily associate that with the XmlData column of the Customer table by using the following syntax:

```
CREATE TABLE Customer(ID int primary key,
  XmlData XML(CustomerSchema))
```

Now when you insert values into the Customer table, the XML data for the XmlData column is validated against the CustomerSchema:

```
Insert into Customer values(1, '<customer id="1"
  xmlns="http://www.wrox.com/books"><name>Joe</name></customer>')
GO
Insert into Customer values(2, '<customer id="2"
  xmlns="http://www.wrox.com/books"><name>Fred</name></customer>')
```

At the time of associating the schema to the XML column, you can use the DOCUMENT or CONTENT flags to specify whether XML trees or fragments can be stored in a typed column. For DOCUMENT, each XML instance specifies the target namespace of its top-level element in the instance, according to which it is validated and typed. For CONTENT, on the other hand, each top-level element can specify any one of the target namespaces in the schema collection. The XML instance is validated and typed according to all the target namespaces occurring in an instance. Say, for example, you execute the following SQL statement that contains invalid namespace declaration:

```
Insert into Customer values(3, '<customer id="3"
xmlns="http://invalidnamespace/books"><name>InvalidData</name></customer>')
GO
```

You should see an error message similar to the following as a result of the invalid namespace in the Insert statement:

```
Msg 6913, Level 16, State 1, Line 1
XML Validation: Declaration not found for element
'http://invalidnamespace/books:customer'. Location: /*:customer[1]
```

Inserting Data into an XML Data-Typed Column

Irrespective of whether the XML column is typed or not typed, you can supply the value for an XML column in the following ways:

- As a character or binary SQL type that is implicitly converted to `XML` data type
- As the content of a file
- As the output of the `FOR XML` with the `TYPE` directive that generates an `XML` data type instance

The supplied value is checked for well-formedness and allows both XML documents and XML fragments to be stored. If the data fails the well-formedness check, it is rejected with an appropriate error message. For typed XML, the supplied value is checked for conformance to XML schemas registered with the XML schema collection typing the XML column. The XML instance is rejected if it fails this validation. Take a look at some examples of the different ways of inserting values into an XML column.

To start with, the following statement inserts a new row into the Customer table with the value 1 for the integer column ID and a `<customer>` instance for the XmlData column. The `<customer>` data, supplied as a string, is implicitly converted to the `XML` data type and checked for well-formedness during insertion:

```
INSERT INTO Customer values (2, '<customer id="2"
xmlns="http://www.wrox.com/books"><name>Joe</name></customer>')
```

As mentioned previously, it is also possible to utilize the contents of an XML file as an input to the `Insert` command. Consider the following XML document stored in a file called Customer.xml:

```
<customer id="6" xmlns="http://www.wrox.com/books">
  <name>Dave</name>
</customer>
```

Now if you execute the following T-SQL command, you will see the contents of the `Customer.xml` file being loaded into the XmlData column:

```
INSERT INTO Customer SELECT 7, xml_value FROM
  (SELECT * FROM OPENROWSET (BULK 'C:\Data\Customer.xml',
  SINGLE_BLOB) AS xml_value) AS R(xml_value)
```

The third option is to utilize the output of the FOR XML with the TYPE directive as an input to the insert command. With SQL Server 2005, FOR XML has been enhanced with a TYPE directive to generate the result as an XML data type instance. The resulting XML can be assigned to an XML column, variable, or parameter. In the following statement, the XML instance generated using FOR XML TYPE is assigned to an XML data type variable @var. Then the variable is used in the INSERT statement:

```
DECLARE @var xml
SET @var = (SELECT XmlData FROM Customer FOR XML AUTO,TYPE)
--Insert the value of the variable into a new table named CustomerOutput
CREATE TABLE CustomerOutput (XmlData xml)
INSERT INTO CustomerOutput (XmlData) VALUES (@var)
```

XML Data Type Methods

Although the XML data type is a built-in data type, it also functions like a user-defined data type (UDT) by providing several methods that let you query and update data stored in an XML variable or column. You can use these methods to query, obtain scalar values from, and modify an XML document that's stored in a variable, column, or parameter. The following table lists the XML data type methods.

Method	Description
Query	Allows you to specify an XQuery against an instance of the XML data type. The method returns an instance of untyped XML and the result type is XML.
Value	Allows you to execute an XQuery against the XML and returns a value of sql type that is supplied in the second parameter. This method returns a scalar value.
Exist	This method allows you to determine if a query returns a nonempty result set.
Modify	Allows you to execute XML DML (Data Manipulation Language) statements against an XML data type column.
Nodes	Allows you to shred an XML into multiple rows to propagate parts of XML documents into row sets.

What Is XQuery?

XQuery is a query language that lets you retrieve data items from XML-formatted documents. The language is not "complete"—it is still a work in progress under the auspices of the W3C's XML Query working group. The current implementation of XQuery in SQL Server 2005 is based on the June 2004 working drafts of the W3C XQuery language. Because the W3C specifications may undergo future revisions before becoming a W3C recommendation, the SQL Server 2005 implementation may differ from the final recommendation.

Indexing XML Columns

XML indexes can be created on `XML` data type columns. It indexes all tags, values, and paths over the XML instances in the column and can result in improved query performance. XML indexing can be very useful in the following scenarios:

- When there is a need to frequently execute queries on XML columns.
- When the values you retrieve from XML values are relatively small compared to the size of the XML column itself. By indexing that XML column, you can avoid parsing the whole data at run-time and be benefited by index lookups for efficient query processing.

There are two types of indexes that can be created on an XML column. They are primary XML index and secondary XML index. As the name suggests, the first index on an XML column is the primary XML index. Using it, three types of secondary XML indexes can be created on the XML column to speed up common classes of queries.

Primary XML Index

This indexes all tags, values, and paths within the XML instances in an XML column. The base table (for example, the table in which the XML column occurs) must have a clustered index on the primary key of the table. The primary key is used to correlate index rows with the rows in the base table. The following statement creates a primary XML index called `idx_xml_data` on the XML column XmlData of the table Customer:

```
CREATE PRIMARY XML INDEX idx_xml_data on Customer(XmlData)
```

Secondary XML Indexes

Once the primary XML index has been created, you may want to create secondary XML indexes to speed up different classes of queries within your workload. There are three types of secondary XML indexes named `PATH`, `PROPERTY`, and `VALUE` that can benefit path-based queries, custom property management scenarios, and value-based queries, respectively.

The `PATH` index builds a B+-tree on the (path, value) pair of each XML node in document order over all XML instances in the column. The `PROPERTY` index creates a B+-tree clustered on the (PK, path, value) pair within each XML instance, where PK is the primary key of the base table. Finally, the `VALUE` index creates a B+-tree on the (value, path) pair of each node in document order across all XML instances in the XML column.

If your workload uses path expressions heavily on XML columns, the `PATH` secondary XML index is likely to speed up your workload. If your workload retrieves multiple values from individual XML instances using path expressions, clustering paths within each XML instance in the `PROPERTY` index may be helpful. If your workload involves querying for values within XML instances without knowing the element or attribute names that contain those values, you may want to create the `VALUE` index.

To create a PATH index on the XmlData column, use the following command:

```
CREATE XML INDEX idx_xml_data_path on Customer (XmlData)
  USING XML INDEX idx_xml_data FOR PATH
```

Working with XML Data-Typed Columns from ADO.NET

You get your first indication that XML is now a first-class relational database type by referencing the relational data type enumerations in ADO.NET 2.0. `System.Data.DbType` and `System.Data.SqlDbType` contain additional values for `DbType.Xml` and `SqlDbType.Xml`, respectively. There is also a new class called `SqlXml` that is contained in the `System.Data.SqlTypes` namespace, and this class acts as a factory class for creating `XmlReader` instances on top of the XML type value.

You can access the XML columns either using in-proc access from within SQL Server 2005 itself or using ADO.NET from your client applications. To start with, let us look at the in-proc access.

In-Process Access to the XML Data Type Column

As mentioned, the integration of CLR with SQL Server 2005 extends the capability of SQL Server in several important ways. In previous versions of SQL Server, database programmers were limited to using T-SQL when writing code on the server side. With CLR integration, database developers can now perform tasks that were impossible or difficult to achieve with Transact-SQL alone. Both Visual Basic .NET and C# are modern programming languages offering full support for arrays, structured exception handling, and collections. Developers can leverage CLR integration to write code that has more complex logic and is more suited for computation tasks using languages such as VB.NET and C#. Both VB.NET and C# offer object-oriented capabilities such as encapsulation, inheritance, and polymorphism.

For the purposes of this example, consider the Customer table that has been used in the previous examples:

```
CREATE TABLE Customer (ID int primary key, XmlData xml(CustomerSchema))
```

Listing 14-5 illustrates how the XmlData column (which is an `XML` data-typed column) can be accessed from the in-proc provider. For out-of-proc access, a new connection to the database must be established.

Listing 14-5: Accessing an XML Data Type Column Using In-Proc

```
using System;
using System.Data;
using System.Data.SqlClient;
using System.Data.SqlTypes;
using Microsoft.SqlServer.Server;

public partial class StoredProcedures
{
  [Microsoft.SqlServer.Server.SqlProcedure]
  public static void GetCustomerNameByID(int id)
  {
```

```
        string retValue = "";
        using (SqlConnection connection = new
          SqlConnection("context connection=true"))
        {
          connection.Open();
          //Prepare query to select xml data
          SqlCommand command = connection.CreateCommand();
          string sql = "SELECT XmlData.query " +
            "('declare namespace ns=\"http://www.wrox.com/books\";" +
            " <Customer Name=\"{/ns:customer/ns:name}\"/>') as Result " +
            " FROM Customer WHERE ID = " + id.ToString();
          command.CommandText = sql;
          //Execute query and retrieve incoming data
          SqlDataReader reader = command.ExecuteReader();
          if (reader.Read())
          {
            //Get the XML value as string
            retValue = (string)reader.GetValue(0);
          }
          else
            retValue = "No Value";
        }
        //Send the output XML back to the caller
        SqlContext.Pipe.Send(retValue);
      }
    };
```

To start with, you import the `Microsoft.SqlServer.Server` namespace so that you can access the types in the in-proc provider. Next, the function is decorated with the `[SqlProcedure]` custom attribute, which is found in the `Microsoft.SqlServer.Server` namespace. On the next line, the stored procedure is declared as a public static method:

```
[Microsoft.SqlServer.Server.SqlProcedure]
public static void GetCustomerNameByID(int id)
```

Then you establish connection to the database by creating an instance of the `SqlConnection` object passing in the appropriate connection string. Note that the connection string passed to the constructor of the `SqlConnection` object is set to `"context connection=true"`, meaning that you want to use the context of the logged-on user to open the connection to the database:

```
using (SqlConnection connection = new
  SqlConnection("context connection=true"))
```

Next you create an instance of the `SqlCommand` object and set its properties appropriately:

```
SqlCommand command = connection.CreateCommand();
string sql = "SELECT XmlData.query " +
  "('declare namespace ns=\"http://www.wrox.com/books\";" +
  " <Customer Name=\"{/ns:customer/ns:name}\"/>') as Result " +
  " FROM Customer WHERE id = " + id.ToString();
command.CommandText = sql;
```

Then you execute the SQL statement by calling the `ExecuteReader()` method of the `SqlCommand` object, and then return the output of the SQL statement directly to the caller:

```
SqlContext.Pipe.Send(retValue);
```

If you are creating this procedure using Visual Studio 2005, you can deploy it with the click of a button. To this end, first build the solution using the Build ➪ Build Solution menu. After that, deploy the stored procedure to SQL Server 2005 using the Build ➪ Deploy Solution menu option.

Now if you execute the stored procedure using the following command in SQL Server Management Studio:

```
exec dbo.GetCustomerNameByID 2
```

you should see the following output:

```
<Customer Name="Fred" />
```

Retrieving the XML Data-Typed Column from the Client

This section focuses on out of process access to the `XML` data-typed column from an ASP.NET page. There are different ways you can retrieve an `XML` data-typed column using a `SqlDataReader` object. Using the methods of the `SqlDataReader` class, you can retrieve the XML data either as a string or as an `SqlXml` object. The next section starts by exploring the steps involved in retrieving the contents of an XML column as a string.

Retrieving the XML Data Type Column as a String

Listing 14-6 retrieves the contents of the XML column as a string value from a client ASP.NET page. To this end, it executes a simple SELECT statement to retrieve the contents of the XmlData column based on the supplied ID value. Finally, it displays the retrieved XML data as a string value in a text box.

Listing 14-6: Retrieving an XML Data Type Column as a String

```
<%@ Page Language="C#" ValidateRequest="false" %>
<%@ Import Namespace="System.Data" %>
<%@ Import Namespace="System.Data.SqlClient" %>
<%@ Import Namespace="System.Data.Sql" %>
<%@ Import Namespace="System.Web.Configuration" %>
<script runat="server">
  void btnReadXml_Click(object sender, EventArgs e)
  {
    int ID = Convert.ToInt32(txtID.Text);
    //Get the connection string from the web.config file
    string connectionString = WebConfigurationManager.ConnectionStrings
      ["AdventureWorks"].ConnectionString;
    using (SqlConnection connection = new SqlConnection(connectionString))
    {
      connection.Open();
      SqlCommand command = connection.CreateCommand();
      command.CommandText = "SELECT XmlData FROM Customer WHERE ID = " +
        ID.ToString();
      SqlDataReader reader = command.ExecuteReader();
      if (reader.Read())
```

```
        {
          //Get the XML value as string
          string xmlValue = (string)reader.GetValue(0);
          txtXmlData.Text = xmlValue;
        }
        else
          txtXmlData.Text = "No Value";
      }
    }
</script>
<html xmlns="http://www.w3.org/1999/xhtml" >
<head id="Head1" runat="server">
  <title>Retrieving an XML data type column as a String</title>
</head>
<body>
  <form id="form1" runat="server">
    <div>
      <asp:Label ID="lblID" Runat="server" Text="ID:"></asp:Label>
      <asp:TextBox ID="txtID" Runat="server"></asp:TextBox>
      <asp:Button ID="btnReadXml" Runat="server" Text="Read Xml"
        Width="118px" Height="30px" OnClick="btnReadXml_Click" />
      <br/><br/><br/>
      <asp:Label ID="lblXmlData" Runat="server" Text="XML:"
        Width="134px" Height="19px"></asp:Label>
      <asp:TextBox ID="txtXmlData" Runat="server" Width="398px"
        Height="123px" TextMode="MultiLine"></asp:TextBox>
    </div>
  </form>
</body>
</html>
```

In this example, you execute the simple `select` query through a call to the `ExecuteReader()` method. Once the results are available in the `SqlDataReader` object, you then retrieve the XML column value as a string, using the `GetValue()`. Figure 14-7 shows the output produced by requesting the page from a browser.

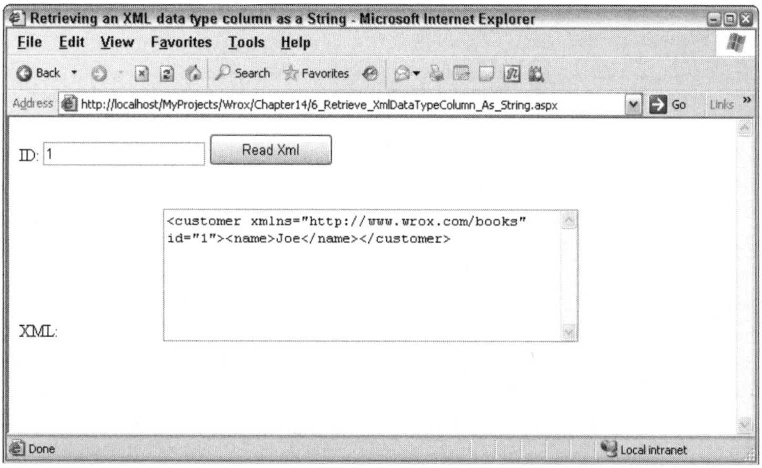

Figure 14-7

Now that you have seen how easy it is to extract the contents of an XML data type column as a string value, the next section focuses on the steps required to extract the output as a SqlXml object.

Retrieving the XML Data Type Column as a SqlXml Object

Before looking at the use of SqlXml object, it is important to get an overview of the properties and methods supported by the SqlXml object. As mentioned previously, the SqlXml class is a new class introduced with ADO.NET 2.0, and it represents the XML data retrieved from a database server. The SqlXml class is exposed by the System.Data.SqlTypes namespace. The following table discusses the properties of the SqlXml class that you will most likely have to work with.

Property	Description
IsNull	Returns a Boolean indicating if this instance represents a null SqlXml value
Null	Represents a null instance of the SqlXml type
Value	Returns the string representation of the XML content contained in the SqlXml instance

The next table discusses the methods of the SqlXml class.

Method	Description
CreateReader	Factory method that gets the value of the XML content of the SqlXml object as an XmlReader
GetXsdType	Static method that returns a string that indicates the XSD of the specified XmlSchemaSet

Now that you have had a brief overview of the SqlXml class, it is time for an example. Listing 14-7 shows how the GetSqlXml() method of the SqlDataReader can be used to get reference to a SqlXml object. Subsequently, it also discusses how to create an instance of the XmlReader object using the CreateReader() method of the SqlXml class.

Listing 14-7: Accessing an XML Data Type Column as a SqlXml Object

```
<%@ Page Language="C#" ValidateRequest="false" %>
<%@ Import Namespace="System.Data" %>
<%@ Import Namespace="System.Data.SqlClient" %>
<%@ Import Namespace="System.Data.Sql" %>
<%@ Import Namespace="System.Xml" %>
<%@ Import Namespace="System.Web.Configuration" %>
<%@ Import Namespace="System.Data.SqlTypes" %>
<script runat="server">
  void btnGetXml_Click(object sender, EventArgs e)
  {
    int ID = Convert.ToInt32(txtID.Text);
    //Get the connection string from the web.config file
```

```
      string connectionString = WebConfigurationManager.ConnectionStrings
        ["AdventureWorks"].ConnectionString;
      using (SqlConnection connection = new SqlConnection(connectionString))
      {
        connection.Open();
        SqlCommand command = connection.CreateCommand();
        command.CommandText = "SELECT XmlData FROM Customer WHERE ID = " +
          ID.ToString();
        SqlDataReader reader = command.ExecuteReader();
        if (reader.Read())
        {
          SqlXml sqlXmlValue = reader.GetSqlXml(0);
          XmlReader xmlReader = sqlXmlValue.CreateReader();
          if (xmlReader.Read())
            output.Text = Server.HtmlEncode(xmlReader.ReadOuterXml());
        }
        else
          output.Text = "No Value";
      }
    }
  </script>
  <html xmlns="http://www.w3.org/1999/xhtml" >
  <head id="Head1" runat="server">
    <title>Accessing an XML data type column as an SqlXml object</title>
  </head>
  <body>
    <form id="form1" runat="server">
      <div>
        <asp:Label ID="lblID" Runat="server" Text="Enter ID:"></asp:Label>
        <asp:TextBox ID="txtID" Runat="server"></asp:TextBox>
        <asp:Button ID="btnReadXml" Runat="server" Text="Read Xml"
          OnClick="btnGetXml_Click" />
        <br/><br/><br/>
        <asp:Literal runat="server" ID="output"/>
      </div>
    </form>
  </body>
  </html>
```

Similarly to the previous example, this example also utilizes the `ExecuteReader()` method of the `SqlDataReader` object to execute the select query. After executing the query, the code invokes the `GetSqlXml()` method of the `SqlDataReader` object to obtain reference to the `SqlXml` object:

```
SqlXml sqlXmlValue = reader.GetSqlXml(0);
```

Then the code invokes the factory method named `CreateReader()` to get an `XmlReader` object from the `SqlXml` object:

```
XmlReader xmlReader = sqlXmlValue.CreateReader();
```

Finally, the `ReadOuterXml()` method of the `XmlReader` object is invoked to display the results onto a browser:

```
    if (xmlReader.Read())
      output.Text = Server.HtmlEncode(xmlReader.ReadOuterXml());
```

Navigate to the page outlined in Listing 14-7 using a browser, enter in an appropriate ID, and hit the command button. You should see an output similar to Figure 14-8.

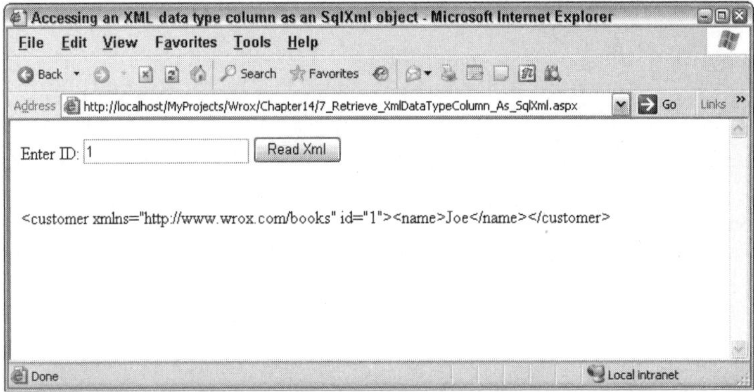

Figure 14-8

Passing Parameters to an XML Data-Typed Column

So far, you have seen how to retrieve an XML data type column from the client ASP.NET page. This section focuses on how to pass parameters to an XML data type column. Similarly to the retrieval, here also you have two options in terms of choosing the appropriate parameter data type.

- Use NVarChar as the SqlDbType, and rely on the automatic conversion wherein SQL Server automatically typecasts the parameter to XML data type.
- Use the SqlXml object.

The next few sections examine both of these approaches in detail.

Passing NVarChar as a Parameter Type to an XML Data Type Column

The classes in the System.Data.SqlClient namespace provide symmetric functionality for XML parameters, meaning that you can also use the String data type with these. Being able to pass in a string (NVARCHAR) where an XML type is expected relies on the fact that SQL Server provides automatic conversion of VARCHAR or NVARCHAR to the XML data type. Listing 14-8 shows you an example of this in action.

Listing 14-8: Automatic Conversion of NVarChar to the XML Data Type

```
<%@ Page Language="C#" ValidateRequest="false" %>
<%@ Import Namespace="System.Data" %>
<%@ Import Namespace="System.Web.Configuration" %>
<%@ Import Namespace="System.Data.SqlClient" %>
<%@ Import Namespace="System.Xml" %>
<script runat="server">
  void btnSave_Click(object sender, EventArgs e)
  {
    int ID = Convert.ToInt32(txtID.Text);
    string xmlValue = txtXmlData.Text;
```

```
    //Get the connection string from the web.config file
    string connectionString = WebConfigurationManager.ConnectionStrings
      ["AdventureWorks"].ConnectionString;
    try
    {
      using (SqlConnection connection = new SqlConnection(connectionString))
      {
        connection.Open();
        SqlCommand command = connection.CreateCommand();
        command.CommandText = "Insert Customer(ID, XmlData) " +
          "Values(@ID, @XmlData)";
        //Set value of parameters
        SqlParameter idParameter = command.Parameters.Add("@ID",
          SqlDbType.Int);
        idParameter.Value = ID;
        SqlParameter xmlDataParameter = command.Parameters.Add("@XmlData",
          SqlDbType.NVarChar);
        xmlDataParameter.Value = xmlValue;
        //Execute and close connection
        command.ExecuteNonQuery();
      }
      output.Text = "Successfully Saved";
    }
    catch (Exception ex)
    {
      output.Text = "Exception : " + ex.Message;
    }
  }
</script>
<html xmlns="http://www.w3.org/1999/xhtml">
<head id="Head1" runat="server">
  <title>Passing value to an XML data type column as a String</title>
</head>
<body>
  <form id="form1" runat="server">
    <div>
      <asp:Label ID="lblID" Runat="server" Text="ID:" ></asp:Label>
      <asp:TextBox ID="txtID" Runat="server"></asp:TextBox>
      <br/><br/><br/>
      <asp:Label ID="lblXmlData" Runat="server" Text="XML:"
        Width="134px" Height="19px"></asp:Label>
      <asp:TextBox ID="txtXmlData" Runat="server" Width="447px"
        Height="153px" TextMode="MultiLine"></asp:TextBox>
      <br/><br/><br/><br/> 
      <asp:Button ID="btnSave" Runat="server" Text="Save Values"
        Width="118px" Height="30px" OnClick="btnSave_Click" />
      <br/><br/><br/><br/> 
      <asp:Literal runat="server" ID="output" />
    </div>
  </form>
</body>
</html>
```

The lines of interest in the above code are where you actually pass in the parameter to the `xml_data` column. As you can see from below, you supply the `SqlDbType.NVarChar` as the second argument to the `Add()` method and rely on the automatic conversion provided by SQL Server 2005:

```
SqlParameter xmlDataParameter = command.Parameters.Add("@XmlData",
  SqlDbType.NVarChar);
xmlDataParameter.Value = xmlValue;
```

Fire up the page in a browser, enter all the details, including the ID and the XML data, and click on the Save button. If everything goes well, you will get a message indicating that the data has been successfully saved. One interesting point to note is that you cannot insert an XML document that is not well formed.

Passing a SqlXml Object to an XML Data Type Column

This section shows you how to utilize a `SqlXml` object to pass parameter to an `XML` data-typed column. To this end, Listing 14-9 creates an object of type `SqlXml` and assigns that to the `Value` property of the `SqlParameter` object that represents the `@XmlData` parameter.

Listing 14-9: Passing a SqlXml Object as a Parameter to an XML Column

```
<%@ Page Language="C#" ValidateRequest="false" %>
<%@ Import Namespace="System.Web.Configuration" %>
<%@ Import Namespace="System.Data.SqlClient" %>
<%@ Import Namespace="System.Data.SqlTypes" %>
<%@ Import Namespace="System.Data" %>
<%@ Import Namespace="System.Xml" %>
<script runat="server">
  void btnSave_Click(object sender, EventArgs e)
  {
    int ID = Convert.ToInt32(txtID.Text);
    string xmlValue = txtXmlData.Text;
    //Get the connection string from the web.config file
    string connectionString = WebConfigurationManager.ConnectionStrings
      ["AdventureWorks"].ConnectionString;
    try
    {
      using (SqlConnection connection = new SqlConnection(connectionString))
      {
        connection.Open();
        SqlCommand command = connection.CreateCommand();
        command.CommandText = "Insert Customer(ID, XmlData) " +
          "Values(@ID, @XmlData)";
        //Set value of parameters
        SqlParameter idParameter = command.Parameters.Add("@ID", SqlDbType.Int);
        idParameter.Value = ID;
        SqlParameter xmlDataParameter = command.Parameters.Add("@XmlData",
          SqlDbType.Xml);
        xmlDataParameter.Value = new SqlXml(new XmlTextReader(xmlValue,
          XmlNodeType.Document, null));
        //Execute and close connection
        command.ExecuteNonQuery();
      }
```

```
      output.Text = "Successfully Saved";
    }
    catch (Exception ex)
    {
      output.Text = "Exception:" + ex.Message;
    }
  }
</script>
<html xmlns="http://www.w3.org/1999/xhtml" >
<head id="Head1" runat="server">
  <title>Passing value to an XML data type column as a SqlXml</title>
</head>
<body>
  <form id="form1" runat="server">
    <div>
      <asp:Label ID="lblID" Runat="server" Text="ID:"></asp:Label>
      <asp:TextBox ID="txtID" Runat="server"></asp:TextBox>
      <br/><br/><br/>
      <asp:Label ID="lblXmlData" Runat="server" Text="XML:"
        Width="134px" Height="19px"></asp:Label>
      <asp:TextBox ID="txtXmlData" Runat="server" Width="308px"
        Height="82px" TextMode="MultiLine"></asp:TextBox>
      <br/><br/><br/><br/> 
      <asp:Button ID="btnSave" Runat="server" Text="Save Values"
        OnClick="btnSave_Click" />
      <asp:Literal runat="server" id="output" />
    </div>
  </form>
</body>
</html>
```

There are two important things that you need to note in the above code listing. First, you supply the `SqlDbType.Xml` value to the second parameter of the `SqlParameter` object's `Add` method:

```
SqlParameter xmlDataParameter = command.Parameters.Add("@XmlData",
  SqlDbType.Xml);
```

Next, you assign an object of type `SqlXml` to the `Value` property of the `SqlParameter` object:

```
xmlDataParameter.Value = new SqlXml(new XmlTextReader(xmlValue,
  XmlNodeType.Document, null));
```

Navigate to the page using a browser. Now enter the ID value of 6 and the following XML as an input argument, and press the Save Values button:

```
<customer xmlns="http://www.wrox.com/books" id="6">
  <name>Joe</name>
</customer>
```

You should get a confirmation message saying Successfully Saved. So far, you have used the XML data entered by the user in the text box as an input to the `XML` data type column. There are times when you might want to utilize an external XML file as an input to the `XML` data type column. Listing 14-10 shows you how to accomplish this.

Listing 14-10: Using XML File Contents as a Parameter to the XML Column

```
<%@ Page Language="C#" ValidateRequest="false" %>
<%@ Import Namespace="System.Data" %>
<%@ Import Namespace="System.Web.Configuration" %>
<%@ Import Namespace="System.Data.SqlClient" %>
<%@ Import Namespace="System.IO" %>
<%@ Import Namespace="System.Xml" %>
<%@ Import Namespace="System.Data.SqlTypes" %>
<script runat="server">
  void btnSave_Click(object sender, EventArgs e)
  {
    int ID = Convert.ToInt32(txtID.Text);
    //Get the connection string from the web.config file
    string connectionString = WebConfigurationManager.ConnectionStrings
      ["AdventureWorks"].ConnectionString;
    try
    {
      using (SqlConnection connection = new SqlConnection(connectionString))
      {
        connection.Open();
        SqlCommand command = connection.CreateCommand();
        command.CommandText = "Insert Customer(ID, XmlData) " +
          "Values(@ID, @XmlData)";
        //Set value of parameters
        SqlParameter idParameter = command.Parameters.Add("@ID", SqlDbType.Int);
        idParameter.Value = ID;
        SqlParameter xmlDataParameter = command.Parameters.Add("@XmlData",
          SqlDbType.Xml);
        string xmlFile = @"C:\Data\Customer.xml";
        XmlReader reader = XmlReader.Create(xmlFile);
        xmlDataParameter.Value = new SqlXml(reader);
        //Execute Insert and close connection
        command.ExecuteNonQuery();
      }
      output.Text = "Successfully Saved";
    }
    catch (Exception ex)
    {
      output.Text = "Exception: " + ex.Message;
    }
  }
</script>
<html xmlns="http://www.w3.org/1999/xhtml" >
<head id="Head1" runat="server">
  <title>XML File input as a parameter to the XML column</title>
</head>
<body>
  <form id="form1" runat="server">
    <div>
      <asp:Label ID="lblID" Runat="server" Text="ID:"
        Width="134px" Height="19px"></asp:Label>
      <asp:TextBox ID="txtID" Runat="server"></asp:TextBox>
      <br/><br/><br/>
```

```
        <asp:Button ID="btnSave" Runat="server" Text="Save Values"
          OnClick="btnSave_Click" />
        <br/><br/><br/>
        <asp:Literal runat="server" ID="output" />
      </div>
    </form>
  </body>
  </html>
```

Listing 14-10 is very similar to Listing 14-9, except for the following lines of code:

```
string xmlFile = @"C:\Data\Customer.xml";
XmlReader reader = XmlReader.Create(xmlFile);
xmlDataParameter.Value = new SqlXml(reader);
```

As you can see from the above code, in this example, the input to the parameter is provided from an external XML file named `Customer.xml`. Note that the worker process account needs to have the necessary permissions to access the external file. This input is supplied to the constructor of the `SqlXml` object in the form of an `XmlReader` object.

Client-Side XML

So far, you have seen how to retrieve and process XML data from the server side. This section will demonstrate some of the XML processing techniques in the client side. One of the issues developers had when they first started to develop commercial web sites was the limitations of using a browser as the interface. For instance, there were many cases where you wanted to retrieve information from the server after the user had performed some action, like entering an employee number in a web page to retrieve the details of an employee. To accomplish this, you would post the current page to the server, retrieve the employee information from the database, and refresh the page with the information retrieved from the server. Although this method of refreshing the whole page is very common today, it is inefficient because the web page refreshes and re-renders the entire page of content, even if only a small percentage of the page has actually changed.

Fortunately, ASP.NET 2.0 provides an efficient approach to invoking a remote function from a server page without refreshing the browser. This new feature is called ASP.NET 2.0 Script Callback, and it builds on the foundation of the `XmlHttp` object library. Using the ASP.NET 2.0 script callback feature, you can emulate some of the behaviors of a traditional fat-client application in a web-based application. It can be used to refresh individual controls, to validate controls, or even to process a form without having to post the whole page to the server. When you utilize a script callback approach to retrieve data, you typically transfer the data in the form of an XML stream from the server side to the client and then load the XML data in a client-side XML DOM object to process the XML.

ASP.NET 2.0 Script Callback Feature

This section will consider an example wherein you retrieve the details of a database log based on the database log ID entered in the web page. To accomplish this, you will leverage the script callback feature and see how to retrieve the database log details from the AdventureWorks database without posting the page back to the server.

Before looking at the example, examine the steps involved in utilizing the callback feature:

1. The client invokes a client-side method that will use the callback manager.
2. The callback manager creates the request to an `.aspx` page on the server.
3. The ASP.NET runtime on the server receives the request, processes the request by invoking a predefined server-side function named `RaiseCallbackEvent`, and passes in the client-side argument to it. The `RaiseCallbackEvent` method stores the client-side arguments in a private variable for later use. After that, the ASP.NET invokes another method named `GetCallbackResult()`, which is responsible for returning the output of the server-side call to the client-side callback manager.
4. The callback manager receives the server response and invokes a callback method located on the client side. If there is an error during the server-side processing, the callback manager invokes a separate callback method.
5. The client callback method processes the results of the server-side call.

Now that you understand the steps, Listing 14-11 shows an example page that implements the callback feature.

Listing 14-11: Retrieving XML Data Dynamically Using ASP.NET 2.0 Script Callback

```
<%@ Page language="C#" %>
<%@ Import Namespace="System.Data" %>
<%@ Import Namespace="System.Data.SqlClient" %>
<%@ Import Namespace="System.Xml" %>
<%@ Import Namespace="System.Web.Configuration" %>
<%@ implements interface="System.Web.UI.ICallbackEventHandler" %>
<script runat="server">
  private string _callbackArg;
  void ICallbackEventHandler.RaiseCallbackEvent(string eventArgument)
  {
    _callbackArg = eventArgument;
  }

  string ICallbackEventHandler.GetCallbackResult()
  {
    try
    {
      int value = Int32.Parse(_callbackArg);
      return GetDatabaseLogDetails(value);
    }
    catch (Exception ex)
    {
      throw new ApplicationException
        ("An Error has occured during the processing " +
        " of your request. Error is :" + ex.Message);
    }
  }

  public string GetDatabaseLogDetails(int databaseLogID)
```

```
  {
    string connectionString = WebConfigurationManager.ConnectionStrings
      ["AdventureWorks"].ConnectionString;
    string returnValue = "";
    try
    {
      using(SqlConnection connection = new SqlConnection(connectionString))
      {
        connection.Open();
        SqlCommand command = connection.CreateCommand();
        command.CommandText = "SELECT XmlEvent FROM dbo.DatabaseLog " +
          " WHERE DatabaseLogID = " + databaseLogID.ToString();
        SqlDataReader reader = command.ExecuteReader();
        if (reader.Read())
        {
          //Get the XML value as string
          string xmlValue = (string)reader.GetValue(0);
          returnValue = xmlValue;
        }
        else
          returnValue = "No Value";
      }
      return returnValue;
    }
    catch (Exception ex)
    {
      throw ex;
    }
  }

  public void Page_Load(object sender, EventArgs e)
  {
    if (!Request.Browser.SupportsCallback)
      throw new ApplicationException("This browser doesn't support " +
      "Client callbacks.");
    string src = Page.ClientScript.GetCallbackEventReference(this,
      "arg", "DisplayResultsCallback", "ctx", "DisplayErrorCallback", false);
    string mainSrc = @"function GetDatabaseLogDetailsUsingPostback(arg, ctx){ " +
      src + "; }";
    Page.ClientScript.RegisterClientScriptBlock(this.GetType(),
      "GetDatabaseLogDetailsUsingPostback", mainSrc, true);
  }
</script>
<html>
<head>
  <title>Retrieving XML Dynamically using ASP.NET 2.0 Script Callback</title>
  <script language="javascript">
    function GetDatabaseLogDetails()
    {
      var n = document.forms[0].txtDatabaseLogID.value;
      GetDatabaseLogDetailsUsingPostback(n, "txtNumber");
    }

    function DisplayResultsCallback( result, context )
```

(continued)

Listing 14-11: *(continued)*

```
    {
      var strXML,objXMLNode,objXMLDoc,objDatabaseLog,strHTML;
      objXMLDoc = new ActiveXObject("Microsoft.XMLDOM");
      //Load the returned XML string into XMLDOM Object
      objXMLDoc.loadXML(result);
      //Get reference to the root Node
      objDatabaseLog = objXMLDoc.selectSingleNode("EVENT_INSTANCE");
      //Check if a valid database log is returned from the server
      strHTML = "";
      if (objDatabaseLog != null)
      {
        //Dynamically generate HTML and append the contents
        strHTML += "<br><br>Event Type :<b>" +
          objDatabaseLog.selectSingleNode("EventType").text + "</b><br><br>";
        strHTML += "Post Time:<b>" +
          objDatabaseLog.selectSingleNode("PostTime").text + "</b><br><br>";
        strHTML += "SPID :<b>" +
          objDatabaseLog.selectSingleNode("SPID").text + "</b><br><br>";
        strHTML += "Server Name:<b>" +
          objDatabaseLog.selectSingleNode("ServerName").text + "</b><br><br>";
        strHTML += "Login Name:<b>" +
          objDatabaseLog.selectSingleNode("LoginName").text + "</b><br><br>";
        strHTML += "User Name:<b>" +
          objDatabaseLog.selectSingleNode("UserName").text + "</b><br><br>";
        strHTML += "Database Name:<b>" +
          objDatabaseLog.selectSingleNode("DatabaseName").text + "</b><br><br>";
      }
      else
      {
        strHTML += "<br><br><b>Database Log not found</b>";
      }
      //Assign the dynamically generated HTML into the div tag
      divContents.innerHTML = strHTML;
    }

    function DisplayErrorCallback( error, context )
    {
      alert("Database Query Failed. " + error);
    }
  </script>
</head>
<body>
  <form id="Form1" runat="server">
    <H3>Error Log</H3>
    <P align="left">
      Enter the Database Log ID:
      <INPUT id="txtDatabaseLogID" name="txtDatabaseLogID" style="LEFT: 149px;
TOP:72px">
      <INPUT id="btnGetDatabaseLog" type="button" value="Get Database Log Details"
        name=" btnGetDatabaseLog" onclick="GetDatabaseLogDetails()">
```

```
    </P>
    <div id="divContents"></div>
  </form>
</body>
</html>
```

To understand the code better, think of Listing 14-11 as being made up of three different parts:

- The part that implements the server-side event for callback
- The part that generates the client-side script for callback
- The part that implements the client callback method

Start by looking at the server-side event for the callback.

Implementing the Server-Side Event for the Callback

At the top of the page, you import the required namespaces by using the `Import` directive. After that you use the `implements` directive to implement the `ICallbackEventHandler` interface. This interface has a method named `RaiseCallbackEvent` that must be implemented to make the callback work:

```
<%@ implements interface="System.Web.UI.ICallbackEventHandler" %>
```

The signature of the `RaiseCallbackEvent` method is:

```
void ICallbackEventHandler.RaiseCallbackEvent(string eventArgs)
```

As you can see, the `RaiseCallbackEvent` method takes an argument of type `string`. If you need to pass values to the server-side method, you should use this string argument. Inside the `RaiseCallbackEvent` method, you store the supplied event argument in a local private variable for future use:

```
void ICallbackEventHandler.RaiseCallbackEvent(string eventArgument)
{
  _callbackArg = eventArgument;
}
```

After that, you override the `GetCallbackResult()` method, as shown below:

```
string ICallbackEventHandler.GetCallbackResult()
{
  int value = Int32.Parse(_callbackArg);
  return GetDatabaseLogDetails(value);
}
```

The `GetCallbackResult()` method is the one that is responsible for returning the output of the server-side execution to the client. Inside the `GetCallbackResult()` method, you first convert the supplied employee ID into an integer type and then invoke a function named `GetDatabaseLogDetails()`, passing in the database log ID as an argument:

```
int value = Int32.Parse(eventArgs);
return GetDatabaseLogDetails(value);
```

As the name suggests, the GetDatabaseLogDetails() method retrieves the XmlEvent column from the DatabaseLog table, and returns that information to the caller. Note that the XmlEvent is an XML data-typed column and contains native XML data.

To start with, you create an instance of the SqlConnection object, passing in the connection string as an argument. Then you create an instance of the SqlCommand object through the SqlConnection object. Then you execute the SQL query by invoking the ExecuteReader() method of the SqlCommand object. Once the query is executed and the results are available in the SqlDataReader object, you then invoke the GetValue() method of the SqlDataReader object to return the XML value contained in the XmlEvent column. The GetCallbackResult() method receives the output XML string and simply returns it to the caller.

Generating the Client-Side Script for the Callback

This section will look at the Page_Load event of the page. In the beginning of the Page_Load event, you check to see if the browser supports callback by examining the SupportsCallback property of the HttpBrowserCapabilities object:

```
if (!Request.Browser.SupportsCallback)
  throw new ApplicationException
  ("This browser doesn't support " + "Client callbacks");
```

Then you invoke the Page.ClientScript.GetCallbackEventReference() method to implement the callback in client side. You can use this method to generate client-side code, which is required to initiate the asynchronous call to the server:

```
string src = Page.ClientScript.GetCallbackEventReference(this, "arg",
  "DisplayResultsCallback", "ctx", "DisplayErrorCallback", false);
```

The arguments passed to the GetCallbackEventReference method are:

- this: Control that implements ICallbackEventHandler(Current Page)
- arg: String to be passed to the server side as an argument
- DisplayResultsCallback: Name of the client-side function that will receive the result from the server-side event
- ctx: String to be passed from one client-side function to the other client-side function through context parameter
- DisplayErrorCallback: Name of the client-side function that will be called if there is any error during the execution of the code
- false: Indicates that the server-side function is to be invoked asynchronously

When you execute this page from a browser and view the HTML source code, you will see that the following callback code is generated due to the above GetCallbackEventReference method call:

```
WebForm_DoCallback('__Page', arg, DisplayResultsCallback,
  ctx,DisplayErrorCallback, false)
```

WebForm_DoCallback is a JavaScript function (introduced with ASP.NET 2.0) that in turn invokes the XmlHttp class methods to actually perform the callback. Then you embed the callback code inside a function by concatenating the callback-generated code with a JavaScript function named GetDatabaseLogDetailsUsingPostback, using the following line of code:

```
string mainSrc = @"function " +
  "GetDatabaseLogDetailsUsingPostback(arg, ctx)" + "{ " + src + "; }";
```

Finally, you register the client script block through the Page.ClientScript.RegisterClientScriptBlock() method call. Note that in ASP.NET 2.0, the Page.RegisterClientScriptBlock and Page.RegisterStartupScript methods are obsolete. That's why you had to take the help of Page.ClientScript to render the client-side script to the client browser. The Page.ClientScript property returns an object of type ClientScriptManager type, which is used for managing client scripts.

Implementing Client Callback Method

In the client side, you have a method named GetDatabaseLogDetails(), which is invoked when the Get Database Log Details command button is clicked:

```
function GetDatabaseLogDetails()
{
  var n = document.forms[0].txtDatabaseLogID.value;
  GetDatabaseLogDetailsUsingPostback(n, "txtNumber");
}
```

From within the GetDatabaseLogDetails() method, you invoke a method named GetDatabaseLogDetailsUsingPostback() and pass in the required parameters. Note that the definition of the GetDatabaseLogDetailsUsingPostback() method is added in the Page_Load event on the server side (through the RegisterClientScriptBlock method call). Once the server side function is executed, the callback manager automatically calls the DisplayResultsCallback() method.

The code of the DisplayResultsCallback() method is shown below. In this example, because the value returned from the server-side page is an XML string, you load the returned XML into an XMLDOM parser and then parse its contents:

```
objXMLDoc = new ActiveXObject("Microsoft.XMLDOM");
//Load the returned XML string into XMLDOM Object
objXMLDoc.loadXML(strXML);
```

Then you get a reference to the Employees node by invoking the selectSingleNode method of the MSXML DOM object:

```
objDatabaseLog = objXMLDoc.selectSingleNode("EVENT_INSTANCE");
```

If a valid error log element is returned from the function call, you display its contents. You display this information in a div tag by setting the innerHTML property of the div element to the dynamically constructed HTML:

```
if (objDatabaseLog != null)
{
  //Dynamically generate HTML and append the contents
  strHTML += "<br><br>Event Type :<b>" +
    objDatabaseLog.selectSingleNode("EventType").text + "</b><br><br>";
  strHTML += "Post Time:<b>" +
    objDatabaseLog.selectSingleNode("PostTime").text + "</b><br><br>";
  strHTML += "SPID :<b>" +
    objDatabaseLog.selectSingleNode("SPID").text + "</b><br><br>";
  strHTML += "Server Name:<b>" +
    objDatabaseLog.selectSingleNode("ServerName").text + "</b><br><br>";
  strHTML += "Login Name:<b>" +
    objDatabaseLog.selectSingleNode("LoginName").text + "</b><br><br>";
  strHTML += "User Name:<b>" +
    objDatabaseLog.selectSingleNode("UserName").text + "</b><br><br>";
  strHTML += "Database Name:<b>" +
    objDatabaseLog.selectSingleNode("DatabaseName").text + "</b><br><br>";
}
```

When you browse to Listing 14-11 using the browser and search for a database log with an ID of 1, the page will display the database log attributes such as event type, post time, SPID, server name, and so on, as shown in Figure 14-9.

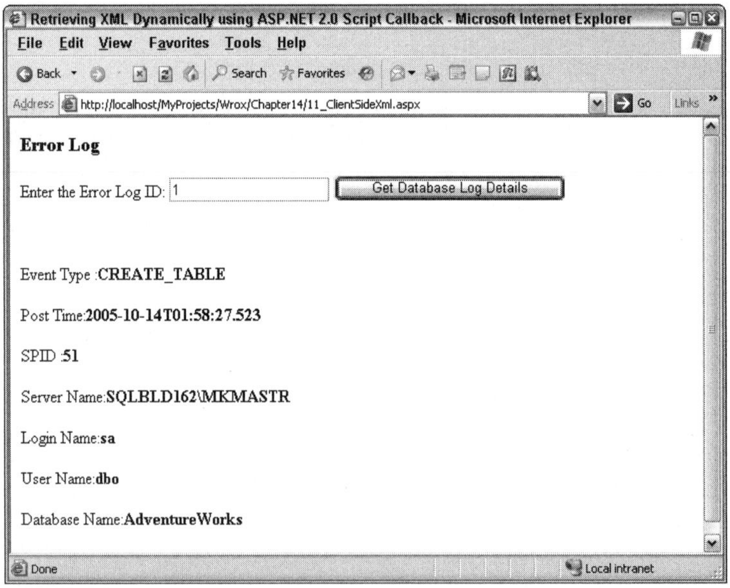

Figure 14-9

When you click on the Get Database Log Details button shown in Figure 14-9, you will notice that the database log information is retrieved from the server and displayed in the browser; all without refreshing the page.

Summary

This chapter took a SQL Server 2005-specific viewpoint. All the features discussed here present an interesting method of architecting your applications that allows you to leverage built-in CLR integration and XML features of SQL Server 2005. Some of the discussed features, such as `FOR XML PATH`, `ROOT`, and the new `XML` data type, are specific to SQL Server 2005.

Since XML is the all-pervasive language of the computer world, it is only logical that SQL Server 2005 and ADO.NET have rich, built-in support for it. This chapter, in presenting an XML-centric view of SQL Server 2005, gives you an interesting viewpoint and methodology to architect your applications. When properly used, these XML features can really make a significant difference in your overall architecture.

In this chapter, you also read about the various flavors the `FOR XML` query can be used in, and how you would leverage that to build flexible ADO.NET applications. You also saw how you can use the new `XML` data type and build applications with ADO.NET that work with such columns.

Finally, you looked at retrieving XML data from the client side using the ASP.NET 2.0 script callback, which is a rather powerful approach of retrieving XML data from the client side without refreshing the browser side.

Now that you understand the advanced features of SQL Server 2005, the next chapter puts them into practice by showing you how to apply those features in the construction of a real-world web site.

15

Case Study: Best Practices for Creating ASP.NET Web Sites

So far in this book, you have understood the various ways of accessing from an external data source such as SQL Server 2005 and displaying them in your ASP.NET pages. With that foundation in place, this chapter will focus on the best practices of creating an ASP.NET web site. Toward this end, this chapter will discuss the following features:

- How to create a scalable n-tier web site using the best practices, including the use of application blocks supplied with Enterprise Library 2.0
- How to create a data access layer class using the Enterprise Library data access application block
- How to implement data binding using the `ObjectDataSource` control
- How to implement data binding with a Generics collection
- How to handle exceptions consistently using the Enterprise Library exception-handling block
- How to transform data from a `SqlDataReader` object into a Generics collection object by using a generic utility
- How to create a consistent site design using master pages in ASP.NET 2.0

Overview of the Case Study

This case study will consider an AdventureWorks trader system. This system provides the subset of features exposed by a trading system. Some of the features include displaying categories and products data contained in the AdventureWorks database.

Architecture of System

Figure 15-1 illustrates the proposed architecture of the trading system.

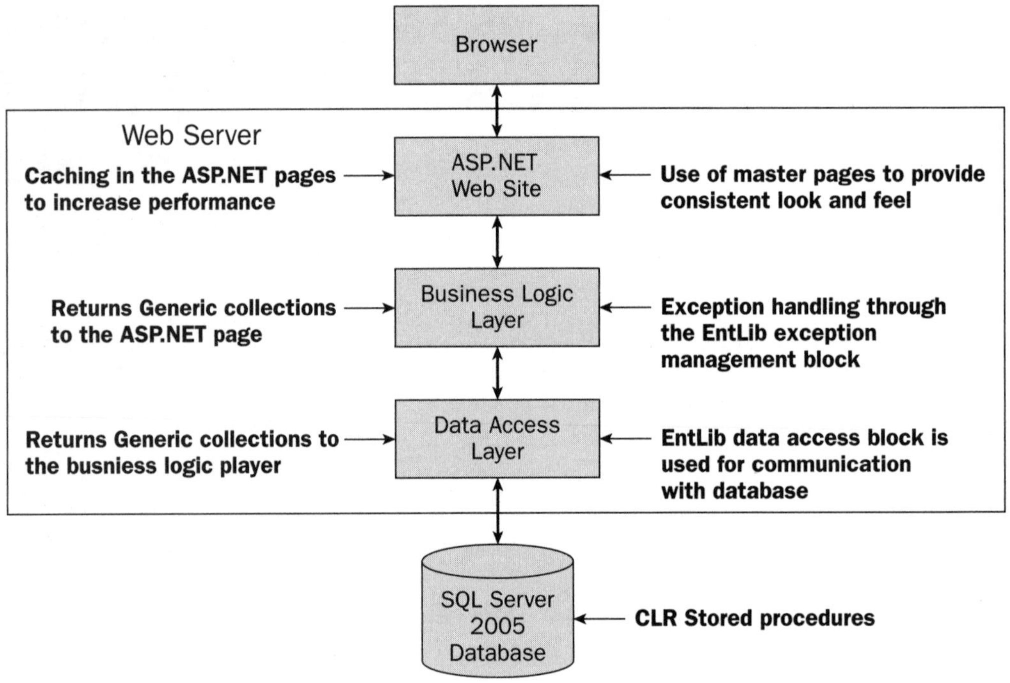

Figure 15-1

As shown in Figure 15-1, the web site primarily depends on the middle-tier .NET components (`AdventureWorksTraderDataAccess` and `AdventureWorksTraderBiz`) for all of its functionality. As the name suggests, the `AdventureWorksTraderDataAccess` component abstracts all the data access functionality, and the `AdventureWorksTraderBiz` components encapsulate the business logic of the application, and this component depends on the data access component for data retrieval. When the user comes to the site and performs operations such as displaying the list of categories, the web site invokes the methods of the business component, which in turn invoke the data access component to carry out those tasks. Some of the important characteristics of the web site are:

- The stored procedures in the SQL Server 2005 database are created using C#. The ability to create stored procedures in managed code enables complex business logic to be executed close to the database, resulting in performance improvement. The compiled nature of the stored procedures also results in increased performance.
- The data access layer classes are encapsulated inside the C# class library named `AdventureWorksTraderDataAccess`, which in turn leverages the Enterprise Library (known as `EntLib`) data access block for executing stored procedures against the database.
- The data access layer converts the data retrieved from the database to the Generics collection, using a generic transformation utility that performs the mapping of data from the database tables object properties.
- ASP.NET web forms in the user interface layer are generated using master pages, providing a consistent look and feel for the entire application.
- ASP.NET web forms utilize `ObjectDataSource` control to directly bind the output of the business logic layer methods to data-bound controls such as a `GridView` control.
- Exceptions generated in the application are handled consistently using policies defined through the `EntLib` exception management block.
- Web forms also take advantage of the caching of database contents to increase the performance and throughput of the web site. This is made possible by the use of the database cache invalidation mechanism that can automatically remove specific items from the cache when the data in the database table changes.

Before looking at the implementation of the architecture, it is important to examine the business processes supported by the web site.

Business Processes

Although the scope of the case study is to demonstrate the best practices for creating high-performance ASP.NET web sites, it is imperative that you review the business processes before choosing the best approach. The business processes that the AdventureWorksTrader system is going to have to enable are:

- **Product Categories display process:** This allows users to display all the categories contained in the AdventureWorks database. From the list of displayed categories, you can click on a specific category to display all the related subcategories.
- **Product Subcategories display process:** Once you have the list of categories, you can then display all the subcategories that are part of a selected category.
- **Products display process:** Each subcategory contains a list of products that are displayed through this process. To get to the list of products in a product subcategory, you click on a specific subcategory.

As you can see, these processes are very simple, since the case study is completely focused on integrating reusable components such as the data access block, the exception management block, the generic transformation of database tables into objects, creating and leveraging stored procedures, and so on.

Implementation

Now that you understand the business processes involved, the following sections examine the individual building blocks that are required to implement this solution. For the purposes of this example, the discussion of the remaining part of the case study is split into the following sections:

- Database design
- Implementation of CLR stored procedures
- Implementation of the data access .NET component
- Implementation of the business logic .NET component
- Implementation of the web site

To start with, consider the database design that is required to support the web site.

Database Design

The AdventureWorks database used in this case study contains a number of tables, but the case study only leverages the subset of that schema that is made of just three tables. The entity relationship diagram for the database is shown in Figure 15-2.

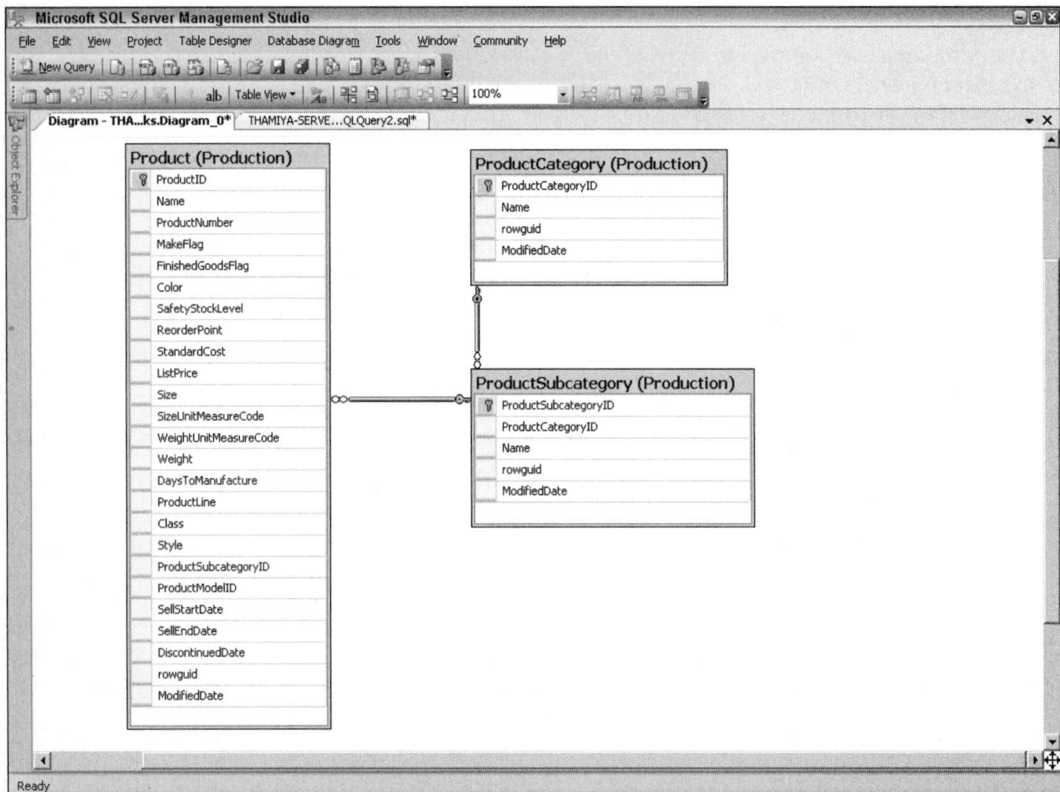

Figure 15-2

The structure of these tables follows, starting with the ProductCategoryID table.

Name	Data Type	Length	AllowNull	Description
ProductCategoryID	int	4	No	Represents the product category ID
Name	nvarchar	50	No	Represents the category name
rowguid	unique identifier	8	No	Represents the unique identifier
ModifiedDate	datetime	8	No	Represents the modified date

The ProductSubcategory table is defined as follows.

Name	Data Type	Length	AllowNull	Description
ProductSubcategoryID	int	4	No	Represents the product subcategory ID
ProductCategoryID	int	4	No	Represents the product category ID
Name	nvarchar	50	No	Represents the name of the product subcategory
rowguid	unique identifier	8	No	Represents the unique identifier
ModifiedDate	datetime	8	No	Represents the modified date

The following table describes the structure of the Product table.

Name	Data Type	Length	AllowNull	Description
ProductID	int	4	No	Represents the product ID
Name	nvarchar	50	No	Represents the name of the product
ProductNumber	nvarchar	25	No	Represents the product number
MakeFlag	bit	1	No	Represents the make flag
FinishedGoodsFlag	bit	1	No	Represents the finished good status

Name	Data Type	Length	AllowNull	Description
Color	nvarchar	15	Yes	Represents the color
SafetyStockLevel	smallint	2	No	Represents the safety stock level
ReorderPoint	smallint	2	No	Represents the reorder point
StandardCost	money	8	No	Represents the standard cost
ListPrice	money	8	No	Represents the list price
Size	nvarchar	5	Yes	Represents the size
SizeUnitMeasureCode	nvarchar	3	Yes	Represents the unit measure code
WeightUnit MeasureCode	nchar	3	Yes	Represents the weight measure code
Weight	decimal	10	Yes	Represents the weight
DaysToManufacture	Int	4	No	Represents the number of days to manufacture
ProductLine	nchar	2	Yes	Represents the product line
Class	nchar	2	Yes	Represents the class
Style	nchar	2	Yes	Represents the style
ProductSubcategoryID	int	4	Yes	Represents the product subcategory ID
ProductModelID	int	4	Yes	Represents the product model
SellStartDate	datetime	8	No	Represents the sell start date
SellEndDate	datetime	8	Yes	Represents the sell end date
DiscontinuedDate	datetime	8	Yes	Represents the discontinued date
rowguid	unique identifier	8	No	Represents the unique identifier
ModifiedDate	Datetime	8	No	Represents the modified date

Now that you have had a look at the required schema, the next step is to create the stored procedures that operate on the schema.

Implementation of CLR Stored Procedures

One of the neat features of SQL Server 2005 is the integration with the .NET CLR. The integration of CLR with SQL Server extends the capability of SQL Server in several important ways. This integration enables you to create database objects such as stored procedures, user-defined functions, and triggers by using modern object-oriented languages such as VB.NET and C#. For the purposes of this case study, the creation of stored procedures will be demonstrated using C#.

To start with, create a new SQL Server Project named AdventureWorksDatabaseObjects, using Visual C# as the language of choice in Visual Studio 2005. Since you are creating a database project, you need to associate a data source with the project. At the time of creating the project, Visual Studio will automatically prompt you to either select an existing database reference or add a new database reference. Choose AdventureWorks as the database. Once the project is created, select Add Stored Procedure from the Project menu. In the Add New Item dialog box, enter StoredProcedures.cs and click the Add button. After the class is created, modify the code in the class to look like the following.

Listing 15-1: Implementation of CLR Stored Procedures

```
using System;
using System.Data;
using System.Data.SqlClient;
using System.Data.SqlTypes;
using Microsoft.SqlServer.Server;

public partial class StoredProcedures
{
  [Microsoft.SqlServer.Server.SqlProcedure]
  public static void GetProductCategories()
  {
    using (SqlConnection connection = new SqlConnection("context connection=true"))
    {
      connection.Open();
      string sqlCommand = "Select ProductCategoryID, Name, rowguid, " +
        " ModifiedDate from Production.ProductCategory";
      SqlCommand command = new SqlCommand(sqlCommand, connection);
      SqlDataReader reader = command.ExecuteReader();
      SqlContext.Pipe.Send(reader);
    }
  }

  [Microsoft.SqlServer.Server.SqlProcedure]
  public static void GetProductSubcategories(int productCategoryID)
  {
    using (SqlConnection connection = new SqlConnection("context connection=true"))
    {
      connection.Open();
      string sqlCommand = "Select ProductSubcategoryID, ProductCategoryID, Name," +
        "rowguid, ModifiedDate from Production.ProductSubcategory " +
        "Where ProductCategoryID = " + productCategoryID;
      SqlCommand command = new SqlCommand(sqlCommand, connection);
      SqlDataReader reader = command.ExecuteReader();
      SqlContext.Pipe.Send(reader);
    }
```

(continued)

Listing 15-1: *(continued)*

```
    }

    [Microsoft.SqlServer.Server.SqlProcedure]
    public static void GetProducts(int productSubcategoryID)
    {
      using (SqlConnection connection = new SqlConnection("context connection=true"))
      {
        connection.Open();
        string sqlCommand = "Select ProductID, Name, ProductNumber,MakeFlag, " +
          "FinishedGoodsFlag, Color, SafetyStockLevel, ReorderPoint,StandardCost, " +
          "ListPrice, Size, SizeUnitMeasureCode, WeightUnitMeasureCode," +
          "Weight,DaysToManufacture, ProductLine,Class, Style, " +
          "ProductSubcategoryID, ProductModelID,SellStartDate,SellEndDate," +
          "DiscontinuedDate, rowguid, ModifiedDate from Production.Product " +
          "Where ProductSubcategoryID = " + productSubcategoryID.ToString();
        SqlCommand command = new SqlCommand(sqlCommand, connection);
        SqlDataReader reader = command.ExecuteReader();
        SqlContext.Pipe.Send(reader);
      }
    }
  };
```

Listing 15-1 starts by importing the required namespaces and then declares a class named `StoredProcedures`. One of the key imported namespaces is `Microsoft.SqlServer.Server`, which contains two important classes that are specific to the in-proc provider:

- `SqlContext`: This class encapsulates the extensions required to execute in-process code in SQL Server 2005. In addition, it provides the transaction and database connection, which are part of the environment in which the routine executes.

- `SqlPipe`: This class enables routines to send tabular results and messages to the client. This class is conceptually similar to the `Response` class found in ASP.NET, in that it can be used to send messages to the callers.

The `StoredProcedures` class contains three static methods named `GetProductCategories()`, `GetProductSubcategories()`, and `GetProducts()`. As the name suggests, the `GetProductCategories()` method simply returns all the categories from the ProductCategory table in the AdventureWorks database, and the `GetProductSubcategories()` method returns all the subcategories that belong to a specific category. Finally, the `GetProducts()` method retrieves all the products contained in a specific product subcategory. The following sections walk you through the `GetProductCategories()` method in detail.

Inside the `GetProductCategories()` method, you start by opening the connection to the database by using the `SqlConnection` object. Note that the connection string passed to the constructor of the `SqlConnection` object is set to `"context connection=true"`, meaning that you want to use the context of the logged-on user to open the connection to the database:

```
using (SqlConnection connection = new SqlConnection("context connection=true"))
```

Here, you open the connection to the database using the `Open()` method:

```
connection.Open();
```

Then you specify the SQL command to be executed. In this case, you retrieve all the records from the ProductCategory table:

```
string sqlCommand = "Select ProductCategoryID, Name, rowguid, ModifiedDate from " +
  "Production.ProductCategory";
```

Then you create an instance of the `SqlCommand` object, passing in the SQL query and the `SqlConnection` object as arguments to its constructor:

```
SqlCommand command = new SqlCommand(sqlCommand, connection);
```

After that, you execute the SQL query by calling the `ExecuteReader()` method of the `SqlCommand` object:

```
SqlDataReader reader = command.ExecuteReader();
```

Then, using the `SqlPipe` object, you return tabular results and messages to the client. This is accomplished using the `Send()` method of the `SqlPipe` class:

```
SqlContext.Pipe.Send(reader);
```

The `Send()` method provides various overloads that enable you to transmit data through the pipe to the calling application.

All the methods in the `StoredProcedures` class utilize the `Send()` method to send tabular results to the client application in the form of a `SqlDataReader` object. Since the implementation of the `GetProductSubcategories()` and `GetProducts()` methods is very similar to the `GetProductCategories()` method, it will not be discussed in detail.

Now that the stored procedures are created, deploying them is very simple and straightforward. Before deploying it, you need to build the project first. To build the project, select Build ➪ Build AdventureWorks DatabaseObjects from the Visual Studio 2005 menu. This will compile all the classes in the project, and if there are any compilation errors, they will be displayed in the Error List pane. Once the project is built, you can then deploy it onto the SQL Server by selecting Build ➪ Deploy AdventureWorksDatabaseObjects from the menu. This will not only register the assembly in the SQL Server, but also deploy the stored procedures in the SQL Server. Once the stored procedures are deployed to the SQL Server, they can then be invoked from the data access layer, which is the focus of the next section.

Before executing the stored procedure, remember to execute the following SQL script, using SQL Server Management Studio to enable managed code execution in the SQL Server:

```
EXEC sp_configure 'clr enabled', 1;
RECONFIGURE WITH OVERRIDE;
GO
```

Although this example uses Visual Studio to create the managed stored procedures, you can easily use a text editor such as Notepad to accomplish the same result.

When to Use T-SQL versus Managed Code

Managed code is better suited than Transact-SQL for number-crunching and complicated execution logic, and it features extensive support for many complex tasks, including string handling and regular expressions. T-SQL is a better candidate in situations where the code will mostly perform data access with little or no procedural logic. Even though the simple stored procedure example in this case study is best written using T-SQL, it uses the managed code approach, mainly to show what it takes to create and use managed stored procedures.

Implementation of the Data Access Layer

This section will discuss implementation of the data access layer, which contains all the necessary classes and methods for communicating with the AdventureWorks database. To start, use Visual Studio 2005 to create a new Visual C# class library project named `AdventureWorksTraderDataAccess`. Once the project is created, change the name of the default class to `ProductCategoryDB`. The implementation of the `ProductCategoryDB` class is shown in Listing 15-2.

Listing 15-2: Implementation of the ProductCategoryDB Class

```
using System;
using System.Data;
using System.Data.Common;
using System.Data.SqlClient;
using System.Collections.Generic;
using System.Text;
using AdventureWorksTraderEntities;
using Microsoft.Practices.EnterpriseLibrary.Data;

namespace AdventureWorksTraderDataAccess
{
  public class ProductCategoryDB
  {
    private DataColumnMapping[] mappings = new DataColumnMapping[] {
      new DataColumnMapping("ProductCategoryID","ProductCategoryID"),
      new DataColumnMapping("Name","Name"),
      new DataColumnMapping("rowguid","Rowguid"),
      new DataColumnMapping("ModifiedDate","ModifiedDate")};

    public IList<ProductCategory> GetProductCategories()
    {
      IList<ProductCategory> list = new List<ProductCategory>();
      Database db = DatabaseFactory.CreateDatabase();
      string storedProcedureName  = "GetProductCategories";
      DbCommand dbCommand = db.GetStoredProcCommand(storedProcedureName);
      using (IDataReader reader = db.ExecuteReader(dbCommand))
      {
        while (reader.Read())
        {
          ProductCategory temp = new ProductCategory();
```

```
                ProductCategory category = (ProductCategory)
                  DataAccessHelper.PopulateEntity(temp, mappings, reader);
                list.Add(category);
            }
        }
        return list;
      }
    }
}
```

The ProductCategoryDB class contains only one method named GetProductCategories, which returns all the categories contained in the ProductCategory table. Under the hood, GetProduct Categories() leverages the EntLib data access block to invoke the GetProductCategories stored procedure, and transforms the output into a generic collection that is made up of multiple Product Category objects. The building blocks used in the GetProductCategories() method are as follows:

- Use of EntLib data access block for accessing data
- Use of a generic utility for transforming the output into a generic collection
- Implementation of ProductCategory objects
- Use of a Generics collection as a way to transmit data

The following sections walk you through each of these building blocks in detail.

Use of EntLib Data Access Block for Data Access

ADO.NET provides many rich features that can be used to retrieve and display data in a number of ways. Even with the flexibility provided by ADO.NET, sometimes you find yourself repeating the same code again and again. For example, every data-driven application requires access to the database, and you need to write code to connect to the database, open the connection, execute SQL or stored procedures, retrieve the results at the client applications, and close the connection. This is plumbing code that you will be forced to write in almost any application you develop and does not really add any value to the core business users. The only things that might be different about this code in each application you develop are the SQL statement or name of the stored procedure, the parameters to the command, and the connection string. As long as you can parameterize these variables, you can abstract most of the plumbing code into reusable classes that can be leveraged across multiple applications. This is exactly what Microsoft has done in the form of the EntLib data access block. This case study will use the data access block for communicating with the database.

What Is the EntLib Data Access Block?

As mentioned previously, the data access block is geared toward addressing the most common tasks developers face when developing database applications. By providing a set of encapsulated methods, the data access block greatly simplifies the most common methods of accessing a database. Each method encapsulates the logic required to retrieve the data and also manages the connection to the database. In addition, the data access block supplements the code in ADO.NET 2.0 by allowing you to write data access code that can work across different database types without rewriting the code. These classes contain code that provides database-specific implementations for features such as parameter handling and cursors.

Moreover, the data access block also provides specific derived classes for SQL Server and Oracle databases. In addition, the `GenericDatabase` class allows you to use the application block with any configured ADO.NET 2.0 `DbProviderFactory` object. You can extend the application block by adding new database types that include database-specific features, or that provide a custom implementation of an existing database.

The data access block 2.0 is an evolution of the 1.0 version and is redesigned to take advantage of the new ADO.NET 2.0 features. You can download the `EntLib` data access block by visiting `www.microsoft.com/downloads` and searching for EntLib.

Steps Involved in Using the Data Access Block

To use the data access block, you need to go through the following steps:

1. Add reference to the `Microsoft.Practices.EnterpriseLibrary.Common.dll` and `Microsoft.Practices.EnterpriseLibrary.Data.dll` assemblies from your solution. You can do this by using the Add Reference option and navigating to the `<Drive Name>:\Program Files\Microsoft Enterprise Library January 2006\bin` folder.
2. Add the necessary configuration entries to `Web.config`, `app.config` or a custom configuration file. To this end, add the following `<configSections>` element under the root `<configuration>` element:

```
<configSections>
  <section name="dataConfiguration"
    type="Microsoft.Practices.EnterpriseLibrary.Data.Configuration.
    DatabaseSettings, Microsoft.Practices.EnterpriseLibrary.Data" />
</configSections>
```

3. Then you also add the `<dataConfiguration>` element directly under the root `<configuration>` element, as follows:

```
<dataConfiguration defaultDatabase="AdventureWorksDB"/>
```

4. This example has marked the AdventureWorksDB as the default database, which is declared separately under the `<connectionStrings>` element:

```
<connectionStrings>
  <add name="AdventureWorksDB" providerName="System.Data.SqlClient"
    connectionString="server=localhost; database=AdventureWorks;UID=user;PWD=word;"
    />
</connectionStrings>
```

5. Import the core namespace of the data access block, `Microsoft.Practices.EnterpriseLibrary.Data`, from within your code.
6. Start writing code against the classes in the same namespace.

Now that you understand the basics of the `EntLib` data access block, look at one of the key classes in the data access block.

Database Object

Any time you work with the data access block, the first class that you will have to deal with is the `Database` class. The `Database` class represents the database and provides methods for you to execute against the database. The `Database` object exposes the methods shown in the following table that you can use to perform CRUD operations against the database.

Method	Description
`ExecuteDataSet`	Executes a SQL query or stored procedure and returns the results in the form of a `DataSet` object
`ExecuteNonQuery`	Executes a SQL query or stored procedure and returns the number of records affected
`ExecuteReader`	Executes a SQL query or stored procedure and returns the results in the form of an `IDataReader` object
`ExecuteScalar`	Executes a SQL query or stored procedure and returns the first column of the first row in the result set
`LoadDataSet`	Executes a command and adds a new `DataTable` to the existing `DataSet`
`UpdateDataSet`	Synchronizes the `DataSet` contents with the database by executing appropriate `Insert`, `Update`, and `Delete` statements

Now that you have an understanding of the methods of the Database class, reexamine the `GetProductCategories()` method of the `ProductCategory` data access layer class to see how the data access block is integrated:

```
IList<ProductCategory> list = new List<ProductCategory>();
Database db = DatabaseFactory.CreateDatabase();
string storedProcedureName  = "GetProductCategories";
DbCommand dbCommand = db.GetStoredProcCommand(storedProcedureName);
using (IDataReader reader = db.ExecuteReader(dbCommand))
```

To start with, you invoke the `CreateDatabase()` method of the `DatabaseFactory` class to obtain an instance of the `Database` object. As the name suggests, the `DatabaseFactory` is a class that contains factory methods for creating `Database` objects. Note that the `CreateDatabase()` method is overloaded and returns a default database when you invoke the parameterless version of the `CreateDatabase()` method. To accomplish this, you set the `defaultDatabase` attribute to the appropriate database configuration key in the `Web.config` file, as follows:

```
<dataConfiguration defaultDatabase="AdventureWorksDB"/>
```

Once you have an instance of the `Database` object, you then invoke the `GetStoredProcCommand()` method to construct an instance of the ADO.NET 2.0 `DbCommand` object. After that, you execute the stored procedure through the `Database.ExecuteReader()` method, passing in the `DbCommand` as an argument.

Use of a Generic Utility for Transforming the Output

Once you have the `SqlDataReader` object as the output, the next step is to transform the contents of that into a Generics collection that can then be sent to the business logic layer. The `GetProductCategories()` method uses a helper class named `DataAccessHelper` (displayed in Listing 15-3) for transforming the contents of a `SqlDataReader` object onto an object.

Listing 15-3: Implementation of the DataAccessHelper Class

```
using System;
using System.Data;
using System.Data.SqlClient;
using System.Configuration;
using System.Data.Common;
using System.Reflection;
using System.Collections;

namespace AdventureWorksTraderDataAccess
{
  public class DataAccessHelper
  {
    static public object PopulateEntity(object entity,
      DataColumnMapping[] mappings, IDataReader reader)
    {
      foreach (DataColumnMapping mapping in mappings)
      {
        int ordinalPosition = 0;
        try
        {
          ordinalPosition = reader.GetOrdinal(mapping.SourceColumn);
        }
        catch (IndexOutOfRangeException ex)
        {
          throw new PropertyColumnMappingException(mapping.SourceColumn +
            " is not a valid SourceColumn", ex);
        }
        object propertyValue = reader.GetValue(ordinalPosition);
        if (propertyValue != DBNull.Value)
        {
          if (mapping.DataSetColumn == "ID")
          {
            Nullable<int> tempValue = (int)propertyValue;
            propertyValue = tempValue;
          }
          object[] param =  { propertyValue };
          try
          {
            entity.GetType().InvokeMember(mapping.DataSetColumn,
              BindingFlags.SetProperty | BindingFlags.Instance |
              BindingFlags.Public | BindingFlags.NonPublic |
              BindingFlags.FlattenHierarchy | BindingFlags.Static,
              null, entity, param);
          }
          catch (Exception e)
          {
```

```
                throw new PropertyColumnMappingException
                  (GetPropertyColumnMappingExceptionMessage(mapping), e);
              }
            }
          }
          return entity;
        }

        private static string GetPropertyColumnMappingExceptionMessage
          (DataColumnMapping mapping)
        {
          return "Could not populate " + mapping.DataSetColumn +
            " property from the " + mapping.SourceColumn + " database column";
        }
      }
    }
```

Inside the `GetProductCategories()` method, you first declare the `DataColumnMapping` array that contains all the mapping information between the ProductCategory table columns and `ProductCategory` object properties:

```
private DataColumnMapping[] mappings = new DataColumnMapping[] {
  new DataColumnMapping("ProductCategoryID","ProductCategoryID"),
  new DataColumnMapping("Name","Name"),
  new DataColumnMapping("rowguid","Rowguid"),
  new DataColumnMapping("ModifiedDate","ModifiedDate")};
```

At the time of invoking the `PopulateEntity()` method, you supply an instance of the `ProductCategory` object, the `DataColumnMapping` array, and the `SqlDataReader` object that contains the output of the stored procedure execution:

```
ProductCategory category = (ProductCategory)
  DataAccessHelper.PopulateEntity(temp, mappings, reader);
```

The `PopulateEntity()` method transforms each row of the `SqlDataReader` object onto a `ProductCategory` object, with its properties populated appropriately.

Implementation of the ProductCategory Object

In addition to the data access and business logic layer components, the case study also contains another project named AdventureWorksTraderEntities that exposes a set of objects that directly correspond to the entities contained in the database. In the case of the ProductCategory table, there is a corresponding class named `ProductCategory` (shown in Listing 15-4) that acts as a container for holding the data related to a `ProductCategory`.

Listing 15-4: Implementation of ProductCategory Class

```
using System;
using System.Collections.Generic;
using System.Text;

namespace AdventureWorksTraderEntities
```

(continued)

Listing 15-4: *(continued)*

```
{
  [Serializable]
  public class ProductCategory
  {
    private int _productCategoryID;
    private string _name;
    private Guid _rowguid;
    private DateTime _modifiedDate;

    public int ProductCategoryID
    {
      get { return _productCategoryID; }
      set { _productCategoryID = value; }
    }

    public string Name
    {
      get { return _name; }
      set { _name = value; }
    }

    public Guid Rowguid
    {
      get { return _rowguid; }
      set { _rowguid = value; }
    }

    public DateTime ModifiedDate
    {
      get { return _modifiedDate; }
      set { _modifiedDate = value; }
    }
  }
}
```

As you can see, the `ProductCategory` class simply acts as a placeholder for a number of properties that directly correspond to the columns in the ProductCategory table.

Use of a Generics Collection

If you remember the return value of the `GetProductCategories()` method, it is simply a Generics collection of `ProductCategory` objects. Here is the code snippet that specifically uses the generic collection:

```
while (reader.Read())
{
  ProductCategory temp = new ProductCategory();
  ProductCategory category = (ProductCategory)
    DataAccessHelper.PopulateEntity(temp, mappings, reader);
  list.Add(category);
}
```

In the previous code, you loop through the `SqlDataReader` object, transform each row of the `SqlDataReader` object into a `ProductCategory` object, and finally add the `ProductCategory` object to the Generics collection.

> **Generics are used to help make the code in the software components much more reusable. They are a type of data structure that contains code that remains the same. The data type of the parameters can change with each use. The usage within the data structure adapts to the different data type based on the supplied variables. Each time the generic is used, it can be customized for different data types without needing to rewrite any of the internal code. Generics permit classes, structs, interfaces, delegates, and methods to be parameterized by the types of data they store and manipulate.**

In the ASP.NET page, the Generics collection returned from the `GetProductCategories()` is then bound directly to the `ObjectDataSource` control. You will see this in action when discussing the web site implementation later in this case study.

Implementation of the ProductSubcategoryDB Class

The `ProductSubcategoryDB` class exposes a method named `GetProductSubcategories()` that simply returns the list of all the subcategories based on a product category. This method is very similar to the `ProductCategory.GetProductCategories()` method in implementation. Listing 15-5 shows the implementation of the `ProductSubcategoryDB` class.

Listing 15-5: Implementation of the ProductSubcategoryDB Class

```
using System;
using System.Data;
using System.Data.Common;
using System.Data.SqlClient;
using System.Collections.Generic;
using System.Text;
using AdventureWorksTraderEntities;
using Microsoft.Practices.EnterpriseLibrary.Data;

namespace AdventureWorksTraderDataAccess
{
  public class ProductSubcategoryDB
  {
    private DataColumnMapping[] mappings = new DataColumnMapping[] {
      new DataColumnMapping("ProductSubcategoryID","ProductSubcategoryID"),
      new DataColumnMapping("ProductCategoryID","ProductCategoryID"),
      new DataColumnMapping("Name","Name"),
      new DataColumnMapping("rowguid","Rowguid"),
      new DataColumnMapping("ModifiedDate","ModifiedDate")};

    public IList<ProductSubcategory> GetProductSubCategories(int productCategoryID)
    {
      IList<ProductSubcategory> list = new List<ProductSubcategory>();
      Database db = DatabaseFactory.CreateDatabase();
```

(continued)

Listing 15-5: *(continued)*

```
        string storedProcedureName = "GetProductSubcategories";
        DbCommand dbCommand = db.GetStoredProcCommand(storedProcedureName);
        db.AddInParameter(dbCommand, "productCategoryID", DbType.Int32,
          productCategoryID);
        using (IDataReader reader = db.ExecuteReader(dbCommand))
        {
          while (reader.Read())
          {
            ProductSubcategory temp = new ProductSubcategory(); ;
            ProductSubcategory subCategory =
              (ProductSubcategory)DataAccessHelper.PopulateEntity(temp,
              mappings, reader);
            list.Add(subCategory);
          }
        }
        return list;
      }
    }
  }
```

As you can see from Listing 15-5, the `GetProductSubcategories()` method leverages the stored procedure named `GetProductSubcategories`, which accepts a `productCategoryID` argument. After that, it does exactly the same as the `GetProductCategories()` method.

Implementation of the ProductDB Class

As the name suggests, the `ProductDB` class, shown in Listing 15-6, provides methods specifically for working with the Product table in the AdventureWorks database. It exposes a method named `GetProducts()`, which returns all the products based on the supplied product subcategory ID.

Listing 15-6: Implementation of the ProductDB Class

```
using System;
using System.Data;
using System.Data.Common;
using System.Data.SqlClient;
using System.Collections.Generic;
using System.Text;
using AdventureWorksTraderEntities;
using Microsoft.Practices.EnterpriseLibrary.Data;

namespace AdventureWorksTraderDataAccess
{
  public class ProductDB
  {
    private DataColumnMapping[] mappings = new DataColumnMapping[] {
      new DataColumnMapping("ProductID","ProductID"),
      new DataColumnMapping("Name","Name"),
      new DataColumnMapping("ProductNumber","ProductNumber"),
      new DataColumnMapping("MakeFlag","MakeFlag"),
      new DataColumnMapping("FinishedGoodsFlag","FinishedGoodsFlag"),
      new DataColumnMapping("Color","Color"),
```

```
        new DataColumnMapping("SafetyStockLevel","SafetyStockLevel"),
        new DataColumnMapping("ReorderPoint","ReorderPoint"),
        new DataColumnMapping("StandardCost","StandardCost"),
        new DataColumnMapping("ListPrice","ListPrice"),
        new DataColumnMapping("Size","Size"),
        new DataColumnMapping("SizeUnitMeasureCode","SizeUnitMeasureCode"),
        new DataColumnMapping("WeightUnitMeasureCode","WeightUnitMeasureCode"),
        new DataColumnMapping("Weight","Weight"),
        new DataColumnMapping("DaysToManufacture","DaysToManufacture"),
        new DataColumnMapping("ProductLine","ProductLine"),
        new DataColumnMapping("Class","Class"),
        new DataColumnMapping("Style","Style"),
        new DataColumnMapping("ProductSubcategoryID","ProductSubcategoryID"),
        new DataColumnMapping("ProductModelID","ProductModelID"),
        new DataColumnMapping("SellStartDate","SellStartDate"),
        new DataColumnMapping("SellEndDate","SellEndDate"),
        new DataColumnMapping("DiscontinuedDate","DiscontinuedDate"),
        new DataColumnMapping("rowguid","Rowguid"),
        new DataColumnMapping("ModifiedDate","ModifiedDate")};

      public IList<Product> GetProducts(int productSubcategoryID)
      {
        IList<Product> list = new List<Product>();
        Database db = DatabaseFactory.CreateDatabase();
        string storedProcedureName = "GetProducts";
        DbCommand dbCommand = db.GetStoredProcCommand(storedProcedureName);
        db.AddInParameter(dbCommand, "productSubCategoryID", DbType.Int32,
          productSubcategoryID);
        using (IDataReader reader = db.ExecuteReader(dbCommand))
        {
          while (reader.Read())
          {
            Product temp = new Product();
            Product prod = (Product) DataAccessHelper.PopulateEntity(temp,
              mappings, reader);
            list.Add(prod);
          }
        }
        return list;
      }
    }
  }
```

The `GetProducts()` method simply executes a stored procedure named `GetProducts` that accepts a product subcategory ID and returns the list of all the products based on the product subcategory ID.

Implementation of the Business Logic Layer

This section will focus on the implementation of the business logic layer, which is encapsulated inside the class library named `AdventureWorksTraderBiz`. To start with, create a new Visual C# class library project named `AdventureWorksTraderBiz` using Visual Studio 2005. After that, add reference to the AdventureWorksTraderDataAccess project created in the previous section. Once the project is created, add a class named `ProductCategoryBiz` to the project and modify it to look as shown in Listing 15-7.

Listing 15-7: Implementation of the ProductCategoryBiz Class

```
using System;
using System.Collections.Generic;
using System.Text;
using AdventureWorksTraderEntities;
using AdventureWorksTraderDataAccess;
using Microsoft.Practices.EnterpriseLibrary.ExceptionHandling;

namespace AdventureWorksTraderBiz
{
  public class ProductCategoryBiz
  {
    public IList<ProductCategory> GetProductCategories()
    {
      try
      {
        ProductCategoryDB category = new ProductCategoryDB();
        return category.GetProductCategories();
      }
      catch (Exception ex)
      {
        bool rethrow = ExceptionPolicy.HandleException(ex, "Log Only Policy");
        if (rethrow)
        {
          throw;
        }
        return null;
      }
    }
  }
}
```

The `GetProductCategories()` method shown in Listing 15-7 acts as a passthrough method, wherein it simply invokes the `GetProductCategories()` method of the data access layer to get the required data. Any exceptions generated in the business logic layer are handled through the `EntLib` exception-handling block in the `catch` block. This is the topic of focus for the next section.

Since the implementation of the remainder of the business logic layer classes (`ProductSubcategoryBiz` and `ProductBiz`) is very similar to `ProductCategoryBiz,` except that they invoke the methods of their corresponding data access layer classes, they will not be discussed in detail. However, you can download the complete code for this case study from `www.wrox.com`.

Quick Tour of Enterprise Library Exception-Handling Block

Every .NET application that you write needs to handle exceptions and recover from those exceptions. Instead of creating, testing, and maintaining this plumbing code in every .NET application, Microsoft has created an application block known as the Enterprise Library exception-handling block (or the EntLib exception-handling block) that provides all of the underlying plumbing code required for handling exceptions. For the purposes of this case study, the EntLib exception-handling block will be leveraged to handle and process exceptions in a consistent and effective manner. Before discussing the steps required to integrate the exception-handling block with the AdventureWorksTrader web site, you need to understand the basics of the exception-handling block.

Key Components of the Exception-Handling Block

There are three main concepts to understand in this block:

- **Exception handling:** The process of doing something with an exception when the exception is detected by your code.
- **Exception logging:** The process of logging an exception, which might include sending formatted exceptions to the event log or sending an email message. The exception-handling block makes use of the Logging and Instrumentation application block for this purpose.
- **Exception policies:** Policies allow you to control the exception-handling and logging behaviors using external configuration files instead of baking the rules into your code. In other words, you can define the exception handling in a policy file and then change the behavior for different testing, debugging, and production scenarios without changing your code.

Using the exception-handling block, there are three things you can do when you detect an exception in your code:

- First, you can wrap the exception in a new exception to add new context information or detail. The original exception is still available as the `InnerException` when the new exception is propagated up the call stack.
- Second, you can replace the exception with a new exception. You typically do this when you don't want the details of the original exception to be propagated across an application boundary.
- The third thing you can do is log the exception. Of course, you can do this in combination with wrapping or replacing the exception, or you can log the original exception and propagate the original up the call stack.

Using the Exception-Handling Block

You can download the `EntLib` caching block, which includes the exception-handling block, by browsing to `www.microsoft.com/downloads` and searching for EntLib. Once you have installed the Enterprise Library, you are ready to start writing code against the exception-handling block. To use the exception-handling block successfully, go through the following steps:

1. Add references to the `Microsoft.Practices.EnterpriseLibrary.Common.dll` and `Microsoft.Practices.EnterpriseLibrary.ExceptionHandling.dll` assemblies from your solution. You do this by using the Add Reference option and navigating to the `<Drive Name>:\Program Files\Microsoft Enterprise Library January 2006\bin` folder. If you decide to use logging in conjunction with exception handling, you also need to add a reference to `Microsoft.Practices.EnterpriseLibrary.ExceptionHandling.Logging.dll`.
2. Add the necessary configuration entries to the `app.config` or `Web.config` file. To this end, you add the following `<configSections>` element under the root `<configuration>` element:

```
<section name="exceptionHandling"
type="Microsoft.Practices.EnterpriseLibrary.ExceptionHandling.Configuration.Excepti
onHandlingSettings,Microsoft.Practices.EnterpriseLibrary.ExceptionHandling" />
```

3. If you are using logging with exception handling, you also need to add the following settings to the <configSections> element:

```
<section name="loggingConfiguration"
  type="Microsoft.Practices.EnterpriseLibrary.Logging.Configuration.
  LoggingSettings,Microsoft.Practices.EnterpriseLibrary.Logging" />
```

4. After that, add the <exceptionHandling> element directly under the root <configuration> element. Inside the <exceptionHandling> element, you add all the exception policies. The following setting shows the <exceptionHandling> element with the policy named Global Policy.

```
<exceptionHandling>
  <exceptionPolicies>
    <add name="Log Only Policy">
      <exceptionTypes>
        <add name="Exception" type="System.Exception, mscorlib,
          Version=2.0.0.0, Culture=neutral, PublicKeyToken=b77a5c561934e089"
          postHandlingAction="ThrowNewException">
          <exceptionHandlers>
            <add logCategory="Default Category" eventId="100" severity="Error"
              title="Exception Management Application Exception" priority="0"
formatterType="Microsoft.Practices.EnterpriseLibrary.ExceptionHandling.
 TextExceptionFormatter, Microsoft.Practices.EnterpriseLibrary.ExceptionHandling"
              name="Logging Handler"
type="Microsoft.Practices.EnterpriseLibrary.ExceptionHandling.Logging.
   LoggingExceptionHandler,
   Microsoft.Practices.EnterpriseLibrary.ExceptionHandling.Logging"/>
          </exceptionHandlers>
        </add>
      </exceptionTypes>
    </add>
  </exceptionPolicies>
</exceptionHandling>
```

5. As these settings indicate, there is a policy named Log Only Policy, which enables you to log the exceptions. Using the <exceptionHandlers> section, you can specify the custom exception handler that will process the exception in an appropriate manner. In this case, the custom handler is implemented in a class named `LoggingExceptionHandler`. The `postHandlingAction` attribute specifies the action to take after the exception is processed, based on the policy. This attribute takes any of the following values: `None`, `NotifyRethrow`, and `ThrowNewException`.

6. Import the core namespace of the exception-handling block `Microsoft.Practices.EnterpriseLibrary.ExceptionHandling` from within your code.

7. Start writing code against the classes in that namespace.

ExceptionPolicy Object

Any time you work with the exception-handling block, the first class that you will have to deal with is the `ExceptionPolicy` class. The `ExceptionPolicy` class exposes a static method named `HandleException()` that lets the client application interact with the exception-handling block, supplying the policy as an argument. The `HandleException()` method uses a factory to create an object of type `ExceptionPolicyImpl` for the supplied policy. The `ExceptionPolicyImpl` object has a collection of `ExceptionPolicyEntry` objects. There is one object for each exception type that is specified in the configuration file for the named policy. For each exception type, the `ExceptionPolicyEntry` object contains a collection of objects that implement the `IExceptionHandler` interface. The collection is ordered and provides the sequence that the exception-handling block uses when executing the policy. Each object that implements the `IExceptionHandler` interface has associated configuration information that is specific to each type of handler.

Exception handlers are .NET classes that encapsulate exception-handling logic and implement the exception-handling block interface `IExceptionHandler`. By default, the exception-handling block includes three exception handlers:

- **Wrap handler:** Wraps one exception around another.
- **Replace handler:** Replaces one exception with another.
- **Logging handler:** Formats exception information, such as the message and the stack trace. Then the logging handler gives this information to the logging block so it can be published.

Now that you have the basics of the exception-handling block, reexamine the code of the business logic layer class to understand the integration with the exception-handling block:

```
public IList<ProductCategory> GetProductCategories()
{
  try
  {
    ProductCategoryDB category = new ProductCategoryDB();
    return category.GetProductCategories();
  }
  catch (Exception ex)
  {
    bool rethrow = ExceptionPolicy.HandleException(ex, "Log Only Policy");
    if (rethrow)
    {
      throw;
    }
    return null;
  }
}
```

Whenever an exception occurs in the `try` block, you catch the exception in the `catch` block where you invoke the `HandleException()` method of the `ExceptionPolicy` object to log the exceptions. After logging the exception, you look at the return value of the `HandleException()` method (which is based on the `postHandlingAction` attribute set in the configuration file) to decide if you want to throw an exception back to the caller. A typical exception logged in the event handler through the exception-handling block looks like the example shown in Figure 15-3.

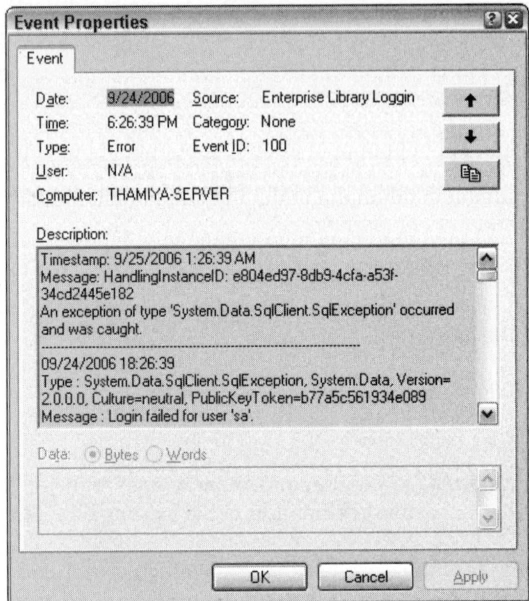

Figure 15-3

Implementation of the Web Site

This section will focus on the implementation of the ASP.NET web site. Create a new web site using Visual Studio 2005. Once the web site is created, add a reference to the business logic layer component, which is `AdventureWorksTraderBiz` in this case. Note that all the configuration settings related to EntLib configuration are stored in the `Web.config` file. The code of the web site will be discussed by considering the different processes involved. Before getting into that discussion, the following section goes over the code of the master page that will be used throughout the web site.

A Look at Master Pages

A professional web site will have a standardized look across all pages. For example, one of the commonly used layouts has its navigation menu on the left side of the page, a copyright on the bottom, and content in the middle. It can be difficult to maintain a standard look if you start duplicating the common logic and look and feel in every web page you build. In ASP.NET 2.0, master pages will make the job easier. You will need to write the common pieces only once in the master page. A master page can serve as a template for one or more web pages. Each ASPX web page only needs to define the content unique to itself, and this content will plug into specified areas of the master page layout.

Listing 15-8 shows the code of the master page named `Common.master` that will be used in the AdventureWorks trader web site.

Listing 15-8: Master Page that Provides Consistent Look and Feel

```
<%@ Master Language="C#" %>
<%@ Import Namespace="System.IO" %>
<%@ Import Namespace="System.Xml" %>
```

```
<html xmlns="http://www.w3.org/1999/xhtml" >
<head runat="server">
  <title>Master Page</title>
</head>
<body>
  <form id="form1" runat="server">
    <div>
      <asp:Table id="tblTop" BackColor="Gainsboro" runat="server" Width="100%"
        Height="108px" ForeColor="DarkCyan">
        <asp:TableRow  runat="server" HorizontalAlign="Center">
          <asp:TableCell  runat="server" ColumnSpan="2">
            <asp:Label id="Label1" runat="server" ForeColor="Black"
              Font-Size="Medium">AdventureWorks Trader System
            </asp:Label>
          </asp:TableCell>
        </asp:TableRow>
      </asp:Table>
      <asp:Table Id="Table6" runat="Server" Width="954px">
        <asp:TableRow runat="server">
          <asp:TableCell runat="server">
            <asp:Table id="Table1" BackColor="Gainsboro" runat="server"
              Width="100%" ForeColor="DarkCyan" Height="290px">
              <asp:TableRow ID="TableRow1"  runat="server"
                HorizontalAlign="Center">
                <asp:TableCell ID="TableCell1" runat="server">
                  <asp:HyperLink runat="server" Text="Product Categories"
                    NavigateUrl="~/ProductCategoryDisplay.aspx"></asp:HyperLink>
                </asp:TableCell>
              </asp:TableRow>
              <asp:TableRow ID="TableRow3"  runat="server"
                HorizontalAlign="Center">
                <asp:TableCell ID="TableCell3" runat="server">
                  <asp:HyperLink ID="HyperLink1" runat="server"
                    Text="Product Sub Categories"
                    NavigateUrl="~/ProductSubcategoryDisplay.aspx" />
                </asp:TableCell>
              </asp:TableRow>
              <asp:TableRow ID="TableRow4"  runat="server"
                HorizontalAlign="Center">
                <asp:TableCell ID="TableCell4" runat="server">
                  <asp:HyperLink ID="HyperLink2" runat="server" Text="Products"
                    NavigateUrl="~/ProductDisplay.aspx" />
                </asp:TableCell>
              </asp:TableRow>
            </asp:Table>
          </asp:TableCell>
          <asp:TableCell runat="server">
            <asp:Table id="Table2" BackColor="Gainsboro" runat="server"
              Width="100%" ForeColor="DarkCyan" Height="290px">
              <asp:TableRow ID="TableRow2" runat="server">
                <asp:TableCell BackColor="#FFFFE1" ID="TableCell2" runat="server">
                  <asp:contentplaceholder id="ContentPlaceHolder1" runat="server">
                  </asp:contentplaceholder>
                </asp:TableCell>
              </asp:TableRow>
```

(continued)

Listing 15-8: *(continued)*

```
            </asp:Table>
          </asp:TableCell>
        </asp:TableRow>
      </asp:Table>
    </div>
  </form>
</body>
</html>
```

The master page encapsulates the header and left navigation information for all the pages of the web site. Now that you have had a look at the master page, the next section discusses the content pages that provide the core functionality. To start with, consider the product categories display process.

Product Categories Display Process

In the product categories display process, you let the user browse through the list of categories contained in the AdventureWorks database. In addition, you also let the users navigate to the product subcategories contained inside a product category. The users can navigate to the product subcategories by clicking on the product category name. Listing 15-9 shows the implementation of the page.

Listing 15-9: Implementation of the Product Category Display Page That Derives from the Master Page

```
<%@ Page Language="C#" MasterPageFile="~/Common.master"
  Title="Product Categories Display" %>
<asp:Content ID="Content1" ContentPlaceHolderID="ContentPlaceHolder1"
  Runat="Server">
  <asp:ObjectDataSource ID="categorySource" EnableCaching="true"
    SqlCacheDependency="CommandNotification" CacheDuration="Infinite"
    TypeName="AdventureWorksTraderBiz.ProductCategoryBiz"
    SelectMethod="GetProductCategories"
    runat="server">
  </asp:ObjectDataSource>
  <asp:Label runat="server" id="lblHeading" Font-Size="Medium"
    Font-Underline="False" ForeColor="#0000C0" >
    Click on the Category to go to the SubCategories
  </asp:Label><br /><br />
  <asp:GridView HeaderStyle-HorizontalAlign="Center" HeaderStyle-Font-Bold="True"
    HeaderStyle-BackColor="blue" HeaderStyle-ForeColor="White"
    AutoGenerateColumns="False" ID="gridCategories" runat="server"
    DataSourceID="categorySource">
    <Columns>
      <asp:BoundField ReadOnly="True" HeaderText="CategoryID"
        DataField="ProductCategoryID" />
      <asp:HyperLinkField HeaderText="Name" DataTextField="Name"
        DataNavigateUrlFields="ProductCategoryID"
        DataNavigateUrlFormatString="ProductSubcategoryDisplay.aspx?
        ProductCategoryID={0}"/>
      <asp:BoundField HeaderText="Name" DataField="Name" />
      <asp:BoundField HeaderText="Row Guid" DataField="Rowguid" />
      <asp:BoundField HeaderText="Modified Date" HtmlEncode="false"
```

```
            DataFormatString="{0:MM/dd/yyyy}" DataField="ModifiedDate" />
        </Columns>
    </asp:GridView>
</asp:Content>
```

Listing 15-9 starts by declaring an `ObjectDataSource` named `categorySource`. Before looking at the code, you need to understand the two important attributes of the `ObjectDataSource` control. The `TypeName` attribute allows you to specify the name of the class you want to bind this control to. The `SelectMethod` attribute allows you to specify the name of the method to invoke in the class. You use these methods to specify the name of the class and its method to bind the `ObjectDataSource` control to. For the `categorySource`, you set these attributes to `"AdventureWorksTraderBiz.ProductCategoryBiz"` and `"GetProductCategories"`. Then you bind the data in this `categorySource` control to a `GridView` control named `gridCategories` by setting the `DataSourceID` attribute of the `GridView` to `categorySource`.

Figure 15-4 shows the product categories display page in action.

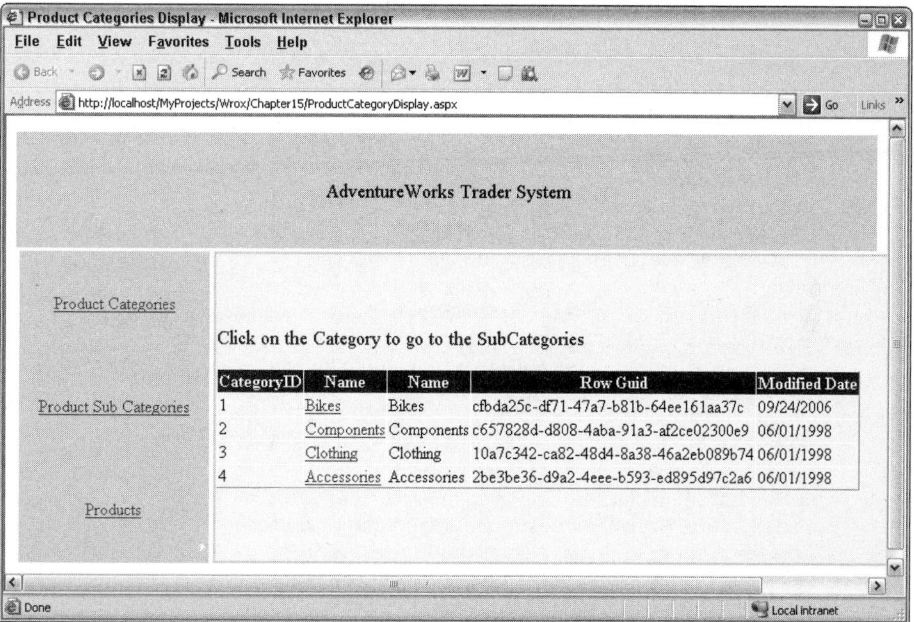

Figure 15-4

Note that the `ObjectDataSource` control also implements caching through the caching attributes, such as `EnableCaching`, `CacheDuration`, and `SqlCacheDependency`. By setting the `SqlCacheDependency` attribute to `"CommandNotification"`, you indicate to ASP.NET that a notification-based dependency should be created for the `ObjectDataSource` control.

> *Note that to leverage the notification-based dependency, you need to invoke the* `System.Data.SqlClient.SqlDependency.Start()` *method somewhere in the application before the first SQL query is executed. This method could be placed in the* `Application_Start()` *event in* `Global.asax` *file.*

SQL Server 2005 cache dependency is more flexible in the types of changes that receive notification. SQL Server 2005 monitors changes to the result set of a particular SQL command. If a change occurs in the database that would modify the results set of that command, the dependency causes the cached item to be invalidated. This allows SQL Server 2005 to provide row-level notification.

The ProductSubcategories Display Process

As the name suggests, the product subcategories page allows users to display the list of all the product subcategories, and then navigate through the list of all the products contained in each of the subcategories. Implementation of the product subcategories page is shown in Listing 15-10.

Listing 15-10: ProductSubcategories Display Page

```
<%@ Page Language="C#" MasterPageFile="~/Common.master"
  Title="Product Sub Category Display" %>
<asp:Content ID="Content1" ContentPlaceHolderID="ContentPlaceHolder1"
  Runat="Server">
  <asp:ObjectDataSource ID="subCategorySource"
    TypeName="AdventureWorksTraderBiz.ProductSubcategoryBiz"
    SelectMethod="GetProductSubCategories" runat="server">
    <SelectParameters>
      <asp:QueryStringParameter QueryStringField="ProductCategoryID"
        Direction="Input" Name="productCategoryID" DefaultValue="1" Type="Int32" />
    </SelectParameters>
  </asp:ObjectDataSource>
  <asp:Label runat="server" id="lblHeading" Font-Size="Medium"
    Font-Underline="False" ForeColor="#0000C0" >
    Click on the SubCategory to go to the Products
  </asp:Label><br /><br />
  <asp:GridView HeaderStyle-HorizontalAlign="Center" HeaderStyle-Font-Bold="True"
    HeaderStyle-BackColor="blue" HeaderStyle-ForeColor="White"
    AutoGenerateColumns="False" ID="gridSubCategories" runat="server"
    DataSourceID="subCategorySource">
    <Columns>
      <asp:BoundField ReadOnly="True" HeaderText="SubcategoryID"
        DataField="ProductSubcategoryID" />
      <asp:BoundField HeaderText="CategoryID" DataField="ProductCategoryID" />
      <asp:HyperLinkField HeaderText="Name" DataTextField="Name"
        DataNavigateUrlFields="ProductSubcategoryID"
        DataNavigateUrlFormatString="ProductDisplay.aspx?
        ProductSubcategoryID={0}"/>
      <asp:BoundField HeaderText="Row Guid" DataField="Rowguid" />
      <asp:BoundField HeaderText="Modified Date" HtmlEncode="false"
        DataFormatString="{0:MM/dd/yyyy}" DataField="ModifiedDate" />
    </Columns>
  </asp:GridView>
</asp:Content>
```

Listing 15-10 consists of an `ObjectDataSource` control named `subCategorySource` that binds to the `GetProductSubCategories()` method of the `ProductSubcategoryBiz` class. As discussed earlier, the `GetProductSubCategories()` method accepts a product category ID as an argument and returns all the subcategories that are part of the product category. To be able to invoke this method, the `subCategory Source` control should be able to pass in the product category ID (retrieved from the product category display page) to the method. In this case, you want to retrieve the value of the product category ID using the `QueryStringParameter` collection. To do this, you set the `QueryStringField` attribute of the `QueryStringParameter` template to the name of the query string field, and the `Name` attribute to the argument name of the `GetProductSubcategories()` method. This allows the selected product category ID in the previous page to be used as an argument to the SQL query. You also set the default value of 1 for the product category ID using the `DefaultValue` property. This default value will be used when the page is requested for the first time.

Figure 15-5 shows the product subcategories' display page when requested from a browser.

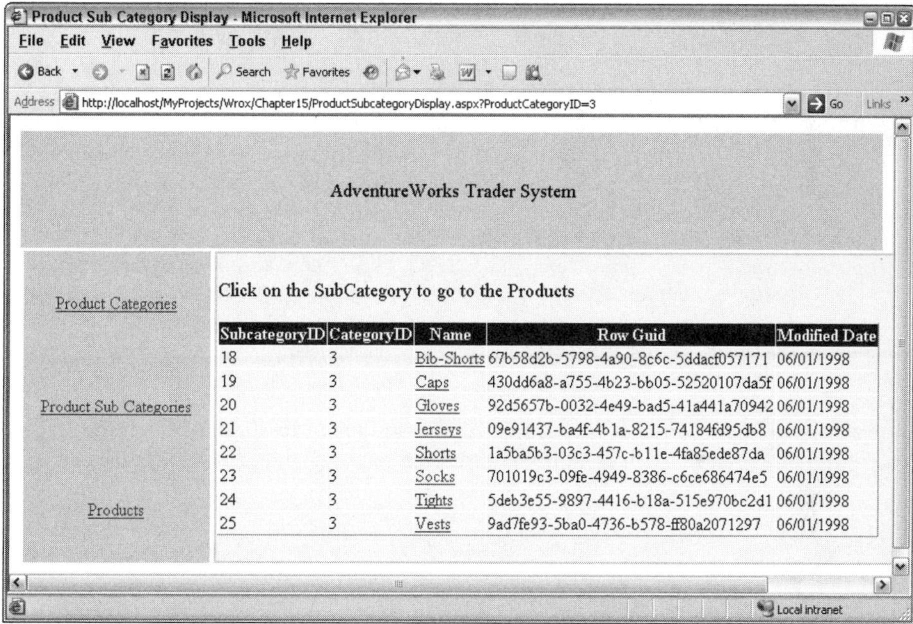

Figure 15-5

Products Display Process

In Figure 15-5, when you click on a specific product subcategory, you are directed to a page that displays all the products belonging to that product subcategory. Listing 15-11 shows the implementation of this page.

Listing 15-11: Implementation of the Products Display Page

```
<%@ Page Language="C#" MasterPageFile="~/Common.master" Title="Products Display" %>
<asp:Content ID="Content1" ContentPlaceHolderID="ContentPlaceHolder1"
  Runat="Server">
  <asp:ObjectDataSource ID="productSource" runat="server"
    TypeName="AdventureWorksTraderBiz.ProductBiz" SelectMethod="GetProducts">
    <SelectParameters>
      <asp:QueryStringParameter QueryStringField="ProductSubcategoryID"
        Direction="Input" Name="productSubcategoryID" DefaultValue="1"
```

(continued)

Listing 15-11: *(continued)*

```
          Type="Int32" />
      </SelectParameters>
    </asp:ObjectDataSource>
    <asp:Label runat="server" id="lblHeading" Font-Size="Medium"
      Font-Underline="False" ForeColor="#0000C0" >
      List of Products
    </asp:Label><br /><br />
    <asp:GridView HeaderStyle-HorizontalAlign="Center" HeaderStyle-Font-Bold="True"
      HeaderStyle-BackColor="blue" HeaderStyle-ForeColor="White"
      AutoGenerateColumns="False" ID="gridProducts" runat="server"
      DataSourceID="productSource">
      <Columns>
        <asp:BoundField ReadOnly="True" HeaderText="ProductID"
          DataField="ProductID"/>
        <asp:BoundField HeaderText="Name" DataField="Name"/>
        <asp:BoundField HeaderText="Product Number" DataField="ProductNumber" />
        <asp:BoundField HeaderText="Color" DataField="Color" />
        <asp:BoundField HeaderText="ListPrice" DataField="ListPrice" />
        <asp:BoundField HeaderText="Modified Date" HtmlEncode="false"
          DataFormatString="{0:MM/dd/yyyy}" DataField="ModifiedDate" />
      </Columns>
    </asp:GridView>
  </asp:Content>
```

The code shown in Listing 15-11 is very similar to that in Listing 15-10, except that the `ObjectDataSource` control in this page invokes a different method to get all the products.

Summary

In this case study, you have learned a wide range of best practices, including the use of `EntLib` application blocks and the new features of ASP.NET and SQL Server 2005 for creating an efficient ASP.NET 2.0 web site. The application discussed in this case study showcased the integration of application blocks in a real-world ASP.NET site, and also discussed the use of Generics collections as a way to transmit data from one layer of the application to another layer of the application. This case study also discussed how the `ObjectDataSource` control supports layered application design by allowing you to directly bind the output of an object's method directly to the controls in an ASP.NET page. The architecture used by the case study provides a number of advantages. They are:

- Changes to the user interface and to the application logic are largely independent from one another, allowing the application to evolve easily to meet new requirements.
- Creating stored procedures using managed code provides performance improvements because of the compiled logic that is executed close to the database server.
- If changes to the middle-layer classes are required, they can be modified and deployed immediately without impacting the ASP.NET pages.
- Using master pages in the presentation layer provides a huge advantage in terms of providing a consistent look and feel across all the pages in the web site.

- Caching of database tables results in increased performance. Also, the new database cache invalidation provides the ability to keep the changes in the database up to date with the data in the ASP.NET cache.
- The ability to transport data using a lightweight, flexible Generics collection can go a long way in increasing the productivity of developers.
- ASP.NET 2.0 facilitates n-tier application design by providing the `ObjectDataSource` control that is specifically suited to consuming middle-tier objects. This new control enables "codeless" data binding by providing the ability to seamlessly integrate the data returned from the middle-layer objects with the ASP.NET presentation layer.

Index

SYMBOLS

A

B

D

E

F

P

Q

R

S

T

U